ASAE HANDBOOK OF PROFESSIONAL PRACTICES IN ASSOCIATION MANAGEMENT

About the ASAE-Wiley Series

All titles in the ASAE-Wiley Series are developed through a publishing alliance between ASAE: The Center for Association Leadership and John Wiley & Sons to better serve the content needs of member-serving organizations and the people who lead and manage them.

ASAE HANDBOOK OF PROFESSIONAL PRACTICES IN ASSOCIATION MANAGEMENT

THIRD EDITION

John B. Cox, FASAE, CAE
Founding Executive Editor and Contributing Author

Susan S. Radwan, SMP, ARM, CAE
Executive Managing Editor and Contributing Author

Published by Jossey-Bass
A Wiley Brand
One Montgomery Street, Suite 1000, San Francisco, CA 94104-4594—www.josseybass.com

Jossey-Bass books and products are available through most bookstores. To contact Jossey-Bass directly call our Customer Care Department within the U.S. at 800-956-7739, outside the U.S. at 317-572-3986, or fax 317-572-4002.

Wiley publishes in a variety of print and electronic formats and by print-on-demand. Some material included with standard print versions of this book may not be included in e-books or in print-on-demand. If this book refers to media such as a CD or DVD that is not included in the version you purchased, you may download this material at http://booksupport.wiley.com. For more information about Wiley products, visit www.wiley.com.

Library of Congress Cataloging-in-Publication Data

Professional practices in association management
    ASAE handbook of professional practices in association management / John B. Cox, FASAE, CAE, Founding Executive Editor and Contributing Author; Susan S. Radwan, SMP, ARM, CAE, Executive Managing Editor and Contributing Author.—Third edition.
        pages cm.— (ASAE-Wiley series)
    Revised edition of Professional practices in association management: the essential resource for effective management of nonprofit organizations, 2nd ed., published in 2007.
    Includes bibliographical references and index.
    ISBN 978-1-118-77539-4 (cloth/website) 1. Associations, institutions, etc.—Management. I. Cox, John B. II. Radwan, Susan S., date– III. American Society of Association Executives. IV. Title.
    HD62.6.P758 2015
    060.68—dc23

                                                                                    2014030720

Printed in the United States of America
THIRD EDITION
HB Printing   10 9 8 7 6 5 4 3 2 1

CONTENTS

Contents

This book is dedicated to the memory of John B. "Jack" Cox, FASAE, CAE, whose vision became Professional Practices in Association Management *and whose passionate leadership guided three editions of this work.*

PREFACE

We come now to the third edition of a book that has become the "go to" reference work in the field of member-organization management. Quite a leap for something with far more modest aspirations, first created almost twenty years ago.

As noted in the two earlier editions, *Professional Practices in Association Management* was first conceived of as the one-stop guide for those studying for the certified association executive (CAE) designation. In a burst of serendipity, the American Society of Association Executives (ASAE) board of directors at the time wished to identify the body of subject knowledge essential to managing the complex entities that nonprofit membership organizations are. It assembled the best and the brightest in this field and set for them the task of creating such a body. That group labored for more than a year, gathering information, opinion, data, and the critical taxonomy needed. As word spread of this endeavor, the effort quickly became known as the Body of Knowledge Project. When completed, it was a sparkling thing of beauty, instantly identifying everything known, and needed to be known, in the field of association management. I was serving on the CAE Commission at that time, and it became obvious to all involved that those creating the Body of Knowledge had just designed a guide for the CAE examination. Thus the fruits of all that labor quickly became adopted as the core framework for future CAE examinations and *Professional Practices in Association Management.* As society at large and nonprofit management in general evolved—sometimes almost to the point of revolution—so did the body of knowledge essential to managing in this field. The second edition of *Professional Practices* reflected those changes when it was published some eight years ago. And in what seems like a twinkling, those changes were surpassed and replaced with still more urgent imperatives, making a third edition absolutely necessary.

There are significant developments in this third edition, which is now titled *ASAE Handbook of Professional Practices in Association Management.* It integrates a focus on helping both CAE candidates and all association staff see how to think like a chief staff executive. Association management is populated with superb subject and functional executives, many of whom would never dream of, nor want, a CSE position. But wise ones know they have to *think* like their CSE in order to succeed in their own area of specialization. Thus the reader will note references in almost every chapter to the CSE perspective approach to management of a program, a project, or the entire organization. By thinking like a CSE, staff specialists will, in brief, be better in their own functional areas and will contribute more to the entire organization. In addition, planning has now been identified as a continuum, with many points across an extensive horizon. Each is sequential on that continuum, and taken together, they are invaluable for realizing optimal association management. And there is a far greater emphasis on the *business* of association management, from building different business models to identifying and acting smartly in the risk-management arena. There are other critical areas of both evolutionary and revolutionary change. Obviously, technology now permeates every aspect of association management, from something at once as simple and complex as social media to how association markets are now identified, how communications work with different audiences, how legislation and regulation are addressed, how financial issues are approached, and on *ad infinitum.* It is hoped that all are more than adequately addressed in this third edition.

In closing, it is a daunting task indeed to attempt thanking all the people involved in producing this work. Guidance was sought with and from other organizations in member-organization management. The work of three individuals, however, has to be recognized, for they were the *sine qua non* in making it happen. Creating the first edition was fairly much a solo act. The second edition was a working partnership between this writer and Baron Williams, CAE, ASAE's director of book publishing. This far more complex and detailed third edition simply would not have been possible without the additional, hands-on participation of Keith Skillman, CAE, ASAE vice president, publications, and Susan Radwan, CAE. Indeed, Ms. Radwan's contributions have been enormous. She helped identify and refine topical areas, coauthored two of the chapters, and wrote sidebars or original passages to still others. As a result of her insight gained in working for many years as an instructor in CAE preparation, she helped identify those issues most important to association executives in the field. Further, she was involved in review and editing of virtually every chapter in the book. But, collectively, it was a team effort, from the initial discussions of a third edition to what the reader now sees in this work.

So whether you are an individual sitting for the next CAE examination, a CSE, an aspirant to the chief staff role, a staff specialist who wants to better acquit your specialty, an individual new to member-organization management, or someone who just wants to "know what you need to know" in association management, it is genuinely hoped that *ASAE Handbook of Professional Practices in Association Management*, Third Edition, becomes the reference, the road map, the essential guide you are seeking to both thrive and succeed in this field.

—John B. Cox, FASAE, CAE

ACKNOWLEDGMENTS

It takes a small army of minds to conceive and assemble a work of this length and complexity. Many, many people have our thanks: most particularly the authors of the individual chapters and those whom they enlisted in reviewing and refining their work; the CAE Commission for its ongoing stewardship of the body of knowledge in association management; and these professionals who, in addition to this book's editors, reviewed the previous edition in detail and provided input to help inform this new book: Carol L. Barbeito; Lauren Hefner, CAE; Sharon Swan, FASAE, CAE; and Nancy Macduff.

ASAE HANDBOOK OF PROFESSIONAL PRACTICES IN ASSOCIATION MANAGEMENT

CHAPTER ONE

A PRESCRIPTION FOR A SUCCESSFUL CSE

Cheryl O. Ronk, CMP, FASAE, CAE, and Susan S. Radwan, SMP, ARM, CAE

The success of chief staff executives (CSEs) can be tied to perspective and focus more than anything else. The CSE's perspective—the way of thinking about himself or herself, others, the team, the organization, and the positioning of the organization—is a key variable for success.

Perspective and focus alone, however, will not carry a leader. The CSE needs knowledge of association concepts and strategies while fostering important connections to provide for long-term success. CSEs must possess qualities that lead others toward a preferred future for the industry or profession. The CSE plays the pivot position to communicate, direct, and manage staff and volunteers, plus work with other entities as partners, collaborators, and contributors toward the preferred future.

What makes a successful chief staff executive? Many individuals who should be very successful, according to their credentials on paper, fail within an association culture. Yet others who did not hold comparative credentials to other candidates identified in the search process grew into very successful CSEs. There is no one magical element or combination. It is a combination of perspective, personal traits, knowledge, experience, communication style, and fit with the organizational culture that results in success.

What Does an Association Buy in a CSE?

When an organization selects a chief staff executive, what are they purchasing? Think about it. A scanner? A planner? A visionary? A leader? Consider the idea that they purchase culture and judgment.

The culture for the organization and the industry as a whole is heavily influenced by the long-term CSE. The CSE is responsible for the aligned values and vision across the whole organization: board, staff, and membership. The CSE's personal and professional values show through and set the tone for ethical behavior and organizational integrity. Staff asks for direction; the board asks for judgment. This judgment influences the culture and ultimately the brand of the organization.

Unique Position

One of the key elements of successful chief staff executives is that they understand their positioning within the organization. The board has primary authority and secondary commitment for the association. The CSE has the primary commitment and secondary authority for decisions made. It is critical for a CSE to understand this dynamic, recognize the appropriate role that needs to be played, and leverage the value that role can provide.

Inside this unique position, a CSE needs to offer the board and staff a skill set beyond being an "expert" in a particular area of association management or industry expertise. Savvy CSEs establish the role in the following ways:

- They evaluate and recommend strategy based on alignment to the mission.
- They collect, evaluate, analyze, and make meaning of relevant data.
- They determine positioning and present recommendations to the board.
- They recognize the role of and plan for an appropriately sequenced process that yields board and member support.
- They build effective work teams and ensure a productive work environment.

These avenues make for better strategic decision making and stronger member buy-in.

Board Partner

The board and CSE are partners, with specific roles inside the partnership. The CSE implements the ideas of the board, which is accountable for its governance to the members.

Appropriately, the CSE brings ideas to the board to advance and position the association. A successful CSE ensures that board members are informed about the direction and achievements within the strategic plan, the capacity and efforts to expand the talent pool, and pursuits to enhance the industry or profession as a whole.

Much of the CSE's role is about working *on* the association so that it is relevant, efficient, and effective. The CSE often facilitates the board's work to create the *what* for the organization (for example, What is the preferred future? What strategies will be most effective? What values are important to our culture? What is member return on investment?) The CSE then works with staff on creating the *how,* or the means, to achieve the outcomes defined by the board. The CSE is the linchpin that keeps both alignment and focus on the right work. In essence, the CSE's role is synonymous with organizational performance.

Changing CSE Role

Not too long ago, to be successful, one had to know the other players in his or her industry; the association connection was the place to do just that. If you wanted referrals, you had to meet and greet. Who you knew was essential for effective communication and partnerships. Being elected to the board of an association equated to being at the top of your field. It was the ultimate recognition in the profession.

Over two decades ago, associations had a unique niche often related to why they were formed. Their "golden-handcuff" (affinity) programs were a guarantee of sustainability. Associations represented their members in the public policy, regulatory, or collective-bargaining arenas. The niche was driven by the members as a collective group, and the association only served specific needs that could be solved better together.

The formula for success was to follow a traditional association business model. For example, an association had to have a communications vehicle, a website, member education, a trade show, a public policy agenda, and the like.

Now we have moved to intensely analyzing what the members need and delivering it. The name of the game is "mass customization." Thus the successful CSE has to know what can be delivered from an entrepreneurial perspective, listen for member needs, and provide solutions.

We live in a nonstop, dynamic environment in which we have few models to follow. It is even more important now to not only listen to members but also "read between the lines" and create member-supported solutions. It is equally important to know what is changing in the environment that will significantly affect members and the association as an entity so that you can prepare to meet the demands of that future state.

This requires a way of thinking that considers the association's relationship to allied associations around the world, regulators, legislators, and global partners. A CSE needs to focus on global competitiveness and strategic positioning of the association.

It is essential to become an organizational designer. How the organization looked ten years or even four years ago may not be right any more. The CSE has to continuously scan the environment, prioritize strategies, and evaluate opportunities. Just because another organization is providing a specific service does not mean it is the right fit for your organization. In fact, if another organization is doing it, what should your organization do differently? What is your differentiated value proposition in the marketplace?

To be an effective organizational designer one has to be open to innovations from other industries or professions. Interacting with peers at the local, state, and national levels, industry leaders and leaders from other sectors through your association executive community, leads to the possibility of cross-pollination. As a CSE, it is essential to learn from others outside the profession you represent. To build on the brilliance of others, you have to reach out beyond your regular networks.

Consider the story of the chief executive officer of Federal Express who, during a business trip, visited a grocery industry trade show. He was introduced to barcode technology at this event, which at the time was primarily marketed to grocers. Tracking packages appeared soon afterward and is still one of the elements of FedEx's success. He saw the innovation as relevant for his own industry and leveraged the opportunity.

Staying within the same circles and hearing the same stories will get you the same results.

Deliver Results

Today, CSEs are asked to deliver results, not just activity—or reports on activity via dashboards or other means. Understanding the return on investment (ROI) for divergent stakeholders and communicating that ROI is essential in today's competitive environment. ROI communication can only be directed from the top of the organization.

Since today is different from yesterday, and tomorrow will be different from today, successful CSEs must have intentional learning about their personal and professional growth. Some CSEs believe they know all there is to learn and could teach other executives about leadership. Really? Do we ever truly master this profession? Savvy CSEs see the value of continual learning. Like the medical and legal professions, perhaps we should "practice" leadership. "Practice" means repetition, learning from the experience, and mastering technique; in other words, continual learning and coaching. Part of that "practice" might include gathering new tools to drive excellence in the field, being curious about how others think and achieve results, and being open to new perspectives that might optimize results.

Beacon to Others

As previously mentioned, the CSE is the linchpin that keeps both alignment and focus on the right work. The long-time CSE is the individual who is often in place longer than any board leader. The CSE must provide for continuity between volunteers and staff members who come and go. The long-term CSE provides stability to the organization and holds its institutional wisdom.

This wisdom recognizes the big picture of how a strategic plan builds upon previous success, and the CSE's perspective, if shared, can assist volunteers and staff in understanding how everything fits together. Leadership is essential in the CSE position, for it is the only position there is to create total alignment among the board, committees, task forces, and staff.

The CSE is compensated for creating the culture to achieve the preferred future, to make the judgments on how to accomplish it, and what opportunities should be considered to maintain the nimbleness of the organization. This high-level thought process is the accountability of the CSE.

Emotional Intelligence

A CSE with high emotional intelligence makes everyone better. That "model from the top" inspires both volunteers and staff to become continually better.

In general, emotional intelligence is the ability to practice ethical behavior, honesty, and integrity with yourself and others. According to social scientists, emotional intelligence includes

1. Knowing one's emotions; in other words, self-awareness.
2. Managing those emotions, which includes handling feelings in a way that is appropriate to the context of your situation.
3. Motivating oneself, operating from a place of emotional self-control—delaying gratification and stifling impulsiveness.
4. Recognizing emotions in others and practicing empathy.
5. Handling relationships, maintaining trustworthiness throughout the course of those relationships.

Those with high emotional intelligence understand the difference between authority and responsibility and expect themselves and others to be accountable for the proper use of authority.

◆ ◆ ◆

Think Like a CSE: How You Think Is How You Lead Is How You Act!

From the top of the operational organization, a CSE has a unique position in the responsibility for the whole organization. To be successful, the CSE must hold the whole organization as his or her primary concern rather than favor one department over another. The CSE needs to be concerned about maximizing the whole by optimizing the parts of the association, rather than maximizing parts only to diminish the impact of the whole.

For example, in the budgeting process, if the CSE allocates funding to the government relations department at the expense of the IT upgrade, will that decision maximize or diminish the overall value proposition to the members? Of course, the answer is, "It depends on the rationale." However, the question posed is a critical one for CSEs to consider in making decisions to allocate resources.

Successful CSEs build an aligned culture. CSEs need to understand the internal culture and strategize what it needs to become for optimal effectiveness in this time and place. Let's break this down in more detail.

The CSE recognizes the interdependent nature of what the organization does. He or she sees how all the parts have to be in good working order and in sync with each other to create the value proposition of the organization.

A successful CSE needs to exhibit advanced leadership skills. These skills go above and beyond the skill set of team-building, trust-building, and personal capacity-building. Advanced leadership breaks through traditional barriers of departments and going it alone. These advanced skills foster cross-functional teamwork and a culture of openness and continuous learning that results in

- Integrating organizational outcomes across all departments, which brings added-value to the membership
- Effective strategic positioning that creates global competitiveness and synergy through partnerships and alliances.

The CSE sets the tone for cross-functional teamwork: the leadership across teams. This is a difficult task because the CSE needs to bridge departmental turf to create an aligned culture that recognizes the interdependence inside the value proposition for members. Core to this culture is valuing diversity of viewpoints and perspectives. Better solutions are devised when different and relevant viewpoints are shared. Whether there is diversity of staff functions at the table or diversity of social experience, the synthesis of these shared perspectives will yield a much richer result.

When there is a shared vision for what creates value for members, positive energy will emerge that will move the organization forward. Savvy CSEs remember that people support what they help to create.

In this collaborative style of work environment, the CSE sets the tone for open communication in which feedback is sought, genuinely considered, and acted upon. This collaborative culture is much more effective than a competitive environment in which one department is intent on winning or dominating at a cost to others. To be effective in making the transition to this cultural style, the CSE has to inspire team leaders to be focused on outcomes for the members every step of the way.

Successful CSEs Master Systems Thinking

Successful CSEs apply high-level thinking to advance the association. This thinking, known as "systems thinking," synthesizes these concepts into an aligned whole:

Focus on value to the beneficiaries, members, and stakeholders rather than the organization itself.

Recognize and embody interdependence rather than independence.

Focus on outcomes and bottom-line results rather than activity results.

Focus on convergent solution-seeking rather than linear problem solving.

Focus on the total organization rather than departmental silos.

Foster cross-functional teamwork rather than siloed solutions.

Foster a culture of openness and feedback rather than a closed environment to which outside influences can't get in.

Foster a culture of communication and collaboration rather than a "not my job" delineation.

Consider systemic changes rather than isolated change.

Adopt circular cycles to foster internal learning rather than linear processes.

Hold the whole organization as the primary concern so that you optimize the parts in order to maximize the whole.

Leadership to Successful Strategy

No CSE is successful without the leadership attribute. However, let's review here a few traits that set the best CSEs apart.

Communicating

Choosing the tone and frame of a message is one of the key elements of communication success. Watch any news program or read the newspaper and notice the tone and frame the spokespersons use to frame a situation so that others understand it.

The process for communication, however, starts with thinking through what you want to achieve. It begins with defining, "What is my desired outcome for this communication?" For example, is it the desired outcome to alarm? To energize action? To inform? To create peace of mind? Once you decide, then consider appropriately framing and crafting the message.

When framing an issue, the CSE needs to think about how to position the issue so that the language chosen and the message crafted connect with the audience and the desired outcome is achieved.

For example, how would you frame a message for your board when a significant segment of membership has not renewed? You might frame the message in terms of comparative results, such as "As many organizations have experienced in this economic downturn, membership has decreased." Or you might frame the message in terms of a crisis to solve, such as, "The drop in renewals is a clear indication that we need to evaluate our relevance to the membership." Or you might frame the message in terms of long-term impact, such as, "If we continue to lose members at this rate, we will need to close our doors or merge." You might frame the situation in terms of a commonly understood metaphor, such as, "We view this loss more like a spring pruning, when we can make room for new growth." Which frame will achieve the desired outcome?

Successful CSEs layer tone in their communication as well. For example, if you have bad news to share, do you create a "just the facts" tone, a "remorseful" tone, a "panicked" tone, or a "serious crisis" tone? There are many options, but the bottom line is that the CSE's communication must always take a professional tone. The choice of tone used will heavily influence the response of the receiver of the message.

The frame and tone you choose are critical to create the desired outcome of the message.

Delegating

To be a leader means there are followers. The job of the CSE is to create an environment in which people can be productive. To be productive, delegatees have to see that they are contributing to the accomplishment of some goal or outcome. This usually requires giving initial guidance, tools, resources, and a degree of autonomy to do the job.

Delegating could be to volunteers, partners, or staff. Communicating about a project, including the rationale and the expected results, clearly allows for more effective delegation. Structuring what is needed, by when, and why can result in better productivity. Of course, appropriately matching talent to the project is part of the assignment as well. Fit your people to the job.

CSEs understand the importance of providing direction and then trusting but verifying that the work is being accomplished. They establish and check in on milestones, not specific tactics, with the delegatees.

Managing Growth and Change

One of the best tools for managing growth and change is business planning with a keen eye on the flow of money, sources of revenue, and the feasibility and sustainability of revenue streams.

CSEs see how all the pieces fit together and what may need to be realigned for new direction and opportunities. Successful CSEs manage the processes that run through the association's departments, rather than the silos created by departmental boundaries. Examples of processes that run through departments include revenue generation, membership retention, and knowledge management.

Aligning with Mission

Shiny pennies. This is a term used to describe distractions that catch the eye of leaders and staff. A program may sound great and be sold as a revenue generator—*but* does it relate to what we do? Is it in alignment with our mission or our strategic plan? When a *shiny penny* does align, it is the CSE, and in larger organizations, the senior team, who sets the tone across departments to make sure the concept is properly vetted, planned, and implemented. As a manager, she or he assesses the impact and opens capacity, if appropriate, by eliminating activities that are no longer productive.

Successful CSEs assess and learn when to say yes and no. They do their homework with a focus on mission. They scan the environment and assess opportunities with clear criteria. They sense when to take risks and assess the level of risk that will be tolerated by the volunteer leaders.

Creating a Learning Organization

The CSE needs to set the tone and lead continuous learning for the industry or profession, the association's members, and the organization as an entity. What does this mean? It means that knowledge is freely and regularly shared and highly valued. It also means that insights of how this knowledge affects work processes, jobs, initiatives, and opportunities is shared. It is learning through each and every interaction and conversation. It is seeking to understand rather than seeking to be understood. A successful CSE models how to listen to shared experience and draws out lessons to be learned, applied, and integrated into the way we think and do, and encourages others to follow in this path.

We live in a nonstop, changing environment. Association leadership not only guides their members through these changes but actively shapes the future and responds to changes that will better the industry or profession.

The CSE Sequence of Thinking

Successful CSEs play out a particular sequence of activities in seeking solutions as they come across problems, challenges, activities, and opportunities that present themselves in day-to-day activities. One such way of framing that sequence is *scan, plan, implement,* and *evaluate,* or SPIE.

This sequence is applicable to any situation, be it a major transformational change for the association, an accusation of wrongdoing at the staff level, or planning for a meeting.

A misconception is that an effective CSE will recognize a problem and quickly jump in and *do* something about it. This command-and-control approach is only effective if the CSE is dealing with a crisis when people and property are at risk, such as there is a fire in your building and evacuation is necessary. However, that "jumping in" impulse is not the best option in most situations. In fact, that *implementation* phase—the *doing something* phase—is really the third step in the desired sequence of action.

A successful CSE is *not* an impulsive player. For success, a CSE knows that one needs to have all the relevant facts to execute appropriate action (*a scan function*). "Knowing what I want out of this situation before I jump in" is the *plan* function.

All four of these steps are process oriented, offering a particular thinking sequence that will lead one to or toward the desired result.

Let's look at each of these steps in the sequence.

Scan

The process of scanning is all about intelligence gathering at whatever level is relevant to the situation. Scanning could include assessing how you feel about an issue, gathering facts about an interpersonal conflict situation, scanning past events to assess where you are today, observing the interactions between managers and their subordinates, conducting a survey with relevant players to understand how they think about an issue or what they need in a solution, environmental scanning to understand the influences at play, and even future environmental scanning to anticipate how change drivers will affect the association and its members.

A successful CSE will scan for the relevant intelligence, including facts, contributing factors, motivations, and pertinent relationships, to fully understand the issue before planning a response.

Plan

Any planning process implies that you wish to make some change in the environment. Identifying the change—beginning with the end in mind—creates an efficiency in the planning, allowing the planner to identify the key steps in reaching the desired goal. Consequently, the first step in any plan of action is to answer the question, "What is the desired outcome?"

It would be important to note that you may desire multiple outcomes. For example, what is the outcome you want to achieve at the end of the process? What is the outcome you want to achieve among the players in the process? What is the outcome you want to achieve as you personally engage in the process? Identifying the outcomes for all the various levels involved will point to certain ways to plan your implementation process.

For example, you have an interpersonal staff conflict that you must address because it is impeding progress of your senior management team. What is the desired outcome you wish for your intervention? *Resolution of the conflict.* What is the desired outcome you wish for the players involved? *Mutual respect, valuing differences, and shared resolution to the situation.* What is the desired outcome you wish for you in the intervention? *Become less reluctant to deal with tough interpersonal issues, better understand the interpersonal dynamics of strong personalities.*

The planning should consider the process to be used, who should be involved, and how you might frame the messaging, all focused to achieve the desired outcome. You may want to pre-think likely objections to your actions and be ready for appropriate responses that will override the objections presented.

The *process* to be used is a critical component of planning. The politics of who gets invited first or who sits next to whom in a high-level meeting at the head table is the stuff that creates hard feelings and political faux pas. For a CSE, designing and sequencing the process is a critical task for effectiveness and success in achieving the desired outcomes.

Implement

Executing your plan is the focus of implementation, rather than impulsively "jumping into the fire" and making things happen. Implementation requires focus on the end prize—your desired outcomes. Effective execution of your plan requires that your actions track with your plan. Of course, there are times when you need to make modifications, particularly when you run into unplanned responses. However, tracking your actions with your plan will likely get you a better overall result versus "shooting from the hip" in the moment.

Evaluate

Evaluation is a space that we tend to forget as a key to process improvement. Evaluation can take place during the process (formative process evaluation) and after the process (summative evaluation).

In formative process evaluation, you continually evaluate your every move and assess whether it advances the likelihood of achieving your desired outcomes. If the planned moves are not leading in the right direction, you have to modify your plan.

In summative evaluation, you debrief on the process used, identify the lessons learned in the experience, and ultimately integrate those lessons into your future activities. This activity is critical to being a learning organization.

The Future

If you are the CSE of an organization or hope to be one in the future, take to heart the importance of continually learning to master the profession of association management. Learn how to stay connected to your leadership, staff, and partners to build trust and avoid surprises.

Be intentional and strategic in your knowledge, relationships, and perspectives. Learn from every interaction. Observe and listen. Align your decisions to be consistent, since this is what sets the culture and brand of the organization and influences the profession as a whole.

The Authors

Cheryl O. Ronk, CMP, FASAE, CAE, is the chief staff executive of the Michigan Society of Association Executives (MSAE).

Susan S. Radwan, SMP, ARM, CAE, is the owner of Leading Edge Mentoring, an international consulting firm based in Grand Ledge, Michigan. Since 1996, Ronk and Radwan have partnered to teach the MSAE-sponsored CAE online exam preparation program, supporting CAE candidate learning around the world.

CHAPTER TWO

MISSION

Kerry C. Stackpole, FASAE, CAE

Mission is the pathway to the hearts and minds of your membership, donors, customers, stakeholders, and the public. Done well, a mission statement illuminates and reflects their values and aspirations. Without those aspirations, your organization is just another business enterprise, jockeying for revenues from a fickle marketplace defined by measures of lesser means and values.

Don't misunderstand. Believing in dynamic capitalism, revenue generation, and spirited entrepreneurship are noble causes. Believing that making money is the core purpose of not-for-profit organizations confuses their essential role of serving, instead of selling. If this is confusing, or seemingly at conflict with your experience, that is completely understandable. Not-for-profit organizations of all shapes, sizes, and purposes have partnered with commercial for-profit interests for decades to deliver perceived value to their members in the form of group buying discounts and other types of benefits.

We live in a world in which commerce crosses over into not-for-profit missions in ways few would have imagined. As just one example, the factories that bake Girl Scout cookies surely benefit financially from the $800 million generated by Girl Scout cookie sales to fund local Girl Scout councils. Cookie sales are the cornerstone of the group's ability to fulfill the Girl Scouting mission at the community level, "to build girls of courage, confidence and character, who make the world a better place."

The U.S. Internal Revenue Service has clear definitions of how it sees the role of tax-exempt organizations, which generally must file an annual Form 990 or Form 990-EZ information return with the IRS. For example,

- 501(c)(3): The exempt purposes set forth in section 501(c)(3) are charitable, religious, educational, scientific, literary, testing for public safety, fostering national or international amateur sports competition, and preventing cruelty to children or animals. The term *charitable* is used in its generally accepted legal sense and includes relief of the poor, the distressed, or the underprivileged; advancement of religion; advancement of education or science; erecting or maintaining public buildings, monuments, or works; lessening the burdens of government; lessening neighborhood tensions; eliminating prejudice and discrimination; defending human and civil rights secured by law; and combating community deterioration and juvenile delinquency.
- 501(c) 6: The Internal Revenue Code provides for the exemption of business leagues, chambers of commerce, real estate boards, boards of trade and professional football leagues, which are not organized for profit and no part of the net earnings of which inures to the benefit of any private shareholder or individual.

A business league is an association of people having some common business interest, the purpose of which is to promote such common interest and not to engage in a regular business of a kind ordinarily carried on for profit. Trade associations and professional associations are business leagues. To be exempt, a business league's activities must be devoted to improving business conditions of one or more lines of business as distinguished from performing particular services for individuals. No part of a business league's net earnings may inure to the benefit of any private shareholder or individual and it may not be organized for profit to engage in an activity ordinarily carried on for profit (even if the business is operated on a cooperative basis or produces only enough income to be self-sustaining).

Your organization can be tax-exempt without being not-for-profit, and vice versa—though most associations are both. The authority for tax exemption derives wholly from the federal government, whereas the categories of nonprofit or not-for-profit are—except in cases of quasi-governmental agencies (such as the American Red Cross)—granted exclusively by the corporate authority granted state government. In its simplest form, the designation of nonprofit or not-for-profit requires that no one who supports or serves the organization make a profit. While state statutes vary, none limit a not-for-profit organization's ability to earn a profit, create reserves, buy property, or otherwise engage in activities to support their mission and purpose. This unique distinction often serves to confuse board leaders, members, donors, stakeholders, and the general public. It is easy to understand why.

Federal law mandates certain limitations. In recent years the Internal Revenue Service has required tax-exempt organizations with gross income of $1,000 or more (gross income is gross receipts minus the cost of goods sold) from a regularly conducted unrelated trade or business to file Form 990-T and to pay taxes on that income. This amount has changed over time, and it's always good to confirm the reporting thresholds with your auditors. IRS regulations clearly define the rules. "Unrelated trade or business income is the gross income derived from any trade or business regularly conducted and not substantially related to the organization's exempt purpose or function (aside from the organization's need for income or funds or the use it makes of the profits)."

So how does a leader reconcile the increasingly blurred border between commerce and commitment—serving or selling—in a marketplace holding high expectations and demands for effective and efficient solutions to the challenges of an industry, profession, community, or charitable cause? As Socrates reminded us, the "beginning of wisdom is the definition of terms." In this case defining your mission is at the heart of it all.

Revisiting Mission

The mission in its most basic form defines why your organization exists and what you as an organization leader are here to do on behalf of all stakeholders.

The purpose of a mission statement is to define the organization's business. What are we are here to do? Who do we serve? How will we accomplish our purpose?

Mission is often intertwined with purpose and values. A scan of the leadership and management literature sometimes uses these words interchangeably.

Unless you were a founding member of your organization, you will most likely inherit the mission. It is exceedingly rare for mission to receive more than passing attention even as organizations grow and change and consider new strategies and directions over the course of their existence. Unlike the vision statement, which is often reworked to calibrate with strategy, mission is viewed as bedrock, underpinning the very reason for the existence of the organization. That need not be so.

One of the chief staff executive's responsibilities is to ensure that mission aligns with strategy, value, and purpose as well as with the activities and initiatives of the organization. If the elements are out of alignment, the task for bringing them back falls to the CSE and the governing body.

On occasion, even with a beneficial and clear mission, a revision or reconsideration may help bring greater focus and deliver significant benefit. One such example is the American Red Cross, whose original 1900 charter articulated the mission, "To furnish volunteer aid to the sick and wounded of armies in time of war, in accordance with the spirit and conditions of the conference of Geneva of October, 1863." In subsequent revisions, the Red Cross came to today's considerably broader mission: "The American Red Cross prevents and alleviates human suffering in the face of emergencies by mobilizing the power of volunteers and the generosity of donors."

Take a moment to consider these two mission statements. More than anything, seen in comparative fashion, they acknowledge the evolving purpose and goals of the American Red Cross in an understandable and clear fashion. While not widely understood, mission is taking on greater significance as members, donors, contributors, and stakeholders consider their decisions to engage with membership and charitable organizations. Research by ASAE explored this question in the course of collecting data from 16,944 individuals to create *The Decision to Join* study, written in 2007 by James Dalton and Monica Dignam.[1]

In their research, Dalton and Dignam point out that associations face a dilemma in answering questions surrounding mission. While individual perspective is a consideration, they point out that the real organization question comes down to, "Who are you and what utility do you offer?" The need for a member, donor, contributor, or stakeholder focus—a customer-oriented view—is critical to overcoming the inherent limitations imposed by a "producer oriented" view.

The reasons this becomes so important are made clear by shifts in the way the next generation of members, donors, contributors, and stakeholders are likely to engage with associations and charitable organizations in the future.

Charitable giving is developing a new face as the new wealth displaces the old wealth as major sources of philanthropy and giving. Where the names Rockefeller, Ford, Mellon, and Carnegie were once the predominant sources of vast giving power, they are being supplanted by new names such as Gates, Bono, Buffett, and Case, and organizations created by celebrities such as Sonja Sohn, whose experience on the streets of Baltimore filming the HBO hit series *The Wire* inspired her to create Rewired for Change to empower at-risk youth, families, and communities living in underserved areas through educational programming, community building support, and media and social advocacy.

There are new philanthropy models emerging as well. Venture Philanthropy Partners (VPP), created by technology moguls Raul Fernandez, Senator Mark Warner, and Mario Morino, invests in high-performing nonprofit organizations that are serving the core healthy developmental, learning, and educational needs of children from low-income families in the greater Washington, D.C., area. Rather than serve as a funder, VPP aspires to serve as a trusted advisor, helping great leaders build stronger, more effective, more enduring organizations to better serve children. The venture fund's investments are not intended to fund program costs. Instead, the focus of every VPP investment is helping leaders build the strength of the organization behind their programs, often referred to as "organizational capacity."

Mission and Leadership

One of the greatest challenges for leaders is honoring the mission of the organization as part of day-to-day leadership. Keeping the reason your organization exists at the forefront of your leadership may seem unnecessary; however, it is shockingly easy for mission to be subverted in the pursuit of competing needs.

Every organization needs resources to accomplish its mission. The two largest are human (members, volunteers, donors, staff) and financial (revenues, contributions) capital. In pursuit of securing these critical resources, leaders wrestle with a daily barrage of opportunities to exchange access to the organization's human capital typically for financial gain. Consider the number of tax-exempt organizations offering health, life, and property insurance programs; group buying discounts; 401K plan administration; bookstore publications; or other professional services to their members, donors, or other stakeholders.

Mark Levin, CAE, CSP, is an association executive and professional speaker who specializes in helping associations grow their membership. When reviewing membership literature as part of his membership workshops, he is fond of asking association leaders the question, "What is all of this stuff?," referring to the myriad programs and services offered universally by organizations. Is your organization's rental car discounting that much better than another organization's? How about book discounts? Can you truly compete with Amazon, and should you try, if it's not a core component of your mission?

As leaders it's easy to rationalize our decisions to add yet another discount program or to justify the next "partnership" because in the broadest form it leans into our mission to educate, advocate, or enhance our member's or donor's interests. The real question is, is it at the core of our mission? Straying outside the strictest interpretation of your mission may be a resource necessity; however, straying too far may bring the unwanted attention of regulators and the sudden departure of valued members, donors, or stakeholders.

In 2012, leaders of the Susan G. Komen Foundation, the nation's largest nonprofit devoted to preventing, treating, and curing breast cancer announced the organization was eliminating $680,000 in funding for breast cancer screenings conducted by Planned Parenthood. The foundation issued a statement at the time saying it cut funding to Planned Parenthood as part of its effort to "evolve to best meet the needs of the women we serve and most fully advance our mission." While Komen ultimately reinstated the funding grant, the damage to the foundation's "charitable brand" and reported declines in contribution resulted in major leadership realignments within the organization and prompted cutbacks in other grant giving.

In 1997, members and outsiders criticized marketing plans by the American Medical Association to allow Sunbeam Corporation exclusive use of the AMA logo on its medical wares. Although the AMA did not plan to test the devices, the deal was expected to bring in millions of dollars for the association. In the resulting furor, there were allegations the AMA was seeking deals with private companies to make up financial shortfalls resulting from declining membership. Ultimately the debacle cost three association leaders their jobs, the CEO stepped down, and the American Medical Association found itself in the midst of a crisis affecting both the board's oversight and the organization's reputation.

While there are likely other situations of similar nature, the real purpose of sharing these stories is to encourage leaders to exert a higher degree of caution and due diligence in decision making when considering activities and services outside the circle of your organization's primary mission.

Aligning Mission with Work

Working to ensure the integrity of mission to the vision and goals of your organization is vitally important to avoid critical missteps. One of the ways leaders ensure the integrity of an organization's efforts and its mission is to conduct a regular audit of the organization's products and services to examine both their value and their alignment with organizational mission. While often described as "mission impossible," sunsetting programs that do not align with your mission is an essential part of overall strategy. In some instances, the shifting needs of your membership, donors, or stakeholders may require a revision to the organization mission. A regular review of the activities of your group gives you a basis to explore, examine, and act as necessary to ensure that you remain on course.

In his research book *Good to Great and the Social Sectors*, author Jim Collins makes the point that aligning purpose and mission relies on asking the right questions. Collins in his work on aligning actions and values suggests leaders ask themselves and those around them, "If these are our core values and this is fundamentally why we exist, what are the obstacles that get in our way?"[2] It is not an idle question.

As a leader you are likely familiar with the idea that you cannot truly motivate anyone to do anything. You can, however, remove the barriers to motivation to encourage forward progress. Determining precisely what allows your organization to thrive and removing the obstacles to success offers a parallel pathway worthy of consideration and implementation.

The Changing World of Mission and Leadership

Over the past century, as businesses and professionals formed not-for-profit organizations to represent, support, and sustain their chosen industry or profession they have more actively engaged in bringing along the operational structures, titles, and frameworks to many not-for-profit organizations. The chief staff executive's title has followed a historical migration from secretary or executive secretary to managing director, then executive director, on to executive vice president and, for many organizations—trade, professional, or philanthropic—finally to president and chief executive officer.

This has led to considerable confusion among board members and other stakeholders who imagine their association or society is aligned with a "bottom line" business-like structure, instead of a more diffuse community service structure addressing and serving the needs of a broad-based group of individuals, organizations, and communities. That confusion often manifests when a board member or stakeholder suggests or attempts to impose structures, frameworks, or policies of the industry or profession they serve on the association, professional society, or charitable entity.

The confusion has also been exacerbated as both privately held firms and publicly traded companies have entered the "membership" space. For many, it began with the charge card company American Express shifting its advertising and marketing messages in 1987 by asserting that cardholders were "card members" with the ubiquitous tag line, "membership has its privileges." They were not alone.

On a growing basis, health insurance providers, Internet service providers, airline loyalty programs, social networks, and commerce platforms are using the term *members* to describe their customer base. Among the largest in the private sector are the warehouse-style stores, including B.J's, Sam's Club, and Costco. For Costco, the high level, "executive member," generates 60 percent of its overall revenues. Costco's mission statement puts its members at the top:

> Costco's mission is to continually provide our members with quality goods and services at the lowest possible prices. In order to achieve our mission we will conduct our business with the following Code of Ethics in mind:
>
> - Obey the law
> - Take care of our members
> - Take care of our employees
> - Respect our vendors
>
> If we do these four things throughout our organization, then we will realize our ultimate goal, which is to reward our shareholders.

A critical responsibility and obligation of the association's chief staff executive is to ensure that all stakeholders have a consensus and understanding with clarity about the mission of the organization.

What's different is that unlike privately held companies or publicly traded corporations that ultimately have one "bottom line"—returning value to the owners and shareholders—trade, professional, or cause-related organizations more often come with multiple "bottom lines." The absence of shareholders' demand for dividends and a return on investment likely comes with myriad different and more demanding expectations.

The Board and the Mission

While it may be unlikely you see yourself as the steward of the mission of your organization, it is a critical role you need to embrace as a leader in the tax-exempt sector and for your organization. If your first thought is "seriously?" you are forgiven. It's not like you don't have enough responsibilities and demands on your intellectual and physical horsepower. Time is a limited commodity, and it's likely your calendar is jammed full of important and pressing appointments and activities.

So pause for a moment to consider just where your board sits in regard to mission. In today's demanding environment, it's unlikely—though not impossible—your board members ever give mission a second thought. Asking board members to write down the mission of the organization often results in looks of confusion, repeated scratch-outs on the paper in front of them, and finally a sigh of resignation when they realize they don't actually know. I'm not being critical of volunteers or governing boards; rather I am pointing out the real importance of your role as a leader and steward.

By the very nature of their roles, board members are not focused on the mission and purpose of your organization on a regular basis. In instances when the board meets only a few times a year, the gap is greater still. As one volunteer director pointed out to me, "Since we only meet face-to-face twice a year, every time I come to a meeting I see the enormous changes in our industry."

Board members are focused on their own professional practices, companies, personal lives, and communities long before they bring their expertise and ideas to the board meeting for their associations. The notion that *where we stand depends on where we sit* can routinely be applied to those who gather in boardrooms. Each person brings his or her own experiences, frustrations, accomplishments, biases, and, in the language of the day, agendas. How those things affect the organization and influence the meeting outcomes are mostly uncertain.

What is certain is that as a leader, you have the ability to influence their thinking, introduce innovative approaches, and present new ways of thinking about how the group can best contribute to and drive forward the organization and its mission. In my own experience, boards regularly struggle with the inherent conflict between the for-profit environment many inhabit ("the selling world") and the not-for-profit tax-exempt environment ("the serving world"), especially when the mission is less than clear or out of step with the direction in which the organization is actually moving.

As leader, you are the chief interpreter of the mission for the board. Board members look to you for the leadership and direction essential to the proper functioning of the organization. Lose sight of the primary mission or fail to engage the board in adapting the mission to new circumstances and you run the serious risks of derailing both your own professional growth and the organization's future.

A critical part of your personal mission has to be to fully comprehend the contexts your members, donors, and stakeholders are bringing into the room whenever you gather together. Your communication on mission and direction must reflect their reality at least in part to garner their attention. In one organization where the board membership was entirely composed of direct marketers who measured the value and response of every promotional mailing or communiqué, failing to demonstrate attention to a corresponding metric for the association's mission resulted in a complete disconnect between the chief staff executive and the board.

Remember, where you stand has a direct correlation to where you sit.

According to the research conducted by ASAE in support of the best-selling classic *7 Measures of Success: What Remarkable Organizations Do That Others Don't*, leading organizations look at membership as constituencies to serve versus markets to sell to. The research data strongly suggest that aligning mission and purpose drives membership, membership retention, and financial results. In Chapter Three of *7 Measures*, the writers note the extraordinary focus leaders in the study group bring to member service, describing it as "an association of the members, by the members, for the members."[3]

Remarkable associations and their leaders work diligently to "build their structures, processes, and interactions—their entire culture around—assessing and fulfilling members' needs and expectations."

Linking your reason for being to the hard work of examining your products and services against the light of fulfilling your mission will create some of the most difficult conversations leaders and their boards will have. Straying too far from mission even when the organization needs the funds has the potential to create a disconnect with the membership and serious declines in member retention. As the authors point out in *7 Measures of Success*, such actions serve only to delay the inevitable rather than bolster true financial strength.

The staff and leaders of the Girl Scouts of the USA consistently ask two questions in examining their new initiatives:

1. How do we need to change to stay true to our mission?
2. What do girls need today for us to achieve the mission we have always had?

While the questions do not preclude change, they bring a laser-like focus to the values of the organization and hold the idea of reconsidering mission at bay until they can be answered fully and completely.

Mission, especially in membership organizations, will likely take on greater importance and significance in the decades ahead than it perhaps has before. The demographics of our organizations are shifting. Where the "baby boom" generation had a strong commitment to belonging, the generations to follow are more wary of political and religious institutions.

The Pew Research Center, examining social and demographic trends of young adults in the eighteen to thirty-three age range, discovered they are relatively unattached to organized politics and religion, linked by social media, burdened by debt, distrustful of people, in no rush to marry—yet remain optimistic about the future.[4] In the future, it's quite likely membership will no longer be about belonging; it will be about believing.

Mission of the Future

So where does the evolving landscape leave the leaders of today's tax-exempt organizations? In part, it leaves you thinking hard about the vitality and relevance of the mission of your organization to its current members, prospective members, donors, and stakeholders. Mission will increasingly be the motivating tool both for membership and for growing commitment to the organization. Success will not come from adapting more "business-like models" for operations or management; rather it will come from providing a platform that serves to inspire and encourage commitment from the generations to come.

In schools across America, the value of community service is integrated into curricula and class activities beginning in elementary school. Helping others in less fortunate circumstances, those affected by natural disasters, and others in need is a common value shared throughout society. Illuminating this shared value and igniting action to bring real meaning to the efforts of members and volunteer leaders is the challenge at hand.

Every association, professional society, and charitable organization has a greater purpose beyond ensuring the continuity of its enterprise. Thinking about horizons is a good metaphor for what is essential for leaders. It has been said, "Good leaders hit targets no one else can hit and great leaders hit targets no one else can see." The notion of things beyond the horizon is a powerful incentive and tool for leaders to use in imagining their organization's mission and future.

So much success in today's tax-exempt environment relies on innovating by shifting the basic rules of that marketplace. While incremental change may garner some progress and offer added rewards, those dreamers, thinkers, and innovators who imagine a totally different marketplace are the ones reaping an increasingly larger share of both community capital and progress. It does not require too much reflection to remember diseases no one believed could be cured, technologies that would never work, or the collapse of long-standing regulatory frameworks. For example, if you are the leader of the Taxi Driver's Association, the technology that allows Uber, the transportation service, to enable passengers to summon a ride using a smartphone app creates a significant and serious competitive threat to your membership and perhaps your mission. The question on the horizon for your association is, What changes or adaptations could you make to give your members more ready means to compete by gathering access to the information they need and want from your organization?

Making your association member-centric is essential to your success. How many times have you found yourself stewing about the "four-hour window" that utilities, repair services, and other vendors require to schedule your service or delivery? Looking closer to home, what systems or processes do you have in place when a new membership application arrives at headquarters?

Responsiveness + Resolution = Return Member

Successful associations find the right metrics and measure, measure, measure. One of the challenges in looking over the horizon is imagining what issues or problems may arise for your members or donors. Some are easy to anticipate and some considerably more difficult because they reflect the unique manner in which your member uses the resources of the association and its products or services.

Associations willing to rethink their member process, consider new approaches, and measure their accomplishments from the member's perspective will gain new insight about potential opportunities and risks on the horizon and ways to solidify and strengthen their mission.

None of this is a guarantee of success. It is more akin to operating a compass. You have to learn how to use it proficiently before it yields any meaningful results. Failure is inevitable at some point along the way. Know it. Work like crazy to avoid it. Prepare for it in any case. Finally, do not get caught in the trap of separating mission from strategy and most certainly not execution. It is a myth these processes could or should somehow be separated. If you haven't taken all of the variables of your culture, organization dynamics, demographics, and attitudes into consideration right alongside mission, you're missing a huge opportunity and a huge point of leverage.

The old axiom, "There is no such thing as a lost opportunity, because someone always finds it"? Believe it. Opportunity, innovation, and success are linked as tools to help organizations grow by standing on the bedrock of their organization's mission. The growing number of for-profit enterprises adopting social missions and membership models increases by the day. While they may not cast a shadow on your organization today, they undoubtedly create an opportunity to create confusion in the marketplace. It is not too early to have begun making certain your mission is optimized to resonate with members, donors, and stakeholder for things to come tomorrow and from well over the horizon.

Notes

1. J. Dalton and M. Dignam, *The Decision to Join: How Individuals Determine Value and Why They Choose to Belong* (Washington, DC: ASAE Association Management Press, 2007).
2. J. Collins, "Aligning Values and Action." June 2000. Web. http://www.jimcollins.com/article_topics/articles/aligning-action.html.
3. ASAE and The Center for Association Leadership, *7 Measures of Success: What Remarkable Organizations Do That Others Don't* (Washington, DC: ASAE Association Management Press, 2006), 24.
4. Pew Research Center, "Millennials in Adulthood." Mar. 7, 2014. Web. http://www.pewsocialtrends.org/2014/03/07/millennials-in-adulthood/.

The Author

Kerry C. Stackpole, FASAE, CAE, is an entrepreneurial association CEO respected by his peers and colleagues for his uncanny ability to solve the toughest business problems. His unique skills of helping associations envision a future no one else sees and inventing concepts not previously imagined powers his work with boards, volunteers, and top executives.

CHAPTER THREE

MANAGEMENT

Mark Engle, DM, FASAE, CAE

Association management requires knowledge and skill sets particular to this business segment, but beginning with a definition of management in a larger context creates a useful foundation for the key principles and practices covered in this chapter.

Peter Drucker, cited by *Business Week* as "the man who invented management," identified the following five basic tasks of managers: (1) sets objectives, (2) organizes, (3) motivates and communicates, (4) measures, and (5) develops people.[1] Simply stated, management means "getting the work done." A manager is someone who leads the charge. In the association arena, management is led by the chief executive officer, also known as the chief staff executive, president, executive vice president, or executive director. (For the sake of clarity, *chief staff executive*, or *CSE*, is used in this book to distinguish the staff executive role from that of the chief elected officer.)

Management of Associations Compared with Nonprofits and Corporations

Although it may be true that all managers should be responsible for handling the five basic tasks cited by Drucker, it also is helpful to understand the subtle distinctions that separate how boards and managers in the association world function compared with their counterparts in the much larger nonprofit and corporate arenas. In the association world, when the chief elected officer (chair) and the CSE are functioning well together there is a correlation of high-quality decision making for the organization.[2] The CSE provides a key support function for the chief elected officer. Research indicates that exceptional chairs had the most impact on (1) clarifying the board's role in the organization vis-à-vis management, (2) setting the broad direction for the organization, (3) helping the board become organized and efficient, meeting its fiduciary responsibilities, overseeing the organization's performance, and attracting top-quality board members.[3] Strategic board contributions were directly linked with organizational performance.[4] The three key functions identified here require the two leaders, the chair and CSE, to work in partnership or the oars will be rowing out of synch with much wasted time and effort. (More about the chair-CSE relationship is covered in Chapter Fifteen.)

One key distinction separating associations, nonprofits, and corporations is the pace of change. According to association governance and leadership consultant Glenn Tecker and colleagues, "Risks tend to occur every two to three years in the association world, but every 30 to 60 days in the corporate world. Members, therefore, are accustomed to much quicker decision processes" (when coming from the corporate world into the association community).[5] Making decisions on key strategic issues in the association world can take up to two years because the process requires achieving consensus among a group of peers.[6] Although the board of directors is the principal decision-making group, its members generally operate by making decisions through a consensus-building process. Getting buy-in usually starts with the board but often requires approval or at least support from the membership to embrace a significant change. The process can be time consuming but ensures support in implementing a decision.

A second differentiator relates to the customer base. In corporate America, the customer has many options when searching for a product or service. Product benefits typically are easy to calculate and compare. Although the face of competition for associations is rapidly changing, "associations are different from such organizations as for-profit businesses (and most other nonprofits) in that their populations of owners, customers, and workforce are one and the same."[7] Members have a relationship with the association because they have already made a financial commitment by paying dues. Associations rely on member input to design, shape, and create product offerings, which they, in turn, purchase.

"A competitive advantage for associations is the aggregate intellectual capital of their memberships, their energy as communities with a common purpose, and their credibility as voluntary institutions."[8] Good management brings together the brightest minds in the whole industry or profession to develop products or position statements. High-performing associations recognize that although competition exists in the marketplace, the association should provide an environment in which professionals support the "greater good" for the industry. In their voluntary roles, volunteers are loyal to the association, not to a specific company or employer.

How Boards Affect Association Management

Key differentiators between corporate America and associations include board turnover, the role of the board, and decision-making hierarchy. In corporate America, turnover in the boardroom generally is viewed negatively. The primary role of the board in the corporate world is to monitor management and guide decisions toward maximizing shareholder wealth.[9] In the general business world, organizational charts indicate decision-making hierarchy, as ultimate authority generally falls to an individual even if a group informs decisions. The rate of risk facing corporate America versus the nonprofit world also greatly affects the decision-making process.

In associations, the steady turnover of board members and officers creates a "rolling culture" that keeps boards in flux[10] yet often stimulates new ideas due to new eyes, ears, and approaches. The result is that management, particularly the CSE, provides constancy and continuity in the larger management processes. The primary role of the board in the association community is to examine the environment, set strategy, and attend to fiduciary functions.[11] Contrasting with corporate America, the legal definition of a nonprofit organization has been expanded to include "any activity or entity that does not involve the distribution of surpluses through dividends."[12]

Differences also exist in decision making between the corporate and the nonprofit worlds. In the association world, it is the CSE's role to bridge the corporate and association environments and promote wise and consequential decision making. Even within the broader nonprofit community, there are role differences for the CSE.[13] With associations, the board is the ultimate authority and is composed of peers.

In the association community, even compared to the broader nonprofit community in which fundraising is key,[14] the primary revenue streams stem from membership dues and conferences or trade shows (associations derive more than 50 percent of income from these sources).[15] Therefore, the CSE's time is invested in building programs and products. As the nature of association work is considered to be knowledge work (for example, the development of practice standards or educational content),[16] volunteering in a professional society is characterized as professional development or continuing education.[17]

The primary role of the board is to govern by setting direction, allocating resources, ensuring compliance, and evaluating the CSE, who reports to the board.

The board must provide clarity of purpose and direction to the workforce, such as task forces and committee members (without performing committee work).

The Role of the CSE

The CSE's role is to position the board for success (which means enabling the board to make wise decisions on consequential issues), implement the decisions, and lead the staff. The board decides the direction and allocates key resources (dollars and time), and the staff executes the strategic direction. To be effective, the CSE must be in lock-step with the board and be seen as a trusted partner in every sense. He or she must inform the board's decisions by providing pertinent data, information, and recommendations, and ensuring that board members adequately understand the key issues at hand.

According to Richard Chait and colleagues, "nonprofit managers have become leaders. CSEs are expected to shape agendas, allocate attention, and define problems."[18] Research indicates that high-performing boards (in conjunction with the CSE) use a filtering mechanism to determine which issues merit board attention and which belong to staff. The following seven questions are useful to consider during this process: (1) Is the issue strategic or operational? (2) Is the issue on mission for your organization? (3) Is the magnitude of the issue consequential? (4) How significant are the potential consequences in making this decision? (5) What is the potential for failure or risk? (6) Is the issue precedent setting? and (7) Is the issue course changing for the organization?[19] Running new issues or opportunities through this filter helps keep distractions from consuming valuable board time. It also empowers staff with latitude to make decisions in an efficient manner.

FIGURE 3.1. CSE CONTINUUM.

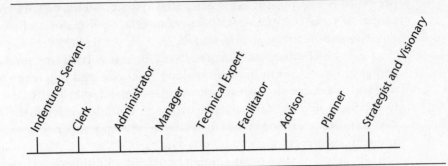

Understanding and distinguishing the role of the CSE in the eyes of the board is empowering to the executive. Glenn Tecker and colleagues use a chart to highlight the CSE role continuum (Figure 3.1), which maps an association CSE progressing from indentured servant to strategist and visionary.[20] Although sometimes a CSE can operate at the two extremes during a board meeting, the chart is helpful in identifying the key role that the board desires of its CSE and that the CSE should attain. Important leadership traits, such as facilitator and advisor, become more vital as you move to the right in the continuum.

Some association CSEs hail from the profession or industry the association serves, while other CSEs come from the field of association management. According to *7 Measures of Success,* both types of CSE have produced high-performing associations.[21] Regardless of the career path, association CSEs, as business managers, need to consider business, human capital skills, and soft skills as part of their daily practice.

Because associations are nonprofit corporations, some leaders discount the need to be profitable and undervalue the programs and services of the association. Managing to margin is a concept that encourages that all costs (including the value of staff time) of the association are adequately covered and also provides reserves at the end of the day for the future growth or survival of the organization. The CSE needs both strategic and financial acumen and an appreciation for best practices in association management. Operating in the strategic realm, the CSE must push the vision but be grounded in reality (for instance, affordability or capacity to achieve), while being action-oriented.

A sound financial understanding is essential to running a business. The CSE needs to consider, Is the organization financially healthy or in need of a turnaround? Do you have sufficient financial strength to invest in new programs or continue offering programs that are subsidized? Are you allocating all costs (including staff time and other overhead) to projects to ensure you fully measure program ROI?

CSEs need adequate financial tools to assess program profitability and assign priorities in decision making. Accurate and timely reports are needed to ensure that there are no surprises for the board. Managing to a budget is important to gain trust and confidence from the board. It is important to deliver any bad news early with accurate assessments and course-correcting recommendations. While the board has a fiduciary responsibility for maintaining financial accountability and exercising due diligence with respect to use of the association's resources, CSEs have financial management responsibilities and are accountable to the board for the financial performance and reporting of the corporation.

Although financial management is covered in detail later, understanding a profit-and-loss statement and providing accurate, pertinent, and timely financial reports are essential to developing trust between the board and the CSE. The CSE must ensure that the board understands that controls are in place and that they have enough financial detail to allocate resources and make key decisions that reflect the financial position of the organization and programs.

The CSE needs to exemplify a constantly learning culture that is creative and self-sustaining. Peter Senge's concept of the learning organization is to create an environment "where people are engaged in their work and committed to the vision of the organization."[22] This goes hand in hand with ASAE's research in *7 Measures,* which encourages CSEs to be idea brokers. The CSE must not only understand the organization's vision but also be able to engage others in defining, refining, and responding to that vision and all it entails.[23] A warning to CSEs who have emerged from the profession or industry that the association serves: the culture of an association may be vastly different than the culture of the field it serves. For instance, emergency room physicians face crisis situations all day long. Constantly managing an association in a crisis environment would be highly ineffective. For many associations, crisis management is not a routine occurrence; however, if you have a significant advocacy agenda, crisis management would likely be a valued skill set for leadership.

The second skill category centers on human capital development and values. Recruiting, supporting, and promoting top staff talent is a necessary ingredient for high-performing associations. This also is reflected in the volunteer element of associations. The CSE should be engaged in the nominations process, not just when the nominating committee meets, by identifying and cultivating future volunteer leaders.

If you are the CSE, the staff reports to you or through you. The CSE is the primary interface with the board and the ultimate staff authority and responsible party. With very few exceptions (perhaps a medical staff officer) all staff report to the CSE. The same theory holds for consultants and contractors. CSEs serve at the pleasure of the board (or executive committee—not just the chief volunteer). The staff and extensions of the staff, such as contractors or consultants, ultimately report through the CSE. The CSE is accountable for performance to the board. An annual CSE evaluation is an important tool to gauge success and performance (see Figure 3.2).

FIGURE 3.2. EXECUTIVE DIRECTOR EVALUATION TEMPLATE (PARTIAL).

First Quarter Evaluation

Management & Leadership

1. Please rate the following:

	Does Not Meet Expectations	Meets Expectations	Exceeds Expectations	Not Applicable
Possesses a good understanding of issues affecting the association and field	○	○	○	○
Serves as a source of knowledge and guidance regarding association and non-profit management practices and principles	○	○	○	○
Performs functions within scope of responsibilities	○	○	○	○
Responds to requests in a timely and appropriate matter	○	○	○	○
Demonstrates resourcefulness, employing an action-oriented approach to management of issues and ideas	○	○	○	○
Utilizes expertise of professional staff and engages outside counsel/consultation when necessary	○	○	○	○
Shares information and encourages dialogue and deliberation as part of decision-making	○	○	○	○

A separate evaluation of association services (that is, staff functions) is a good management tool to guide the CSE in determining if service issues or staff issues exist. The sample evaluation in Figure 3.3, while framed in an association management company context, is adaptable and useful whether such services are provided by external or internal sources.

The third skill category is the soft skills of leadership. In his seminal study on great companies, Jim Collins introduced the concept of Level 5 leadership (the highest level in a hierarchy of executive

FIGURE 3.3. 2013—AMC'S EVALUATION OF SERVICES AND OUTCOMES PROVIDED BY AMC.

2013 - AMCs Evaluation of Services and Outcomes Provided by AMC

Page description:

This evaluation is intended to elicit your level of satisfaction with the quality of service you receive from Association Management Center. Your candid feedback and suggestions will help ensure that AMC is continuously improving its professional services and value to meet *XXXXX* evolving needs. Respondent identification is optional should you wish to comment anonymously.

This survey should take less than 15 minutes to complete. We ask you to submit it by *XXXXXXX*

1.

BOARD/COMMITTEE SUPPORT

	Exceeds Expectations	Fully Meets Expectations	Meets Most Expectations	Meets Some Expectations	Does Not Meet Expectation
Board Support *	○	○	○	○	○
Board Meeting Support*	○	○	○	○	○
Committee Support*	○	○	○	○	○

capabilities identified during Collins's research). "Level 5 leaders blend the paradoxical combination of deep *personal humility* with *intense professional will*."[24] By crediting others for their organization's success and taking blame for poor results, Level 5 leaders are able to manifest humility.[25] Humility is a key trait in successful association managers. The concept of ensuring that the board and volunteers receive credit for success is a recipe for success in this profession.

The variable terms of board members versus the longer tenures of staff often result in a tension between the CSE and the board regarding authority. Two attributes of a CSE are elemental to reducing tension in the board-CSE relationship—self-denial and respect for authority. Self-denial in the form of humility means not owning an idea, project, or the podium (taking responsibility is different than feeling a sense of ownership). Decisions are more readily accepted and easily implemented when volunteer leadership has ownership rather than when staff is seen as driving the bus. Regarding respect for authority, this means acknowledging that the organization belongs to members and their elected board, as opposed to being "owned" by the staff or CSE. It is often said that the quickest way to get fired as a CSE is to make the mistake of thinking the organization is "yours."

Attributes such as being a good listener and good communicator also rank high as traits of high-performing CSEs. Being politically astute is a valuable asset. Determining whether the CSE is out in front of the association may be necessary but also may make the CSE a target. Defining the parameters of CSE spokesmanship and ambassadorship with volunteer leaders is an important issue to navigate. Additional desirable traits of high-performing CSEs include being authentic, relational, and trustworthy. Being a consensus builder helps the board maintain high performance. The last and perhaps most important of the primary responsibilities of the CSE is to guard the values of the organization, which are dictated and articulated by the board.

Association Management Models

According to ASAE, there are four primary staffing options for associations, each with its own advantages and disadvantages.[26] The four options are

- All volunteers
- Volunteers with a skeletal staff
- Association management company
- Stand-alone association

Volunteer efforts can be erratic and difficult to control or predict. In addition, there is little continuity as officers and board members rotate quickly, and even the phone number and address of the organization may have to be updated yearly. A better management option is to have volunteers working with a skeletal staff. Usually this means a paid administrator works on a part- or full-time basis, either in an office or out of his or her home.

Another management option is contracting with an association management company to manage the association, including services and benefits such as a headquarters location, professional staff with association management expertise, program management, and so forth. Many groups are not aware that such companies exist, but they can be found in most major cities.

When making arrangements with a management firm, certain areas need to be investigated by the board or search committee. It is most important that the board investigate the financial stability of the firm because the association may be expected to pay association expenses in advance. In addition, they should learn how the financial accounts of separate clients are handled (for example, is there pooling of funds?); check the depth of staffing to ensure that it's adequate to carry out all association operations; and understand how the firm makes its profits (for example, in management fees, markups of products or services, commissions, or some other manner). Finally, the board should have a clear understanding of the terms of the agreement under which they would work. The AMC Institute provides an accreditation program in conjunction with ANSI (http://www.amcinstitute.org/?Accreditation) that establishes standards of good practice for the association management company community.

A stand-alone organization means a fully operational office staffed by full-time professional and support employees. Obviously, this is the most expensive option, but it has advantages. You can locate the office wherever you wish, and choose exactly the kind of people you want working on organization activities. You have direct control over employees, costs, and purchasing decisions.

You will have large expenses to get an office up and running, regardless of whether you lease or purchase equipment. Your board must devote a considerable amount of time to hiring and evaluating your chief staff executive. Furthermore, you must have expert help to file the necessary papers to employ staff, withhold Social Security, provide benefits, and so on. This means that you may have to pay for more staff than you really need to.[27]

Alignment and Execution of Operations with Mission, Goals, and Core Competencies

The guiding instrument that helps focus the management of an association is a strategic plan. A strategic plan defines what an organization will do in the next three to five years to move closer to their vision of what they want to be and is addressed in Chapter Eleven. It is designed to be a living document for a learning organization, and it should be updated annually. Properly conceived, supported, and implemented, a strategic plan is a critical tool for the alignment and execution of the time, talent, and treasury available to an association. Figure 3.4 indicates how integral the plan is to determining action plans and budgets, driving committee or task force work groups, and organizing board meeting agendas.

FIGURE 3.4. INTEGRATION OF STRATEGIC PLAN.

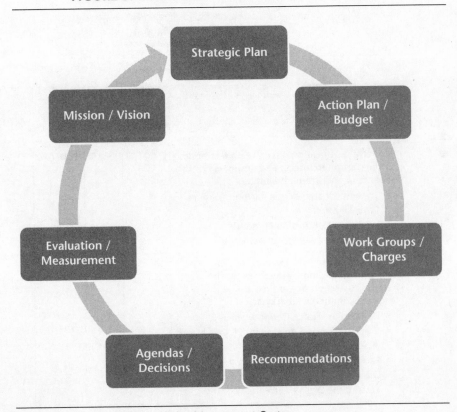

Source: Anne Cordes, CAE, Association Management Center.

While the board should access a summary plan, the CSE should lead the staff through development of action plans, complete with tactics, budget detail, staff assignments, and timelines.

Figure 3.5 is an example of a partial action plan.

In addition to driving the day-to-day operations of the staff and organization, the budget process, and evaluation of performance against the strategic objectives or goals, the plan should also drive board meeting agendas. (See sidebar sample, "MCA Vision.") To address key visionary issues, it is important to focus energy and board meeting time on the larger issues rather than fine details, which can prevent a board from seeing the big picture and a vision for the future. The plan prioritizes and communicates strategic objectives and aids in the allocation of budget dollars and staff time. Effective managers create operational plans to

FIGURE 3.5. SAMPLE ACTION PLAN.

NATIONAL FRAME BUILDING ASSOCIATION

Strategic Action Plan

Goal 1: Building decision-maker predominantly select post-frame construction because of its advantages: versatility, cost-effectiveness, durability, and sustainability.	Timeline	Lead	Cost	Status
Objective 1. Education: Increase understanding on the part of architects and engineers of the benefits of post-frame building. • Trade show attendance: 4 Wood Solution Fairs, Regional AIA • Webinars: Conduct 3 per month • Develop new webinar presentation	Q4 2103	John R	$116,089	
Objective 2. Research: Increase use of post-frame building by overcoming the barriers to acceptance of post-frame in targeted commercial markets. • Update Post-Frame Design Manual • Conduct Thermal Analysis for PF Ceiling and Wall Assembles • Package and present data from the Diaphragm and Shear Wall Performance Tests to the Design Community	Q4 2013	John R	$108,444	

achieve the strategic objectives and align the work with the goals and objectives of the organization (see sidebar "Board Meetings Focused on Strategic Objectives").

◆ ◆ ◆

MCA Vision: Metal Is the Construction Material of Choice for the Building Envelope

    I. Call to Order—John Miller, Chairman—8:00 A.M.

   II. Welcome and Opening Remarks—Miller

  III. Antitrust Briefing—John Kelly, Esq.

  IV. Generative Discussion

      a. Future Skilled Workforce Shortage (How are member companies impacted—their employees, their customers' workforce? Will there be enough skilled workers to install our high-end products?)

      b. Implications of Commercial Construction Rebound in 2015 (Where is MCA vulnerable with the forecast of another year of no growth in the market: membership, trade show, and other programs? What are the implications of no growth to member companies?)

   V. Financial Overview—John Smith, Treasurer

      *August Statement and 2013 Year-End Forecast

  VI. Strategic Objective 1—Market Development

      All significant stakeholder groups within the construction industry are convinced of the advantages of using metal in the building envelope.

      a. Residential Issues and Opportunities—(Council chair and staff liaison)

      b. Commercial Issues and Opportunities—(Council chair and staff liaison)

      c. Insulated Panels Issues and Opportunities—(Council chair and staff liaison)

  VII. Strategic Objective 2—Advocacy/Public Policy

      MCA is the recognized leader influencing public policy affecting the use of metal in the building envelope.

      a. Legislative Update—(Committee chair and staff liaison)

      b. Research and Code Initiatives—(Committee chair and staff liaison)

 VIII. Strategic Objective 3—Membership

      MCA's membership has grown in quality and engagement through penetration of new and existing industry segments.

      a. Membership Report—(Committee chair and staff liaison)

      b. Communications Report—(Committee chair and staff liaison)

  IX. Council and Committee Initiatives

      Issues requiring board direction or decisions.

      a. Product Council A—(Council chair and staff liaison)

      b. Product Council B—(Council chair and staff liaison)

      c. Governance—(Committee chair and staff liaison)

      d. Program—(Committee chair and staff liaison)

      e. Statistics—(Committee chair and staff liaison)

   X.   2014 Budget Discussion/Approval
   XI. Consent Agenda
       a. Approval of Minutes—May 11, 2013
       b. Committee Appointments
       c. Trade Show Report
       d. Committee Reports
       e. Future Board Meetings Schedule
   XII. Other Business
       *Board Evaluation Discussion—Miller and Engle
   XIII. Adjournment—11:30 A.M.

◆ ◆ ◆

Board Meetings Focused on Strategic Objectives

During its strategic planning, the Metal Construction Association's (MCA's) board articulated three goals—grow the market, advocate for favorable codes and standards, and be the home for all manufacturers in the metal construction community. The strategic plan influenced the development of each board meeting agenda. All of the programs and activities were measured against the three goals; if something didn't fit, it was terminated. The success statement for each goal was the lead statement on each section of meeting agendas (identified by italics). All of the work of the association was aligned with a strategic goal. This encouraged generative conversation around the changing landscape in commercial construction and the implications for the marketplace and association.

During budget preparation, resources were allocated across the three goals to help focus the board's attention on top-line issues in their meetings. This process encouraged the board to focus time on strategic and environmental issues, without spending much time in the weeds. (See sample agenda from board meeting in the previous sidebar.)

The board articulated two specific value statements—doing the right things well and serving quality product manufacturers—which was helpful in focusing attention on detail and quality statements (about the association and the industry MCA represented). This focus also helped the association elevate the goal of creating codes and standards set at a high level for the industry versus at a commodity or low level. This discouraged some companies from participating; however, MCA ultimately was successful in producing a value statement to the industry. The value statement also helped support the pursuit of certification and accreditation programs and empowered the CSE to carry these values throughout all components and programs of the association.

◆ ◆ ◆

Establishing and Managing to Performance Metrics

According to *7 Measures of Success*, remarkable associations constantly gather data (environmental, product, and so on)—qualitative, quantitative, or anecdotal. They use data to modify a product, introduce a new service, or initiate change through board dialogue and deliberation. The executive committee of one organization assigned metrics to each strategic goal. Their metrics included statistical performance of publications and conferences (attendance, readership scores, abstract submissions), membership numbers (satisfaction scores, retention), customer service metrics (call center waiting times, web access), and financial performance (revenue growth, revenue diversification). Each quarter, leaders evaluated the metrics against the goals.[28]

Similarly, ASAE utilized a strategic direction dashboard (see Table 3.1) for measuring performance in key outcome areas. Areas for measurement were determined by staff under the guidance of the strategic objectives articulated in the plan. Agreement was reached between the staff and board on what was measured, how items were measured, and how often items were measured.

Agree on which key metrics to monitor with the board and, where practical, tie these metrics to staff performance so each staff person knows how his or her position or function supports achieving the strategic plan. The partial action plan previously reviewed provides a clear approach to assigning strategic plan initiatives to key staff members. Deliver bad news to your board when you are aware of the problem and have solutions to offer. Don't give the board a problem without solutions or options. Don't overwhelm the board with detail (for example, although financial statements may be ten pages each month, the board gets the overview, and the treasurer gets the full ten pages).

Succession Planning to Ensure Continuance of Progress to Goals

Volunteers

Because staff members often are the primary interface with committees and task forces, they should continuously be identifying and cultivating future leaders. Staff should have considerable input into the nominations

TABLE 3.1. STRATEGIC DIRECTION DASHBOARD.

Overall Measures	Frequency	Goal	Status
1. Overall member satisfaction	A		
2. Gross revenue	Q		
3. Net income	Q		

Knowledge Outcome: ASAE and The Center are the first choice for knowledge and information for the association profession.

4. User satisfaction index (compilation of user evaluations of Knowledge Center, *Associations Now* journal, newsletters, books, knowledge resources)	A		
5. Innovation index (based on survey responses)	A		
6. Number of Knowledge Center inquiries	M		
7. Number of website knowledge resource page views	M		
8. Number of CAEs	A		

Learning Outcome: Those in the association community attribute their enhanced performance to ASAE and The Center's learning experiences.

9. Total attendance	M		
10. Attributed performance (in follow-up survey)	Q		
11. Attendee satisfaction based on immediate survey	M		

Community Outcome: ASAE and The Center are the professional community of choice for association professionals and industry partners.

12. Number of members in three main categories	M		
13. State of community assessment index	A		
14. Volunteer satisfaction index	A		
15. Diversity index	Q		

Advocacy Outcome: The legislative and regulatory climate is favorable to associations, and the general public recognizes the valuable role that associations and association professionals play in advancing society.

16. Number of media placements in which associations are quoted as an authoritative source	Q		
17. Percentage of CEO hires who come from Associations	Q		
18. Grassroots participation index	A		

of future leaders. Staff are able to identify and recommend those volunteers who support with time, talent, and treasure as opposed to those who just have the loudest voice during meetings and online forums. Although staff may not be the best to determine content expertise, neglecting their wisdom in identifying leadership and participation would be unwise.

Typically, a chief elected officer submits committee and task force rosters for board approval. One technique to accomplish staff input is to ensure that the process of committee and task force appointments allows for adequate inclusion of staff input prior to circulating the recommendations to the board for final approval.

On a related note, one of the most important functions of a CSE is to suggest or vet names for leadership positions, particularly officers and directors. Caution should be had in taking public positions relative to individuals. However, with proper finesse, sharing factual information about volunteer engagement is appropriate and important to the future success of the organization and performance of the board. As Collins reports in *Good to Great*, "Attend to people first, strategy second. Get the right people on the bus and the wrong people off."[29] Ensuring continuity of the association's business case is facilitated by lining up future leaders who are smart, are well respected, meet deadlines, and are resourceful.

CSEs and Senior Staff

Being prepared for a senior staff change is good management. For a small association, what if the CSE has an immediate exit? Who provides leadership and continuity? Having a disaster recovery plan that identifies interim executives can be hugely helpful and reassuring for the leadership. Such a plan would include references for qualified interim executives and search firms. There are firms that specialize in disaster recovery plans for associations and may serve as fine resources for volunteer leaders should the need arise. Share a copy of the disaster recovery plan with each member of the executive committee and your key staff. Be sure to update it annually.

For organizations with larger staffs, the senior management team should be fluent in interim and mid-term options should the CSE become unable to perform his or her duties. It would be a shame for an organization to flounder because of executive leadership changes. At an association management company, the burden of identifying interim staff leadership generally falls to company management, removing the burden from volunteer leaders.

FIGURE 3.6. DUES DOLLARS DISTRIBUTION.

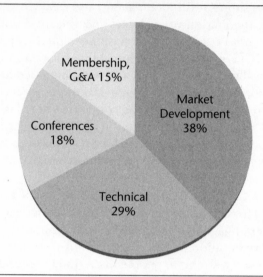

Systems to Promote Innovation, Management to Goals, and Adaptability

As Collins identified, pursuing a relentless culture of discipline separates good from great organizations. "A culture of discipline is not a principle of business; it is a principle of greatness."[30] Channeling and vetting new ideas and programs requires discipline. Sharing with the membership your expenses by strategic objective is a tool to indicate how you are managing to goals. Figure 3.6 provides one example of how this information was presented to the membership of a trade association that had three primary strategic objectives (market development, responding to regulatory and technical challenges, and serving the community of manufacturers—conferences and membership).

Seeing where the dues dollars go is a compelling story to current and prospective members.

One tool that fosters good discipline is to prepare a business case, or charter, for each initiative, program, or product (see Figure 3.7). The charters become the basis for the business plans that support achieving the strategic objectives. Charters also support the development of detailed budgets (including staff time) and progress monitoring.

Completing the business case or charter requires discipline. Going through the process encourages organization of ideas and thoughtfulness

FIGURE 3.7. CHARTER TRACKING TOOL.

PROJECT CHARTER: **DATE:**

EXECUTIVE PROJECT SPONSOR: **PROJECT MANAGER:**   **PROCESS OWNER:**

Sept   Oct   Nov   Dec   Jan   Feb   Mar   Apr   May   June   July   Aug

OVERVIEW	PROGRESS TO DATE (Key Stakeholders, Team Members)
Opportunity Statement:	
Goal Statement:	
Project Vision:	
Benefits:	
Scope:	
Resources Needed:	
KEY METRICS	**NEXT STEPS**

to what you are trying to accomplish—and is best accomplished when partnering a volunteer's wisdom with staff's counsel and legwork.

Through the goal statement, the program or activity is tied back to the strategic goal, while the executive sponsor, project manager, and process owner depict staff accountability. This tool provides clarity of purpose and tie-in to the tactical plan with budget and metric implications and staff assignments. Charting the progress to date also serves as a resource during annual staff evaluations and chartering progress toward the overall plan achievement.

Human Capital Management

Association management requires wearing many different hats. If you are in a smaller association (for example, with a budget of less than $2 million) and you are the staff expert in negotiating hotel contracts, balancing the books, ensuring database security, and writing the newsletter, your association's success likely is limited to (and by) your personal strengths. Hiring staff professionals or outsourcing some of these functions will likely increase the levels of expertise, and thus performance, of your association. Naturally, current budget and business plan projections are key factors in staffing decisions.

When you have identified your action plans and resources to achieve your strategic objectives, hiring the best available talent who can conceive and execute the tactics necessary to ensure success likely requires hiring talent smarter than you. A leadership style of equipping and encouraging has proven effective in achieving results. Fostering an environment of cooperation and support, for example, gathering your team to discuss how to respond to a hotel attrition situation, ensures focus on the larger issues instead of placing blame on individuals. Some CSEs find that weekly senior staff meetings encourage proper communication across boundaries and help remove obstacles to achieving the objectives.

Winning the "Best Places to Work" award for our team at my company, Association Management Center, indicated that our staff was fully engaged with the mission of the associations we serve. In competing for this award, it was a humbling experience to see how our policies, benefits, and staff morale compare in competing for top talent. If your staff are happy and engaged, your members are likely being well served.

Leading an association is rewarding work and requires passion, humility, intelligence, and patience. There is no profession that can have a greater influence on transforming society. How exciting is that?

Notes

1. "How-To Guide," adapted from *The WSJ Complete Small Business Guidebook* (New York: Three Rivers Press, 2009), available at http://guides.wsj.com/management/developing-a-leadership-style/what-do-managers-do.

2. M. Engle, *The Strategic Decision-Making Process of the Board and Its Impact on Decision Outcomes (Quantitative Research Report for Doctor of Management Program)* (2011). Retrieved from http://library.case.edu/digitalcase/datastreamDetail.aspx?PID=ksl:weaedm377&DSID=weaedm377.pdf.

3. C. Cornforth and W. A. Brown, *Nonprofit Governance: Innovative Perspectives and Approaches* (Abingdon, Oxon: Routledge, 2014).

4. W. A. Brown, "Exploring the Association Between Board and Organizational Performance in Nonprofit Organizations," *Nonprofit Management & Leadership 15,* no. 3 (2005): 317–339.
5. G. H. Tecker, P. D. Meyer, B. Crouch, and L. Wintz, *The Will to Govern Well: Knowledge, Trust & Nimbleness* (Washington, DC: ASAE Association Management Press, 2010), 46.
6. M. Engle (2011).
7. Tecker, Meyer, Crouch, and Wintz, *The Will to Govern Well,* xi.
8. Ibid., 36.
9. M. Huse, *Boards, Governance and Value Creation* (Cambridge, UK: Cambridge University Press, 2007), pp. 45, 46.
10. N. Axelrod, "In the Boardroom, 'Culture Counts,'" *Journal of Association Leadership* (Fall 2004): 7.
11. R. P. Chait, W. P. Ryan, and B. E. Taylor, *Governance as Leadership: Reframing the Work of Nonprofit Boards* (New York: John Wiley & Sons, 2011).
12. A. Gardon, "Strengthening Boards of Nonprofit Organizations," *Journal for Nonprofit Management 5* (2001): 2.
13. Tecker, Meyer, Crouch, and Wintz, *The Will to Govern Well.*
14. Axelrod, "In the Boardroom."
15. ASAE and The Center for Association Leadership, *Operating Ratio Report,* 14th ed. (Washington, DC: ASAE Association Management Press, 2012).
16. M. Niederpruem. (2014). Situational Factors Influencing Sustained Volunteer Commitment in Professional Associations. Retrieved from http://library.case.edu/digitalcase/DatastreamListing.aspx?PID=ksl:weaedm431.
17. Ibid., 19.
18. Chait, Ryan, and Taylor, *Governance as Leadership,* 2.
19. M. Engle (2011).
20. G. H. Tecker, Presentation conducted at the Chief Staff Executives and Chief Elected Officers (CEO Symposium) of the American Society of Association Executives, Scottsdale, Arizona, February 2014.
21. ASAE and The Center for Association Leadership, *7 Measures of Success: What Remarkable Associations Do That Others Don't* (Washington, DC: ASAE Association Management Press, 2006).
22. P. Senge, "Management Theory of Peter Senge," available at http://www.business.com/guides/management-theory-of-peter-senge-15935.
23. ASAE and The Center for Association Leadership, *7 Measures of Success.*
24. J. C. Collins, "Text Excerpts from … *Good to Great and the Social Sectors,*" available at http://www.jimcollins.com/books/g2g-ss.html.

25. J. C. Collins, *Good to Great and the Social Sectors: A Monograph to Accompany Good to Great'* (New York: HarperCollins, 2005).
26. ASAE and The Center for Association Leadership, *Starting an Association*, available at www.asaecenter.org/Resources/whitepaperdetail.cfm? ItemNumber=24445.
27. ASAE and The Center for Association Leadership, *Starting an Association.*
28. ASAE and The Center for Association Leadership, *7 Measures of Success,* 41.
29. Collins, *Good to Great and the Social Sectors,* 13.
30. Ibid., 1.

The Author

Mark Engle, DM, FASAE, CAE, principal of Association Management Center (Chicago), has been a CSE for nearly thirty years. Engle recently earned his doctor of management degree from Case Western Reserve University with his research in nonprofit governance; Engle is an ASAE fellow and chair of the ASAE Services Board.

CHAPTER FOUR

MANAGING THE COMPLEX ASSOCIATION ENTERPRISE

Gary A. LaBranche, FASAE, CAE

Associations come in all shapes and sizes. The budgets of most associations are less than $7 million with a median of $3.5 million.[1] But some associations have budgets in excess of $25 million, and a few generate more than $1 billion. Larger budgets are associated with larger scope and scale. Greater size, scope, and scale impose complex management challenges and demand responses that are proportionate to the situation.

A $2 million budget, 10-staff association with one office and one board is a different environment from a $40 million, 150-staff association with boards for five different entities and subsidiaries and offices in Chicago, London, Shanghai, and Sao Paulo. Add several dozen chapters, special-interest groups, and other units, and management challenges grow exponentially.

Scope—the breadth and depth of an enterprise—and scale, the operating systems, impose unique demands on structure, staff, and governance and produce multifaceted relationships and dynamics.[2] Aligning the work of multiple governing bodies and dispersed staff is just the start. Alliances, coalitions, and ventures with third parties add the challenge of working with groups outside of the association structure, affecting the association's ability to coordinate efforts. Adding a variety of components, subsidiaries, and other organizational units ensures communication challenges.

The complex association enterprise is one of the most challenging environments in the field of association management. You'll need a thorough understanding of strategy, management, and organizational development to ensure that the resources of the association are focused in the right direction and applied to achieving the intended outcomes. Failure to do so delays goal achievement and fosters confusion and conflict. Most associations have resource constraints and must "do more with less." To achieve its mission and serve the evolving needs of members, an association can't afford to waste time, effort, and resources.[3] Alignment, coordination, and communication are vital for the complex association enterprise to succeed.

The association chief staff executive is best positioned to lead the complex enterprise. The CSE has a comprehensive view of all facets of the organization: people, resources, structure, and strategy. With longevity, the CSE develops institutional memory and perspective, along with critical intelligence and insight on the internal and external environments.[4] But while the CSE plays a critical role, the complex association enterprise imposes limitations on what the CSE can know or do, especially in a time of continuous and rapid change. As association members become increasingly engaged in co-creation of customized products and services, the ever-changing environment is a standard reality for association managers. Adapting to, compensating for, and embracing such limitations, challenges, and opportunities is the crucial skill set for the CSE in complex association enterprises.

This chapter provides the current or prospective association CSE with a broad review of the challenge of managing the complex enterprise, along with a sampling of tools and techniques. Complex enterprises are examined using four frames of reference:

The Manager: Applying fundamental concepts of management from the manager's point of view provides a baseline starting point for understanding.

The Enterprise: Using a framework to analyze how each organizational element contributes to organizational health.

The Tools: Techniques and tools are available to assist management in alignment, coordination, and communication with the complex enterprise.

The Lenses: This refers to a set of perspectives that provide a unified vision for integrating the requirements of today and the opportunities of the future.

Managing any association is a challenge due to the unique realities of mission, governance, and membership. The basic structural components of an association—structures, programs, members, committees, board, and staff—can quickly multiply as associations grow in size and scope. Complex association enterprises may include a variety of components in addition to boards and committees. Examples include

- Chapters, which provide a local means of organizing members and connecting them
- Allied organizations, or local or regional groups that do not have formalized or official "chapter" relationship
- For-profit subsidiaries, often established for the pursuit of activities outside the association's exempt purpose (such as for group purchasing programs or investment service offerings)
- Foundations, or legally separate but related 501(c)(3) organizations
- Houses of delegates, or assemblies of member representatives that serve as "legislative" branches in association governance systems
- Member communities, or groups (online or otherwise) created to facilitate the exchange of knowledge, sharing of expertise, and networking activities
- Certifying, accrediting, or standard-setting bodies, which support activities that accredit people, institutions, places, or equipment to designate levels of proficiency, performance, accuracy or achievement relative to established standards, as well as for other reasons
- Strategic alliances, which are voluntary relationships with one or more independent organizations established for purposes such as advancing mutual goals or coordinating efforts
- Joint ventures, for sharing risk and collaboratively pursuing new initiatives
- Political Action Committees, or vehicles that enable associations (except 501(c)(3)s) to participate in the electoral process at the U.S. state or federal level
- Coalitions, or often loosely organized groups of organizations or companies to work on specific legislation, regulations, or other issues
- Special-purpose programs, funded by special dues, assessments, or contributions from an interested member segment to address the needs of a small but vocal group willing to put resources into a project that is not as widely embraced by other members

Mergers

Associations consider mergers as an option to achieve strategic goals and respond to changes in their environment. While publicly traded companies can be subject to unsolicited takeover bids, associations are far more insulated from being compelled to act by outside forces. Because association boards have no personal economic interests in a merger transaction, they have different motivations than found in the for-profit sector.

Association mergers are often driven by members, customers, or strategic objectives. The most common reasons that associations consider mergers include

Adjacency: Substantial overlap in membership or customer base

Expansion: Access to new markets

Capacity: Opportunity to add capacity or capability

Financial: Consolidation or competition that has created economic or operational inefficiency

Associations can acquire other associations, for-profit entities, or specific assets of either. Not all acquisitions result in mergers, as acquired units can be operated independently.

Mergers are complicated and challenging due to the many legal and financial hurdles. While legal and financial issues are many, association mergers most often fail because of "people" and cultural issues. Issues such as which board members will serve on the new board, which CSE will emerge to lead the new organization, and how any differences in values and behaviors will be handled are among the considerations that may de-rail association mergers. It is always important to remember that mergers are really between people, not institutions.

Merger partners typically proceed through several distinct stages:

Precursor partnering: Working together in real partnership can help in moving toward common objectives.

Informal discussions: Often occurring between members or other stakeholders, discussions reveal opportunities and challenges and "test the waters" for resistance and acceptance concerning merits and benefits of a merger.

Formal negotiations: Involving officially designated leaders from each party, formalized discussions may lead to negotiations and due diligence and conclude with formal merger.

Implementation: Integrating governance, staff, systems, style and other elements are critical to completing a successful merger.*

*J. A. Pietroburgo and S. P. Wernet, *Investigation of Association Mergers* (Chicago: The William E. Smith Institute for Association Research, March 2007).

Much has to be right and go right for association mergers to succeed. Some mergers have taken decades to achieve; others have been completed in months. However, the more compelling the reasons, the more likely those merger discussions will resolve with a new, combined organization.

◆ ◆ ◆

Organizational units proliferate because they provide specific responses or capabilities to address specialized and focused tasks. Diverse units and supporting systems are needed to meet member needs, exploit opportunities, pursue innovation, manage risk, grow revenue, create and share knowledge, and deliver value. Some of the units mentioned earlier may be incorporated or domiciled in countries far from the association's headquarters. An association may also have offices or representatives around the world, with a workforce composed of staff, consultants, or third-party administrators.[5] Each component or unit within the association faces its own unique environment and is positioned at a specific point on its own lifecycle continuum, requiring strategy, leadership, and management corresponding to the situation.[6] Complex enterprises are complicated in every sense.

The Manager

Mastering the fundamentals of management, strategy, and operational systems is essential; to succeed as an executive or manager in a complex environment, your first task is to manage your mind-set.

Peter Drucker, considered by many as the most influential thinker on management, shaped much of what is currently taught about management. What he had to say about the work of managers and management continues to resonate today:

- Management is about people—maximizing their performance in a collaborative setting.
- Management is embedded in culture—how managers manage depends on the culture in which they operate.
- Focus and commitment to shared goals and values are essential. Management's first job is to ensure that the enterprise has simple, clear, and unifying mission and objectives that are widely shared and held.
- Every enterprise is a learning and teaching institution. Management must support each person in the enterprise to learn and grow.
- Every worker is unique and diverse, but within the enterprise each is interdependent. Management's task is to ensure that everyone is valued and supported while focused on the work in common.

- Performance can be measured in many ways, but it has to be measured and continuously improved.
- The result of an enterprise—its value—exists only on the outside, most often in the mind of a customer, client, or member.[7]

Drucker's view of management provides a blueprint for a managerial mind-set. Explicit in Drucker's approach is that your responsibility is to think about the perspectives of others. That understanding, when married to clarity of purpose and focus objectives and outcomes, is what management is all about. This managerial mind-set provides a strong foundation for leading the complex enterprise.

Another way of approaching the context of managing a complex enterprise is to imagine "standing on a balcony" while observing the entire organization. Having such context is critical to appreciating and analyzing all the forces that have an impact on an organization. While standing on the balcony, the manager looks for patterns of work, struggles over values, and leadership, as well as functional and dysfunctional behaviors.[8]

Management theorists call this "sense making": synthesizing information, patterns of behavior, and other clues to inform analysis and judgment.[9] Sense making is a critical skill for the manager of a complex enterprise.

"Standing on a balcony" may suggest the manager as a distant figure, but it is just the first step to understanding the complex organization. One of the first things that a manager realizes while taking in the view is that there are real limitations to any specific vantage point.[10] The manager must get closer to the action and must have the means to make sense of the situation from multiple vantage points, without actually being there.

Making Sense of Complexity

Few endeavors in human history were more carefully planned than the invasion of Normandy on June 5, 1944. Countless hours were devoted to planning, preparation, and coordination. Vast stores of equipment and detailed schedules of logistical support were organized. Battle plans were laid out, with clear, specific objectives detailed, along with alternatives and options. Enormous human and capital resources were concentrated on the task, the biggest endeavor of World War II.

And then D-Day began. Plans went immediately awry. The weather was miserable, the troops were wave-tossed and sea-sick. Paratroopers were dropped miles from their targets. Landing craft drifted off course. Shells and bombs missed their targets. Equipment failed or didn't perform adequately. Communications systems failed. The enemy was stronger in some places than expected. Men died in horrible ways. Aboard the USS Augusta, eleven miles out to sea, Lieutenant General Omar N. Bradley, the senior tactical U.S. commander, stood helpless in the fog of war. From the moment of engagement, Bradley and his allied comrades in arms had to improvise, adjust, regroup, counter, and change as circumstances required.[11]

While managing a complex association enterprise doesn't rise to the life-or-death struggle of D-Day, it shares with it the fundamental challenge of complexity: too many variables. You will rarely have enough information, or resources, or time. Things happen faster than expected, or slower, or not at all, or in ways not imagined. People behave as people will: in uniquely human ways.[12]

Few plans ever totally survive the clash with implementation. The reality that no plan is ever perfect, or perfectly implemented, does not render planning obsolete or irrelevant. Rather, it suggests that the power of planning is found in the process of thinking. Thinking strategically involves a synthesis of analysis, forecasting, testing, and responding.[13]

Complex enterprises also behave differently because they consist of multiple, independent, and self-reinforcing systems. In such complex enterprises

- Obvious solutions don't often produce intended outcomes; in fact, intended solutions often backfire.
- Cause and effect aren't as closely related as they may at first seem.
- Resistance is embedded in complex systems. Complex systems strive to maintain internal balance—status quo—against external forces (which can include the CSE).
- Changing a complex system requires a deep understanding of the organization and its environment as a unified system. Achieving change or affecting behavior requires learning and depends on fostering a systems-thinking approach to leadership.[14]

Management challenges are magnified by size, scale, and scope. Complexity forces limitations on a manager's knowledge and imposes realities on implementation. Accepting the limitations of what a manager can reasonably do, know, or anticipate is an essential element in mastering complexity thinking.[15] Peter Drucker repeatedly focused on the role that ignorance plays in management.[16] Compensating for such limitations by developing supporting systems is critical to managing the complex enterprise. These systems and tools are designed to augment "sense-making" and provide continuous intelligence and insights from throughout the enterprise.

The Enterprise

Managers have long sought the means to compensate for the dynamic variability of complex organizations. A number of tools, models, and frameworks have emerged to bring order to chaos and create mental maps to guide comprehension. And no wonder: complex enterprises almost defy comprehension because they are so dynamic:

- The complex organization didn't just arrive as it appears today—it has history. But hindsight does not lead to foresight because the conditions constantly change.
- The elements of a complex organization interact with each other, often in unpredictable ways.
- The interaction of a large number of players with differing roles and goals creates ever-evolving alliances and motivations.
- The whole is greater than the sum of its parts, and solutions can't be easily imposed.[17]

Faced with such dynamic variability and unpredictability, your task is to distill the foundational elements of the organization to understand how the whole comes together. Theoretical models are often used to provide baselines for understanding.

While no model is perfect, some are helpful in providing context to a situation or environment. The McKinsey 7-S Framework (Figure 4.1) is one such aid in thinking about complex organizations. Developed by Tom Peters and Robert Waterman, then with the McKinsey consulting firm, the 7-S framework was first outlined in the June 1980 edition of *Business Horizons*. It was also shared in *The Art of Japanese Management* (1981) by Athos and Pascale and, most famously, in *In Search of Excellence* (1982).[18]

The 7-S Framework describes seven elements that are essential in effectively organizing and operating an enterprise. Each element is equally important; there is no priority or hierarchy. All elements are important to ensure alignment and organizational effectiveness.

FIGURE 4.1. THE MCKINSEY 7-S FRAMEWORK.

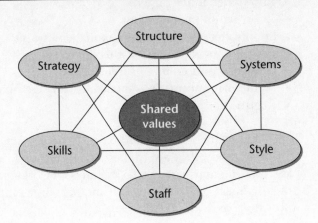

- Shared Values

    Shared values are at the interconnecting center of the 7-S model. Shared values are commonly held beliefs, mind-sets, and assumptions that shape how an organization behaves, its culture. Shared values are critical to developing and maintaining trust. Values express an organization's central ethics, beliefs, and attitudes. These values must be explicitly stated and exhibited as both organizational objectives and individual values. How employees treat one another, and members and customers, is a key focus on shared values.

- Strategy

    Strategy defines what is to be accomplished to reach a desired outcome or range of outcomes.

- Structure

    Structure outlines how people in an organization relate to each other and how tasks are both divided up and integrated. In other words, structures describe authority and accountability in an organization.

- Systems

    Systems define the procedures, processes, routines, and support systems involved in the ongoing operation of the enterprise. Some of the systems found in an association are

    - Compensation and performance management
    - Human resources, development, and training
    - Accounting and financial management

- Asset management
- Knowledge management
- Information management
- Supply chain and contracts management
- Program, product, and service delivery
- Customer and member service
- Member recruitment, onboarding, engagement, renewal
- Registration, fulfillment

- Staff

    Staff refers to the number and types of personnel within the organization and how they are trained and developed. In today's complex association enterprise, "staff" includes all workers who contribute to the organization, including full and part-time employees, outsource providers, and volunteers.

- Style

    How management acts is more important that what management says. Thus, "style" has immense symbolic power and is a critical component of managing, as it expresses acceptable and expected behavior in achieving the organization's goals.

- Skills

    Skills are the distinctive capabilities and core competencies of staff as individuals as well as teams within the organization.

The McKinsey 7-S Framework provides context to analyze the essential elements of every enterprise. You can use the tools shown in Table 4.1 to apply the framework to a specific association.

The Tools

The working tools of management in any enterprise are also fundamental to the complex enterprise: plans, budgets, performance measures, human resources, IT and data management, and others.

However, size, scale, and scope, coupled with dynamic variability and limitations on knowledge, require you to emphasize organizational focus and effort. As a CSE or senior staff member, focus on the key leverage points for driving performance and outcomes:

- *Alignment:* Ensuring that each organizational component is aligned toward objectives that support the guiding strategic vision. Articulate and emphasize the importance of alignment regularly with leaders and staff throughout.

TABLE 4.1. MCKINSEY 7-S FRAMEWORK KEY QUESTIONS.

7-S Element	Application	Sample Key Questions to Ask and Answer
Strategy	Decide what is to be done to achieve specific outcomes.	Are we focused on the right things? Is our effort aligned and concentrated appropriately? Do we need to adapt and change? How do we engage all stakeholders in sensing our environment and co-creating strategic responses?
Structure	Define each organizational unit's authority, responsibility, and accountability.	Does our structure support the annual "Plan of Work"? Are responsibilities and accountabilities clear? Is our team engaging across boundaries?
Systems	Ensure that systems are designed to reinforce desired behaviors; systems are not obstacles to work.	Do our compensation and bonus plans support the desired outcomes—both short term (annual) and long term (strategic)? Does the annual "Plan of Work" align with the "Strategic Plan"? Does the annual "Plan of Work" drive the budget? How do we gather and interpret data and information? Do we have technology that facilitates collaboration and knowledge management? How can we use social media systemically to engage in conversations and feedback with staff and stakeholders?
Staff	Determine which staff positions are required to achieve tasks, goals, and desired outcomes.	Have we considered all forms of "staffing," including Insourcing versus outsourcing? Does our staffing approach allow for flexibility? What is our recruitment and retention plan? How do we ensure diversity? Do we have the right people in the right jobs? How do we develop and train staff? Do we have succession development and contingency plans? What is the right mix of employee and volunteer staff? Do we have the right staff in-house, or do we need to acquire resources from outsourced providers? Are compensation systems aligned with and supportive of goals and plan? How are we building capacity and developing capability? How can we eliminate distractions?

(continued)

TABLE 4.1. CONTINUED

7-S Element	Application	Sample Key Questions to Ask and Answer
Style	Consciously exhibit behaviors and practices that set standards and influence others.	What do we believe are the most important behaviors to demonstrate? How do we demonstrate them? What do we do if someone exhibits nonproductive behaviors? Are we authentic? How much risk are we comfortable with? Are leaders seen as visible champions for improvement? Are leaders available to front-line staff, in order to solicit ideas and ensure that work is aligned with objectives?
Skills	Specify distinctive capabilities of key staff as well as specific skill sets of team members.	Are job descriptions accurate? Do they reflect sound HR practices and provide for appropriate accommodations as needed for differently abled persons? What are our training and development goals for each position? Is there a skill-development path for each position and each person?
Shared Values	Express the guiding values of the organization.	What do we believe in as an organization? Are these values communicated consistently throughout the organization? Are our actions guided by ethical considerations? What is our responsibility to society?

- *Coordination:* Concentrating resources and work effort on key performance outcomes. Ensure that high-priority items are not subverted by distractions unrelated to the plan and desired outcomes. Make mid-course corrections and adjustments as a result of continuous learning and process improvement.
- *Communication:* Building and nurturing an environment in which data, information, and knowledge are transparent, accessible, and shared; critical conversations and honest dialogue are encouraged and expected; leaders listen and engage with both internal and external stakeholders; leaders are visible champions of improvement.

Numerous tools are available to aid in alignment, coordination, and communication. You're encouraged to find those that fit your needs. The 7-S Framework is one such tool that can be adapted to facilitate alignment. In addition, embracing a more open, inclusive approach to strategic thinking and planning is one of the new capabilities needed within the complex association enterprise—and one that can help address the challenge of communicating the plan and gaining alignment and commitment throughout the enterprise.

As an example, the American Institute of Architects (AIA) has designed a strategic planning response to fit its complex environment. AIA shares its strategic plan along with an online toolkit to help components to align their plans and programs with the national vision.[19] The objective isn't compliance or an attempt to command AIA's hundreds of components, but to inspire conversation throughout the system. Another benefit is the stimulation of a continuous cycle of strategic thinking.

The Association for Corporate Growth (ACG) utilizes a two-pronged effort to engage stakeholders in strategic planning. A global, chapter-centric association, ACG chapters are the front-line providers of member service and value and are guided by their own strategic plans—each on their own time frame. Chapter boards often utilize the services of the ACG global staff team in facilitating chapter plans. This provides for cross-pollination of perspectives and ideas and has resulted in closer coordination and collaboration. Engaging with chapter boards also informs and enriches the strategic planning effort for the global organization. In addition, chapter leaders and executives provide direct input to and feedback on the strategic plan for the global organization. The ultimate objective is to engage the ACG community in co-creating a desired future, while respecting and validating the diversity and independence of all units.

These "open source-association" approaches to strategic planning depend on co-creation and collaboration rather than centralized, controlled planning.[20] Relying on "crowdsourcing" of perspectives and potential responses, such an approach creates a learning dialogue throughout the enterprise. This "unorthodox" approach to strategy development matches well to the complex organization's environment. An open-source planning approach recognizes that the "center" of such a complex enterprise simply can't know everything, control everything, or predict everything. By inviting strategic conversations from a variety of perspectives, this approach serves as both an early warning system and an idea cultivation process. By harvesting strategic thinking from many sources, including those at the fringe, the association can accelerate creating, learning, prototyping, and adapting.[21] Open-source strategic planning is a key means of "sense making" in complex association enterprises.

Integrated Dashboard

As a CSE or staff manager, you cannot personally know everything. Given that, some kind of reporting system is essential. Dashboards have become a common practice. Dashboards can be very simple or highly complex, even integrated with real-time reporting, with constant online updates. They are essential tools for coordination and communication.

These tools take their name from the various dials or meters seen on an automobile or aircraft "dashboard." Customized for the needs of each association, dashboards can be shared throughout the organization. They are typically designed to share a great deal of information on a single sheet of paper or screen, as shown in the sample in Figure 4.2.

Dashboards are essential tools in managing a complex association enterprise and can be a key component in "sense making." When shared widely throughout the organization, dashboards promote transparency and help to hold all team members accountable for deliverables.

The Lenses

Ensuring congruence between management and governance is one of the keys to alignment in complex enterprises.

FIGURE 4.2. SAMPLE DASHBOARD: ABC ASSOCIATION.

ABC Association
Six months ending June 30, 2014
Issued July 26, 2014

($'000s)	Actual YTD	Budget YTD	LY YTD	Latest Forecast	Annual Budget
Revenue:					
OPERATING - Revenue	12,577	12,000	11,575	24,150	24,750
NON OPERATING - Revenue	685	700	696	1,400	1,475
Total Revenue	13,262	12,700	12,271	25,550	26,225
Expenses:					
OPERATING - Expenses	6,118	6,500	5,998	12,990	13,781
NON OPERATING - Expenses	120	125	174	375	227
Total Expenses	6,238	6,625	6,172	13,365	14,008
Inc/(Dec) in Net Assets - Association only	7,024	6,075	6,099	12,185	12,217
PAC - Revenue	457	600	0	1,150	1,150
PAC - Expenses	140	145	0	247	247
PAC - Surplus / (deficit)	317	455	0	903	903
FOUNDATION - Revenue	200	225	212	425	450
FOUNDATION - Expenses	289	225	196	483	552
FOUNDATION - Surplus / (deficit)	(89)	0	16	(58)	(102)

Net Assets/Reserves/Designated
in thousands of dollars

Net Assets, Total 12/31/14	$6,870
Net Assets, Designated	$6,420
Net Assets, Total as at 1/31/14	$6,431

**Annual Convention
ABC Association
Chicago, IL - Sept 2014
$k**

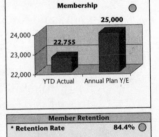

**Paid Registration Goal of 2,315
Registration opened in April 2014**

Commentary:

Association revenue is ahead of plan as membership continues to grow and sponsorship & exhibit sales remain strong for the annual convention in September. The overall results for the six months ending June 30 are $949k favorable to budget. Exhibit sales is $124k ahead and sponsorship $842k above budget. Expenses are favorable mainly due to the timing of spend for the new AMS. Expect to achieve budget targets. The PAC is slightly behind its financial goals. The Foundation, in its twelfth year, continues to struggle. A strategic review of the Foundation is scheduled for September ahead of next year's budget cycle.

FY 2014 Priorities	Status
1. Achieve Membership Retention Rate of 85%	◐
2. Grow Membership to 25,000	◐
3. Achieve Dues Revenue of $10,241k	◐
4. Achieve Convention Profit of $2.6M	◐
5. Launch Foundation Capital Campaign	◐
6. Achieve passage of HR 8899	●
7. Achieve 500 certifees with new launch in China	◐
8. Revenue of $800k in content sales	◐
9. Launch New AMS on time & on budget	○

● - Risk   ◐ - Caution   ○ On Track

Membership

```
             25,000
24,000
        22,755
23,000

22,000
      YTD Actual   Annual Plan Y/E
```

Member Retention

* Retention Rate   84.4% ◐

* 1955 members renewed in June
which is 154 more than last year

Advocacy	Achievements	Issues
* HR 8899 passed the House on a vote of 422-0 * 13 Members of Congress scheduled to attend Policy Summit * 150 registered to attend Summit/Fly-in * Policy Agenda being updated by Committee *PAC fund raiser set for next month in Chicago * Quarterly Lobbying report (LD-2) filed	* 9 Webinars held for 3,543 attendees * AMS go-live delayed by one month * Orientation held for new chapter executives * FY16 Editorial Calendar set * For-profit subsidiary launched new liability insurance product * Achieved 50% milestone for Sponsorship Revenue * Chapter executive conference program developed by committee	* Content sales soft in European markets; additional marketing efforts will be added for next quarter; sales strong in other markets * Two Foundation staff accepted new jobs; search underway * CFO announced retirement date of 12/31/16 * Retention rate dipped by .3%; Membership Dept evaluating

Source: J. O'Loughlin and G. LaBranche (March 17, 2014).

Among the many concerns that must be addressed between staff leadership and governance are the following:

Alignment: Do we share mental models and values? Do we share the same level of knowledge and understanding of our environment, opportunities, and challenges? Are we focused on the same strategy and objectives? Do we share values and styles?

Coordination: Are our systems, staff, structure, and skills working toward the same goals?

Communication: How do we monitor performance and check and adjust as needed? How do we solve problems and ensure teamwork across components?

The *3 Sight Lens* (3SL) approach is a framework to support governance alignment. The framework provides three "lenses" through which the governance and management team can view the total enterprise. Each lens provides a vantage through which to view the organization in the past, present, and future.

The Stewardship Lens: The lens of *oversight* is a popular viewpoint in governance. And it should be: boards have a fiduciary duty to provide oversight. By its nature, this viewpoint primarily utilizes lagging data: financial reports, committee reports, membership statistics, and so on. Oversight uses a *microscope* to discern anomalies, exceptions, and disruptions. The Stewardship Lens focuses on ensuring the sustainable continuity of the enterprise.

The Membership Lens: By contrast, a *periscope* is employed to look through the Membership Lens. A periscope is designed to look over and around the scene and gain immediate, current data. This lens is used to gain *insight* on the needs, wants, and desires of members and other stakeholders. Member and prospect research, data on member engagement and participation, sales of products and services, and so on help to provide needed metrics. The Membership Lens is used to ensure the currency and relevancy of the business that the enterprise is in today.

The Leadership Lens: This is the viewpoint of *foresight*. Imagine using a *telescope* to see far ahead. Peer through the Leadership Lens to "define the meaningful outside" and discover emerging needs.[22] Trend-watching and forecasting, predictive analytical tools, and environmental scanning are among the tools used to gain clarity on coming changes, opportunities, and threats. The objective is to use this lens to drive the generation and exploration of new ideas.

The 3 Sight Lens model highlights the triple challenge in leading the complex enterprise:

- Ensure sustainable continuity
- Deliver current and relevant value
- Plan for the future

When overlapped, the three lenses bring into focus a balanced view of the organization and its environment, as shown in Figure 4.3.

The 3 Sight Lens approach encourages the leadership team—both staff and volunteers—to balance the realities of today with both the near-term possibilities and long-term opportunities. Engaging the leaders and managers of key organizational components in thinking about the world through the lenses is a useful technique in shaping mental models; creating shared values; and fostering alignment, coordination, and communication. Associations can apply the 3 Sight Lens approach in governance practices. For example, board agenda items can be coded

FIGURE 4.3. THE 3 SIGHT LENS APPROACH.

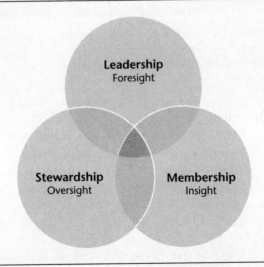

or noted as Leadership, Stewardship, or Membership. This will help to balance effort as well as place focus on areas where it is most needed.[23]

The Enterprise Coordinating Body

Achieving unified, enterprise-wide synergy while changing as needed to compete and thrive is essential to success. Some associations have provided an ongoing mechanism for such discussions through "enterprise" coordinating bodies. While independent boards may govern specific components (association, foundation, subsidiary, and so on) a coordinating body is formed outside of formal corporate structures. Usually advisory, such "umbrella" groups provide a platform for ongoing strategic dialogue that slices through and affects the complex enterprise in unexpected ways. The senior volunteer and staff leaders from the key components, units, subsidiaries, and so forth should be included in the enterprise coordinating body. If executed well, such a body can enhance nimbleness, trust, and knowledge, the key attributes of effectively governed associations.[24]

The association's CSE, as a "broker of ideas," is uniquely positioned to shape and grow the enterprise.[25] Complex association enterprises will increasingly empower CSEs to provide the professional management needed to ensure success in the future.[26] Because the CSE role is so central to aligning, coordinating, and communicating, the CSE should serve as the "executive chair" of the enterprise coordinating body.

Engaging, Sensing, and Responding

All associations are complicated organizations. Those complications are compounded in associations with larger budgets, broader scope, and greater scale. Few environments are more challenging for the association professional. Managers of complex association enterprises must master a comprehensive array of strategies, tools, and techniques to succeed in such environments. Leading a complex association demands CSEs and managers who can thrive in open-source environments, live with ambiguity, and succeed in the face of dynamic and discontinuous change. The reality is that complex enterprises are not managed by a "command and control" culture but by an "engage, sense, and respond" culture that provides opportunity for people throughout the organization to contribute.

Notes

1. ASAE, *Benchmarking in Association Management: Financial Operations* (Washington, DC: ASAE Association Management Press, 2012).
2. J. C. Panzar and R. D. Willig, "Economies of Scale in Multi-Output Production," *Quarterly Journal of Economics* (March 1977): 481–493.
3. H. Coerver and M. Byers, *Road to Relevance* (Washington, DC: ASAE Association Management Press, 2013).
4. Coerver and Byers, *Road to Relevance.*
5. ASAE, *Benchmarking in Association Management.*
6. G. LaBranche, "Situational Governance: Suiting Style to Stage," *Leadership* (January 1991): 33–36.
7. P. F. Drucker, *The Essential Drucker* (New York: HarperCollins, 2001).
8. R. A. Heifetz and D. L. Laurie, "The Work of Leadership," *Harvard Business Review* (1997): 124–134.
9. S. Clegg, M. Kornberger, and T. Pitis, *Managing & Organizations* (London: Sage, 2008).
10. G. Sargut and R. G. McGrath, "Learning to Live with Complexity," *Harvard Business Review* (2011): 3–10.
11. R. Atkinson, *The Guns at Last Light: The War in Western Europe 1944–1945* (New York: Henry Holt, 2013).
12. H. Mintzberg, *The Rise and Fall of Strategic Planning* (New York: The Free Press, 1994).
13. Coerver and Byers, *Road to Relevance.*
14. P. M. Senge, *Systems Principles for Leadership* (Cambridge, MA: MIT Sloan School, 1985).
15. K. A. Richardson, "Managing Complex Organizations: Complexity Thinking and the Science and Art of Management," *E:CO* (2008): 13–26.
16. J. E. Flaherty, *Peter Drucker: Shaping the Managerial Mind* (San Francisco: Jossey-Bass, 1999).
17. D. J. Snowden and M. E. Boone, "A Leader's Framework for Decision Making," *Harvard Business Journal* (2007): 69–76.
18. T. Peters, Tompeters.com/dispatches, January 9, 2011, available at Tompeters.com: http://www.tompeters.com/dispatches/012016.php.
19. J. Notter and M. Grant, *Humanize* (Indianapolis: QUE, 2012).
20. G. A. LaBranche, "The Open Source Association," *This Week at Association Forum* (March 26, 2007).

21. J. De Cagna, "Associations Unorthodox: Six Really Radical Shifts Toward the Future," *Chief* (2012).

22. A. Laffey, "What Only the CEO Can Do," *Harvard Business Review* (2009): 54–59.

23. G. LaBranche, "Meaning, Relevance and the Future of Associations," presentation at the Special Libraries Association, July 16, 2012.

24. G. Tecker, P. Meyer, L. Wintz, and B. Crouch, *The Will to Govern Well*, 2nd ed. (Washington, DC: ASAE Association Management Press, 2010).

25. ASAE and The Center for Association Leadership, *7 Measures of Success: What Remarkable Organizations Do That Others Don't* (Washington, DC: ASAE Association Management Press, 2006).

26. Coerver and Byers, *Road to Relevance*.

The Author

Gary A. LaBranche, FASAE, CAE, is the president and CEO of the Association for Corporate Growth. His thirty-plus-year career in association management includes serving as chief staff executive of three associations.

CHAPTER FIVE

BUSINESS MODELS AND ECONOMIC DRIVERS

Paul Pomerantz, FASAE, CAE

Many association CSEs have found themselves in the following situation. Things have gone well for years. Suddenly, revenues have flattened. You watch as the income begins to dip and slide gradually (or quickly deteriorates). The board is concerned. They say "Try harder" or "We need to market more." Some say a new strategic plan is the answer, but the new plan, when all is said and done, is a continuation of the past, with emphasis on "member value" and improvements to current programs, such as the annual meeting. You know the answer is far more fundamental. It goes to the very core of what you do, how you attract customers (members) and generate revenue.

In fact, the oversight of your business model is one of the most important responsibilities of the chief staff executive (CSE). It is your responsibility to optimize its performance and your responsibility to recognize when improvements and changes are necessary.

Associations are businesses, distinguished from others only by their purpose and tax status. Businesses, to exist, must have customers, and, in the case of associations, these are usually, but not all the time, members. To attract customers, associations must provide value, defined as benefit over cost. The process of generating revenue to support the organization's value proposition is often referred to as the business model.

The association business model is a bit of a paradox. In many ways it is very standard and predictable, usually driven by membership and events.

Each association, however, is different. Moreover, the business drivers for associations are rapidly changing.

Business Model Defined

A business model describes the rationale of how an organization creates, delivers, and captures value.[1] The process of business model construction is part of business strategy. "In theory and practice, the term *business model* is used for a broad range of informal and formal descriptions to represent the core aspects of a business, including purpose, target customers, offerings, strategies, infrastructure, organizational structure, trading practices, and operational processes and policies."[2]

Business model design includes the modeling and description of an organization's

- Value propositions
- Target customer segments
- Distribution channels
- Customer relationships
- Value configurations
- Core capabilities
- Partner network
- Cost structure
- Revenue model

The concept of the business model is captured by Peter Drucker in his classic, "The Theory of the Business."[3] He describes three key assumptions that drive the business model.

- Assumptions about the environment of the organization and its market
- Assumptions about the specific mission of the organization
- Assumptions about the core competencies needed to accomplish the organization's mission

Drucker then defines four specifications for a valid theory of the business:

1. The assumptions about the environment, mission, and core competencies must fit reality. Assumptions must be based on the realities of the market and the capacity of the organization to address market needs.

2. The assumptions in all three areas have to fit one another. Drucker gives the example of General Motors, whose core competencies in financial control of the manufacturing process fit with its mission to manufacture cars geared at virtually every customer segment.

3. The theory of the business must be known and understood throughout the organization. The theory becomes a part of strategy, culture, and the discipline of decision making.

4. The theory of the business has to be tested constantly. Drucker stipulates "It is not graven on tablets of stone. It is a hypothesis. And it is a hypothesis about things that are in constant flux—society, markets, customers, technology. As so, built into the theory of the business must be the ability to change itself."

The Association Business Model

An association is, by definition, a group of individuals or organizations organized around common interests. Associations will often define their activities around services to individuals, organizations, or interests including community, networking, information resources, education, standards, or advocacy. Accreditation of institutions and certification of individuals also represent primary activities.

Similarly, revenues are derived from a limited set of sources. Membership is at the core of associations and, for most organizations, is the single largest activity and revenue source. In addition to membership revenue, according to ASAE's *Operating Ratio Report*, other large revenue sources come from meeting registration and exhibits, certification programs, contributions, subscriptions, and advertising.[4]

The ASAE report points out some important trends:

While membership dues have constituted a decreasing proportion of association revenue over the long term, in recent years this proportion has stabilized. For example, in 1953, the first year of the *Operating Ratio Report,* dues represented 95.7 percent of association revenue, by 1977 it represented 52.3 percent, and in the most recent survey, 37.7 percent. However, dues have represented, as a percentage of revenue, 37.5 percent, 37.7 percent, and 37.7 percent in 2003, 2007, and 2011, respectively.

The extent to which membership dues contribute to an association's revenue varies by type. Trade associations tend to rely more heavily on dues than individual membership organizations. This is also the case for 501(c)(6) organizations when compared to 501(c)(3) organizations, which rely more heavily on donations and contributions. When looking at geographic scope of the association, regional or state and local organizations tend to rely more heavily on dues than those with an international or national scope. Size is also important, with larger organizations less reliant on membership dues than their smaller counterparts.

As a consequence of decreasing reliance on dues income, associations are continuously striving to develop nondues revenue streams for their organization. According to the *Operating Ratio Report,* the largest nondues revenue areas are meeting and convention registration fees (11.4 percent of total revenue), exhibit and trade show booth fees (7.8 percent of total revenue), and educational program fees (6.1 percent of total revenue.) Table 5.1 lists the top five sources of nondues revenue for trade associations and individual membership organizations.

A core and unique concept of associations is volunteerism. This generally refers to the voluntary donation of time to do the work of an association. Activities may include governance, program planning, speaking or teaching, standards development, and advocacy. Many associations, particularly small associations, are staffed and driven by volunteers.

TABLE 5.1. TOP FIVE NONDUES REVENUE SOURCES BY MEMBERSHIP TYPE.

Rank	Trade Associations	Individual Membership Organization
1	Meeting and convention registration fees (10.4 percent)	Meeting and convention registration fees (12.5 percent)
2	Exhibit and trade show booth fees (9.7 percent)	Educational program fees (7.5 percent)
3	Certification, accreditation, and standardization evaluation revenue (5.0 percent)	Contributions, grants, and contracts—non-government (7.2 percent)
4	Meeting sponsorship revenue (4.6 percent)	Exhibit and trade show booth fees (6.0 percent)
5	Educational program fees (4.5 percent)	Certification, accreditation, and standardization evaluation revenue (4.7 percent)

As associations get larger and more complex, professional staffs are employed and volunteers and staff work in a partnership to accomplish the aims of the association.

From a business perspective, associations are unusual in that members govern, develop content, and form the market for their offerings. For many organizations, this was a predictable and relatively stress-free business model.

Reimagining the Association Business Model

In years past, CSEs and their staffs need not have minded the business model. Sources of revenue and the value provided were very predictable.

However, the world of associations is rapidly changing. Many factors are driving this, including the impact of technology, the economy, changing demographics, globalization, and competition. Many of the services that once defined associations, such as community and information, can now be obtained by consumers at no charge via the Internet, social media, and mobile technology. Meanwhile, the corporate world is adopting "membership" and "engagement" as part of their business models. Businesses as diverse as LinkedIn and Zipcar are examples and illustrate the evolving concept of membership and community. Nonprofit web-based resources, such as Coursera, the Khan Academy, and edX offer educational programs for free or at nominal cost.

While competition increases, demands on associations are increasing along with costs for programs, technology, and staff.

Harrison Coerver and Mary Byers, CAE, in their book *Race for Relevance*, point out six trends that are having a dramatic impact on the business of associations.[5]

1. Time pressures

    The traditional association model is time insensitive, with expectations for volunteerism, meeting attendance, and reading of materials. Yet people are busier than ever with demanding jobs; two-income households; and many other factors, including a twenty-four-hour stream of news, information, and entertainment clamoring for attention.

2. Value expectations

    Membership was considered a professional obligation of professionals or of business for organizations. Today, "individuals and companies expect return on their dues investment."

3. Member market structure

> Associations are challenged to serve markets that are vastly different from those they were initially designed to serve. Industry consolidation and professional specialization require a rethinking of the member market the association can competitively and realistically serve. The threat is real. Some associations have lost members, have merged, or have ceased to exist.

4. Generational differences

> Coerver and Byers quote from the 2006 report "Generations and the Future of Association Participation," "the difference between Generation X and Baby Boomers is not the propensity to join associations but in their expectations about what membership means and the return it provides." There are real differences between the generation leading the association and the succeeding one.

5. Competition

> As noted, competition for associations is emerging from nontraditional firms, including universities and for-profit businesses. Areas of competition include education, tradeshows, online community, and certification and accreditation.

6. Technology

> Coerver and Byers point out that "a tidal wave of technologies has evolved to offer virtually every association deliverable and function: education, information, networking, fundraising, grassroots mobilization, and more." Associations frequently lack the financial resources and human talent to respond to the rapid influx of new technologies that are disrupting business models in every industry.

Indeed the question of relevance is one that consumes boards, CSEs, and their staffs. The role of associations and the business models that support them must change.

What is an association to do? Strategic planning is not enough. Strategic planning is the process of defining an organizations' strategy or direction, and making allocations of people, technology, and other resources in order to achieve its vision and goals. As noted earlier, the strategic plan usually does not test the assumptions surrounding the business of your association.

However, the design of the business model or theory of the business is in fact more basic. It involves disciplined research and decision making combined with innovation, creativity, and experimentation.

When should the business model be assessed? From a practical perspective, the business model cannot be changed frequently. You have based the very structure and operations of your organization on it. In some aspects, the answer might be, when it no longer works. However, it may work, but not as well as that of your competitor, or it may not be able to reach its potential. The following represent "warning" signs that should drive business model assessment.

- Maturity or flattening or decline in major sources of revenue
- Failure to penetrate a large percentage of your target market
- A dramatic change in the industry or profession you serve, such as demographic shifts, consolidation, or technology disruption
- The emergence of new competitors

Coerver and Byers, in their follow-up book, *Road to Relevance*, suggest five steps that can be applied by an association to assess and develop their business model.[6] All of these areas require focus and discipline and can be compared, in some ways, to the hedgehog principle outlined by Jim Collins in *Good to Great*,[7] The hedgehog always wins because he is doing what he was born to do and what he is best at doing. Collins encourages individuals and companies to create their hedgehog bases on the intersection of three circles:

- What are you best (and equally important, what you cannot be the best) in the world at?
- What drives your economic engine?
- What are you deeply passionate about?

Coerver and Byers recommend that associations do the following:

1. *Build on strength:* The authors stress that to compete you begin assessing your strengths in terms of customer base, member base, or both; programs; delivery channels; and core competencies.
2. *Concentrate resources:* Associations of all sizes tend to be spread thin. However, resources should be focused on the most impactful programs and strategies in terms of member value and for competitive advantage.
3. *Integrate programs and services:* The authors agree with strategy guru Michael Porter, who has written that one of the most critical aspects of competitive strategy is *fit*, in which all parts of strategy or portfolio of programs are mutually supportive and fit together seamlessly.

4. *Align people and processes for efficiency:* In general, there is significant waste in associations. The authors advocate that associations adapt the techniques of lean production to understand processes, to optimize value, and to eliminate unnecessary resources.

5. *Abandon services and activities when necessary.* Purposeful abandonment of obsolete or underperforming programs is viewed as essential activity to create capacity for innovation.

Examples of Emerging Business Models

Many associations are successfully transforming their business models. In each case, the approach is unique to the market served by the association and its environment. Following are a few examples.

Freemium

"Freemium is a pricing strategy by which a product or service (typically a digital offering such as software, media, games or web services) is provided free of charge, but money (premium) is charged for proprietary features, functionality or virtual goods."[8] In a freemium model, the key metrics to watch are (1) the average cost of serving a free user and (2) the rates at which the free users convert to premium (paying) customers.[9]

One example of this is the Drug Information Association (DIA), a global association serving professionals in the life sciences. DIA offers access to regulatory information and industry news before the member "wall." Viewers must trade up to membership to get full access to publications and more in-depth information.

Consistent with this is the notion of low-cost, virtual membership. The 2012 edition of *Benchmarking in Association Management: Membership and Components Policies and Procedures* reports that 13 percent of associations have a virtual or e-membership category.[10]

Moving from Membership to Cause-Based

The Healthcare Information Management Systems Society (HIMSS) started in 1961 as an individual membership serving IT and informatics professionals in the United States. Rapid changes in health policy, technology, and globalization have caused a reshaping of the business. Today, HIMSS describes itself as a cause-based, not-for-profit organization focused on better health through information technology. It focuses on its goals through leadership, education, events, market research, and media services. While headquartered in the United States, it has evolved to a global organization with offices in Europe and Asia.

Leveraging Certification

Certification and accreditation are major drivers in health care, engineering, education, and other areas. The Project Management Institute has leveraged global trends and demands to make certification its primary driver of association services. Certification drives membership, education, and PMI's global strategy. There are now 2.9 million PMI-certified individuals globally.

Quality as a Business Driver

The College of American Pathologists represents about fifteen thousand individual members, yet generates revenue in excess of $100 million. Its primary revenue driver is a set of resources directed at supporting, measuring, and demonstrating quality in laboratories and accreditation. This has grown in recent years to become a worldwide business and generates nearly two-thirds of its revenue.

The Association as Market Creator

AARP, originally the American Association of Retired Persons, was founded in 1958, in part as a vehicle to sell insurance, including Medicare supplements, to aging Americans. It has over time rebranded itself and refocused its market on individuals over the age of fifty and reframed its audience as active and vital. Today, AARP has thirty-seven million members and earns annual revenue approaching $1 billion, primarily from royalties and advertising on a wide range of insurance, financial, travel, and lifestyle products. Dues are only $16.

While AARP is an extreme example, other associations have leveraged their membership to create additional value for members and an additional stream of revenue.

The Business of Big Data

Associations are unusually positioned in that we capture significant data on our market segments. These data are often captured in our association management systems and may represent basic demographic data, but increasingly also represent transactional data. With increased computing and analytical power, several associations are developing businesses around "big data." This trend is very evident in medical societies, such as the American College of Cardiology and American Society of Anesthesiology, in which new regulatory requirements are incentivizing members to provide clinical data to large registries. These societies, in turn, can monetize the large data through the sale of analytics and data files to members, health care systems, and industry. The National Association of Realtors uses its multiple-listing service in a similar way.

Converting Your Network and Knowledge into Consultative Resources

A number of associations, including the American Optometric Association, the American Academy of Family Practice, and the Medical Group, either directly or through related organizations have built their business around consulting services. These businesses successfully leverage members' search for solutions in a changing environment, the association's reputation and network, and the assets of its database and knowledge resources.

Knowledge Management and Content Strategy

Associations are redesigning and restructuring on the basis of their approach to knowledge management and content strategy. Packaging and monetizing curated content drawn from all levels of the organization, including co-created offerings from communities of practice, offers new possibilities as an economic driver in a global environment.

The Power of Globalization

A common theme in most of these examples is globalization. Modern communications technology has removed physical limits on your market and amplified association opportunities on a global scale. U.S.- and European-based associations typically have more knowledge resources and knowledge assets than counterparts in Asia, Latin America, the Middle East, and Africa. Of course, globalization as part of your business model requires considerable thought as to focus, market development, cultural competence, and the management of business transitions.

Considerations in Business Model Assessment and Development

As you assess your current or new business model, here are some questions to consider:

1. Does the business model represent a platform for growth or does it build on an already mature market? What are the implications of your current or proposed business model on your competitive position?
2. Does the business model address the needs of your core membership market segments? Does your business model address changing demographics of your members?
3. Does your business model optimize the use of technology, including mobile platforms, social media, and big data?
4. Does the business model fit with strategy and culture? It may make good business sense, but may not be consistent, for instance, with the core values of your membership.
5. What capabilities or competencies are needed? Do you have these? If not, how can these be acquired?
   - Should you build, outsource, partner, acquire, or merge?
   - If you decide to build, can you afford to recruit and retain the right staff?
6. What are the legal and tax implications of your business model? Are you organized properly from a legal perspective? Will your business model create tax liabilities, and how can these be addressed? Are there other compliance areas such as privacy or intellectual property that need to be considered?

Conclusion

The business model is one of the most rewarding aspects of association work. To get the model right, real discipline, expertise, and leadership are required. Done correctly, it will yield the largest rewards in terms of customer satisfaction, member value, market growth, and organizational sustainability. You can get the rest right, but you cannot survive as an organization or an individual without a business model that works.

Notes

1. A. Osterwalder, Y. Pigneur, and T. Clark, *Business Model Generation: A Handbook for Visionaries, Game Changers, and Challengers* (Hoboken, NJ: John Wiley & Sons, 2010).
2. "Business Model," Wikipedia, available at http://en.wikipedia.org/wiki/Business_model.
3. P. Drucker, "The Theory of the Business," *Harvard Business Review* (1994).
4. ASAE, *Operating Ratio Report,* 14th ed. (Washington, DC: ASAE Association Management Press, 2012).
5. H. Coerver and M. Byers, *Race for Relevance: 5 Radical Changes for Associations* (San Francisco: Jossey-Bass, 2013).
6. H. Coerver and M. Byers, *Road to Relevance: 5 Strategies for Competitive Associations* (San Francisco: Jossey-Bass, 2013).
7. J. Collins, *Good to Great: Why Some Companies Make the Leap . . . and Others Don't* (New York: HarperBusiness, 2001).
8. "Freemium," Wikipedia, available at http://en.wikipedia.org/wiki/Freemium.
9. Osterwalder, Pigneur, and Clark, *Business Model Generation,* 96.
10. ASAE, *Benchmarking in Association Management: Membership and Components Policies and Procedures* (Washington, DC: ASAE Association Management Press, 2012).

The Author

Paul Pomerantz, FASAE, CAE, is chief executive officer of the American Society of Anesthesiologists. He has worked as an association CSE for over twenty years and has served in volunteer leadership positions with ASAE and the ASAE Foundation, as well as health- and medicine-related organizations. He speaks and writes frequently on association leadership and business strategy.

CHAPTER SIX

IDENTITY AND BRANDING

Mark N. Dorsey, FASAE, CAE

What are the promises your association makes to its members or the public? What can stakeholders expect from your association, and how do they distinguish you from your competitors? What is the idea—the mission and foundation of your association—that you and your staff can commit to and build upon? These questions touch upon the intangible essence of branding. Fundamentally, branding is a feeling about your organization based on experience.

If branding is about someone's experience with you and your organization, then *every touch point* related to your organization reflects and contributes to your brand. Everything from advertising, messaging, public relations, presentations, product and service availability and quality, education programming, certification processes, emails, and governance to how the phone is answered influence the perception of your brand. Like the discipline of marketing, the evolution of branding is customer- or audience-centric, not "sender" centric. Often confused with each other, branding and marketing (covered in more detail later in this book) are not the same thing, nor should branding be relegated to simply a design function or logo.

Branding and marketing are closely intertwined and depend upon each other, but the disciplines are distinct. Marketer and entrepreneur

Seth Godin's approach to branding paints a broader picture more relevant to today's sensibilities:

> "A brand is the set of expectations, memories, stories, and relationships that, taken together, account for a consumer's decision to choose one product or service over another. If the consumer (whether it's a business, a buyer, a voter or a donor) doesn't pay a premium, make a selection or spread the word, then no brand value exists for that consumer.
>
> …
>
> "A brand used to be something else. It used to be a logo or a design or a wrapper. Today, that's a shadow of the brand, something that might mark the brand's existence. If you've never heard of it, if you wouldn't choose it, if you don't recommend it, then there is no brand, at least not for you.
>
> …
>
> "Design is essential, but design is not brand."[1]

Think of branding as what goes into your choice of store or service—as well as the feeling after you've made your purchase—and marketing as all the activities that help you narrow your decision to the point of purchase. In the association world, one can make the case that associations define marketing as the acquisition and retention of "members." Being responsible for the happiness of a market is far bigger than member acquisition and retention. Arguably, so much focus on attracting and retaining members is a bit like a store focusing on the point of purchase—the cash register or the online checkout—instead of focusing on the offerings and experiences that entice the purchase in the first place. To summarize, brand is how you and your organization connect emotionally with customers.[2] Marketing is a disciplined array of activities putting buyers (the market) and sellers together.

While everyone in your organization has an influence on its brand, senior managers—particularly the chief staff executive—are primarily responsible for building and cultivating a loyal, enthusiastic following. At a minimum, this means having

- A coherent identity that stands for your organization's value
- Brand standards to ensure that clear identity, and that define the benefits, features, and value offered by your association
- An ability to integrate the brand across all association programs, services, and activities
- A means to evaluate the strengths and weaknesses—the effectiveness—of your brand

Ultimately, you should be able to clearly answer the questions "What do we do?" and "Why would anyone want to do it with us now or in the future?"

The CSE's Role in Branding

If sound strategy sets a company apart and puts it in a unique position, and if developing unique positioning is a branding function, then branding, by definition, is a strategic function. Taking this idea a step further, if one of the roles of the CSE is to work with the board to chart strategy—along with securing relationships and resources to enable the organization's mission—then the role of the CSE is to support branding as strategy. Along these lines, publications, professional development (education, credentialing, or both), information technology, finances, the physical office space, the telephone system—*everything*—communicates in some way about the association and has a role in strategy.

If these things are all true, then the CSE has a responsibility to ensure that staff are aligned with the culture of the organization to focus and communicate the organization's messages, to guarantee that the organization has the capacity and desire to listen to stakeholders, and to prevent branding activities—or any other function—from becoming a silo.

The CSE is ultimately on the hook to the board for this success, and the CSE is only as good as the staff. Microsoft's Bill Gates and Steve Ballmer, United/Continental's Jeff Smisek, Apple's Steve Jobs, GE's Jack Welch, and any U.S. president are all examples—for better or worse. However, many companies are famous for their performance and culture without a very famous chief executive officer as figurehead. Nordstrom, REI, Google, Edward Jones, Zappos, and Intuit come to mind as shining examples of this strategy. While the CSE has an obligation and ability to shape and support culture to the benefit of the organization and its stakeholders, it's everyone's job to deliver.

Branding Is Dead

Branding has been dying a very slow death because traditional strategies are no longer viable. Gone are the days when a brand was tightly controlled by advertisers and distributed one way via your local paper and a handful of television and radio outlets, and potentially supplemented with a handful of direct mail pieces.

Earlier in the chapter we noted that branding and marketing are intertwined, and perhaps no more closely than the evolution of branding and marketing. Marketing once was—and in some companies still is—product focused. Much like radio and television broadcasting in the mid- to late twentieth century, marketing theory embraced one-way communication on the premise of developing products with the broadest possible appeal at the lowest price. Branding, in this era, was developed to provide a common identity to support this activity. In this regard, branding was a subset of marketing.

Branding concepts broadened to include customer-centric ideas. Lifestyle marketing took hold in the 1960s when markets began responding to consumer demands. Target and segmentation marketing, positioning, and services marketing evolved in the 1970s, with increasing focus on the customer leading the way to experiential marketing, cause marketing, and sponsorship marketing through the 1990s.[3] The common denominator during this time is that, despite improvements in technology and market research, the customer is still viewed as passive. The increased use of lifestyle factors and causes to differentiate companies is the beginning of a broader definition and application of branding.

What's the result of more of the same as companies spit out increasing numbers of messages, easily developed and broadcast through ever-growing numbers of channels to oversaturated audiences?

- Organizations are creating shiny new tactics of the day rather than pursuing strategy. For example, just as companies in the 1990s created websites without really knowing why they wanted or needed one, so too are companies doing the same thing with social media platforms, mistakenly believing social media are simply another form of static, web-based content.
- In the frenzy to keep up, organizations are failing to identify metrics to help measure the success or failure of branding implementation. Can your organization identify the behaviors of customers or members? What is your reputation, on the basis of news and user-generated content? How does this compare to your competitors? What are they talking about? What is the likelihood someone will recommend your product or service?
- Dull and uninspiring creative content lists features rather than focusing on the *value* of the offering: anyone can offer resources, continuing education, information, discounts, and networking. Will what you offer give me a competitive edge or make me more successful? Will I get a raise or be a better human being by taking your education and certification offerings? Can you save me money? Many associations use the

generic "You have access to an array of programs that allow you to enjoy group discounts," as opposed to "Cut your equipment costs through members-only offers from dozens of association suppliers you won't find anywhere else."

Glum tidings indeed, and what's a brand manager to do? For many associations, it would seem that products and services often seem to sell despite our best branding and marketing, not because of it.

Long Live Branding

If branding is "the set of expectations, memories, stories and relationships that, taken together, account for a consumer's decision to choose one product or service over another,"[4] then modern views of competitive strategy should be music to an association executive's ears. Harvard business professor Michael Porter asserts three strategic principles that apply perfectly to branding:

1. It's not just a matter of being better at what you do, it's a matter of being *different* at what you do.
2. Good strategy differentiates your company and positions it as unique.
3. It's not good enough to be different; you have to trade off with other ways of being different (another way of saying you can't be all things to all people).[5]

Associations may struggle to adopt this approach because it means they have to make choices—something they generally are not good at, especially if it means disappointing a member. Further, this philosophy subtly presumes one-way communication, from producer to customer, removing important feedback aimed at enabling members to feel their voice is heard and depriving the organization of information about its performance.

Seize the Opportunities

How can we benefit from these new trends? Consumers' behavior and expectations of their relationship with a brand has changed. These days, customers trust one another more than the brand itself. Customers are increasingly engaged, informed, and communicative about their consumer experiences. Peer-to-peer referrals and relationships, even those online, are more trusted than brand messages.[6] As a result, organizations "no longer have full control over their brands because they are now competing with the collective power of consumers." In other words, you no longer own the channels of communication. Ignore this at your own peril.

Instead, it's important to create environments to encourage user-generated content and to recognize that individuals will communicate with each other about your organization *outside* those channels, whether you like it or not. For example, social media enables opportunities to rate your products and services, share video about your products and services, talk about your initiatives, and tell stories about interacting with your brand.

Recognize that customers co-create their experience with the brand. This goes beyond the idea of self-service. It may be a given that customers have always defined value for themselves. Now, customers define deeper relationships—which is one reason why Starbucks is piloting tea-only stores where customers can develop personalized blends of teas,[7] why purveyors of kitchenware are offering cooking classes, and why Porsche offers free driving improvement classes.

Authenticity rules, posers lose. Authenticity is based primarily on whether or not your organization delivers on what it says it will deliver. But almost as important, authenticity is about communicating in ways that come across as real and honest. Far too often, we really do have great things to offer our members and talk about them in ways that come across as utterly inauthentic. Although most of us have grown up hearing a near constant stream of it, no real human speaks "marketing speak." And, increasingly, no one believes it. Are we communicating in ways that are compelling? Or are we using the bland, less-than-compelling language of business?

Here's an example:

> "Why come to our event? Because professionals need access to
> high-quality information, professional networking, and professional
> development resources that only fellow members can provide."

Does that sound like an authentic, compelling message that promises a unique experience that you cannot do without? I don't think so either.

Instead, try making a topic like ceramics engineering interesting:

> Every day, materials professionals use ceramics to pioneer energy
> solutions, advance medicine, improve the environment, support
> manufacturing innovations, and make life better.

Often hidden, ceramic components are critical in nearly everything that makes modern life possible—from computers, cell phones, jet engines and armor, to skis, tennis rackets, and hip replacements.[8]

Or how about trees?

What do we do? We plant trees.
Why? Every time a tree is planted, our environment improves.
American Forests works to spread the word about the many benefits that forests provide for the health and well-being of the entire planet. With a greater understanding of what forests do for us all, we can encourage greater support to protect and restore these valuable resources.[9]

Or becoming a ski or snowboard instructor?

What we do: We get people excited about skiing and snowboarding.
Our culture: Connecting to people and ideas in unexpected ways and places.
Our direction: To be the first place people come for information about skiing and snowboarding, teaching, and the industry.
The value of membership: Access to people, resources, and more of the mountain environment that infuse excitement about skiing and snowboarding.

In other words, do your messages help paint a compelling picture and spark conversation about what you do, or do they merely emit "white noise"? Do they sound like the way a real person would talk about what you offer?
Authenticity is also based primarily on whether or not your organization delivers on what it says it will deliver. It's one thing to paint a compelling picture, and it's another to actually follow through. If you promise to plant trees, be ready to prove it. If the promise is to get the public and members more excited about skiing and snowboarding, then the experience had better do so. Customers will quickly judge whether or not your brand is authentic.[10] Tell a compelling, authentic story, engage your audience, and keep your promises—it's a simple, but effective combination.
Somewhat related to the issue of authenticity is uniqueness. Taking Michael Porter's comment about being different a step further, what

makes your organization *indispensable* to the marketplace? Do you offer a certification, research analysis, or a service to a population that no one can match? If not, chances increase every day that some other group or free service will successfully compete against you.

Being indispensable is another way of saying the utility your brand offers is unique, and you are known for providing high value and removing friction and pain points in ways that people will support by paying for what you offer. Authentic value is not simply a question of dollar cost, especially when we have shifted from people spending time to save money to spending money to save time.[11] "Actually giving consumers something valuable seems counterintuitive to most marketing departments because they equate 'value' with 'cost,' and the last thing a marketer wants to do is give something that costs them more money to fewer people than they are reaching with their traditional advertising. The truth is that great utilitarianism marketing doesn't have to cost more. It just has to be useful."[12]

Acknowledge that social responsibility is becoming a given within more and more market segments. This takes authenticity one step further. As increasing numbers of consumers educate themselves about what companies do beyond increasing value to shareholders, organizations that want to be more successful than their competitors must demonstrate they are stewards of their community and environment, not just the balance sheet. It isn't new that for-profit entities have tried to emulate the behavior or appearance of nonprofits. Some are genuinely committed to social responsibility, others less genuinely so.

Technology Changes the Playing Field

Many of the trends cited in the previous section are the result of rapid technological evolution, or revolution, if you prefer. We've moved from having the ultimate reference library at our fingertips—in which we are challenged with the task of organizing and consuming vast amounts of information pulled from or pushed to us—to a virtual world that is more expressive and collaborative.[13] People, not just institutions that employ them, generate news, information, ideas, and entertainment in unprecedented volume. And this content appears to be created with the purpose of sharing experiences, many of which include the experience one has with a brand. Under the cautionary note of "be careful what you wish for," word-of-mouth advertising has exploded, thanks to technology.

In one sense, we're moving toward that economic idea in which the market has perfect information available to customers whenever they want it (minus the perfect part, of course). As best-selling author

FIGURE 6.1. HUMAN COMMUNICATION.

Sender   Channel/Noise   Audience

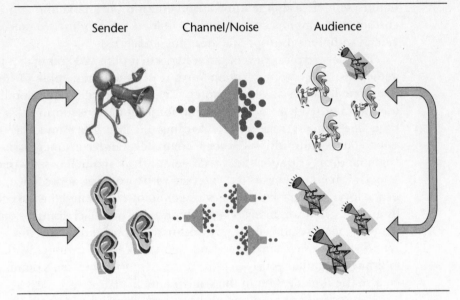

Daniel Pink notes in his book *To Sell Is Human*, it used to be true that sellers owned most of the information relevant to negotiation.[14] Now the information gap between buyers and sellers is about dead even. Increases in the exchange of information create a more level playing field as the flow of goods moves more seamlessly across borders due to lessening transportation and information costs.[15]

Communication Defines the Relationship

One can make the argument that branding is another view of human communication. An image of human communication may look like this: a message is sent by someone such as you (the Sender) through a Channel (verbal, physical gestures and expressions, written, electronic, and so on) (see figure 6.1). Your message is interfered with or distorted by Noise (as in irrelevant or meaningless data accompanying the desired information). The message may or may not be received by someone (the Audience). The audience may or may not send Feedback, subject to more noise, to the sender, who may stop the loop or adjust the message and resend. As feedback is sent and received, a communication loop ensues, which, with any luck, will continue.

For the record, this communication model is as applicable in education, credentialing, marketing, mass communications, and branding as it is in the study of one-to-one communications. And it would be a mistake to define "sender" as limited to your organization or marketing effort. Your customers, members, and other stakeholders are senders (as well as individuals with their own specific ideas and concerns).

The stereotypical view of branding is that of broadcasting to a passive audience—the communication version of matching supply to demand mentioned earlier in this chapter. That's more of yelling loudly one way, and not really a communication loop. In database terms, this would be a one-to-many relationship. During the late 1990s and early 2000s one-to-one relationships between companies and customers came into vogue and organizations learned a great deal about how different customer segments behave and interact with products and services. Thus began loyalty programs. Changes in technology facilitated the next change by enabling many-to-many relationships to become increasingly common. Many-to-many relationships provide new opportunities for the organization's employees, advocates, and detractors to be in touch with many customers simultaneously—and the many customers can communicate back to the organization in the same manner.

If the essence of branding is to predispose an audience or stakeholders to a certain relationship with an organization, then the roots of that relationship are in your organization's communication at every level—right down to how the phone is answered—and the proof of the relationship is in the audience's reaction to that communication. In other words, the audience, not you, ultimately defines the brand relationship.

Speaking of Engagement . . .

Brand relationships run the spectrum of engagement, with the spectrum defined by Forrester Research as "involvement, interaction, intimacy, and influence."[16] As one might expect, the qualitative elements of engagement change as one moves from involvement (for example, tracking site visits, page views, search, logins) through to influence (for example, Net Promoter Score, content sharing, blog posts). Understanding these forms of engagement and identifying the extent to which customers and stakeholders are actively or passively engaged with your brand is critical to developing insight about your markets. Forrester relates this understanding to four potential branding objectives: creating awareness, driving transactions, building brand preference, and increasing loyalty and a host of broader implications.

Simply assigning points for engagement is not enough. You need to meet customers where they are. And simply following the channels you create—an old-school notion—isn't sufficient. Why? Because 70 percent of Baby Boomers and 84 percent of Millennials say that user-generated content influences a purchase decision, with at least one in five saying this influences their decision "a lot."[17] And 51 percent of Americans trust user-generated content of information over that from a company website (16 percent) or news articles about the company (14 percent).[18] The point is, branding depends on factors outside your control as much, if not more, than those factors within your control.

Assessing Brand Effectiveness and Equity

Financial resources are critical to sustaining organizational activity, no matter how big or how small, which brings to mind the association adage "no margin, no mission." Volunteer efforts and in-kind contributions can be included as important financial resources as well. Measuring and reporting association progress toward achieving the mission along with stakeholder support toward—and their experiences with you in—achieving the mission is a key branding concept.

Examples of these measures may include the following:

- Financial measures
  - Changes in dues and renewals
  - Nondues revenue from all sources, including events, advertising, sponsorship, grants, and donations
  - Purchase behavior
- Nonfinancial measures
  - Likelihood of a stakeholder to recommend your organization to others (Net Promoter Score)[19]
  - Your brand's standing and importance compared to direct and indirect competitors
  - Use of and satisfaction with association print and electronic publications
  - Acceptance of, utility of, and satisfaction with certification programs
  - Unique products and services compared to formal and informal competitors
  - Identification and measurement of media content (social media and otherwise) about your industry or organization
  - Understanding of why members leave or stakeholders speak poorly of your organization

- Identifying brand attributes[20]
  - Prestigious
  - Loyal
  - Trustworthy
  - Credible
  - Effective
  - Scholarly
  - Innovative
  - Useful
  - Important
  - Practical

Ultimately, these and other measures contribute to brand equity. Multichannel marketing expert and author Akin Arikan offers a concept of brand equity that relates nicely to the definition of branding: "potential energy that has been stored in buyer's minds and that still needs to transform into actual purchases and increased shareholder value."[21]

Predictors of Behavior

Philip Kotler, as noted earlier, says that "(executives) today no longer have full control over their brands because they are now competing with the collective power of consumers."[22] He goes on to suggest that organizations that embrace this paradox, among others, will ultimately derive more revenue as the organization engages consumer emotions, which is the essence of contemporary branding. Profitability will increase as the cost of reaching more consumers decreases because the influence and importance of word of mouth—or perhaps word of keyboard—becomes more prominent. As a key influencer in your association, your role is critical in helping to identify stakeholder behaviors, identify factors that influence them, and answer the critical underlying question of "Why?" behind the results and behaviors. Too often, managers rely on frequency distributions and cross-tabulations to assert predictors of behavior rather than using the array of data available through their association's database, combined with more sophisticated analysis to identify the variables that are relevant and important.

Branding Is Everyone's Responsibility

Too often all responsibility for branding is kicked over to the marketing department. While someone has to shepherd an organization's messages, images, and customer experiences, this creates a tricky set of organizational issues.

If an organization has a chief marketing officer or chief relationship officer, does that let the rest of the organization off the hook for attracting and maintaining customer relationships? Of course not, but where does the responsibility lie? With everyone, because meaningful customer relationships and experiences are, and should be, part of the organization's culture. Left to a silo, the care and feeding of these critical activities becomes someone else's job. Therefore, an association executive's role, particularly the CSE and anyone in marketing, becomes one of staying in touch with and influencing the organizational culture. It's also the brand advocate's role to work with colleagues to ensure the association captures relevant, timely information about marketplace behavior, enables the organization to adapt to changes in that behavior, and helps the organization to remain true and authentic within the markets it serves.

The Rules

Consistency Still Matters

The importance of consistency as it relates to branding is contained within the definitions of integrated marketing communications (IMC), wherein IMC "is the development of marketing strategies and creative campaigns that weave together multiple marketing disciplines (paid advertising, earned media/PR, promotion, owned assets and social media) that are executed across a variety of media, and selected to suit the particular goals of the brand."[23] Or, put another way, IMC is "a strategic marketing process specifically designed to ensure that all messaging and communications strategies are unified across all channels and are centered around the customer."[24]

The case for consistency is straightforward.[25] If you tout the prestige and exclusivity of certain products and services to one audience on your website, and then turn around and promote sweeping discounting as a way to attract members via the same medium, you risk confusing your audiences and your brand proposition. This isn't to say you can't adopt these tactics via different media, only to take care not to send inconsistent and confusing messages to the broader audiences.

To this end, consistency of design and identity still facilitates strong branding. This means that logo use guidelines, editorial style guides, and easy-to-access resources must be available to those who might represent your organization's brand. Part of maintaining a brand also includes working with legal counsel specializing in intellectual property to ensure that rights regarding copyrights, trademarks,[26] trade dress,[27] and other forms of intellectual property are protected.

Embrace the Mission

Successful businesses start with the relentless, organization-wide pursuit of a mission and purpose, not with planning financial returns.[28] The mission should be clear and concise, define the organization's fundamental reason for being, and connect with the customer's ideas about how to make a difference.[29] They derive their mission from core values and beliefs, and examine policies that might weaken those values. They create a mechanism that directly links actions with values.[30] Embrace the mission, and members, financial results, and other support will follow.

Be Authentic and Deliver Real Value

Your audience determines the value, not you. It's important to note that members are likely to have the highest belief in the value of their purchase at the time they join an association, meaning associations start with high credibility to squander, if they're not careful. Also realize that perfection is a myth. Be ready to deal with it when your organization makes a mistake and your audiences communicate with each other, and with you, in ways you might not like.

Ask Five Key Questions

1. What do you *do*? (You should be able to answer this in one sentence.)
2. What makes your offering unique (or, better yet, indispensable)?
3. Why do you do it, and why do your constituents engage with you? (If you can't answer this, why should anyone care?)
4. How do you know what you know? (Are you relying on solid data and testing hypotheses, or are you just guessing? And if you can't answer this, how are you tracking the effectiveness of your brand?)
5. Do you like your customers, or are you focused on trying to get them to like you?[31] (The latter comes from a place of seeking validation as opposed to creating a relationship and, frankly, is not all that attractive.)

The Care and Feeding of the Brand Is Everyone's Job

Every contact with your brand is a chance to increase or decrease an individual's support of your organization. And as noted earlier, the role of the CSE as brand steward is critical in this regard. This individual will need to maintain focus on the mission and culture, break down any internal resistance to branding, and support marketing and communication efforts to ensure that branding isn't a sideline.

Utility, Utility, Utility

As we said earlier, being indispensable is another way of saying the utility your brand offers is unique. Or, put another way, what indispensable product or service would be lost if your association were to go away?

In conclusion, viewing the association from a branding perspective, you're in a unique position to help focus the organization and connect the outside with what's happening inside it. Many of the tried-and-true brand strategies of yesterday will always be relevant, but it's a new world, and organizations that seek to gain customers or members, engender loyalty, and build a solid financial structure need to ensure the association's brand maintains the emotional tie to mission and values.

Notes

1. Seth Godin, "Seth's Blog," n.d., available at http://sethgodin.typepad.com/seths_blog/2009/12/define-brand.html.
2. Brandstoke offers nine criteria to help in assessing brand essence, because articulating how customers feel about your brand in an authentic and meaningful way is often challenging. The features of a brand, for example, "lightweight," "fast," or "blue," are tangibles. They are easy to sense, describe, measure, and compare. The essence, on the other hand, is felt. Lacing up a new pair of Nike running shoes feels inspirational. Riding a Harley-Davidson motorcycle feels liberating. Experiencing Walt Disney World with your children feels magical. Strong brands have well-defined, easily grasped, simply obvious essences. Test your essence against these criteria: (1) single-minded, (2) intangible, (3) unique, (4) experiential, (5) consistent, (6) authentic, (7) sustainable, (8) meaningful, (9) scalable. Brandstoke, February 9, 2009, available at

http://www.brandstoke.com/2009/02/09/9-criteria-brand-essence/#sthash.eH80Wk6s.dpuf.

3. Philip Kotler, Hermawan Kartajaya, and Iwan Setiawan, *Marketing 3.0: From Products to Customers to the Human Spirit* (Hoboken, NJ: John Wiley & Sons, 2010).

4. Godin, "Seth's Blog."

5. Rowan Gibson, "Michael Porter on Strategic Innovation—Creating Tomorrow's Advantages," Innovation Excellence, December 29, 2011, available at http://www.innovationexcellence.com/blog/2011/12/29/michael-porter-on-strategic-innovation-creating-tomorrows-advantages.

6. Nielsen, "Global Advertising Consumers Trust Real Friends and Virtual Strangers the Most," July 7, 2009, available at http://blog.nielsen.com/nielsenwire/consumer/global-advertising-consumers-trust-real-friends-and-virtual-strangers-the-most.

7. Kelly Blessing, "Starbucks to Open Tazo Tea Store," Bloomberg, June 20, 2012, available at http://www.bloomberg.com/news/2012–06–20/starbucks-to-open-tazo-tea-store.html.

8. The American Ceramic Society, "Learn About ACerS," n.d., http://ceramics.org/about/learn-about-acers.

9. American Forests, n.d., available at http://www.americanforests.org/why-it-matters.

10. James H. Gilmore and B. Joseph Pine II, *Authenticity: What Consumers Really Want* (Boston: Harvard Business School Press, 2007).

11. "What is utilitarianism marketing? It's not about advertising, it's not about messaging, and it's not about immediate conversions. It's about providing a true value and utility: something consumers not only would want to use—constantly and consistently—but would derive so much value from it that it would be given front-and-center attention in their lives. Do you think your brand has the ability to create that kind of interest and attention in this media-saturated and ads-everywhere world in which we live?" Mitch Joel, *Ctrl Alt Delete: Reboot Your Business. Reboot Your Life. Your Future Depends on It* (New York: Business Plus, 2013), 33.

12. Joel, *Ctrl Alt Delete*, pp. 33–34.

13. Kotler, Kartajaya, and Setiawan, *Marketing 3.0*.

14. Daniel H. Pink, *To Sell Is Human* (New York: Silverhead Books, 2012).

15. Kotler, Kartajaya, and Setiawan, *Marketing 3.0,*

16. Brian Haven, with Josh Bernoff and Sarah Glass, "Marketing's New Key Metric: Engagement," Forrester Research, Inc., August 8, 2007, available at https://www.adobe.com/engagement/pdfs/marketings_new_key_metric_engagement.pdf.

17. Bazaar Voice, "Talking to Strangers: Millennials Trust People Over Brands," January 2012, available at http://resources.bazaarvoice.com/rs/bazaarvoice/images/201202_Millennials_whitepaper.pdf.

18. Ibid.

19. The Net Promoter Score, or NPS, is based on the fundamental perspective that every company's customers can be divided into three categories: promoters, passives, and detractors. By asking one simple question—How likely is it that you would recommend [your company] to a friend or colleague?—you can track these groups and get a clear measure of your company's performance through your customers' eyes. Customers respond on a 0-to-10-point rating scale and are categorized as follows. Promoters (score 9–10) are loyal enthusiasts who will keep buying and refer others, fueling growth. Passives (score 7–8) are satisfied but unenthusiastic customers who are vulnerable to competitive offerings. Detractors (score 0–6) are unhappy customers who can damage your brand and impede growth through negative word of mouth. To calculate your company's NPS, take the percentage of customers who are promoters and subtract the percentage who are detractors. Frederick F. Reichheld, "The One Number You Need to Grow," *Harvard Business Review*, December 2003, available at http://hbr.org/2003/12/the-one-number-you-need-to-grow/ar/1.

20. Sheri Jacobs, *The Art of Membership: How to Attract, Retain and Cement Member Loyalty* (Hoboken, NJ: John Wiley & Sons, 2014), 47–49, 62–63.

21. Akin Arikan, *Multichannel Marketing: Metrics and Methods for On and Offline Success* (Hoboken, NJ: John Wiley & Sons, 2008), 118–121.

22. Kotler, Kartajaya, and Setiawan, *Marketing 3.0*, 10.

23. Stir, "It's Time to Redefine Integrated Marketing," Stirology, April 16, 2013, available at http://blog.stirstuff.com/2013/04/16/time-to-redefine-integrated-marketing.

24. Journal of Integrated Marketing Communications, n.d., available at http://jimc.medill.northwestern.edu/what-is-imc.

25. Arikan, *Multichannel Marketing*, 16.

26. U.S. Patent and Trademark Office, "Trademark, Patent, or Copyright?" n.d., available at http://www.uspto.gov/trademarks/basics/definitions.jsp.

27. Cornell University Law School, Legal Information Institute, "Trade Dress: Definition," n.d., available at http://www.law.cornell.edu/wex/trade_dress.

28. Peter F. Drucker, "What Businesses Can Learn from Nonprofits," *Harvard Business Review*, July 1989, available at http://hbr.org/1989/07/what-business-can-learn-from-nonprofits/ar/1.

29. Kotler, Kartajaya, and Setiawan, *Marketing 3.0*, pp. 40–41.
30. Jim Collins and Jerry Porras, (New York: Harper Collins Publishers, Inc., 2004).
31. "(Businesses are) asking consumers to 'like' them on Facebook while few actually make an effort to connect to those individuals on their own spaces. Here's a hint: Instead of asking people to like your business, why doesn't your business start liking these people first? They're asking customers to subscribe to the RSS feeds of their blogs or share their content, while the brand editors spend zero time engaging in the comments on the blogs being created by their customers. Here's a hint: Be active on every blog that serves your industry. Don't expect everyone to come to you. They're looking for customers to follow them on Twitter, but don't actually push beyond their own tweetstream to build affinity and loyalty. Here's a hint: If your Twitter feed is nothing but announcements about your sales or service upgrades and nobody is retweeting or sharing your content, it may be time to start thinking about adapting your content strategy." Joel, *Ctrl Alt Delete*, 16–17.

The Author

Mark N. Dorsey, FASAE, CAE, is executive director and CEO, Professional Ski Instructors of America (PSIA) and the American Association of Snowboard Instructors (AASI). He entered the association field in 1989 and served as PSIA-AASI's marketing director and later as COO. He is recognized for expertise in developing and presenting innovative corporate and association strategy with positive, quantifiable results, and an emphasis on change management, turnaround strategies, and revenue growth.

CHAPTER SEVEN

FINANCIAL MANAGEMENT

Rob Batarla, MBA, CPA, CAE

Money matters. Some people don't like to talk about it. And in the world of nonprofit (which includes charities and associations—both trade and individual membership), there is often focus on the mission and organizational accomplishments pushing finances to the back burner. However, deep down inside everyone knows that without the money, the mission and major accomplishments would not exist.

With increased scrutiny on nonprofits from the Internal Revenue Service and charity watchdog organizations, making sure the money is in good proper order is essential. From budgeting to financial reporting to auditing and tax preparation, following best practices can make all the difference.

Strategic Budgeting and Financial Planning

Most nonprofit entities start financial planning with a budget. Simply put, a budget is a financial roadmap of how an organization wants its finances to look. Budgets are typically done toward the end of the previous fiscal year. As organizations plan activities to come, knowing how the money is going to be spent—and how it is going to come in—is essential. And since the future cannot be predicted, budgets are oftentimes wrong the minute they are finished. So budgets should be looked at as a guideline and not a doctrine.

Types of Budgets

As you start planning, using different types of budgets can provide different perspectives in how the association's finances are viewed. Here are some different types of budgets:

- *Program budget:* Part of the operating budget, detailing out a specific program of the association, for example, the conventional budget, the magazine budget
- *Functional budget:* Equivalent to a "department budget," encompassing all activities and overhead expense of a specific department, such as the education department budget
- *Operating budget:* For a specific period, covers the revenue and expense of the day-to-day operations of the association
- *Capital budget:* Estimates all capital asset acquisitions and summarizes all expenses and costs of major purchases for the next year
- *Cash budget:* Covers the ins and outs of cash for the association.

The creation of the annual budget can be a lengthy process that involves many people in the organization. Once the association leaders set the strategies and priorities for the near future, the budget usually starts with the program managers that are responsible for specific areas of the association and then goes back "up the chain" to senior management, the chief staff officer, a volunteer finance committee, and finally the organization's board of directors. The entire process can take months.

Understanding the financial landscape of the association more than one year out is a good practice. Some organizations actually choose to do two-year budgets and just make refinements in the off year. For associations operating with a multiyear long-range financial plan, two-year budgeting may not be that difficult.

Some organizations use zero-based budgeting—a technique in which the "budgeteer" starts from scratch in building the budget. This technique may be a good idea if you want to eliminate wasteful spending or you are completely redesigning your benefit package or business model. But at most times, incremental budgeting is applied when the numbers are based on prior-year information and adjusted. Be mindful not to befriend the budget's worst enemy: "SALY," which is short for "same as last year." Although prior-year information is a great place to start, make modifications as needed. For example, if your annual conference changes cities year to year, that may have an impact on attendance revenue and conference or travel expenses. Budgeting the same amount for meals in Las Vegas as you did for meals in Charlotte would definitely cause a variance.

Budgeting techniques also work well for doing some financial planning with new initiatives. As your organization embarks on new projects, creating a business case with pro-forma financial statements or future budgets helps determine if the project is viable. Your organization should have standards as to how long the new initiative needs to be supported by other revenue streams, the level of growth desired, and so on. By using estimates and future planning on new initiatives, decision makers can better evaluate how and when—from a financial perspective—the organization should launch new programs. (See "Business Planning," Chapter Thirteen.)

Ideally, budgeted revenue would exceed budgeted expenses (or at least break even), but that isn't always going to be the case. Sometimes, perhaps due to an economic downturn or some specific priority, a deficit (expenses exceeding revenue) is budgeted. Assuming there are ample reserves (which will be discussed later), budgeting to lose money is not a bad thing. For example, let's say that there is a strong public awareness need and the only way to accomplish that goal is to purchase a Super Bowl ad. If that one-time expense causes a deficit budget, but accomplishes a much-needed goal (and the organization has the money), then using the reserves is a good thing to do.

◆ ◆ ◆

Capital Expenditures

Capital expenditures are large cash outlays in one year that will affect future budgets. When investing in fixed assets or some types of software, the useful life or benefit extends beyond the year of the operating budget. And thus those expenditures are capitalized and depreciated over the useful life of the assets. For example, if an organization spends $4 million on a building that has a useful life of forty years, although $4 million worth of cash may go out the door in year one, the organization will only incur $100,000 worth of expense each year for the next forty years. That $100,000 needs to be factored into the operating budget for many years to come. But that should make sense since the organization is using the assets during that time anyway!

◆ ◆ ◆

Tying money to goals, objectives, or so on is the basis for strategic budgeting. If, as in the previous example, public awareness is a top priority, then funds, like the Super Bowl ad, should be allocated to it. If your organization has a strategic plan, then the budget should be a compendium piece to it. Resource allocation to the plan should take priority over nonplan spending. Of course, there will be nonplan expenses that need to occur. And not every expense can or should be tied to the plan. Saying that "everything we do" is strategic is simply not true, and the budget supporting the plan becomes artificial when this forcing of expenses occurs. Moreover, there is not an industry standard on how much of your expenses should be included in the strategic plan. But setting an organizational benchmark or level and then monitoring it year after year is a good practice. One calculation to consider is how much of the discretionary funds are going toward the plan. So take out expenses for "must-do" activities (such as finance, HR, IT, and so on) and calculate the percentage of expenses resourcing the plan.

> "A strategic plan without a budget is just a dream and a budget without a strategic plan is just spending."

◆ ◆ ◆

Budget Use

Strategic budgeting and financial planning lay the groundwork for the organization to follow. Again, the actual results will be different than the budget, but the budget provides one objective barometer for measuring financial performance. Many times organizations like to adjust the budget as the year progresses. As the budget is usually a board-approved document, it should only be changed if the board wants or needs to have officially revised numbers. This would likely be requested when there is a significant variance in revenue or expenses with negative impact to cash flow and the association has no reserves. Otherwise, using forecasted numbers and variance analyses should get you through the year. Remember that budgets are history once you have actual numbers.

◆ ◆ ◆

Financial Reporting and Analysis

There are three main financial statements for a nonprofit organization: the statement of financial position (that is, the balance sheet), the statement of activities (the income statements), and the statement of cash flows.

The statement of financial position is a point-in-time statement that lists the entity's assets, liabilities, and net assets. Assets are what the organization owns, such as cash, investments, receivables (money owed to the association), and fixed assets such as furniture and computers. Liabilities are what the organization owes, such as payables (bills not yet paid), deferred revenue, and debt. Net assets are the difference between assets and liabilities and are essentially what the organization is worth. To put it in personal terms, let's say you own a house that has a market value of $400,000. You have a mortgage on that house for $275,000. So your equity in the house is $125,000. Your house is an asset; your mortgage is a liability; and your equity is your net assets.

Usually prepared at month-, quarter-, and year-end, the statement of financial position presents the balances at that specific point in time. So on December 31, for example, an organization has a certain amount in cash. If the next day, they pay a huge bill, that cash number would be different.

Here are a few things to look for when reviewing the statement of financial position:

- Assets are valued at market value, which is the price the asset would get on the open market (except fixed assets, which are valued at depreciated cost).
- Assets should be listed in order of liquidity, with cash always listed first.
- Organizations that keep their books on a cash basis (instead of accrual) will not show any liabilities. Organizations with modified cash or modified accrual will probably show payables.
- Net assets are broken up into three classes: unrestricted, temporary restricted, and permanently restricted. Restriction in net assets results from funds that come in through "non-exchange transactions," when money changes hands without any expectation of a return, like a donation. These are "donor transactions" and are restricted on the basis of the donor's intent.

The statement of activities is a period-of-time statement that shows the entity's revenues and expenses. Assuming accrual basis accounting, revenue represents what has been earned, not necessarily collected. And expenses represent costs that have been incurred regardless of whether payment has been made. There are many different ways to present the statement of activities. In fact, how the statement looks month to month may vary with how auditors present an audited financial statement. Although the statement generated from your accounting software may be cumbersome to work with, it is recommended that your financial statements be presented in a standard format drawn from your accounting software rather than manually created statements. This reduces the risk of transfer errors.

The statement of activities reports results over a period of time, for example, "three months ending March 31" or "twelve months ending December 31." In contrast to the statement of financial position, which is a point in time, the statement of activities spans a period and is usually cumulative during the year.

The difference between revenue and expenses is known as the "change in net assets." In the for-profit world this would be known as "net income/loss." And the two statements are linked. See Table 7.1 for an example.

Although the example is simplistic, it illustrates the point. The change in net assets in 2015 from the revenue and expense is $5,000, meaning that the organization increased its net worth by $5,000 in that given year with revenues exceeding expenses. To further illustrate the point, you can see that net assets on December 31, 2016, are $5,000 higher than on December 31, 2015. This is the only line item that links the balance sheet and the statement of activities.

When reviewing the statement of activities, if the expenses exceed the revenue, then the organization has a net loss. It is the statement of activities that you use for actual-to-budget comparison.

See Table 7.2 for an example.

The budget was a break-even budget with $130,000 in revenue and the same amount in expenses. However, revenue came in below budget by $5,000, but expenses were also under budget by $10,000. The overall result is that instead of breaking even, the organization made $5,000.

Looking at budget variances helps with financial planning in future years. There may be many reasons the actual results are off from budget—including bad budgeting! As the budget is just a guide, there isn't any reason to panic when there are budget variances. Understand what causes them and use that knowledge going forward. Being under budget, like in the preceding example, may look great on the bottom line, but perhaps the money allocated to other expense that was not spent may mean that an important activity didn't get done. And that isn't good.

When you think about the budget as a plan, comparing the actual results to the budget is just a way to see how your plan was executed. Periodically checking the budget-to-actual variance helps in seeing if things are still on the track you projected.

The last statement to mention is the statement of cash flows. The statement takes the change in net assets and uses it to show the change in the cash position from the beginning of the year to the end of the year using three sections: changes in operating activity, changes in investing activity, and changes in financing activity. The statement of cash flows used by audits can be somewhat confusing to the general users of financial statements, and many associations choose to create their own versions to show the cash position throughout and at the end of the year.

TABLE 7.1. SAMPLE FINANCIAL STATEMENTS.

Statement of Financial Position		Statement of Financial Position		Statement of Activities	
December 31, 2015		December 31, 2016		Jan 1, 2016–Dec 31, 2016	
Assets		**Assets**		**Revenue**	
Cash	$10,000	Cash	$15,000	Dues	$100,000
Investments	$50,000	Investments	$55,000	Other	$25,000
Total Assets	$60,000	Total Assets	$70,000	Total Revenue	$125,000
Liabilities and Net Assets		**Liabilities and Net Assets**		**Expenses**	
Accounts Payable	$5,000	Accounts Payable	$7,000	Salaries	$80,000
Deferred Revenue	$15,000	Deferred Revenue	$18,000	Other Expenses	$40,000
Total Liabilities	$20,000	Total Liabilities	$25,000	Total Expenses	$120,000
Net Assets	$40,000	Net Assets	$45,000	**Change in Net Assets**	**$5,000**
Total Liabilities and Net Assets	$60,000	Total Liabilities and Net Assets	$70,000		

TABLE 7.2. SAMPLE BUDGET-TO-ACTUAL VARIANCES.

	Budget	Statement of Activities	Budget Variances
For 201_x_		Jan 1, 201x–Dec 31, 201x	For 201x
Revenue		**Revenue**	**Revenue**
Dues	$115,000	Dues $100,000	Dues ($15,000)
Other	$15,000	Other $25,000	Other $10,000
Total Revenue	$130,000	Total Revenue $125,000	Total Revenue ($5,000)
Expenses		**Expenses**	**Expenses**
Salaries	$75,000	Salaries $80,000	Salaries ($5,000)
Other Expenses	$55,000	Other Expenses $40,000	Other Expenses $15,000
Total Expenses	$130,000	Total Expenses $120,000	Total Expenses $10,000
Change in Net Assets	$0	Change in Net Assets $5,000	Change in Net Assets $5,000

Metrics for Financial Analysis

Besides comparing actual results to the budget, there are other ways to read financial statements. Table 7.3 offers seven easy metrics to look at when determining an organization's financial health.

These seven metrics, together, give an overall snapshot of the organization's financial health. It makes most sense to look at these metrics on a quarterly basis and compare them to an industry or organizational benchmark and a year-to-year comparison for trending. However, be careful with benchmarks. All organizations are different, so understanding how your organization compares to a benchmark is important.

To illustrate the point of benchmarks, let's dive into the current ratio. The current ratio divides current assets into current liabilities to show that

TABLE 7.3. KEY FINANCIAL METRICS.

Metric	Where to Find or How to Calculate	What the Metric Will Tell You
Revenue growth	From the statement of activities, divide the difference of YTD current year and YTD prior-year revenue by YTD prior-year revenue.	Is the organization growing year after year?
Revenue diversification	From the statement of activities, divide the difference of total revenue and your largest revenue stream (perhaps dues) by total revenue.	Does the organization rely too heavily on one revenue stream?
Programmatic expense percentage	From the statement of activities, divide programmatic expenses by total expenses.	Do most of the funds go toward the mission?
Current ratio	From the statement of financial position, divide current assets by current liabilities.	Can the organization pay its bills?
Profitability	From the statement of activities, divide the change in net assets by the total revenue.	Is the organization making money?
Liquid reserves	Divide the unrestricted net asset balance (from the statement of financial position) by the annual expense budget.	Does the organization have money in investments?
Total reserves	Divide total investments (from the statement of financial position) by the annual expense budget.	Are the net assets adequate?

there is enough money to pay the bills. The industry benchmark on this is two, meaning a healthy organization should have twice the current assets as current liabilities. So an organization with $300,000 in cash and $150,000 in accounts payable would be fine as opposed to an organization with only $160,000 in cash and the $150,000 in accounts payable. But since assets and liabilities are pulled from the "point-in-time" statement of financial position, the below-benchmark current ratio may really only be a timing issue.

In the preceding example, let's assume that the $160,000 in cash is as of March 31st, and the organization calculates its ratios at the end of each quarter. The organization is going to have a below-benchmark ratio on that date, but perhaps with the way cash flows, they get a huge influx of cash on April 3. The first quarter current ratio may look bad, but it is just a timing issue with the organization's cash flow. And assuming that the cash flow is similar year after year, seeing a below-benchmark current ratio on March 31st becomes common and essentially is not an issue. Having a solid understanding of the metrics and benchmarks and knowing how to apply them is equally as important.

As each organization is different, perhaps there are other ratios and metrics that make more sense for your organization. If there is significant revenue from product sales, then inventory turnover would be good to look at. If donations are large, diving into the restrictions of the net assets would be important. It is also important to look at the trends of the numbers. Variances may be minor, but continual decreases over time, for example, can tell more of a story.

Another good evaluating tool, especially for specific initiatives and programs, is your return on investment (ROI). By dividing the difference of the gain and the cost of the investment by the cost of the investment, you can see if the initiative is yielding a fair return. For example, if you invest $50,000 in new software that earns the organization $60,000, then the ROI would be 20 percent. Given that most investment doesn't have double-digit returns, the 20 percent ROI is quite good. The trick to getting a complete ROI is making sure you include *all* the costs included in the investment, including staff time if applicable.

So what does one do with financial statements and ratios and financial analysis? All this information should be presented to those who make decisions in the organization, from program managers to senior management to the board of directors. Programmatic financial information should be given to program managers monthly, no later than fifteen days following the end of the month. Association-wide financial data and benchmarks should be distributed to the board and senior management on a quarterly basis, again, no later than fifteen days after quarter-end. Financial information should be prefaced with some qualitative information about the association's activities for the quarter, and it may also be helpful to add some nonfinancial data (such as membership count, conference attendees, and so on) to create a more complete picture.

Do not send too much information, as that overload could be too much for nonfinance people to digest. Less can be more, but smartly presented financial information will help. At the end of the day, providing the right information with proper analysis that helps association leaders make good financial decisions is the ultimate goal of financial statement reporting and analysis.

Internal Controls and Attestation

To ensure that the finances run smoothly, there are certain procedures and protocols that the finance department follows. Ever wonder why they need certain signatures or proper coding? Your financial department is trying to create an environment that has good, solid controls.

Internal controls work to prevent fraudulent activities. For example, think about what it takes to pay a vendor. First, someone needs to initiate funds going out the door. Then that initiation needs to be approved. Next, someone who has custody of the checks needs to cut a check, and then that check needs to be signed. The check needs to be recorded properly in the accounting system and ultimately mailed out to the vendor. Those are a lot of steps during which error or manipulation could occur. However, with a solid internal control system, checks and balances are created and the potential for something to go wrong is reduced. So the person who initiates the check shouldn't be the same person who signs or authorizes the check because then that person could just cut themselves a check. Good internal controls would segregate those duties so risk can be mitigated.

Other types of good internal controls, besides segregation of duties, include

- Proper safeguarding of assets to prevent fraud, misuse, and waste (in other words, keep the checks locked up!)
- Timely reconciliations of bank accounts
- Processing controls that allow for an audit trail of what occurred

At the end of the year, it is a good idea to have an external review of the financial statements. There are three options from which an organization can choose:

- *Compilation:* When an external professional just compiles the financial information provided by the client but doesn't provide any attestation
- *Review:* When an external professional does limited testing on the financial information
- *Audit:* When an external professional (that is, a certified public accountant) does testing based on general accepted auditing standards in order to form an opinion to say that the financial statements are free of material misstatements

Certainly the audit is the highest level of attestation. The audit process starts with a review of the internal controls. If the organization can prove there are good internal controls, then the audit testing can be reduced. Auditors do not look over every transaction and do not state that the numbers are perfect. It is a common misunderstanding that "audited financial statements" are perfect. They are, instead, free of material misstatements. For example, in a $10 million organization, if there is a $40 expense reimbursement for travel that is coded to supplies, it is possible that the audit would not pick that up. It might be a symptom of bad internal controls, and the auditors will test for that.

Auditors give an opinion on the financial statements. Options are unqualified, qualified, adverse, and disclaimer of opinion. Organizations strive to get an unqualified ("clean") opinion, whereas a qualified opinion indicates there is an issue that the auditor has concerns about. An adverse opinion indicates there is a serious issue to address. The auditors will also provide a management letter to the board of directors with suggestions on improvements to internal controls, if there are any.

Every association should have written policies that address the process of handling financial transactions and decision making, including the receipt and recording of cash, payment of bills, authorization of disbursements, payroll preparation, account reconciliation, investments, and journal entries as well as requirements to initiate payments, who has authority to authorize or approve check requests, verification of assets shown on the books, audit frequency, lines of authority for financial decision making, bonding, and training required for anyone involved in handling the association's money.

Tax Exemption

Corporation status is determined through your organization's home state. Being a tax-exempt entity is something granted by the Internal Revenue Service (IRS). Once incorporated, an organization can apply for tax exemption from the IRS. By filing Form 1023 or 1024, a nonprofit corporation can achieve tax exemption, most often in the form of a 501(c)(3) or 501(c)(6). There are twenty-nine types of tax exemptions under the code, but (c)(3) and (c)(6) are the two most common and are described in detail in other chapters.

Being tax exempt doesn't mean that the organization won't pay any taxes. It means that income earned by the entity within the scope of its stated purpose isn't subject to state or federal tax. However, tax-exempt entities will still pay

- Payroll taxes
- Sales tax (unless they have a sales tax exemption—which varies by state)
- Food and beverage tax
- Hotel taxes
- Taxes on income earned from unrelated activities

The last one is commonly known as UBIT, or unrelated business income tax. Net revenue generated from activities that are not part of the organization's exempt purpose is subject to taxation. Common examples include advertising, rental income, and royalties. The IRS code lists specifically what is and what isn't unrelated business income. However, you should be careful because there are nuances.

- Advertising income is taxable; sponsorship income is not. The IRS views sponsorship as publicly acknowledging their donors and thus is not the same as advertising, although many see it as very similar.
- Rental income from debt-financed properties is considered taxable, but rental income from finance that is debt-free is not.
- Royalty income is not considered taxable if the association isn't actively generating the revenue. Staying passive and letting a third party handle the business (where you just then get a royalty check) keeps the activity tax exempt.

Despite the title, tax-exempt entities are required to file an annual return with the IRS. The Form 990 (or the Form 990-EZ or Form 990-N postcard—dependent on the organization's size) is due on the fifteenth day of the fifth month after fiscal year-end. For organizations with fiscal years ending December 31, that puts the return due on May 15th. Like your personal return, it can be extended by request, and the extensions can push the return's due date six months.

The Form 990 has grown in size over the past several years to include more than just financial information. At its core, the Form 990 presents financial information similar to the statements of financial position and activities, albeit in somewhat of a different format, as well as many other schedules from international activities to related party transactions to information on gaming activities to endowments.

Form 990 statements are public documents, and many are available online for review. Because the filings are public, many organizations take the opportunity to use the form as a marketing tool. The form does provide the ability for an organization to talk extensively about its activities.

Reserves

Much like we hold money in savings, smart organizations have reserves. Whether they are saving for a new IT system or a big project, or just being cautious in case the economy crashes, having ample reserves is essential.

Reserves can be defined in many ways. Two simple reserve definitions are "liquid" and "total." Liquid reserves equal what is held in the investment account. And total reserves equal unrestricted net assets. Reserves are often presented in percentage form with either investments or net assets as the numerator and total budgeted expenses as the denominator. For example, if an entity with a $15 million expense budget has $7.5 million in reserves (either in investments or in net assets), then you would say their reserves are at 50 percent.

So what is the right answer as to how much should be in reserves? It depends. There actually isn't a right or wrong answer; it depends on your organization. Per a recent study, nonprofits were averaging around 55 to 60 percent in reserves. This is not a benchmark but rather where the industry sits currently. Here are some reasons to have higher-than-average reserves:

• Revenue streams are not very diverse (that is, all your eggs are in one basket).
• Revenue streams are not very stable.
• There is uncertainty in the marketplace.
• There are large expenses coming up.

It is possible to have too much in reserves as well. As nonprofits are not banks, hoarding members' money doesn't go over too well. When you have 300 percent in reserves it would be hard to justify a dues increase! The best way to handle this is to have a board-approved reserve policy that sets out the target for the level of reserves.

Organizations use their reserves (using the total reserve definition) when they have a negative change in net assets. Sometimes this loss is budgeted—a planned use of reserves. Sometimes the loss is not budgeted, resulting in an unplanned use of reserves. For example, holding the annual conference in Hawaii sounded like a great idea but attendees did not want to travel there due to the increased costs. Conference revenue was way down, and the organization suffered a loss for the year. Essentially they ate into reserves. The conference was planned but the poor attendance was unexpected.

Sometimes things don't go according to plan and having a safety net or a cushion is helpful.

To ensure the future viability of the organization, you will likely use reserves. Associations cannot rest on their financial laurels and sometimes need to take some risks. To stay current, investments into new revenue streams need to occur. Creating new revenue streams may be costly at first, but by using the good planning tools talked about before, you will know what your loss tolerance is and when to "cut bait."

Investment Management

Liquid reserves are defined as what an organization has in its investment portfolio. Investments can be a very small or a very large portion of the total assets. All investment advisors would tell you to have a good diversified portfolio with the goal to reduce risk as much as possible while still maintaining some return. The funds put in your investment accounts are, in essence, from members or donors, and the last thing an organization wants to do is lose that money on bad investments.

There are many ways to set up a good diversified portfolio. With a mix of equities and fixed income investments, the organization's risk tolerance level will determine how much of each should be held. It is advisable to use an investment advisor who can help. Always make sure that the organization has a sound, board-approved investment policy for any advisor to follow. Your advisor can help in determining if the best route is mutual funds, individual stock and bonds, or a blend of both.

This is a great place to involve a volunteer investment committee that focuses on effective investment strategies in consultation with your advisor, the investment policy, and examining the risk tolerance of the board. Having your investment advisor meet with the board on an annual basis is recommended.

Summary

From budgets to metrics, finances are an integral part of a nonprofit's existence. Making sure the books are clean and the financial plan has been charted out are steps to ensuring a well-run organization. With all that being said, remember that there are external factors that can make or break an organization. The financial markets are increasingly more unpredictable. Government regulations, societal changes, and globalization are all playing into the financial health of an organization. Although many things are beyond the organization's control, being prepared and fiscally healthy through sound financial management will help you to successfully maneuver through what may lie ahead.

The Author

Rob Batarla, MBA, CPA, CAE, is currently vice president, finance and business development, and chief financial officer for the American Physical Therapy Association in Alexandria, Virginia. He is a former member of the AICPA's Exempt Organizations Expert Panel and the Not-For-Profit Audit Committee Toolkit Task Force.

CHAPTER EIGHT

GLOBALIZATION

Dick Blatt and Donna Hasslinger

More and more associations are considering or engaging in globalization efforts. Some associations are just starting to take a serious look at them. Many associations are realizing that whether by plan or by natural evolution they have already undertaken some level of globalization. It is incumbent upon every chief staff executive (CSE) to be informed about the opportunities and challenges associated with an increasingly globalized world. The CSE should work to determine if the association should be more international by selling its products and services abroad or be global by bringing people together around the world to advance the industry or profession.

Some associations are well along in implementing and managing globalization and are enjoying the benefits, including opportunities to

- Enhance the association's relevance to its domestic and global community.
- Exercise thought leadership on behalf of its industry or profession on a broader stage.

Note: The content and concepts shared in this chapter are specifically or generally derived from the book *A Practical Guide to Globalization for Associations* by Donna Hasslinger and Dick Blatt, published by the ASAE Association Management Press in 2012.

- Provide growth for membership, or for products and services, including education, or for the elevation of standards.
- Increase support for the association's mission.
- Share information globally to enhance the member value proposition.

On the other hand, the primary risk of not expanding globally is potential loss of industry or profession thought leadership. The association also risks loss of value to members. Many organizations around the world are aggressively making competitive inroads into associations' traditional programming.

Globalization is not a linear process where you start at point A and then go to B and complete the effort at point C. There are four phases of globalization that represent a continuum of efforts and commitment over time. The nature of globalization often requires an association to be actively involved in different phases of globalization in several countries at the same time.

Thinking about globalization in the following four phases helps to segment efforts and makes a global effort manageable and achievable:

1. Deciding whether to expand globally.
2. Developing a plan for global expansion.
3. Implementing the globalization plan.
4. Managing, evaluating, and sustaining globalization.

Phase 1: Deciding Whether to Expand Globally

The key elements of this phase are

1. Determine whether the association's mission is applicable globally.
2. Establish the exploratory process.
3. Include all appropriate individuals.
4. Define the existing status of the association's global efforts.
5. Define what the association means by globalization.

Determine Whether the Association's Mission Is Applicable Globally

The most fundamental starting point for any global thinking is to ensure that the association's mission is applicable globally. Do the association's mission and goals have meaning that can constructively be acted upon outside of the United States? Is the industry or profession active or represented in other countries?

If the association's mission is applicable globally, then there is a viable starting point to consider expanding globally.

Establish the Exploratory Process

For all organizations, a strong exploratory process gives the organization the best opportunity to reach optimal decisions. That process should

1. Ensure consistency with strategic goals.
2. Define all terminology.
3. Identify what information is needed to make a decision.
4. Identify who is responsible for gathering and communicating the information, including the process's "point person."
5. Set a timeline for the process.

To make these determinations, an association can use its existing strategic planning process or establish a "globalization task force" to ensure that its most strategic thinkers with the most global expertise are the individuals considering globalization.

Include All Appropriate Individuals

Often within associations, specific individuals or groups within the association advocate for globalization. While it is always good to have advocates speaking on an effort's behalf, it is also important to engage people with expertise, which may include

- Knowledge of the industry or profession both domestically and internationally.
- Knowledge of the association and its decision-making processes.
- Domestic and international members who will weigh the value proposition.
- Knowledge of how decisions should be carried forward by the association, especially related to staff.
- Potential "point people" from targeted expansion countries.

An inclusive and transparent exploratory process usually serves the association best. It is especially important to have the support and active engagement of the CSE in the process. The more inclusive the group, the better chance the process has of delivering a well-rounded and properly weighed recommendation for the board. Inclusivity can also help minimize any oversights that could negatively affect the association in the future.

Define the Existing Status of the Association's Global Efforts

Whether or not they have in place formal plans mandating some global effort, many associations have initiated some level of global activity. An association may have taken advantage of an operational opportunity when it had presented itself. It may take the short-term form of accepting members from outside the country of the association's headquarters, holding a meeting or conference in a different country, or perhaps selling a product or service elsewhere.

It is important to recognize the status and magnitude of any existing global efforts and to integrate such efforts into a more comprehensive long-term strategy that relates to both mission and strategic goals. Learnings from any efforts to date should be shared with the exploratory group. The financial implications of the existing global efforts should especially be considered to

1. Define return on investment expectations.
2. Identify risk factors.
3. Find financial resources for expanded efforts.
4. Establish metrics by which to measure success.

Applying the knowledge of what efforts have already been undertaken and worked, as well as why efforts may have fallen short, should be part of assessing the existing status of the association's global efforts.

Define What the Association Means by Globalization

It is important that consensus be reached on the definition of *globalization* for the association. Some associations use an international approach that focuses on developing relationships with specific countries that benefit U.S. members. A trade association may want to expand business opportunities for its companies, while a professional membership association may be interested in increasing members and adding markets for its current products and services. International expansion is typically a U.S.-centric model that benefits the association through interactions with other countries with the oversight of a predominantly U.S. board.

Some associations choose an integrated global approach with a goal of sharing and exchanging information among countries and bringing people together worldwide to raise industry or professional standards and improve best practices. A global organization benefits members worldwide and eventually may include multiple, relatively equal entities in different countries or regions with oversight from a global board. Some associations begin expansion efforts with an international approach, and as they become more active in new countries, they develop a more integrated, global-centric structure.

◆ ◆ ◆

Tips from Those Who Know: A Non-U.S.-Based View from Field Experience

Alfons Westgeest and Dani Kolb

One mistake often made by U.S. associations is the assumption that going global is always beneficial and at least worth a try. In fact, deep investment (over three to five years) is usually needed in order to expand successfully. In some cases, your research may conclude it is better staying with a mission focused on North America as the target market for your products and services.

We offer these additional tips for your consideration:

1. Study the landscape before you enter the market.
   - *Tap into local experience and expertise:* Local help will bring opportunity while investigating, benchmarking and scanning the options.
   - *Manage expectations:* For an American, *long term* might mean one to three years, for a Chinese it means five to ten years, but for a Japanese, it's a lifetime. Scenario planning is considered a useful method to help forecast and become more ready to tackle unexpected issues.
   - *Don't underestimate:* There is significant complexity involved when going global. Launching in more than one "country" at a time will increase complexity exponentially. Building relationships in the respective country and setting priorities is more important than structure. Misconceptions do exist in terms of what an (nonprofit) association is, what volunteering means, and what role other stakeholders may play.
2. Consider the impact of government intervention.
   There are different models around the world for which stakeholders need to prepare, discuss, and finally set the strategic direction of an association.

   When considering whom to involve, European leaders are supportive with government involvement because the European Union, for example, prepares or decides in the far majority of rules that have an impact on business and professions. On the other hand, in Asia, government dialogue is anticipated, as associations are usually funded and staffed by government departments. Some changes are afoot, however. Japan has taken a more liberal approach with new legislation in 2008, and China is working on allowing independent associations.
3. Differentiate. It is a key to success.

When establishing criteria to choose one country or region over another consider how (dis)similar another country is in regard to accepting the products and services, not only in terms of language. For example, if the technology standards or practices and regulatory code are more comparable to, or even based on, U.S. technology, this means "accessibility" and the potential gain (in time and money) is much greater.

Guidance and leadership by staff are essential, as personal agendas are being pushed forward and misunderstandings of language and context occur. If staff are guiding the process in a neutral manner, progress can be made faster.

4. Go local and global at the same time.

Work with local staff, consultants, and volunteers who live outside the United States. They can provide a reality check when you believe you have found a worthwhile product or service to "export." They can tell you if your "find" is rather useless in countries that have even better or deeper knowledge.

Oftentimes, locals claim they cannot afford the member dues and fees that the U.S.-based association asks. Is this truly the bottom-line message, or is this a negotiation technique? Any association that wants to enter a new market needs to have this local connection to ensure understanding of local business practices, abiding by all rules and laws and understanding the need of the market. "Build it and they will come" applies to exceptional products (iPhone) or services experience (Starbucks); usually associations do not have such breakthrough services.

However, global outreach for education and certification is seen as a way to expand for professional societies. The demand for education by non-U.S. audiences remains important in spite of increased online competition. Experience has shown that professional associations only discover this option once they see a lack of growth or even decline in North American markets and want to compensate for that loss this way.

Trade associations are increasingly exposed to global developments in the regulatory environment. In other words, a new law or regulation in Europe, Asia, or Latin America may affect a "national" industry much more and faster than previously. Many trade associations set up global monitoring projects by having an "ear on the ground" in different parts of the world to listen for what is emerging that in time might potentially have an impact on them as well.

Phase 2: Developing a Plan for Globalization

The key elements of this phase are

1. Identify the process and timeline.
2. Identify criteria for the plan.

3. Differentiate between short- and long-term considerations.
4. Evaluate global opportunities.
5. Choose the business and governance models.

Identify the Process and Timeline

As with the first phase of reaching a decision to expand globally, careful planning of the process will help ensure a stronger implementation plan. Like the exploratory process, it should be inclusive, transparent, communicated, and measured.

The group tasked with developing the plan should include the people most likely to implement the plan, as well as people with a good grasp of the strategic implications of the plan for the association. It could be the initial exploratory group or it could be a staff-driven operational effort. Again, it is also important to establish and observe a timeline for delivery of the plan. Normally, the timeline should be a six- to twelve-month period for delivery of the plan.

Identify Criteria for the Plan

With the board-approved definition of globalization from Phase 1, criteria need to be identified to be included in the plan. The planning group should identify the criteria with board oversight.

Criteria often include, but are not limited to

- What is the level of risk tolerance for the board, staff, and association?
- What return on investment is required?
- What does quantitative success look like? Examples would include, but not be limited to, increases in membership, increases in product sales, increases in programming participation, or the number of countries in which efforts exist.
- What does qualitative success entail regarding the association's values and extension of the brand?
- What resources are available for implementation of the plan, and how can capacity best be increased? Resources include monetary and human considerations.
- Have short- and long-term schedules been set for the rollout to countries with types and levels of activity identified? Examples of factors for the short term include to what countries efforts will be expanded first or in how many countries per year efforts will be undertaken. Examples of long-term factors include how many countries the association ultimately looks to be in.

- Is there a shared understanding of the expectations of potential working colleagues and participants from other countries?
- What data should be tracked, and what technologies will be needed for globalization? Examples include what form a global website will take, what social media will be used to communicate, and how and how much data about members and their participation should be gathered from the beginning.
- On the basis of all of the criteria identified, what are the optimal business and governance models for the association to pursue?

Differentiate Between Short- and Long-Term Considerations

Attempt to differentiate between the initial notion of being global and what the ultimate goals of globalization are for the association. Ultimate goals could include how many countries and how much programming will be undertaken in all countries. In other words, it is one thing to make the decision to expand globally and another to develop the plan for it. The application of resources are different for each of the four phases identified.

The plan should include a long-term commitment, which is critical for a successful globalization effort. To put this in perspective, consider the evolution of the association domestically with its growth and sophistication of programming over the years. Consider that evolution relative to undertaking the business of the association in a number of countries, each of which will have a different pace or stage of development.

Evaluate Global Opportunities

Developing a list of countries or regions to consider for global expansion and providing the following information for each market can help the association compare and rank the countries for globalization:

- Competitors
- Related organizations and potential strategic alliances
- Revenue models and mixes of products and services
- The extent to which language may be an issue and what resources will be needed to address any language barriers
- The business, professional, or regulatory climate
- Whether payments will be handled in U.S. funds or local currency and what financial accommodations will have to be made

- The size of the market and the potential for market penetration
- What existing members think about investing in globalization
- A vision of what the future looks like for the industry or profession

Choose the Business and Governance Models

Recommendations on the criteria to be included in the globalization plan should drive the choice of business model for Phase 3 implementation.

The business model that is currently successful for associations in the United States may not be the most promising model for launch in a new country. Associations now have a variety of models as options which may be better suited for expansion and the association's capacity to manage and fund the initiative. Those business models include the following:

1. Forming a strategic alliance with a similar organization in a new country, which can provide a local presence, introduce the association to potential members and volunteers, and immediately add value for current members.
2. Joining a loosely organized federation of independent organizations with a common interest, which can allow an association to collaborate on important issues and enhance thought leadership.
3. Licensing individuals or organizations in other countries to provide services in the name of the association, including certification testing, local-language publishing, and translation.
4. Identifying and naming a local country representative to oversee the association's preliminary engagement, assess demand, recommend expansion strategies, and assume a leadership role if the association decides to establish a greater presence.
5. Establishing representative country chapters by selecting leaders in new countries and entering into agreements that allow those leaders to operate on behalf of the association and replicate the U.S. model or execute a new, more appropriate model.
6. Opening national or regional offices to allow the association to offer a wide variety of products and services, especially if the association has identified robust potential.

Some associations may streamline their efforts and offer the same business model in each new area. However, the number of members in areas outside of the United States may differ widely, so some associations may use different business models for new countries if their goals, the stage of development of the industry or profession, and the opportunity in each new market differs widely.

As an example, a professional membership association may prefer to open regional offices to serve local members in more active areas and use country representatives to build a presence in areas with fewer members. The association's leadership may either manage the operations from the United States, engage local colleagues or staff to oversee new operations, or hire an association management company. A trade association may find that representative country chapters or loosely structured federations with shared control offer the most cost-effective benefits for their companies. Both types of associations may also use strategic alliances and licensing agreements from time to time.

Table 8.1 summarizes the models. The return on investment should especially be noted.

In addition to choice of business model, the approach to governance affects global expansion significantly. That approach may change over time as the association learns from its expansion or environmental factors change. The association's governing body will be determined by addressing the following questions:

1. Does the association's existing board want to maintain all authority over all operations through all time, often referred to as a U.S.-centric model?
2. Does the association want to provide some level of governance autonomy by country?
3. Does the association want to provide some level of governance autonomy by region?
4. Will there ultimately be a global board of directors empowering all global members, often referred to as a global-centric model? Will non-U.S. board members have a voice in U.S. policy and operations?
5. What will the structure and composition of the board be and when?
6. How, when, and where will the board meet? Do bylaws need to be revised to accommodate different forms of decision making?
7. How does the association best nurture a working relationship among global colleagues?
8. Should global committees or task forces be established to better account for good ideas about the operations of the association in all countries, or how will the voice of non-U.S. members be heard in the association?

TABLE 8.1. GLOBALIZATION BUSINESS MODELS

Business Models	Financial Investment	Resource Commitment	Control	Return on Investment
Strategic Alliances	Minimal	Minimal	Shared	Mission and member benefit
Federations	Minimal	Minimal	Shared	Mission and member benefit
Licensing	Minimal	Minimal	Varies by contract	Mission and member benefit at reduced cost
In-Country Representatives	Minimal—Part-time salary	Small	Full	Market testing Building relationships in new countries Gradual expansion
Representative Country Chapters	Moderate	Medium	Contractual control of brand	Mission and member benefit Repayment of investment Shared financial benefit
National or Regional Offices	Moderate to significant	Significant	Full	Mission and member benefit Repayment of investment Significant long-term growth Significant financial benefit

Phase 3: Implementing the Globalization Plan

The key elements of this phase are

1. Choose the right people to work with in-country.
2. Address legalities and financial implications.
3. Plan and manage the three evolving levels of country activity.
4. Communicate appropriate information to target audiences.
5. Document processes, operating parameters, and guidelines for operations.

Choose the Right People to Work with In-Country

It is very important to choose the right people to represent the association in new countries, whether the association is selecting local colleagues to start a representative country chapter, engaging with a strategic partner, or hiring employees to staff a local association office. The local leaders should respect the association and its mission, vision, and values. They should have a prestigious reputation in their community and be able to represent the brand, strategically position the association, offer guidance, and oversee the expansion of activities in the area. To take immediate advantage of the association's broader outreach, staff can be encouraged to collaborate with colleagues in new countries to develop conferences, trade shows, magazine articles, book chapters, and website content that offer a perspective from outside of the United States.

The association's choice of business and governance models will drive what roles and responsibilities people in-country will have. Success depends in no small part on trust to be mutually earned in the working relationship between country and headquarters.

Address Legalities and Financial Implications

Legalities include but are not limited to

- Registration of the association to conduct business
- Intellectual property protection of name, trademarks, owned assets, and website URL
- Tax implications
- Employment laws

- Trade issues
- Lobbying

The best starting point for protecting all legalities and financial positions is to work with the association's legal counsel and its tax and financial advisors. In general, intellectual property rights are governed by the laws of the local country. The association needs to take steps to protect all of its intellectual property before undertaking activity in any other country. It is the best way to minimize any legal challenges after launch into a country.

Plan and Manage the Three Evolving Levels of Country Activity

At any point in time the association's level of activity in any one country will take one of three forms:

1. An introductory level of activity
2. A moderate level of activity
3. A robust level of activity

Each level of country activity, like the phases of globalization themselves, requires different management dynamics. Keep in mind which phase of globalization the association is in, as well as which level of activity each country has reached. At any point in time, an association's global efforts will likely entail all three levels of activity simultaneously. In time the association may establish working groups representing countries with similar levels of activity to help them learn from one another to facilitate progress. This type of networking, however, would not take the place of continued guidance and support from headquarters.

Communicate Appropriate Information to Target Audiences

The association should develop and communicate its message for globalization to all target audiences. For example, conveying the benefits of expanding globally is especially important for domestic members.

Audiences include

- The board of directors
- Staff
- Domestic members
- International members
- Prospective members

- Competitive or allied organizations
- Media
- Industry and profession voices of influence, including leaders and academics
- U.S. government officials (when the activity of members has implications for U.S. security or foreign policy)

Dependent upon the phase of globalization or level of country activity, communication should include

1. The plan and general reason why it is being pursued.
2. The status of progress for the plan, including both successes and challenges.
3. Always, the benefit and value of implementing and achieving the plan.
4. Any cultural or language considerations when at all possible.

A comprehensive communication plan is essential for both the implementation phase and going forward, including

1. How will publications be shared? How will translations be handled?
2. What website adjustments will need to be made?
3. How will communications take place?

Sharing information should be encouraged from country to country for both volunteer leadership and staff as well as between headquarters and individual countries. There are geographic and cultural commonalities that can benefit operations, if shared. Also, share challenges that arise in individual countries with all countries, if it will be constructive. It may help others avoid similar challenges and to identify potential solutions for all. Forums for sharing and addressing these challenges can vary, but may include the governing body in-country, a committee to address operations, simple coordination and communication among country staffs, or even a "global" committee of representatives from all countries.

Document Processes, Operating Parameters, and Guidelines for Operations

Just as the contracts negotiated with in-country partners are important to global efforts, documenting processes and procedures between headquarters and operations in new countries can ensure a smooth transition and speed the assimilation of new colleagues. It is also a constructive, cooperative mechanism to maintain leverage and consistency across multiple country efforts.

Guidelines that focus on management and governance can provide support for in-country colleagues. Documenting the requirements for the protection of intellectual property, the ethical and legal protocols expected for conducting the association's business, and the timing and content for marketing and financial reports can define general responsibilities. If approval processes for new entities are prepared and communicated with charters documented and shared, the association has taken important steps to ensure the success of global expansion.

Requirements and operating parameters should be established at the outset of a launch into a new country. This is the best time to establish procedures and guidelines so that new colleagues around the world understand their responsibilities and agree to pursue the association's strategic goals.

Phase 4: Managing, Evaluating, and Sustaining Globalization

The key elements of this phase are

1. Recognize indicators and patterns of success.
2. Reorient target audiences as turnover occurs.
3. Remind all colleagues continually of the commonalities of the association.
4. Establish processes by which to objectively assess and adjust problem areas.
5. Maintain flexibility.

Recognize Indicators and Patterns of Success

In addition to ensuring the strongest initial plan to expand globally, each new country provides opportunity for learning how to do it better. Those experiences can be used over time to identify indicators and patterns of success that can optimize new country launches going forward.

Indicators and patterns of success may include

- Seeing growth patterns and setting critical mass for activity.
- Recruiting a solid core of people and members to be involved and increasingly engaged.

- Attracting and receiving consistent, positive media coverage.
- Developing a three-year plan for program expansion.
- Developing a plan for how funding will occur over at least three years.
- Achieving specific regulatory goals.

Reorient Target Audiences as Turnover Occurs

From the beginning, orient all target audiences with a global mind-set. The orientation might include training in cultural competency and should also include communicating what the global expansion plan is and how it is being implemented. It could also include encouraging the board to travel to other countries, participate in the association's activities abroad, and meet other country colleagues. The board of directors should also be meaningfully engaged. Go beyond reporting of results to nurturing the board's appreciation of globalization's contribution to the association's success.

As turnover among the board and among country staff and volunteer leadership occurs, newcomers should be thoroughly oriented. All of the association's audiences should be as constructively informed about the association's strategy and progress as possible. This could include testimonials from domestic and global members about how they have benefited from the global efforts.

Remind All Colleagues Continually of the Commonalities of the Association

The more people around the world that become involved with the association, the more varied opinions will surface about what is best for the industry or profession and the association. Sometimes these opinions will conflict. Acknowledge and consider these opinions while reminding people that with all of the differences that might exist, there remain commonalities that brought people and efforts together in the first place. The dialogue should be as constructive and objective as possible, focused on what is best for the common good. Final decisions should provide for local customization when possible, but always remain consistent with that common good.

Establish Processes by Which to Objectively Assess and Adjust Problem Areas

Challenges will always unexpectedly arise. If the association can establish a process that is communicated to all involved and which objectively addresses challenges, then those challenges can be minimized.

Challenges can take the form of

- Problem leaders or problem members
- Competition from other organizations
- Falling short of economic or participation projections
- Potential legal or ethical violations
- Lack of consistency in management or progress from country to country

Whatever the challenges, address them promptly and let people know the outcomes. Share the issue involved, the association's position and why the association assumes that position, and what action is being taken. The processes and positions should reflect the association's core values, uphold its established standards, and parallel its strategic goals.

Maintain Flexibility

Even the best-laid plans are subject to change. Especially in expanding globally, be pragmatic about changes that might benefit the efforts. There will be new learnings from each country that can be applied forward, especially when they concern the business model and governance.

Recognize what is working from country to country and share that information with all. In-country colleagues should feel free to utilize that which they deem is relevant to them. Good ideas should be acted upon regardless of origin at any and all times.

Summary

Recognizing that every association is unique and needs to apply its own thinking to goals and programming, this chapter has attempted to provide a checklist approach to the most salient points in expanding globally.

Be inclusive, think broadly and long term, remember that the future belongs to those who bring people together on the basis of their commonalities, and realize that global expansion is achievable and rewarding.

Resources

Axtell, R. E., and Parker Pen Company. *Do's and Taboos Around the World.* New York: John Wiley & Sons, 1993.

Glassie, J. C. *International Legal Issues for Nonprofit Organizations.* Washington, DC: ASAE Association Management Press.

Hasslinger, Donna, and Dick Blatt. *A Practical Guide to Globalization for Associations.* Washington, DC: ASAE Association Management Press.

The authors also recommend the extensive archive of globalization articles on ASAE's website as well as use of the site's Collaboration for the International Section and any general readings on the global economy and international politics.

The Authors

Dick Blatt has served as the executive director of the Information Systems Security Association, a client of the Drohan Management Group, which has over 150 chapters in nearly seventy countries. He is the former CEO of POPAI, The Global Association for Marketing at Retail, where he led global expansion to Europe, Asia, Latin America, Australia, and Africa over seventeen years. Dick was a member of the U.S. Chamber of Commerce's Committee of 100 for ten years.

Donna Hasslinger served as vice president of worldwide member services for the National Geographic Society where she had responsibility for offices in North America, Europe, Asia, and Africa; vice president of the Council for Advancement and Support of Education, which has offices in North America, Europe, and Asia-Pacific; and worldwide director for the Drug Information Association with offices in North America, Europe, Japan, India, and China.

Sidebar author *Alfons Westgeest* is group vice president of the Kellen Company, and an ASAE Fellow; and *Dani Kolb* is manager, Kellen Europe, and has served as chair of the ASAE International Section Council.

THE PLANNING CONTINUUM

Susan S. Radwan, SMP, ARM, CAE

Strategic planning isn't what it used to be. It has evolved from the ponderous exercise every five years that resulted mostly in a weekend away from work and a nicely bound plan on the shelf. While retreats can indeed be of value in allowing time for focused leadership thinking, modern strategic planning is an essential step in strategic management, establishing the foundation upon which tactical and business planning and evaluation rest. It engages the staff and membership, along with other stakeholders, in consideration of their association and how it should work to serve them. It forces the leadership to make the important choices about what is important to do and, at a high level, about the best way to accomplish it. It is communicated effectively and efficiently throughout the staff and volunteer ranks so that everyone can pull together in support of shared priorities. Strategic planning, done well, is the glue that can hold a successful association together in pursuit of its mission and vision. However, strategic planning is only the first step of a much larger strategic focus called "strategic management." Strategic management recognizes that a primary job of leaders is planning and change. The whole point of planning is to effect positive change.

Effective execution of a strategic plan involves a continuous cascade emanating from ongoing environmental scanning (see the figure).

STRATEGIC HIGH-LEVEL PLANNING.

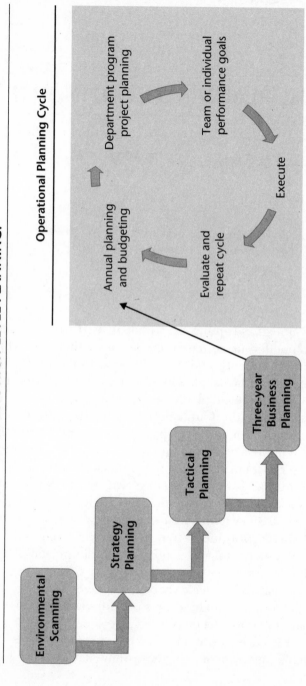

Operational Planning Cycle

Department program project planning

Team or individual performance goals

Execute

Evaluate and repeat cycle

Annual planning and budgeting

Three-year Business Planning

Tactical Planning

Strategy Planning

Environmental Scanning

Source: Graphic by Susan S. Radwan, SMP, ARM, CAE.

The continuous cascade evolves from ongoing and periodic environmental scanning, which informs the long-term strategic plan, which informs the broad tactical plan, which informs the multiyear business or financial plan, which informs the organization's annual plan and budget, which informs departmental and program planning, which informs tactical or project management planning, which informs team and individual performance goals. All of these levels of planning are reviewed, renewed, tweaked, and sometimes overhauled on a systematic basis to respond to changes and emerging trends in the environment.

In the context of this comprehensive strategic management system and with the results of an ongoing external and internal environmental scan, strategic planning is a valuable tool from which tactical and business plans can be derived, and it can serve as the guiding star for the association's many constituencies. The following chapters highlight key parts of the cascade.

The Author

Susan S. Radwan, SMP, ARM, CAE, is the owner of Leading Edge Mentoring, an international consulting firm focused on governance and leadership issues, based in Grand Ledge, Michigan. Radwan holds the Strategic Management Professional designation, which focuses on the entire planning continuum.

CHAPTER NINE

ENVIRONMENTAL SCANNING AND FUTURES ANALYSIS

Bruce Butterfield, APR, FASAE

When we were learning to drive, we were taught to watch the traffic ahead of the car in front of us and to shift our gaze from side to side so we could anticipate and avoid a crash. Will the vehicle three car lengths in front of me slam on the brakes? Will the truck at the intersection pull out in front of me? Will the child run between those parked cars?

Being a defensive driver is all about preparing for a potential future outcome. Association leaders should use that same principle when wrestling with how to respond to the accelerating pace of change.

Anticipation is not forecasting. Forecasts tend to assume that the future will be like today only more so. But the future doesn't run in a straight line from today. It spins out in all directions at once, and assumptions about it can be knocked askew by events. The late management guru Peter Drucker was once asked how he made such accurate predictions. He said, "I don't forecast. I identify what's visible but not yet seen."[1]

Drucker understood that many of the clues to the future exist now but are often missed or ignored. The purpose of an ongoing futures analysis process is to identify what is visible but not yet seen to avoid being blindsided, to head off adverse outcomes and take advantage of opportunities. A major component of that analysis is environmental scanning, which is the process of assessing the forces that affect the organization's future. According to the American Society of Association Executives (ASAE), an environmental scan focuses your association on what is relevant to its strategy and its future. By driving a team toward inventorying what is new, emerging, and important, scanning and trend analysis help team members reach consensus on new policies.

Categories of Change

The effectiveness of an environmental scan is a function of *what* is being scanned and *for what purpose.* The more outlets, the richer the scan and the greater the likelihood of correctly identifying critical change drivers. But scanning volumes of information is a daunting task. There are several different areas of change, with two—emerging issues and trends—being the most crucial to identify in a scanning process, as these are the change areas most effectively leveraged. There are four categories of change that an environmental scan may address:

> *Cycles:* Changes that occur over an observable time period and are rather predictable (for example, seasons, El Nino and El Nina, solar storms, economic cycles).
>
> *Trends:* Changes that move in a direction over time. Trends are not new; there are a lot of data and information about them and they have been observed for a period of time (for example, climate change, demographic shifts, and political polarization).
>
> *Wildcard events:* Sudden, discontinuous change; unexpected, unpredictable (for example, the Asian tsunamis, the Arab Spring uprisings, the National Security Agency spying revelations). Even wildcard events have precursors that could help mitigate them if identified soon enough.
>
> *Emerging issues:* Seeds of trends; the changes that will initiate a trend over time. This is the type of change that futurists are most interested in. Sniff out an emerging issue and you have the potential for real leverage in how that issue eventually affects the organization.

To prepare for the future and to implement any positioning strategy, associations must understand how their members' needs will change, not in the murky and distant future but in the years that lie immediately ahead. To determine what is driving the future, associations must examine not just their members and customers but also their members' customers. The very best one can expect from a study of one's own members and customers is

FIGURE 9.1. ANTICIPATING EMERGING NEEDS.

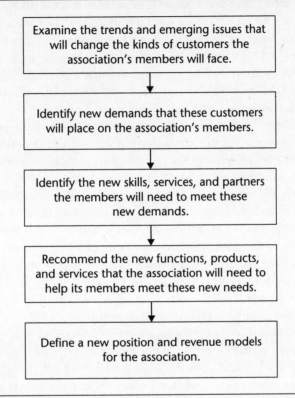

Examine the trends and emerging issues that will change the kinds of customers the association's members will face.

Identify new demands that these customers will place on the association's members.

Identify the new skills, services, and partners the members will need to meet these new demands.

Recommend the new functions, products, and services that the association will need to help its members meet these new needs.

Define a new position and revenue models for the association.

Source: The Forbes Group.

to *react* to changes sooner. However, by studying its members' customers, an association can *anticipate* the emerging needs of its own members and customers. Schematically, the process can be described as shown in Figure 9.1.

The result of this approach is a proactive, market-driven solution that responds to the long-term needs of the members' market rather than solely the short-term concerns facing today's members.

Components of Futures Analysis

Associations have always been information gatherers and producers. But there are many other sources of information today, so associations no longer have the franchise. Now they need to be intelligence digesters, abstracters, analysts, connectors, and curators. This has high value because their members often are too busy to do this for themselves. The members' cry for help is, "Just tell me what I should pay attention to and what it means!" This requires futures analysis. Note the use of the word *futures*, not *future* analysis. There is no one future to be divined from the vantage point of today. To attempt to do so leads to forecasting and predicting, which usually are wrong.

There are five primary activities involved in futures thinking. The first four are part of the environmental scanning function; the fifth activity moves the analysis into a planning and implementation phase. They are identifying and monitoring change, considering and critiquing the impacts of change, imagining alternative possible futures, envisioning a preferred future, and planning and implementing desired change.

Identifying and monitoring change involves assessment of patterns of change in the past as well as collecting baseline data on current conditions. These efforts provide a context within which an organization can look for ongoing cycles, trends, or emerging issues such as technological innovations or value shifts. The most successful tool used to identify and monitor change is environmental scanning.

Considering and critiquing the impacts of change means both assessing the effects that cascade from ongoing change throughout the macro environment and also evaluating what impact those effects have on an organization. How will this change affect day-to-day activities? Who has been newly advantaged or disadvantaged by the advent of this change? What trade-offs might we face as a result of change? One way to critique and consider impacts of change is to benchmark another industry or profession to study how they were affected by similar changes in their environment. Benchmarking is a powerful tool for learning what was successful and unsuccessful in other organizations with regard to how they dealt with changes in the macro environment.

Imagining possible alternative futures follows naturally from the extrapolation of trends and the consideration of the long-term effects and impacts of emerging issues. Scenario building serves two purposes: first, scenarios of alternative futures allow organizations to explore possibilities and uncertainties so they can create contingency plans for the surprises the future might bring; second, exploring alternative possible futures heightens the creativity and flexibility with which an organization imagines its preferred future. There are many different scenario methods available to organizations.

Envisioning a preferred future means creating a model of the ideal future an organization would like to create as the first step in transformational planning and in leadership. It requires careful, explicit articulation of long-term ideals and goals, and the values that contribute to them.

Planning and implementing desired change require a commitment to act from the highest levels of the organization to champion actions that contribute to the creation of a preferred future and implementation plan.

The means of accomplishing these activities are, in addition to environmental scanning, identification of change drivers, scenario planning, and strategic planning.

Components of an Environmental Scan

Typically, environmental scans identify changes in the sociodemographic, technology, environmental, economic, and political arenas that may affect the organization's future. These areas are called STEEP categories by futurists for the acronym spelled by the first letter of each area. There is some debate about whether there should be more or fewer categories, but the biggest consideration is what is most important to track given an association's financial and human resources. Also, the categories do not stand alone; they are part of a fluid and interconnected web where trends and emerging issues in each affect the others.

Changes in this macro environment web will affect the working environment of an organization's industry or profession, the internal environment of an organization, and any decisions and actions taken with regard to critical issues facing an organization. For example, women increasingly are the majority of students in medical, dental, and law schools. That sociodemographic shift affects the economic and political environments and ultimately the associations serving those professions. The lingering economic effects of the Great Recession influence sociodemographics and politics as the income disparity gap widens and associations deal with more parsimony from members seeking to cut costs. Technology advances affect the political, sociodemographic, and economic environments, as workers at all levels are required to be tech savvy and younger workers question the need for association-type networks.

Environmental scans can lead to meaningful revelations that generate short-term responses. In one example, a dental association learned that its members could be tapped in a pandemic to fill in for casualties among nurses and physicians who would be first responders to the crisis.

This revelation caused the association to immediately launch a pandemic response training program for its members. In another example, a medical association recognized that it could not wall off its members from competition from other disciplines and began a successful path to become a recognized subspecialty in their field with newly designed education and training programs. In yet another example, an organ transplant association created an outreach program after realizing that it had ignored the fast-growing Latino community in seeking organ donations and providing information on transplants.

Do It Yourself (DIY) Environmental Scanning

Ideally, environmental scanning should be an ongoing process rather than an event. But scanning is labor intensive and can be difficult for hard-worked staff and part-time volunteers to perform well. More often than not, associations retain a consultant to help them with the design and creation of the scan, usually in the form of a report. But unless they have extensive resources, it can be hard to keep the scan refreshed as assumptions about the future change. Nonetheless, it is possible to do scanning in house. The trick is to track only the most critical sub areas of the STEEP categories to avoid being overwhelmed. One association in the medical distribution industry hired a consultant to conduct their initial scan then created a system of refreshment that involved staff information gathering vetted quarterly by a panel of experts from within and outside the industry. Their work product was a quarterly summary for the membership.

Scanning resources abound. The U.S. Bureau of Labor Statistics has a wealth of information and data about population and employment trends. Most public libraries offer free online access to proprietary databases. All you need is a library card. A few of the resources usually available are EBSCO Host, more than 375 full-text and secondary research databases and over 420,000 e-books; ERIC, the online library of education resources; Medline, which taps the National Library of Medicine and the National Institutes of Health; Infotrac, a family of databases with full-text articles from academic journals and general circulation publications; Reference USA, a database of business information, and Papers First, a database of papers from congresses and conventions worldwide. Of course, there's always Google and the association's own databases and trade publications.

Any futures analysis system should have these extremely important objectives: that issue or trend identification and analysis be ongoing, that implications be determined, that implications lead to actions, and that the futures analysis process yields marketable products. On that final point, too often associations give away their best intelligence for free or on the cheap. Intelligence has real value.

Scanning the *internal environment* will identify the association's strengths and weaknesses so that it can successfully address its external opportunities and threats. The internal environment consists of leadership, members, management, and staff. It can be expressed in terms of three factors—structure, culture, and resources.

Structure

The association's *structure* means how it is organized in terms of communications, authority, and work flow. It deals with the chain of command and table of organization. Examples include

- Relationship between volunteer leaders and staff (chain of command)
- Relationships among departments and peer groups
- Relationships with members

Culture

The association's *culture* consists of its beliefs, expectations, and values. Examples include

- Strong top-down direction
- Consensus driven
- Innovative or risk taking
- Conservative or follower

Resources

The association's *resources* include both financial and human assets. Examples include

- Volunteer leadership
- Staff, managerial talent, facilities
- Dues, contributions, earnings, investments

Identifying Change Drivers

Through the environmental scanning process, decision makers can identify emerging forces able to reshape or overwhelm existing institutions and, consequently, promote different behaviors that may not appear rational within today's structure. The output of environmental scanning can be a daunting array of these change drivers. It is important to narrow the number of change drivers because they will be used to define alternative future scenarios. For example, a health care organization created a list of more than sixteen health care change drivers but winnowed it down to two: what kind of care will be delivered and by whom, using a "blue ribbon" scanning panel of several senior staff and select members.

Scenario Planning

When change drivers have been identified, they can be used to create potential future worlds in which planners can work at minimum risk. This methodology was initially developed by The Rand Corporation and refined by Royal Dutch Shell. It has been successfully used worldwide by companies, governments, and associations.

It is human nature to restrict our thinking to the known and the comfortable. However, history has demonstrated time and again that profound change comes in surges and jerks instead of sustained moderate trends. Scenarios let decision makers play out alternative futures. Scenarios are not stories about the way things are but alternatives about what they could be.

The Value of Scenarios

Scenarios stories are told from a particular point in time and look back to the present. Scenario planners work with them by adding their thinking about how the stories might evolve and then creating strategies that will advance desirable futures and prevent undesirable ones. While the real future will emerge from all of the scenarios and more, scenario planning helps leaders to move past barriers and, as Peter Drucker said, identify what is visible but not yet seen.

Scenario planning is an approach to strategy development and decision making that acknowledges then addresses the inherent uncertainty in the societal, public policy, and business environments and aims at achieving maximum feasible resilience in strategy. It is predicated on the fact that, in an uncertain environment, single-point forecasts, which most leaders tend to rely on, are inherently inaccurate and strategies based on them will almost certainly be misdirected.

Scenarios are not predictions; they are carefully structured descriptions of alternative possible futures. They are not just variations around a base case; they are significantly, often structurally, different views of the future. And they are not generalized views of feared or desired futures; they are specific "decision focused" views of the future. The benefits of scenario planning, properly conceived and executed, are that the scenarios provide

- A more thorough understanding of the dynamics of change
- Better consideration of the full range of opportunities and threats
- Reduced vulnerability to surprises
- More resilient, flexible strategy
- Better assessment of risks

Scenario Principles

There are two principles required for scenario planning to work:

- Planners must agree that the scenario stories are only plausible, not probable.
- They must be willing to suspend disbelief when confronted by stories that challenge their current thinking.

The word *never* should not be used when developing and working with scenarios. For example, people once thought that the United States homeland would *never* be attacked, that the housing market would *never* collapse, and that the United States could *never* nearly experience another depression.

Creating Scenarios

Because there are unlimited possible combinations of the effects of facts, issues, and trends, scenarios usually are limited to a manageable number—two to four, with four being ideal for richness and nuance. Two scenarios lead to a best case–worst case, either–or type of approach, which is limiting. Three scenarios lead to a best case–worst case–most likely approach that encourages planners to take the easy and familiar "most likely" path. More than four scenarios are unmanageable and often lack sufficient contrast to be useful.

Scenarios can project far out into the future, fifteen years or more. Long-term projections are essential for longer-term investments such as factory locations, drug development, hospital construction, and road building. But scenario building takes practice, and long future projections can be difficult. Longer-term scenarios risk playing guessing games and injecting "wildcards," the unexpected events that disrupt the scenarios.

Scenarios also are three dimensional. Like the Rubik's Cube puzzle with its movable facets that was popular years ago, scenarios can be changed by changing assumptions, drivers, or the facts and trends chosen to describe them. In fact, scenarios are not static. Once developed, they need to be constantly refreshed as new facts, trends, and issues emerge, and the strategies that grow from them should be reviewed for continuing relevance and updated.

Scenario development begins with selection of two powerful and intersecting change drives identified in the environmental scan. Each change driver becomes an axis that defines a four-pronged matrix of alternative future worlds. Each axis has opposite poles that have an equal chance of occurring. Two significant drivers of change in the association world are technology and sociodemographics. Using them, we can create a matrix that looks like the one in Figure 9.2.

The quadrants of the matrix create future worlds. Each one contains a story. In creating scenario stories for each of these alternative future worlds, a five-year timeline makes sense. Within that period, there will be flashpoints of technology advancement that will make today seem antique, and new generations will be flooding that job market and the membership that have very different gender, ethnic, and cultural characteristics.

Scenario stories should be short—no more than one or two pages—compelling, and bold. The stories should have short, memorable names. It is difficult to write scenario stories in planning sessions. It is best if the consultant and staff create the stories offline and vet them in a facilitated session. At that session, the planning team should identify strategies that might work in several scenarios. Such strategies enable the association to quickly respond as the real future evolves because they have been thought through in advance.

Using the scenario matrix, an association could create a strategy of phased-technology adoption funded by sponsorships, grants, or reserves that would satisfy younger members without putting off older members and straining tight budgets. In other words, that strategy would work in all four futures. Another strategy might be a two-way mentoring program that would allow younger members to share their technological expertise

FIGURE 9.2. SCENARIO DEVELOPMENT MATRIX.

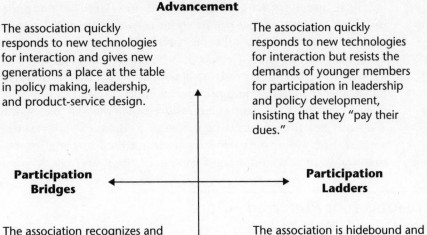

**Technology
Advancement**

The association quickly responds to new technologies for interaction and gives new generations a place at the table in policy making, leadership, and product-service design.

The association quickly responds to new technologies for interaction but resists the demands of younger members for participation in leadership and policy development, insisting that they "pay their dues."

**Participation
Bridges**

**Participation
Ladders**

The association recognizes and meets the participation needs of younger members but is slow to acquire the new tools of interaction because of budget constraints or difficulty in persuading older members to relinquish reliance on older means of interaction.

The association is hidebound and fails to respond either to changing means of interacting or the needs and demands of their young, technology-savvy members.

**Technology
Resistance**

with older members and older members to share their organizational expertise with younger members. This would increase understanding among the member generations and would work particularly well in the two right-hand matrix quadrants.

Working with Scenarios

Because scenarios identify strategies, they feed naturally into the association's strategic planning process. Scenarios expose gaps in the association's policies, value equation, and organizational structure that should be addressed in the strategic plan. Take, for example, the lower-right quadrant of the association scenario matrix in Figure 9.2. One could argue that it describes a bleak potential future filled with dissatisfaction and, perhaps, dissolution. Viewed through a different lens, it can be a harbinger for change. A task force of traditional and newer member cohorts could look at ways to address apparently colliding desires. Here is a place for younger members to mentor older ones about the value of new technologies for interaction and older members to mentor younger members about how to approach policy setting. Conversely, the upper-left quadrant of the matrix appears to be Nirvana. But is it? If associations in this world jump on new technologies, are they being thoughtful and prudent in use of resources? Are new generations' needs being addressed at the expense of older ones'? The same task force addressing the bleak scenario can address the Nirvana scenario. It is well to have people work in conflicting scenarios to challenge their conventional wisdom and encourage them to think differently.

Creating Your Preferred Future

Alternative future scenarios are the means for determining a preferred future for an organization. Too often, associations indulge in the creation of meaningless vision statements, such as "be the premier association for (fill in the blanks)." Such so-called visions offer no direction to staff and leaders about how to proceed. On the other hand, preferred futures are a series of ends that create a timeline of milestones to achieve by a date certain. Here's an example that is a composite of several real-world preferred futures:

By (date), the Association

- Has defined the discipline as a specialty
- Is a catalyst for improving procedural outcomes and safety
- Has a global reach
- Is sought by policy makers in making decisions about products, procedures, and compensation
- Defines best practices

Preferred futures are a set of milestones for the association to achieve at a defined future point. Steps to accomplish them can be arrayed on a timeline—usually covering two planning cycles or six years—that defines the association's work. In this way, the preferred future directly connects to the strategic and operational plans of the association instead of being removed and ambiguous. Each element of a preferred future is an outcome. Between these milestones, or outcomes, objectives can be inserted to define specific ends and deadlines. With this timeline, staff and volunteers can create implementation strategies to accomplish the objectives, which must be achievable, measurable, and timely.

American baseball legend and cracker-barrel philosopher Yogi Berra, once advised, "When you get to the fork in the road, take it." The futures analysis process does just that. It enables associations to explore pathways to the future risk free. It creates valuable intelligence that is marketable and exciting for participants. Moreover, it puts you in charge of designing your future rather than being defined by it.

Notes

1. R. Lenzner and S. S. Johnson, "Seeing Things as They Really Are" (cover story). *Forbes* 159, no. 5 (1997): 122–128.

Resources

Heijden, Kees van der. *Scenarios: The Art of Strategic Conversation*, 2nd ed. Chichester, UK: John Wiley &Sons, 2005.

Heijden, Kees van der, Ron Bradfield, George Burt, George Cairns, and George Wright. *The Sixth Sense: Accelerating Organizational Learning with Scenarios*. Chichester, UK: John Wiley & Sons, 2002.

Shell Global. "Shell Scenarios." available at www.shell.com/futureof-energy/shellscenarios.

The Author

Bruce Butterfield, APR, FASAE, based in Sarasota, Florida, is the president of The Forbes Group (www.forbesgroup.com), whose mission is to chart your future by helping you think, plan, and act strategically.

Butterfield has decades of experience as an association and public relations executive and has worked with scores of trade and professional groups, with a focus on the health care sector. He is a leading association futurist and strategic thinker who has written and spoken extensively about association and organizational management issues and the future of "associating." He has served as an executive in seven trade and professional associations and created four for-profit associations.

CHAPTER TEN

ENVIRONMENTAL SCANNING

A Chief Staff Executive's Perspective

Susan E. Avery, CAE

A critical exercise for any association CSE to guide his or her board and volunteer leadership through is environmental scanning. As noted in Chapter Nine, scanning is used for multiple purposes, but the most relevant point made is to "identify what is visible but not yet seen to avoid being blindsided, head off adverse outcomes, and take advantage of opportunities." However, no existing model fits all associations. Just as there are many strategic planning models and methodologies, there are also nearly unlimited models and methodologies for environmental scanning.

Multiple Models and Methodologies

As a CSE, it's important that you identify the model and methodology that best meets your association's needs. You must take into consideration your board and association culture—as your association type (professional membership or trade association), the levels and types of professionals who serve on your board (for example, c-levels, mid-management practitioners, administrative level), your association internal resources, and other factors have a bearing on your choice of model and methodology.

Environmental scanning is not a one-time exercise. Whether you use a third-party consultant or an internal resource, such as a board member, member, or staff person, the initial scanning process simply sets up what will eventually become a process that is maintained and kept fresh and relevant.

Developing a Strategic Radar Screen

One model I have used for years is the strategic radar screen,[1] which identifies ten to fifteen issues. The radar screen should be composed of at least 80 percent of issues (trends, signs, and other items noted in Chapter Nine) that affect, or have the potential of affecting, your industry or profession, and the remaining issues may be geared toward issues to improve your association (for example, governance models and infrastructure, limitation of resources, membership resistance, and so on). Consultant Jim Dalton often said members do not pay dues for the association to solve its problems, but for the association to solve their problems.

The radar screen issues are categorized into (1) issues that we must and can address; (2) issues that we cannot affect, but should keep on our radar screen; and (3) issues for which we will create strategies to address. It requires a clear understanding of the priority issues and whether the association can do anything about them—and also an appreciation for those for which viable strategies can actually be developed and executed.

One benefit of this methodology is that the radar screen of strategic issues becomes a communication tool for current and prospective members. If you have the right issues—those that have now or have the potential to have an impact on the members' world—then the radar screen can be an effective tool to demonstrate what the association is doing for the members. When a member asks, "What value am I getting for my membership?" a great way to convey that value, beyond the standard benefits of membership, is to share the radar screen and show that the association is working on issues that address the membership's current and future professional or business needs. If at least a few of those issues resonate with the member, you have most likely retained a member or attracted a new one.[2]

Illustration of a Radar Screen

Association Management Professional Trends

1. Family and employment pressures are reducing the amount of time volunteers are willing to commit to their trade and professional associations.

2. The assumptions many elected leaders make about their knowledge of the customers they represent leads many associations to underestimate the value of customer research and the need for diverse means of two-way communication with the membership.

3. The demand for organizational transparency will generate growing demand for information on the
   - Value of membership
   - Ethical implications of the organization's decision-making process
   - Process for becoming involved in the organization

4. The rapid development of technology for meetings and education will
   - Increase the delivery of online learning and networking
   - Put growing pressure on meeting and education professionals to keep up with the changes
   - Draw new competitors into the marketplace
   - Change traditional relationships with the hospitality industry

5. Exploding amounts of information available to trade, professional, and consumer sectors will pressure associations to validate the credibility of the information and facilitate the ability to use it reliably.

6. Consolidations in many industries are causing greater separation between those who appreciate the value delivered by trade associations and those who make the financial decision to maintain the membership.

7. The expanding development of performance metrics in many industries is increasing the demand for similar applications in associations and highlighting the unique challenges of measuring performance in not-for-profit organizations.

8. Speculation concerning the viability of the traditional dues-based, member-oriented model is driving a growing demand for evidence-based testing and verification of a variety of association operating models.

9. The risk-averse nature of associations puts them at a disadvantage with respect to growing competition from the private sector and the need to invest in capital-intensive communication technologies.

10. Volunteer leadership in many associations is shifting from prominent people who have achieved success to career builders who come with a different set of motives and expectations.

11. Economic uncertainty and rapid rates of change will increase the demand for tracking and forecasting market dynamics.
12. An increasing understanding of the way adults learn will alter the way continuing education programs are developed and expand the competencies necessary for associations to remain competitive.
13. Factors thought to have the greatest influence on the effectiveness of board governance are shifting from representational demographics to board member competencies and access to accurate information on the needs of distinct member segments.
14. The growing impact of global competition on associations will drive an increasing need for skills in developing international relationships with foreign counterparts and understanding the trends affecting global markets.

After the radar screen issues are identified, categorized, and prioritized, the next step is to assign them to committees, task forces, staff, or a combination thereof. The board's role is to set the outcomes and guiding principles. The strategy development and execution group's role is to set the major milestones and the how to's. Ideally, no more than three or four strategies are in play at any given time. Once a strategy is completed, or becomes part of the traditional operations, new strategies are developed to address the next issues in order of priority.

Elements of a Strategy

To understand how to best create a strategy from a strategic issue, first we must explore the composition of a strategy. Strategies are composed of (1) a strategic issue, or issues, from your strategic radar screen (the radar screen being an end-result of your environmental scanning process; (2) strategic outcomes that the board or visioning body identifies as what they want to achieve by addressing the issue(s) and the implementation of the strategy; (3) guiding principles, or "the parameters we must act within or considerations to keep in mind when developing the strategy," which should also be set by the board or visioning body; and finally (4) the event sequences that represent the major milestones or key execution steps that are outlined. The development of the event sequences creates a great time to set project due dates and reporting timelines to allow the board or visioning body to monitor progress on the strategy execution. Figure 10.1 shows Dalton's four elements that compose a strategy.

FIGURE 10.1. FOUR ELEMENTS OF STRATEGY.

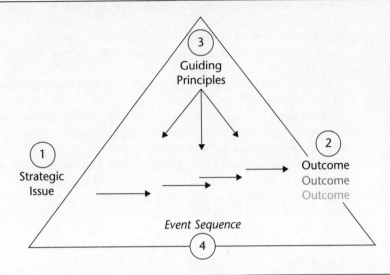

Source: J. G. Dalton, J. Jarratt, and J. B. Mahaffie, *From Scan to Plan: Integrating Trends into the Strategy-Making Process* (Washington, DC: ASAE Association Management Press, 2003).

To best illustrate how an issue, or issues, from a strategic radar screen is addressed by a strategy and integrated into an overall strategic plan, I have provided a sample strategy we developed at International Association of Plastics Distribution around multiple radar screen issues. It is important to note that a strategy may address a single or multiple issues and an issue may be addressed by multiple strategies.

◆ ◆ ◆

Sample Strategy

Radar Screen Issues

Issue #3: The negative environmental perception of plastics limits the growth of the industry.

Issue #4: Plastics are being outpaced for recognition in the marketplace by alternative materials that have industry marketing initiatives in place.

Issue # 5: There is an opportunity to educate the plastics industry and end-using communities on the benefits and applications of plastics, thereby expanding the use of plastics.

Desired Outcomes

1. Generate leads from engineers, OEMs, and specifiers for member companies to pursue.
2. Generate focused lists of engineers, OEMs, and specifiers who actually create demand. Achieve 15,000 new leads in 2009, 15,000 in 2010, and 15,000 in 2011.
3. Business growth as reported by members in an IAPD annual benchmarking survey; doubles in five years.
4. Establish baseline and increase by 10 percent annually the use of IAPD's website by engineers, specifiers, designers, and OEMs. Measure by number of hits on critical content pages and leads captured through the website.
5. Increased membership of resin manufacturers, fabricators and pipe, valves, and fittings companies in IAPD. Increase by 3 percent annually.
6. Specifying engineers recognize IAPD and members as a source for information on selecting materials. Establish baseline from *Market Insight Report* metrics and raise the percentage of respondents who rate themselves as having an average or above level of awareness of IAPD by 5 percent annually. Baseline metrics are 9.38 percent, 7.81 percent, and 15.62 percent, respectively.
7. Educate the market on the validity of the distribution channel.
8. Create recruiting materials for presentation and distribution in schools and post-secondary institutions.

Guiding Principles

When planning the marketing strategy, the staff and the marketing committee should consider the following questions:

- What specific populations have the greatest potential to increase demand of plastics' use?
- What information do they need to convince them to do this?
- How should IAPD reach them with this information?
- How will IAPD know if these initiatives are making a difference?

Event Sequence

Timeline: First three steps = four months; Step 4 = ongoing

1. Determine the target populations that meet two critical criteria: (1) they can be reached in a reasonable manner and (2) they are apt to provide the greatest return on investment.
2. Identify specific strategies for reaching desired outcomes, including short-term and long-term measures of success.
3. Conduct research to provide baseline data for use in measuring awareness-building efforts.

4. Develop promotional plans for products key to success in meeting outcomes (for example, certificate program, convention and exhibition, membership promotion and renewal).
5. Implement, evaluate, and revise on an ongoing basis.

I am currently exploring a new model, the Two-Curve Future.[3] It is an emerging methodology identifying signs from areas such as technological foundations or disruptive technologies and new ways of publishing, learning, and associating. Part of the analysis and outcomes is to determine how those areas may affect the way that individuals or companies interact with the association, develop different needs that the association may fulfill, and discern whether there is competition from nontraditional sources or disruptive technologies that could alter the very way we operate.

Regardless of the methodology, you must first vet it to ensure that it fits with the culture of your association and also have a plan for how to maintain, prioritize, and use the information. The downside of not doing this prework is that your leadership may become overwhelmed by the information, avoid prioritizing, and try to address all issues or signs, become too focused on the methodology and process and not the information and data, do nothing as it seems too big to take on, or focus too much on the scan and forget that there still is an association to govern and current programs and services to maintain.

Understanding Your Limitations

In a perfect world, we would love our associations to be able to identify and address all of the current and future issues or trends that will most likely affect our members. But associations do not have unlimited resources. Time, money, staffing capacity, and maintaining current operations, programs, and services limit how much we can do. Resources are finite, which requires us to prioritize how much we will allocate to maintaining the association's current operations and offerings and how much we dedicate to planning and executing strategies for the future. At a minimum, I recommend dedicating at least 20 percent of resources and focus toward the future.

Many associations recognize the need to have resources to plan for the future and develop different reserve funds to provide the financial backing in various areas, such as operational, strategic, and information technology.

The *operational reserve* is your rainy day fund. The *strategic fund* is a method for setting aside some of the reserves for development of long-term strategies, which may span multiple years and are for developing the future of the association. The *information technology fund* sets aside resources to prepare the association for major enhancements to infrastructure, website, association management software systems, and other vital IT resources. Even though its function is fairly administrative, the technology fund can serve to add capacity or set the stage for future innovations.

Maintaining the Environmental Scan

Again, scanning is not a one-time event, but an ongoing process. When you decide what methodology or model to use, it is vital that you determine not just what you will do with the information, but how you will keep it fresh. I recommend keeping it as part of your strategic planning or strategy management process, board governance, and, minimally, your annual operational planning process. Always question what is new, still relevant, missing, or no longer an issue. Further, if used correctly, it can be a tremendous resource to develop new programs and benefits, create greater value for your members and professions or industry, as well as ensure the relevancy of the association.

Avoiding the Whiplash Effect

As CSEs, we must be extremely careful about what we put in front of our boards and avoid taking the latest and greatest methodologies and mistakenly presenting them as a prescription to fix all of our problems. So many boards experience the whiplash effect, in which every few years they are changing governance, strategic planning, and other models. If not vetted and thought through, a new methodology can disrupt the association and veer it off on a different path, only to change course when the next methodology is introduced. There is no quick fix to problems and no one-size-fits-all methodology. This same philosophy should be employed with the environmental scanning process.

Our roles are to be partners in setting vision and strategy with the board. We must keep abreast of new thoughts, processes, and methodologies applicable to managing associations. However, when introducing a new methodology, including a proposal to implement an environmental scanning process, vet the methodologies and any third-party firms you bring to your board. You know your association the best and, intuitively, you should know what feels right. Be protective, but also be bold. A great environmental scanning process, followed with a solid strategic planning or strategy development process, can give you the best chance at making your association relevant for the future.

Notes

1. J. G. Dalton, J. Jarratt, and J. B. Mahaffie, *From Scan to Plan: Integrating Trends into the Strategy-Making Process* (Washington, DC: ASAE Association Management Press, 2003).
2. J. Lampel and H. Mintzberg, *The Strategy Process: Concepts, Contexts, Cases,* 4th ed. (Harlow UK: Pearson Education, 2014).
3. Institute for the Future and the ASAE Foundation, "Sustaining and Growing Association Knowledge and Learning Workshop," 2014.

The Author

Susan E. Avery, CAE, is the CEO of the International Association of Plastics Distribution. She began her career in association management in 1998 as the deputy executive director/CFO at ARMA International, a professional association. IAPD, also owns and operates an AMC, and Susan also serves as executive director for a couple of their clients, one of which is a European-based trade association. She is an experienced association management executive with both trade and professional associations and is known for her work with governance, strategic planning and strategy development, data-driven decision making, financial and strategic turnarounds, and building professional and competent staff teams.

CHAPTER ELEVEN

STRATEGIC PLANNING

Robert H. Rich, PhD, CAE

In a recent study, highly successful associations and other nonprofits reported that strategic planning has high impact on overall organizational success.[1] These organizations conduct strategic planning as a routine periodic process. Low-success organizations, by contrast, don't think strategic planning is as important.

Strategic planning is both a powerful tool and a much-maligned symptom of industrial-age management practices. How can both of these be true? It comes down to definitions. When done well, strategic planning

- Aligns the association from top to bottom
- Is agile and responsive to the latest external trends
- Focuses limited resources on the most important outcomes
- Represents a common, agreed-upon basis for making key decisions shared by volunteers and staff
- Supports performance measurement
- Enables leaders to make the difficult decisions about scaling back or terminating programs and activities

When done poorly, strategic planning

- Locks associations into inflexible plans for extended periods
- Drains creativity and innovation

- Is an enormous administrative drain for the association staff and volunteers to administer
- Focuses on minutiae, misses the big picture
- Spends more time debating the process to be followed than considering the key strategic issues

Strategic planning is no longer what it used to be. It has evolved from a cutting-edge concept in the early 1960s, through calcification into a fixed template that inadequately addressed the need for flexibility, to today's modern approaches, which put a premium on agility, efficiency, inclusive participation, and making the tough (but important) decisions. There was a point in the not-too-distant past when everyone used a similar approach to planning, but there is no longer a uniform understanding of how it should work. Still, it is essential that associations maintain some way of anticipating the future and building consensus around what should be done. An understanding of available strategic planning tools and methods is a vital competency for a chief staff executive.

What Is Strategic Planning?

The nature of the word *strategic* implies there will be trade-offs and decisions on priorities. Most associations cannot continue to do all the things they have been doing and then pile on new direction-setting initiatives. Being "strategic" implies that choices will be made so that the association will become more relevant or more competitive, or will achieve a desired positioning in the global marketplace.

Naturally, strategic planning involves strategy. *Strategy* is the intentional effort by an organization's leaders to achieve a desired set of outcomes. In the marketplace, it is directed at finding the best approaches toward the creation of maximal stakeholder value.[2]

Strategic planning also is a form of *planning* and evaluation. A plan without specifics is too ethereal to make a difference; therefore specific outcomes must be targeted, specific champions should be assigned to lead the efforts, and specific strategies should be applied to reach the desired outcomes. Plans serve to align people but can become rigid if not constantly reassessed. As an evaluative tool, tracking and measuring plan progress can help maintain management focus and discipline.

In today's dynamic environment, associations should engage in strategic planning on at least an annual basis. Even though the time horizon for a strategic plan may cover three to five years, it is valuable to look out at the next period each year using a mechanism to revisit or shift the focal points of the plan nimbly in response to internal and external changes. That way, each year's annual plan will be firmly grounded in a long-term focus.

It Is Not Primarily About the Plan, It's About the Planning

Strategic planning can be a great opportunity for leaders to step back a bit from everyday concerns, put on a big-picture perspective, and consider the most valuable ends to seek. As the discussion proceeds from vision and mission through preferred future to goals, objectives, and success measures, every attempt should be made to circle back and inform planning participants about the thinking behind the chosen path. Where there is disagreement, taking time to discuss and debate before making a clear decision will help everyone work in maximum alignment, the ultimate aim of strategic management. Certainly, a written plan document will result from the process, but the most valuable result is management and leadership consensus on the big picture outcomes to be pursued.

Even in the written work product, modern practice is to use a variety of media (for example, websites, pocket cards, posters) as the primary vehicles for communication with the association's staff, members, and other stakeholders, rather than old-fashioned bound printed reports. Dynamic planning software can also make it easier and more efficient to regularly update the plan as the external and internal realities change.

Strategic Planning in a Nutshell

Every planning function revolves around these five questions:

1. Where are we now?
2. What is changing in our environment that will affect us?
3. Where do we want to be?
4. How do we get there?
5. How will we know when we get there?

◆ ◆ ◆

Charter, Mission, and Vision

The cornerstone of strategic planning is the association's charter (or purpose), mission, and vision. Most associations begin with a charter (presented in the articles of incorporation), which establishes the purposes of incorporation and serves as a constant reminder of the original intent. A mission statement describes the primary purpose of the organization. This should be carefully crafted, concise, and unambiguous. It defines why the association exists. Management guru Peter Drucker suggested that "only a clear definition of the mission and purpose of the business makes possible clear and realistic business objectives. It is the foundation for priorities, strategies, plans, and work assignments."[3] It can also serve as the basis for brand taglines, emblems, and catch phrases.

Built upon the mission, the vision is an aspiration of what the world will look like when the association is successful. It is a shared understanding of what the overall impact of the organization will be. It is a rallying cry that can mobilize action into its realization. A good vision is not a list or enumeration of different outcomes to be achieved; rather, such lists of priorities should be included as goals within the strategic plan.

The mission and vision are typically reviewed by the board annually, and should only be edited when substantial change to the association's direction is needed. A mission statement can last for decades unchanged, and the vision equally as long, provided that the main focus of the association remains unchanged. Any changes to these critical statements should be subject to extensive discussion by representatives of all of the association's stakeholders.

◆ ◆ ◆

Illustrations of Charter, Mission, and Vision for the American Chemical Society (ACS)

Charter: The purposes of the corporation are

1. To encourage in the broadest and most liberal manner the advancement of chemistry in all its branches
2. To promote research in chemical science and industry
3. To improve the qualifications and usefulness of chemists through high standards of professional ethics, education, and attainments
4. To increase and diffuse chemical knowledge
5. By its meetings, professional contacts, reports, papers, discussions, and publications, to promote scientific interests and inquiry to foster public welfare and education, aid the development of our country's industries, and add to the material prosperity and happiness of our people.

Mission: Advance the broader chemistry enterprise and its practitioners for the benefit of Earth and its people

Vision: Improving people's lives through the transforming power of chemistry

◆ ◆ ◆

Core Values

Every association has core values, whether they are formally articulated in a strategic plan or not. These are the assumptions that staff and members bring to how they are expected to complete their work. For example, the association could value autonomy or collaboration, excellence in efficient operations or innovation, member satisfaction or service to society broadly. By including explicit consideration of the desired core values in a strategic planning process, the leadership can focus on areas where change would be desirable or stability a continuing strength. They provide a standard against which the culture can be assessed and developed.

Desired core values move energy and focus in the organization. For example, a desired core value might be innovation, adaptability, or long-term perspective. Such value choices become a filter for decision making in the organization.

Care should be taken around several key issues in creating such a list. First, inclusion of overly broad and universal statements that could apply to almost all organizations (for example, being financially sustainable or providing excellent offerings) is essentially meaningless and detracts from the overall plan. Second, leaders must be prepared to "walk the walk," exemplifying the desired core values in their own interactions. Hollow words expressed in the strategic plan are worse than saying nothing at all. Finally, culture change is hard and takes time. It is only through the continual application of leadership throughout the association that the current core values can be transformed into the desired ones.

Challenges and Opportunities

Most strategic plans include reference to the environmental scan through the inclusion of challenges and opportunities that provide a rationale for the goals and objectives. This should be a short list, selected by the leadership from the most significant internal and external forces that could help or hinder the association's work toward the preferred future. Challenges and opportunities may be considered as they affect the association as a whole or in the context of each of the strategic goals.

Strategic planning is all about closing the gap between where you are now and where you want to be. It should be noted that the value of the internal SWOT (strengths, weaknesses, opportunities, threats) analysis is optimal only in relation to identifying the gap between your current state and where you want to be as defined in your mission and vision. Strategies and tactics need to be chosen to close the gap.

The Language of Planning

In strategic planning, there is much debate over the meaning of the items that support organizational goals. It seems that every practitioner has their own lexicon. There are goals, objectives, strategies, tactics, sub-objectives, milestones, and targets. The important thing is to clearly define a specific meaning to each term and to avoid debate over the language (instead of an exclusive focus on the substance of the plan). For the purposes of this overview, goals are general outcomes (a general what), objectives are more specific outcomes (for example, engage 10 percent of members in online professional development this year), and strategies are the approaches used to reach the objectives (for example, develop a series of online resources relevant to leadership skills enhancement).

Goals

Perhaps the most important phase in strategic planning is the development and selection of organizational goals. Goals form the basis for detailed objectives for the organization as a whole, and for its constituent parts. Since these should establish the highest-level outcomes to be sought by the association, careful consideration should be given to select those which will maximize the mission impact for stakeholders and relevant value for members. Resist the temptation to simply organize the association's existing activities and call them "goals." Rather, goals are intended to drive change and create a future state in which the mission is most significantly advanced.

There should only be a limited number of such goals, perhaps three to six, forcing prioritization and decision making. One of the common pitfalls in strategic planning is the selection of too many goals. With a long list of goals, not all can be a priority. The association's impact is diluted, trying to be all things to all people, and the paid or volunteer staff responsible for implementation can be overwhelmed.

Another mistake to avoid is making the goals so broad and vague that almost anything could conceivably be seen as supporting it. Done right, vigorous debate within the board (or planning committee) about goal selection can result in powerful goals that inspire and motivate the necessary work. Setting strategic goals may be the most important work that a board undertakes.

In practical terms, goals should be broad but clear and focused, without specifying how the desired outcomes will be attained (that is the role of objectives and strategies). They should represent the most important work that the association seeks to do. In an annual (or more frequent) strategic planning cycle, it is likely that there will be a need to refine or replace one or more of the goals. Priorities and opportunities shift, so the goals must be changed along with them to keep the plan focused and relevant.

Objectives and Strategies

Objectives should represent the most important outcomes that will aid in the realization of the goals. For each goal, perhaps three to seven objectives are optimal. They should be specific, measurable, achievable, realistic, and time-determined. These can be remembered with the acronym SMART. To develop SMART objectives, it is most common to brainstorm about possible draft objectives first, narrow them down through prioritization, establish specific targets (of how much and by when), and finally refine the language to make them as clear and unambiguous as possible. When setting goals and objectives, the question to ask is "what?" not "how?"

Identification of strategies should follow agreement on the objectives. This is when the "how" discussion is useful. In other words, design activities and programs to reach objectives, instead of creating objectives that justify existing or pet activities (that is, those which are of great interest to only a very limited, but influential, segment of the membership or volunteer leadership). Strategies can be identified by asking how the association can best reach the objectives. Be creative. Sometimes the preconceived notions going into strategic planning may not be the highest value or lowest cost strategies. To have a chance of successful execution, strategies require identification of a lead "champion" to oversee each one, allocation of specific resources of money and time, and a commitment of sufficient leadership attention. Tactical planning and business planning will proceed to flesh out the details that will enable successful execution of strategies.

Who Does Strategic Planning?

Strategic planning is not just an activity for the top leaders of the organization. To maintain an effective strategic focus, leaders should develop a continuous "parallel process" that involves a wide range of members, staff, and other stakeholders in scanning the internal and external strategic environment, identifying key challenges facing the membership, considering the implications for strategy, and suggesting potential goals and objectives. In an ideal situation, every member and stakeholder would have the opportunity to participate meaningfully in helping to shape the association's developing strategic direction.

A recent innovation is "appreciative inquiry"—a powerful parallel process that engages large numbers of members and stakeholders.[4] Based on the work of David Cooperider, appreciative inquiry summits enable hundreds or thousands of participants to "discover" what currently works well, "dream" of potential goals, "design" objectives and strategies to reach the goals, and reach the organization's "destiny" through the leadership of all summit participants in realizing the possibilities around which they are most excited. A growing number of associations have used appreciative inquiry to empower members and other stakeholders in support of shared strategic goals and objectives.

The planning process needs to be owned by the leadership of the association. Usually, this means the board of directors and senior staff leadership. If this is too large a group (more than approximately twenty-five people), a planning committee that represents both sides of the association leadership can engage in the actual planning, with the final outcome refined and ratified by the full board. The assembled perspectives from the parallel process, any research available on external trends, and awareness of the organization's recent accomplishments should be brought to bear in framing any planning discussions.

Staff participation, especially that of the CSE, is vital to successful strategic planning. Insights relayed from frontline staff can prepare the volunteer leaders to be grounded in the member's true needs, so that they can plan on the basis of more than just their own perspectives. Staff should serve as custodians of the environmental scan information, and remind leaders of the current understanding of relevant factors prior to any planning discussion. Once a plan is adopted, the management team must work to see that the goals and objectives are met through the work of staff and volunteers. Of course, this is made easier if the key implementers are also involved in the parallel process of planning, since people naturally support what they help to create. The CSE can also draw attention of the board (or planning committee) back to strategic planning in the event that a dramatic change in the environment occurs that suggests a different strategy. It is useful to build regular checkpoints on the strategy into board meetings to ensure that the plan remains directionally correct.

◆ ◆ ◆

Strategic Planning from a CSE Viewpoint

Mark W. Light, CAE

Simply hearing the words *strategic planning* may send shivers down your spine. We've all heard horror stories about strategic planning retreats and meetings going amok, and the CSE spending untold hours trying to fix the plan. This often results in the plan being shelved and the participants developing a negative impression of a critical management and leadership tool.

The CSE's role is to ensure the process fits the organization and has the full support of the board and staff leadership. Designating top-level staff, such as the COO, as the internal champion, sends a message to the entire organization that the process is important. Even when the responsibility for implementation is transferred to the COO, the CSE must continue to support the process and show commitment to incorporating the results into future actions of the association.

The CSE must decide early in the process how the strategic planning process will be facilitated. If staff or volunteers possess the skills to manage strategic projects, will they be the best advocates to push the organization to think differently? Will they challenge elected leaders and executive staff when putting forth unconventional ideas or when the group goes off track? As the CSE, your role is to see that the process cannot be hijacked by a weak facilitator.

Another option is to hire a consultant or professional facilitator to lead the process. This approach will most likely result in someone that is not a subject matter expert in your arena, but that is not necessary. A facilitator's role is to push the group to look at new opportunities, question, and keep the process on track. They are there to help you achieve good results and can often say things that someone internal to the organization could never say.

The key consideration for hiring consultants is to make sure they understand what you want and, more important, what you don't want. If you don't want your mission statement rewritten and hours are spent doing that because it's the normal process, no one will be satisfied. All players should agree on terminology up front and agree on what defines a goal, an objective, a strategy, and an action item. You can waste valuable time in the group process arguing over whether a statement is an objective or a strategy. In addition, make sure the consultant is open to adjusting the approach during the process, so if the CSE sees it going off track, it can be changed swiftly rather than waiting until the next step to make corrections. CSEs can never forget that the process is as important as the outcomes. Make sure the process sets the stage for great results.

In evaluating the plan, ask yourself, Was the process successful? Does the plan positively move the organization forward? Does it position the organization for future challenges? Is it accepted by the membership and staff? Does it accomplish what the board and executive leaders wanted? If the answers are yes, then the hard part begins—implementing your new strategic plan.

◆ ◆ ◆

How Is Strategic Planning Conducted?

The standard two- to three-day strategic planning retreat can be effective to focus attention on strategy each year. Increasingly, though, strategic planning conversations are broken down into the component parts and spread over a much longer period. For example, environmental scanning data may be shared in the first meeting, with discussion on what the data mean for the association. The vision and mission might be reviewed and core values updated at the second meeting, goals decided upon at a third, and objectives and strategies defined and assigned to champions and resources at a fourth. A major advantage of this approach is allowing leaders to pause and take stock of what has been decided after each stage. Independent and collaborative consideration of what might come next in the process can then lead to a much more considered, informed, and thoughtful discussion and results. It also allows strategy to be dynamic, always in focus, and responsive to ongoing events.

The need to reconsider our understanding of strategy making under rapidly changing conditions is captured by James Brian Quinn, a management guru from Dartmouth's Tuck School of Business, in what he calls logical incrementalism.[5] Quinn's thesis is that the development of strategy in successful organizations is fragmented, evolutionary, and intuitive. Good strategy evolves over time in a stream of activities that include conversations, planning, serendipity, failed initiatives, persistence, more conversation, and technique. In this modern "strategic management," a rational-analytical technique is applied to the information flow that percolates through a wide variety of events and yields strategies.

In fact, it is useful for the board to consider key strategic issues (such as how an emerging technology may be affecting members) as a part of each of its meetings. This often helps to refine the organization's ability to achieve its goals and objectives. Sometimes such a focused discussion will also lead to refinements in the next year's strategic planning. These strategic discussions keep the board focused on the future, appropriately leapfrogging ahead of current plan implementation.

Role of the Facilitator

It is very difficult to proceed through a strategic planning process without a skilled facilitator. Facilitators can either be drawn from the association itself or hired as a consultant; however, it is ill-advised for the CSE to facilitate the process. Insiders can apply knowledge of the organization's history, culture, and the personalities involved. If the facilitator is internal, care should be taken to make sure all voices are heard and to avoid pushing a personal agenda. The advantage of an outside facilitator is that outsiders ask different questions, apply an impartial process, and play an objective role. If the facilitator is external, it is important to invest time in familiarizing him or her with the norms, preferences, and record of strategic planning within the association to avoid conflicts over expectations. Regardless of the origin of the facilitator, the planning group itself and its leader (for example, the board chair) must "own" the results of the process, buying into the decisions made and being prepared to communicate them broadly among the volunteers and staff.

Communicating Strategy

If strategy, as embodied in a strategic plan, only resides in the awareness of the association's senior leadership, its realization is highly doubtful. Once the mission, vision, core values, challenges and opportunities, goals, objectives, and strategies are identified, a concerted effort is needed to share them with all of the volunteers and staff who will make them a reality. Since the process of strategic planning is becoming more continual, this communication also needs to be much more frequent than in the past.

Perhaps the best way to communicate strategy is leading by example. If leaders explicitly consider all of their important decisions in light of the strategy, others will naturally start to do the same. They must make the effort to explain the strategy and what it implies for the tactical and operational issues at hand.

The association website is an excellent place to share the strategy broadly with staff, volunteers, and members. Though some details of a proprietary and confidential nature may need to be withheld, it can be empowering for members to know that their association's strategy is publicly and readily available (for example, American Chemical Society at http://strategy.acs.org). Such a website could also include information on relevant ongoing activities, recent accomplishments, and how members can help to reach the goals. Short videos that highlight the goals and objectives also help to cement them in the thinking of stakeholders.

Psychological research has shown that people have difficulty remembering long lists of priorities and strategies. Certainly, the multipage, bound strategic plans of yesteryear are not likely to be recalled and applied to daily work. Constant reminders of just the top-level mission, vision, and goals will make an impact in increased awareness of and engagement with the plan. Some effective approaches include the use of trifold pocket cards and framed posters of the goals, with a weblink to access the plan's details when needed. Other engagement activities can include presentations at meetings and so-called "strategy cafes," which allows groups of grassroots volunteers to consider in small groups the association's goals and how they'd like to help achieve them.

Once the strategic plan is constructed, the next step is to create the tactical plan that will connect the dots between broad strategy and actionable execution of the plan.

Notes

1. Association for Strategic Planning, "Strategic Planning for Non-Profits," n.d., available at http://www.strategyplus.org/Non-Profits.shtml.
2. Michael E. Porter, "What Is Strategy?" *Harvard Business Review* 11–12 (1996): 61–78.
3. P. Drucker, *Management* (New York: Harper & Row, 1974).
4. See Appreciative Inquiry Commons, "Definitions of Appreciative Inquiry," n.d., http://appreciativeinquiry.case.edu/intro/definition.cfm.
5. James B. Quinn, *Strategies for Change: Logical Incrementalism* (Scarborough, Ontario, Canada: R. D. Irwin, 1980).

The Authors

Robert H. Rich, PhD, CAE, is the director, strategy development, at the American Chemical Society. He holds a PhD in chemistry from the University of California, Berkeley, and has extensive association experience as an executive and as a volunteer leader. He is an active member of the Association for Strategic Planning and was a cofounder of its Not-for-Profit Center of Excellence.

Sidebar author *Mark Light, CAE,* is the chief executive officer of the International Association of Fire Chiefs.

CHAPTER TWELVE

HIGH-YIELD TACTICAL PLANNING

John B. Cox, FASAE, CAE

It is all well and good—and critically important—to do environmental scanning, strategic planning, and business planning, but the fruits of those exercises will go unrealized if execution is poor. That's where the discipline of tactical planning comes in.

Except in entirely volunteer-run associations, tactical planning is a staff function. The chief staff executive leads the staff, and those staff members who think like chief staff executives, who focus on the issues of greatest strategic import, are those who distinguish themselves by understanding and playing a part in the CSE's most preoccupying concern: how to turn the vision of the association's leadership into reality, which is the role of tactical planning.

When it comes to tactical planning, the wise CSE thinks through questions like these:

- Do the tactics fully support the strategic direction approved by the board?
- Can the tactics be adequately resourced, and are they achievable?
- What are the risks of implementing, or not implementing, the tactical plan?
- What are the obstacles, and how will we overcome them?

By using proven tactical planning steps, association staff can exceed their leaders' visions, realizing growth and accomplishment not previously attempted or even considered. Developing the tactical machinery to drive the dream is the focus of this chapter.

With that said, please note that there are as many different approaches to tactical planning as there are associations. As long as they lead to the same result, they are all worth the effort. The following model is proffered because in use after use, it has yielded the absolutely highest return on the investment of association time and human and financial resources. It is what the sciences call radially adaptive (in other words, highly malleable); it can be freely employed for almost any application an association needs—single-purpose or organizationwide. In the latter regard, the tactical plan is most valuable. In its creation, obvious synergies among various operational functions, programs, and activities will surface, and it is in recognizing and cross-fertilizing these opportunities that the highest yields will occur. Stated simply, no association activity occurs in a vacuum. When various operations such as continuing education, annual meetings, publications, political activities, and press and communications programs are linked together in a tactical plan, a multiplier effect kicks in and the return on investment is far greater than on any activity undertaken alone.

Keep that multiplier effect in mind as you read the planning steps that follow.

◆ ◆ ◆

Some Helpful Tips Before You Begin Tactical Planning

This book contains many references to environmental scanning. And almost all refer to the external environment. It is just as worthwhile, and sometimes more so, for the association to do an internal environmental scan. Jack Welch, arguably the most famous CEO in GE's history, developed a unique business model. In it, he postulated the need to "destroy your organization." Sounds radical, but it helped propel GE to the greatest growth in its history.

The same can and does work in nonprofit organizations. This author has witnessed and participated in exercises that literally deconstruct an association, its programs, and its operations. The overarching, guiding principle was to ask who did what, and why, and how that contributed to the organization's mission. In one astonishing example, a prominent association, using that exercise, realigned almost every staff function and operation. Older, tired programs, products, and some services were jettisoned, staff in some areas assumed responsibilities for activities and programs in other areas, and, most important, more than three dozen in-house functions were either discontinued or outsourced, some within a matter of days. Net result: within seventy-two hours of effort put into tactical planning, the association dropped a tidy six figures on its bottom line simply in realized savings. More than one prominent executive in association management has noted that nonprofit organizations rarely "plan to plan." Except for some leadership strategic exercises, internal planning is too often by happenstance. It should not be this way. It is imperative, in fact, to set aside specific times and dates, with appropriate staff, to do tactical planning. Moreover, involve as many staff as can be spared in tactical planning. It is often the staff least expected—who do the same tasks routinely, such as mailroom and reception—who have the most unexpected and valuable contributions; they serve in the trenches, and hear firsthand what the member audiences want, and are looking for. This phenomenon becomes even more obvious in smaller and mid-sized organizations.

Don't be afraid of "blue sky," out-of-the-box thinking in tactical planning. It is often the ideas from left field that are the most productive, and yield the absolute highest return to the association. Time and again, the author has seen ideas shot down as untried, tried and failed, too bold, too new, too retro, too something to be done or considered for the association. Tell your planning participants, loudly, that this is nonsense. Some ideas that may not have worked in the past may now be ideal for the association. Some ideas that seem to be too bold may actually lead the association into the future. There are no bad ideas in tactical planning, only ideas that haven't been tested. Important: do not limit yourself or your organization in tactical planning. Its reach can often exceed the association's goals.

It should become obvious almost immediately that tactical planning is completely linear. It is one of those rare enterprises in which each step logically follows the last, in sequence. If the planner develops or refines knowledge in each step, then the next step will logically follow, and so on to completion. When viewed in its entirety, it is clear that, say, Steps 2 and 4 could not have been possible without first completing Steps 1 and 3, respectively.

The most valuable thing for all involved is to realize that tactical planning belongs to the staff. They are responsible for its creations, its content, and its execution. It begins where the board's planning ends. A handy reference is that if strategic visioning and planning is the province of the board, then realizing that visioning and planning's product tactically is the province of the staff.

Step 1: Setting Goals and Objectives

This step will already be accomplished in the aforementioned strategic planning exercise that many associations engage in. But if not, please do understand that it is the prerequisite to tactical planning. Quite simply, it must answer questions such as, What does the association want to accomplish? Why? What strategies will take it there?

If you haven't already defined your goals and objectives, do so now. Even if you have, revisit them. Ignore the obvious. Kick your way out of the box. In other words, avoid the predictable, easy-to-attain goals. Maybe it's time to think of a global presence. Of starting a for-profit subsidiary. Of opening that branch office in Tierra del Fuego.

In any case, in Step 1 you define what you want to attain, your goal(s) in planning. Then you define why you think you want to achieve them, and what your objectives are for goal attainment. Finally, you think of the gross strategies to get you there. Metrics are key components. For example,

- The World Wide Widgets Association (WWWA) establishes a *goal* to have the greatest possible number of members, to represent the entire industry.
- Its *objectives* are to generate 20 percent additional revenue in twenty-four months to increase its political clout; to become the real voice of the industry; and to provide more programs, services, benefits, and activities to its constituents.
- WWWA's *strategy* will be to design and implement a major, ongoing member recruitment and retention program focused on converting to membership the 30 percent of the identified market not currently represented in the membership.

If you are thinking that looked rather easy, you are right. Tactical planning really is as easy as it appears. It is just a question of recognizing its necessity, and then following the simple linear steps to achievement.

In a couple of steps or so, we'll look at how tactics are required to drive strategies. But first plan to plan. Setting goals and objectives is best done in an atmosphere devoted to the enterprise. A retreat is usually the best venue and vehicle. Wherever and whenever, allow thinking to roam free. That's when breakthroughs occur.

Step 2: Situation Analysis and Problem Definition

Remember those references to tactical planning being linear and sequential? Here is where it begins to become obvious.

WWWA now has a goal, objective, and even a strategy. Before it can set about attaining its goal, it needs to carefully analyze its current status, its market position, the impediments to goal and objectives attainment, its strengths, and, most important, its weaknesses. Does it have the resources to proceed? If not, can it acquire them? What will be required to succeed?

As, and after, it has analyzed and defined its current status, WWWA needs to define its problem areas—those impediments to achieving its goals. This is actually a two-part exercise.

Internal Problems

What elements will preclude WWWA from realizing its goals? It is imperative to be brutally honest in this exercise. In a nutshell, if there are road-blocks, identify them.

Typical references here include insufficient staff, insufficient financial resources, lack of the electronic resources that would make coordination of a member campaign possible, lack of real time to devote to the effort, and so forth. If you don't candidly identify the barriers here, don't proceed with planning. The effort won't be successful. A cautionary note: revealing internal problems can sometimes be very discomfiting to certain staff. If the earlier-mentioned deconstructing exercise has been performed, this problem will have already been obviated. If not, it is the planner's task to anticipate and alleviate possible concerns at this point.

External Problems

External factors must be recognized and overcome. In marketing, it can be thought of as identifying and measuring the competition. Suppose there is a larger, stronger, longer-established association that predominates in member share, or your association is not well recognized in the marketplace, or a social networking site is undermining your historical competitive advantage by offering free means of connecting. Perhaps the association didn't prevail in an important political battle. Possibly, potential and former members consider its dues too high. Whatever the problems are, they must be identified, confronted, and, if possible, overcome to clear the way for any success with stated goals.

Something important will have transpired at this point. Staff of an association engaged in tactical planning and following the just-described steps will have established goals and know why they want to achieve them. They will know the strategies it will take to get there and will have analyzed the association's current status including what is going right and where there are challenges and problems—internal and external—that must be addressed to realize the dream. In short, the association's leadership and staff may know more about the organization than ever before. Armed with the knowledge gained to this point, those engaged in the planning exercise can create the future of the association.

First, of course, must come the next essential and sequential steps in tactical planning.

Step 3: Identification of Key Audiences

Audiences in our context may also be thought of as publics, markets, and campaign targets. In brief, these are the members, buyers, nonmembers, potential members, legislators, funders, and consumers that the association wants and needs to reach with products, services, benefits, and programs.

On a global scale, a list of the audiences includes virtually everyone with whom the association wants or needs to interact. For a specific, single-purpose campaign, the list would be narrowed to those audiences relevant to the purpose or goal at hand.

Surprisingly and too often, some associations define their universe too narrowly. When asked how many media would be on a key audiences or target list for a public information program, they might respond with six or eight, having thought primarily about trade media covering their industry or profession; considered in a broader context, though, a minimal list could include more than twenty, and the author has seen successful and ambitious media lists with forty separate kinds of media targets. Similarly, a membership recruitment and retention campaign target list might yield half a dozen different types of audiences. However, there are so many different audiences involved in a proactive campaign that any good list should extend well into double digits. The same point could be extended to lists of audiences for fund-raising campaigns, legislative and governmental initiatives, conference and meeting development plans, and more. Here is another time when blue sky thinking on the part of all involved can produce surprising results. And only when an association defines all its possible audiences for any given outreach can it achieve the full potential envisioned in its campaign. Indeed, I participated in one such audience-identification exercise in tactical planning that spanned an entire association, and the yield was almost two hundred potential campaign targets, across a vast array of categories (such as governments; funders; media at the national, state, and local levels; groups of foundations; groups of different regulators; groups of different general-population types; and so on, seemingly ad infinitum). No one has ever erred in identifying too many potential users and buyers of association programs, products, service, and benefits.

All that said, an important consideration is that the organization will be better-equipped to reach some audiences than others. Go for those first. Some audiences you may know you can reach because you have experience doing so. Others might require more effort and time to reach. Others may be aspirational, potentially reachable only as the execution of the plan gets traction and achieves success. The point is to start by identifying the prospective universe and then prioritizing your approach on the basis of importance, effort, and resources related to reaching each audience. Once you've finished this exercise, it's time to plan how to go about reaching them. That would be Step 4, logically enough.

Step 4: Identification and Development of Vehicles and Tactics

In our tactical-planning context, the ideas of vehicles and tactics are almost interchangeable. Once an association has defined all of its audiences, it must define and determine the best ways for reaching them. And as with audience definition, on a global tactical plan the association must list every possible, conceivable method of reaching the targets in its plan—and then go through the prioritization process done with audiences. Newsletters, meetings, workshops, social media, email, blogs, podcasts, testimony, letters, speeches, trade press coverage, general-interest media, annual conferences, and so forth must be listed. Even if an approach or vehicle isn't being used currently, it should nonetheless be listed; it is something to be aspired to, or ruled in or out, and may eventually prove to be a key element in achieving success.

On a cautionary note, the same concern expressed in Step 3 pertains in Step 4. Namely, associations regularly underestimate the number, breadth, and range of vehicles and tactics for reaching their intended audiences. If a list of audiences can extend well into double digits for any given tactical campaign, the methods, tactics, and vehicles possible for reaching these publics should, at the minimum, match it. The only limits here are self-imposed. Nonetheless, practicality and available resources demand a process of prioritization.

Step 5: Creating the Tactical Plan: "A Matrix of Opportunities"

The tactical plan puts the pieces together.

If the staff of an association have set its goals and objectives, determined what obstacles it has to overcome, and identified its audiences and the vehicles needed to reach them, they need only match the audiences and vehicles, calendar the activities, and put a cost line on the enterprise.

Let's look at three brief examples of single-purpose tactical campaign planning. It is important to bear in mind that if we were looking at a global, organizationwide plan, the audiences and vehicles would be integrated in their respective steps, or columns, and that all activities would be intertwined synergistically. This, of course, would produce the aforementioned multiplier effect. When one or two elements in audiences and vehicles are cross-linked with others, they become worth four or five times their value alone.

For simplicity, think in this step of just matching the right audiences for any campaign with the right vehicles and tactics to reach them effectively. So, you want to use vehicles and tactics 2, 6, and possibly 8 in your list to effectively reach audiences or publics A, C, and probably E. In matching the right vehicles—now tactics—with the right audiences, synergy and the multiplier effect will kick in, and the yield will exceed the goal.

Example One

The Ozone Society decides it wants to create a tactical membership recruitment and retention plan. It has conducted all the preliminary steps outlined to this point. In Steps 3 and 4, it identified its key audiences and the vehicles and tactics required to reach them as the following:

Step 3 Audiences or Publics	Step 4 Vehicles and Tactics
• Potential members	• Social media presence in key forums
• Former members	• Personal visits, telephone calls, or letters to the best prospects
• Students	• Direct mail letters to the remainder of the list
• Affiliated organizations	• Telemarketing to the remainder of the list
• Those ineligible, but nonetheless interested	• Member-get-a-member and other campaigns
• Corporations	• Special offers: for example, a "two months for free" offer to prior members who have allowed their memberships to lapse
• Foundations	• A "free whitepaper" content marketing campaign designed for prospecting
• Auxiliary members	• Discounts for joining in conjunction with book purchases, workshops, and annual meeting attendance
• Retired members	• Special campaign-only rates
• Inactive members	

Example Two

The American Ethereal Association wants to design and mount a major fundraising or endowment building campaign. It successfully navigated all steps to this point and has identified its targets and methods as the following:

Step 3 Audiences or Publics

- All members
- Foundations
- Corporations
- Potential donors
- Former donors
- Known benefactors
- Most likely individual contributors
- Medium-to-least-likely contributors
- Program sponsors for annual meetings or workshops
- Government funding sources

Step 4 Vehicles and Tactics

- Individualized letters to all members defining the purpose of the campaign
- Direct marketing targeting the most likely prospects for giving, on the basis of historical giving and the level of current engagement with the organization
- Funding proposals
- Grant proposals
- A "like us on Facebook" campaign designed to build a community passionate about the mission of the organization
- Telemarketing to a wide audience
- Personal visits to identified prospects for highest contributions
- Gifts or acknowledgments for participation or contributions
- Formal recognition programs
- Electronic campaign information and targeting
- Planned-giving campaigns, such as estate funding

Example Three

The National Sea Shells League (NSSL) wants to pump attendance at its annual conference. It has identified its key publics and vehicles/tactical methods as the following:

Step 3 Audiences or Publics

- Current members
- Interested nonmembers
- Those who always attend

Step 4 Vehicles and Tactics

- Meeting program promotions and brochures targeted to those most likely to attend
- Letters to past attendees

Step 3 Audiences or Publics	Step 4 Vehicles and Tactics
• Those medium-to-least-likely to attend	• Magazine and newsletter articles reaching the entire membership
• NSSL book and periodicals buyers and subscribers	• NSSL website plus all appropriate social media to reach prospective nonmember attendees
• All workshop attendees	• State and chapter newsletters
• Current exhibitors	• Press releases
• Potential exhibitors	• Media wires
• Former exhibitors	• Feature articles targeted to interested publications
• Members of affinity organizations	• Postage-meter cancellations or indicias
• Members of affiliated organizations	• Buck slips
• General public	• Stuffers or flyers for book orders
• Press	• Blow-ins and tip-ins for NSSL publications
• Students	• Stationery legends or logos
• Spouses	• Cross-marketing with membership campaign
	• Early-bird discounting campaigns

At this point, tactical planners would simply draw synergy lines between the audiences, targets, and publics identified in Step 3 with the vehicles, tactics, and methods needed to reach them as listed in Step 4. For ease of purpose, it can be helpful to create a "matrix of opportunities," with audiences listed on one axis and vehicles—now considered tactics—on the other; contacts and activities would then fall into the grid of the matrix. In Step 4, it is important to remember that some vehicles will reach only one public; others will reach all. Similarly, some audiences are continuously key, while others have value only once or twice. Identifying who is to be targeted and when, and with what vehicle, can produce the earlier-referenced multiplier effect, when multiple vehicle hits with various target publics can produce excellent results with modest efforts.

◆ ◆ ◆

Technological Tactics

You will have recognized that in the three examples given, there were almost no references to specific electronic vehicles and tactics. The playing field has changed dramatically in tactical planning and association growth opportunities, and it is evolving faster than almost anyone's ability to keep pace. It is quite possible for a medium-sized or even a small association to have a worldwide portal and presence, reaching audiences not even conceived of a mere decade ago. New methodologies, vehicles, and social-media platforms are emerging almost instantaneously, only to be replaced in a blink by still newer ways to reach key audiences.

At this writing, the latest high-utility tactics for reaching vast publics include content marketing, viral marketing, blogs, message boards, social networking, and others. Before the ink dries here, there will be still newer, better, faster, farther-reaching technologies to reach key markets. The wise planner will try to keep an eye one or two clicks above the horizon and see which of these new methods, these singularly valuable vehicles, will be most beneficial in reaching what audiences to achieve specific goals.

◆ ◆ ◆

Step 6: Scheduling the Plan

Having identified *who, what, where,* and *how,* the final step is focused on identifying *when.* In years past, strategic planning—along with the tactics needed to support it—could be thought of in multiyear terms, with typical plans stretching out four or five years and beyond. That is no longer practical or wise today. Events simply move too rapidly. A good tactical plan will max in the twenty-four-month range, with a top-end reach of thirty-six months. And if viewed globally, and not only for discrete activities, the collective tactical plan *becomes* the organization's plan of work.

Many associations use the "NASA" approach to tactical plan calendaring—identifying the goal and then working backward on the steps it will take to get there. In real terms, if an association wants to increase membership attendance at its August annual meeting, it needs to identify its target audiences several months earlier, perhaps in October or November of the preceding year—or maybe much sooner if the market demands innovative and longer-term changes to the meeting—and then begin applying its tactical steps and employing its vehicles at calendared intervals in January, March, May, and so on.

A Handy Shortcut

For those new to the tactical planning process, creating a matrix of opportunities and linking various vehicles with numerous audiences may be a bit daunting. It gets easier with each plan created. If the reader feels somewhat stymied at this step, there is an easy shortcut to creating the plan and moving forward in Step 6.

Simply look over the list of vehicles identified in Step 4 and prioritize them numerically in Step 5. What will yield the greatest return from the most beneficial publics quickly? The most successful plans the author has been involved with developing have always identified the "low-hanging fruits" first, targeted them, and reaped the benefits to go on and finance later activities in the plan. For example, radically increasing annual meeting or workshop attendance will provide the monies to greatly increase essential publications and other revenue-producing information services. Then, high yields from those activities will finance, perhaps, new technologies that will in turn help recruit new members and retain existing ones. Every part of the plan interlocks with others and yields additional benefits and returns in still other listed activities and goals.

So, about that shortcut: continue numbering the vehicles and tactics in Step 4, from highest return to most modest, until the entire list is prioritized. Then, match these numbered items with the publics you want to reach (also prioritized) in Step 3. You now have the next step in your tactical plan. If you have taken this shortcut approach just noted, simply start creating your schedule and your tactical plan calendar with those first-identified, high-yield tactics and vehicles, and keep sequencing them in until all tactics and vehicles are matched with intended target publics and audiences. Next, allot specific time periods for accomplishing the outreach and actions required, and the calendar is complete.

A very important consideration in the calendaring step is that all tactical plans should contain a lot of air. Do not think of any tactical plan as a finished document. Rather, with ongoing evaluation, the plan will continuously be tweaked. Certain vehicles will be dropped while others are being added, and new or additional target audiences will replace existing ones. Most important, with sufficient malleability or air built into the plan, it will be possible to add and maximize opportunities not thought of or included in the plan during its design phase.

Step 7: Budgeting to the Plan

In the current climate, everything is thought of in economic terms, including and especially planning. To add the validity a serious tactical plan will require, a column should be added to the right of the matrix of opportunity or in the shortcut form just described, and in every place where an action is being calendared—where a vehicle or tactic is being used to reach a targeted audience—its economic impact must be indicated. On a happy note, not every reference connotes cost. That is, positive economic consequences should be listed as well. In brief, think in terms of a "monies out–monies in" column.

Not only will you have an accurate idea of what your effort will cost in human and financial resources, you will also be able to show the benefit to be derived. And that promotes buy-in by all the stakeholders in the plan, including other staff, boards, leadership, and interested volunteers.

A final benefit of budgeting to the plan is that it forces the planner(s) to focus and prioritize. When costs are added to the wish lists, those involved usually become a little more serious and begin to look at such things as return on investment before expending precious association resources.

Step 8: Evaluation

Evaluation is the *sine qua non* of tactical planning. It is the essential step.

In prior days, evaluation checkpoints could be built into a plan at longer intervals. In today's rapidly evolving climate, opportunities present themselves at a moment's notice, and the longest possible interval between evaluation points should be six months, and preferably three months or less for twelve- to eighteen-month plans.

In brief, evaluation is a snapshot of your progress at a given moment. It tells you where you've been, where you are, and where you appear to be going. It can tell you what to add, what to drop, what needs additional reworking, and where some tuning would help. It allows you to prevent failure and to measure success. Evaluation should focus on progress versus the metrics—whether in financial, growth, or other terms—developed when setting goals and developing the plan.

Most important, periodic evaluation guarantees that your tactical plans won't suffer the fate of most strategic and tactical plans: growing dust on a shelf. As noted at the outset, many associations think it is quite enough just to create the "strategic" plan; somehow implementation will take care of itself. By evaluating the tactical plan at specific intervals and making the changes required to ensure its success, you also ensure that the plan becomes a living, working blueprint for accomplishments. You institutionalize accountability, and that is a powerful motivator.

Well, all of this sounds fine and good. A matrix of opportunity. Budgeting to plan. Vehicles and audiences. Accountability.

But does it all work? Yes. In one association with which I am familiar, such planning increased net revenues on member professional development from $150,000 to $800,000 in a three-year period and more than doubled annual meeting attendance—from 4,500 to 9,700—in the same window. In another association, it produced a 10 percent increase in membership that costs a high three figures each year, and in still another association, generated a 6 percent increase in membership that costs four figures a year. A fourth association quadrupled its nonperiodical publishing output and income within a four-year period, while tripling its advertising revenues. The list goes on, but the point is made.

Everyone can plan strategically, and many do. It is those association professionals who knowledgeably back up their strategic plans with tactical planning who guarantee achievement. In a nutshell, high-yield tactical planning is the engine that can drive an association's success. And everybody wins: the planners, the association, its members, volunteers, and leaders. Very few other association activities can make that claim.

The Author

John B. Cox, FASAE, CAE, retired from a three-decades-plus career in association management and consulting, most recently as principal and CEO of Association Growth and Income Builders, LLC, and previously as chief staff executive of multiple associations. He mentored more than two dozen CAE candidates.

CHAPTER THIRTEEN

BUSINESS PLANNING

Brian Birch, CAE, and Susan S. Radwan, SMP, ARM, CAE

The business side of the association environment is taking on more and more importance to boards of directors, CSEs, and senior staffs. There is a demand for greater understanding and accountability for the financial picture of our complex organizations. New business model development, major product launches, and investments in technology infrastructure all require thinking through the flow of money that will justify the investment the association is about to make. The business plan is all about the flow of money in the organization.

Whether you are preparing to implement your multiyear strategic plan or exploring new options for the association, business planning is a crucial step in managing the assets of the association. Keep in mind that solid business planning is two-fold. First, it is an ongoing process that enhances team buy-in and connects directly to the strategic plan. Second, it is an outcome, a physical (digital) plan that can be used to communicate, inform, remind, and align all stakeholders through a given period of time.

We have all heard the statement, "You have to run the association like a business." That mandate means that we need to carefully and intentionally keep our eye on and manage the flow of money in and out of the association. We need to understand the financial impacts of the decisions we make.

We need to anticipate where money will come from to invest in new initiatives and infrastructure and understand when the association will receive a return on the investment (ROI). An association can no longer assume its long-term sustainability. CSEs need to study the financial prospects of the slate of services offered, the financial impact of investments into programs that are intended to keep the association relevant, and project financial health.

At the same time, we need to understand that we cannot fully run the association exactly as if it were a business; the governance, leadership, and influence from the membership make associations fundamentally different. Instead, a business plan for an association needs to incorporate these complexities and help staff manage through them.

There was a time when businesses were happy when they received a financial ROI ten years after the initial investment. Today, the ROI expectation is twelve to eighteen months from the point of investment. To achieve that kind of return, CSEs need to be attuned to the mid- and long-term financial decisions requiring investment of association dollars. The balance is the sweet spot at which financial growth and ROI on specific programs match well with completion of bigger-picture strategic goals. Creating a solid business plan is key to understanding the investment, and at the same time the core way strategic success is achieved over the long term.

◆ ◆ ◆

Distinctions in Terminology: Feasibility Study Versus Business Case Versus Business Plan

Feasibility Study

When considering a new innovation, it is wise to do a feasibility study to explore whether the idea has the potential for success in your marketplace. A feasibility study will yield an assessment of who the target market is, whether your idea is technically feasible within a projected budget, the viability of your new product or service in that market, and whether the initiative will likely produce a positive impact either as a revenue generator or in social impact. If the feasibility study indicates your new product will likely be successful, then a business case is developed. The feasibility study becomes the first section of the business case document.

Business Case

A business case typically focuses on a specific project or initiative. The document provides an objective rationale for why the initiative should be pursued. It examines the financial impact, the ROI of the pursuit, and how the initiative adds to the value proposition for members. When there are competing opportunities for investment in new initiatives, the business cases offer comparative information for association leaders to prioritize the decision to pursue. A business case must always be looked at in the context of the overall business plan.

For example, in a given year, you have competing proposals from various departments for the association to invest in (1) a technology upgrade, (2) development of the knowledge management system, (3) a major redesign of the website, and (4) a new publication. Each of these initiatives will require significant investment. The association cannot do them all and must choose the most desirable opportunity. Developing a business case for each of these initiatives will assist decision making by assessing the comparative deliverable value to the membership, the investment necessary to realize the full functionality of the project, and how long it would take to realize the return on investment.

Feasibility studies and business cases are prepared in the exploration of new initiatives.

Business Plan

A business plan is the overarching process and vision to accomplish financial success tied to defined strategic outcomes. The business plan is connected to the strategic planning processes, focusing on sustainability of your chosen business model.

◆ ◆ ◆

What Is a Business Plan?

The business plan is a critical step in the planning continuum. Once you have your strategic plan developed, then you have to attach dollars to it. This is not a budgeting process, but it is a study of how the association will perform financially. The business plan assesses the programs and services you offer in terms of financial projections for revenue generation, long-range funding needs, and revenue generation plans. The business plan ultimately identifies whether your association is a viable and ongoing business concern. The difference between budget plan and business plan is key here; a budget is the financial roadmap of how an organization wants its finances to look. The business plan should be optimized to enable staff and the CSE to plan, organize, and achieve goals. A good business plan is not something that is created and left on the shelf; it is a continuous work-in-progress that must adapt to change over time. It should project financial targets out further than one year, as opposed to the budget, which typically focuses on one fiscal year.

Business planning starts with identifying business goals—the revenue and profit goals for the association. The plan assesses how the current slate of products and services will contribute to those revenue and profit goals (a financial SWOT analysis) as well as how the current resources (human, infrastructure, and financial) will be used to produce the revenue and profit goals. Conducting a proper business plan will identify your long-term funding needs.

Ideally, the process for staff in creating a business plan is an iterative part of both planning and strategy; the business planning process should be ongoing, and insight gained from it should in turn influence long-term strategic discussions led by the CSE.

◆ ◆ ◆

Assessing Organizational Capabilities

As the plan is developed, it becomes essential to understand the complex dynamics that compose the organization. Understanding strengths and limitations is key, including the following:

- *Core strength:* What is the one thing the association does better than anyone else?
- *Personnel:* What skills and talents do current employees hold that could enable success? Are all staff engaged with the mission and culture of the association?
- *Infrastructure:* What is the current association management system? Can it track the data needed to offer insight into business success? Are there significant investments in technology or resources that must be made?
- *Governance:* Are there special rules or limitations that apply on the basis of governance? Are there funding issues that could arise due to board-related decisions?

◆ ◆ ◆

Content of a Business Plan

One way to think about the content of a business plan is to write it as though you were seeking investors in your association. Those investors would need to see background information about the association; who the players are; what you have as going concerns (revenue generators); and what you are proposing for the future in terms of new product development, who your potential business partners are, pro forma financial projections, timelines for rollout, and conclusions. The numbers developed should be based on conservative projections. Remember that any plan like this will require some assumptions to be made, and the role of the lead developer of the plan is to obtain as much feedback as possible so that the financial projections are sound estimates that can be achieved in the marketplace.

Playing with Numbers

As the business plan takes shape, financial projections must be made. This is the most essential time in the creation of the plan, and the process of establishing financials should not be seen as the end of the process. Instead, at this stage, use financial projections for various programs or products and take some time to "play" with the numbers; use them to creatively explore plan tactics. Here are some ways to play:

- *Organize outcomes:* Review core revenue streams and plug in different potential revenue outcomes. What is the impact on the bottom line if a specific price is changed for a product? For example, what if we discounted the fees for all members for that new event? What if we charged a fee that was somewhere in between break even and what a for-profit organization would charge?
- *Explore expenses:* What resources would be available if you added more investment into an area of the plan? What expense-related areas are things that have "always been done"? Are these expense projections based on real-world quotes? Which areas of the expenses will be hardest to keep under control? Which expenses can be directly related to revenues?
- *Collaborate with staff:* Invite key staff to provide their own independent financial projections, then compare notes. This encourages them to take a leadership role in developing certain aspects of the plan, and it will be highly informative, especially for key areas that don't have long-term revenue histories tied to them, like new products.
- *Understand the impact of failure:* Use this time to consider failure and its impact on the overall plan. What if the new product revenue projections are actually 50 percent of what is in your projection? How does that affect other expense-related items? Are there board-mandated controls if net profits are down? What if the new product website costs 30 percent more than originally projected in two years because of an unforeseen technology-related demand by consumers?

No matter how sound or insane an idea might look on paper, the numbers don't lie. Use projections to plan at the beginning of the process, then refine them as core tactics take shape before finalizing them in the "official" plan.

Your business plan opens with a *brief review of your organization*: its history, its entrepreneurial success, and its current state. What is your current business model? How do you make money?

You want to include a profile of your management team, how long they have been together, and their relevant abilities with particular focus on the entrepreneurial strengths of the team.

To ensure credible projections, the business plan provides *a market analysis* for the products and services your association offers as well as what the marketplace needs. What is the association's relationship with the marketplace? What is its market share? Who are your competitors?

Why is this analysis important? If your association has captured 90 percent of the potential market of members and has retained that market share over time, then your market credibility is well established. This can make it easier to launch new products without intense sales efforts. However, if your association has only 35 percent of the potential market of members, the sale of new products will require significantly more marketing effort in the marketplace to reach customers who don't already know you. More effort translates into more marketing investment from the association to get similar results.

Be wary of the "hire a salesperson" trap that can occur when launching new products. If the plan depends on a magical salesperson to achieve success, a red flag should be raised. The market assessment and a more fundamental understanding of market dynamics are a much better strategy to rely on for plan success; keep in mind that while sales is the final step prior to fulfillment of revenue generation, many other items must fall into place in order to enable sales success.

It should also be noted that business plans not only consider the external marketplace but also the internal marketplace. For example, if you are considering a major upgrade in technology infrastructure, your primary audience is the internal marketplace. However, any internal solution has got to be connected to the value that the upgrade will contribute to the membership as a whole.

The third section of the business plan identifies what you are proposing as solutions in that marketplace.

Your proposal should address the needs of the marketplace and how you plan to address those needs. This proposal can be as broad or narrow as is appropriate. The issue for this section is, What is the need and how are you going to address that need? Who is your target market? How will you reach them? From where could you experience the greatest profitability?

Remember that solutions need to be focused on real-world deliverables but tied to overall strategic objectives. It is important that the plan reflect language and references from the overarching strategic plan. This will aid in keeping the CSE and staff organized and focused on the bigger picture the board has laid out for the organization.

The fourth section of the plan is the financial forecast for what you are proposing. Can you quantify your real costs and establish a reasonable margin per each sale? Clearly identifying the investment with the projection of sales over time, on the basis of credible projections, illustrates the potential for revenue generation. Often the financial forecast is presented against a background of three scenarios, such as conservative estimates and aggressive estimates and somewhere in between. This style of proforma budgeting assists in understanding where the association might focus its marketing efforts for a larger return on investment. Pro forma budgets are definitely not guarantees of performance, but one can learn about revenue potential from this exercise.

The fifth section of the plan is identification of potential strategic partners that could contribute credibility, expertise, or market value to the project. What vendors or suppliers will you be working with? What are their track records for success? Are there potential strategic partnerships that could be involved to achieve a larger market share, reach a larger target audience, or share the risks of investment? Who would be likely partners for this proposal?

The sixth section of the plan is an assessment of what could impede the successful launch of the products proposed. An investor needs to know the risk of investing in the pursuit proposed. If you only tell the upside and never look at the potential downside, you can't assess if the investment is worth it. It would be irresponsible to ignore the downside of such an investment.

The final section summarizes and draws conclusions about the wisdom of the investments proposed in terms of the payoff to the association, the ROI of the project(s), and the overall impact to the association and the marketplace.

◆ ◆ ◆

Business Case Example: Snow & Ice Management Association

Initiative: Social Media Planning

The Snow & Ice Management Association created a specific business case tied to its social media efforts. Here is a recap of one area of the plan, with some examples tying to the overall business plan and the association's strategy as a whole.

Objectives

1. Share quality, simple statistics, and information that prove the value of professional snow and ice management to consumers and the public.

2. Increase awareness of SIMA as an organization, its mission, and the value it offers to the marketplace as a whole, as well as to professionals within the industry.

3. Drive positive brand association by providing relevant, valuable information and exchanges in appropriate contextual settings and create better SEO results for SIMA long term.

Core Audience(s) by Priority

General public

Friends of snow professionals

Snow professionals

Current State at the Beginning

- 891 current followers (majority industry-specific), who have 300,000+ friends on Facebook
- Most shared post reached >2,000
- Less than $500 per year tied to social media expenses
- No relationship with social media efforts and association strategy
- No metrics identified from social media that determine success

Tactics to Employ

- Focus efforts on one social media space, Facebook, due to current engagement in the space and limitations of staff time
- Create five or six core messages, with a focus on simple messages with a strong visual tied to association brand
- Align messages and visuals with the overarching "Impact of Snow Public Relations" awareness campaign occurring at the same time
- Monitor the "engagement" metric in Facebook that focuses on the number of shares

Projected Year 1 Results

- Direct revenue = $0
- Expense = $2,000
- 44 percent growth in number of "likes" to the organizational Facebook page in year one
- 10x increase in peaks of the engagement metric—"Impact of Snow" campaign (major strategic initiative) messaging reached 10,000+ people via Facebook in four months
- Traffic to association web property GoPlow.com rose to the number 2 referrer of traffic. GoPlow.com is a revenue-generating website tied to advertising.

- Association-specific benchmark created for engagement levels that can be monitored long term
- Highly valuable insight into which messages were most valued by industry professionals

Ties to the Business Plan

- Core messaging from this initiative is absorbed into overall "Impact of Snow" campaign
- Members are provided detailed reports of success of the "Impact of Snow" campaign, including the successful reach of many people via Facebook.
- Overall growth in number of followers on Facebook lead to more reach for other messages or information shared via that social platform for other items
- No direct revenue generated from the effort on Facebook, but efforts support revenue streams in excess of $50,000 that are part of the overall business planning process

Organizing the Plan

Taking on the creation of a dynamic business planning process should be approached with care and a solid investment of time. The good news is that most organizations do the majority of what is in such a plan, but typically more informally. The task then is to formalize the process that ties overarching strategy with common-sense business savvy. Since strategic ties are essential to a quality business plan, the best way to start is at the end, with the association's strategic plan.

Use the strategic plan as a set of guideposts that look out long term, and begin working backward from those points. Identify the major steps that would need to occur in order to get to the end result, and walk back one step at a time until the goals are well-defined and of a much shorter time frame than the typical strategic plan defines.

Example: Strategy, Objectives, and Tactics Defined

Consumer Awareness and Education

Strategic vision: Association will establish itself as the leading resource to consumers looking to hire a service provider in the industry.

Long-term goal: Three to five years—consumer awareness expands to include the referencing of best practices and association-governed credentials in bid specifications.

Mid-term goal: Two to three years—consumers across North America learn about best practices for purchasing industry services.

Tactic: Create a group of ambassadors and train them in presenting information related to best practices.

Short-term objective: One year—finalize and provide the best practices document for consumers on purchasing services in the industry.

Tactic: Create a list of trade press for associated industries and message consistently about the availability of best practices.

Tactic: Organize a task force of subject matter experts to review survey results and generate a rough draft set of best practices.

Tactic: Survey a statistically valid sample of the industry to determine a working list of best practices in service.

Unfortunately, simply setting goals is not enough. Cash is king, and long-term revenue must be a major part of the equation.

Driving Long-Term Revenue Success

Many associations have been in business for a long period of time, or at the least will have some core revenue-generating programs and membership products that keep the doors open. The business planning process will grow from these foundations, but should also always seek to amplify existing programs or create completely new revenue streams. A thorough analysis of assets and revenue streams should be conducted, including a review of items such as the following:

- *Diversity:* Before a business plan can be built, the association must understand its revenue diversity. If over-reliance on membership revenue or annual conference revenue exists, then diversification of revenue streams becomes more of a priority.
- *Cash flow:* A cash flow analysis is essential to the process of business planning. If the plan calls for cash outflows in two years for infrastructure investments but cash is not available, the plan's success will stall. Conducting a review of annual cash flow tied to business cycles is key.

- *Strategic fit:* It may seem counterintuitive, but some revenue streams may not be in the long-term strategic interest of the association. The CSE and leadership team should be open to putting any product or program on the table, reviewing them in the context of the current strategic vision, and doing a deep look at both the actual expenses and the "opportunity" costs (what are we *not* doing because we are doing X) associated with such programs.

After a solid review of assets is in place, good discussions can begin about driving long-term revenue growth. Associations run into some big challenges in this arena, most typically tied to the "nonprofit" nature and mentality of many staff and board members engaged in the association. It is important to note that no association can thrive without long-term solvency and fiscal health.

Brainstorming about funding sources should be a creative process with no initial limits on ideas (Table 13.1). As discussions move forward, the goal is to understand core strengths and overall strategy, and develop product- and revenue-generating concepts that synergize between the two. It is much easier to build on existing success than to create it out of thin air.

Planning for Long-Term Expenses

Where business planning provides critical support to the association is in the space of long-term funding needs. Plotting out long-term projects with their accompanying funding needs assists in annual budgeting and in decision making for unbudgeted projects.

Think about the long-term funding needs your association may need to plot out in the business plan. Here are some examples:

- Upgrading your technology infrastructure with a focus on turning it into a strategic asset
- Investing in a platform for your knowledge-management initiative
- Conducting a major mission-related public education campaign
- Purchasing new carpet and furniture for your office
- Renovating or adding a new wing to your office space
- Replacing property that you are currently depreciating
- Replacing the windows in your building for energy efficient impact
- Purchasing a large flat-screen TV for your training center

TABLE 13.1. FUNDING SOURCE PROS AND CONS.

Funding Source or Business Model	Pros	Cons
Sponsorship	Can support new initiatives, provide access to a market to suppliers; low risk of "failure" to start	Line between sponsorship versus advertising must be monitored, staff time invested in sales process
Foundation	Designates funding often for highly specific purposes; tax deductible for donors, potential for estate planning gifts and so on	Initial investment in time and funds to get started, ongoing staff oversight and potentially separate governance needed
Advertising	Commonly understood method of revenue generation; recurring revenue stream per month, quarter, or year based on product	Staff time invested in sales process; will likely need to pay UBIT
Grants and Government Funding	Significant potential for 501(c)3 organization for cause-related projects	Staff time invested in writing and managing; potential of oversight or influence from a third party providing the grant; no guarantee of recurring revenues long term; significant program evaluation or report writing
Events	Often builds on core strengths of associations; potentially good fit for members who already represent an "engaged" audience	High financial risks tied to food and beverage, attrition, and so on; large investment of staff time to plan, implement, review
Certification and Credentialing	Certification programs once established can provide ongoing annual revenue	Major investment in time and money to establish, manage, and govern
Subscription Services	Bundled specialized services create just-in-time education for members; members will pay for the convenience of access to valuable information	Distinguishing content for general membership access versus subscription services may be political
Content as a Revenue Generator	A solid content strategy can create new possibilities for revenue generation; What will you give away for free? What will you charge for?	Distinguishing content on a fee-for-service basis may be political
Other Business Models	See Chapter Five for other viable approaches to revenue generation	

One way to ensure funding for the replacement of items you already own and are depreciating is to actually fund the depreciation. Rather than treating depreciation as a "paper expense," if you actually save that amount in an interest-bearing account, you will accumulate the money over time to pay for the replacement.

Creating a rolling three-year business plan is a great tool to ensure good financial management and sustainable cash flow.

Business Plan Accountability

The CSE is accountable to the board, and the staff are accountable to the CSE. Who is accountable to the business plan? Every staff member.

The ongoing process of business planning should be tied directly to department goals. It is the job of the CSE to connect the dots for staff; the revenue projections in the business plan should speak the language of the staff, not the CFO. The CFO, CIO, and other staff, especially in leadership and management positions, need to be familiar with the entirety of the plan and experts in the areas that they are responsible for producing—they need to have a seat at the table. Furthermore, the entire staff and the CSE should make all efforts to be accountable to the membership for performance tied to the plan.

◆ ◆ ◆

Business Plan Accountability

Once a business plan is set in motion, the money of the membership is invested in the plan. It is very important that the CSE leads the way to ensure accountability of the organizational business plan both for the staff and to the membership at large. This includes the following:

- *Staff performance:* Staff performance evaluations should in some way be tied to overall success at implementing areas of the business plan, either formally or through one-on-one discussions.
- *Day-to-day:* An organized method of enabling staff to monitor and report on performance tied to business plan goals is extremely important. Quick weekly meetings with a focus on outcomes or monthly monitoring by departments are useful for this purpose.
- *Communication:* The association should communicate the most important aspects of the business plan to the membership. The members need to see sound business practices taking shape at the association, and naturally will become more aware of what the association is trying to accomplish, creating more membership buy-in.

- *Transparency:* Leaders hold themselves accountable to an audience. Be transparent with staff, the board, and members about failures or areas of the plan that aren't working, and seek to understand why.
- *Action:* As the plan unfolds, things will change. Review successes and build on them. Act in areas that are working. At all stages of the ongoing process, seek feedback and collaboration from staff and members to ensure decisions aren't made in a vacuum.

Accountability cannot be achieved without clearly defined goals and the tracking of progress. Dashboards, scorecards, contests, and other methods of visually tracking success are paramount. The team must be able to see what they are achieving together, or it will get lost in the daily demands of busy association professionals.

The Authors

Brian Birch, CAE, serves as chief operating officer for the Snow & Ice Management Association, where he oversees marketing, sales, and technology for strategic initiatives.

Susan S. Radwan, SMP, ARM, CAE is the owner of Leading Edge Mentoring, an international consulting firm focused on governance and leadership issues, based in Grand Ledge, Michigan. Radwan holds the Strategic Management Professional designation, which includes business planning as a function of strategic management.

GOVERNANCE: AN INTRODUCTION

Beth Gazley, PhD

Those familiar with boards of directors know that many elements related to a board's structure and its human relationships make governance work. The two chapters that follow this introduction complement one another in their ability to jointly address these characteristics of effective boards: *structure* and *culture*. Chapter Fourteen addresses the fundamental design of boards, including its governing documents, and Chapter Fifteen describes the ways in which association boards and staff members build relationships that make governance work.

Structure describes the nature of the board's organization and membership, its formal control mechanisms, and its rules, per bylaws and policies. Boards may devote a good amount of time to developing an effective structure. But, as governance experts Richard Chait, William Ryan, and Barbara Taylor have pointed out, organizations are led by human beings who also shape the culture within which boards operate.[1] An organization's *culture* includes the traditions it values, the norms of behavior it tolerates, and the incentives it puts in place to drive high performance. Any association professional or board member who has tried to change a board has probably encountered a surprising cultural roadblock or two until he or she realized change strategies were not aligned with the way the organization was accustomed to doing business. It seems counterintuitive, but it does seem to be true that to change norms of behavior, one begins by working within prevailing norms of behavior. Indeed, in my pre-academic career as a consultant, when asked "Where do I start if I want to implement x, y, or z structural changes in my organization," my frequent response was, "Let's start with what your leadership is (culturally) prepared to do and then work from there."

Jim Collins wrote more about culture than anything else in his analysis of high-performing businesses in *Good to Great*.[2] ASAE did the same for membership organizations in *7 Measures of Success*.[3] And so did Leslie Crutchfield and Heather Grant in a 2007 nonprofit best-seller, *Forces for Good*.[4] In the governance context, simple policy questions such as "Which decisions remain with the board and which belong to staff?" have a cultural dimension that must be addressed first. This lesson was brought home in my two most recent collaborations with the ASAE Foundation, a 2013 study and research report on high-performing boards[5] and a follow-up study on governance change currently under way. The first book—covered in greater detail in Chapter Fourteen—benchmarks the practices of high-achieving boards. The second book will be about the journey rather than the destination—the catalyzing events and paths taken that have led dozens of association boards to become high achieving.

We discovered something interesting as we analyzed high-achieving boards during the past three years. They all had strong structures in place—clear policies, good bylaws—but the specific tools or practices they employed were, in the end, no more important to success than were overarching norms of behavior that drove a healthy board culture. So our principal findings were less about the perfect size, committee structure, election process, or meeting schedule and much more about how boards create strong cultures of learning, assessment, and innovation.

These findings help us understand something crucial about good governance in that achieving it may require more profound cultural and structural changes than some participants may anticipate. Indeed, many of our study participants refer to a process of many years to align structure in a way that will support the culture they are aiming for. Those aiming to improve their boards should also understand that changes to structure and culture support one another. Simply put, you can't accomplish one without the other. Here's an example: applying just four elements from BoardSource's "Twelve Elements of High Performing Boards"[6] (the full list is on pages 23–25 of BoardSource's *Handbook of Nonprofit Governance*, a book that should be on every association leader's bookshelf), we begin to understand that active investment in a "strategic thinking" board requires a structure (in the way board meetings are organized) to support such a strategically oriented culture. A "culture of inquiry" and "continuous learning" requires, again, an (structural) investment of time and resources in board development. And building an "ethos of transparency" in an organization may require (structural) bylaws changes to enforce strong expectations of disclosure and accountability.

Given this complex relationship between structure and culture, it is not surprising then to observe the academic research on governance taking an increasingly "systems oriented" view of boards.[7] Recent scholarship addresses boards as complex, multi-actor systems whose success is contingent on many internal and external factors. Internal factors include such practical considerations as the nature of board-staff relations or a board member's preparedness for the responsibilities of governance. External factors include numerous characteristics of the association environment that put pressure on boards and staff, including membership and budgetary health, and the volatility of their markets. Despite the complexity of circumstances, however, the scholarship is clear that no nonprofit organization thrives without a strong board at its head.

As you review the following chapters, taking away lessons and benchmarks for your own associations, this idea of your board as part of a larger organizational "system" may help to reinforce not only how many moving parts there are to good governance but also how crucial good governance is to the overall health of your association.

Notes

1. R. P. Chait, W. P. Ryan, and B. E. Taylor, *Governance as Leadership: Reframing the Work of Nonprofit Boards* (Hoboken, NJ: John Wiley & Sons, 2005).
2. J. Collins, *Good to Great: Why Some Companies Make the Leap . . . and Others Don't* (New York: HarperBusiness, 2001).
3. ASAE and the Center for Association Leadership, *7 Measures of Success: What Remarkable Associations Do That Others Don't* (Washington, DC: ASAE Association Management Press, 2006).
4. L. R. Crutchfield and H. M. Grant, *Forces for Good: The Six Practices of High-Impact Nonprofits* (San Francisco: Jossey-Bass, 2007).
5. B. Gazley and A. Bowers, *What Makes High-Performing Boards: Effective Governance Practices in Member-Serving Organizations* (Washington, DC: ASAE Association Management Press, 2013).
6. BoardSource, *The Handbook of Nonprofit Governance* (San Francisco: Jossey-Bass, 2010).

7. See, for example, C. Cornforth and W. A. Brown (eds.), *Nonprofit Governance: Innovative Perspectives and Approaches* (New York: Routledge, 2014); and J. L. Miller-Millesen, "Understanding the Behavior of Nonprofit Boards of Directors: A Theory-Based Approach," *Nonprofit and Voluntary Sector Quarterly* 32, no. 4 (2003): 521–547.

The Author

Beth Gazley, PhD, is associate professor in the School of Public and Environmental Affairs at Indiana University-Bloomington, where she teaches in the nation's top-ranked nonprofit management program. Her research addresses nonprofit management capacity, volunteerism, and nonprofit-government relations. She is coauthor of ASAE's *The Decision to Volunteer* and *The Decision to Give.*

CHAPTER FOURTEEN

GOVERNANCE STRUCTURES, PROCESS, AND CULTURE

Christine McEntee, FASAE

Governance. It's not the sexiest word you will ever hear, but it's certainly one of the most important. Good governance is one of, if not the most, important factors in the success of any association or not-for-profit. It's what allows organizations to achieve their strategic goals and meet the needs of their members, while at the same time handling the unexpected challenges the organization encounters along the way. A high-performing board is a strategic asset of a member-serving organization. High-performing boards guide member-serving organizations to achieve their strategic vision, reinvent themselves as their external and internal environment changes, and provide ever-increasing value to their members and stakeholders. This requires ongoing development and support, a prime responsibility of the chief staff executive.

What Is Governance?

According to *Merriam-Webster's* dictionary, *governance* is defined as the way that a city, company, or so forth is controlled by the people who run it. However, as noted by the Institute on Governance, "the complexity of governance is difficult to capture in a simple definition." Each organization has unique governance needs, practices, and accountabilities. Regardless of form or structure, governance is composed of

- *Authority:* The body or group of people with ultimate fiduciary and legal responsibilities of the organization
- *Decision making:* The body that sets the strategic direction of the organization and ensures that the organization's resources—people, staff, and time—are appropriately allocated to achieve that direction
- *Accountability:* The body or group of people responsible for ensuring that the organization is fulfilling its fiduciary, legal, and moral obligations as articulated in nonprofit law, the organization's governing documents, and governance policies

Governing Documents

Nonprofit law at the federal, state, and local levels and the association's governing documents serve as the legal and fiduciary bases for the responsibilities and accountabilities of the association's governing body.

There are many classifications for obtaining a nonprofit tax status designation under federal law. In general, though, associations and cause-related organizations obtain one of three classifications:

501(c)(3): Organized to promote charitable, scientific, educational purposes

501(c)(6): Organized to promote business and professional interests

501(c)(4): Organized to promote social welfare of their members or constituency

The articles of incorporation are the primary rules governing the organization and are filed with the applicable and regulatory authorities to obtain a tax designation. The articles contain elements such as the name and address, mission, tax designation, and the board directors. The bylaws are the rules the entity establishes for regulating itself. They are more specific to how the organization governs itself. In general, the bylaws need to be specific enough to clearly outline roles, responsibilities, duties, and procedures but not so specific that they require constant change to effectively govern and manage the organization. The general elements contained in the two documents are listed in Table 14.1.

TABLE 14.1. KEY ELEMENTS OF ARTICLES OF INCORPORATION AND BYLAWS.

	Articles of Incorporation	Bylaws
Name and purpose	x	x
Time duration of organization—time limited or in perpetuity	x	
Geographic location	x	
Principal office, name of registered agent	x	
Membership Organization—yes or no	x	
General board authority and list of initial board directors	x	
Dissolution of assets upon termination of the organization	x	
Tax designation and provisions supporting compliance with designation	x	
Name, address, and registered agent	x	
Board—size, structure, duties, terms, meeting requirements		x
Membership structure and rights		x
Committee structure		x
Duties and authority of board, officers, committees, chief staff executive		x
Board indemnification and insurance		x
Bylaws authority—amendments and changes		x

Board Policies

In addition to the required legal and regulatory documents, boards establish policies to govern their conduct and the conduct of the organization. Such policies include the following:

1. *Conflict of interest policies* (recommended, and required by law in some states) designate what constitutes a conflict of interest and how conflicts are to be identified, designated, addressed, and managed on an ongoing basis.
2. *Whistleblower policies* designate the process and procedures for how a whistleblower can raise a legal or ethical concern, along with how confidentiality will be maintained and what the process is for addressing and resolving any whistleblower allegations. The Sarbanes-Oxley Law of 2002 provisions prohibiting retaliation against those who report federal violations apply to associations.

3. *Document destruction policies* designate what documents are to be maintained, how they are maintained, and what cannot be destroyed if a legal investigation ensues. The Sarbanes-Oxley Law provisions prohibiting destruction of documents in connection with federal investigations apply to associations.

4. *Risk management policies* designate the types of risks that could occur, what insurance levels if any are needed to insure against such risks, and how risk management occurs in the organization. This would include directors' and officers' liability insurance along with other insurance needs, such as general liability and property insurance.

5. *Fiscal policies* designate the procedures for the use of organization assets and any required reserve funds and investment policies.

6. *Chief staff executive review and compensation policy* designates the process and procedure for the annual review of CSE performance, how compensation is to be determined, and any bonus structure.

7. *Ethics policy* designates the ethical code of the organization and its members and the process and procedures for addressing any allegation of an ethical violation, including what sanctions may be applied by whom if an allegation is found to be true.

Board Authority and Responsibilities

A board of directors is a collective, meaning the authority and responsibility resides in the entity: the board. No one individual board member has individual authority and accountability. Three fundamental legal responsibilities of boards are encased in law, and it would be determined in a court of law whether a board has acted improperly.

As written in *The Governing Board Key Responsibilities for Association Boards and Board Members,* the fundamental legal responsibilities of a nonprofit board are as follows:

Duty of Care: to be reasonably informed and to use sound information and judgment in making decisions on behalf of the organization

Duty of Loyalty: to put aside personal interests and act in the best interest of the organization

Duty of Obedience: to act in compliance with the organization's mission, bylaws, and policies, as well as legal and regulatory requirements [1]

Boards are also the ultimate fiduciary of their organizations. As such, they are entrusted to ensure that the financial, human, and capital assets of the organization are managed and used appropriately according to their legal status. For example, 501(c)(3) organizations have limits on the percentage of total budget that can be used for lobbying activities, and are prohibited from using funds for political campaign purposes. In all types of nonprofits, they are also responsible for ensuring that those assets are properly reported to the appropriate authorities, that sound financial controls are in place to prevent fraud and theft, that required tax filings are completed and submitted correctly, and that the organization is ethical in its work and operations.

What Makes a Board Effective?

The most effective and high-performing boards don't stop with the basics described earlier. In 2013, the ASAE Foundation published the results of a research study: *What Makes High-Performing Boards: Effective Governance Practices in Member-Services Organizations.*[2] More than fifteen hundred associations were studied and evaluated according to the measures in Table 14.2. As summarized in the January 2013 *Associations Now Leadership Issue,* boards that ranked in the top 10 percent had the following characteristics:

- A strong strategic orientation
- A culture of self-assessment and accountability
- Healthy attention to board member recruitment and retention

If one takes the basics of board responsibilities and marries them with the characteristics of high-performing boards, the functions of an effective board can be summed up in what Nancy Axelrod, an independent governance expert, would call oversight, insight, and foresight.[3] Oversight is ensuring the organization is well managed and run and in legal compliance and that its resources are used appropriately in advancement of its mission. It is what Axelrod would call "eyes in, nose out," meaning that oversight is provided but boards refrain from actually engaging in operational implementation. Insight is taking the time to fully understand the membership, their environment, the risks and opportunities facing the members and the organization, and the organization's capacity to provide valuable services according to its mission. Foresight is looking ahead, anticipating what will affect the membership in the future, and

TABLE 14.2. PERFORMANCE MEASURES YOUR BOARD SHOULD CONSIDER.

Stewardship	Strategic Performance	Internal Accountability	Chapter Relations	Member Relations
Overall quality of board relations with staff	Effectiveness at strategic rather than operational thinking	Board's ability to set performance standards for itself	Overall quality of board-chapter relations (if applicable)	Overall quality of board relations with the membership
Overall quality of relations among board members	Board participation in advocacy, public policy	Board's record of enforcing self-imposed performance standards		Accountability to the members
Stewardship over the organization's resources	Effectiveness at aligning the organization's resources with strategic needs	Board's securing feedback on its own performance from key constituencies		Direct outreach and engagement of members
Willingness of the board to take responsibility for difficult decisions	Ability to serve as a catalyst for change			
Ability to make decisions based on organizational interests not self-interest	Understanding the organizational external environment			
Collegiality of board atmosphere	Ability to promote achievement of the strategic plan			
Leading the organization in a way that maintains the public trust in nonprofits				

Source: Associations Now Volunteer Leadership Issue (January-February 2014): 57.

strategically positioning the organization to prepare for and adjust itself to meet future opportunities and challenges. The sidebar gives a brief case example of a board exercising foresight.

◆ ◆ ◆

Exercising Foresight: A Case Example

The main source of revenue for a large global membership organization was publishing revenue, comprising more than two-thirds of its annual gross revenues. From its inception, the organization had self-published, meaning it provided editorial and peer review support for its editors as well as handled all aspects of production, sales, marketing, and fulfillment. An early adopter of converting print-based publications to digital publications, the organization had developed and maintained a proprietary technology platform for hosting its digital publishing content that was becoming obsolete. The board engaged a consultant to undertake a strategic review of its publishing operation that included scanning the external environment for publishing and a SWOT analysis of its editorial quality and operational effectiveness. The review found that the advent of open-access publishing would continue to challenge the publishing revenue model. In addition, the review found that the investments needed to maintain technological competencies and operational effectiveness would require significant and ongoing investments that would be difficult to maintain in a membership organization over time in order to remain competitive in the publishing space. As a result, the board explored the potential of securing a publishing partner that could provide the production, sales, marketing, and technology infrastructure that would be needed over time for the organization to remain relevant and competitive in an uncertain and evolving publishing marketplace. Using strategic foresight, the board decided to enter a publishing partnership that resulted in significant technology improvements, revenue stability and growth in a changing marketplace, new product launches within the first two years, and improved publications development time that are now industry leading.

◆ ◆ ◆

An effective board is situational; that means the group effectively balances its work in oversight, insight, and foresight as needed depending on the current state or needs of the organization. For example, early in the life of a nonprofit, when staff resources are limited or when an organization is in an operational crisis (sudden departure of the chief staff executive, legal action, or so on), the board may spend more time as a working board ensuring effective day-to-day management, oversight, and stewardship of the organization. When the organization is successfully operating and well managed by staff, then the board can shift its emphasis to insight and foresight while still engaging in appropriate oversight.

Governance Structure

How Big Is Too Big?

The governance structure in any organization is specified in its bylaws. It consists of the decision-making units; how they are constituted; and their defined roles, responsibilities, reporting relationships, and accountabilities. While the board of directors in a membership organization has the ultimate governing decision-making authority, many boards use formal and informal committee structures to assist them with their governing work.[4] The adage of "if you have seen one board, you have seen one board" applies to the composition of boards of directors in membership organizations.

Boards come in a variety of sizes. There has been little scholarly research about how board size relates to board effectiveness. The ASAE study *What Makes High-Performing Boards* found that boards with membership ranging from twelve to twenty were more likely to have effective board practices in place compared to smaller or larger boards.[5] BoardSource and other governance experts also argue that there's a sweet spot related to board size. But the ASAE study also found that larger boards were rated higher by association chief staff executives on some performance measures. The results seem to suggest that larger boards, if properly designed, can offer the capacity to accomplish more. In the end, each organization must balance its unique needs, its requirements in terms of sufficient diversity to generate multiple perspectives and varied points of views, its place in its lifecycle (newer versus well-established organizations), the numbers needed to accomplish the work so that no one board member is overly burdened in terms of time requirements, and its requirements to be agile and nimble while being deliberative and thoughtful.

The Players

How boards are constituted also varies along a continuum of primarily representative from various member constituencies to ones that are purely competency based to everything in between. However, according to Tecker and colleagues,[6] "the subject of constituency vs. competency-based boards … is, in reality a false issue." Boards need to be both "credible," meaning that they have the required skills; expertise; competencies; and effective, rational, and transparent processes, and "legitimate," meaning that they are viewed by constituencies and stakeholders as having the voices and interests that represent the diversity of their views and perspectives.

Officers of the board are elected to lead the work of the board. In general, the officer roles are

- The president or chair of the board, with responsibility to preside at board meetings and ensure that the board is governing appropriately
- The vice chair or president-elect, who assists the chair and can preside at board meetings in the absence of the chair; in addition, this position usually succeeds the chair or president when his or her term ends
- The secretary, who is responsible for ensuring required documentation of board meetings
- The treasurer, who is responsible for ensuring that the board appropriately carries out its fiscal duties, oversight and obligations.

Sometimes these officer roles are combined. For example, an organization may choose to combine the secretary and treasurer roles into one position. In addition, some organizations have additional officer roles (that is, vice presidents) that are assigned specific program, functional, or geographic areas of oversight.

The chief staff executive or executive director is also often a board officer and can be either nonvoting or voting. The ASAE 2013 study found that 57 percent of chief staff executives are nonvoting ex officio board members.[7] BoardSource recommends the ex officio, nonvoting role as good governance to avoid any potential conflict of interest between governing (exercising independent judgment about strategy and finances) and executing operations.[8] For example, the board may want to explore moving the headquarters of the organization to a different geographic location that would be undesirable to the chief staff executive who would be unwilling to relocate there.

Many but not all member-serving organization boards have an executive committee. When they do, the board officers typically constitute the board executive committee. In addition, some organizations add committee chairs to the executive committee. The role of the executive committee vis-à-vis the board is determined by the board and codified in the bylaws, and it varies by organization. In some organizations, the executive committee meets only if a critical and urgent action is needed in a time frame in which the board cannot be convened. The executive committee may also serve as the body that oversees the annual chief staff executive performance review. If a board is very large, the executive committee may meet regularly to prepare information and strategic discussions for full board deliberation. However, in this regard, care needs to be taken that the executive committee not become "a petite board" surpassing the authority and responsibilities that are entrusted to the entire board.

◆ ◆ ◆

Developing Board Agendas and Meetings That Work

Creating and designing board meetings and agendas that enable a high-performing board do not occur by accident. Meeting materials and agenda development requires careful thought, planning, and development so that the board can contribute to advancement of the organization's mission and strategy and focus their limited but valuable time on those issues that matter the most. Some general tips include the following:

1. Dividing the agenda topics into three categories: strategic conversations (What is the future of our membership? What critical issues are facing us as an organization and how should we assess their associated risks and opportunities? What capacity exists to pursue our organization, or do we need to build or partner to create the needed capacity? What are our success factors, and how should we assess our success? and so on) for which no action is required; operational oversight for which action may or may not be required (financial and investment reports, annual audit, and so on); and board development (governance education, board assessment, guest speakers, and so on)
2. Allocating a majority of board time to strategic conversations
3. Using consent agendas for routine matters such as committee information reports, program updates, and approval of minutes
4. Conducting a regular board assessment and using the results to continue to improve board performance
5. Applying decision rules when needed, such as *Robert's Rules of Order* for developing and considering motions
6. Preparing background materials for agenda items that focus the conversation at the governance level, summarizing key take-aways and important data and information that are pertinent to the conversation and posing questions that focus on what we need to know, what we want to accomplish, and what success would look like rather than tactical implementation
7. Providing time for open mic conversations during which board members have time to bring up topics not on the agenda
8. Confining executive sessions to those items that are truly sensitive, confidential, or both

In addition to the executive committee, the board may also appoint standing committees and ad hoc task forces to assist with the organization's work. According to governance consultant and author Douglas

Eadie, success depends upon organizing their responsibilities for aiding in governance and the work of the board, rather than program or administrative oversight.[9] Standing committees are those that remain in place year after year. They focus on longer-term and ongoing governing needs such as budgets, finances, investments, and audits; nominations or governance; planning and program development; and membership and external relations. Ad hoc task forces tend to be formed for time-limited tasks such as developing the (strategic) objectives of a new education program or specific membership service. Committees and task forces are accountable to the board. An effective board will carefully construct objectives for a committee or task force that advances and contributes to the work of the board, not supervise the staff. For example, the board may recognize a member need to develop a certification program. The board will convene a committee or task force to analyze the need and develop a set of strategic objectives, product concepts, and risk and success factors for board consideration. The board will then consider the committee work and decide whether to proceed with development of a business plan. If the answer is yes, the staff would then be charged to develop a business plan for board approval.

Two additional governing bodies that may exist include a house of delegates and special-interest groups. A house of delegates operates similar to a publicly elected legislative body whereby delegates are elected by a specific membership or geographic constituency with powers designated in the bylaws. The powers can range from purely advisory to electing the board. Special-interest groups are groups of members who form a community to focus programs and communications specific to their specialized area of interest within an industry or profession.

Governance Management

Recruitment, Selection, and Term Limits

Serving on the organization's board of directors either as a board member or as an officer is one of the most cherished volunteer roles in an association. It also requires the skill set and expertise to be able to successfully work as part of a collective rather than as an individual, since organizational authority resides within the board as a unit, not in any one board member.

Increasingly, membership organizations are using governance committees to fulfill two interrelated functions: identify, recruit, and select nominees for board and officer positions, and conduct ongoing leadership and board development.[10] The ASAE Foundation study found that 70 percent of organizations in its study had a committee with nominating responsibilities.[11] Once nominees are identified, a slate of candidates can be prepared in a variety of means. Options include a slate with one nominee for each open position, a slate with two choices for each open position, and a slate of nominees from which directors are selected with those receiving the most votes being elected. The election can be done by the board itself, by the general membership, or through a "House of Delegates" or representative body of the membership. In addition to elections, some boards have designated positions for representatives of a special interest group or membership constituency, certain committee chairs, and at-large seats to access expertise outside of the organization's membership.

Orientation, Development, and Self-Assessment

High-performing boards invest in themselves through instituting a culture of learning, participating in orientation and ongoing board development, and conducting periodic board assessments of their performance (see Figure 14.1). As stated in the ASAE 2013 Foundation study "A high-functioning board may not have all of the answers, but it is willing to invest in learning them—and to asking good questions about its role along the way."[12]

A formal board orientation provides information about the organization overall—its mission, vision, strategic plan, key issues, strategic initiatives, and programs, and operational and financial overview—along with the basics of governance duties, responsibilities, and policies.

Orientation to the role is just the beginning. A culture of continuous learning to deepen the board's understanding of the organization, its members, its external environment, and key stakeholders is also important. Continuous learning can be fostered by incorporating some aspect of board development in every meeting, whether it is something specific to a governance role or bringing in an outside expert on a strategic issue that the board or organization is facing. Books and articles both about the industry or profession represented by the organization and environmental factors such as the changing nature of social media and best practices in governance can also contribute to continuous learning.

A periodic board assessment, whereby the board completes a survey and answers open-ended questions about its own performance, and then

FIGURE 14.1. AMERICAN GEOPHYSICAL UNION'S MODEL OF ORIENTATION, DEVELOPMENT, AND SELF-ASSESSMENT.

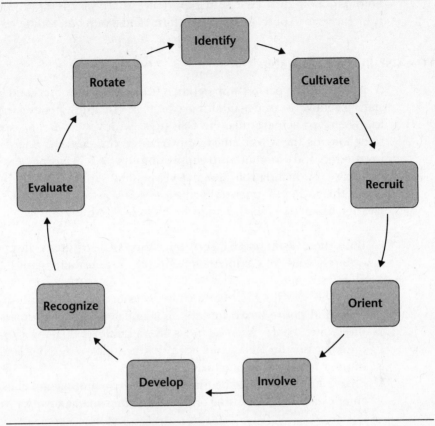

Source: Developed by Cheryl Enderlein, AGU staff.

uses the results to improve the board's performance, rounds out the three elements of board development.

Term Limits

The time period in which board members can serve before a reelection and the total number of years any one person can remain in a board position, otherwise known as term limits, are defined in an organization's bylaws and are considered best practice. While some continuity across board terms provides stability to strategy, term limits allow for fresh thinking and new ideas; additional diverse viewpoints can be brought to the board. They also help to avoid volunteer burnout. In the ASAE Foundation study, 61 percent reported a three-year term, 25 percent a two-year term, 5 percent a one-year term, and 9 percent, four to six years.[13]

The CSE-Board Partnership

A strong trusting partnership between the board of directors and the chief staff executive is an essential ingredient in creating effective board performance. To achieve this, the CSE must be invested in and committed to enhancing the work and capacity of the board, and the board must be invested in and committed to supporting the CSE in his or her role and ongoing growth and professional development. While Chapter Fifteen discusses this in depth, a few critical success factors for forging an effective partnership between board and CSE include the following:

1. Both the board and CSE see each other as peers and colleagues with different and yet complementary roles, responsibilities, and accountabilities.
2. The CSE sees the board as a strategic asset and works with the board chair and entire board to develop agendas, board performance measures, and board work agendas that enable the board to focus its thinking on the issues and tasks that are most consequential to the future success of the organization
3. Boards hold the CSE accountable through an annual and constructive chief executive goal-setting and performance-management process.

Conclusion

Effective and high-performing governance doesn't just happen. It ensures that the basics are well attended to and then moves beyond the basics through systems and processes in order for the board to "add significant value to their organizations, making discernable differences in their advance on mission."[14] The association's CSE is a critical player in ensuring that the board and governance structure has the capability and means to be truly effective in exercising its governance responsibilities. He or she is responsible for ensuring that the organization has policies, systems, and processes that enable the board to focus on the strategic issues that matter most to the organization's current and future viability and that provide the information regarding finances, programs, and operations that allow the board to exercise appropriate oversight.

Notes

1. N. Axelrod, *The Governing Board: Key Responsibilities for Association Boards and Board Members* (Washington, DC: ASAE Association Management Press, 2013), 14–15.
2. B. Gazley and A. Bowers, *What Makes High-Performing Boards: Effective Governance Practices in Member-Serving Organizations* (Washington, DC: ASAE Association Management Press, 2013), 29.
3. N. Axelrod, *The Governing Board,* 32–33.
4. G. H. Tecker, J. Frankel, P. D. Meyer, and the American Society of Association Executives, *The Will to Govern Well: Knowledge, Trust, & Nimbleness* (Washington, DC: American Society of Association Executives, 2002), 15.
5. Gazley and Bowers, *What Makes High-Performing Boards,* 29.
6. Tecker, Frankel, Meyer, and the American Society of Association Executives, *The Will to Govern Well,* 22.
7. Gazley and Bowers, *What Makes High-Performing Boards,* 41.
8. BoardSource, *The Nonprofit Board Answer Book: A Practical Guide for Board Members and Chief Executives,* 3rd ed. (San Francisco: Jossey-Bass, 2011), 65.
9. D. C. Eadie and L. Daily, *Boards That Work: A Practical Guide to Building Effective Association Boards* (Washington, DC: ASAE Association Management Press, 1994).
10. Tecker, Frankel, Meyer, and the American Society of Association Executives, *The Will to Govern Well,* 27.
11. Gazley and Bowers, *What Makes High-Performing Boards,* 35.
12. Gazley and Bowers, *What Makes High-Performing Boards,* 102.
13. Gazley and Bowers, *What Makes High-Performing Boards,* 43.
14. BoardSource, Preamble. *The Source 12, Twelve Principles of Governance that Power Exceptional Boards* (Washington, DC: Author, 2005).

Resource

Associations Now Volunteer Leadership. Washington, DC: ASAE Association Management Press, January-February 2014.

The Author

Christine McEntee, FASAE, is executive director and chief executive officer of the American Geophysical Union, a worldwide scientific community of sixty-two thousand members that advances the understanding of Earth and space for the benefit of humanity. Ms. McEntee has made her mark as an association leader and innovator, building a record of achievement in leading large organizations through changes in strategy, governance, membership, programs, and the fluid public policies that confront them.

CHAPTER FIFTEEN

GOVERNANCE RELATIONSHIPS

The CSE and the Board

Richard Yep, CAE, FASAE

Overseeing the organization's budget, project management, finding the right mix of staff, and ensuring that the trains run on time may once have been the main purview of the successful association CSE. However, with the evolution of a much more sophisticated and engaged volunteer leadership, coupled with a competition to attract and retain organizational and individual members, today's CSEs must focus on the relationships they maintain with those in their volunteer leadership in order to ensure organizational success.

The traditional organizational chart delineates the CSE as subordinate to the governing body of the organization. In actuality, the board is dependent on the CSE for guidance, information, wisdom, and assistance in the decision making with which they are entrusted. Most board members understand the value that their CSE brings to the organizational equation. They respect the knowledge and guidance that is offered. In the modern world of association management, the board-CSE relationship is a partnership. Each member of the team is confident in knowledge and expertise, but also cognizant of what he or she needs from the other in order to accomplish strategic organizational success.

To build strategic capacity, ensure organizational and programmatic success, and carry out the association's mission, the CSE must establish positive, open, and mutually respectful relationships with those who serve in governance. Understanding and being able to overcome the challenges of the board-CSE relationship is key to a successful partnership. If either the board or the CSE is unable to establish or maintain respect for the other, a schism forms from which no amount of organizational development will heal.

This chapter explores the unique relationship of the CSE and the board. For some CSEs, this might include a small board of directors and an even smaller executive committee while others have both a board and a "house of delegates" numbering in the hundreds. The concepts of this chapter are applicable to either.

Providing Advice and Guidance

Building relationships is a key responsibility for the association CSE. This is a skill, an art, and may require a great deal of patience. However, learning what makes someone "tick" and finding ways to communicate with the volunteer leader will, in the long run, make for a more enjoyable and rewarding experience for both parties.

Many who serve on boards, including the chief elected officer (CEO), have great stature in their profession or industry. Lending their time and expertise to serve as a volunteer leader is admirable. However, their knowledge and understanding of the intricacies of managing an organization of volunteers may be starkly different from how they operate in their "day job." The CSE understands this and finds ways to draw parallels in order to illustrate both the similarities and the differences for the volunteer leader.

The CSE ensures that the board understands its role, responsibilities, and reason for being. This occurs through training, resources, and board discussion. The CSE does not "lecture" the board members about how they should operate and conduct their business; rather it is the executive's role to find experiences and education in which the board gains this knowledge, learning about exemplary practice as policymakers and how to evaluate their strengths and overcome deficiencies.

Tact and diplomacy are skills that the CSE must practice. Letting the volunteer chair know that he or she ran a terrible board meeting must be handled in a manner that allows that person to acknowledge what they were challenged by in hope that they will commit to improving. For example, rather than saying, "Wow, I have never witnessed such a bad board meeting. I think that was a train wreck," ask the chair a question about his or her impressions. This could include something like, "Well, it is clear we didn't get through our agenda in the way you had hoped. What thoughts do you have on how we all could have made this more productive?"

If the chief elected officer or members of the board persistently do not see how they contribute to unproductive meetings, the CSE may wish to ask a governance expert from outside of the association to assist. The outside expert can often say things that might be difficult for the CSE or staff to say to a board that is in need of governance capacity-building.

A CSE's success is best measured when his or her board emerges as a high-performing entity that excels at its role as a policymaker that thinks, talks about, and acts on strategic areas of focus. In essence, governance is about making the most critical and important decisions that will determine the direction of the association, or as governance pioneer John Carver has defined it, governance is seeing to it that the organization achieves what it should and avoids unacceptable situations.[1]

◆ ◆ ◆

Collaborative Leadership in Governance

Gabriel Eckert, CAE

Collaborative leadership is central to effective nonprofit governance. It extends beyond the relationship between the chief elected officer and chief staff officer. It is about creating a culture of collaboration between members and staff at all levels of the organization. With it, organizations increase their likelihood of creating a sustained level of success, increase the speed at which they are able to adapt to change, and build a stronger sense of community. Without collaborative leadership, organizations often drift, unable to clearly articulate a consistent value proposition for member engagement.

The Building Owners and Managers Association of Georgia (BOMA Georgia) has built an effective culture of collaborative leadership. This trade association, serving the management and operations segment of real estate, has defined four strategies that have proven to be essential in creating a sustained culture of collaborative leadership.

Clearly Define Roles and Responsibilities

It is easy for there to be misunderstandings about the roles of members and staff, particularly in associations. This misalignment of views generally occurs as a result of differing expectations of who is responsible for carrying out different aspects of the work of the organization. To build collaborative leadership, it is critical to understand and define the unique skills, knowledge, and relationships both members and staff bring to the organization.

BOMA Georgia accomplished this by evaluating the competencies of members and staff and then creating a set of written objectives for each of its committees and task forces. The objectives outline the role members play in their volunteer efforts and leverage their unique skills, knowledge, and relationships. Areas of committee or task force work that fall outside of the written objectives are delegated to staff. For additional clarity, the association also often provides a written description of staff responsibilities that align with committee or task force work.

This approach has greatly reduced the amount of misunderstandings between members and staff and has also aligned the efforts of both groups with their competencies. Since the charges are updated annually, it also provides a unique opportunity for the association's governing body and senior staff to collaborate—and achieve consensus—on the role of members and staff on a regular basis.

Be Transparent

In addition to a sixteen-person board of directors, BOMA Georgia also has a five-person executive committee, which operates alongside the full board. Before committing to a conscious effort of collaborative leadership, the executive committee was viewed with suspicion by most board members. They were perceived as a mysterious group of leaders who were above the board and who made most of the important decisions on behalf of the organization. With the implementation of collaborative leadership, the committee was repositioned and made more transparent. Minutes of their meetings are shared with the full board of directors, and the executive committee no longer makes most decisions on behalf of the board. The committee has become the servant of the board. It now acts as a sort of think tank, helping to ensure strategic alignment of board meetings and providing background information related to board agenda items. This gives the entire group a base of consistent working knowledge when engaging in strategic conversations and making decisions.

Agree on How to Measure Success

BOMA Georgia's board of directors creates a shared understanding of how to measure success—in writing—in advance of each year. The association keeps its benchmark of success simple: implementing two new strategic priorities each year. The leaders know they can't accomplish everything in the association's strategic plan in the plan in a single year, so they choose two new strategic initiatives each year on which to focus. This approach matches the capacity of the organization's members and staff and creates heightened focus for each year. Furthermore, the association's leadership doesn't get too hung up on operational metrics as a measure of success in a single year. The philosophy of BOMA Georgia's leadership is that if the organization successfully implements the right strategy, over time all metrics—membership, event attendance, education enrollment, and other measures—will trend upward.

Celebrate Success

Celebrating success is one of the most important—and overlooked—elements of creating a culture of collaborative leadership. Members give a tremendous amount of time volunteering for associations, and staff often go above and beyond expectations. As a result, it is critical for leaders to look for opportunities to celebrate the success of member volunteers, staff, and the organization as a whole. BOMA Georgia also sees celebrating success as another opportunity for collaborative leadership, with elected leaders and senior staff working together to recognize efforts and accomplishments. This is particularly true when celebrating success with the board of directors, as it reinforces the link between board governance and the results achieved by the association.

Results

BOMA Georgia saw tremendous results after implementing these strategies. The association became more collaborative in decision making at all levels, member engagement increased, and quantitative results can be easily measured. Over a five-year period, despite the real estate industry suffering from a deep recession, membership increased 16 percent, event attendance grew 29 percent, education enrollment increased 290 percent, and the association's financial reserves expanded by 251 percent.

◆ ◆ ◆

Roles and Responsibilities

The CSE ensures that all stakeholders, including volunteer leaders, understand how they contribute to the association's strategic capacity. The board and the staff maintain a certain amount of authority over specific areas of the organization. Because clarity of roles and responsibilities is critical to determine an appropriate balance of power in the organization, the CSE ensures that both the board and the staff understand the delineation of roles.

The CSE manages and coordinates the association's resources to implement the policies adopted by the board. It is critical that the CSE keep the board updated as to the legal, regulatory, and operational issues so that the body is in compliance with all local, state, and federal laws and regulations having an impact on not-for-profit organizations. In addition to providing guidance and sharing information about the operational "nuts and bolts," the effective CSE is valued for his or her knowledge and insight.

Beyond this, the CSE also has the responsibility to support the board in being as effective and efficient as possible in carrying out its own responsibilities. This task is accomplished by building a rapport with the board that allows it to understand that exemplary governance includes an ongoing review and assessment of policies, practices, procedures, and the group process of the board itself.

More important, the CSE must have the ability to understand what motivates the individuals that compose the association's board. The CSE knows board members by their names, what they do for a living, and the length of their board terms. However, the exceptional CSE will establish a professional relationship with each that provides insight as to why the person chose to serve, what they see as their role on the board, what they want to accomplish during their service, and what their plans are once they leave the board. Why? Because having this knowledge allows a CSE to have more open, honest, and transparent conversations with those volunteer leaders. This can be especially helpful when tough issues face the board, or decisions that are uncomfortable need to be made. It also demonstrates that the CSE cares about the success of the association's volunteers. This demonstration of concern contributes to trust-building.

To begin building this relationship, the CSE must "do some homework" as new board members are elected or appointed. Communicating with board members upon their election or appointment prior to their first meeting is a good initial step. New members on the volunteer leadership team often have questions but do not know who to contact. The CSE can be proactive by sending a message of congratulations, can meet in their office, and can call them between board meetings to simply check in and get their "read" on issues facing the association. This one-on-one orientation is about establishing a professional relationship.

According to nonprofit governance expert Nancy Axelrod, the four main roles of the board are

- Setting direction
- Ensuring and protecting resources
- Providing oversight
- Engaging in outreach[2]

In addition, BoardSource's *The Source: 12 Principles of Governance That Power Exceptional Boards*[3] state that eight characteristics of exceptional boards are

- Good stewardship
- Constructive relationships

- Intentional governance policies and practices
- Being data-driven and results-oriented
- Organizational adaptability
- Board development and renewal
- Having a culture of respect and inquiry
- Strategic thinking

With these items in mind, the CSE must find ways to convey the importance of these concepts and how to operationalize them, and assist the board in creating a culture around these roles and characteristics. With agreement on, training in, and practice implementing these items, the CSE enjoys a cooperative board that seeks to be high performing. Characteristics of such performance can be seen in a board's understanding of strategic oversight and how it conducts its business toward that endeavor.

Relationship building with current and potential volunteer leaders is based on some basic tenets. The CSE understands that these volunteers are committed to their profession or industry, and that those who volunteer want to know that their contributions of time and expertise are valued. The savvy CSE recognizes the value contributed by volunteers and shows appreciation for their efforts.

Keeping these points in mind when working with current and future leaders of an association will provide the CSE with the basic building blocks of creating a relationship with these individuals. Building and maintaining mutual trust and respect between the volunteer leadership and the CSE makes a major impact on achieving the association's strategic goals.

Nurturing Future Leaders

Being in tune with the needs, wants, and rewards of current volunteer leaders is important. However, the savvy CSE also scans the organization and other societal factors that may have an impact on the association on both the short- and long-term horizons. The purpose of this scanning function is to understand and plan for capacity-building for future leadership.

The CSE understands that the volunteer leadership of an organization does not contain a finite group of people who are "appointed for life." Rather, due to term limits and other commitments in a volunteer leader's life, the CSE realizes that it is increasingly important to be on the lookout for emerging leaders who may be able to serve in the future. Filling "the pipeline" with dedicated and hardworking members who may aspire to a board position is critical to the organization in meeting its strategic goals and objectives. CSEs realize that in today's association world, it is no longer "business as usual." Today's members and potential leaders have different expectations than those who came into the leadership ranks previously. The CSE brings these thoughts to the board so that volunteer leadership can discuss how the organization may need to change or adjust if it is to survive.

The effective CSE also engages current leadership in reaching out to possible successors. As the talent pool of leaders is identified, a plan is developed wherein both the board and the staff have responsibilities to engage, nurture, and prepare those future leaders, such as leadership development programs and special "leadership" tracks at conferences or other meetings.

In the traditional association model, it was unusual to structure volunteer activities on the basis of the time someone was willing to devote to the association. Rather, the volunteer was simply "expected" to take on a role and complete it regardless of how much time it might take to accomplish. Today's association must be more cognizant of how best to build the relationship between the organization and the volunteer, and it may be through virtual efforts, micro-volunteering, or short-term task forces. For a healthy future, the CSE must facilitate various types of leadership assignments that are based on varying levels of time commitments and other factors. Ideally, members will be presented with a choice as to the level of their involvement.

One challenge that the CSE may encounter is current board members and volunteer leaders who are unable to see the value in a diverse pool of candidates for leadership. While this is somewhat attributable to human nature since people are more comfortable with those who reflect their opinions and style, the CSE must communicate to the board the need to include new voices. The CSE does this by sharing information, statistics, member demographics, and societal indicators that support the position with the board.

Intentionally scanning for and making connections between the CSE and potential volunteer leaders is prudent and forward-thinking.

Providing Role Clarity to the Board

It is the responsibility of the CSE to ensure that the board is complying with its policies as well as with legal, tax, and corporate regulations.

This requires that the CSE and staff regularly conduct a review of governance documents to ensure that they support the organization's strategic direction and that the organization is in compliance.

The CSE has the responsibility of managing and coordinating the resources to pursue the association's mission and vision and fully implement the board's policy. It is important for the CSE to clearly understand the wishes of the board so that subsequent direction to staff and others will be in line with fulfilling the board's vision.

There will be times when the CSE realizes that improvements and adjustments need to be made to increase the efficiency of the board. This is when careful thought on the part of the CSE must be exercised in how best to present findings and possible solutions to the board. For example, the CSE may need to recommend changes to the board that will result in supporting and maintaining an effective, representative governance system to guide the organization toward accomplishing its mission. This type of presentation should be done with supporting evidence as to why a change is necessary, along with the possible repercussions if the changes are not implemented. It is most diplomatic to get buy-in for these ideas first from your volunteer officers before presenting to the board. It is even more effective to identify and engage a respected volunteer champion who might present the ideas to the board peer to peer or at least promote or support the ideas among peers on the board.

The CSE is at the nexus between the board and the staff. Today's associations comprise professional staff who identify with the association management profession. With the combination of an elected or appointed board of industry professionals along with professional staff with specialized skills and expertise, tensions may arise around the priority of various projects. The CSE communicates and manages the unique roles and responsibilities of each group to ensure an appropriate balance of power, empowerment, and the alignment of duties with the organization's mission and strategic goals.

The CSE helps the volunteer leadership fine-tune its vision and identify common goals. This occurs through utilizing consensus-building skills. The CSE works to establish a relationship with the board that helps the group with collective decision making. In this role, the CSE supports the board to look at and process multiple viewpoints. The skillful CSE provides advice, counsel, training, and guidance in a manner that facilitates the board to effectively and strategically discuss, deliberate, and decide on issues facing the association. To accomplish this, an understanding of human and group dynamics is necessary.

Facilitating Continuous Process Improvement

Effective boards are ones that engage in ongoing training and implement a regular process of self-assessment for the effectiveness of both individual members and the group as a whole. The CSE provides advice about issues facing the association but has a responsibility to facilitate improvement in the group process skill set of those who sit on the board. It can be challenging for the CSE to assist the board in how the group evaluates overall board performance.

In establishing a positive working relationship with the board, the CSE is positioned to assist the group in developing its own expectations for board service, the value of self-evaluation, and how best to implement such a process. That process could include a focus on key responsibilities and relationships and boundaries that board members maintain with each other, with staff, and with those whom they represent.

To maximize the board's ability to move forward on its strategic priorities, the CSE is called upon to help leadership assess what is working and what adjustments need to be made. The assessment of board competence goes beyond the understanding of fiduciary responsibility. While that is a core component of the skill set of a good board, the move to becoming an exceptional board is in the culture that is created and practiced. As a group, the board might evaluate the degree to which a majority of its meetings focus on discussion and decision making relative to strategy and policy. Other questions for reflection and exploration might include

- Are board members encouraged to speak their minds?
- Is the board welcoming of diverse opinion and discussion?
- Does the chief elected officer facilitate meetings in a way that creates an environment in which individuals come together to work for "the good of the whole association"?
- Is the CSE encouraged to share both the positives and negatives of projects, issues, or other situations affecting the association?
- Do volunteer leaders understand how their decisions relate to other units of the organization (committees, task forces, and so on), as well as with other organizations?
- When it comes to discussion at the board level, do the directors allow time on the agenda to hear a broad range of thoughts, while not allowing any individual to take up most of the time?
- Following up on this, is the board able to make informed decisions on matters that are supported by data? If so, does the board seek or demand the most relevant data in order to ensure sound decision making?

Board evaluation or capacity-building can be a touchy subject for those who are acknowledged experts and leaders in their profession or industry—a status most often achieved by singular efforts. Yet we must recognize that effective board work requires the ability to think together in a collaborative group process. This gap between thinking alone and thinking together is an opportune space for discussion.

Board assessment is not a static activity. In other words, simply conducting and implementing an assessment will not reap rewards unless it occurs with regularity and the lessons learned are integrated into the practice of board governance. The fact that many boards welcome new members every year, while the more "seasoned" ones rotate off, means that recruiting, orienting, training, and assessing are multifaceted and ongoing.

Putting the CSE-Board Relationship in Perspective

Board meetings do not begin when the chair gavels the leadership to order. Rather, there is much planning, discussion, coordination, and strategizing that leads to the moment when the chair calls the meeting to order. In essence, the start of a governance meeting is the summation of weeks, if not months of work. The CSE knows that the efforts of committees, task forces, professional staff, and direct conversation with the CEO are the linchpins to ensuring a successful gathering of the governing body. In other words, governance is not just the board meeting. Rather, it is how the volunteer leadership and staff work together prior to and after the board meeting in order to advance the association in a strategic manner. The CSE is called upon to use many skills to ensure that projects move along and issues are addressed in a timely manner regardless of whether the board is meeting or not.

The exemplary CSE ensures that the CEO and board are not caught off guard by issues or potential controversies. Keeping the CEO informed is especially important as project plans are launched and milestones established. Many CSEs seek out ways to regularly and predictably communicate in the most effective means possible with their board. Some provide monthly written or telephonic management updates to the board while others might find that posting to a leadership listserve works best. Some CSEs choose to use a variety of communication channels in order to reach the board. It is important for a CSE to ascertain what his or her board members identify as preferred methods of communication.

Chief elected officers sometimes need to develop skills to "run" a meeting and follow an agenda. The truly good CEOs have the ability to facilitate gatherings of the board in which there is a general feeling of inclusiveness, respect for divergent opinions, transparency, and accomplishment in carrying out the association's mission. The CSE has an important role to play in helping the CEO meet these goals.

Early in the relationship, a savvy CSE finds ways to better understand the personality, knowledge, and interests of the CEO. While the CSE has likely been with the association for more years than those serving in volunteer leadership positions, it is critical that one use the wisdom of experience to figure out how best to connect with the current leadership. There may be times when the CSE has to be very creative in ensuring that the CEO and other volunteer leaders understand what needs to be accomplished in order to be successful.

Attending programs, such as those conducted by the ASAE, that are designed to have the chief elected officer and CSE understand how to create, and agree upon, a common vision of success is one example of building one of the most important partnerships in the association. The result of a fruitful professional relationship is evidenced by board meetings and the general practice of governing, both of which lead to meeting short- and long-term strategic objectives.

The CSE works at the pleasure of the board with focus on the good of the association's membership. Regardless of how many years one has devoted to the organization and no matter how personally close the CSE may become with the CEO or members of leadership, the CSE must never forget that he or she is the board's employee. The unique aspect of the CSE's role is that he or she often brings to the table more association experience, financial acumen, human resource skills, and history of the organization than those who are elected to serve as CEO and board members. The CSE is key to the organization's success, but that does not always equate to receiving accolades or "the spotlight" for such actions.

The CSE should not assume ownership of the association (that is, consider it "my association"), but rather should demonstrate servant-leadership to the board. The CSE must acknowledge that the board may not always accept advice offered. This can be challenging to some CSEs, but at the end of the day, it is the governing body that has the authority to make final decisions on issues that come before the leadership.

A CSE needs to know where "the line" is in terms of how to let the board know you disagree when a board is about to make a contrary decision. Regardless of how decisions are arrived at, the CSE works with leaders to ensure that their structure of governance can be responsive, is nimble, and has the best possible data in order to vote on issues that come before them. A CSE needs to keep an open mind and realize that, regardless of the board's vote, once you have done your best to communicate the pros and cons of an issue, the job then moves to implementation of the will of the board.

Savvy CSEs will always see to it that the CEO and the board look good—even when their actions may not necessarily deserve recognition. The work in the background to achieve this perception is important for the CSE to orchestrate.

◆ ◆ ◆

How the CSE Creates a Beneficial Working Environment with the CEO

The relationship between a CSE and CEO can be a very special partnership. Both individuals have a great responsibility to the organization and its members. To make the most of their year together (or for however long the term lasts), it is incumbent on both the CSE and CEO to understand some things about each other.

The CSE must be able to create an atmosphere of trust and be committed to the CEO and the board's success. There are various ways to build this relationship that include learning together at any number of workshops or conferences that focus on an effective relationship between the CSE and CEO. The CSE may also wish to book some one-on-one time, perhaps even visiting the new CEO at his or her place of employment or in his or her home.

When both the CSE and CEO share mutual understanding of their respective roles, responsibilities, and authority within the association, the work toward finding and applying solutions can occur in a more expeditious manner. In an era when situations can arise and be communicated instantaneously via the Internet, it is critical that the CSE and CEO know how to reach each other. Both need to understand preferences for communication and protocol for crisis situations.

Ongoing and regular communication from the CSE to the CEO can help to ensure that important information is shared to avoid surprises. Whether it is via phone, email, or face-to-face meetings, the routine can be agreed to early in the relationship. Make this communication a regular part of the job, and it will result in a better working environment that can support open communication.

In addition to communication on a regular basis, the CSE might review and orient the CEO to the association's annual calendar, and offer guidance on how to book travel and seek reimbursement. While these things may seem basic, they are important concerns for someone who has never held the CEO position. The CSE should make a reasonable effort to ensure that the CEO is not "surprised" by any policy, procedure, process, or communication that may occur during his or her term.

Of growing importance in the association industry is ethical conduct. It is incumbent that the CSE is well versed in this topic and can converse on this subject with the new CEO. The CSE may wish to discuss this topic with the entire board as well, so that exemplary ethical behavior is the behavioral norm of the organization's leadership.

The importance of establishing credibility, trust, and an understanding of responsibilities ranks high on the list of many successful CSEs and CEOs. During their time together, events or issues facing the association may arise. By creating a positive working environment, the CSE and CEO will be able to openly discuss problems and think together to find the best solutions.

Some organizations have created a "handbook" for each of the positions of CEO-elect, CEO, and then immediate past CEO. Regardless of the medium in which this information is provided, the key is to ensure that the CEO has a thorough understanding of the "job" in its various phases.

◆ ◆ ◆

Knowing When and Who to Engage—the CEO, Executive Committee, or Full Board

Each association must establish in writing, either in bylaws or board policy, the distinctive roles of the board, the executive committee, and the CEO. The CSE understands that despite a very close working relationship with the CEO, some matters must be discussed with the entire board. If the CSE confides or shares information only with the CEO, this could result in excluding the executive committee or full board on issues and areas in which they actually have jurisdiction. The CSE must work to ensure that this does not occur.

Rather than a list of "dos and don'ts" (although those can be helpful for some), the CSE must be able to explain the rationale for the way in which the CEO, executive committee, and board will operate. The CSE helps the CEO establish an environment that is open to inquiry and clarification on these matters. The CSE must understand clearly what is within the purview and responsibility of the board, the executive committee, and the CEO so that agreed upon authority is not usurped.

There will be times when the CSE is faced with an issue in which the leadership will need to be advised, included in a discussion of options, or both. In some associations, the executive committee acts as a sounding board and advisor to the CSE, whereas the full board is focused on strategic issues. Most bylaws that contain provisions on executive committees state that the entity is empowered to act between meetings of the full board.

It deserves note that the executive committee does not have higher authority than the board. The board holds all legal authority. The executive committee is actually a subset of the board, with its authority established in the bylaws and by direct delegation from the board.

There are various reasons to empower an executive committee to act in the absence of a full board. For example, the executive committee may be called upon to brainstorm with the CSE on strategic issues facing the association between the times that the full board may meet. There may be a need to address a decision required about a real estate transaction that cannot wait for the action of the full board. In many associations the board delegates the performance evaluation of the CSE to the executive committee.

Savvy CSEs establish the proper channels of communication among leadership. To honor the proper hierarchy, a good practice is that all governance communication should be shared equally with the full board, rather than being held exclusively by the CEO or executive committee.

Clarity of roles include the rule of thumb that chief elected officers should intervene with volunteer concerns; the CSE deals with staff concerns. When there is a difficult interpersonal issue involving volunteers, the CSE should facilitate addressing the problem with the smallest group possible. First, start with informing, empowering, and perhaps coaching the CEO to intervene. If the issue can't be resolved there, then the executive committee or officer group might be the next stop. If the issue can't be resolved there, then the issue would likely go to the full board.

Notes

1. J. Carver, *Boards That Make a Difference: A New Design for Leadership in Nonprofit and Public Organizations* (San Francisco: Jossey-Bass, 2006), xxvii.
2. N. Axelrod, *The Governing Board: Key Responsibilities for Association Boards and Board Members* (Washington, DC: ASAE Association Management Press, 2013), 17.
3. BoardSource, *The Source: Twelve Principles of Governance That Power Exceptional Boards* (Washington, DC: BoardSource, 2005).

The Authors

Richard Yep, CAE, FASAE, is the chief executive officer of the American Counseling Association, the largest membership organization of professional counselors in the world with over fifty-five thousand members.

Sidebar author *Gabriel Eckert, CAE,* serves as executive director of the Building Owners and Managers Association of Georgia. He is also coauthor of the book *From Insight to Action: Six New Ways to Think, Lead, and Achieve,* published by ASAE.

CHAPTER SIXTEEN

VOLUNTEER LEADERSHIP DEVELOPMENT

Holly Duckworth, CMP, CAE

Volunteers are the energy engines of most associations. As they engage with their associations, volunteers bring with them creative ideas and action that maintain and move our organizations.

In the past, volunteers have been told what to do, how to do it, and why do it. As the next generation of leaders chooses to volunteer in their associations, they will require a much different type of invitation, development, and experience. Volunteer leadership development is the approach to educating, connecting, and inspiring your volunteers. In volunteer leadership development, you may set a framework for what needs to get done and advise, but do not tell the volunteers how to do the job. Today's volunteers want to be empowered to co-create solutions to their organizational projects.

Association CSEs realize that the very fabric of association leadership is changing. It is in that energy that we share this chapter of board and volunteer leadership development. We hope to highlight the critical role that a CSE plays in setting the tone for designing an efficient and effective volunteer leadership culture. This requires cultivating leadership skills and abilities in individual members to feed board leadership. Leadership succession is one of the most critical imperatives to keep our organizations thriving in a new volunteer climate.

A Critical Understanding

Susan S. Radwan, SMP, ARM, CAE

Let's make a critical distinction about members as volunteers. People who are willing to invest their time and energy into an organization are really making an "ownership" investment in the association. Members-as-owners make those investments because they care about the big picture, they care about the future of their profession or industry, and they care about the contribution they can make to that future. "Members-as-customers" are receiving or seeking to receive a specific benefit or service from the organization. Members-as-customers want something today; members-as-owners value something about the future and are willing to invest themselves to realize that future.[*]

The distinction between members-as-owners who are focused on "us" and members-as-customers who focus on the "me" is absolutely influenced by the communication from the organization. In general, association marketing practice has done a great job of training our members to be customers; however, we tend to ignore the messaging that gets to the ownership side of the equation. The association's ability to activate the ownership mind-set of members is the key to creating a healthy volunteer network.

Key findings from ASAE's *Decision to Join*[**] research identified that the individual decision to join does not hinge on a cost-benefit calculation but rather reflects an appreciation that goes beyond self-oriented assessment to include an assessment of value generated for a community of interests. One's decision to volunteer builds on this idea where we move members from customer (me) mind-set to an owner (we) mind-set by correspondingly moving them from "an appreciation" to a place of active investment.

Notes

[*]Owner-customer distinction is inspired by J. Carver, *Boards That Make a Difference: A New Design for Leadership in Nonprofit and Public Organizations* (Hoboken, NJ: John Wiley & Sons, 2011).

[**]J. G. Dalton, M. Dignam, ASAE, and the Center for Association Leadership, *The Decision to Join: How Individuals Determine Value and Why They Choose to Belong* (Washington, DC: ASAE Association Management Press, 2007).

The Volunteer Pathway

Volunteerism is a uniquely American activity in which one in four Americans participate.

The volunteers of tomorrow wish to be inspired to lead and not be managed. With the Gen-Xers and Gen-Ys, we must recognize that co-creation is the name of the game with our volunteers, while, at the same time, the 24/7/365 nature of our world makes it often harder for volunteers to serve. To address this condition, association leaders must consider new roles, new processes for leadership development, and new structures to capture the imagination of these volunteers. The old forms of standing committees, rotating through the chairs, and committees without clear functionality are gone. Volunteer recruitment practices must change to attract and inspire members to engage in the volunteer ranks of the association.

Volunteer pathways are being recast and redesigned in consideration of the lifestyle and career paths of membership. For example, is it realistic for a board member to serve for six years before being eligible to become an officer? Is it realistic for a volunteer to rotate through all officer chairs before becoming the chief elected officer? In our dynamic society, many members will move, retire, or change professions before they get to the sixth year!

Volunteers are choosing their own futures in their associations on the basis of personal wants and needs. Some choose to serve without ambition to higher levels of leadership. Others choose to move up into the ranks of board or advanced leadership. Mapping out the potential volunteer pathways can visually demonstrate to volunteers that they can choose their own course according to what they wish to learn, hone, or develop. Volunteerism is no longer a "giving back"; today it is a "learning laboratory" for leadership skill development.

Volunteer Leaders Need A Why

For successful volunteer recruitment, each volunteer needs a clear understanding of *why* the organization exists and *why* he or she should give time and talent to the organization. However, the ultimate choice of which cause to support is incredibly personal for most volunteers.

A common practice in volunteer leadership development is asking and listening to volunteers share their "why"—why they choose to volunteer and work with the organization. Once the association staff understands the motivation, it's incumbent upon staff to place each volunteer in a role that relates to the volunteer's area of passion. For example, if a member is passionate because a credential she worked to attain from your organization has helped her to obtain a highly desired job, you may want to place her in a volunteer role that supports the credentialing program.

A CSE must recognize the importance of knowing and living the organization's vision or mission. These directional statements are the guiding force in volunteer and board leadership. Volunteers need strong inspiration and a sense of meaningful purpose in the work they do.

Designing Volunteer Leadership Structures

Leading volunteers in the new economy of technology, globalism, and association change requires association leadership to design programs to meet the needs of today's sophisticated audience.

First, consider your structure. Does your volunteer structure align with your business model? Which structure will serve you better—a hierarchical structure or a flat structure? Traditional associations have a hierarchy with project volunteers, ad hoc and standing committees, task forces, directors, vice presidents, and executive committees reporting up the chain of command. It is not unusual that a hierarchical structure would require a year or more to make a decision about a new program or service. That hierarchical structure creates "speed bumps" so that things don't change too fast.

Many organizations have restructured to become flatter organizations. Why? First, they needed to become more nimble and flexible in decision making. In the twenty-first century, opportunities appear and are lost within three to six months. Associations need to have the ability to scan for, assess, analyze, and decide on opportunities within a matter of a few months. Second, the flattened structure is designed in response to fewer volunteers willing to make the time commitment required.

It is also important to note that the vitality of an association is directly related to the vitality of active members engaged in the cause of the association. When flattened volunteer structures override this reality, it is critical for the association to create new opportunities for volunteers to actively engage in a "member as owner" capacity.

Volunteer Job Descriptions

As associations evolve from a volunteer management paradigm to a volunteer leadership paradigm, clear job descriptions for each volunteer committee should be integrated into your organizational structure. Job descriptions should be one page or less. Making the description accurate and succinct so that a volunteer knows what is expected and what defines success is very important.

For example, a project management committee job description would include

- Duration of project: What are the start date and the end date?
- Membership on the committee: How many people will serve? What are the required skills or talents? What are the highly desirable skills or talents?
- Resources available to complete the project: Are other volunteers, staff, money available?
- Outcomes: What are the overall desired outcomes of the project?
- Project goals: Raise money? Awareness? Attendance?
- Key success measures: How would we know the project was successful?
- Time commitment required: How many meetings? How much travel?

Please note: this style of job description is connected to the strategic and business plans and is focused on aligning volunteer efforts to advance the plans. In general, it is not efficient for volunteer committees to decide what projects they want to do; valuable volunteer time is wasted in the wandering and exploration. Alignment is the key to an effective use of time.

Some organizations create a committee charter approved by the board to accomplish this task; others integrate committee job descriptions into their committee handbooks.

Types of Volunteer Opportunities

A well-designed volunteer leadership program will have many levels of leadership and types of volunteer opportunities to meet the needs of the volunteer and the organization, as illustrated in Table 16.1.

It should be noted that as the association staff grows with expertise, volunteer decisions must move away from logistical and operational "how to" and move toward analysis and sense-making from the field to ensure relevance to the membership. Many organizations have eliminated standing committees from their bylaws to ensure a more flexible committee structure, on the basis of "What do we need to get done?" rather than "We have to have an education committee; what can we give them to do?"

As you can see, there are many levels of volunteerism and new ones emerging that are adapting to available time and technology. Not every

TABLE 16.1. VOLUNTEER OPPORTUNITIES, TRAINING, AND FOCUS.

Type of Opportunity and Duration	Level of Training Required	Focus
Micro-Volunteering (also known as ad hoc or episodic volunteering) Duration: variable: one hour per month to three hours and done Often requires the volunteer to be able to accept an invitation and start contributing on a moment's notice	Training is minimal, as long as assignments are made in connection with a desirable skill set.	Assignments focus on tasks that do not need committee involvement, such as mentoring, assistance in recruiting a specific member, writing for association publications, routinely checking the website for outdated material, tweeting during your annual conference.
Ad Hoc Committee Duration: can be projected on the basis of the assignment; generally from one to six months	Training is minimal, since volunteers generally step forward, willing to champion the assignment.	Ad hoc committees are generally formed to assist the board in intelligence gathering and framing issues. For example, you might form an ad hoc committee to explore the feasibility of restructuring the governance of the association, search for a new office location, or develop criteria and process for a new CSE search.
Project Management Committee Duration: generally one year or less	If the project is perennial, volunteers will need to study the lessons learned from past experience as well as review the procedures developed by past project teams.	This is a volunteer team to support key operational initiatives each year. For example, a volunteer conference committee might identify and select speakers and session topics and assist with marketing, registration, meeting logistics, and a myriad of other tasks required to pull off the event. A project management committee generally has a specific start time and end time and one role in the organization.

Standing Committee

Duration: generally on a termed basis of one to three years, with renewable terms

Generally, there is a learning curve to be successful on a standing committee. The curve involves understanding the function and the environmental context to be successful. Knowing the players is often critical for success.

Standing committees are identified in the bylaws and focus on a specific function of the association. They engage in several projects or issues related to that function. For example, a fundraising committee might host a golf tournament, conduct an annual fund campaign, and conduct a capital campaign in the same year. Typical standing committees include government relations, fundraising, education, governance, bylaws, and nominating.

Board

Duration: generally terms of service of two to three years; ideally, to preserve momentum, three-year terms with one-third of the board rotating off or renewing each year

Considerable training is required in strategic thinking, strategic fit in the context of the professional environment, understanding the culture of the association, learning how to function in group process, and thinking and acting as a collective body.

Boards govern the organization as its highest authority, setting direction; developing broad policy; ensuring relevance of the association to overall membership; recognizing emerging trends from the field; fulfilling the fiduciary duties of care, loyalty, and obedience; and ensuring operational performance through CSE evaluation and monitoring as well as governance performance by undertaking board evaluation as a continuous process improvement. An effective board will add value to the organization, rather than act as a "super CSE."

volunteer you recruit will need access to the same resources. It is important that they recognize where the assigned tasks fit into the overall strategic and business plans that are driven by vision and mission.

A CSE dedicated to volunteer leadership will ensure that a volunteer orientation exists. Such an orientation addresses context, policies, procedures, and culture of the organization before the volunteers start on a project or step into a particular role. The volunteers need to know what is expected and for what they are accountable to be successful.

Volunteer Selection

In 2001, Jim Collins published seminal research[1] on what distinguishes a good organization from a great organization. Getting the right people on the bus was one of five tenets identified for greatness.

There is a commonly held misconception in many associations that you have to take every volunteer that walks through your door. Association executives know from experience that it's better to have an empty volunteer role than have to work with the wrong volunteer on a project.

With today's online programs, an application process to volunteer can be automated. As you build your volunteer pathways, be clear and transparent about the skills and fit you are looking for in your recruitment efforts and *whether* you will place everyone. If there is an appointment approval process or a screening process, you need to clearly state the selection criteria and the process for notifying both those selected and those not selected. It is important to identify when, how, and by whom you will notify those not selected.

Recommended practice mirrors the corporate sector's human resource practices. Check credentials and references, interview, and select volunteers on the basis of demonstrated skill sets and fit for critical leadership roles. In addition, since many volunteers are participating to hone their leadership skill sets, highly effective organizations incorporate performance appraisal as part of the capacity-building process and as a requirement for additional leadership assignments.

Designing a Volunteer Leadership System

There are five critical underpinnings to develop vital volunteer leadership: recruitment, retention, review, recognition, and reward.[2]

Recruitment

Association volunteer managers all have one thing in common: they have a core group of people doing a majority of the work. It is not unusual that volunteers get so busy and excited doing the work they forget to ask other people to help them. Sometimes they don't know who to contact or how or when to ask for help. Sometimes volunteers will say, "Bringing people up to speed on a project takes more time than if I do it myself." And then there are others who have built their identity around a specific project and how they want it done; they simply can never see anyone else doing the project as well as they do it. When volunteer recruiting shuts down, associations tend to become cliquish and insular and eventually enter into accelerated deterioration.

In the 2007 ASAE study *The Decision to Volunteer,* key findings included the top methods by which members were recruited into volunteer activities.[3] Among the top methods was participation in a chapter or annual meeting by virtue of a request by staff or another volunteer. The study affirmed that passive techniques such as website postings and emails are not as effective. The key learning from this research is that we must ask people to volunteer, yet we do not provide training on how to "tap people on the shoulder."

Logically, then, one key to successful recruiting is to train your volunteers and staff how to directly invite someone to volunteer. When we start to tap people on the shoulder, good things happen: we reach new volunteers, which results in more diversity of volunteers in terms of generations, backgrounds, ideas, and industry experience.

A direct "ask" may go something like this. "Hey, Amanda, I am volunteering for the JCC association, and we are working on a new communications project. Our goal is to increase our member participation via social media. We would like to leverage LinkedIn and Facebook. I see that you post regular updates on behalf of your company. Would you be willing to share your skills with the JCC for three months so we can get this initiative under way?"

An "ask" to someone who may want to learn a skill could look like this. "Hi Nate, this is Frank. I am a volunteer on the board for the LFC association. We have a strong committee of event professionals who are working to promote our gala. You mentioned a few weeks ago that you wanted to learn about event promotion so you could promote a company event you are working on. Would you be interested in helping us for July and August?"

In both of these examples we are recruiting the volunteer in a very personal way. When people receive such a personal invitation, it is very hard to say no.

With five generations in the workforce, some organizations also have five generations volunteering. If you look around your association and see only one or two age demographics volunteering, now might be the time to reach across the age divide and recruit new volunteers. Also remember that age is only one consideration of diversity. Examine the demographics of your volunteers. Do those demographics resemble that of the membership? If not, plan for recruitment accordingly.

Recruitment takes on a variety of forms. We know the direct ask as just illustrated has the greatest success rate. This does not mean it should be your only recruitment strategy. A mix of recruitment tools may be most effective in your membership. Assess where your membership is actively communicating and start asking there. If your members are active on LinkedIn, participate there. If Facebook or Twitter is where your people are actively building community, converse on those platforms. Video is also emerging as a medium to share current volunteer success stories and to inspire others to get involved. Of course, local chapters feed into statewide affiliates, which feed into regional components and ultimately the lead organization.

The CSE must factor in the vitality of the volunteer structure to ensure a healthy future for the association. The volunteer leadership system must be driven by a recognition that the whole of the organization is at risk without that volunteer connection. Volunteers should not have to find their own colleagues to build a functional team. Generally, volunteers only know a handful of people across the breadth of the association. When they are solely responsible for recruiting, they will recruit people like themselves, creating a homogenous team. Staff on the other hand are in regular communication across the entire membership. When volunteer efforts are built into an operational system, diversity is more likely.

Retention

Research shows that it costs more to gain a new member than to keep a current one. The same is true of volunteers. The key to retaining volunteers is building a solid personal relationship with the volunteers as they work in their association. Associations need to focus on helping volunteers to grow professionally and personally, rather than to "chew them up and spit them out." Volunteerism should be life-giving, not life-draining.

Appropriate placement of volunteers has a direct impact on longevity of service. Would you place a high-level strategic thinker on the conference committee? Similarly, would you encourage a hyper-detail-oriented person to serve in a strategic capacity? Both of these situations are prescriptions for volunteer frustration and dissatisfaction. Placement should be intentional, based on a match between the skill set and job to be accomplished.

Properly training volunteers plays an important part in volunteer effectiveness and growth. Volunteer training can take many forms. A common method is the volunteer orientation and training meeting. Each volunteer is invited to a common place or a webinar to be briefed on the organization and the project or role to be played. In some cases, mentors are offered and matched with new volunteers to pass down key knowledge on how to accomplish the task at hand.

Training is also critical to address association risk management. Because of the impacts of the legal and financial complexities that underlie many decisions made by volunteers, risk management is becoming a much more prominent issue in volunteer leadership development. Risks include contractual liability, antitrust exposure, libel, slander, conflicts of interest, and making financial decisions that the association cannot easily fund. The risk management solution is to design volunteer positions, roles, and jobs to avoid or reduce the exposure to adverse loss as much as possible. Then, train, supervise, and monitor volunteers to effectively handle the remaining risks with backup and contingency systems in place. Continue to monitor for new exposures to risk and respond accordingly.

Review

A common belief among association staff is, "We can't hold our volunteers accountable because they are just volunteers." The reality is that when volunteers do not fulfill their promises, it affects the association—sometimes critically. Enabling poor performance is a problem built into our current volunteer structures.

To create accountability, review the skill sets, abilities, and effectiveness of each volunteer, or at least each volunteer project. Such a performance review process should be based on clear criteria that contribute to high-performing associations. A review process might take the form of an evaluation survey, a brief conversation, or ongoing coaching by an assigned mentor. Remember, however, that such an assessment is about professional and personal growth and capacity-building, rather than judgment and criticism. When dealing with poor performance, it is important to always ensure that volunteers "save face" in the presence of their peers. Diplomacy and tact must be applied at all times.

It is recommended that associations keep a database of volunteers, why they volunteer, which projects interest them, and what skill sets they possess, along with assessments of their reliability, leadership, and actual performance in their specific assignments. This type of database can be very helpful to ensure that future assignments are appropriate given past performance. For example, your database indicates that a particular candidate for the board bullied committee members as the chairman, did not follow through on promises, and was absent for a majority of meetings when assigned as a committee member. Why would you encourage or even allow that candidate to run for the board?

Quantify the Value of Volunteers

As a part of the volunteer review process, it is a good exercise for organizations to calculate the value of the volunteer effort in financial terms. There is a growing awareness of just how much volunteers can "add value" to the organizations they serve. The notion that volunteers can contribute in significant and substantive ways to advance the association is a key "learning." Quantifying that contribution is a valuable statistic to build on your volunteer efforts, to demonstrate that the association is connected to its membership, and to show that the association could not do its work without the contribution of and partnership with volunteers.

◆ ◆ ◆

Recognition and Reward

In the fast pace of association life, it is critical that we take time to recognize and reward those who are doing the work. Volunteer recognition is life-giving to many, for most people do not receive the affirmation in their daily lives that they have made a difference. When such affirmation comes from the association, it builds an emotional bond.

Today, organizations are building ongoing recognition systems in which volunteers are getting thanked more frequently and recognition is personalized. For example, associations personalize rewards with gift cards or gift items in the area of a volunteer's interest. Many organizations ask permission to send thank you letters to the volunteer's boss in acknowledgment of the support the company has given to volunteerism.

Recognition does not have to be expensive, but it does need to be systematic. To achieve this, you may need to employ a volunteer coordinator or manager to ensure that each volunteer gets a pat on the back and recognition immediately after a project concludes instead of waiting for the annual awards dinner. Longer-term volunteers should systematically get kudos every sixty to ninety days. In addition, keep in mind that April's National Volunteerism Week is a simple reason to recognize volunteers and be a part of a movement.

Trends in Volunteer and Board Leadership

Skill-Based Volunteering

Many organizations look at volunteerism through the lens of human resources. For many organizations that have geographic-based boards, it is clear that filling seats with warm bodies does not work. Board members need strategic and group process skills to move the organization forward. Thus more and more organizations are changing to skills-based recruitment. Amending your bylaws and policies to remove requirements of specific geographic representation on your board so you can recruit on the basis of skills may be needed. Review your bylaws and work with legal counsel to make any necessary amendments.

Keep in mind that the primary job of leaders is planning and change. Organizations moving to a strategic board structure will need to identify the key individual skills necessary to be an effective board leader in this context. Assess the group's collective skills to make sure that the needs of the organization and entire membership are met. Collective skills may be industry experience, association history, global mind-set, group process, chapter experience, governance, or strategic planning. The board should be directly involved in identifying the leadership criteria for qualified candidates to govern toward a relevant future state. Board conversation about the desired skills, necessary skills, and essential skills to advance the association is the beginning of becoming a strategic board.

Aging Volunteers

As the demographics of our population shifts, so does the population of our volunteers. Associations today need to consider how they will attract and retain active younger volunteers into an environment in which senior members are the prevalent demographic. Members and volunteers are attracted to organizations in which they can "see themselves" around the table. If a thirty-something joins a board or committee on which all the members are sixty or older, he or she will not likely stay for long. Demographic diversity and seamless transition from one generation to the next has been and will be a challenge for many associations.

Micro-Volunteering and Virtual Volunteering

Every organization struggles to fill volunteer slots. Progressive associations are adapting by offering micro-volunteering opportunities, also known as episodic volunteerism. Micro-volunteering focuses on opportunities for volunteers from their smartphone devices or in small segments of time. Micro-volunteering allows for quick, easy commitments from members to support the organization. This pathway requires solid database management to ensure that all micro-volunteer efforts are tracked and recognized.

Due to the rapid advancement of technology, it is critical that you integrate technology into your volunteer opportunities when possible. You want to consider fewer face-to-face meetings and integrate virtual conference technology into volunteer work sessions. Virtual volunteering allows you to expand your reach and the pool of volunteers who may not attend regular events.

Associations might learn from websites such as www.sparked.com, where you can post the microtasks you need completed by volunteers. When members know what you need and they can imagine themselves being able to do that task, it can result in a volunteer matchup.

Global Volunteering

Volunteers are now participating in global projects ranging from contributing funding to physically going to another country to volunteer with groups. CSEs should recognize that the membership may have broad experiences in terms of skills and talents that they can bring to your organization.

As the CSE, you work with your staff and volunteers to deliver on the desired results of a volunteer board of directors. Much of your success hinges on your ability to build, inspire, facilitate professional and personal growth, and retain vitality in your volunteer workforce.

FIGURE 16.1. LIDC PROCESS AND THE LEADERSHIP PIPELINE CYCLE.

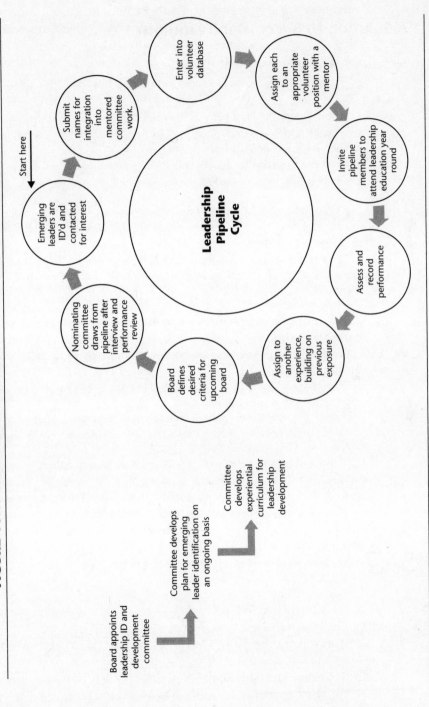

A Solution to Succession Planning

by Susan S. Radwan, SMP, ARM, CAE

Succession planning by definition is a deliberate and systematic effort to

- Ensure leadership continuity in key positions
- Develop and retain intellectual and knowledge capital for the future
- Encourage individual advancement
- Build bench strength
- Develop a pipeline of leaders

Systematic association succession planning occurs when an organization *adapts specific procedures to ensure* the identification, development, and long-term retention of talented individuals.

Progressive associations are replacing or augmenting their nominating committees with leadership identification and development committees (LIDCs). The purpose of an LIDC is to

- Be a continuous radar scan to identify people in the membership who are emerging as potential leaders
- Get those emerging leaders involved in committee work to test out their leadership skill
- Offer opportunities to emerging leaders to further develop skills that support group process, leadership, and governance
- Ensure that volunteers running for the board have appropriate orientation to the work of your organization and skills that will contribute to its governance

The LIDC creates a defined curriculum of leadership education, experience, and mentorship that builds individual capacity that will serve the professional growth needs of the volunteers and the association's leadership succession needs.

The LIDC engages in a process represented in Figure 16.1.

Notes

1. J. Collins, *Good to Great and the Social Sectors: A Monograph to Accompany Good to Great* (New York: HarperCollins, 2005).
2. Drawn from the ASAE Online University Program on Volunteer Management.
3. B. Gazley, M. Dignam, the American Society of Association Executives, and the Center for Association Leadership, *The Decision to Volunteer: Why*

People Give Their Time and How You Can Engage Them (Washington, DC: ASAE Association Management Press).

Resources

Volunteerism research is continuously being updated. For more on this topic you should reference the following works.

American Society of Association Executives and Center for Association Leadership. *7 Measures of Success: What Remarkable Associations Do That Others Don't.* Washington, DC: ASAE Association Management Press, 2012.

Dalton, J. G., Dignam, M., the American Society of Association Executives, and the Center for Association Leadership. *The Decision to Join: How Individuals Determine Value and Why They Choose to Belong.* Washington, DC: ASAE Association Management Press, 2007.

2008.

Web Resources

Corporation for National & Community Service, "Volunteering and Civic Life in America 2013," n.d., available at www.volunteeringinamerica.gov.

Leadership Solutions International, "52AssociationTips.com," 2014, available at www.52associationtips.com.

Points of Light: Dedicated to Volunteer Service, n.d., available at www.pointsoflight.org.

USA.gov, "Public Service and Volunteerism," n. d., available at http://www.usa.gov/Citizen/Topics/PublicService.shtml.

The Authors

Holly Duckworth, CMP, CAE, is the CEO of Leadership Solutions International, based in Denver, Colorado. Duckworth is a frequent contributor to *Associations Now,* ASAE's Great Ideas Conference, and is on faculty to ASAE Online University.

Sidebars author *Susan S. Radwan, SMP, ARM, CAE,* is the owner of Leading Edge Mentoring, an international consulting firm focused on governance and leadership issues, based in Grand Ledge, Michigan.

CHAPTER SEVENTEEN

COMPONENT RELATIONS

Lowell M. Aplebaum, CAE

Creating community is a traditional strength of associations and is a fundamental factor in the reasons "components" exist and succeed. In many cases, a national or global association first started with a small group of local professionals who found that by forming an association they created a community of colleagues that could learn and grow from each other's strengths and pooled resources. These chapters, as they are known today, still exist in the majority of national and international associations. As technology continued to evolve so did the corresponding means by which to form community—and today associations may have their traditional geographic chapters or sections, virtual communities united around a discipline or area of interest, or global alliances uniting multiple associations under a single umbrella. All together, these various community segments are referred to as "components."

Why Components?

An association's decision to start a new class of components, or new individual components in an established class, is not one that is easily made. From legal and financial considerations to volunteer management and leadership development, there are many areas to consider. If created and run well, a successful component program can be a huge boon and area of value for any association.

Following are some association enhancements that come from components:

- *Targeted value to members:* Components create communities that speak to a member on a more personal level—whether that is by where he or she lives or works or by a specific discipline.
- *Extended avenues of knowledge:* Many components have professional development programming as a key activity, enhancing the overall efforts of the organization.
- *Greater association value awareness:* Associations that ensure that their component leaders are treated as high-value partners can essentially create association spokespeople, able to make a greater impact than any brochure.
- *Leadership pipeline:* Many components are run to some extent by volunteers, building a path by which leadership of the organization can first get "on the ground" training.
- *Ability to "do" more:* The programs, products, networking, and community that an association's components produce add to the whole of how an association works to provide opportunities for greater success of its professionals and investment in the profession.

With all the good that can be accomplished, an association still must first assess its resources and areas of strategic focus to determine what type of component(s) is the right fit for its efforts.

General Types of Components

Components fall into one of several general categories.

- *Geographic:* This "traditional" model can range in size from a city-subsection to a country. Geographic components allow members to meet and network in person more frequently, as well as address topics of regional interest. It is important to note that models of domestic geographic components may not be identically transferable to their international counterparts. Depending on the culture, social norms, developmental progress, and even the local laws, international components may require unique leadership and governance structures or alternative programming models. Are volunteers unpaid? Do those that typically serve on a board actually "do" or just "advise," and is a separate committee needed for action? What are the specific educational needs of professionals in the area? The balance of a structure that feels "local" but which still retains organizational branding and connection is a delicate one to make.

- *Topical:* Often virtual in nature, components that are formed around an area of interest can allow professionals from around the globe to share, discuss, and learn from one another. These components will find the majority of their activity in online community learning platforms, and some will still organize a newsletter or specialized conference. These components can range from those with a formal governance structure, often called councils or communities of practice, to those that are simply discussion forums, such as special interest groups. The line of demarcation between this as a component and a simple avenue for dialogue is dependent on the intent and formation of community within the model.
- *Allied partners:* To better serve a profession, associations will often choose to combine efforts in alliance relationships. In most cases there is the retention of organizational independence, but an agreement of terms of shared access and benefits to each member population. The balance of power in these relationships may vary depending on the size or scope of resources of the organizations involved.
- *Others:* There are a number of other types of components that exist—the virtual chapter, institutes and academies, even some leadership entities that are subdivisions of the whole association and a community in their own right.

As an association evolves so will its component needs. It is important to review not only the types of components that exist but the structures under which they are functioning as well. What might have once made sense when they were originally formed may no longer align with organizational objectives or capabilities.

Financial and Legal Considerations

When establishing components, associations need to make a clear decision whether their components will be separate legal entities. Components that are separate legal entities give the association a line of defense against any liability originating from the component's actions. The incorporated component is responsible for its own tax filing, and there is an inherent level of protection to the association's tax-exempt status. Of course, with independence comes—well, independence, and associations whose components are separate legal entities also give up a measure of control. These components, which are often volunteer led, may miss filing tax forms with the government, as things are often lost in translation in leadership transition. In addition, unless addressed in an affiliation agreement, if the component does dissolve and is an independent entity, its remaining funds and reserves could very likely not revert back to the lead association.

An association can preempt many legal and governance questions of clarity by creating a standard affiliation agreement. While some of the details of these agreements may occasionally need to be modified under unique circumstances, in general these agreements give a standard of establishment that cuts across each component type of the organization. While this list is not comprehensive,[1] such agreements should be sure to address the following:

- *Trademarks:* How an association is willing to allow its brand and logo to be used must be explicitly agreed upon and enforced. It is the inherent nature of any community to want to have a "unique" identity and the length to which an association is willing to go to meet this need while still making sure that every component is part of the organizational brand needs to be consistent.
- *Geographic boundaries:* For those components that are formed around a place, agreement on what area they cover can help them target membership drives and outreach while ensuring from early on that later-forming components won't overlap as competitors.
- *Membership status:* Is membership in the lead organization a requirement for joining the component? Can a component have independent membership? Is there a minimum requirement of the component leadership belonging to the association? This is one of the potential "hot spots" for rifts between an association and its components and needs to be a clear expectation from component creation.
- *Reporting requirements:* Is there a single annual report that the association requires each component to submit? With full financial information? Are the minutes of each board meeting required? It is critical that the association not only knows what information it wants from each component, but that it in turn will be able to demonstrate how it is going to use that information. Otherwise, volunteers who have spent their limited

time working hard to create the requested data may walk away feeling frustrated and less inclined to make the same effort in the future.

In addition, to avoid any miscommunication, clear guidelines should also be set for financial considerations. For example, most associations will require their components to operate on the same fiscal year as the lead organization. In addition, many components will look to open their own bank account. Guidelines for proper fiscal oversight, such as number of required signatures, who should have signing authority, and the process of transferring authority in years of leadership transition should all be outlined. Some associations publish such guidelines in a component handbook; others include these guidelines as an addendum to the affiliation agreement.

While certainly your organization as a whole has a budget, each of your components should have one as well. A companion to its strategic plan (to be addressed shortly), the budget can tell the story year over year of what a component wanted to accomplish through its expenditures and investments and where it succeeded, exceeded, or fell short. While it might not answer the why of those trends, it can point later generations of leaders to knowing when to ask that question. A component budget can provide insight to the organization on what the component is trying to accomplish and to future leaders of the component who might not have served (or even belonged!) when the current leadership was in office.

Strategic Alignment

How does your organization align its vision and resources, measure its results, and take corrective action in its efforts year after year? For the majority of associations the solution is a strategic plan—a singular place where the mission and vision of an organization are translated into what it is trying to achieve and what efforts it will put forth to reach those achievements. Strategic plans serve the three-fold need of a historical account of an organization's path, an agreement on current efforts, and a projection of where the association wants to go.

Since many components do not have dedicated staff, a strategic plan at their level is even more essential to ensure that efforts are focused and connected to the ongoing goals of the community. Intentional connection between the organization and component strategic plan is the ideal path to a stronger partnership and greater overall achievement and recognition. Here are four areas to consider as relates to strategy:

- *Strategic consultants:* Many lead associations act in a consultant role to their components when it comes to strategy formation. At a minimum, this can mean having "strategic planning resources in a box" available online so any component can run its own session. Creating a set of materials and guidelines for forming a plan can help ensure that there is consistency in format among an association's components. When available, associations will also offer to act as in-person strategy facilitators, running a full session for the component. Issues such as cost, limited staff time, and expansive number of components can be hindrances to this, but when it is possible the results go beyond a stronger strategy—it can elicit a feeling of investment by the overall association in the component.

- *Strategy requirements:* How can you help guide a component strategy so there are connections to the overall organization? Though there may be some divergence when it comes to the tactics, the mission and vision of a component should closely align with the association. The objectives they are trying to meet would then ideally align with the larger objectives of the organization, generating forward movement on all fronts. For the best overlay, if an organization has categories that provide the framework for its strategic plan, a component should use the same categories.

- *Strategy sharing:* An organization should be intentional in how it chooses to share its strategic vision and plan. Is it available for public viewing on its website? For member viewing behind a firewall? This passive display is a good step toward transparency, but for true component buy-in there should be an intentional process in place to connect with all parties. An annual strategic plan conversation with component leadership will allow all parties to hear from fellow colleagues and leaders what the organization is trying to achieve, ask questions about their role in that plan, and have the added benefit of a personal touch in recognizing the importance of components to the organization.

- *Component presence:* If components are a key factor to the organization's success, whether through creating community, knowledge, or content, or acting as marketing spokespeople for the organization, there should be aligned representation given to the component role in the strategic plan of the organization. Their intentional inclusion will only enhance the component-lead relationship and be a tangible vision of how they affect the success of the association.

Program evaluation in any form seems to only happen when funders require it. But here is a case study about an association that proactively committed to organizational evaluations of its entire network.

◆ ◆ ◆

Case Study: Organizational Reviews and Strategic Planning for State Associations

Luis A. Rivera, MBA, CAE

In efforts to better align and enhance the strategic partnership *between* state associations and *among* state associations, the American Association of Nurse Anesthetists (AANA) focused its attention on a rigorous organizational review of all state associations plus the facilitation and development of a comprehensive strategic planning process for all state associations.

Following a thorough evaluation process, AANA contracted with three association management consulting firms to conduct this work over a four-year period. Small, medium, and large states were randomly assigned to each firm.

The project is divided into three major phases: (1) Interview and data collection, (2) presentation of the report and governance and leadership development, and (3) strategic planning process and development of a strategic plan. In a final project closure phase, the consultants remain available for a nine-month period to coach the state leaders through the implementation of recommendations and execution of the strategic plan.

The business objectives for this project are

- Perform a comprehensive review of several state association documents and volunteer structures, such as bylaws, policies and procedures, strategic plan, mission or vision statements, audits, BOD and committee charters.
- Submit recommendations to foster board relations and ensure effective and seamless volunteer succession planning.
- Evaluate contracts for contracted services and assess the services provided by contracted individuals or firms (for example, lobbyist, legal counsel, association management).
- Assess each individual state association's organizational functionality, efficiency, and governance model and member engagement and make recommendations for improvement.
- Assess financial decision making and make recommendations on the process that each individual state association should follow to effectively identify the resources needed before engaging in long-term legislative initiatives.
- Assess and make recommendations regarding the appropriate mechanisms that should be in place to ensure that each individual state association has a sound financial position and appropriate financial processes (for example, a budget, formal financial reviews, IRS Form 990).
- Facilitate a strategic planning process and prepare a plan that incorporates the recommendations from the organizational review.

- Assess state associations' ability to follow AANA's *Guidelines for State Organizational Health* (a list of organizational components that state associations should have in place to function effectively).
- Analyze common issues and make recommendations for national support services and education on leadership development.

The data obtained from these reviews and the development of strategic plans for the state associations has helped the organization as a whole have a better understanding of the opportunities and challenges related to infrastructure and governance. In addition, the lead organization has a better understanding of the legal, legislative, regulatory, and practice-related initiatives that states are contemplating so the national organization is able to more effectively collaborate with those efforts.

With a better understanding of the opportunities and challenges related to infrastructure and governance, leadership and management have started addressing those needs. Here are some examples of resulting initiatives:

- Development of leadership development toolkits for new board members to address needs identified
- Development of a sample comprehensive board policy manual
- Development of video modules on parliamentary procedures
- Development of a bylaws model template for state associations; language that could be tailored to meet the needs of organizations on the basis of their size is identified throughout the template
- Development of sample board roles and responsibilities emphasizing expectations and time commitment
- Development of sample state association budgets, financial reports, and policies and procedures
- Development of sample requests for proposal (RFPs) to assist in the selection of association management and lobbyists services
- Development of evaluation forms and scope of services for association management companies and lobbyists

Component-Lead Relationship

Component "management" could really be rephrased as component "relationship building." Clear expectations of roles and responsibilities, open communication, and leadership investment are the keys to stronger relationships. Since many components function as associations in their own right, there is often ongoing tension between competition and cooperation with the lead association. Working to build a synergistic relationship where there is strength in the partnership between the component and lead organization should be the ideal. In short, it should be an "us" and not an "us versus them."

1. *Roles and responsibilities:* How does the association support the component, and does it support every component the same? Greater support of course means greater resource needs, but also translates to stronger component ties, a broader insight for the association into its communities, and often more latitude for component volunteers to focus on richer experiences for its members rather than logistical necessities with their limited time.

   For instance, will members join the component through the lead association or through the component directly? By joining through the lead association, there are database and reporting, join and renew processes, and dues collection and distribution needs, to name just a few. These are not inconsiderable in cost or staff time and resources. On the other hand, an association then knows which of its members belong to a component for greater segmentation and personalization of marketing.

   In addition, there should be some broad expectations about the role of the component. What services are they providing that add value to its constituents? For example, there may be the expectation that the component is responsible for prioritizing topical needs for its "local" professionals while the lead association is expected to provide avenues by which components can share their best practice models of how they address those needs with each other. There may be the expectation that the lead association is going to supply the marketing and train local leadership on the importance of membership while it is the expectation of the component leaders to then translate that learning into action and increase engagement and membership.

2. *Open communication:* An association should have standards of communication with its components so that there is regular dialogue. If a component "goes quiet," this should be a red flag that there is a potential issue, whether in component activity and leadership or in a fraying relationship with the lead organization. In addition, a lead organization should be mindful not only to rely upon staff for ongoing communication with the component but also to integrate opportunity for additional touches from association volunteer leadership. Peer-to-peer conversations can create a strong bond between the component and organization that is different than staff-only contacts. Altogether this can clearly paint the

communication path and points of contact for a component if they have a question, a problem, or a success they want to share.

There is, of course, the technical side of communications. From the service question above, what communication platforms will the lead association support on behalf of the component? Website hosting? Private online social communities? Moderating public social media communities? Email blasts to the component membership? These questions go beyond the simple service considerations since there is real risk of a lead association and a component both going out to the same member with communications multiple times in the same time period, lessening the impact of any effort.

3. *Leadership investment:* As mentioned earlier, most components are run by volunteers. While often these volunteers will be experts or masters of their field, it may be their first time leading in a nonprofit association environment. If an organization recognizes the impact that these members make on the association through their component work, that recognition must lead to an investment in leadership development. This investment is essential for component success.

Volunteer Management

Volunteer management is a key issue in component management because not only does the association need to manage its component volunteers, it also needs to help its components with its volunteer management structures. This onus is actually an opportunity—if an association does a great job in its volunteer management practices, its components can look to those patterns and emulate them on a local level. At a high level, here are five areas of volunteer management that can be used as reflection points when evaluating a volunteer structure, whether at the organization or component level.

1. *Structure:* Given its current work plan and its goal in raising the level of involvement of its members, what are the volunteer needs of the entity (either the lead or the component)? Are there smaller, micro-volunteering opportunities that can then lead to broader exposure to executive leadership opportunities? Creating a path for volunteer involvement inherently produces a pipeline for volunteer training and identification that forgoes the assumption that the only way to volunteer is by making a one- to six-year commitment. Once the

scope of volunteer positions has been identified, there should be clear position descriptions written for each. Defining the expectations of the position and the time commitment involved informs the leader stepping into the role with what he or she is actually committing to do.

2. *Recruiting:* Asking for volunteers should start with clear identification of who the entity is, what is to be accomplished, and the role the available volunteer position(s) play in achieving that goal. The "ask" should then be taken to the appropriate medium—whether in person at a meeting, passively on a website, or actively posted in social media. An entity should know what audience to recruit and then connect its request for volunteers with the right place to find that audience.

   There should be an easy path for a volunteer to raise his or her hand and be nominated. There is also great value in current leaders identifying "rising stars" and tapping them for further involvement. Many associations are moving to a leadership identification and development committee to discover emerging leaders and engage them into a leadership pipeline rather than a nominating committee solely creating a slate of officers. Once the volunteer applicants have been collected, a formal selection process should ensure that not only are the volunteer posts filled, but the right candidate is chosen for each position—"right" defined as someone who may not necessarily have every single expertise needed, but has the "fit" needed for the team or the community, for insight and for where the entity is headed. Skills can be taught; someone who has vision, is a team player, or is dedicated has something inherent that is more than can necessarily be taught.

3. *Training:* Touched on briefly earlier, it is not enough to express expectations of position accomplishments. An entity also needs to work to help its volunteers develop their knowledge and skill sets so it is easier to succeed in meeting those objectives. This may include a formal start-of-term orientation, ongoing leadership resource sharing, quick exercises at leader meetings, or a full-on leadership retreat. In all methods an entity chooses to use, it should start from a mind-set of "If I was the volunteer, would this be what I need?" For example, an eighty-page leader handbook may serve as an excellent reference tool, but will it provide the "training" needed for true resource or skill development?

4. *Ongoing support:* Throughout the term of volunteer commitment there should be regular touch points at which either staff or more senior volunteers are checking in to make sure the component volunteers have what they need, are not running into problems, are still aligned, and are creating impact through their collaborative efforts.

5. *Recognition and evaluation:* Key to the volunteer experience is for the entity to recognize accomplishments and efforts. This can be done during the volunteer process as milestones are met or exceeded and should be done at the conclusion of a volunteer commitment. Recognition, whether private through a thank you message or public through a public acknowledgment or actual citation at an event is essential for a number of reasons. First, it reinforces for the volunteer that the time and energy he or she gave to the entity was noticed and appreciated. This in itself sets the stage for positive reflection on the work volunteers have done and how they would like to stay involved. Perhaps just as important as the impact on the volunteer is the impact on the community. Volunteer recognition inherently serves as volunteer modeling—showing other members how they can get involved, the importance of what they would want to do, and even someone they can speak to about the value of volunteering.

    Finally, on a regular basis an entity should evaluate the work of its volunteers, the roles they are playing, and whether that work and structure are aligned with the objectives of the entity as a whole. A volunteer position should exist only as long as the impact it is supposed to make is still an organizational need.

Global Considerations

As more associations develop international growth strategies, looking to enhance the professional audience that can partake in the value offered, the question of an international component structure is an important piece of the puzzle. "Going global" doesn't necessarily mean that an association suddenly is expanding to every corner of the world—researched focus on the areas with the greatest alignment to the organization's strengths and offerings can evidence a list of initial expansion regions. Once these are identified, analysis should be conducted to assess the needs of those regions, and how those needs are currently being met (if at all). Before establishing local geographic-based components, is there already a local association that is acting in the same fashion? If so, will the best-case scenario play out from the association establishing its own group in direct competition? Or will the ROI be maximized by forming an alliance with the local entity, supporting its efforts in return for branding, market placement, and expanded community? Since most components are volunteer led, does the organization have the local leader threshold to initiate and sustain a local community? And, of course, what are the logistical considerations, including any language or cultural barriers and local legal and fiscal confines?

Global components can be a powerful tool to establish brand recognition and new member or customer bases where the association is yet to be discovered. Yet if the components that are established are not on equal footing with those that are in closer proximity to the association's central member base, the results are often a feeling of disconnect and that the organization truly is not invested in the success of the community. When establishing these components, careful planning should be given to how they will actively be kept as part of the larger association community, with intentional communication, recognition, and in-person visitation when possible. Those associations that are able to establish local overseas offices can help mitigate this problem to some extent, but those options often demand a much higher fiscal return to justify their existence. In many cases, the key to the component feeling a strong part of the whole is an intentional relationship with its leadership. If the leaders of the component are kept in the loop, if they feel that they have a voice and a colleague back at the lead organization who will listen to their questions and concerns and in turn is working with them for success, those leaders will bring back that feeling of association investment.

Struggling Components

The path to component dissolution should be one that has multiple warning signals and intervention strategies along the way. Not all components will succeed. Some will be formed around a professional discipline that in itself evolves and is no longer relevant. Some will be formed around a location where there was a hub of professionals but, because of economic shifts, there are now few if any left. And, sadly, some will not succeed because of the combination of a decline in strong leadership, vibrant programming, and member participation.

An association should be clear in the warning signs to watch for, and know when enough signals have been triggered to raise a flag and take action. Here are ten warning signs to look for:

1. Declining number of members
2. Expenses exceed revenues
3. Breakdown of communications

4. Poorly designed meetings
5. Outdated or nonexistent strategic plan
6. Absence of supportable goals
7. Insufficient support from the lead association
8. Lack of accountability
9. Widespread apathy among members
10. Insufficient number of enthusiastic leaders[2]

Supportive steps that a lead association might take includes making coaching calls with local leaders, running a strategic planning or check-in meeting, outlining milestones that should be met on the path to recovery, and even in some cases making a financial investment to help the component get back on its feet.

When the component's path continues to decline, an association is obligated to review eventual endgame options to best serve the component membership and the mission it was tasked to achieve. In some cases, this may mean joining the component with another local or discipline-aligned group. It may mean the dissolution of the component. This is a difficult decision and process for the remaining component leadership, for those members who remain that may have belonged through the times of strength and vibrancy, and for the association as a whole as it closes the door on one of its segments. All efforts should be made to help the component make the transition in a respectful way, honoring its past. Communication should be clear on how remaining members can continue to be involved. There are also the legal and fiscal implications of folding a component, including disbursement of its assets and retention of previous tax filings. An association should have established standard operating procedures, though it is hoped rarely used, to make sure that all steps are fulfilled and the failed component is appropriately dissolved or merged.

A Hopeful Path Ahead

Components are a key to success on the future paths of associations. Within their volunteer and programming models, as well as with a focus on engendering community and the ability to speak "local" while making "global" impact, there are a number of strengths that associations can tap with the right intent and structure:

- *Global partnerships:* As associations look to better align their efforts with their core areas of strength and to partner on those areas where others could enhance their own offerings, alliances, partnerships, federations, and even mergers are all rising component models. These models may not follow the traditional "chapter" practices, but can lead to expanded customer and member bases with minimal additional staff and resource needs.

- *Niche organization partnerships:* On the domestic front, there are often organizations already in existence to address subdisciplines of a larger association. Instead of creating a separate internal community, more associations are looking for ways to partner with these already existing organizations. From simultaneous conferences to shared educational opportunities to the larger association potentially serving the database or back-office needs of the smaller, there are many paths that can create an integrated end-user experience for the member while still returning a positive bottom line.

- *Directed sources of knowledge:* Most components will have a major focus on creating professional development opportunities for their members. Whether these are in-person meetings or online webinars, they should be part of the overall knowledge-management strategy of the organization. Can they add to the expansive library of content the association offers so that global members could benefit from that "local" learning? If a stellar presenter is discovered, how can the component feed that teacher into the overall association pool for a conference session or regular education efforts? When an association evaluates the knowledge opportunities it creates for its members, the work of its components should be part of that consideration.

- *Leadership pipeline:* Volunteers who have had past leadership experience often bring more to the table when they serve at the lead-organization level. Components can serve as that training ground—as a leadership pipeline for the overall organization. When outstanding leaders rise to the top, the association should have intentional paths that shepherd them on to greater organizational opportunities.

- *Core piece of value:* As organizations continue to refine and redefine their value proposition, the role and vitality of components are key factors in the value delivered. The decision to belong is influenced by an organization being able to provide solutions, connections, and opportunities that enhance one's career, field, and professional life. This is the task that each component, in a targeted fashion, tries to accomplish. Including the component story in the association value narrative is an important message for professionals. Components play a unique role in speaking to current and prospective members by tangibly demonstrating pride in "who we are" rather than "what we do."

Membership is a relationship as much as, if not more than, a product. That relationship, the reason people and companies belong, is founded on being able to address core issues, identify professional-enhancement opportunities, and empower member voices through connection to the benefit of the individual and to shape the field. Components as communities, created around a factor of similarity, naturally fulfill the needs of the member relationship. The voice of each component as a unique community coupled with the lead association enhances the overall impact on its aligned field and in the lives of its individual professionals.

Notes

1. A full listing of affiliate agreement considerations can be found in L. Aplebaum and T. S. Mitchell (eds.), *Component Relations Handbook: A Guide to Successfully Managing and Motivating Chapters, Affiliates, and Other Member Groups*, 2nd ed. (Washington, DC: Association Management Press, 2012). Samples can be found in ASAE's Component Relations Collaborate group. Collaborate is ASAE's online private community. Access to the Component Relations group within Collaborate is free for all ASAE members.
2. Aplebaum and Mitchell, *Component Relations Handbook*, Chapter 12.

Resources

Mariner Management. *Component Structure and the Value Proposition*. Laurel, MD: Mariner Management & Marketing, 2006, available at http://www. marinermanagement.com/resources/white-paper/2006–01–01/component-structures-value-proposition.

E. W. Engel and P. Hoffman. *The Mission Driven Volunteer*. August 2013, available at http://getmespark.com/wp-content/uploads/MissionDriven-Vol.pdf.

The Authors

Lowell M. Aplebaum, CAE, is senior director of membership and professional development for the Society for Neuroscience. He served as chair of ASAE's Component Relations Council in 2013–2014. He is the co-executive editor of and a contributing author to the second edition of the *Component Relations Handbook.*

Sidebar author *Luis A. Rivera, MBA, CAE,* is the senior director, state management affairs division of the American Association of Nurse Anesthetists (AANA).

CHAPTER EIGHTEEN

MEMBERSHIP RECRUITMENT AND RETENTION

Jay L. Karen, CAE

Associations by their very nature are membership organizations, designed to serve and represent the interests and needs of a section of our society, such as a trade, profession, industry, hobby, cause, and so on. So it is often the case that "membership" is the hub of the organizational wheel, for example, the membership department (if there is one), membership staff, membership volunteers, membership programs, membership communications, and so on. Those who work in membership often feel acutely responsible for the success of the organization because so much is centered in membership. If membership numbers are good, it must mean the association is doing well; they must be doing the right things. If membership numbers are down, those who work in the hub of the wheel feel the weight of it. Strong recruitment and retention numbers are the responsibility of the membership professionals, right? Yes. But, ultimately, membership recruitment and retention results are greatly affected by the spokes, the tires, the pedals, the handlebar, and others. Just about everyone who works at the association—staff, volunteers, outside contractors—has an impact on the success of membership.

How would you answer this question: If your association's membership numbers showed consistent growth and strong retention numbers, would you say the association is successful? Are good membership numbers music to the ears of the CSE and the board of directors? The answer is obviously "yes" to both of those questions. Good membership numbers equal good membership dues income. There is no question that membership dues is a vital income stream to any association. In addition, other areas of the operation may rely upon strong membership numbers to be successful, such as sponsorship, advertising, events, advocacy, and more. Again, membership is the hub of the wheel.

The purpose that underpins an association is not to simply be a vessel that holds a group of members but rather to accomplish things—big things! "Membership" as a function and construct helps the association achieve those big things. When thinking about membership you need to ask yourself, "Is membership the ends or the means?" Within the walls of a membership department, having valued benefits and great numbers seems like it should be an end. But from the CSE position, selling and retaining memberships is really a vehicle by which an association accomplishes great things for the collective.

◆ ◆ ◆

Evolving Parameters

The association's bylaws should have clear definitions of the types, categories, and kinds of people, companies, or entities who are welcome behind the proverbial "member wall." You should be circumspect for opportunities to broaden (or narrow, as it may be) your definition of members. As industries and professions evolve and change, associations should be sure their membership definitions reflect that evolution.

◆ ◆ ◆

Serving, Leading, and Connecting

People join associations for all kinds of reasons, and the professionals directly responsible for membership and recruitment must do their best to determine motivating factors and provide corresponding services. In ASAE's *The Decision to Join*, we learn that people join associations as much to support a common good for their profession or industry as they do for the individual benefits that may be received.[1] This is incredibly important to remember as you develop programs and services, as well as in what and how you communicate to your membership and prospective members.

There are really two ways you can approach serving your membership base: asking your members what they want or need or anticipating the needs they don't know they yet have. The difference between the two could mean the difference between mediocrity and greatness from an accomplishment or member value standpoint. It was automobile inventor Henry Ford who said, "If I had asked people what they wanted, they would have said 'faster horses.'"

Most associations conduct periodic customer surveys, asking members what they want out of the association or what they think of the existing portfolio of services. The survey results become the mandate for future planning. Matching services to desired needs positions you as "responsive to the membership."

But what about being innovative or progressive in how you approach serving your members? Your members, like Americans in the early twentieth century when answering Henry Ford's question, don't know what they don't know. Association leadership should be doing their best to look around the corner to see what's happening in your members' lives and professions, and anticipate what they may need down the road. If you're able to do that successfully and be ready to meet those needs, your association will be seen as progressive and innovative, or maybe even clairvoyant!

Your retention efforts will be greatly helped if you are able to find ways to meaningfully connect with your members. Connection and value may be seen very differently by your members. If the primary purpose of joining your association by one person is to receive information and education to be more proficient at a job, that member may indeed be satisfied without feeling "connected" to the association. She may be perfectly content and feel there is great value received for her dues by receiving and reading your emails, magazine, journals, or social media posts. She may not need to feel connected. Another member may get more satisfaction out of contributing, being invited to do things and having his voice heard. He may not need the information or education as much. This distinction is similar to the difference between someone who is an active participant in an online discussion group and one who "lurks" in the forum.

In addition, the need for connection may change over time. For example, a member, early in her career, may want to be overloaded with information, but ten years down the road may crave connection with her colleagues and peers more than anything. The connection desire may also be driven by a person's location. Someone who doesn't have the opportunity to network locally with industry peers may seek connection through your association.

Connection through volunteerism can be very meaningful. Members who volunteer often receive great satisfaction and fulfillment knowing they are shaping the organization in significant ways. Involvement can weave a strong fabric of relationships with other members and build loyalty to your association. Plus, your volunteers are more likely to refer others to your organization. A solid volunteer program is a double bonus for both recruitment and retention!

If you have multiple generations in your existing or prospective membership, you will need to think about diverse methods of connecting people to each other and with the association. The most traditional form of connection is when your members see each other, face to face, at events, such as an annual convention. A section of your members might not even be able to imagine your association existing without a face-to-face event like this, while other members may feel perfectly connected through a mobile device that fits in their pockets.

Either way, it's important to establish and maintain meaningful connections with as many members as possible.

Recruitment

Recruitment is, in association lingo, synonymous with "sales and marketing." Membership staff may coordinate recruitment tactics and ensure that they are executed, but your sales and marketing efforts should be a shared responsibility among all staff or volunteers who come into contact with prospective members.

The old saying that "you should fish where the fish are" holds true with membership recruitment, and there are usually two big ponds full of fish: your database of former members and your database of prospective members. Too many associations neglect their list of former members, thinking they left for a reason and that attempts to get them back may be futile. You may or may not know the reason they left, but membership staff should engage recruitment strategies to get them back. Pick up the phone and call them. Send them a hand-written letter or an email with an invitation to come back. Utilize your happy members to reach out to former and prospective members. Consider offering "come back to us" specials for your former members.

Looking toward prospective members, be sure your database is as clean and accurate as possible. This may mean engaging people to help build and scour the database, so that your marketing efforts are fruitful. Marketing and sales is where you can experiment with all kinds of tactics—everything from time-limited price promotions to storytelling, and partnerships to phone calling. You will need to employ messaging and content strategies that make your pitch very compelling. How compelling is the subject line in your email? Do your membership ads, email content, or social media postings look simple and meaningful to your audience? Above all else, *ask* them to join! You'll get 0 percent of the people you don't ask to join. Be sure every recruitment tactic has a bold and clear message to take action and join.

Here is a sampling of the kinds of things any association could be doing to attract potential members and seal the deal:

- Many associations allow nonmembers to subscribe to free daily or weekly email newsletters, which provide some meaningful content. By doing this, you're staying on their radars and enticing them (hopefully) to buy the full meal by giving them an appetizer.
- Similarly, some associations send complimentary issues of their print or digital magazines to prospective members. Advertisers love the broader audience, and prospective members get a taste of the association.
- Attend conferences and events at which prospective members will also be in attendance. Exploit opportunities to promote your association, but also seek to provide valuable information and content to demonstrate your value. Getting out on the road demonstrates your commitment to your profession or industry.
- Partner with other organizations or companies who have the audience you want. Execute joint promotions or even dual memberships.
- Split test your recruitment ideas. Instead of sending the same direct mail piece to five thousand prospects, print two or three different versions and see which resulted in the best return. And maybe send those mail pieces to five hundred prospects first, before investing in the five thousand. Sampling and testing can save the association a great deal of money, as well as help ensure the best return on investment.

Be aware that providing complimentary information and education as a way to entice membership—known as the "freemium" model of membership—may also be the very reason some people never pay membership dues. If you give them enough information to satisfy their needs, they may see no reason to pay dues. Here is where developing a content strategy would be useful.

Consider giving them just enough to whet their appetite, but no more. And then employ tactics to move them up the engagement ladder. Consider allowing free access to your valuable information for a limited amount of time or a limited number of articles, and then require them to join if they desire more. Have volunteer opportunities for your "free" members, with the plan in mind to build greater loyalty and interest. Also consider requiring your free members to respond to periodic surveys (that glean valuable information for your strategies and goals) in order to continue receiving free benefits.

Measuring success in recruitment can be pretty simple: did you bring in more members this year than last year (or it can be analyzed by week, month, quarter, or so on)? It is helpful to measure and break down your recruitment results by membership categories or other qualifiers. The more scientific you can get with analyzing your data, the more insights and opportunities you might uncover.

Retention

Membership retention involves systems, strategy, and tactics. Strong membership retention is possible and will happen if the association's strategic objectives and the delivery of benefits and services are in alignment. The CSE must provide leadership to ensure consistency, cooperation, and understanding of how the association's activities affect retention.

Retention is a year-round effort, but where the rubber hits the road is at renewal time. Association professionals must ensure that members hit the "Renew Now" button in their emails or on the website. Ultimately, you need to take action and have systems that make it easy and compelling for members to pay their renewal fees. Here are some examples of systems and tactics you may use to keep members under the tent:

- In your renewal appeals, be sure you are able to tell a compelling story of exactly what the association has accomplished, what you are working hard on, and what your goals and vision are. The more you can personalize this to the specific member, the better; for example, "John, you've told us that advocacy is the most important thing we do. You should know that we have accomplished XYZ this year. In addition, we are in communication right now with members of Congress about ABC...."
- Offer automatic billing on members' credit cards either as a payment plan option or to be charged at the anniversary renewal date. This kind of "set and forget" payment approach may be something your most satisfied members are willing to do. (This doesn't mean you shouldn't reach out and personally thank them for their renewal, simply because they said to just charge their Visa each year!)

- Get staff and volunteer members to email or call other members who are up for renewal or who are at risk of not renewing. Be strategic about this and get the right members to reach out to peers with whom they have something in common. Make this personal, rather than the "Dear (Enter First Name Here)" shotgun approach. A member will first like to hear something such as, "Hey Sarah! How are things in St. Louis? We understand things in your market have been difficult this year. Tell me about what's happening…" Establish connection before you make your appeal to renew.

In *The Art of Membership,* by Sheri Jacobs, we are told that members want their associations to be problem solvers.[2] Your retention results will be commensurate with your ability to show members how you are solving problems for them personally, as well as for the group to which they belong. Don't assume the members up for renewal know what problems you have solved or are solving—tell them.

Membership Models

With the advent of the Internet and the new "knowledge economy," people have unprecedented access to information and education, which was for decades the bailiwick of the association. Associations have competition in the twenty-first century that did not exist in the twentieth century. This has caused associations to rethink how they serve members and how they structure their membership offerings. Correspondingly, members have been rethinking the value proposition of associations as they frequent the Internet search engines to find the information and education they desire. The search engines don't always lead them to the doorstep of an association!

Some may say these changes have turned "members" into "customers" who focus more on return on investment (ROI) than ever before. Others say that gone are the days when people felt it was their civic duty to join organizations. Even though *The Decision to Join* indicates that people join associations as much or more for the common good than for personal benefit, association executives have been moved to make changes. Many associations have been disrupting the old membership model of everyone paying the same price to join and get the same benefits. They've been experimenting and moving to new ways of engaging members, including segmenting, unbundling, tiered pricing, and even "freemium" models of membership (offering free benefits to anyone in their industry or profession as a way to bait and hook them).

Your model of membership is nothing more than how you package access to and price your benefits and services. The most traditional membership model is having members pay dues for a complete package of benefits—an all-inclusive approach. You may charge additional fees for attendance to events and webinars or for supplementary publications. But the core model is one price for your core members. The "unbundled" membership model is more of an a la carte setup. Members may pay a base set of dues—or nothing—and only pay for the benefits they consume. The advantage of this may be that members get as much—or as little—as they desire out of an association, rather than an all or nothing requirement.

To gauge whether or not your membership model is the most effective one for your association, be sure to engage both members and nonmembers in any focus group or reviews of the model. Generally, your members believe the membership model is just fine. It's your nonmembers who may have an issue with how you sell access to and price your benefits; their input may be more valuable than the chorus who already bought in. Following are some key questions the CSE might ask in a review of your membership model:

- Given the typical resources of our members (and nonmembers), the benefits we tout, and what our competition may offer, are we priced fairly?
- Are there opportunities to base pricing and access on different variables, such as benefits received, when someone is in the career path, size, or scope of organization, payment methods, or engagement levels?
- What new ways can you dream up for experimenting with the membership model?

Defining and Measuring Success

People vote with their wallets. If the association is doing the right things, people will join and renew. But there are many hairs to be split once you start analyzing recruitment and retention numbers. Remember that membership is a construct and function that supports the larger goals of the organization. Good membership numbers in and of themselves do not mean the organization is successful. Membership numbers are only one of many instruments on a dashboard that are critical to organizational health.

What Constitutes Good Membership Numbers?

Recruiting may be strong, but as new members are coming in the front door, are current members slipping out the backdoor? Good membership numbers require both solid recruitment *and* retention to build the breadth and depth of your member base.

Another key metric comes from segmentation of your membership by demographic, such as age range, gender, line function, ethnicity, member category, and so on. Your overall membership may reflect an 80 percent market penetration, but when you segment by age demographic, you discover you have 95 percent of the over-fifty-five market, 75 percent of forty- to fifty-year-olds, and only 30 percent of the twenty to forty market. Analyzing market penetration through segmentation will inform where you need to focus recruitment efforts. Analyzing retention rates by demographic informs strategic retention efforts.

Segmentation is also very helpful in strategically targeting recruitment efforts. If you were to focus on a specific category of member, what demographic offers you the most revenue potential (dues plus fees)? Strategic membership marketing has the power to optimize your revenue production.

As CSE, think strategically about what you need from membership efforts. Revenue production? Market penetration (to be the voice of the industry)? Strength in certain geographic areas (for legislative impact)? Once you define your desired outcomes, ensure that a strategic marketing plan is developed and implemented with results monitored.

◆ ◆ ◆

A rudimentary way to measure membership success is simply by looking at your membership numbers and the trajectory of your growth or market penetration. In other words, if you have two thousand members at the beginning of the year and had a retention rate of 80 percent the prior year, and end the current year with twenty-two hundred members and an 82 percent retention rate, you must be doing well! Or, let's say there are 16,000 potential companies in your market that are eligible for membership (let's use golf courses as an example). At the beginning of the year, if you count 4,400 of those golf courses as members of the association, your market penetration is 27.5 percent. If by the end of a one-year membership cycle you count only 4,300, should you be disappointed? It depends. If the total number of courses in the market remained at 16,000, you might be a little deflated. But what if the number of courses eligible was only 15,500 (due to business closures)? Then in actuality, your market penetration (27.7 percent) is slightly better in the most recent year.

Be mindful of the fact that market conditions out of the association's control, as well as actions like industry mergers or acquisitions, may have an impact on the market penetration numbers. Beyond market penetration, you can monitor dues income as a sign of success. After all, associations need that revenue, so you can deploy resources to get the work done. It doesn't necessarily help to have stronger market penetration but also see a decline in dues income. Success in membership can be defined as membership's financial contribution to the overall enterprise, which is a vital way to ensure the work of the organization's strategic plan can be done.

Another way to measure membership success is to look at the lifetime value of your members. You could do this for all members or segments of your membership. The lifetime value of a member is the average financial impact a member has on the association. If you can measure the average tenure of a member (say, seven years is typical) and then determine what that average member pays per year in membership dues ($400 per year), annual conference fee ($750), and other nondues programs ($75), then you can calculate the lifetime value. In this example, the average lifetime value of the average member is $8,575 ($1125/year times 7 years). That number is interesting to glean, especially when considering the budget and planning for membership recruitment and retention activities. Retention efforts might focus on increasing that lifetime value number—either in the annual spend with the association or the average tenure to eight or nine years, or both.

◆ ◆ ◆

Other Strategic Membership Considerations

Whose Feedback Is Most Important?

Association professionals typically are obsessed with feedback and input. Hearing from your members can validate what you are doing, or instruct you on what you should be doing. Too often, though, membership may look to your most involved volunteers to give you this feedback. This would be akin to the management of the Chicago White Sox asking only their season ticketholders if they are satisfied with the organization. Don't let your association's board be the voice of your members when it comes to satisfaction levels. The most involved volunteers are the first people to say, "I don't understand why more people aren't members!" Voila! That phrase alone should tell you that these folks are not the best to give you the feedback you need. Find ways to dive into the brains of former members, those who have never been members, and the least engaged of your members.

All Things to All People?

Association professionals tend to be people-pleasers. We want to make our members and supporters happy. We don't like using the word *no* in any fashion. Who likes saying "no" to members when they need help? Because of our propensity to want to please everyone around us, we often allow "mission creep" to occur in our organizations. Mission creep is when we start adding stuff to our plates that are outside the scope of our core objectives. The most ardent people-pleasers have the unique talent of being able to justify working on any request a member throws their way. A slippery slope, indeed! What results is the inability to get the "real" work done.

Consider Figure 18.1 and assess your association's current approach to member service.

It is futile to try to be all things to your members. Rather, focus on a select few objectives and priorities that deliver member value and be the best you can be at those. If it is well known that your association is incredibly effective and meaningful with only the most important issues facing your industry, and your communications make it clear that this is all you do, the members and industry can be conditioned to realize this and not make erroneous requests of you.

Collecting and Using the Right Data

Every association—large and small—is collecting data on its members. It might be as minimalist as contact information and when the person paid his or her dues, to as complex as tracking demographics, purchase history, communications received by the person, conversation notes from phone calls with the member, volunteer history, speaking history, data on his or her business, certifications, and the list could go on and on. Knowing your members is incredibly important. Being able to slice and dice

FIGURE 18.1. WHAT IS YOUR ASSOCIATION TRYING TO BE?

Some things to all people	All things to all people
Some things to some people	All things to some people

your membership data and take a targeted approach to serving and engaging your members is quite an advantage over seeing your membership data as one amorphous blob of information. Tracking information and observing trends and changes in that data over time may be important to you or outside interests, such as the media.

If you are to keep track of dozens of bits of information on your members, be sure to think about how you plan to use that information before you develop all those custom fields in your database. One person in your office may argue it is critical to know the gender of each of your members, and it may indeed be important. But more important is getting a good answer to the questions—Why do we need to track that information, and what do we plan to do with it? Mentioned above are the media. Trade or consumer media may be interested in knowing whether more women are practicing the profession you represent today than ten years ago, and they may go to you as the source of that information. A great deal of time and energy can go into data collection and maintenance. Be sure to have a strategy and plan for using the data to support your membership recruitment and retention efforts.

Considering All Membership Types

Many associations have multiple membership types or categories, but they may have a "primary" member type. Take the Professional Association of Innkeepers International as an example. The "core" member may be the innkeeper—the person or people who own bed and breakfasts and inns. There are also membership categories for aspiring innkeepers and vendors who sell goods and services to innkeepers. The name of the association is not the "Association for Aspiring Innkeepers," so it may be easy to see why aspiring innkeepers could feel less important to PAII than the innkeepers. To combat this in your association, be sure that association staff offer the best possible experience for all membership categories, even if the name of the association shines the spotlight on one category. Involve all member types in volunteer opportunities. Construct councils or committees around membership types, if that makes sense for you. Mention all membership types in your communications. Employ different recruitment and retention strategies by membership type. Make sure your website (in both design and content) has a place or home for each member or prospective member type. Consider recognizing members by category or type through an awards program. The bottom line is that everyone who pays dues to an association wants to feel as important and welcome as any other member.

◆ ◆ ◆

Notes

1. J. G. Dalton, M. Dignam, the American Society of Association Executives, and the Center for Association Leadership, *The Decision to Join: How Individuals Determine Value and Why They Choose to Belong* (Washington, DC: ASAE Association Management Press, 2007).

2. S. Jacobs, *The Art of Membership: How to Attract, Retain and Cement Member Loyalty* (San Francisco: Jossey-Bass, 2014).

Resource

Jacobs, S., Assante, C., and the American Society of Association Executives. *Membership Essentials: Recruitment, Retention, Roles, Responsibilities and Resources.* Washington, DC: ASAE Association Management Press, 2008.

The Author

Jay L. Karen, CAE, is the chief executive officer of Select Registry. He was also the director of membership for the National Golf Course Owners Association and has served ASAE on both the Membership and Executive Management Section Councils.

CHAPTER NINETEEEN

STANDARD SETTING

Dorothy I. Mitstifer, PhD

Standard setting is a huge field of practice in the United States, and it opens doors for global enterprise. Standards are all around us. They include codes of ethics, definitions of practice and management in a particular field, requirements for sporting equipment, technical standards for manufactured goods, and criteria for admission into some exclusive organizations. Standards are the reason we can buy a light bulb and it fits a "standard socket." Standards level the playing field, eliminating proprietary approaches for any product that has to work with another product.

Standard setting is important in determining how well performance requirements are met. Standards are guideposts for quality. This chapter will define standards and discuss the foundation and building blocks of standards (rationale, values, content, and assessment) before describing the practice of standard setting. Beyond the standards themselves, there are often additional steps of developing assessment tools, designing implementation activities, promoting the standards, and enhancing professional development to enhance performance or professionalism to meet the standards. These follow-through steps often become stumbling blocks to full dissemination. Commitment to the full rollout of standards is essential to the practice of standard setting.

Definition and Rationale for Standards

According to the Council for Advancement of Standards in Higher Education (CAS), a *standard* is an example of something measured; a principle of propriety, honesty, and integrity; a level of quality of excellence. Standards guide practice and preparation for specific roles as well as guide mastery; they become the basis for the way individuals are mentored, choose personal and professional development, and are evaluated. Standards promote a culture of professionalism. Standard setting is a systematic process by which leadership and members improve organizational effectiveness in the accomplishment of mission and goals.

According to the American National Standards Institute (ANSI), a standard is a document, established by consensus, that provides rules, guidelines, or characteristics for activities or their results. Standards play an important role in everyday life. They may establish size or shape or capacity of a product, process, or system. They can specify performance of products or personnel. They also can define terms so that there is no misunderstanding among those using the standard.

The process of standard setting identifies the specific tasks that must be performed to meet a desired level of performance. In this way, standard setting moves away from the command-and-control emphasis in organizations toward a facilitation model of leadership.

Certification for individuals and accreditation for organizations are based on standards. The CAE competencies and ASAE's Code of Ethics are examples of standards for professionalism in the association environment. These two approaches were created "to elevate professional standards, enhance individual performance, and designate association professionals who demonstrate the knowledge essential to the practice of association management... It helps drive professional self-confidence, opens doors, creates connections, and offers widespread value and recognition for certificants."[1]

◆ ◆ ◆

Standard-Setting Organizations

There are many organizations that engage in standard development. Following are some of the leaders in the field:

The American National Standards Institute (ANSI) has served as coordinator of the U.S. private sector voluntary standardization system since 1916. Its mission is to enhance both the global competitiveness of U.S. business and the U.S.

quality of life by promoting and facilitating voluntary consensus standards and conformity assessment systems and safeguarding their integrity. Through its members, staff, constituents, partners, and advocates, ANSI responds directly to the standardization and conformity assessment interests and needs of consumers, government, companies, and organizations.

The International Standards Organization (ISO) ensures that products and services are safe, reliable, and of good quality. For businesses, ISO standards are strategic tools that reduce costs by minimizing waste and errors and increasing productivity. They help companies to access new markets, level the playing field for developing countries, and facilitate free and fair global trade.

The National Information Standards Organization (NISO) is where content publishers, libraries, and software developers turn for information on industry standards that allow them to work together. Through NISO, all of these communities are able to collaborate on mutually accepted standards—solutions that enhance their operations today and form a foundation for the future.

Founded in 1979, the Council for the Advancement of Standards in Higher Education (CAS) is the preeminent force for promoting standards in student affairs, student services, and student-development programs. CAS creates and delivers dynamic, credible standards, guidelines, and self-assessment guides that are designed to lead to a host of quality programs and services. CAS aims to foster and enhance student learning, development, and achievement.

Values Underlie Standards

Standard setting is often driven from a sense of ethics, a philosophy of excellence or quality, or a desire for standardization.

As an example drawn from CAS documents, here are some guiding principles for standard setting that could contribute to the quality of association management. *You might note that they are grounded in theoretical models of human development, educational theory, and organization management.*

Health engendering environment: Associations benefit from an environment that features adequate facilities, human resources, and fiscal support to create positive influence on the development of association personnel. This reinforces the notion that standards require an effective environment conducive to learning and development.

Diversity and multiculturism: This value affirms the importance of diversity and multiculturism in creating a culture that offers justice and respect for differences. Multicultural awareness and positive regard for differences is essential to the development and maintenance of a health-engendering environment.

Strong leadership and management: Association success is dependent upon capable and experienced personnel who exhibit knowledge and credibility. The association and its programs and services must be based on a clearly defined mission and purposes that are published and well understood. Defined duties and job responsibilities and policies and procedures to guide quality practice contribute to association success and document outcome expectations.

Ethical practice: Fundamental ethical expectations ensure fair and equitable practice and guide the behavior of association personnel and members to enhance the overall integrity of the association and its programs. A code of ethics provides guidance for establishing and maintaining an appropriate level of moral and ethical behavior.

Self-regulation toward quality: Standards to guide practice are essential to the evolution of associations and must be developed and promulgated by and for those working in that arena. Furthermore, a cycle of review and refinement should be established so that the standards represent currency of practice. New challenges require practices to shift and evolve to reflect change.

Statutory and regulatory requirements: To protect the association's reputation, assets, intellectual property, and trademarks, as well as to comply with antitrust laws, standards may be necessary to guide policies and procedures for compliance with applicable laws.

Government-Mandated or Voluntary Standards?

The wisdom of self-regulation should always prevail. However, sometimes industries are not able to work together cooperatively or effectively to address issues revolving around unethical practices, such as promises of service (bait and switch), false advertising, and misleading claims. When the public complains, the government often steps in and threatens to mandate standards to protect the public good. It is always more desirable for the industry to regulate itself rather than respond to governmental mandates. When the industry regulates itself, the standards are usually less stringent than governmental mandates.

Content of *Professional* Standards

Professional standards provide a comprehensive and valid set of criteria for judging practice. They are written to apply to a specific role or program and represent quality practices that can be reasonably achieved and measured. Defining quality is the first hurdle to overcome in establishing a convincing link between standards (input) and quality (output).[2]

Theoretical principles: A research orientation to developing content ensures that new practices and developments are identified. Independent, external advisors are valuable in providing insights, experience, and ideas to improve the quality of standards and the standard-setting process. Thus the content of standards should represent the literature and experience of insiders and outsiders.

Measurable performance statements: Construction of standards includes four steps:

1. Identifying and clarifying essential functions
2. Organizing essential functions into "actions" and "objects of actions"
3. Answering the right question of how you can tell the essential function has been performed properly
4. Reviewing job standards to ensure they are measurable

No amount of learning about constructing standards can replace the actual work of writing, rewriting, and examining the standards in light of the four steps described here.

◆ ◆ ◆

Examples of Categories for Professional Standards

Sets of standards are organized to meet the needs of the organization, profession, or industry. The Council for the Advancement of Standards in Higher Education uses the categories of (1) mission; (2) program; (3) organization and leadership; (4) human resources; (5) ethics; (6) law, policy, and governance; (7) diversity, equity, and access; (8) institutional and external relations; (9), financial resources; (10) technology; (11) facilities and equipment; and (12) assessment and evaluation. These standards are intended to raise performance, professionalism, and quality in functions and departments in the higher education community.

CAE uses the domains of (1) organizational management; (2) leadership; (3) administration; (4) knowledge management and research; (5) governance and structure; (6) public policy, government relations, and coalition building; (7) membership development; (8) programs, products, and services; and (9) marketing, public relations, and communications.

A new self-assessment model developed by the Michigan Society of Association Executives (MSAE) determined that "the demands on association leaders to maintain relevance require deeper and broader knowledge, more effective relationships, and clear perspectives." These three dimensions describe the multifaceted association leader. The MSAE model was further organized to develop capacities and mastery in three facets: personal awareness, association knowledge, and mastery in the association's industry.

◆ ◆ ◆

Process for Development of Standards

Prior to pursuing a development process, it is important to obtain consensus about the need for and interest of members in developing (or revising) standards. Substantial organizational commitment is required for standard setting, so the source of the initiative to set standards should be considered and evaluated:

- What is the need to clarify expectations?
- Is there a need for a cultural change toward consciousness of quality?
- Is there a concern for consistency in hiring and evaluating?
- Is there interest in shaping the future?

It should be noted that some standards have an impact on product design. This type of standard setting impedes proprietary products and marketplace choice, which can cause anti-trust liability if the standard setting process isn't inclusive to non-members. Is the association willing to accept this risk?

The development of standards should be a broad-based and inclusive process, encompassing internal and external association members, leaders, and experts. Although the internal leaders direct the process, the insights of other internal and external stakeholders supply important information to strengthen the standards. Standards, to be of real and lasting value, must be developed by people who function in the setting in which they are intended for use.

Selection of task force: A development task force of three to five should represent various stakeholders in the profession or industry so that a variety of experience and skills can be offered in the standard-development process. The credibility of the product may very well depend upon the quality and reputation of task force members, so selection of the task force is a critical decision. Because this commitment often takes on a life of its own, individuals who accept the responsibility should know that the time commitment might be more than expected.

Charge to the task force: Although not mandatory, a discussion paper serves as background for the charge to the task force by defining the history of standards in the association, sharing previous standards, documenting outcomes, sharing research findings, explaining the present need, and generally discussing the rationale for the present charge. The charge should establish a comprehensive overview of expectations and preliminary views of the authorizing body, propose possible approaches for process (including environmental scanning), set a sample timeline, identify chair and task force members, and describe authorization of the charge. In setting the agenda for development of standards, the task force should consider the relevance and reliability of information provided, whether other sources are available, and resource constraints.

Development of standards: The first step in the development of standards is to conduct an environmental scan to search for available research and literature to provide resources for the task force.

The second step is to define what quality looks like in terms of characteristics or behaviors exhibited or outcomes produced. It should be expected that input in the beginning of the development process will be messy; extraneous information will be included with the nuggets of sound elements. The danger is that important notions will be excluded if brainstorming and small-group work are restricted during the early developmental phase. Elements can be refined, combined, and structured at later stages of the process.

It is important to acknowledge that standards have certain qualities. They must be

- As explicit and precise as possible
- Justifiable and logically sound
- Acceptable to the stakeholders
- Validated
- Practicable
- Written in plain language

That's a big order!

After a first draft is developed, the task force should solicit an internal stakeholder review. When careful review and refinement has been conducted after receiving feedback, the task force should solicit external review by a variety of experts or leaders in the field. The second draft by the task force will take advantage of the further feedback and be ready for the next stage in standard setting.

Checking your standards: With rigorous internal scrutiny, plus internal and external consultation, the standards are ready for one last check against these questions: Are they realistic? Are the standards specific? Are the standards based on measurable data, observation, or verifiable information? Are the standards consistent with organizational goals? Are the standards challenging? Are the standards clear and understandable? Are the standards dynamic? If the answer is *yes* on these criteria, the standards are ready to be submitted for the approval process.

Approval process: The authorizing authority for the standard development task force has the responsibility of approving standards. Because the task force has yet another responsibility of developing the assessment instrument that may require financial resources for implementation, a request for approval of a budget for that purpose should be included with the submission of the standards.

Development of assessment instrument: Assessment tools should be designed in accordance with the competencies and the evidence criteria necessary to judge quality. The more aligned the instrument is to the objectives for assessment, the more direct the inferences to effectiveness. When alignment is poor, the results of assessment provide weak or limited information about effectiveness. Assessment outcomes should provide information for comparison with a standard, for monitoring of processes, and for development of a feedback loop. (See "More on Assessment Choices" further on.)

Pilot testing: A pilot test is a method that is used to test the design of an instrument before carrying out the implementation plan. This process helps a task force find the difficulties in using the instrument or understanding the language of the standard or the descriptive statements of levels of performance. Using data from the pilot test, refinement of the standards and assessment instrument can proceed. This is the last step in standard setting. The task force and the authorizing body should consider copyrighting the standards and assessment instrument to protect the intellectual property.

Implementation: The development of a systematic approach to implementation is important to the success of the standards, as well as a worthy endeavor to recognize the tremendous contributions of volunteers in the standard-setting process. After completion of the task force responsibility, the authorizing body then has the obligation to promote and shepherd the use of standards to produce the desired outcomes regarding ethical practice, quality performance, and professionalism.

Analysis and refinement: The cycle of continuous improvement and review continues through research and collection of data to analyze and refine standards. At some point, perhaps on a cycle of seven to ten years, a new task force should be assigned to review and refine the standards to meet the needs of the future. Standard setting is never done!

More on Assessment Choices

"Assessment is, at its core, as much a mind-set as it is a practice. It begins in curiosity and a desire to know that our hard work is yielding the results we intend."[3] *Professional* standards of practice provide content for assessment instruments to measure level of mastery, including knowledge, skills, values, perceptions, and interactive capacities. The main focus of assessment is on learning rather than on accountability.

There are other standards, however, that are designed to be "enforceable" standards. Particularly in the health care field, peer review committees adjudicate patient complaints against codified professional standards. Being found in gross negligence of a violation of a professional standard could result in the withdrawal of one's license to practice. Enforceable standards inherently carry much more liability exposure for due process and a fair hearing.

Assessment Tools

The choices of assessment instruments for standards include checklists, rating scales, and rubrics.

Checklists: Checklists usually use yes–no or complete–not complete responses, and they provide structure for respondents. Checklists are often used for quality inspections and accreditation processes.

Rating scales: A rating scale includes standards and degrees of performance and is a simple format for making judgments. The scales typically include terms that have point values or descriptive words, for example, exemplary (5–4), satisfactory (3–2), needs improvement (1–0).

The disadvantage of rating scales is that rating is subjective. Please note Table 19.1 as an example of a rating scale.

Rubrics: Rubrics are an explicit set of criteria used for assessing performance against a predetermined set of criteria.[4] This assessment instrument offers a more nuanced assessment and increased validity because the rubric includes descriptive statements. The component parts of rubrics include the standard and explanation of three or more levels of performance. See Table 19.2 as an example of rubrics.

TABLE 19.1. SAMPLE RATING SCALE. CAS SELF-ASSESSMENT GUIDE (SAG)—ALCOHOL AND OTHER DRUGS PROGRAMS STANDARD: INSTITUTIONAL & EXTERNAL RELATIONS.

ND Does Not Apply	0 Insufficient Evidence/Unable to Rate	1 Does Not Meet	2 Partly Meets	3 Meets	4 Exceeds	5 Exemplary

Criterion Measures	Rating
8.1 The Alcohol and Other Drugs Program (AODP) reaches out to internal and external populations to	
8.1.1 establish, maintain, and promote understanding and effective relations with those that have a significant interest in or potential effect on the students or other constituents served by the programs and services	
8.1.2 garner support and resources for programs and services as defined by the mission statement	
8.1.3 disseminate information about the programs and services	
8.1.4 collaborate, where appropriate, to assist in offering or improving programs and services to meet the needs of students and other constituents and to achieve program and student outcomes	
8.1.5 engage diverse individuals, groups, communities, and organizations to enrich the educational environment and experiences of students and other constituents	
8.2 The AODP has procedures and guidelines consistent with institutional policy to	
8.2.1 communicate with the media	
8.2.2 contract with external organizations for delivery of programs and services	
8.2.3 cultivate, solicit, and manage gifts	
8.2.4 apply to and manage funds from grants	
8.3 The AODP gathers and disseminates information to the campus community on ATOD problems, risk-reduction strategies, resources, and related topics	
8.4 The AODP maintains effective working relationships with campus offices and community groups and agencies to promote a healthy environment in which the use or abuse of ATOD does not interfere with learning, performance, or social aspects of college life	

TABLE 19.2. SAMPLE RUBRICS. ASSOCIATION/ORGANIZATION KNOWLEDGE CAPACITY (MSAE).

Perspectives Dimension Standards	5–4 Exemplary	3–2 Satisfactory	1–0 Needs Development	Score
Mission	Examines the role of the association in society	Understands the role of the association in society	Lacks perspective on the role of the association in society	
Strategic Plan	Analyzes the alignment of the strategic plan to the association position in the community	Understands the role of the association strategic plan in the community	Does not understand the value of strategic plans	
Members	Examines member participation in the association	Understands the role of members in the association	Lacks perspective on the role of members in the association	
Strategic Partnerships	Examines the association relationships with a variety of external groups and people	Understands how others can influence the association	Lacks focus on the value of external groups	
Board of Directors	Analyzes the effectiveness of the roles of the volunteer board and committees	Understands the value of an effective board and key volunteer leaders	Views relations with the board as extra work	
Staff	Examines the role of staff in participatory leadership	Understands staff role in leadership	Believes staff members should be told what and how to do their work	
Individual	Analyzes servant leadership in the association	Understands the role of servant leadership	Lacks understanding of the role of each individual in governance of the association	

Source: Copyright © 2013. Michigan Society of Association Executives. Reprinted with permission. No part of the MSAE Association/Organization Knowledge Capacity Standard may be reproduced or copied in any form, by any means, without written permission of the Michigan Society of Association Executives.

About Self-Assessment Rubrics

A self-assessment instrument supplies data for the development of a plan for professional growth. One of the values of self-assessment is the empowerment of an individual to use those findings to intentionally choose direction for professional development, ultimately becoming the master of one's own growth. Associations can support professional development by gathering self-assessment data to inform educational programming and construct pathways to engage individuals in their ongoing professional development journeys.

Summary

Associations are generally in the business of leveling the playing field and raising the bar of practice, performance, and professionalism. To help associations consider their future agendas for standard setting, association members and staff could be asked to identify, review, and raise issues that might warrant attention through standard setting. The organizational framework and governance may become potential items in light of comments from members and other interested parties. In any profession, it is important for practitioners to understand the standards of good practice. To practice effectively, they must know what quality looks like.[5] This is important not only so the public knows what to expect but so the professionals themselves can use widely accepted and well-informed benchmarks to assess whether they are doing good work.[6]

Notes

1. ASAE. (2014). Certified Association Executive Program. 2014. Available at http://www.asaecenter.org/YourCareer/contentcae.cfm?ItemNumber=16097&navItemNumber=14985.
2. J. Arminio and D. Creamer, *Promoting Quality in Higher Education: The Council for the Advancement of Standards (CAS) Celebrates 25 Years* (Washington, DC: NASPA Leadership Exchange, 2007), pp. 18–21.
3. L. A. Dean, "Using the CAS Standards in Assessment Projects," in E. J. Whitt (series ed.) and J. H. Schuh (ed.), *Selected Contemporary*

Assessment Issues, New Directions for Student Services, no. 142 (San Francisco: Jossey-Bass, 2013).

4. R. Robbins, *Developing a Rubric as Part of an Overall Assessment Program for Academic Advising* (Manhattan, KS: NACADA, 2013).

5. B. Jacoby and L. A. Dean, "What Does 'Quality' Look Like? Why Higher Education Should Care About Standards for Student Programs and Services," *About Campus* 15, no. 3 (2010): 29–32.

6. L. A. Dean and G. M. Jones, "The Council for the Advancement of Standards in Higher Education and the Role of Standards in Professional Practice, in S. Freeman Jr., L. S. Hagedorn, L. F. Goodchild, and D. A. Wright (eds.), *Advancing Higher Education as a Field of Study: In Quest of Doctoral Degree Guidelines—Commemorating 120 Years of Excellence* (Sterling, VA: Stylus, 2014) pp. 93–109.

Resources

CAS. *Protocol for Developing New CAS Standards and Guidelines.* n.d. Available at http://cas.wiki-neon.adaptavist.com/display/DirectorsReview/PROTOCOL+for+DEVELOPING+NEW++CAS+STANDARDS+and+GUIDELINES.

Lusthaus, C., and others. *Organizational Assessment: A Framework for Improving Performance.* Washington, DC: International Development Research Centre/Inter-American Development Bank, 2002.

The Author

Dorothy I. Mitstifer, PhD, is executive director of Kappa Omicron Nu and the Association of College Honor Societies, East Lansing, Michigan, and served as editor of the *CAS Professional Standards for Higher Education* publication. Appreciation is extended to Laura Dean and Gavin Henning for serving as reviewers.

CHAPTER TWENTY

LEGAL ISSUES IN ASSOCIATION STANDARD SETTING, CERTIFICATION AND ACCREDITATION PROGRAMS, AND CODES OF ETHICS

Jeffrey S. Tenenbaum, Esq., and Beth A. Caseman, Esq.

Association standard-setting programs, certification and accreditation activities, and member codes of ethics provide valuable benefits, not only to associations and their members but also to industry, government, and the general public. However, to successfully establish, operate, and enforce such programs, association executives must have a basic understanding of, and take measures to protect the association from, the potentially significant legal risks.

Although clearly in the public interest and of benefit to members and others, standard setting by associations raises risks of legal liability under antitrust law; copyright and patent law; and common law theories of due process, negligence, and warranty, among others. An association's certification and accreditation programs and code of ethics also may incur risk of legal liability under antitrust law and under theories of due process, negligence and warranty, and defamation. Courts generally are extremely reluctant to second-guess the reasonableness of an association's standard-setting and certification programs and member codes of ethics. Yet the costs, burdens, and distractions of mounting a defense to a lawsuit can be overwhelming. Fortunately, there are steps associations can take

---

Note: This chapter is not intended to provide legal advice or opinion. Such advice can only be provided in response to specific factual situations.

in structuring and administering such programs to minimize the risk of being sued in the first instance, and, if a lawsuit does materialize, to ensure that the association will prevail. In addition, appropriate errors and omissions insurance can help protect the association against the financial burdens of such litigation.

Outlined in the following are the principal areas of legal risk that associations encounter in connection with the operation of standard-setting programs, certification and accreditation programs, and member codes of ethics: antitrust; intellectual property; due process; negligence; defamation; compliance with the Americans with Disabilities Act; and federal tax exemption. Other theories of liability exist as well—such as theories of warranty and enterprise liability—but the areas of legal risk outlined here make up the majority of claims filed against associations in connection with standard setting, certification and accreditation programs, and codes of ethics. Note that not all of these forms of liability apply to all three types of programs; for instance, the Americans with Disabilities Act applies to certification programs (that is, testing), but not to standard setting or codes of ethics. The forms of liability as they apply to specific programs are made clear in each section that follows.

Antitrust

Antitrust laws generally prohibit anticompetitive acts in restraint of trade. The primary federal antitrust laws that affect associations are Section 1 of the Sherman Act and Section 5 of the Federal Trade Commission Act. Section 1 of the Sherman Act states, in part, "Every contract, combination in the form of trust or otherwise, or conspiracy, in restraint of trade or commerce among the several States, or with foreign nations, is hereby declared to be illegal." Associations are, by definition, combinations of competitors and thus particularly susceptible to allegations of antitrust abuse.

The key factor in an antitrust challenge to an association's standard setting, certification activities, or code of ethics is whether the association's actions in establishing or enforcing standards or rules of conduct are unreasonably anticompetitive within the meaning of the antitrust laws. Any standard or rule adopted by a group of competitors (for example, a trade or professional association) that discriminates against, excludes, or damages other competitors may potentially violate the antitrust laws. Under the rule of reason, courts will look at all of the facts and circumstances to determine whether the association's program, on balance, restrains competition in the relevant market more than it promotes it.

For example, unsuccessful applicants for certification, or those whose certification is revoked, may seek to use the antitrust laws to obtain certification or to obtain damages for the failure to certify. An association may be held liable under the antitrust laws if the challenger can demonstrate that (1) certification is essential in order to effectively compete in the market, and (2) the program's exclusion was the result of unreasonable or invalid standards or criteria or of unfair or inappropriate procedures.

Certifying bodies generally have broad discretion in setting and implementing certification requirements. Courts are reluctant to second-guess technical standards—such as those used as the basis for certification decisions—as long as the standards are objectively established and substantively justifiable. A certification program that is designed to, and does in fact, protect and promote the economic health of a particular industry or profession or the welfare of the industry's or profession's customers or clients generally will be deemed to be more pro-competitive than anticompetitive—even though those who fail to achieve certification may find it more difficult to compete in the market.

In contrast, certification programs that are anticompetitive, discriminatory, unrelated to objective standards, or implemented without fair procedures are likely to attract antitrust challenges. In addition, certification programs that charge an unreasonably high price to apply for or receive certification or recertification or that require membership in the sponsoring association as a prerequisite to obtaining certification ("tying arrangements") are subject to antitrust challenge.

Similarly, standards for conduct contained in an association's code of ethics, which seek to guard against immoral or unethical behavior, must be reasonably tied to a pro-competitive purpose, such as discouraging fraud or deception in the profession, and also must provide procedural fairness to affected members or applicants. An association's membership restriction may have strong pro-competitive justifications, but if the restriction is applied arbitrarily or subjectively, the association still may be at antitrust risk. The association's code of ethics and the process for enforcing the code should be stated plainly and objectively in publicly available association documents. A well-drafted code of ethics will put members and applicants on notice not only of rules of ethical conduct all members must follow but also the procedural steps the association will follow in resolving alleged violations of those rules.

In the standard-setting context, antitrust laws and enforcers acknowledge that standard setting is generally pro-competitive. However, standard-setting bodies may provide a forum for collusion among competitors. For example, courts have found violation of the antitrust laws where members of an association conspired to release an interpretation of a standard that was unfavorable to a competitor and where an association recruited new members to vote for a standard that excluded certain competitors in the industry.

Intellectual Property

It is often necessary to incorporate intellectual property into standards. Standard-setting bodies are thus challenged with balancing (1) the individual ownership rights recognized by patent and copyright laws, (2) the competition values protected by the antitrust laws, and (3) the need for compatibility of competitors' products.

The law of patents requires an inventor seeking a patent to prove that the inventor has developed a novel, useful, and non-obvious process or product. The grant of a patent gives one the right to exclude others from making, using, or selling the claimed technology for twenty years from the date of application filing. Patent applications are secret during the period of review, which can take years. Typical types of patents include utility patents, design patents, plant patents, and the business methods patent, which has taken on tremendous importance in the digital economy.

Copyright law provides narrower protection than patent law—it merely protects "expression," defined as the original arrangement of symbols of communication based on the creative choice of the author. It does not protect ideas, processes, methods of operation, or facts.

There is a fundamental conflict between the exclusive rights granted to an inventor by patent or copyright law and the necessity of interoperability in the digital economy. Patent issues are implicated in standard setting when patented material is "essential" to a standard (that is, those adopting the standard would not be able to implement it without infringing on the patent). The "essential facilities" doctrine says that denial of access to a resource essential to competition in a downstream market may violate the antitrust laws.

For example, an industry member's failure to disclose ownership of a patent design incorporated into a standard, when participating in the standard-setting process and promoting a standard that incorporates that design, may be seen as an anticompetitive act in direct violation of antitrust laws, particularly when the patent holder then seeks to enforce the patent against infringers adopting the standard.

This conflict can be reconciled at the outset of any standard-setting process by making sure that the process is fair, access to proprietary information is not unduly limited, and the standards adopted have good technical support. Standard-setting bodies should require members (and any other participants in the standard-setting process) to disclose any patents or pending patent applications involving a contemplated standard, and require either free licensing of intellectual property incorporated into a standard, or at minimum, licensing on "reasonable" and "nondiscriminatory" terms.

Due Process

As noted earlier, in addition to antitrust issues, associations also may incur legal risk for failing to afford members and others "due process" based on a lack of either substantive or procedural fairness. Substantive fairness requires the use of objective standards reasonably related to a legitimate organizational purpose, while procedural fairness requires the uniform application of such standards.

To minimize the risk of liability, it is critical for associations to carefully establish and strictly, consistently, and objectively follow their own written rules and procedures for the administration of any standard-setting or certification program or code of ethics. Associations are legally bound to follow their own rules and regulations in setting professional and product standards.

Courts usually will defer to substantive standards established by an association. However, standards set and decisions made by an association in applying those standards may be overturned if the standards, or the association's decisions in applying them, are arbitrary, capricious, or discriminatory, where they are influenced by bias or prejudice, or where they lack good faith. Courts are likely to scrutinize the fairness of the procedures (as opposed to the standards themselves) more closely because these are matters with which they are more familiar.

At minimum, procedural due process requires associations to provide notice of a potential adverse decision to a member, prospective member, or applicant for certification, to provide an opportunity for the affected individual to respond, and to provide the individual with an opportunity to appeal any adverse decision. Of course, it is incumbent on an association to both have the relevant procedures in place and actually follow all due process obligations it places on itself through such procedures. In addition, fundamental fairness requires that similarly situated persons and entities be treated the same.

Negligence

Reliance on the fact of membership, certification, or accreditation of a professional, entity, product, or service can, in some cases, cause the association that granted the membership, certification, or accreditation to be held liable when a patient, client, or customer suffers harm (physical, financial, or otherwise) at the hands of the member or certified individual, entity, or product. The most common claim is that the association was negligent in granting membership, certification, or accreditation and should therefore be liable for resulting injuries.

This liability risk to third parties generally means negligence liability (a form of tort liability), but it is sometimes couched in claims such as misrepresentation, failure to warn, warranty, strict liability, and enterprise liability. For instance, the injured party may allege that the association warranted or guaranteed the individuals, entities, products, or services certified or granted membership by the association and therefore should be responsible (under a breach of warranty theory) for resulting injuries to those who purchase, utilize, or participate in them.

Court decisions holding associations and certifying bodies liable for negligence in the context of self-regulatory programs and certification programs are relatively rare. This type of liability is subject to a number of conditions and remains infrequent, although there have been several high-profile cases in recent years holding associations liable for negligence arising from their self-regulatory programs. In short, an association generally will be found liable under the tort of negligence only if the injured party can prove all of the elements of negligence liability:

> *Duty:* The first question courts ask is whether the association owed a duty of care to the third party (the injured plaintiff who utilized the services of a certified vendor, for instance). While there is generally no duty of care owed to third parties, some courts have held that

once an organization undertakes to set standards or inspect, test, or otherwise certify individuals, entities, products, or services, it should reasonably know that third parties might rely on those standards or certifications, and therefore must exercise reasonable care in doing so.

Breach of duty (negligence): The court will next determine whether the certifying body failed to act with reasonable care (that is, acted negligently) in granting the certification or in setting a particular standard. In other words, the association is obligated to use due diligence and reasonable care in promulgating the certification standards and in applying them to applicants for certification. For instance, a mail-order certification program that establishes no meaningful standards or that exercises no real scrutiny in evaluating applicants could be at risk for breach of its duty of care.

Reliance: It must be proven that the plaintiff relied upon the association's certification in utilizing the certified individual, entity, product, or service. It generally is not sufficient for a plaintiff merely to show that the association certified a vendor, for instance, and later an injury occurred; the plaintiff must establish that it was because of the association's certification that the vendor's products or services were utilized. If the association can establish that the plaintiff did not know of the association's certification or that the certification was not a material factor in the decision to utilize the vendor's product or service, then it may be able to avoid liability.

Causation: The negligence of the certifying association must be considered to be a "proximate cause" of the injury to the ultimate user (the plaintiff). While the most direct cause of the plaintiff's injury generally is the negligence of the certified party or product—not the certifying association—where the certifying body expects the public to rely upon the certification, and the injured party does just that in selecting the certified party or product, the causation and reliance criteria both may be met. In other words, if reliance is established, causation likely will be as well.

If any one of these four elements cannot be established, then liability generally will not result. Finally, there must be measurable injury (physical, financial, or psychological) to the plaintiff for any damages to exist.

Defamation

Defamation is the oral utterance (slander) or written publication (libel) of false or misleading facts or false or misleading implied facts that are derogatory or damaging to an individual's, entity's, or product's reputation. Accusing someone of dishonesty or other moral deficiency or of professional or business deficiency raises significant risk of defamation liability.

The risk of defamation is likely to arise in the context of certification activities and codes of ethics (1) when an individual, entity, or product is denied certification or when an individual or entity is denied or expelled from membership, and then damaging statements are made (to one or more third parties) by a representative of the certifying body or association about the individual, entity, or product; or (2) when sensitive, potentially damaging information about a member or an applicant for membership or certification becomes known to the certifying body or association during the certification or ethics enforcement process, and that information is subsequently disclosed to one or more third parties (intentionally or unintentionally).

Even those who believe they are communicating the truth may commit defamation. For a statement to be defamatory, it must be actually communicated to someone other than the speaker or author. The defamed individual or entity may sue anyone who publishes, prints, or repeats the defamation, and, depending on the circumstances, may recover from the speaker(s) or author(s) money damages to compensate for the harm to reputation and to punish the speaker(s) or author(s) as well. Truth is an absolute defense to any defamation claim.

In some circumstances, legal "privileges" apply that may protect the speaker or author from liability even where a statement might otherwise be defamatory. The three principal privileges in the association context are (1) where the speaker takes reasonable precautions to ensure the statement's accuracy, including making reasonable inquiry; (2) where the statement concerns a public official or figure, the speaker will not be liable unless the speaker actually knew the accusations were false and made the statement in reckless disregard of its truth or falsity; and (3) publication or communication of a derogatory statement within an association's governing body—for the purpose of promoting a common interest—may be protected by a "qualified privilege." For example, deliberations among a certification board concerning certification-related proceedings are likely protected by this qualified privilege. Where this privilege applies, statements may give rise to defamation liability only if motivated by spite or ill will or if communicated to persons outside of the management or governing group.

Compliance with the Americans with Disabilities Act

Associations sponsoring and administering certification and accreditation programs are subject to the requirements of the federal Americans with Disabilities Act (ADA). The requirements of the ADA of most relevance to certifying bodies are the specific and extensive standards contained in the law for private entities that conduct examinations and courses relating to applications; licensing and certification; or credentialing for educational, professional, or trade purposes. The U.S. Department of Justice's regulations require that certifying bodies "offer such examinations or courses in a place and manner accessible to persons with disabilities or offer alternative accessible arrangements for such individuals."

Note that the ADA does not apply if an individual seeking certification does not have a covered disability. For instance, U.S. Supreme Court decisions have clarified that available corrective and mitigating measures, such as medication or medical aids, must be considered in determining whether or not an individual has a disability under the ADA. Thus, for example, the Court held that correctable myopia is not a disability, nor is high blood pressure that is controlled with medication.

A certifying body is responsible for selecting and administering the certification examination in a place and manner which ensures that the examination tests what the examination purports to measure, rather than testing the individual's disability, such as impaired sensory, manual, or speaking skills (unless those skills are what the examination is designed to test). This means ensuring that (1) testing places are accessible to individuals with disabilities and (2) auxiliary aids and services are made available to enable individuals with disabilities to take the examination, in accordance with the ADA's requirements.

For example, for individuals with hearing impairments, oral instructions or other orally delivered materials could be provided through an interpreter, assistive listening device, or other applicable means. For individuals with visual impairments, the examination and answer sheets could utilize large print or Braille, could be provided via audiotape, or could be provided through the use of qualified readers and transcribers to read questions and record answers.

A certifying body does not have to provide auxiliary aids and services in all cases. If providing a particular auxiliary aid or service would fundamentally change the examination or result in an undue burden on the certifying body, it does not need to be provided. This determination is case specific.

Regarding who decides what type of auxiliary aid or service should be provided, when possible, the individual with the disability should be consulted to determine the type of aid or service that may be needed. When more than one type of auxiliary aid or service will enable a person with a disability to participate effectively, a certifying body may choose what aid or service to make available.

Aside from auxiliary aids or services, other types of modifications may be required. For instance, it may be necessary to modify the manner in which the test is administered. For example, if an individual has an impairment that makes writing difficult, it may be necessary to give that individual more time to complete the exam or to permit the typing of answers.

The individual with a disability may not be required to bear the cost of the aid or modification. The certifying body must bear the cost of the aid or modification. However, a certifying body is only required to provide auxiliary aids or modifications that do not pose an undue burden on the certifying body and do not fundamentally change the examination.

Examinations must be administered in facilities that are accessible to disabled individuals, or alternative accessible arrangements must be made. If the facility in which the examination is offered is not accessible, the exam may be administered to an individual with a disability in a different room or another location. The alternative location should provide conditions comparable to the conditions in which the test is administered to others.

All testing locations need not be accessible and offer specially designed exams; however, if an examination for individuals with disabilities is administered in an alternative accessible location or manner, it must be offered as often and in as timely a manner as other examinations. Examinations must be offered to individuals with disabilities at locations that are as convenient as the location(s) of other examinations.

Individuals with disabilities cannot be required to file their applications to take the examination earlier than the deadline for other applicants in order to enable accommodations to be made. However, a certifying body may require individuals with disabilities to provide advance notice to the certifying body of their disability and of any aids or modifications that might be required, so long as the deadline for doing so is not earlier than the deadline for others applying to take the examination.

A certifying body may require applicants to provide documentation of the existence and nature of the disability as evidence that they are entitled to an aid or modification, so long as the request is reasonable and limited to the need for the modification or aid requested. Appropriate documentation might include a letter from a doctor or other health care professional or evidence of a prior diagnosis or accommodation (such as eligibility for a special education program). The applicant can be required to bear the cost of providing such documentation, but he or she cannot be charged for the cost of any modifications or auxiliary aids provided for the examination.

Finally, the rules for courses (such as educational seminars of any type offered by associations) are similar to those for examinations. They generally require that modifications be made in courses offered by private entities to ensure that the place and manner in which the course is given are accessible to individuals with disabilities. The most significant difference is that the general rule for courses applies to all individuals with disabilities, not just those with "impaired sensory, manual, or speaking skills." Modifications in courses may include changes in the length of time allowed for completing the course, substitution of course requirements, or adapting the manner in which the course is conducted or materials are distributed. Advance notice of the opportunity to obtain materials in alternative formats must be provided to disabled individuals. Appropriate auxiliary aids also must be provided, unless to do so would fundamentally alter the course or create an undue burden. If courses cannot be administered in a facility accessible to individuals with disabilities, comparable alternative arrangements must be made. Such arrangements may include offering the course through the Internet, DVD, CD-ROM, prepared notes, or some other alternative means. The selection or choice of courses available to individuals with disabilities may not be restricted.

Federal Tax Exemption

It is conceivable, although very unlikely, that an association that is exempt from federal income tax under Internal Revenue Code (Code) Section 501(c)(6) could run afoul of the Code restrictions that prohibit such organizations from providing substantial "particular services" to members. Such a restriction might apply in the event that the Internal Revenue Service (IRS) reviewed an association's code of ethics enforcement program and determined that in fact, the program's primary purpose is the mediation of intra-membership business disputes, as opposed to the promotion or furtherance of the industry or profession as a whole. Even if that were the case, an association would only be in danger of losing its tax-exempt status if the IRS were to determine that the activity constituted greater than 50 percent of the association's total activities. However, if the questioned activity accounted for less than 50 percent of the association's total activities, the IRS still might seek to tax fees received by the association in exchange for the provision of such services as (taxable) unrelated business income.

For associations (with certification or accreditation programs) that are not exempt from federal income tax under Section 501(c)(6) but rather are exempt under Section 501(c)(3), special considerations come into play. In a 2004 Private Letter Ruling, the IRS held that the certification program of a nonprofit membership association exempt from federal income tax under Section 501(c)(3) was not consistent with such tax status. That ruling, which has been consistently followed by the IRS since then, has led most nonprofit tax advisers to advise their clients that except in rare instances, certification and accreditation programs should be operated by associations exempt from tax under Section 501(c)(6)—where the income from such programs generally is fully consistent with tax-exempt status—instead of Section 501(c)(3). Failure to do so can generate taxable unrelated business income for a 501(c)(3) association, and can even jeopardize the organization's tax-exempt status if the certification or accreditation income is significant compared to total income. Many 501(c)(3) associations have now created or used affiliated 501(c)(6) associations to carry out such certification and accreditation activities.

Steps to Minimizing Risk

Court decisions involving association standard setting, certification and accreditation programs, and codes of ethics suggest that taking the following steps in connection with such activities will significantly limit the association's liability risks and protect its interests.

Ensure that valid, objective bases support each standard, certification requirement, and code of ethics provision, to the extent possible. Standards, certification and accreditation requirements, and codes of ethics should be clear and unambiguous, reasonable, fair, and objectively grounded. If used in connection with a certification program, standards should be based on supporting data or on a respected body of industry or governmental opinion linking each particular standard to the qualities that the certification purports to measure. Where possible, standards should be directed at, and focus on, the ends, not the means. Where the means are specified, they must be legitimately, demonstrably, and directly related to the objectives. Equivalent standards or alternative paths to certification should be established wherever possible. As with the standards themselves, the determination as to whether requirements for certification have been satisfied should focus on the ends, not the means. There must be valid, demonstrable, and reasonable bases upon which to determine that applicants for certification have met the requirements. Standards, requirements for certification, and code of ethics provisions should never be arbitrary or capricious, or vague or ambiguous. Procedures should be developed that document the reasonableness of, and the objective basis for, the proposed standards, certification requirements, or code of ethics provisions.

Make sure that standards, certification requirements, and code of ethics provisions are no more stringent or rigid than necessary to ensure that the specified competency or quality levels have been attained or to ensure that minimum acceptable levels of conduct are met.

Specific commercial or economic considerations should play no role in the setting of standards or certification requirements or in the setting or application of code of ethics provisions. In addition, standards, certification programs, and codes of ethics should never be created or used for the purpose of raising, lowering, or stabilizing prices or fees, excluding competitors from the market, or limiting the supply of products or services.

Prior to finalizing standards, certification requirements, and code of ethics provisions, provide interested parties with notice of the proposed standards or provisions and an opportunity to comment on them. Fairly and objectively consider such comments in finalizing the standards, certification requirements, or code of ethics.

Periodically review and update all standards to ensure that they are current and reflect new legal, technological, and other developments. The association's code of ethics also should be reviewed and updated periodically to ensure that it is current. Provide appropriate opportunities for public notice and comment whenever standards or code of ethics provisions are modified, and carefully consider such comments in the revision process. In addition, document any and all complaints or concerns about the standards or code of ethics, and revise the standards or ethics provisions accordingly if appropriate.

Administer each process objectively and uniformly without subjectivity, favoritism, or discrimination. There must be no bias, partiality, or inconsistency in establishing or operating the association's standard-setting, certification, or code of ethics program. Those administering the program must scrupulously, consistently, and objectively follow the rules governing the process.

Require full disclosure by those involved in the standard-setting, ethics enforcement, or certification process of any factor that might be considered bias or a conflict of interest. Require recusal or removal if a bias or conflict is particularly severe or pervasive. Full disclosure and appropriate checks and balances generally are effective mechanisms for safely managing most potential conflicts of interest. In addition, reduced volunteer involvement and increased association staff involvement may assist in objectivity and the absence of bias in the ethics enforcement and certification process.

Require participants in the standard-setting process to disclose any patents or pending patent applications involving a contemplated standard. Require either free licensing of intellectual property incorporated into a standard, or, at minimum, licensing on "reasonable" and "nondiscriminatory" terms.

Before discipline is enforced or certification is denied or revoked, individuals who would receive such discipline or who seek certification should be provided due process. This includes providing these individuals with (1) notice of an adverse decision and a meaningful opportunity to respond to the notice; (2) a hearing before a panel of peers, none of whom has a direct economic or personal interest in the outcome of the proceeding; (3) the right to be represented by another person, including an attorney, and to submit evidence and arguments in defense; (4) the right to examine the evidence and to cross-examine witnesses (if applicable); (5) the right to a written decision explaining the reasons underlying it; and (6) the right to appeal an adverse decision to a higher-level decision-making body within the association.

Base decisions with regard to certification and ethics enforcement completely and exclusively on the record of review and not on extraneous, anecdotal, subjective, or other outside sources of information. The proceedings and all adverse allegations, complaints, and actions that arise in connection with the process should remain strictly confidential. While nothing prevents a certification program from publicizing the names of, and information about, those who are certified, care should be taken to avoid any explicit or implicit disparagement of those who are not certified. While it is acceptable for a certifying association to verify that an entity is not currently certified, no further details should be provided.

Use a copyright notice on all standards and related materials (that are subject to copyright protection) and register such standards and materials with the U.S. Copyright Office. With regard to standard setting and certification programs, this will minimize the risk of copyright infringement, maximize copyright rights, and facilitate enforcement of such rights. Be sure that the association owns or has the right to use the entire contents of such materials (for example, obtaining written copyright assignments from all non-association employees that participate in the standard-setting process). In addition, as listings of certified entities generally are not protectable under U.S. copyright laws, use a shrink-wrap license or other form of contractual commitment to place explicit, binding limits and conditions on the use of the list. The shrink-wrap license also can be a useful vehicle to disclaim any endorsement or guarantee of the certified entities by the association.

Widely publicize the availability of the association's certification program and permit application to all who choose to apply. Do not limit participation in the certification program to only members of the sponsoring association. Certification programs should be open both to association members and to nonmembers on the same terms and conditions. Moreover, nothing in excess of a reasonable price should be charged to apply for or receive certification or recertification. However, fees charged to nonmembers for certification may be higher than those charged to association members to reflect any membership dues or assessments that contribute to funding the program.

Avoid "grandfathering" of those who do not meet all current certification standards. Require regular recertification as appropriate to ensure that those who are certified continue to meet the program's standards. In addition, review the certification process itself on a periodic basis to ensure it is being properly administered.

Comply with the Americans with Disabilities Act. Ensure that all certification examinations—as well as all courses that prepare applicants for certification exams—are administered in strict compliance with the specific requirements imposed by the federal Americans with Disabilities Act and implementing regulations.

Maintain strict security regarding all aspects of the association's certification process. Any missing, stolen, or copied examination booklets, for instance, can have a severe impact on the integrity of the certification process.

Use a trademark notice in connection with any certification logo or seal, and register the mark with the U.S. Patent and Trademark Office (either as a certification mark or as a service mark). Registering will minimize the risk of trademark infringement, maximize trademark rights, and facilitate enforcement of such rights. Be sure the association's use of the mark does not infringe anyone else's trademark rights. In addition, codify the terms and conditions of, and limitations on, use of the mark by certified entities in a written agreement, possibly as part of the certification application form or in connection with distribution of the mark. Be sure to include provisions, among others, designed to prevent false or misleading use of the mark and to prohibit any further use upon decertification. Note that the federal Lanham Act, and similar state laws, prohibit the use of any false or misleading terms, names or symbols, or any other false or misleading descriptions or representations that are likely to deceive the public with respect to the affiliation of the user with a particular organization.

Include binding limitation of liability and indemnification provisions in the certification application form (or other document) to absolve the association from liability to those who are certified and to hold the association harmless from lawsuits by those injured by the acts or omissions of certified entities.

Make it clear that it is voluntary. Ensure that participation in and use of standards or a certification program is completely voluntary.

Do not limit participation in the standard-setting process to members only.

Invite nonmembers of the sponsoring association to participate in the process.

Use written disclaimers. Where appropriate, use written disclaimers to clarify the association's limited role with respect to the use of, and responsibility for, the standards and to clarify the association's limited role with respect to lack of responsibility for, and absence of, guarantees or warranties of certified products, services, or entities. If and where appropriate, require use of similar disclaimers by those that receive certification.

Where appropriate and feasible, consider utilizing and participating in the standard-setting procedures of the American National Standards Institute (ANSI). Where a certification program is involved, consider obtaining accreditation of the certification program by ANSI.

Maintain sufficient insurance to cover the liability risks of the standard-setting or certification program. Some association professional liability insurance (APLI) policies provide coverage for certain (but not all) claims arising from standard-setting and certification programs as part of the basic policy, although some with coverage sublimits. Other APLI policies will not cover such activities without an endorsement to the policy. Be sure to fully disclose the association's standard-setting and certification activities in the insurance application. Of importance, APLI policies do not cover bodily injury or property damage claims arising from these programs. Stand-alone standard-setting and certification insurance policies are available and may be necessary to insure against these particular risks. Adequate insurance should be a prerequisite to the operation of any association standard-setting or certification program.

Avoid any implicit or explicit guarantee or warranty of certified products, services, entities, or individuals, including members. To this end, avoid "puffery." Do not overstate how a product, service, professional, or company performs, and do not use superlatives such as "never fails" or "safest" in describing those that are members or certified. Do not allow members to express or imply that they are endorsed by the association by virtue of being accepted as a member.

Resources

Jacobs, J. A., and American Society of Association Executives and Center for Association Leadership. *Association Law Handbook: A Practical Guide for Associations, Societies, and Charities.* Washington, DC: ASAE Association Management Press, 2012.

Tenenbaum, J. S. *Association Tax Compliance Guide*, 2nd ed. Washington, DC: ASAE Association Management Press.

The Authors

Jeffrey S. Tenenbaum, Esq., is a partner and chair of the nonprofit organizations practice at the Venable LLP law firm. *Beth A. Caseman, Esq.*, is assistant general counsel at Volunteers of America.

CHAPTER TWENTY-ONE

DEVELOPING AND MANAGING PROGRAMS, PRODUCTS, AND SERVICES

Mariah Burton Nelson, MPH, CAE

People who have a bad habit of accumulating too much stuff are called hoarders. Organizations that have a bad habit of accumulating too much stuff are called—associations.

That's a little joke—but isn't there a ring of truth? Associations do tend to "hoard" programs, products, and services, even outdated and unpopular ones. Associations sometimes make undisciplined decisions about what to create in the first place. It's not easy knowing what to add to a portfolio of products, what to discard, and when.

Why is wise product management difficult?

First, unlike corporations, associations do not consider the bottom line the most important criterion. That's appropriate; associations do not exist to accumulate profit. But without that profit motive, other factors—anecdotal member interest, board-member beliefs, and volunteer passion—often drive product-development decisions, for better and sometimes for worse.

Second, there are no data about the future. Despite our best market assessments, we can't be sure how many people will purchase (or even appreciate) anything we produce. Companies tend to have budgets devoted to testing potential products before launching them. Associations more often wing it, with mixed results.

Third, associations serve multiple constituents: members, volunteers, sponsors, vendors, advertisers, and other customers. By attempting to please everyone, we sometimes end up with a "messy house" filled with things that were once valuable, things that were never valuable, and things that are still valuable—but might be difficult to uncover, given the clutter.

A new product development (NPD) framework solves these problems—and helps associations establish a strong financial footing in the midst of a torrent of technological and social change. An NPD framework is a strategic, disciplined, data-informed process for developing new products, evaluating and pruning legacy (existing) products, and balancing the entire portfolio. It's a decision-making process designed to help organizations focus on what matters. Other terms used to describe related processes include *innovation, idea generation, product management, product lifecycle management, portfolio analysis,* and *Stage-Gate,* a trademarked corporate process designed by NPD expert Robert G. Cooper.

At ASAE, we call our process NPD (and joke that it stands for "Never Produce Duds"). Exxon Chemical uses the term *PIP,* for Product Innovation Process. The United States Army uses the militaristic acronym TARGET (Tank Automotive Research, Development, and Engineering Center Grated Evaluation Track). Any name will do, as long as people understand what it means.

The way we use this term, new product development encompasses idea generation, product review (of new and legacy products), and portfolio management. This unified framework strengthens organizations by helping them select and retain "the right stuff." In associations, the "right stuff" should be superior, differentiated programs, products, and services that align with the mission; meet member needs; sell well; provide net revenue that can be invested in other projects to stimulate growth; position the association in a positive light; and keep pace with ever-changing technologies and demographic and cultural shifts.

Given the pace of change, we need to continually scan the environment, see what competitors (including companies) are doing, take a hard look at what we're doing, and try new approaches. Yet many associations play small, offering leftovers and copycat products that promise minimal returns.

Why such risk aversion? Consider the principle of inertia: bodies at rest tend to stay at rest. Associations that have discovered a core business that works for them tend to become reluctant to experiment with new strategies that might help them adapt to new environments. "Start-ups know how to start, but most struggle with scale," notes David Butler, vice president for innovation and entrepreneurship at the Coca-Cola

Company. "Big companies know how to scale, but not how to start."[1] So if your association is in startup mode, you may welcome innovation. If you've been around for decades, you may find it harder to try new things.

Identifying exactly what your "right stuff" is will depend on many things, including member needs, competitive offerings, pricing considerations, technological capacities, the availability of startup funds, and the board's tolerance for risk. The beauty of NPD is that it helps associations answer the question "What's the right stuff for us?" repeatedly over time.

As far as we can tell, most associations do not yet have in place a systematic process for selecting and sunsetting products. (By contrast, about 74 percent of for-profit companies do, according to the American Productivity and Quality Center.) For that reason, this chapter explains what a chief staff executive needs to consider when orchestrating the creation of a new product development framework.

First, this context: you may have heard the phase, "No money, no mission"—meaning that no matter how worthy the mission, organizations will fail if they fail to raise revenue. NPD frameworks force an association to pay attention to the money. The organization may still offer programs, products, and services that do not generate revenue, but those choices become apparent, with an understanding that for every product that loses money, others must make money.

This is not to minimize the importance of mission. Even businesses need a *raison d'être* beyond money. As Henry Ford put it, "A business that makes nothing but money is a poor business." In other words, both mission and money matter. While businesses sometimes focus too much on money, associations sometimes focus too much on mission.

Why must associations become better businesses *now?* The answer can be summarized in one word: Internet. Before the Internet, physicians, for instance, who sought professional development and networking needed the American Medical Association to provide lectures, advice, updated information, and professional camaraderie. These resources were fairly difficult to locate or obtain elsewhere. Post-Internet, the physician who seeks to keep up in the field and meet like-minded colleagues need only open a web browser. With the world at our fingertips, all the information and contacts we could possibly want seem just a few clicks away.

Associations are still relevant. We offer quality professional development, exceptional experiences, and unique opportunities for networking with leaders in our fields. We offer advocacy, credentials, cutting-edge conferences, and other benefits. But we need to work harder than ever to attract members. We can't afford to produce unpopular programs, irrelevant books, or extravagant awards ceremonies—not if they drain our resources. No money, no mission.

Fortunately, along comes NPD to save the day—or at least to introduce a business process that can help you make good decisions.

◆ ◆ ◆

ASAE's Story

In 2013, ASAE launched its NPD framework. Here is how this works for us. Idea generation (also known as the discovery phase) happens within or across departments. Once an idea has been selected, developed, and (ideally) market-tested with at least a few potential customers, a product manager submits a two-part (narrative and budget) proposal to the NPD team. This group scores the proposal on the basis of preapproved criteria and issues a go or no-go decision, which we refer to as green or red lights. (Corporations often call this go/kill, but we prefer a traffic metaphor.) All legacy products are also reviewed, with the same results: green or red lights.

Companies using a Stage-Gate system employ about four gates (decision points). Each one asks, "Given what we know now, shall we move this product toward launch or stop here?" With simplicity and efficiency in mind, ASAE built its system with just one official gate. Our NPD team answers what for others is the final question: "Shall we launch (or continue) this product?"

We encourage product developers to involve the NPD team in their planning process, so they receive as much guidance as possible during that discovery phase. They may encounter some unofficial gates during that time, and may appropriately abandon or drastically revise their efforts.

Even when issuing a green light, the NPD team often recommends minor revisions. That way, a product manager can make final refinements to improve the product before it launches.

We instituted an evaluation system so applicants can review the reviewers; created an "Idea Portal" to serve as a pipeline for new ideas across the organization; and sorted our ASAE Product Portfolio into meaningful categories so it can be evaluated for patterns, omissions, and redundancies.

ASAE's NPD framework represents a challenging, exciting, and so far successful journey for us. Like all good NPD frameworks, it will evolve over time. We hope it also serves as a model, or at least inspiration, for other associations.

Key Considerations

When building a new product development framework, the three key considerations are people, priorities, and process.

People: Build the Team

Choosing the right person to lead the team, staffing the team appropriately, and involving the board and staff are essential. Therefore, the first question is, How will you build this team?

Begin with the board. In mid- to large-sized associations, the board should not get involved in go/no decisions, but the board will need to approve directional decisions, including adding an NPD staffer if needed. In small associations, the board or other volunteers may be the ones serving on the NPD team.

The chief staff executive must be publically committed. A recipe for failure would be a CSE or board members who subvert the process by ignoring the decisions of the NPD team.

After making sure the board and chief staff executive are on board, the question becomes, who will lead the team? What staff member (or, in small associations, volunteer) will facilitate the creation and implementation of the process? Nothing happens if no one takes responsibility, so someone needs to be in charge. This person should be a respected, patient, persistent leader who receives a clear mandate to develop an NPD process that takes into account such things as the organization's budget, portfolio size, and readiness to change. Whether you need to staff this position anew will depend not only on the skills of your current staff, but on the demands of the job. At ASAE, NPD startup tasks kept one full-time vice president busy for about a year.

Yet responsibility for this system must not rest on an individual's shoulders. Who else will take responsibility for ensuring that this process becomes an integral part of the fabric of your organization—and improves the way you do business? The NPD leader needs a team of other people who possess relevant skills and share a sense of ownership. This is where the value of a centralized function lies. Instead of decisions being made by individuals or small teams, decisions are made by a group of people with broad expertise and a holistic view of the organization.

Important traits for the NPD team include business acumen, strategic thinking, creativity, and people skills. A team will be stronger if its members have expertise in functional areas such as marketing, meetings, membership, technology, education, publications, and research. The team should include people who are willing to try new things, people who are willing to make unpopular decisions—and people authorized to make such decisions. This might be an executive team or senior management team that's already in place. Or you might create a subset of that team, or a new team based on expertise, interest, authority, and availability. In small-staff associations, volunteers need to step up. For volunteer NPD groups, succession planning becomes especially important to ensure that institutional knowledge of product review, idea generation, and portfolio analysis are successfully passed from one generation of volunteers to the next.

In organizations with a large enough staff to support it, NPD should be a staff function, because it involves labor-intensive business decisions. In these cases, staff will be the ones who will implement new product ideas that get approved, have some of their proposals rejected, and adjust to planning products in this new way.

Whether the NPD team is composed of staff or volunteers or a combination, these people may not embrace the new structure initially. They may resist change simply because many human beings do; they may have legitimate concerns about any aspect of the new process; and they may feel confused or worried if the plan does not seem clear, well thought out, or user-friendly.

At ASAE, we ensured board and chief executive buy-in first, then took pains to involve the whole staff throughout our development phases. The NPD team conducted a "listening tour," asking every staff member for input about how to design an NPD process that would stimulate innovation, serve members, and strengthen ASAE. We then designed a system with their suggestions in mind. Later, during the launch phase, we provided departmental trainings, during which we explained how the process would work and how we had incorporated staff input into the plan. Now that we're under way, NPD team members still listen to staff concerns, assist with budget preparation and proposal-writing, and help staff navigate the proposal process.

Priorities: Decide What's Important

Establishing clear priorities will help you sort through options, make good decisions, and figure out where to start building your framework. Given your association's situation and goals, should you begin by building a product-review process? Or should you begin by assembling and analyzing your product portfolio? Or should you begin by generating ideas for new products?

One of these three elements probably offers the best place for your association to begin, all things considered. If your programs, products, and services seem stale, you might want to start with idea generation—but keep in mind that you'll soon need to somehow sort and select the good ones.

If your organization tends to say yes to mediocre ideas, you'll probably want to establish a product review process first, to create go/no gates. If you're suffering from product overload, "clean your closet" first with a portfolio analysis that leads to sunsetting the poor performers—but if you don't yet have a product-review process established, you might have difficulty removing products from that portfolio.

At ASAE, we started with product review—while simultaneously building and beginning to analyze the portfolio of all of our products to look for gaps and overlaps. Already robust and routine idea generators, we calculated that formalizing that part of our process could justifiably happen last. There is no one right place to start—but clarifying your problems and priorities will help you figure out the best starting place for you.

To review products—both new and existing—you will need to answer the question, what is a product? The question seems straightforward. *Product* generally serves as an umbrella term for programs (such as educational conferences), physical or virtual products (such as books), and services (such as consultations).

But what about free articles? Should a typical annual convention count as one product (one primary location, one main marketing effort); or two (education program plus expo); or more, considering receptions, lounges, fitness and fundraising outings, virtual streaming to remote locations, and so on? If you're going to insist that all new products must be approved by the NPD team before launching (as we do at ASAE), the definition of product becomes important.

At ASAE, we define product this way: "anything we create and distribute, for free or for a fee." That doesn't resolve all of the gray areas, but it excludes things that we do not "create and distribute." The activities of governance, executive management, finance, IT, web, marketing, and social media, for instance, are generally exempt from NPD review.

However, NPD principles and processes can be used to evaluate *projects*: initiatives that are not *products* but nevertheless compete for an association's time, attention, and money. For instance, you might put any new technology purchases through a rigorous review process before deciding which platforms to purchase or install. You can create a portfolio of current marketing channels to assess whether they constitute the right choices, or the right combinations. And you can brainstorm ideas to improve office efficiency, then carefully evaluate those ideas based on predetermined criteria. NPD is fundamentally a decision-making process, and it can be applied widely. For the sake of simplicity and focus, ASAE has found it helpful to exclude *projects* from our rigorous NPD process, at least for now.

How you define *product* is up to you—and will depend on your priorities. If the programs, products, and services you sell seem to need the most attention, you can exempt everything else from the "product" definition to help you focus on what's important.

Your starting point also depends on your priorities. Will you start by evaluating all products, or just new ones? At ASAE, we review all products. Because new-product review was a high priority for us, we implemented the "all *new* products must go through NPD review" policy first, then started working our way through legacy products. In some cases, we review these one by one; in other cases (especially with publications, because they are so numerous), we batch them.

Be careful not to overwhelm your NPD team with demands for too many reviews at once. Staff resources, number of products, and sense of urgency will dictate how you handle the review flow. Is the influx of new, unvetted products the bigger problem, or do you feel a more urgent need to prune the portfolio of underperforming products? You can start in either place—or both places at once.

Process: Create an Efficient Method

There is no one-size-fits-all NPD framework. Here are some principles to guide your efforts to create an effective one:

1. *Keep it simple:* No one welcomes bureaucracy.
2. *Share ownership:* People who help develop a process are more likely to support it.
3. *Drive toward implementation:* An imperfect, flexible process that can evolve over time is better than no process.
4. *Think holistically:* How will NPD affect other people and processes?
5. *Protect innovation:* A strategic process for selecting and sunsetting products can inadvertently squelch innovation. Build into your system a way to support innovative efforts, even if they're not perfected or revenue-generating right away.

Figure 21.1 presents an overview of the product development process.

Idea Generation

Often called the fuzzy front end, idea generation is probably the most important and least understood part of the process. If you have no good ideas for products, or no good way to differentiate good ideas from the

FIGURE 21.1. KEY ELEMENTS OF THE PRODUCT DEVELOPMENT PROCESS.

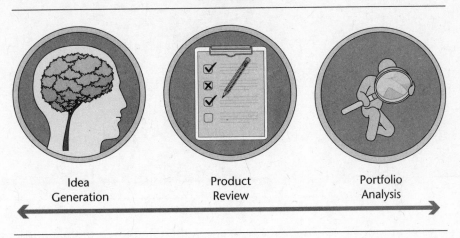

Idea Generation   Product Review   Portfolio Analysis

many ideas available, your products will not be very valuable, your members will not be very pleased, and your organization will not be very strong.

Yet where do good ideas come from? How can you cultivate and test them?

Unfortunately, there is no guaranteed formula; otherwise, every book would be a best-seller. But the most significant driver of innovative products is not an innovative CEO, an innovation strategy, or even innovative individuals, but an innovative *culture* that encourages and celebrates experimentation without many constraints.

To develop such a culture, an organization needs to get comfortable with ambiguity, indecision, and uncertainty. Idea generation can be chaotic, and could just as easily be dubbed the messy front end. Fortunately, staff can be trained to appreciate and even welcome the messiness.

At the same time, staff can be given tools to test those messy ideas on potential customers, sort the ideas into strategic categories, weed out the weak ones, and re-test revised prototypes or minimally viable products to continually receive feedback on what might work. Robert G. Cooper, the innovation and NPD expert who coined the term *Stage-Gate*, calls this a build-test-feedback-revise loop (Figure 21.2).

When people trust that their ideas will be respected and even rewarded, they will propose lots of ideas, some of which may ultimately provide great value to your association and its members. A spin-off benefit: people thrive when they feel connected to a community that's rich with possibilities, so an

FIGURE 21.2. ROBERT G. COOPER'S NEW PRODUCT LOOP.

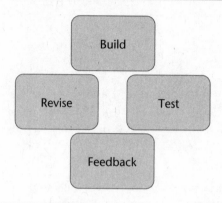

innovative culture is likely to strengthen employee morale and enhance member retention.

◆ ◆ ◆

Best Practices in Idea Generation

1. *Think many:* To find one good idea, gather lots.
2. *Channel the ideas:* "Strategic buckets" can focus idea-generation efforts on new markets or certain problems.
3. *Be encouraging:* People who hear appreciative responses to their first ideas will bring other ideas forward.
4. *Assign responsibility:* While "good ideas come from everywhere" is a philosophy that can invite contributions, successful ideas usually emerge from small dedicated groups committed to success.
5. *Cultivate curiosity:* Ask, What if? Might we—? Even failed experiments can fascinate: What worked? What didn't? What can we try next time?
6. *Get out of the office:* At least one association (the American Registry for Diagnostic Medical Sonography) has created an offsite skunkworks lab. Skunkworks refers to an enriched environment intended to foster innovation by taking a small group of idea generators out of the normal workspace and freeing them from bureaucratic constraints. The term was first used by Lockheed Martin during World War II; the company built a secret offsite lab near a plastics factory, and the bad smell brought to mind the moonshine factory ("Skonk Works") in Al Capp's *Li'l Abner* comic.

7. *Bring diverse minds together:* According to research, the most productive teams combine a few people who know each other with a few outsiders.

8. *Co-create with potential customers:* "Market research" can sound daunting, but it can be as simple as asking people who might buy your product what they think of it.

People like being asked for their opinion. Start with a sketch, prototype, or minimally viable product—an early incarnation of the thing you hope to build—to test on potential customers. Show it to people, listen to their feedback, revise to improve its value or design, and repeat. Not only will the product improve, you'll build a database of potential customers who feel a sense of ownership and pride, since they helped to create it.

◆ ◆ ◆

Product Review

Has your association ever created a new program, product, or service simply because one person thought it might fly? As Phil McGraw (of the TV show *Dr. Phil*) might say, "How's that working for you?"

The NPD product review phase is designed to increase the likelihood of product success. It takes decision making out of the hands of one person with a hunch and places it in the hands of several people equipped with information, expertise, and an assessment tool. The same process can be used for new and legacy products.

Tools for product review are available for sale online. Associations may find that it's best to design their framework first, then select software to support that system. That was the path ASAE chose. For small associations, basic Microsoft Office tools (Word and Excel) may suffice.

Product review tools should include

- A narrative proposal form that requires the applicant to explain the product's value
- A budget proposal form
- Clearly defined scoring criteria
- Agreed-upon interpretations of scores
- Well-defined next steps after a go/no decision has been made
- An opportunity for applicants to "review the reviewers" to provide feedback on the system, so it can be continuously improved

What criteria will you use to determine if this product is worth the time and money it will take to develop, launch, and market? This is a central question. It merits careful consideration and, as noted earlier, a clear sense of your priorities.

According to David Matheson, who teaches strategic portfolio management at Stanford University and cowrote *The Smart Organization,* the criteria should answer these three questions:

1. Does anyone care? (What's the market need?)
2. Should we do it? (What's the strategic and economic value?)
3. Can we do it (given our existing or available technology)?[2]

After much pilot-testing on legacy products, ASAE chose the seven criteria below, which are based on corporate best practices and ASAE priorities and are defined on every ASAE proposal form. We ask applicants to comment, and we ask reviewers to rate the first five on a scale of 1 to 5, with 5 indicating, "strongly agree":

1. Strategic fit
2. Member needs
3. Market viability
4. Feasibility
5. Innovation
6. Projected net income (first year)
7. Red flags

Products that score high on innovation but low on other criteria are given special consideration, to ensure that we're cultivating innovation. "The best ideas are often the most fragile ones," notes NPD pioneer Robert G. Cooper in *Winning at New Products.*[3] So we want to nurture these fragile, embryonic ideas.

ASAE's sixth criterion is projected net income. We consider the net budget number itself as part of our overall deliberations to determine whether the product will provide a valuable return (financial or otherwise) on our investment.

Finally, "red flags" provides a way for reviewers to quantify (on the five-point scale) any concerns; there is also room on the form for comments.

Your criteria may be different, but don't choose too many; six to eight should suffice. Most important is that they effectively measure what you hope to measure: the product's chance for success.

Sunsetting Products

To everything, there is a season. Even conferences, seminars, books, and professional journals have "a time to be born and a time to die." This is called the product lifecycle.

An interesting thing happened after ASAE created its NPD framework. Staff members started "euthanizing" low-performing products—without NPD review. The simple act of the NPD team's setting up shop and beginning to educate people about product lifecycles and the need to make good business decisions resulted in product managers' taking responsibility for decluttering their own departments. This reduced the workload of the NPD team and had a ripple effect throughout the organization as people learned that, "naturally," some products were being composted to make room for others to grow.

After ASAE's NPD team has carefully read a proposal and budget, scored it according to our criteria, and (often) discussed it at a team meeting, we consider that sufficient analysis to render a final decision. When we were building our framework, some staff members requested an appeals process, but we did not want to establish a judicial-type atmosphere.

The NPD team is empowered to make two decisions: green light (often with accompanying recommendations) or red light (accompanied by an in-person explanation.) The chief staff executive retains veto power over the NPD team's decisions. To us, this makes sense: the CSE might have information or a perspective that we do not have. However, if a CSE vetoed decisions on a regular basis, this would indicate a problem with the system.

Because early staff concerns included the extra time it takes to write a proposal and await NPD review, we have expedited the process as much as possible. Our turnaround time is three to four weeks. Knowing this, product managers build a month into their own planning process.

In the nonprofit arena, rushing to market to beat the competition is not usually a valid concern—most associations are not in that sort of highly competitive, time-sensitive environment—but people are understandably eager to share their new program, product, or service with members or other customers, so it's considerate to move as quickly as possible, without skimping on the time the team needs to vet proposals. We also believe that the time it takes the product manager to think through the questions on our application forms (narrative and budget) and to test the product with potential customers is time well spent.

Product Portfolio Analysis

Like a financial portfolio, an association's product portfolio should be balanced. Some products will probably be free, some at the higher end of the price scale. Some should be for early-career professionals, others for seasoned veterans. To identify the gaps and overlaps, all product information needs to be organized. Often this begins with a "monster spreadsheet" filled with data (revenue, expenses, target audience, market segment, number of attendees, evaluation scores, department, lead staff member, price, and so on).

Once the relevant information is available in one database, the analysis begins, with questions such as

- How many products do we have?
- Who are our products for (which markets or market segments)?
- Which are the strongest and weakest financial performers?
- Which are the most popular?
- What percentage are more than five years old?

These questions eventually lead to more qualitative ones, such as

- Do we need so many products on one subject?
- Why are we offering products that almost no one is buying?
- Why aren't we doing more for a certain segment of members, or to address a current need or problem?
- What could we create that would "surprise and delight" our members, as Starbucks CEO Howard Schultz puts it?

"The cost of doing too many small, unproductive projects is not the financial cost; it's that you dilute and distract resources away from doing big, great things," says product-portfolio expert David Matheson.[4] Taking a good look at your portfolio is an important step toward decluttering and making room for big, great things.

Implementation and Evaluation

The staff and volunteer leadership should be involved and informed, and the chief staff executive should be supportive, but actual implementation of a new NPD framework should be in the hands of the NPD leader and team. Unambiguous definitions about what is and is not a product, technical user-friendliness, clear expectations and deadlines, and an open-door policy so that staff feel comfortable dropping by to ask questions will be some of the early hallmarks of success. The later hallmark, of course, will be product performance.

The first moment of truth may occur when a new-product proposal receives a red light. Does the product manager understand and respect the metrics that were used to evaluate potential success? Careful treatment of applicants will have a big impact on the larger cultural acceptance of this change.

Another milestone comes when a legacy product—especially one that is near and dear to someone's heart—is discontinued. Disappointment is inevitable, but David Matheson's paradigm for measuring success in such cases can be helpful: The "gold standard of persuasion," he says, is when the political loser comes to the same conclusion as the NPD team, realizing that the product is not viable or outdated. The "silver standard"—second best, but also a sign of success—"is when the political loser accepts that process was fair and accurate."[5]

Find out whether you achieved the gold or silver standard by asking for feedback on an evaluation form distributed to applicants shortly after decisions have been rendered. Feedback should be used to improve the process over time.

While an NPD framework aspires to be data-driven, projections (such as, is this a good fit for us? How many people will buy it?) are made by human beings, as are go/no decisions. The most industrious planning, calculating, and scoring still comes down to this: people decide a product should move forward, or not. There's no way to know "the right answer" for sure. Therefore this is fundamentally a human process. Start by choosing the right people, involve lots of people, and revise the process according to feedback from the people, and you'll be well on your way to creating an effective, efficient, trusted, accepted process that can spark innovation, serve members, and strengthen your organization.

Notes

1. David Butler, Presentation at the Business Innovation Factory conference, September 2013, Providence, Rhode Island.
2. David Matheson, "Portfolio Management: Driving Innovation in Your Portfolio" at the Product Innovation Management Conference, October 22, 2012.

3. Robert G. Cooper, *Winning at New Products: Creating Value Through Innovation* (New York: Basic Books, 2011).

4. David Matheson, "Portfolio Management."

5. Ibid.

Resources

Kahn, Kenneth B. (ed.). *The PDMA Handbook of New Product Development.* Hoboken, NJ: John Wiley & Sons, 2005.

The Author

Mariah Burton Nelson, MPH, CAE, serves as vice president for innovation and planning at ASAE: The Center for Association Leadership. She previously served as executive director of the American Association for Physical Activity and Recreation. She's the author of six books about gender and sports (most notably *The Stronger Women Get, the More Men Love Football*), and played basketball at Stanford University and in the first women's pro league in the United States. This chapter is excerpted and adapted from a forthcoming ASAE workbook, *Focus on What Matters,* copyright 2015 by ASAE.

CHAPTER TWENTY-TWO

FUNDRAISING AND DEVELOPMENT

Todd Wurschmidt, PhD, CFRE, FASAE, CAE, and
Erin M. Fuller, MPA, FASAE, CAE

Fundraising—a topic and function that can strike fear into the heart of even the most seasoned association professional. Fundraising is largely viewed as asking people for money, and early experiences of selling cookies and car washes door-to-door make many feel uncomfortable and untrained in this key area.

As association executives, we consistently ask people and organizations to invest in our mission, programs and services. Each membership contribution, each event registration, and each education class or credential application are all the result of creating a compelling value proposition in which the investor believes giving his or her funds to you will result in mutual gain. Although fundraising is different from a purely transactional relationship, the elements of research, marketing, budgeting, and assessment are all fully present.

We often hear that the chief staff executive is also the chief membership officer—here, we argue that he or she should be the chief fundraising executive as well. No one is more familiar with the organization's strategy and direction, understands the area of need and opportunity, and can leverage the skill and expertise of volunteer leadership like the association CSE.

Although fundraising is commonly thought of only in the province of the 501(c)(3) organization—raising money around a cause, research, scholarship, or education—501(c)(6) organizations have ample opportunity to leverage resource development as both a key means of nondues revenue and support for key initiatives that advance the strategic plan.

Let's review the key reasons why people, corporations, or organizations choose to invest in your association:

1. There is an alignment between values, ideals, and goals.
2. There is a deep feeling of connection and gratitude toward benefits and services received from your association.

Despite consistent reporting and touting of tax advantages, people seldom give for tax benefits alone.

The principle of linkage, ability, and interest (LAI) is helpful when evaluating a funding source and the potential for investment.

*   *Linkage* is any contact or access through a peer to a potential donor. (For instance, who do your board members know?)
*   *Ability* is an assessment of whether the donor is able to make a contribution.
*   *Interest* assesses the connection between your association's cause, programs, services, and market with the donor's areas of interest and support.

Five Stages of the Fundraising Cycle

Your relationship with your donors usually follows a time sequence through five stages:

1. *Identification:* You identify possible donors either through prospect research or as a result of someone recommending a possible funding source.
2. *Qualification:* Before approaching a possible donor for money, your fundraising staff will need to conduct background research in order to ensure the prospect has ability to give at any level, and then to drill down further in order to see what is the best category of giving amount the prospective donor might consider. You do not want to ask for a small gift to only find out that the giver would have been motivated to give a much larger gift had they only been asked.

3. *Cultivation:* Part of tactical planning is to determine the best approach to nurture a two-way relationship with prospective donors.

4. *Solicitation:* This is the part of the cycle where and when the "ask" is made. Careful planning will pay dividends in creating relationships and in securing needed gifts.

5. *Stewardship:* Part of stewardship is ensuring your foundation consistently expends the donors' donations according to agreed-upon terms. In addition, consistent communication with your donors on the results being achieved as a result of their charitable gifts will likely bring ongoing and future support and appreciation from your donors.

◆ ◆ ◆

Margin of Excellence: Why Fundraising Is Important for Associations

Paulette V. Maehara, CFRE, CAE (ret.)

Many associations have learned that augmenting their traditional sources of revenue with additional fundraising efforts provides a "margin of excellence" that they otherwise would not have been able to provide. The margin of excellence is creating new programs, providing scholarships, providing memberships, and so on for those who may not be able to financially afford participating in educational programs or membership programs.

Developing the additional fundraising expertise is one that requires commitment and continuity, as most new fundraising programs do not immediately pay for themselves. The associations that conduct additional fundraising efforts consistently will have success, and these funds are a critical resource to the association.

I encourage all associations to consider developing your margin of excellence and recommend hiring a fundraising consultant to assist with this effort. All too often, fundraising efforts fail without the direction and roadmap needed to build a new fundraising program. The success of any fundraising effort requires the sustained commitment of both the association board and staff.

◆ ◆ ◆

Essential Considerations

The Association of Fundraising Professionals (AFP) has both a code of professional ethics and a donor bill of rights that are both useful policies to incorporate into association operations. The key areas of ethical consideration are as follows:

Donor acknowledgment: From an early age, we learn that saying "thank you" is an integral part of the art of giving and receiving. Your donors deserve the same—not only should you acknowledge the gift amount and purpose (useful for tax purposes and expense tracking), but it should outline the results of the support, as well as provide copies or links to any recognition received.

Honoring donor intent: Just as there are different motivators for people and organizations to give, there are different areas of interest for each donor. Although there may be political pressure to apply designated funds to another area of interest or need, all funds held should be applied to their designated purpose. It is important to officially document donor intent—especially of major gifts, bequests, or endowments that extend long after your tenure ends with the association.

Compensation of fundraisers and grantwriters: Many assume, incorrectly, that fundraising professionals work on a commission basis. This practice goes against the AFP's Code of Ethics, and should be reviewed and understood by both CSE and fundraising staff. The AFP recommends compensation based on goals, allowing fundraisers to maintain a commitment to the association's mission over personal gain.

Financial considerations: Your fundraising plan should support both programmatic and revenue goals. Skilled fundraisers set appropriate goals on the basis of past performance or programs on the horizon, and by integrating the environmental scanning data referenced in the sidebar.

The more tangible the benefit, the easier it is to predict fundraising success. Booths, advertisements, and lower-level event sponsorships build upon relationships created year over year, and provide a direct opportunity to sell and connect to the sponsor. Funding opportunities that are more broad, involve new programs and initiatives, and require a new source of revenue are more challenging to predict—it takes longer to demonstrate the value proposition without data on past performance and success.

Fundraising is essential to having a balanced portfolio of revenue sources in your association, and often integrates other areas of success—building upon member and leader relationships, leveraging content in new ways, allowing for new research, expanding existing programs. It is critical that the staff and leadership that "touch" those areas are engaged and enlisted in fundraising efforts to ensure success.

Contractual considerations: Every sponsorship, grant, or bequest should include a written contract, executed by both parties. The contract should explicitly detail the amount of the investment, how and when it should be paid, and any associated benefits or recognition. A consistent contract process supports a transparent and ethical operation, and ensures information continuity and relationship management in the case of a staff departure.

Legal Aspects of Association Fundraising

Jeffrey S. Tenenbaum, Esq., and Kristalyn Loson, Esq.

Whether for a trade association, professional society, or related foundation, association executives are regularly involved in charitable fundraising. Therefore, it is important for association executives to have a grasp of the potential legal issues inherent in these activities.

Approximately forty states require that organizations register with the state prior to conducting solicitations for charitable purposes. The definition of charitable purposes is not confined solely to requests by organizations exempt from tax under Section 501(c)(3), and could potentially encompass requests for a specific charitable or educational program of a trade or professional association.

States also require professional solicitors, or those who solicit on behalf of a charitable organization for compensation, to register prior to conducting solicitations. If the association itself receives compensation for solicitations, it may need to register with the state, when applicable.

Approximately twenty-five states also have regulations specific to commercial coventurers, or for-profit entities that conduct promotions in which it is advertised that the sale or use of a good or service will benefit a charitable purpose (for example, $1 from your purchase of X will benefit ABC charity).

Association executives also should be aware that many states have specific regulations for charitable raffles and gaming activities, such as imposing residency requirements or requiring a charity to file a raffle registration prior to conducting the raffle.

Finally, on the federal tax front, organizations that collect tax-deductible charitable contributions must provide written substantiation to donors if goods or services are received in return for the donation. If the organization is exempt under an Internal Revenue Code section other than Section 501(c)(3), the organization must inform donors that contributions to the organization are not tax deductible as charitable contributions (although they may be tax deductible as business expenses).

Role of Technology in Successful Fundraising

Ensure accurate memory: Unless your foundation has but one benefactor, your fundraising efforts will likely involve hundreds if not thousands of details over periods of time. Donors appreciate and expect that your professional foundation will be, well, professional. Thus efficiency, accuracy, timeliness, and a personalized touch are critical ingredients to being successful in raising donations. Whether you seek personal donations, corporate sponsorships, or government or foundation grants, each contact you make requires research and remembering details. The only feasible and efficient way to accomplish remembering is through your ardent embrace of technology—your partner in fundraising.

Record field notes: Each and every time you meet in the field with current or prospective donors, you need to commit to promptly and formally documenting your interactions and observations, and the follow-ups you mutually agreed. Big money fundraising is personal business. There is nothing worse than misspelling a donor's name, or getting their spouse's name wrong, or forgetting to list a donor in your annual report. Details matter, and you rarely get a second chance at correcting a bad impression. Commit to the discipline needed to consistently write or dictate your field notes soon after field experiences. Then file your field notes into your database for future reference.

Keep your database current: Given the competing demands of daily to-do lists, inputting into your database can be one task easily put off. This will become a big mistake quickly. You and your staff must commit to viewing the task of updating databases as critical to the functioning as is your case statement, strategic plan, or leave-behind marketing literature. Inputting information when it is fresh in memory should be a staff policy and enforced practice. This will pay dividends to the success of your fundraising efforts.

Research for large personal assets: Your foundation can subscribe to commercial products that will give you access to enormous databases of publicly held data about individual assets. Either through targeted searches or searches undertaken using relevant criterion, you have the capacity to discover individuals who might be considered prime prospect donors for your cause.

Leverage social media: Social media permit your organization to reach unlimited numbers of people across the United States and around the globe. Your association most likely combines your website pages with social media linkages. This linking process can also be used to tell your fundraising story and to raise funds. Perhaps your social media messages include links to donation webpages, or quick text messaging can automatically designate a donor's intentions to give a fixed amount. If donors take the time to click and give, know these same donors may be believers in your cause and could become great active volunteers.

Crowdsource and crowdfund: Several web services offer opportunities for you to raise initial capital and donations for a particular foundation's mission or program. Donors have the opportunity to express their support of your cause by offering to invest and donate after learning about your foundation's work via these web crowdsourcing and crowdfunding websites. Increasing numbers of success stories are being communicated by the media and philanthropic publications.

Strategic Planning: Articulating Foundation Goals in the Context of the Whole Organization

Money as a means to an end: Money raised through philanthropic and charitable efforts is a means to an end, not an end in and of itself. This is very important to keep at the forefront of all efforts relating to fundraising. What is your association hoping to accomplish? How will your organizational mission be enhanced if charitable donations are pursued? What are the programs and services that your association feels can best become reality if your membership organization could raise additional monies using techniques and strategies articulated within fundraising communities? You and your organization need more money to do what? Why? How will your mission be advanced?

The feasibility of implementing a new program or service is solidly dependent on your ability to raise initial and ongoing revenues. Great ideas require the fuel of funds to enable continuous offering, and wither quickly if initial funding dries up.

Comprehensive strategic planning: When your parent membership association conducts formal strategy planning, the philanthropic component of the organization should be integrally included in these discussions. The 501(c)(3) board should be represented in order that ownership and approval of decisions on overall strategic priorities will be wholly embraced. Of course, once the membership association's strategic plan has been approved by the parent association, the full foundation board should be accorded its fiduciary role in formally accepting the parts of the strategic plan relating to the foundation's mission.

Articulating goals prior to seeking donations: Associations diversifying revenues via philanthropic fundraising can easily lose sight of the fact that donors want to know why and how their donations will be making a difference. Donors also highly appreciate being kept informed on what has been accomplished and may in fact expect this. All associations are eager to experience increased revenues, but knowing what you want to accomplish and writing the case statement to detail what, how, why, when, and who are required first steps in order to be successful.

Case statement: Core to successfully initiating fundraising efforts is articulating the "internal case" and the "external case." Organizations must articulate why a fundraising effort is needed and needed now. The target audience for the external case is potential donors and the larger community. Ask questions such as, "Why is our cause and program so critical and to whom? How will implementing this program, made possible by your donation, save lives or make lives better?" Donors will want to know what resources are needed and how they will be used efficiently. Internal case statements address operational, policy, and procedural issues. Case statements force staff to prepare "the case" prior to going public or ever asking for money.

Keeping the strategic plan fresh in content and in the minds of the governing body: Keeping all important parties up to date on progress toward organizational goals and objectives is key to ongoing support. Regularly scheduled update reports provide opportunities to notice that certain objectives need addressing or are no longer relevant, or have morphed in some way significant to the organization. A periodic status report should be designed and disseminated to the board, executive staff, and committee chairs that provides an executive summary overview of progress on the plan's goals and objectives, as well as a dashboard report on key metrics to keep everyone focused on (and no one to escape from) the importance of fundraising initiatives.

Further, the foundation's strategic plan should be formally refreshed on an annual basis, perhaps at the last board meeting of the year.

Tactical Strategies and Work Plans

Tactical work plans: Once your foundation has adopted the organizational strategic plan, with articulated goals and objectives, staff need to detail tactical work plans that think through

- Steps required for accomplishing each objective
- Deadlines (both start dates and finish)
- Person(s) primarily responsible for undertaking
- HR, volunteer, and budgetary resources required
- A Gantt Chart with time progress bars
- Notes for updating highlights of issues and discussions of importance

Vilfredo Pareto's 80–20 rule: It is probably the most frequent and instinctive solution for someone on your board, committee, or task force to assert, "If we just get everyone to give $1.00 (or $5.00 or $100.00 each), we will meet our goal." We can only assume this flawed assertion comes from the fact that it is easy to conceive of this approach as "a strategy driving toward a solution." And doing this math is quite easy—# of people × identical $ gift = total $ goal. You must resist this thought process and instead think "pyramid." In fundraising, it is a commonly accepted principle that 20 percent of your donors give 80 percent of your campaign goal. This is known as the insightful "Pareto Principle—The 80–20 Rule." These top 20 percent of donors have the capacity and wherewithal to give *more* per donation (that is, larger gift amounts). Thus, early on in our planning process, we need to devise gift categories.

Gift pyramid charts: Using the Pareto 80–20 rule, construct a gift pyramid chart that articulates the gift-giving categories, number of gifts needed per gift category, and number of prospective donors you need to make "asks" in order to meet your fundraising goals. Shown in Figure 22.1 is a sample pyramid gift chart that includes a variety of instructional pieces of information.

Following is how to interpret the gift pyramid illustration:

1. There are five gift ranges listed in the first column on the left-hand side.
2. Next is the pyramid illustration with the number of gifts needed for each of the five gift ranges.
3. The third column combines the first two columns to calculate the sub-goals and thus the total campaign goal.
4. Columns four to eight present five years of historical data for this sample fundraising campaign for comparative analysis.
5. The box on the bottom gives insight into the number of campaign volunteers needed.
6. Last, you identify *prospective donors* that you believe your research shows might be able to donate at one of the five gift categories. For this sample campaign and this pyramid gift chart, we show our need to solicit eighty total gifts. To successfully solicit eighty gifts, we would need to make perhaps two hundred to five hundred "asks," depending on this being our first campaign or our having a collection of past (and hopefully repeat) donors.

Power of the friendly face: As you involve your foundation board members and fundraising volunteers, a prime consideration is "who knows whom,"

FIGURE 22.1. A PYRAMID GIFT CHART.

Some -Foundation. Inc.
Some -Place Campaign
Gift Pyramid and History

No. of Gifts
6
7
17
20
30

80 Gifts

Gift Range	Goals	Year 1	Year 2	Year 3	Year 4	Year 5
$10,000—	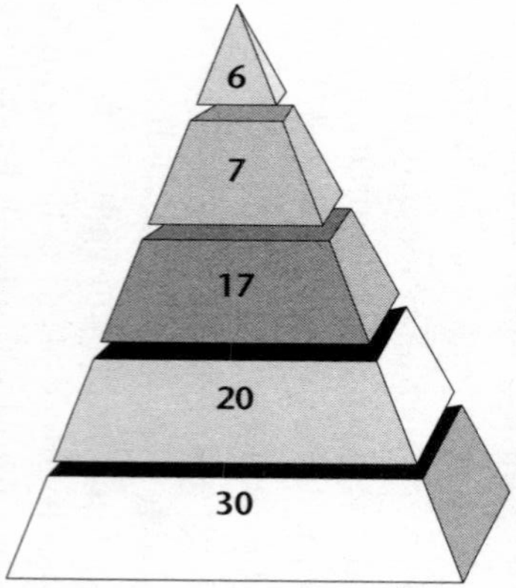 6 $60,000	6 $90,000	6 $90,000	6 $87,000	5 $75,000	5 $75,000
$5,000—$9,999	7 $35,000	6 $32,500	7 $37,500	7 $35,500	6 $35,000	5 $21,000
$2,500—$4,999	17 $42,500	5 $13,900	7 $19,500	5 $14,000	8 $24,500	9 $29,500
$1,000—$2,499	20 $20,000	19 $21,500	16 $20,500	16 $20,250	10 $14,000	12 $15,000
Under $1,000	30 $17,500	18 $5,675	29 $9,930	35 $12,875	24 $9,275	18 $6,550
Totals	$175,500 80 Gifts	$163,575+ 54 Gifts	$177,410 65 Gifts	$170,125 69 Gifts	$157,775 53 Gifts	$146,550 49 Gifts

The Chair is to recruit 10 Team Captains @ 5 Prospects each - 50 Prospects.
Each Team Captain will recruit 2 Team Members @ 5 Prospects each - 100 Prospects.
This covers 150/200 area prospects with personal contact from campaign volunteers.

or relationships. Passion for your mission can carry you a long way, but the ability to have your foundation friends open doors to their wealthy friends or friends in high decision-making places is key. The maxim commonly refrained is, "People don't give to causes; people give to people with causes." This maxim is well worth remembering and repeating often. You normally have one opportunity to make an ask, and you need to make your ask maximally impactful. Friends of friends, or the power of the friendly face, is part of the network nexus that you conduct during your planning and preparatory phases. As well, most corporate and foundation offices have assistants who are well trained as "gatekeepers." And asking a subordinate to open the door of their superior can be uncomfortable with lower probabilities of return. Thus taking time to identify who knows whom is homework worth doing as a critical tactical step in fundraising and mapping the nexuses.

Thank you, thank you, thank you: In the art and science of fundraising and dealing with people, you cannot say "Thank you" often enough. Instill into all of your foundation's board and staff the importance of offering thanks to donors, personally and often. And, when lists of donors are printed in your annual reports or listed on walls, make certain you have 100 percent of donors listed and their names printed correctly. What is the first thing most donors do with your annual report? They look for their name and check that it is listed accurately. Your foundation culture must include expressing personal and frequent appreciation to those who make your foundation financially feasible. And, don't wait until a year later when you want to ask for more money.

Implementation of Fundraising Strategy and Campaigns

Fundraising takes different forms to serve different purposes and timelines. Each of the categories outlined below take research, marketing, and program development and evaluation abilities that match the donor's vision and goals.

Annual funds: An annual fund generates money for ongoing support and seeks to enroll new donors in order to continually expand that base of support, in addition to both renew and upgrade existing contributors. Contributions usually support existing programs, and funds are typically unrestricted.

Major gifts: As the term implies, major gifts are sizeable donations as defined by their impact on the total amount of funds needed. For one organization, $1,000 may be a major gift while another may perceive $25,000 as a major gift. Major gifts can be a component part of the top of a gift pyramid, while for other campaigns, a special or major gift may be sought if the program or service has an appeal to a single donor, family, private foundation, company, or so on. Major or special gifts can be one-time gifts to enable the program or service to be accomplished, or represent a large percentage of the total.

Capital campaign: Funds are raised to accomplish a key objective, for instance, constructing or renovating a building, or purchasing equipment. Increasingly, capital campaigns are seen to assist in a large investment in technology. The appeal is typically time-limited and encourages gifts via multiyear pledges.

Planned giving: Another source is the solicitation of gifts from a person's current assets or estate, with the bequest received as a trust, contract, or gift. Many states regulate the solicitation of planned gifts, and a CSE should ensure that his or her association (or affiliated foundation) is appropriately registered in the states that require that type of compliance.

Grants: Whether from government or private foundation sources, the grantsmanship skills required to solicit, implement, and evaluate received funds are similar. Grants are given after a thorough solicitation process, with a defined request-for-proposals (RFP) process that is typically vetted and scored by a number of evaluators. The proposal typically contains the following elements:

- Organization qualifications (proving the ability to execute on the proposal)
- A problem statement (why funds are needed)
- Program goals and objectives
- Methodology (detailed explanation of how the program will be executed)
- An evaluation process
- A budget
- Appendices (can include prior research, staff qualifications, list of prior grant-funded projects)

Due to the RFP process, and response and evaluation time needed, the grant cycle can be extremely lengthy, and because there is usually competition for funds, results are uncertain. In addition, traditional multiyear grants have evolved into one-two year funding cycles, or if multiyear, with evaluation at the end of each completed year to evaluate whether funds will continue.

Corporate sponsorship: Although some think of corporate sponsorship only through the lens of event-related support, there are a variety of ways for corporations to invest in an association's programs and initiatives.

- *Year-round partnership:* Allows for consistent visibility and a demonstrated support for the association's members and mission.
- *Special events:* Allows opportunities for direct connection between the sponsor and the program, with the added benefit of providing a memorable, fun, or impactful experience to attendees while allowing the sponsor direct contact with their desired market. Benefits are usually standardized at lower levels, with greater ability to customize as levels of investment increase.
- *Program support:* Targeted, time-limited support for a specific initiative, such as a curriculum, research project, or scholarship program. This is easily customized to serve a sponsor's needs in terms of market visibility, recognition, and area of impact.

Marketing: Each association promotes the opportunities for investment as well as program results in a variety of ways—and all of these are effective marketing tools for fundraisers. Most associations have a prospectus—a document that clearly outlines opportunities for investment throughout the organization. Sometimes these opportunities are segmented by program area—for instance, a separate prospectus for the annual meeting. At other times, they may be separated by investment level, as sponsors or donors may want to evaluate the different areas of recognition, impact, and market access they have for a given amount.

In addition to the prospectus, the association's other publications and products serve to demonstrate the association's market and reach, quality of prior work, and examples of how sponsors have been integrated into programs and recognized in the past.

Your case statement is a critical marketing communication tool.

Metrics: To know if you are successfully accomplishing goals and objectives, you need to identify quantitative measures that let all involved know whether you are on track. Like all association program areas, establishing and tracking metrics is an essential part of fundraising and resource development. At first glance, it would seem that tracking key revenue categories would be sufficient—if the funds are raised, metrics have been clearly met, yes? But that doesn't tell the full picture.

Metrics will be priceless if undertaken. The number of prospects, the number of conversations, and the number of off-season inquiries are all good indicators of a healthy pipeline. In addition, actively reviewing the sources of all leads and successful relationships is important. If, as with many associations, the majority of relationships come directly from or as a result of your volunteer leaders, it makes sense to provide fundraising training as well as updates on how sponsorships and investments are helping the organization.

Resources

Association for Fundraising Professionals, available at www.afpnet.org /ethics. See in particular the links to the Code of Ethics, the Donor Bill of Rights, and FAQ's about ethics.

Association Foundation Group, an organization of 501(c)(6)-affiliated 501(c)(3) organizations and their staff leadership, available at www. associationfoundationgroup.org.

IEG, the global authority on sponsorship trends, research and valuation. Available at www.sponsorship.com.

Jacobs, J. A. *Association Law Handbook: A Practical Guide for Associations, Societies and Charities,* 5th ed. Washington, DC: ASAE Association Management Press, 2012. Give special attention to chapters 75 and 78, which cover unrelated business income tax and corporate sponsorship income.

National Council of Nonprofit Boards. Available at www.councilof nonprofits.org.

The Authors

Todd Wurschmidt, PhD, CFRE, FASAE, CAE, holds a doctorate in human and community resource development, The Ohio State University, and has served many volunteer roles with ASAE. Wurschmidt has been involved in association management business at the state, national, and international levels. Wurschmidt currently serves as executive director of the U.S. Farmers and Ranchers Alliance, and is the account executive for AMR Management Services, an AMC accredited by the AMC Institute.

Erin M. Fuller, MPA, FASAE, CAE, is the president of Coulter, an AMC Institute charter-accredited nonprofit management and consulting firm that works with more than twenty associations and affiliated foundations on setting and achieving goals around marketing, membership, events, and fundraising.

Sidebar author *Paulette V. Maehara, CFRE, CAE (ret.),* is the former president of the Association of Fundraising Professionals, and has served as chair for both ASAE and the ASAE Foundation.

Sidebar author *Jeffrey S. Tenenbaum, Esq.,* is a partner and chair of the nonprofit organizations practice, Venable LLP; *Kristalyn Loson, Esq.,* is an associate and member of the nonprofit organizations practice, Venable LLP.

CHAPTER TWENTY-THREE

MEETING AND EVENT MANAGEMENT

Dawn M. Mancuso, MAM, FASAE, CAE, and
Natasha J. Ross, CMP

E vents and meetings play a key role in an association's ability to fulfill its
mission. Meetings bring together members to conduct personal, professional, and association business; provide for the delivery of educational
programs to members; and establish forums for the development of industry and association policies or for the airing of controversial issues and
concerns. Meetings offer opportunities to recognize volunteers, reward
excellence, enhance member relations, educate members' customers, provide a showcase for products and services, and engage donors. Meetings
create opportunities for prospective members to "test drive" the association before making the decision to join. They also provide moments to
nurture a sense of community among the members.

In addition, meetings provide the mechanism through which the association meets the requirements set by its own bylaws, which usually call for
at least one annual business meeting of members. At these meetings, board
members may be elected and votes may be held on bylaws amendments.

The chief staff executive's (CSE's) role is to *see to it* that the association
achieves what it should from meetings and that unacceptable situations
are avoided. When there is such a vast array of activity and impact wrapped
into an event, the CSE must ensure professional staff are available to plan
your major meetings. The CSE and planning staff must hold a shared
vision of what the desired outcomes are for major association meetings
and events, including financial impact as well as a general timeline

involved for planning and marketing. Once defined, the CSE's role focuses on monitoring to ensure that the plan is on track and progressing appropriately. The CSE may need to be involved in problem solving if the plan is not being realized.

This chapter offers an overview of meeting planning for large events with the intent that a CSE might provide oversight with some knowledge of all the elements involved in planning for a successful meeting.

◆ ◆ ◆

Meeting Planner Competencies

With a wide variety of event types, functions, venues, and objectives, the expectation for today's planners is that they play a key role in their association's ability to deliver on its mission. Thus a successful meeting planner has to be adept at a number of different skills. No longer is it enough to be an organized and efficient manager of logistics. He or she must now be able to

- Assess and integrate technology enhancements into event operations as well as the content of learning opportunities
- Identify and track trends within the members' industry or profession in order to provide educational programming and events that are timely and worthwhile
- Build and execute budgets, marketing plans, crisis management plans, and strategic plans (complete with mission, goals, objectives, and strategies) for conferences and events
- Expand upon current revenue streams and generate new ones
- Develop and utilize a facility with analyzing and reporting statistical and financial data, and producing evaluative systems that will guide a continual improvement process and maximize return on investment (ROI)
- Cultivate both written and verbal communications skills, and understand how to incorporate multiple communication channels into both the marketing plan and the program for the event
- Foster an entrepreneurial spirit that enhances the organization's ability to identify and respond to opportunities present in a quickly changing external environment
- Maintain knowledge of current legal and ethical issues surrounding supplier contracting and meeting or event planning in order to minimize risk
- Develop negotiating skills to help with all aspects of the event-planning process—from contract negotiations to personnel management
- Design a planning process using project management concepts and tools in order to maximize productivity and available resources
- Facilitate and manage teams made up of paid staff, volunteers, and third-party vendors so that all work together seamlessly and effectively

◆ ◆ ◆

Program Development

What makes an event, a meeting, or a convention successful? Factors often cited as indicators of a successful event include stimulating programs, a format well-suited to the target audience and the message(s) to be delivered, well-planned and executed logistics, knowledgeable moderators and chairpersons, a comfortable and attractive physical environment, and sufficient opportunity to meet one's colleagues and exchange ideas.

The key to hosting a successful meeting lies in the advance work. Adequate planning will deliver higher-quality programs, streamline costs, maximize revenues and participation, and simplify the onsite logistics.

The objectives of the meeting should be clearly delineated and aligned with the association's mission. Around these objectives, the association should develop a program and a format that meet participants' needs, elicit excitement, and entice attendance.

The most common method for deciding on a meeting's program and format is to use a volunteer committee or task force. Volunteers are well-suited to participate on content and speaker selections and awards—specifically the areas where field knowledge and intimate knowledge of what members value is critical to the decision-making process. However, if you have conference staff, leave logistical, print materials, and meal-function decision making to the professionals.

Program content should be based on information gathered from a range of sources, including program or education committees, surveys, evaluations of previous events, calls for presentations, crowdsourcing, and association departments that have special insight into "hot" topics or new trends.

Choosing Your Format

The next step in planning is to design a meeting format that will deliver the chosen content in the most interesting and effective way. Consider the learning objectives identified during the needs-determination process, how interactive the format should be to foster this learning, the demographics of the participants, the meeting's overall objectives, the character of the destination (once chosen), budget, and available delivery systems.

Format options for in-person meetings vary greatly, but typically include general or plenary sessions, educational breakout sessions or workshops, and scientific assemblies or poster sessions. Other options include hands-on demonstrations, simulations, competitions or competitive games, and so on.

Digital technology delivery options have expanded the reach and impact of association-sponsored events and programming. More and more, associations are using mobile technology and apps to host meetings and provide value-added services to event participants. In addition, the use of technology in delivering virtual conference programming via webinars, video conferencing, and discussion forums on social media outlets has grown exponentially.

Tours and other social events provide meeting delegates with social or networking time mixed in with the educational or business events. For instance, receptions offer attendees a means to network with old and new friends and colleagues. Sometimes a professional educational component is added when study tours are conducted of business operations of local members, suppliers, and more. Fundraisers, sporting events, and guest programs are a few more options to consider.

Once you have decided on the right mix of events, you need to create a schedule or agenda that includes the number of days the meeting will be held, the start and end times for each event, and the program format for each event.

Budgeting

The basic components of a meeting budget are income (or revenue), expenses, and net return.

It is crucial to set reasonable goals and track results for each revenue source: delegate registration (number of participants, minus any complimentary registrations offered, multiplied by the registration fee), special event ticket sales (including tours and guest program), exhibit space rental, exhibitor registrations, sponsorships, and other miscellaneous income (such as sales of convention proceedings, often via streaming video or mp3 file). Detailed historic information about past meeting results will provide a good basis for setting realistic goals.

Meeting expenses typically fall into one of two major groupings: direct or indirect. Direct expenses are those owed for goods or services provided by outside suppliers. These include food and beverage costs (paid to the hotel, convention center, or an outside caterer), audiovisual equipment and labor, staff travel and accommodations, speakers' fees, entertainment, photography, decorations and signage, exhibition decorating services, printing of convention materials, facility rental, security, and insurance.

Indirect expenses are incurred by allocating salaries, benefits, and office expenses against the event. Indirect expenses are as much a part of the cost of putting on any event as direct costs; they must be taken into account to get an accurate picture of an event's effect on the association's bottom line.

It is also important to understand the basic differences between fixed and variable costs of a meeting. Variable costs are those that change depending on the number of participants. Some typical variable costs are food and beverage charges and the costs for registration materials. By contrast, fixed costs are those that do not change depending on the number of participants attending an event. These costs are borne by the association whether 250 or 500 people attend, so it is important to watch these costs carefully and work to minimize them whenever feasible.

Your net return is the difference between income and expenses.

The budget, along with information gathered about expenses during the logistics planning stage, should be used to set participant prices for the meeting. Calculate full registration (which includes all events), individual event ticket prices, meal prices, optional tour prices, guest program prices, and exhibit booth rental. You may wish to factor in the impact of sponsorship dollars that can significantly help to reduce registration costs. Alternatively, you can use that revenue to build a healthier bottom line.

Site Selection

Identifying the most appropriate facility type, location, and time of year to hold a meeting requires some basic information on the potential meeting audience. Does the group comprise corporate CEOs looking for opportunities to network or individuals very interested in sports? A resort facility would offer lots of informal activities to foster that networking or fulfill recreational needs. A trade association with members who conduct much of the buying for their businesses at its trade show should entertain using a convention center or hotel with substantial facilities to house exhibits. Airport hotels offer the convenience of location for smaller, shorter meetings. A five-star hotel in a large city would probably not be the best choice for a budget-conscious group.

Locale, too, plays a big part in site selection. Many national groups rotate their conventions around the country so that no one group of members is required to travel long distances every year. Some regions of the country may hold special significance to the members of a group; for example, the members may wish to visit an area where business is growing rapidly or where they hope to vacation after the meeting has concluded.

Timing may come into play as well. For example, conventions for educators may need to be held during the summer months or school breaks.

Historical data will be crucial in determining whether a facility is right for a meeting, and those data may also have an impact on the facility bids you receive. Collect information such as the number and type of sleeping rooms used per night; the number and types of food and beverage functions held; the number and size of meeting rooms used each day; the number of hospitality suites utilized; the amount of space required for registration, ticket sales, and information desks; the number and size of exhibit spaces rented (your gross versus net square footage of exhibit space); and any statistics you can get about attendee spending while at the meeting.

The local convention and visitors bureaus (CVBs) or destination marketing organizations (DMOs) can assist in your quest for an appropriate meeting facility. Compile all the information on the meeting's schedule, format, history, and preferred locations and dates into a request for proposal (RFP) and distribute it to the CVBs or DMOs. These agencies will identify and contact the most appropriate facilities for your meeting.

When selecting a meeting site, consider rates (prices for sleeping rooms, meeting rooms, food and beverage costs, exhibit space, and ancillary charges), dates (exact days for which sleeping rooms and meeting space are available to the group), and space (amount and configuration of meeting space being offered and the flow of that space from one event to another).

Meetings held outside the United States pose special challenges: language and cultural differences, substantial mailing and shipping costs, longer lead times, customs and immigration regulations, duties and taxes, currency exchange rates, special insurance requirements, electricity and other utility systems disparities, and labor union regulations. Because of these added concerns, planners usually lengthen their planning timetable considerably and seek outside help from U.S. consulates, customs brokers, freight forwarders, professional conference organizers, and travel agencies. Members residing in the host city and local convention bureaus are generally good sources of additional assistance.

Conducting a Site Inspection

The next step is to personally visit the most promising facility(ies). The point of a site inspection is to ensure that the facility chosen has the appropriate amenities to address your needs. Site inspectors want to consider the ambience, quality, cleanliness and amenities of the sleeping rooms, meeting and banquet rooms, and gathering spaces, as well as what accommodations are available for special needs attendees. The ultimate question is about the *fit* of the facility with your members. Will they be comfortable, happy, and proud of their association in this venue? Most planners prefer to conduct their own site inspections, but when others must be involved, be sure to assign only those who are qualified, dependable, and as impartial as possible. When volunteers are selected to participate in site inspections (a practice we do not recommend), be sure there are explicit job descriptions as well as written and enforced policies on ethical considerations for these volunteers.

Finally, it is always wise to talk with other meeting planners who have held events at the facility you're considering, to hear first-hand how the property performed and what challenges can be expected onsite. The hotel, convention center, or CVB can provide the names of planners who have held recent meetings at the properties in question. Reach out to your professional network to get an unbiased opinion of a facility or contractor.

Contracting

With the site inspections completed, it is time to narrow the field to one or two top choices, place a tentative "hold" on the space, and start contract negotiations. Final contract negotiations should always remain a staff function, and may involve the association's legal counsel.

Negotiate fairly with a hotel or other property so the contract provides a fair profit for the services and facilities provided. Some planners have discovered that driving a property to agree to a one-sided contract results in poorer quality service during the convention or a lack of interest in hosting future meetings. Remember, everything is negotiable: concentrating on additional services and amenities can be a good alternative to strictly focusing on price.[1]

Every meeting should involve a formal letter of agreement or contract (preferred), signed by representatives of both parties (the hotel or facility and the association). Putting the agreement in writing helps clarify the terms and makes the terms binding and enforceable. A clear offer must be made and accepted by both parties involved in the agreement, including details about what the hotel or facility will provide and what the association or its members will pay. As with all contracts, consult legal counsel before signing any agreement on behalf of your association.

Most associations set up a master account at the host hotel or meeting facility by filling out a credit application and getting approval from the property in advance of the meeting. Against this master account, they charge meeting expenses such as food, meeting room rental, and labor. Be explicit with the hotel about what will and will not be charged to the master account and who has authority to charge items. Once onsite, review the charges made to the master account each day.

Specialized Services

Many planners contract with additional suppliers, such as airlines, car rental agencies, destination management companies, travel agents or tour companies, caterers, entertainers, audiovisual companies, and trade show decorators for specialized meeting services.

Because most planners are not experts in audiovisual equipment, they typically hire an audiovisual firm to provide, set up, and operate the equipment. When choosing a firm, ask about inventories, the firm's location (an in-house firm is likely to have a larger supply of labor and equipment available on the spur of the moment), labor costs, overtime policies, and any additional charges incurred for use of the hotel sound system.

Working with entertainers requires special expertise as well. Booking agents can recommend appropriate acts and offer additional services such as onsite coordination. They can also be helpful in emergency situations when a last-minute replacement is needed. Always preview the act before confirming the booking. Be sure the performers receive your guidelines for appropriate entertainment (such as acceptable language), background information on the audience, the event start time and length of performance, and any expenses covered by the association beyond the arranged performance fee.

The use of copyrighted music anytime during your event will require the necessary performance licenses from organizations such as the American Society of Composers, Authors and Publishers (ASCAP) and Broadcast Music International (BMI).

Booking Speakers

One group of service providers—speakers—merits special attention. The ability of the speaker to engage the audience is critical for success. Consider whether the speaker's message will help the association satisfy the meeting's objectives, if the speaker's participation will stimulate attendance or press coverage, if the audience will recognize and respect the speaker's expertise, and whether the speaker's style of delivery will hold the audience's attention.

Associations who use practitioners as speakers should take steps to ensure presentation content aligns with published learner objectives and program descriptions, the approach to the content aligns with adult learning principles, and the presentation skills of the speaker will connect to the target audience.

Many associations find talented speakers through speakers' bureaus that represent both the famous and the not-so-famous. Other speaker sources include local chapters of the National Speakers Association and referrals from your meeting planning or member communities. Whenever possible, preview the speaker by seeing him or her give a presentation or by sending a committee member to do the preview.

For any speaker to be successful, he or she needs to be briefed on the audience—its demographic profile, perspective on the topic, the industry's or profession's general concerns and jargon, and topics to avoid. In addition, educate the speaker about the meeting itself, such as its theme, format, and program.

Speaker contracts should cover the usual items as well as the following, as appropriate: liability issues (copyright or slander), security requirements of high-profile speakers, substitute speakers provided by the speakers' bureau, expenses covered in addition to the arranged speaking fee (for example, coach versus first-class airfare), whether the speaker may market any ancillary products (books or CDs), preferred attire, audiovisual equipment needed, approval to record or webcast the presentation, cancellation by either party, and the type of background information to be provided to the speaker.

Marketing Your Event

An association may host the best event in history, but it won't be a success if no one attends. An association's market data will help determine how much promotion to do and how best to do it. The planner should partner with the association's marketing team to assess options and develop a plan that is appropriate for the event in question. Be aware that lead times for national and international meetings need to be much longer so that participants can plan for expensive and potentially complex travel arrangements.

Regardless of how the message gets out, meeting promotions should include the value an attendee can reasonably expect to gain by attending; the schedule of events, including their exact time and location; registration instructions and fees; information on air travel, sleeping room accommodations, airport transfers, car rentals, and other travel arrangements; recommended attire; other local activities or attractions that may prompt a person to want to visit the meeting location; and where to find more information.

Exposition Management

If an exposition or trade show accompanies the meeting, a basic tenet must be understood: a buyer-seller relationship exists between the companies exhibiting and the people attending (or the companies they represent). The stronger that relationship, the greater the odds that the exposition will be a valued part of a meeting.

Big or small, trade shows should not be treated as an afterthought in the meeting planning process. From the beginning, the exposition should be an integral part of the meeting's objectives and site selection.

Keeping exhibitors happy requires delivering a good supply of buyers to them on the exhibit floor. That means designing the meeting agenda so delegates have time to visit the trade show without the interruption of other sessions or seminars. To ensure high buyer turnout, many associations conduct advance marketing promotions and offer incentives (such as free meals, prize drawings, and giveaways in the exhibit hall) for delegates to walk the show floor and place orders.

The marketing materials sent to potential exhibitors should include details about the show's logistics and exhibitor procedures, a buyer profile, an exhibit space rental agreement, and show rules. The contract should cover space price and payment terms, restrictions, rules of participation, plus the usual terms of a contract. Once again, consult legal counsel when developing this contract.

U.S. courts view exhibiting privileges as a competitive advantage, so restricting exhibit space rental to members may expose the association to the risk of an antitrust violation. In light of this, it is important to note that it is legal to charge nonmembers a premium price if supplier dues are regularly used to defer exhibit show costs. In addition, associations are not obligated to solicit nonmember exhibitors to participate in the trade show.

Meeting planners generally hire a trade show decorator, or exhibition service contractor, to assist in the planning and onsite logistics management. These contractors provide and set up the pipe and drape or walls (that create the individual booth spaces on the exhibit floor), aisle carpeting, signage, lounge and booth furniture, registration counters, and special decorations. In addition, the decorator creates and distributes a manual for exhibitors, which highlights the rules associated with show move-in and tear down and markets a number of services, such as drayage, furniture and equipment rental, and labor. Make sure that contracted services are fairly priced and meet the association's quality standards for service.

Housing

There are several ways to handle the sleeping-room reservation process: allowing participants to reserve rooms directly; providing a rooming list (where the association submits a list of meeting participants and their arrival and departure dates directly to the hotel); or working with a housing bureau (or centralized reservation service operated by the association or its contractor).

Whatever the housing process used, the meeting planner should assign any VIPs (including sponsors) to special rooms (upgrades or suites) before the room block becomes available for general reservations, and make sure that those who register receive confirmations. In addition, the planner should consider reserving a few extra sleeping rooms before the room block cut-off date in case a speaker, staff person, board member, or other participant forgets to make a hotel reservation for the meeting.

Food and Beverage Functions

Food and beverage (F&B) events often prove the most visible and memorable of functions. They also require close scrutiny on the part of the planner in order to safeguard the meeting budget.

Here are a few tips to get the most out of your F&B functions:

- Rooms holding meal functions should be the appropriate size: not so small that participants are uncomfortable, but not so large that empty space in the room overshadows the event.

- If an event is scheduled for outdoors, have an indoor location reserved in case of inclement weather.
- Local attractions often provide unique and memorable backdrops for a meeting function; be sure to alert the host hotel not to include the off-premise function in the list of meals it will provide.
- Selecting appropriate menus requires a good understanding of the meeting delegates. Menus can be tailored to match an event theme or fit any type of age demographic, cultural or religious profile, and food restrictions.
- The catering staff can assist with menu design and planning, the most effective room layouts, and ways to get the most amount of food for the association's budget.
- Remember to include taxes and gratuities when calculating cost—and find out if gratuities are taxable.
- Because hotels usually require guarantees forty-eight to seventy-two hours in advance, the planner needs to guarantee the exact number of people to be served so the association doesn't pay for meals that aren't consumed. If the planner underestimates attendance, however, the hotel may not have sufficient food or table space to serve everyone wishing to attend. Hotels usually prepare a small number of meals over the guaranteed figure, but you should ask about the exact percentage before deciding upon the guarantee.
- It's the planner's responsibility to make sure adequate dining facilities exist to serve delegates when meal functions are not planned. Is there sufficient restaurant capacity for a mid-day luncheon? Can the hotel accommodate a heavy demand for breakfast room service? Be sure to communicate these on-your-own moments to the hotel so that it can prepare in advance to meet your members' needs.

Registration

The first experience participants have with a meeting is the registration desk. Long lines, misplaced registration packets, and missing tickets or materials will not give delegates a positive first impression. Be sure to staff your registration desk adequately, offer separate areas for preregistrants and onsite registrants, provide training for the desk staff, streamline registration procedures as much as possible, and make sure all participants are treated courteously.

Security

As a security measure, associations often require meeting participants to wear a name badge at all events. Some event planners use radio-frequency identification (RFID) tags to support continuing education tracking functions or digital lead retrieval programs offered to exhibitors; these can also be a valuable tool for admission control and security.

By hiring a security company, you can provide a secure environment for exhibitors during move-in, exhibit days, and tear down. Get competitive bids, check references, and ask about company policies on overtime, breaks, employee longevity, dress code, and whether the guards are armed.

To minimize the possibility of theft, use bonded personnel, put all receipts in a safe deposit box, and reconcile registration receipts and other sales at least every evening.

Printed Materials

A plethora of printed items are produced for most meetings. They range from imprinted specialty items (registration portfolios, bags, and pens) to direct mail marketing materials, from exhibitor contracts and manuals to printed meeting programs, directories, convention proceedings, and evaluation forms.

Over time, associations have adopted digital technologies as alternatives to these traditional printed materials, including making promotional information, online registration, and speaker handouts available via download on the association's website. Mobile devices and applications have become the newest way of providing everything from conference schedules and exhibitor listings to speaker handouts and evaluation tools.

Leading the Team

Meeting planners require the assistance of many people—other association staff members, committee members and other volunteers, hired temporaries, hotel and facilities staff, and staff from other suppliers such as show decorators and tour companies. Orchestrating all these people so that events run smoothly requires a lot of time, attention to detail, and coordination of resources.

Before the meeting begins, the planner should develop job descriptions for the team members involved onsite with a clearly stated mission and list of activities for which they are responsible. If you are using volunteers onsite, these job descriptions help them understand and accomplish their goals in relation to the meeting and clarify the working relationships with staff.

Both volunteers and staff should know exactly what to do should an emergency strike. The emergency plan should include the chain of command, actions to take for various situations, and important telephone numbers to use onsite. The staff of the meeting facility needs to be involved in developing the emergency plan.

Onsite Management

It would be impossible for one person to personally handle all the details of a large meeting. Because the planner cannot be everywhere at once, associations typically rent mobile phones, tablets, pagers, or portable radios to keep staff in touch during the meeting, especially when concurrent events are taking place.

A detailed plan of action that assigns specific duties to individuals helps ensure that all meeting events go smoothly. To implement this plan of action, the CSE must give the planner the authority to direct the onsite operations.

Meetings place association staff in a highly visible position, where members and nonmembers alike watch and evaluate how the staff interacts with volunteers, customers, and each other. Staff's behavior becomes a reflection of the association itself. It is important that all staff attending the event are well prepared and well informed. With the CSE in the lead, a preconference staff meeting is essential to communicate expectations of quality service and professionalism, responsibilities, and logistics. It is most helpful for key onsite staff and the CSE to have access to all function sheets, speaker intros, and speeches compiled in an easily accessible format.

Evaluating the Meeting

An effective evaluation process will tell the association not only what happened, but why it happened. Include each audience segment—delegates, exhibitors, speakers, and volunteers—in the evaluation process.

Methods of evaluating a meeting range from small, single-event surveys distributed and collected onsite to comprehensive, post-convention surveys distributed digitally to meeting participants. Others include special focus groups, an evaluation team or committee, and personal interviews conducted onsite or afterward by telephone or email.

As you design your evaluation tool(s), consider all aspects of the meeting, but also be clear about how the data collected will add value. Consider the tolerance of those responding to lengthy and detailed surveys, especially if the instrument is being completed days after returning home.

The evaluative data collected and processed, along with the financial results and statistical data from the event, should be compiled into a meeting history report. These data will prove useful when planning future meetings.

Emerging Trends

Association meetings are becoming more environmentally friendly and socially conscious: associations are using digital tools to make their events paperless, using recycled paper and products, encouraging recycling of discarded materials, conducting fundraising and community service projects in the host locale, and distributing remaining meeting items left over from event functions to area charities.

Ethical principals have also become a focus of conversation in meeting planning circles. Because of the industry's focus on hospitality and the competitive relationship among suppliers, professional organizations of meeting planners have established guidelines related to accepting familiarization trips, free site inspections, gifts, and rebates.

On the legislative and regulatory front, the challenges include government's decreasing support of travel by government officials to attend association events, local governments' increasing taxation of tourists to offset general budgetary deficits, the deductibility of meeting and travel expenses for meetings held abroad or on cruise ships, and the increasing difficulty for participants from countries outside North America to acquire visas to come to meetings held in the United States. These threats, among others, have spurred planners and their professional societies to become proactive about educating legislators and the public about the role associations play in American society.

Economic downturns often result in a downturn in event participation, and can prove to be a formidable challenge to associations that are increasingly called upon to justify the return on investment for participants and their employers. Associations will be further stressed by the quickening pace of changes in their members' external environment, requiring quicker response times to take advantage of opportunities and often less lead time for planning events.[2]

Access to the Internet and the ever-continuing miniaturization of digital technology have brought innumerable opportunities to creatively incorporate these advances into current programs. It has been said that the digital economy is all about creating new patterns of personal activity. Associations are playing a pivotal role in designing these new patterns, extending the life and scope of their programs while serving more people.

Notes

1. Contracts contain a host of issues that can be negotiated. For a complete review on contracts with hotels and other properties and suppliers, the editors refer readers to J. A. Jacobs, *Association Law Handbook*, 5th ed. (Washington, DC: Association Management Press, 2012).
2. American Express, "American Express Meetings & Events Forecast Predicts Stabilization of Meetings & Events Activity in 2014," October 14, 2013, available at http://about.americanexpress.com/news/pr/2013/amex-meetings-events-2014-activity-forecast.aspx.

Resources

ASAE. "Conventions, Meetings, Education and Professional Development Policies and Procedures." In *Benchmarking in Association Management*, vol. 4: 9. (Washington, DC: ASAE Association Management Press, 2012).

ASAE and Center for Association Leadership. *Operating Ratio Report*. Washington, DC: ASAE Association Management Press, 2012.

Convention Industry Council, "APEX—Accepted Practices EXchange." n.d. Available at http://www.conventionindustry.org/standardspractices/apex.aspx.

Convention Industry Council, *Fact Sheet: 2014 Economic Significance of Meetings to the US* (Washington, DC: Convention Industry Council, 2014).

Ramsborg, G. C. *Professional Meeting Management: Comprehensive Strategies for Meetings, Conventions and Events*, 5th ed. (Dubuque, IA: Kendall/Hunt, 2006).

The Authors

Dawn M. Mancuso, MAM, FASAE, CAE, is the CEO of the Hydrocephalus Association, a national health charity headquartered in Bethesda, Maryland. Formerly, she served as the executive director and CEO of the Association of Air Medical Services and the MedEvac Foundation International.

Natasha J. Ross, CMP, is the director of education and events at Association of Air Medical Services and MedEvac Foundation International.

CHAPTER TWENTY-FOUR

CERTIFICATION PRINCIPLES

B. Denise Roosendaal, CAE, and Anjali Weber

Just as the world has increased in complexity in general, the workplace environment is also gaining in complexity. Employers are requiring workers to obtain more specialized skills in order to be ready for all that employment demands. Government entities and the public are demanding ways to recognize workers who demonstrate these skills and knowledge. Credentialing offers one solution for answering these demands and ranks among the top reasons for why an association may consider developing a certification program. The top five reasons for credentialing are to

- Create safeguards for protection of the consumer or the public
- Elevate the industry or profession
- Recognize professionals with requisite skills, knowledge, or competencies
- Identify and recognize a specialty area of practice
- Distinguish the association or its members from the competition

Because developing and maintaining a certification program involves careful research and long-term investment, it is important to be aware of the primary considerations before undertaking such an endeavor to help ensure success of the program. It is also important to clearly define the desired outcome to determine whether a certification program is appropriate, or whether needs may be better met with a different offering, such as a certificate program.

Credentialing Definitions

There is often confusion in the terminology used to identify different types of credentials, which includes academic degrees as well as certifications and certificate programs.

Credentialing (specifically academic and professional) is a term applied to processes used to designate that an individual, program, institution, or product has met established standards recognized as qualified to carry out this task. The standards, set by a governmental or nongovernmental agent, may be minimal and mandatory or above the minimum and voluntary. Licensure, registration, accreditation, approval, certification, recognition, or endorsement may be used to describe different credentialing processes.

Accreditation is the voluntary process by which a nongovernmental agency grants a time-limited recognition to an institution, organization, business, or other entity after verifying that it has met predetermined and standardized criteria.

Professional or personnel certification is a voluntary process by which a nongovernmental body grants time-limited recognition and use of a credential to individuals who have demonstrated that they have met predetermined and standardized criteria for required knowledge, skills, or competencies.

A *certificate program* is a training program on a topic for which participants receive a certificate after attendance or completion of the coursework. Some programs also require successful demonstration of attainment of the course objectives by examination. When an organization issues a certificate of attendance or participation without any assessment of knowledge, this is not considered a credential.

Licensure is the mandatory process by which a governmental agency grants time-limited permission to an individual to engage in a given occupation after verifying that he or she has met predetermined and standardized criteria and offers title protection for those who meet the criteria.

Registration refers either to the professional designation defined by a governmental entity in professional regulations or rules, or to a listing or registry of practitioners.

Source: J. Knapp and C. Wild, *Certification: The ICE Handbook*, 2nd ed. (Washington, DC: Institute for Credentialing Excellence, 2009).

Needs Assessment

Before considering offering a certification program, it is important to conduct a needs assessment that takes into consideration the following concerns.

Is there a need that is not currently being met in other ways or by other organizations? Is there sufficient capacity to create an additional program within the industry? Because of the long-term nature and expense of implementing and maintaining a certification program, the needs assessment should begin with a thorough understanding of the marketplace. The larger and more well-defined the target audience and the knowledge of how their skills are currently recognized, the better the prospects are for continued success. Are there safety risks or calls for public protection to be addressed? Are the arising complexities due to technological shifts or new knowledge about the profession?

While credentialing programs can be a source of healthy revenue, the cost of implementation and operation are often underestimated. Therefore, spending the time up front on performing a strong market analysis will pay immense dividends in the long run.

Abandoning a certification program once there are practicing certificants in the industry may violate a promise or trust. The promise to the certificant is that the program will be sustainable and provide ongoing support and value to their certification. To the public or user to whom the certificant provides services, there is an ongoing need for the skills, enhanced competency, and ethical practice, all of which are built into a good certification program. And to the employer, earning and maintaining certification demonstrates a grasp of critical knowledge and skills and an ongoing commitment to maintain or enhance those skills.

Does offering of a certification program align with the association mission and vision? A strong alignment between the membership organization's mission and vision with the purpose of the certification is an important element to success. Addressing this question in the beginning avoids creating a mismatched program. Just because a membership organization is stable and has a strong reputation is not a sufficient reason to carry a certification program if the mission and vision are not in alignment. Would a partnership between several organizations serve the purpose better by creating a larger pool of potential certificants? Could such a partnership also expand industry expertise and the pool of potential subject matter experts? Could such a partnership also allow for sharing of the expense and risk?

Many credentialing programs may start under a membership organization umbrella but then become separate entities in order to satisfy the stakeholder needs of members. In this move, however, the needs of the organization's nonmembers will also need to be considered since this population will be part of the certificant candidate pool. Therefore, the membership organization should not build a credentialing program with the anticipation that doing so will drive growth in membership or other ancillary membership products. Educational programs offered by the membership organization are only one source of such information and programming.

Who are the relevant stakeholders? Stakeholders are not just the members of the association or certificants and potential certificants (members and nonmembers). Employers of credential holders are also important stakeholders since they will need to understand the meaning and distinction of your certification in their marketplace. Legislators and regulators may rely upon the credential for public protection or require a specific certification in lieu of licensing. Certification exams may also be used for licensure.

The consumer who purchases goods or services from the certificant would be considered a stakeholder. In the case of health-related services, the insurance companies and third-party payers may be considered stakeholders. Casting a wide net when identifying and defining potential stakeholders will enable the program to consider many perspectives.

What value does the certification bring to the association, its members, and the broader community of prospective certificants as well as those benefitting from their services? Professions that are expanding in numbers or growing in complexity often can benefit from a certification program. The value of a certification program for the certificant (perhaps related to career path and recognition) will differ from the value offered to a member of the public using the services (such as safety or peace of mind gained from working with a professional possessing attested skills and knowledge). These various stakeholders will come to rely upon the certification and its value. This public stakeholder aspect increases the pressure to ensure that the program is thoughtfully built from the beginning.

Is there sufficient capacity to support a certification program? Conducting market research and assessing (current and potential) competition are key elements of determining the likely success of a program. Relying upon a large association membership base as the sole source of potential candidates does not necessarily guarantee success of a certification program. Skill development and knowledge assessment are growing employment trends in the marketplace that can attract many competitors. There are many sources of information that offer data on professions and employment trends (Department of Labor, employment related associations, and so on, which can supplement an organization's primary research). If there is not sufficient capacity to support a certification program or when there is need to address an ongoing skill or knowledge gap, education and training programs offering certificates may better suit the industry's needs. Such certificate programs have very different purposes and goals from certification programs (see "Credentialing Definitions" sidebar).

Assessing Resource Needs

Developing and maintaining a certification program requires significant resources. A long-term commitment is needed to develop and grow a program as well as to honor the obligation to its certificants.

Adequate financial resources are needed for sustainability of the program. The up-front investment costs are substantial, as is the time frame that should be allocated for adequate research and development. Expenses will include staffing, exam administration, exam development, public awareness and marketing, general overhead, legal fees, administration of recertification programs, and exam preparation products. Certification revenue will vary depending upon the size and scope of the program, and it may take a number of years to realize a profit.

Sufficient qualified personnel must be dedicated for program management and daily operations. Some organizations approach this aspect by simply assigning staff involved in education to the credentialing functions; however, this approach carries significant challenges:

1. To mitigate security and conflict of interest concerns, staff involved in credentialing should not be involved in education or exam preparation products.
2. The job analysis for a credentialing professional identified three primary domains:
   - Operations
   - Issuing, maintaining and renewing the credential
   - Test development, administration, scoring, and analysis[1]

The tasks in these domains may vary depending upon role and level in the organization. As a program grows, analyzing functions and structure will dictate the kinds of staffing required.

According to research by the Institute for Credentialing Excellence (ICE), the median staff size is six, but the exact size fluctuates dramatically (from 1 to 2,000 full-time equivalents) depending upon the size, scope, and number of the certifications offered by an organization.[2]

Appropriate technology should be used for record keeping, application processing, and tracking requirements for recertification. A variety of technology is available to serve as or supplement existing database management systems that allow for adequate record keeping required for quality data management. Data is an important component to an overall program that will affect marketing and future strategic growth. How the data are collected, managed, and secured is an important aspect and should be factored into the costs of implementation and ongoing operations.

Subject matter experts (SMEs) may be volunteers or paid consultants and are needed on an ongoing basis for item development, review, and validation of examination content. Technology exists for aiding in item development and tracking. Still, nothing substitutes for the knowledge gained and shared by your profession's SMEs. The costs (meetings, travel, software) and time associated with item development should be factored into the budget. The item-writing process will require training of the SMEs, including appropriate security policies.

Expertise is needed for examination development and delivery. Services may exist in-house for larger or more established programs, but most often services are contracted for research, strategic development, examination development, delivery, maintenance, and psychometric evaluation. This includes psychometricians, who specialize in the science of measurement and help to create and maintain valid and reliable examinations that are fair to candidates. If in-house expertise is not available, consultants may also be needed for activities such as creation of strategic and business plans, outlining and guiding development activities, marketing of the certification program, and developing website content.

A definition of what constitutes success is important from the onset, as well as identification and tracking of relevant metrics to evaluate performance of the program. Including the organization's governing body in this discussion will help ensure that the tracked metrics are a reflection of success.

Legal Issues

Credentialing programs (in policy and execution) aim to be reliable, valid, and legally defensible. A well-run, carefully developed, and diligently conducted certification program should not give rise to significant legal liability. In reality, however, certification programs are subject to legal risks, but there are many ways to mitigate these risks.

Separate Incorporation

Certification programs are often started under a parent association. Over time, it may make sense to separately incorporate the certification program as a distinct organization for the following reasons:

- To meet legal and taxation requirements
- To separate from other priorities of the association (like member recruitment and retention) to protect the integrity of the certification program
- To prevent undue influence that could affect the integrity of the certification

Most credentialing bodies are tax exempt (either $501(c)(6)$ or $501(c)(3)$ but a growing number are created as for-profit organizations.

Governance

The governance structure should be addressed through the articles of incorporation and bylaws. Board or certification governance members need to understand that they have legal fiduciary duties, including duties of care, loyalty, obedience, and confidentiality. As a function of the duty of loyalty, any conflicts of interest should be disclosed, with recusal from decisions enforced.

Boards should be composed of appropriate stakeholder audiences (which may include certificants, employers, third-party payers, students, and so on), who would provide valuable input for the direction of the program and should include certificants and members of the public.

Public members are valuable because they bring a unique perspective to a board by representing the consumer or user of the services provided. Their input may be focused more on protection of the public, transparency of policies and procedures, and continuing competence of certificants, rather than elevation of the profession or recognition.

Boards should also have autonomy in essential certification decisions and be protected from undue influence from the association itself, as well as other relevant entities within the profession or role.

Policy Review

The policy manual would address nominations and elections of board and commission members, exam eligibility, process for exam development and review, appeals and discipline of certificants, employment policies, whistleblower policies, document retention, and so on. Legal review of organizational policies is critical to maintain defensibility of the program, especially those that relate to fairness and equivalence to candidates (such as prohibition or discrimination, accommodations for testing). The policy manual might also address the various forms used (paper or electronic) for implementation of the policies and procedures.

Candidate Handbook

Treating all elements of candidate processing in a standardized manner is a key aspect of creating a legally defensible program. Communication to credentialing candidates can be achieved through a candidate handbook, which would include policies, eligibility requirements, exam content outline, preparation for the exam, exam process details, fees, communication of exam results, appeal process, and so on.

Federal Legislation

Certification programs must comply with the following:

1. The *Civil Rights Act of 1991*, an extension of Title VII of the Civil Rights Act of 1964. The Uniform Guidelines on Employee Selection Procedures (1978) published by Equal Employment Opportunity Commission, Office of Personnel Management, Department of Justice, and Department of Labor.
2. The *Americans with Disabilities Act of 1990*. It requires that organizations provide "reasonable accommodations" to individuals covered by this legislation.

Due Process

Due process is the most important legal principle for certification programs. It requires notice of a hearing and a fair and objective hearing any time an organization wishes to withdraw something of value from an individual or entity. Due process ensures transparency and reasonable application of policy and fairness. The principle applies to the consistent use of policies and procedures with the certification candidate throughout the process (before, during, and after the exam).

Antitrust

The antitrust issue also applies to the certification design process itself if created in such a way that it unfairly excludes some professionals in the marketplace. An association must also beware of potential tying claims (for example, requiring association membership in order to be eligible for certification), boycott (concerted refusals to deal under antitrust), or price-fixing

Intellectual Property

A certification program needs to consider protection of its intellectual property, which includes copyrights and trademarks. These protections may include copyright of examinations and websites, or trademarking of certification marks (such as designations or logos).

Contracts

Many organizations opt to contract out discreet portions of the credentialing process such as exam development or test development and delivery services. When establishing vendor support, such relationships should be governed by explicit written agreements

Insurance

Legal actions are a real risk, so it is important to carry insurance to cover general liability, as well as a directors' and officers' liability coverage, both of which will provide legal defense if the organization is sued.

Developing a Certification Program

Whether or not an association pursues third-party accreditation for its certification program(s), it is wise to use accreditation standards as a framework to build and maintain a quality program. Accreditation standards help to identify appropriate structure and governance, fair policies, valid and reliable examinations, and continuing competency requirements for the certifying body itself.

The foundation of your certification program rests in the validity and reliability of your examination.

Research must be conducted to determine the requisite knowledge, skills, or competencies for which you are testing. These types of studies (usually referred to as job analyses) require representative sampling of those practicing in the profession, role, or specialty area and a validation of results by subject matter experts to determine what needs to be assessed. Then, a determination must be made for how to assess these essential knowledge, skills, or competencies and to what level, whether by written examination, or performance-based or practical examination, and the minimum qualifications for a candidate. Then, determination should be made of how a certificant will maintain or enhance his or her competency, whether by retesting periodically or by continuing education and other requirements.

Proper governance and oversight of each step in program development and maintenance help to ensure integrity of the certification program. Consideration must also be given to use of technology (for example, content management systems) and need for upgrades for testing, secure storage of confidential records and exam items, records retention, test administration, and recertification.

Evaluating Performance

Defining what constitutes success for the certification program will assist an association in determining appropriate next steps. Success may be measured in a number of ways, including profit, recognition by the industry, preference or requirement for certification by employers, and adoption into legislation or regulation.

As mentioned earlier, many programs do not realize a profit in the initial years following launch of a new program. Certification programs require significant investment initially to conduct research and to develop an examination. Maintenance also requires investment for updates to examinations for currency and relevancy, as well as updates to policy, marketing and communications, updates to technology, and other related expenses. Consequently, economic performance is not an appropriate metric for success in the early phases of implementation.

Tracking relevant metrics and collecting feedback from candidates and the industry will provide guidance as to whether to continue a certification program, grow it, partner with similar entities, or perhaps develop additional certifications in other core or specialty areas. In some cases, certification may bring substantial revenue; in other cases, it may be value added to the association or industry and deemed important enough to maintain even though it does not bring in significant revenue.

Credentialing Trends

Predicting the future is always difficult. The trends in the credentialing field will largely be driven by the following:

- Rapid pace of technological change
- Pressure on workplace skills development and specialization
- Globalization
- Increased competition

Rapid Pace of Technology Change

Technology is having a significant impact on the operations of credentialing and how assessment instruments are designed and delivered. There are more robust content-management systems as well as configurable and customizable software for recertification management and auditing. Technology in various professions is also growing in significance and has an impact on how tasks are performed and evaluated. Technology is also a factor in what is being tested by certification agencies, so it is important that they be aware of the currency and relevancy of the knowledge and skills tested.

Technological advances can affect the rate and kinds of security intrusions into the testing environment. A credentialing body and its testing facility need to ensure that the highest security measures are employed to stay abreast of the changing technology employed by those with an intent to cheat or sell the test content.

Workplace Skill Development and Specialization

With the cyclical nature of the economy and status of job growth, workplace skill development is continually analyzed and discussed in the public at large as well as with policymakers. Employers also play a role in how desired skills are identified and classified in the workplace. Credentialing programs may need to evolve and respond to those changes within the particular profession in order to remain relevant to the employer and certificant. Certificate programs are playing a growing role in workplace skill development. Furthermore, employment trends will continue to fluctuate over time as generations enter and exit the job market.

International Opportunities

Depending on the profession, the international arena can be a profitable marketplace. Expansion can take one of two pathways: centralized (U.S.-based model exported as a prefabricated package); or localized (customized to the country or region involving a local sponsor). Either model will require strategic alliances to create licensing or partnerships in international locations. However, many aspects of the program should be thoughtfully considered before expanding: language issues, cultural differences, financial and payment-processing considerations, differences in regulatory and legislative environments, various workplace dynamics, and differences in ethical and legal considerations. Intellectual property rights and copyright concepts may vary broadly internationally.

Increased Competition

The Internet offers many opportunities for reaching unmet markets and expanding the potential candidate pool. However, the Internet also means an expanding potential competitor base as well. Because the Internet allows information to be freely and easily shared, it is fertile ground for competitors seeking profit without the requisite foundational work that a legitimate credentialing program requires. The Internet is also an environment in which reputations are built or scarred. Staying aware of what is being reported on your certification is part of any ongoing marketing plan.

The word *certification* is broadly used across the credentialing industry and in training to mean different things, and this adds confusion to the public about what the credential really represents. Table 24.1 outlines primary differences between certificate programs and certification, because these terms are often used interchangeably but have a very different purpose. It may aid stakeholders in making the business decision about program to pursue, as discussed in the section on "Needs Assessment."

◆ ◆ ◆

Consider Accrediting Your Organization

Melissa Sines

Your association might seek accreditation for your certification program.

Higher education institutions seek accreditation for technical programs so that their students can qualify for jobs in accredited institutions such as hospitals or schools,

TABLE 24.1. FEATURES OF QUALITY CERTIFICATION AND ASSESSMENT-BASED CERTIFICATE PROGRAMS.

Feature	Certification	Assessment-Based Certificate Program
Primary Focus of Program	Certification is accomplished through Independent assessment of the knowledge, skills, or competencies required for competent performance of an occupation or profession or specific work-related tasks and responsibilities.	The program facilitates the accomplishment of intended learning outcomes. It provides education and training that support the accomplishment of intended learning outcomes.
Content of the Program and How It Is Identified	Certification is based on the knowledge, skills, or competencies required for competent performance of an occupational or professional role or specific work-related tasks and responsibilities as identified through a formal study (such as job or practice analysis, role delineation).	The program may include knowledge, skills, or competencies related to (1) An occupational or professional role or specific work-related tasks and responsibilities (2) General-interest or leisure pursuits (such as first aid, sailing) Intended learning outcomes and associated knowledge, skills, and competencies are identified through a systematic analysis of the needs of (1) Participants (2) Industry (3) Consumers (4) Other identified stakeholders
Program Oversight	A governing body with representation from relevant stakeholders is charged with oversight of the certification program. This body is legally or administratively autonomous from other entities and maintains control over all essential decisions related to certification activities.	A governing-body with oversight responsibilities for the assessment-based certificate program is *not* required; however, the program should function with input from subject-matter experts and qualified individuals who assist in development, delivery, and evaluation of the program.

(continued)

TABLE 24.1. CONTINUED

Feature	Certification	Assessment-Based Certificate Program
Provider Role in Education and Training	The certification program provider conducts the certification program independently of any educational or training programs. The assessment is *not* linked to a specific class, course, or other education or training program or to a specific provider of classes, courses, or programs. The assessment is *not* designed to evaluate mastery of the intended learning outcomes of a specific class, course, or program	The certificate program provider conducts or sponsors the education or training that is required for the certificate. The assessment is aligned with the education or training and is designed to evaluate accomplishment of the intended learning outcomes that the provider has identified for the class, course, or program.
Education and Training Requirements and Prerequisites	Eligibility requirements may include completion of specific education or training; however, the certification program provider is *not* the sole provider of any education or training that may be required for certification. Nor is the certification program provider responsible for accreditation of educational or training programs or courses of study leading to the certification.	The program requires completion of education or training offered or sponsored by the certificate provider. There may be other prerequisites in addition to the education or training required to attain the certificate.

Note: Other distinguishing factors include: validation of assessment content, standard setting, evaluation of assessments, credential maintenance, identification of individuals who have completed the program, statement of program purpose.

Source: Institute for Credentialing Excellence, *Defining Features of Quality Certification and Assessment-Based Certificate Programs*, 2010. Complete and complimentary copy available online at www.credentialingexcellence.org/programdifferences.

qualify for a higher pay-grade because they completed an accredited program, or, for those who serve(d) in the military or are employed by government institutions, qualify for government-funded tuition reimbursement.

For-profit entities such as laboratories might seek accreditation to gain a competitive edge, demonstrating that a standard of quality control exists and is consistently delivered.

Some organizations mandate accreditation for providers of their content. Others seek accreditation on a voluntary basis.

In general, accreditation translates into pubic credibility, meeting standards set by a profession or governmental body, and quality execution of those standards.

This sidebar addresses a unique application of accreditation—getting your own charitable organization accredited. The context of general accreditation practice is woven throughout.

Nonprofits face increasing pressure from the public, donors, and stakeholders to ensure transparency, accountability, and effectiveness. In response, many have turned to the common standards or benchmarks offered by accreditation as a way of measuring and demonstrating the efficacy of their policies and practices. A number of accrediting bodies in the nonprofit sector offer a third-party review of an organization's management, governance, operations, and programs.

Accreditation programs differ from "watchdog organizations" that exist to inform prospective donors about business practices of charity organizations in three specific ways:

1. Accreditation programs are voluntary. Organizations may choose to apply and may choose to withdraw their application with no penalty.
2. Accreditation programs typically charge a more substantial fee to complete the organization review and to license the accreditation logo.
3. They often include a peer-review component, meaning that the organization's application is reviewed by several nonprofit experts. This gives the organization the benefit of advice and feedback from some of the best minds in the industry.

Accreditation can be a multiyear process, and most accreditation programs require renewal on a regular schedule. It is not as simple as writing a policy and letting it sit on the shelf, or training staff once and then letting training fall to the back burner the next year. Accreditation bodies will ask to see evidence that best practices are being regularly implemented across the organization. The goal of representing to a third party that your organization is at the top of its game will demand a regular habit of top-to-bottom evaluation of leadership, practices, and programs.

Because of this, organizations that complete an accreditation process report that the biggest benefit is a stronger organization overall. There are several benefits to accreditation that make it worth the time and effort that is needed by a nonprofit's leaders. When done correctly, it can increase the engagement of the board, build bench strength in middle management, engage new volunteers, and build the confidence of leaders in the competence and effectiveness of their organization.

Accreditation can also be a risk. There is always the risk that after spending valuable time and resources on the application process, the organization's application will be rejected. When required to meet an outside standard of practice or benchmark, current operations or management may be found lacking. Another risk is that in-depth reviews and evaluation have the potential to uncover festering issues or hidden weaknesses in an organization's leadership, programs, staff, or operations. An honest and thorough evaluation can delay the application process as the organization works to mitigate the issues revealed in the process.

An organization should not pursue accreditation as a marketing ploy to attract donors with another bright logo on their website. Research on donors consistently reports that they are most likely to donate to causes that are personal and because someone they know has asked them to give. Few donors do research on an organization before giving. The point of accreditation, as with any improvement process, is to better meet the mission. When an organization is meeting its mission in the most effective, efficient, transparent, and accountable way, that will make a community of members, supporters, and donors stop and take notice.

Notes

1. Institute for Credentialing Excellence, *Job Analysis Study for the Certification Professional*, 2010; revalidated 2012.
2. Institute for Credentialing Excellence, *Business of Certification*, 2012.

Resource Organizations

ANSI

Washington, DC, Headquarters

1899 L Street, NW, 11th Floor

Washington, DC 20036

Tel: 202.293.8020

ASAE

1575 I Street NW

Washington, DC 20005

Tel: 202.950.2723

ATP

601 Pennsylvania Ave., NW

South Building, Suite 900

Washington, DC 20004

Institute for Credentialing Excellence

2025 M Street, NW

Washington, DC 20036

Tel: 202.367.1167

International Organization for Standardization

ISO Central Secretariat

1, ch. de la Voie-Creuse

CP 56

CH-1211 Geneva 20

Switzerland

National Commission for Certifying Agencies

2025 M Street, NW

Washington DC 20036

Tel: 202.367.1167

Department of Labor

Certification Finder (www.careeronestop.net)

The Authors

B. Denise Roosendaal, CAE, is the executive director for the Institute for Credentialing Excellence (ICE) in Washington, DC. She has served in this capacity since 2011. She has also served on the CAE commission in the past.

Anjali Weber is the director of accreditation services at the Institute for Credentialing Excellence (ICE). In this role, she provides strategic and operational leadership and management expertise to advance ICE's accreditation programs for certification and assessment-based certificate programs.

Sidebar author *Melissa Sines* joined Maryland Nonprofits and the Standards for Excellence Institute in March 2011. As accreditation manager, she works directly with organizations applying to earn the Seal of Excellence, helping them reach the highest standards of ethics and accountability in nonprofit governance, management, and operations.

CHAPTER TWENTY-FIVE

AFFINITY PROGRAMS

Susan Moseley, CAE

In recent years, nondues revenue has been at the forefront of association strategies to support and supplement overall income growth. At the core of these nondues-income-driving activities can be affinity programs. These programs involve a relationship between three parties: the association, an external business, and the association member. The premise of the relationship is based on the association providing the business with access to its name or brand and its membership, in order to promote a wide variety of commercial products and services (for example, insurance, credit cards, payroll, marketing). The business compensates the association for this access and in return expects greater sales, at a lower marketing cost, as a result of the member loyalty to the association. The member benefits by receiving lower pricing, an enhanced level of customer service they would not receive outside of an association program, or both, as well as the knowledge that they are supporting their association.

The Changing Landscape

Affinity programs within the association space are evolving significantly as a result of changing business models and diminishing profit margins within the businesses that participate in affinity programs. In the past, associations were typically sought out by these businesses that believed access to the association brand and membership would result in significantly increased sales and reduced costs. In addition, the business typically invested heavily in marketing the program utilizing both association and external marketing channels to drive member awareness. Now as affinity programs have saturated the market, and association programs have matured, there are fewer choices and options due to a contraction of the number of businesses participating in association affinity programs. And a new business model is emerging in which many businesses require associations to provide more support and sales leads than they did in the recent past. Associations now need to carefully consider all aspects of affinity relationships before they proceed in order to ensure long-term success.

Program Types or Categories

Associations offer various programs depending upon their strategies and the needs of the members. Typical affinity programs reflect this variety (Table 25.1).

Many associations have their own insurance agency or hybrid company to support their affinity insurance programs. It's important to note that insurance is an industry highly regulated by state governments and will require a great deal of association and insurance expertise to oversee and manage.

Value Proposition

There must be a *win-win-win* scenario for all three parties for a program to have long-term success.

TABLE 25.1. EXAMPLES OF AFFINITY PROGRAM TYPES.

Categories	Product or Service Examples
Business and financial services	Credit cards, credit card processing, shipping, computers, payroll, uniforms, prepaid legal aid
Insurance - Property and casualty - Employee benefits	Commercial, home, auto, workers compensation, life, liability, disability, long-term care
Personal products	Discounts: hotels, cellular phone, mortgages, identity theft protection, car rental
Marketing	Website development, e-marketing

The Association

Most associations strive to achieve a dual mission in their affinity programs.

1. *Member value:* First and foremost, they want to drive greater member value, which can be measured on a number of levels including increased member acquisition, retention (both in terms of longer membership tenure and higher dues) and a more engaged, committed, and satisfied member.
2. *Nondues revenue:* Second, and no less important as ensuring member value, is the ability of the affinity program to generate revenue for the association. Revenue generation purposely follows member value in the sequence of the mission because without member value, the association will not derive revenue needed for long-term success. It's important to emphasize that *member demand* for an affinity product or service should be the *primary driving factor* in the association's decision to launch a program.

The Business

Businesses usually have a single goal when entering into an association affinity program. Put simply, they want to drive profitable sales. The business often bears the majority of costs, including administering, operating, and promoting the program. The premise behind an affinity program is that the loyalty a member has for an association will translate into greater sales, customer satisfaction, and credibility for the business, thereby offsetting the revenue paid to the association.

The Member

For the members, these affinity products and services translate to both tangible and intangible benefits. In some cases, the association program may be differentiated in the market with lower or better pricing. In other cases, the members may receive enhanced customer service by participating in an association program. In all cases, members benefit from the vetting, research, and due diligence the association performs to find a business, product, or service that's a "good fit" for the needs of membership. In addition, they can receive the advocacy of the association staff to aid in any difficulties or issues the member may experience with the business once they become a customer.

In professional associations, there are research and experience that suggest it's harder to deliver "the value," as these members are not looking for modest discounts on car rentals or credit cards. Instead they want customized, meaningful programs that meet their defined member need.

Criteria for Success

As associations evaluate affinity opportunities, they should consider these criteria:

- Include products and services that align with the organization's mission.
- Ensure the product or service has unique value and is not easily found in the market.
- Perform rigorous due diligence and develop a strong business case.
- Balance the tax and expense implications against the member value and revenue derived.
- Feel confident that member demand will drive a minimum threshold of qualified leads and subsequent sales.

◆ ◆ ◆

Choosing a Program: Guiding Principles and "Must Haves"

Associations can receive hundreds of inquiries each year from individuals and companies that feel they have a product or service that would benefit the association's membership. Often these companies have no affinity or association experience, do not understand the association's mission, and are simply looking for a new, low-cost channel to promote awareness of their product. It's easy for associations to be flattered and excited by these opportunities. It's up to the association staff (or committee) to bring "reality" to these discussions and take a leadership role in determining whether a program can truly be a viable long-term success for the organization. Each product or service should be strategic in nature, contributing tangible member value, as well as have its own business case, thereby creating an integrated suite of products that are bundled together for a strong affinity program. Several steps should be undertaken to aid in this important decision:

1. *Member need:* There must be a need and therefore member demand by a large majority or targeted segment of the membership before an association should embark on the development and launching of a program. Determining need can be done in a number of ways. Research can be conducted to validate member interest For example: an electronic survey emailed to a portion of the membership or collected at a tradeshow is a good way to obtain direct member feedback.

2. *Due diligence:* Association staff should invest a good deal of time to vet the business, review the product or service, and evaluate the likelihood of the program's long-term success. Staff should "kick the tires," to determine if the company is "walking the talk." Due diligence can be a lengthy process, and the following should be evaluated as part of the process:

    - *Affinity experience:* Entering into a program with a business that has extensive affinity experience is advantageous. It means they understand that every association program is unique and requires customized management and execution. Working with an inexperienced business that has little or no affinity experience means there is a steep learning curve for the business, and the association staff will likely have to devote more time to the launch and management of the program.

    - *Financial:* Financial due diligence should include requesting a copy of audited financial statements from the business. If the business does not have audited financials or won't share them because they are a private firm, the association should be wary. If the association obtains financial statements, their finance team should be asked to evaluate and provide an assessment of the financial health of the company.

    - *Operational:* The association should consider making a site visit to the customer service center of the business being evaluated for certain significant or important products. Reports on customer satisfaction and call answer times should be requested. Association staff should sit side-by-side with a customer service representative to observe exactly how members will be treated. The association should understand the typical customer lifecycle and the steps and timing members would go through within the cycle.

    - *Marketing:* It's important for the association to gain perspective on the business's marketing capabilities. How has the business utilized targeting and segmentation strategies? What marketing channels does the business intend to use and with what frequency? What does the business anticipate spending annually on marketing? What does the business expect the association to provide with regard to marketing the program? The association should ask for samples of marketing the business has developed for other clients and see if the business knows how the marketing performed (for example, through the use of data and analytics, performance such as response rates, conversion from lead to sale, renewal rates, and the average time a consumer remains a loyal customer).

- *Reference checks:* For the association, an ideal scenario is to enter into a new relationship or program with a business that has affinity experience and a robust roster of affinity relationships. Association staff should have in-depth discussions with the business's existing clients to determine if the business has a proven track record as a reliable program administrator, providing accurate reporting, timely payment, excellent product competitiveness, product fulfillment, marketing, and customer service.

3. *Business case:* Typically, a business-case document or proposal that provides a compelling reason for launching a new affinity program should be developed and provided to the association's management (committee or board). The reason for the business case is to justify the program and document how it will be a good use of association resources. The business case should include information such as background for the program (for example, the results of an RFP), the expected association and member benefits, and the possible risks. Most important, the business case should include a pro-forma that sets forth expected costs of the program, the level of member participation, and the minimum sales and revenue thresholds required for the program to succeed for both the business and the association.

4. *Ability to track and monitor:* The association should determine whether the business has the ability to track and quantify a lead originated by the association. The business should be able to provide the association with periodic reports regarding the performance of the program. To avoid privacy concerns, these reports can be aggregated and do not need to be member specific. Examples of key metrics to track can include sales volume (the number of units sold), average sale price in dollars, and the number of units renewing.

Handling Inquiries

Associations often receive frequent inquiries from companies or individuals asking to utilize the association to promote its product or service. A good way to handle these inquiries in a timely and professional manner is to develop a document that educates the inquirer on the opportunities for external companies to have a relationship with the association (such as advertising, sponsorship, affinity programs). This document can be featured on the association's website or emailed to the individual making the inquiry. The document can include an overview of the association's membership, parameters for advertising and sponsorship, and the "must have's" for a successful affinity program with the association. Typically, the inquirer will appreciate the professional overview and minimal staff resources that will be spent handling these inquiries.

Structuring the Program

As the new affinity model emerges, more performance pressure is being placed on the association now than in the past. Businesses may require associations to drive *qualified leads and quantifiable sales* (as determined by both parties). And they may shy away from the heavy marketing investments made in the past. Ultimately, access to the association's name or brand and membership may no longer be all that's required. Associations must now be prepared to ensure a threshold of qualified leads and invest their own resources to promote awareness and market affinity programs to their members.

There are many ways to structure and support an affinity program, and the newly emerging model may have an impact on how this is done. Often the strategies, goals, and objectives of the program help determine how it will be structured. The following commentary introduces some of the fundamentals of the various structures.

A tax-exempt association may owe taxes, which are an expense to an association, if it receives income from certain business activities not related to the purposes for which the association was granted tax-exempt status. This is referred to as "UBIT" (unrelated business income tax). Three criteria generally dictate if income derived from an association's activities will be liable for UBIT:

1. Income from the activities are *considered a trade or business.*
2. The activities are *regularly carried on,* are *substantial,* or both.
3. The unrelated business activity is *not substantially related* to the *exempt purpose* of the association.

Without getting into great detail, here are a few concepts that are helpful to know:

- *Passive versus active involvement:* If an association is licensing its intangible property (name, logo, membership list) and receiving royalty as payment, its involvement must be passive. If the association has active involvement, it will need to structure the program accordingly. The association can "bifurcate" contracts as described further on or it can establish a for-profit subsidiary or other type of subsidiary to address the association's active and passive involvement in the program.

- *Contracts:* There are different types of agreements to support an association's involvement in an affinity program. There are contracts that address an association's *passive* involvement in a program (such as agreeing to license its logo to a business). The payments made to the association under these types of agreement are generally *not taxable*. Following are two examples of these types of agreements:
  - *Royalty agreement:* This is the most common type of agreement and allows the 501(c) organization to license its intangible property (name, logo, and membership list) and receive a royalty payment for passive involvement.
  - *License agreement:* This is the same as the royalty agreement. It has similar parameters and focuses on the license of the association's intangible property. However, there are also separate contracts that address an association's *active* involvement in a program (that is, when the association is providing some level of service for the program). The compensation received from the services being provided by the association under this type of contract is generally *taxable.* Following are examples of these types of agreements:
    - *Marketing agreement:* This agreement defines the marketing activities or services the association will provide in support of the affinity program.
    - *Services agreement:* This agreement more broadly defines services the association may provide. For example, helping in the administration of the program is a service.
    - *Program agreement:* This agreement is similar to the services agreement noted above.
- *Bifurcated contracts:* Agreements can be bifurcated (or split) to allow the 501(c) organization to receive tax-free royalty for passive involvement of licensing intangible property (name, logo, member list) in one contract. A second contract is used to outline the association's active involvement in the program for which the payment to the association may be subject to UBIT.

- *Entities:* Associations may set up different entities to support affinity programs and to protect the exempt status and liability exposure of the lead organization.
  - *For-profit subsidiary:* This organizational structure is established, owned, and controlled by the lead 501(c)(6) organization to operate affinity programs. It's generally set up to protect the exempt status and liability exposure of the lead organization. The organization pays taxes on *net income earned* from affinity programs.
  - *Insurance agency or captive insurance company:* Some associations may establish an insurance agency or a captive insurance company to handle the complexities of the highly regulated insurance industry. These typically are subsidiaries of the for-profit subsidiary. The value of establishing these types of structures is that they allow the association to participate in larger revenue opportunities. However, they can also result in increased responsibility for administration of the program as well as risk of revenue loss.
- *Compensation:* There are a variety of structures that are utilized to remunerate associations. The strategies, goals, and objectives of each program determine how the association may be paid. Payments can be structured on a fixed or variable basis, taxable or nontaxable.
  - *Royalty:* This is the most common type of compensation. The business pays the association to license intangible property (name, logo, member list). This is generally tax-free income and requires passive involvement by the association. However, marketing, services, or program income would result with a bifurcated agreement discussed prior. This would require active involvement by the association, and the income is generally taxable. The next two types of compensation occur when the association establishes an insurance agency or captive insurance company.
  - *Commission:* This type of payment is variable and typically is based on a predetermined percentage of the insurance policy premium.
  - *Contingency commission:* This type of payment involves the association sharing in the profitability of an insurance program. The formula for the payment is company specific, but is usually based on the amount of sales, the quality of the business, and the loss experience of the book of business.

Responsibilities

Prior to drafting the agreements for the program, it is important for the parties to discuss, define, and agree upon expectations about each party's responsibilities related to the program. In addition to legalities, it's critical that the party's marketing responsibilities and other requirements are clearly outlined in the agreements related to the program.

The Association

The association should enter into an affinity relationship with a full understanding of the commitment and responsibilities required. Some typical responsibilities follow:

- *Marketing:* The structure of the program will determine how passive or active the association can be in promoting the program. The business will likely expect the association's marketing channels (website, e-newsletters, and events) be available for marketing and promoting the program.
- *Staff support:* Typically, an individual (title only, such as Program Manager) from the association's staff will be identified as the primary point of contact for the business to aid in any administration of the program. This individual or a team of association staff serves as the liaison between the association and business and is responsible for the successful launch and ongoing management of the program.

The Business

The association should also define the responsibilities for which it expects the business to commit. Typical responsibilities may include the following:

- *Administration and fulfillment:* The business is responsible for delivering the product or service to the member. The specific steps involved in providing such product or service to the association's members, along with the time frames associated with such steps, should be outlined in the agreement relating to the program.
- *Marketing:* The level of investment the business makes to market a program to membership is as important as the revenue the associations will

receive from the program. If the association doesn't create awareness, it won't drive the leads and sales needed to create a successful program. Associations should consider asking the business to commit to some level of quantifiable marketing activity. This may include setting an annual marketing budget or defining a number of activities (for example, four direct mail campaigns, one print advertisement, and attendance at an annual event). Ideally, all aspects of marketing, including channels, timing, and frequency, should be established in an annual marketing plan that both parties agree to.

- *Member verification:* Both parties should decide whether the program is available only to members. If so, a method for verifying membership at both the time of acquisition and on an annual cycle is required. Member verification may be difficult for some businesses to administer.

- *Performance expectations:* While not necessarily included in a contract, it's important for the association to understand where the "break-even" point lies for the program to be considered a success for the business. Once this is determined, it can be monitored by the parties. Neither party should be surprised about whether or not sales expectations are being met.

- *Reporting:* It is important to set expectations in the contract about the type of reporting the association will receive from the business. The contract should specify the types of metrics that will be provided and the format and frequency of the reports.

Marketing

From a marketing perspective, the premise of an affinity program is *co-branding*. A business co-brands its name with the association. This differentiates the product or service of the business from its competition. The trust and loyalty the members presumably have with the association give a "foot in the door" to drive greater awareness and sales. The business gains access to a target market it might not otherwise reach. Time and again, co-branded marketing experiences result in higher open and response rates than non–co-branded promotions.

What many associations are finding is that an integrated marketing plan and strategy is necessary to drive awareness and sales for the program. The key is integration of as many marketing channels and activities as possible to achieve broad awareness within the membership. Often the business wants to rely solely on the association's digital marketing channels (such as website or e-newsletters). However, digital marketing alone does not typically create enough awareness. Multiple internal and external channels, including direct mail, outbound telemarketing, print advertising, digital advertising, events, and sponsorship, should be utilized. Which organization funds and executes marketing activities is something that needs to be negotiated and defined in the contract.

Associations should use member segmentation and targeting strategies to customize marketing messages and offers. Messages can be more relevant when communicated to a specific member segment than when mass marketing the entire membership.

Drafting the Agreements for the Program

When entering into a relationship and agreement for a new or existing affinity program with a business there are some helpful guiding principles an association may want to consider:

1. *Legal counsel:* The assistance of experienced legal counsel is essential.
2. *Contract development:* If the association has a number of programs, and the luxury of legal resources, it may be advantageous for the association to take the lead in developing the agreement(s). By doing this the association can achieve standardization across all contracts and makes it easier for staff and legal counsel to monitor and manage multiple contracts. Often the terms can be more favorable and less onerous to the association if they lead the development efforts.
3. *Terms:* Associations may want to steer away from language such as "agent" (an agent of the other), "partner" or "partnership," or "joint venture" (this is not a partnership or joint venture in the legal sense).
4. *Termination:* It's never easy to discuss the end of a program; however, it is critical that association staff give significant thought to the impact the program termination will have on the association and its members.
   - *Cause:* Should a party be able to terminate the agreement without cause? Or should a party only be able to terminate the agreement for cause? Either approach may have certain advantages or disadvantages to the association.
   - *Servicing or disposition of member accounts:* The method of notifying members of a program termination and the possible continuation of a program's pricing and service to members after termination should be considered.

- *Post-termination compensation:* Associations may be able to negotiate a wind-down of payment of fees over a period of time so as to prepare the association for the gradual loss of income from the program. This should be considered while negotiating the terms of the program.
- *Notice:* The duration of the termination process should be comfortable for both parties. Typically, 60 to 120 days allows ample time to execute the steps needed to end a program.
- *Post termination:* The contract should include a provision terminating the rights of the business to use the association's logo and membership list upon termination of the program. In addition, the contract should identify what provisions (for example, confidentiality and indemnification provision) will survive termination of the program.

5. *Legal obligations and liability:* The association's legal counsel will make recommendations about how to protect the association. An indemnification clause will likely be included and may be extensive.

6. *Third parties:* It's important for the association to know which outside entities (third parties, affiliates, or assignees) the business will involve in the administration of the program. The specifics of the outside entities' responsibilities should be understood. This is an important aspect for many reasons. The association will want to ensure the protection and proper use of the membership list and association brand by these third parties, and determine if the association needs to contract directly with these parties.

7. *Marketing:* The contract should stipulate that all marketing and promotions bearing the association's name or logo must be approved with plenty of lead-time by the designated association contact prior to publication. Both the business and association's marketing commitment and the requirement for a mutually agreeable annual marketing plan should also be outlined in the contract. Last, the association will want the right to include certain legal disclosure(s) on marketing promotions.

8. *Fees and reporting:* Advice from the association's legal counsel will determine the entity structure and association fees. The agreement should specify how the business will quantify a lead and sale driven by the association. In addition, the frequency and format of performance reporting for the association should be defined.

9. *Insurance:* The contract should set forth the type and amount of insurance both the business and association must maintain during the contract term.

Ongoing Management and Relationship

Once the relationship is established with the business and the program is launched in the market, there are best practices to consider in terms of effective ongoing management of the program:

- Ensure there is solid oversight of each product and the entire program by association staff.
- Results should be monitored on a quarterly basis or more frequently if it's a significant program or just launching in the market.
- Depending on the significance of the program, the association and business should review the performance of the program at least twice a year. If the association staff is actively involved, in all likelihood discussions about performance and execution are taking place much more frequently.

When to Pull the Plug

With the right due diligence and up-front evaluation, most affinity products will have a long life in the market. However, some associations may need to shed a product or service. This can happen for a number of reasons: the market changes significantly and the product is no longer relevant to the membership; member interest diminishes, and therefore leads and sales; the association is no longer comfortable working with the business, for example, because of customer service issues; the product or service comes in conflict with the mission or goals of the association. Whatever the reason, it's important for the association and business to work closely to develop an appropriate wind-down or termination plan, and if possible for the association to delicately communicate the termination of the program to members who are existing customers of the business.

Role of the Chief Staff Executive

Depending on the scope and structure of the affinity program, the chief staff executive's (CSE's) role can vary. As with any other member benefit, the CSE should be knowledgeable about the general performance of the program and the contribution to the organization. When there is a separately incorporated for-profit subsidiary or captive insurance company, the CSE would likely hold a seat on the board of directors.

The Future

Affinity programs will continue to play a vital role in enhancing member value and supporting nondues revenue growth as associations seek to expand beyond their traditional roles. Today, many members' participation in affinity programs generates a great deal of goodwill and profits for associations. But the association responsibilities are expanding with the opportunities. The affinity model has evolved beyond the simple arrangement of an association granting a business access to its brand and membership. It now includes the responsibility and investment required to promote, grow, and maintain a program. Associations must have a high degree of confidence that there is a member need as well as the demand to drive leads and sales to the business. Without these, the program may be short-lived.

Resource

Jacobs, J. A. *Association Law Handbook: A Practical Guide for Associations, Societies, and Charities.* Washington, DC: Association Management Press, 2012.

The Author

Susan Moseley, CAE, has managed two for-profit subsidiaries for the American Dental Association (ADA) and The National Federation of Independent Business as chief operating officer and vice president.

CHAPTER TWENTY-SIX

OPTIMIZING PROFESSIONAL DEVELOPMENT

Donald R. Levy, MEd

One need not look too far below the surface of most associations to find the rationale for their involvement in the professional development of their constituents. Virtually every organization has a mission statement that sets out the lofty goals for the enterprise, and they certainly all have articles of incorporation filed with their home states and which lay out the purposes for which they have been organized. The professional advancement of members is frequently among the first components of the organizations' guiding principles. If we do nothing else, certainly providing learning resources that enhance our constituents' ability to be successful while improving the flow and quality of goods and services they deliver are justifications enough for our associations' existence.

This centrality of the education mission confirms that virtually everything the association does serves a learning purpose. In addition to the traditional menu of learning resources (workshops, seminars, webinars, books, tapes, podcasts, and so on), many other association venues serve as learning channels: journals, magazines, newsletters, topical conferences, committee meetings, membership campaigns, standards development, online community networks, leadership development programs—all these, and more, are situations in which high-value member learning occurs. Research by the Society for Human Resource Management concluded that U.S. enterprises spent about $21.3 *billion* on "conferences, seminars, workshops, professional organizations, webinars, and other online training"[1] (programming typical of associations). Clearly, it's an important line of business for the association community.

Responding to Change

The importance of the education mission can best be understood by asking and answering three key questions:

1. In the past five years, has anything changed in the way your members do their work? Are there any changes in technology, materials, or workflow processes? Are there changes in the regulatory, social, political, commercial, or physical environments in which they operate? (Obviously, the answer is, "yes.")
2. What is the likelihood that change will continue? (It's reasonable to expect that change will continue to affect virtually every aspect of our working lives. "Constant change" is the new normal.)
3. Generally speaking, is it better to be organized, or disorganized? (Organized.)

Learning is how we respond to change. It is the process on which our very survivability depends. It enables us to adapt to the continual evolution of an increasingly complex and unpredictable world, making it possible for us to not only survive but thrive. Learning makes it possible to succeed in the face of change.

What Is Professional Development?

Professional development (PD) is the broadscope term applied to an individual's evolving preparedness for a working life, a growth model that includes the full range of knowledge, skills, and attitudes (KSAs) that, together, constitute a solid foundation for vocational achievement. Workplace success is based on a critical mass of all three elements: knowledge without application is useless; application without knowledge is inept. And exemplary knowledge and skills alone are insufficient for a successful career; having the "right attitude" is a key component of success in virtually every field.

A robust PD program therefore includes resources aimed at enhancing all three components, and addressing each of these components brings with it unique and important considerations. It is the goal of this chapter to provide an overview of those considerations, and the roles they play in an association's success.

Since the lives of our members are constantly changing, it follows that their associations must also continue to adapt and evolve. Successful associations will be those that go beyond a traditionally passive "market basket" involvement; forward-acting associations have developed a much deeper understanding of and a more tightly integrated relationship with their members. This reinforces the assertion that it is the association's responsibility to deliver the goods and services its dues-payers desire; only by developing a clear understanding of and responsive relationship with its constituents can associations evolve in ways consistent with member interests.

Motivation to Participate

Why do people participate in continuing education? Why do they sign up for conferences, attend seminars, buy books, read journals, watch videotapes, participate in webinars, seek collegial interaction in networks? Why do they spend hard-earned money and precious time, and defer important work or leisure, in pursuit of learning?

I often ask this question in my seminars, and flipchart the responses. Invariably, the responses include, "to get ahead, keep current, get a new job, keep the job I've got, avoid making mistakes, improve practice, take a tax-deductible vacation, see old friends, learn new things from the field's experts, find a mate or date, and the dreaded, 'because the boss said so—'"[2]

All of these are right answers, of course, and there are likely many more. We can summarize these correct answers by substituting one word for them all: "*benefit.*" Our participants have a legitimate expectation that they will benefit from their involvement. Not only do our participants have this expectation, but so do the employers who provide support (in cash or kind).

Our resource development efforts therefore ought to be clearly focused on delivering the benefits our prospective audiences seek. What *we* think, what our bosses think, what our boards of directors think, what the professional development committees think, is only of marginal interest here; what our *audiences* think is the key element. If we fail to deliver the benefits our constituencies want, they will stay away in droves.

Our success depends upon understanding the nature of those benefits, and if they are less than the cost, people won't participate. The brand equity you develop over time is based on your ability to consistently deliver on that benefit promise. Ignore this at your peril.

Goals of Professional Development Programming

Mission statements define and guide the activities of the PD department, consistent with the organization's mission. These statements serve as useful devices to help provide a framework for ensuring that resources are expended in the most effective way possible, as shown in the following examples.

It is the goal of the (association's) PD program to

- Help members (and others) be better consumers of continuing education
- Increase the likelihood that rightful learning will occur and workplace performance will be improved
- Remediate deficient practice, and optimize the merely adequate
- Become the resource of choice for continuing education programs, products, and services
- Maintain and enhance professional knowledge and technical proficiencies of our members
- Improve professional practice by advancing member education and supporting research
- Increase the expertise of industry professionals by providing quality education programs that are integral to their work

The association fulfills this mission by providing education, training, mentoring, research, credentialing, and so on.

Key Education Principles for the Non-Educator

Every senior executive should have at least a basic understanding of the key tenets of the field. Herewith are the "big ideas" that undergird this critical subject.

Adults Are Different from Children and College Students

In the 1960s and 1970s, Malcolm Knowles codified the key elements of effective adult education, and contrasted them with the principles then typical of teaching children and college-age learners. Knowles asserted that the processes undergirding K–16 education (kindergarten through college) were insufficient in framing education methods for working adults. In K–16 education, content is transmitted by the knowledgeable instructor to the untutored student, who is expected to absorb it exactly as delivered. Adults, however, bring components that substantially affect instructional design, possessing significant workplace experience that constitutes a context for the new content. Knowles refers to this as "active learning." Figuring out how to *apply* the new content is referred to as "reflection," a feedback loop in which the new content is mapped to individual situations and modified to fit local conditions (see Figure 26.1).

FIGURE 26.1. KNOWLES'S MODEL FOR ADULT EDUCATION.

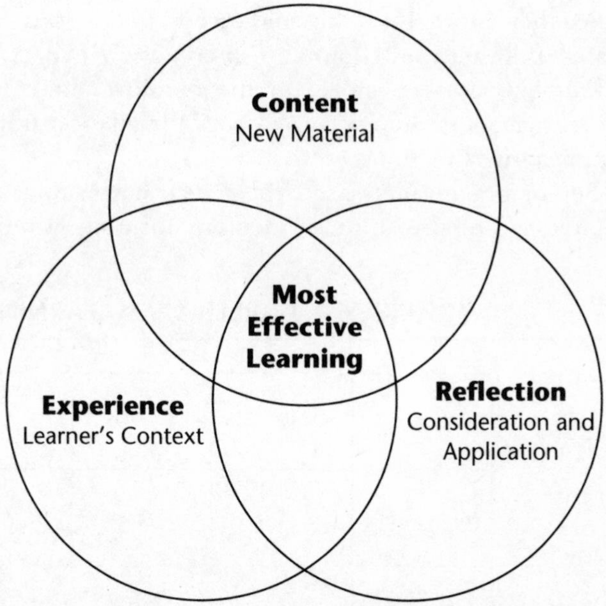

Source: Graphic by Donald R. Levy, © 2014 The Rochelle Organization, Inc.

Association education *must* acknowledge and leverage *all three* elements (content, experience, reflection) if adult learning is to be effective; didactic lecturing alone is insufficient. Programming must provide opportunities for the learners to integrate new material with their experience, and to consider how to apply it to their own work. If learners can't figure out what to do with the new material, the educational intervention has failed.

Learners' Needs Change Over Time

Associations serve a range of members, and association programming necessarily includes a range of resources. Figuring out what kinds of resources to provide for each audience segment is *the* key educator task.

Research with a national engineering organization produced a useful illustrative model based on career stages. We see in Figure 26.2 that junior practitioners focus on the acquisition of the technical material of their field—they're novices, learning the basics: doing the work, being part of a team, acquiring entry-level techniques, working with essential tools, materials, and processes, all of which provide the foundation of successful practice.

As they move into the mid-career phase, they're working toward technical mastery, and some are increasingly expected to acquire managerial skills as they move up the employment ladder. They become project managers; supervise new staff; or take on training, coaching, or administrative functions.

Senior practitioners are expected to have achieved managerial mastery, and can be thrust into leadership positions, whether that be leading

FIGURE 26.2. CAREER-SPAN LEARNING.

Junior	t		
Mid-Career	T	m (↗ T ↘ M)	
Senior	t	M	L

a department, division, organization, or profession. Interestingly, we often discover that as their management and leadership skills evolve, their technical repertoires atrophy, and that junior staff are often more conversant with current technical material. This disconnect can prove to be a substantial management challenge.

This research revealed a dynamic that was unrealized in the professional press and professional schools. Midcareer practitioners were often confronted with choice points for which they were unprepared: they could be channeled (willfully or not) into a management track, or they could be directed into a senior technical track. This career fork was a surprise to many, including the professional society. When we catalogued available learning resources, we found much technical information but little of the management education support needed by engineers who were thrust into these unexpected roles. The organization was advised to develop management resources, which provided a framework for the association's programs and a welcomed resource for the field.

Not All Learners Share the Same Perspectives

There are many jobs within a particular professional or trade arena. Association programming must address this range of needs if it is to serve all its members—"one size does *not* fit all." Different learners have different KSA requirements, experiential frames, employment settings, personal aspirations, and a host of other issues that set them apart from others. While it's virtually impossible to custom-craft a suite of resources for each individual, it's essential to develop an effective segmentation model that can help focus resource development so that audiences can individualize selections.

Segmentation models take a variety of forms, but typically include differentiating clusters of members on the basis of demographics—career phase, length of service, vocational role(s), the nature of employment, and the career paths pursued by members. Other factors also affect their learning needs—general economic conditions; workflow processes and situations; the nature of the knowledge, skill, or attitude (KSA) content of the resource; and so on.

It is useful to develop a segmentation model used by all association departments to quantify and qualify each segment. By establishing a common framework, the collected multiple flows of information describe each segment and can be enhanced by each department, working collaboratively, to create a well-informed understanding of each cohort.

We Work in a Crowded and Unruly Marketplace

Few education resources are delivered into markets absent competition from other providers. Competing without understanding the competition is ill-advised, at best, and foolhardy at worst.

Primary and secondary research provide an understanding of the competition faced in each segment. A robust understanding of your arena can include "market-basket analyses," in which promotion and marketing material are collected and analyzed. Other approaches include direct engagement (interviews, surveys, focus groups) and secondary research (competitive intelligence directly from competitors or other sources).

Environmental scanning develops a sense of the most frequently cited (most popular) programs so that you understand the kinds of programs the marketplace buys. Do not develop programs that are simply clones of others' products, a process which, by definition, stifles innovation and breakthrough thinking. Understanding what kinds of resources have been successful in a marketplace can improve programming; building products that mimic others' successful ventures is no guarantee of success, but developing products that replicate others' failures is a prescription for disaster. A robust understanding of the competitive forces in your markets is a key element in staving off erosion of your audiences. You can't beat the competition if you don't know what they're doing.

Effective Continuing Education Standards Are a Half-Century Old

A 1970 national task force developed guidelines for this emerging specialization (continuing workplace education). That work gave rise to the International Association for Continuing Education and Training (IACET), and resulted in the "continuing education unit" (CEU), a model that continues to guide the field. In 2007, IACET combined with the American National Standards Institute (ANSI) to publish the *ANSI/IACET 1–2007 Standard for Continuing Education and Training.*

The ten criteria for the CEUs (below) are distilled from the more extensive *IACET Principles of Good Practice.* Many educators consider the CEU criteria to be the minimum quality standards for responsible continuing education. Although a full explication of the *Principles* would be useful, a brief discussion of the more compact CEU criteria and guidelines will have to suffice. The criteria are presented below in italics, each followed by this author's notes to place it in an association context.

> "A CEU is comprised of ten contact hours of participation in an organized continuing education experience under responsible

sponsorship, capable direction, and qualified instruction."[3] (The CEU was developed to quantify involvement in learning, and the team that created it drew on the collegiate model, in which a three-credit course includes forty-five to forty-eight hours of instruction. The notion of "CEU" has acquired various meanings in the interim, many of which no longer bear a direct relation to the original *Guidelines.* In some cases, "CEU" now refers to a "fifty-minute hour," or sixty minutes of learning activity of whatever kind, or, in at least one case, a generic term describing a resource of any kind and duration that awards a corresponding amount of CE credit.)

1. *Each activity is planned in response to educational needs which have been identified for a target audience.* Activities should be based on thoughtful, authoritative needs assessments; research should direct development, not board, committee, or staff guesswork.
2. *Each activity has clear and concise written statements of intended learning outcomes.* Explicit statements establish participant learning goals; guide resource development; and serve as the armature around which program promotion, marketing, and evaluation are structured.
3. *Qualified instructional personnel are involved in planning and conducting each activity.* Adult learning expertise should be employed in resource design, drawing on the content expertise of subject matter specialists.
4. *Content and instructional methods are appropriate for the intended learning outcomes of each activity.* Instructional methods should be appropriate for the outcomes—lectures are adequate for knowledge development, skill development requires supervised practice, and attitude change typically requires multiple interventions.
5. *Participants must demonstrate their attainment of learning outcomes.* Demonstrations can include Q&A, quizzes, projects, case studies, final exams, and so on. These provide for the assessment of learner success, enable instructors and staff to refine methods and materials, and suggest additional resources. Demonstrations of learning achievement are especially critical in situations in which continuing education is a credentialing requirement.
6. *Each learning activity is evaluated by the participants.* Rigorous methods should be employed to evaluate instructors, methods, materials, settings, and so on. Prudent practice also includes ways to segment responses as market research.
7. *The sponsor has an identifiable unit, group, or individual with clearly defined responsibilities for developing and administering learning activities.* Having the education program housed within the membership or

meetings department (or elsewhere) detracts from the credibility of the programs. Continuity, capability, and accountability are important.

8. *The sponsor has a review process and operation that ensure that the CEU criteria are met.* Have an appropriate system to monitor activity and ensure process integrity; all providers should be held accountable to maintain standards. Your organization's brand equity and budget are at stake.

9. *The sponsor maintains a complete record of each individual's participation and can provide a copy of that record upon request for a period of at least seven years.* This is particularly important when participants are required to prove successful participation in credible continuing education for credential maintenance. It's also important in fields in which job mobility is accelerating.

10. *The sponsor provides an appropriate learning environment and support services.* While learning can occur in a wide variety of settings, concern has been raised regarding the efficacy of programming in resorts, or the provision of technical skills training in online or recorded formats, and so on. The venues in which learning resources are delivered must pass a "reasonable person" test.

There are well-established methodologies for effective adult education. Too often providers create programs that are merely entertaining, but doing so at the expense of learning is inappropriate at least, and unethical at worst. The time and expense necessary to develop resources and support participation are both limited and valuable (for participants, providers, and employers), and expending those precious commodities on anything but the best resources is a disservice to all. The true success of programming is measured by behavioral change and enhanced workplace performance, not by the number of widgets sold or dollars generated.

"Professional" Has a Distinctly Narrow Definition

Many vocational groups aspire to professional status; fewer achieve it. In *Continuing Learning in the Professions,* Professor Cyril O. Houle developed a model that displays the nature and evolution of continuing learning in the professions.

Houle's model (Figure 26.3) includes three phases of preparation: general education (K–16), specialized preservice education (graduate programs and advanced study, often including internships), and continuing education. Entry into professional work typically includes three elements: education, experience (internship), and a demonstration of competence—a licensing examination—as well as meeting post-licensure requirements for continuing education.

FIGURE 26.3. AN EMERGING MODEL OF PROFESSIONAL EDUCATION.

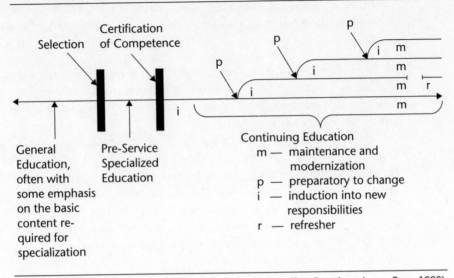

Source: C. O. Houle, *Continuing Learning in the Professions* (San Francisco: Jossey-Bass, 1980), 106.

Houle's model suggests that education resources developed for a given field may spread across these three components, and there are opportunities to address all three with association resources.

The Basic Building Blocks of Education

KSA describes the DNA of learning; it's the acronym for knowledge, skills, and attitudes, and is used as the categorizing device for learning. This tripartite model was first articulated by educational psychologist Benjamin Bloom, who concluded that learning is segmented into

> *Knowledge:* Things you *know* (information, data). Knowledge development can be demonstrated by recitation. ("You either know it, or you don't; tell me.") Bloom referred to this as the Cognitive Domain.
>
> *Skills:* Things you *do* (physical application of knowledge). Skill development requires application. ("You can do it, or you can't; show me.") Bloom termed this the Psychomotor Domain.

Attitudes: Things you *are* or *believe* (integrity, perseverance, tolerance of ambiguity or risk, appreciation of diversity and inclusivity, sense of humor, flexibility, trust, creativity). ("You're either like this, or you're not; we'll have to wait and see.") Bloom termed this the Affective Domain.

Most association programs focus on knowledge development because it's easiest to manage and measure. Skill development requires supervised practice, and attitude refinement can encompass significant time spans and is more difficult to measure.

Bloom's research team delineated the components of the Cognitive Domain in what has become widely known as "Bloom's Taxonomy," concluding that learning proceeds in a stepwise fashion, from the concrete and rote on the lowest end to the abstract and creative on the highest. Successful progression up this learning ladder depends on the achievement of prior levels; one cannot develop highest-order thinking skills—judgment and creative thought—without first achieving the lower levels. No skipping.

Figure 26.4 portrays the six levels of the taxonomy and includes (underneath the steps) words that describe intellectual activities within each level. The upper portion illustrates teaching strategies that could be employed to achieve the outcomes.

Providers should clearly state the outcomes learners can expect to achieve. For example, it's inappropriate to suggest that one will become an expert practitioner after a single two-hour experience. Bloom's Taxonomy provides a ready framework that can inform outcome statement development by reminding planners to specify where on the "stepwise ladder" the participants will arrive. Articulate outcome statements provide a clear definition of the target at which the learning activity is aimed, and provide objective, measurable criteria for evaluating success.

Learning Styles Differ

We know that people are different and that they are attracted to different things for differing reasons. So also are they drawn to different kinds of learning resources, on the basis of their learning style preferences and situations. Some people prefer to read quietly by themselves, others prefer lively debate; some enjoy online interactions, others prefer individualized instruction.

There are useful models that can help planners understand the implications of these differences and direct development that recognizes

FIGURE 26.4. MATCHING INSTRUCTIONAL STRATEGIES AND BLOOM'S TAXONOMY.

Strategy	Level					
	REMEMBERING	**UNDERSTANDING**	**APPLYING**	**ANALYZING**	**EVALUATING**	**CREATING**
	lecture	discussion, Q & A	exercises	problems	simulation analyses	projects
	audio/video	review	practice demo	exercises	assessment exercises	case study solutions
	visuals	test	project sketches	case studies	critiques	creative exercises
	examples	assessment reports	simulations	critical incidents	appraisals	develop plans
	illustrations	learner presentations	role play	questions, tests		simulations
	analogies	writing				

Outcome						
	count	associate	apply	analyze	appraise	combine
	define	compute	calculate	arrange	assess	compile
	describe	convert	change	breakdown	compare	compose
	label	defend	classify	combine	conclude	create
	list	discuss	complete	detect	contrast	derive
	match	distinguish	compute	develop	criticize	design
	outline	estimate	demonstrate	diagram	determine	integrate
	quote	explain	examine	differentiate	grade	modify
	read	extrapolate	graph	discriminate	interpret	order
	recall	generalize	interpret	illustrate	judge	organize
	recite	give examples	manipulate	infer	justify	plan
	record	paraphrase	modify	relate	measure	prescribe
	repeat	predict	operate	select	rate	propose
	reproduce	rewrite	prepare	separate	support	relate
	select	summarize	produce	subdivide	test	reorganize
	write		show	utilize		revise
			solve			transform
						specify

Note: The precise, literal differentiation between some of these words can depend on local custom, context of use, and other factors. They are presented here to illustrate the range of behavioral results anticipated —the knowledge gained or skill developed —as a result of the learning episode. Dr. Benjamin Bloom headed a group of educational psychologists that developed this classification of intellectual behavior important in learning (the cognitive domain) in 1956; the taxonomy was revised in 2001 by Anderson and Krathwohl.

Source: Adapted from L. Phillips, *The Continuing Education Guide: The CEU and Other Professional Development Criteria,* 2nd ed. (Louis Phillips, 2009. Graphic by Donald R. Levy). © 2009 The Rochelle Organization, Inc. All rights reserved.

these learner preferences. For example, research conducted with a surgical organization used the Kolb Learning Style Inventory (KLSI) to assess members' learning preferences.

The model portrays learning style preferences on two spectrums: "perceiving"—how an individual takes on new information—and "processing"—what they do with the information once acquired. Figure 26.5 shows Kolb's basic model, and one would expect a random sample of learners to be evenly distributed across all four quadrants. But when 166 surgeons completed the KLSI, the results were clearly *not* uniformly distributed around Kolb's model (Figure 26.6).

Given this evidence, planners were advised to create programs featuring acknowledged national experts presenting current business school material, the applications for which would be discussed by participants' peers in an academic environment far from the distractions of their jobs. This program is contrasted with "touchy-feely" explorations of feelings led by senior practitioners in resort settings, or published as breezy short articles in popular journals to be read on an airplane or viewed online.

FIGURE 26.5. KOLB'S FOUR-QUADRANT LEARNING STYLES MODEL.

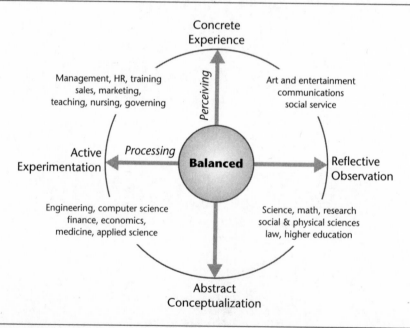

Source: Daniel A. Kolb, *Kolb Learning Styles Inventory, LSI Workbook, v. 3.1.* (Boston: Experience Based Learning Systems, Inc., 2007). See http://www.haygroup.com/downloads/au/misc/lsi_sample.pdf.

FIGURE 26.6. LSI DISTRIBUTION FOR 166 SPECIALIST SURGEONS.

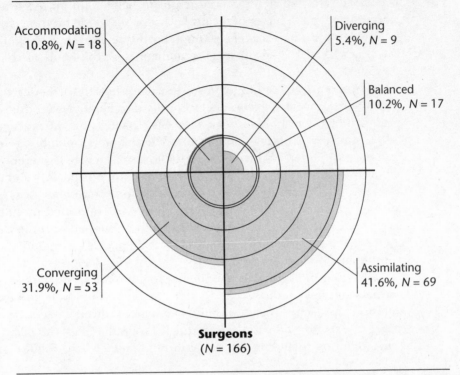

Accommodating
10.8%, N = 18

Diverging
5.4%, N = 9

Balanced
10.2%, N = 17

Converging
31.9%, N = 53

Assimilating
41.6%, N = 69

Surgeons
(N = 166)

Source: American Orthopaedic Association, *Leadership Development Research Project* (Rosemont, IL: Author, January 2001).

Recognition of learning style preferences and an understanding of audience trends should inform development; programming should acknowledge audience preferences. However, individuals rarely have a single, dominant preference, and the same is true for larger groups. Program planners should develop resources consistent with and proportionate to the preferences of the target audiences; differentiated treatments of the same material are often necessary.

Models of Programs, Products, and Services

Many associations use a mechanism that produces a distorted view of the learning enterprise, issuing an annual "call for presentations." The proposals submitted are then cobbled together to form the program menu. Unfortunately, this process presents programs that the instructors want to teach, not necessarily the ones learners want to attend. The IACET *Guidelines* state that development ought to begin with an assessment of learner need, not a survey of faculty favorites. Many organizations respond to overtures from providers without having a clear understanding of the issues faced by the prospective audiences or the kinds of resources they seek.

Planners are advised to first issue a "call for heartburn"—descriptions of the vexing problems learners face every day. Planners can then solicit presentations that address those interests. (As a matter of practice, this is but one piece of the larger puzzle; evaluations, member research, summaries of letters to the editors, bookstore sales records, reference desk inquiries—all combine to provide insight into prospective audiences' thinking. These multiple flows of information, continually assembled, analyzed, and integrated, collectively undergird "informed intuition," a framework wherein planners become so fully enmeshed with the *meaning* of the data that they can intuitively—and quickly—respond to their constituents' changing world.)

Effective professional development programs are focused more on the learners and less on the teachers; educators should innovate and explore delivery approaches that respond to audiences' diverse needs, learning style preferences, and vocational settings. Program design can take a wide range of forms, including, but certainly not limited to, the following:

A. Events
  1. National workshops or seminars
  2. Convention or conference programs:
    Plenary programs
    Professional programs
    Consultation sessions
    Local case studies and tours
    Technical case studies and seminars
    Pre- and post-event workshops
    Networking programs
    Exhibitor education
  3. Focus groups
  4. Users' groups
  5. Nonconference networking opportunities
  6. Specialty breakfast, lunch, and dinner speakers
  7. Business meetings presentations and discussions
  8. Chapter programs
  9. Short courses
  10. Symposia
  11. Institutes
  12. Forums
  13. Online presentations (synchronous)
  14. Online presentations (multimodal hybrid or blended)

B. Products
1. Audiotapes (with or without workbooks)
2. Videotapes (with or without workbooks)
3. Correspondence courses
4. Self-study materials
5. Group-study materials
6. Computer-based training (CBT)
7. Topical newsletters or periodicals
8. Information databases
9. Online presentations (asynchronous recordings)
10. Journals, newsletters, books, monographs (print, online)

C. Services
1. Credentialing or certifications
2. Provider accreditation and program standards
3. Research and development
4. Assessment, diagnostic, and referral services
5. CEU credit record-keeping or transcripting
6. "Consulting support" for other departments, state and local chapters; allied organizations; members and members' organizations
7. Awards and juried recognition programs (disseminating best practice models)

A Few Notes on Technology

We're big fans of the Next Big Thing. We're drawn to novelty and innovation, to "new and improved" versions of old stuff, and to things we've not seen before. Smaller, smarter, faster, better, newer, different, updated, revised—we're quick to move forward, eager to get to the future, impatient with the present, and only moderately tolerant of the past.

Regrettably, the education business is often subject to the same fascinations. But just because something is new does not mean it's *better.* Planners are advised to maintain a sober understanding of this realization as they respond to pressure to adopt technologies before effectiveness is proven and prospective audiences identified. Rose-colored participation levels (and revenues) often fail to meet projections.

In the 1980s, we became convinced that videotape would revolutionize the education business. The 1990s witnessed the advent of CBT—computer-based training. The twenty-first century brought the Next New Big Thing: Internet-based e-learning. For each advance, the tech-savvy few who liked the technology thought it a fun way to spend some time. But for many others, the technology holds little attraction, and successful learning is always subject to the vagaries of local distractions.

There's been a surge of interest in e-learning; many organizations are rushing headlong into this platform. While the technology holds much promise and can provide affordable support to a wide range of people, virtually anywhere, and at different times, associations must remember that it is but one delivery channel amongst a variety of other *proven* approaches. While it is appropriate for some learners and subjects, planners mustn't forget that it is *not* useful for those to whom the approach is not attractive. If they're not interested in the offer—in either the content or the technology—they simply won't show up; if they don't like to read, they won't buy a book.

Executives must consider four key issues when adopting any new technology:

1. *Prove the market:* Prudent management requires thoughtful analysis of potential markets. Has the target market adopted this technology via other providers? At what prices, and with what results? Does the medium match the material? What percentage of prospective audiences will respond to this overture, and what will be the adoption rate for the full membership? ASAE research showed that association members overwhelmingly prefer in-person learning, ranking it highest in a twelve-choice list, and ranking distance learning lowest, suggesting that people choose it because it's cheap and convenient, but they clearly don't like it, and would prefer alternatives.[4]

2. *Manage expectations carefully:* Developers should present realistic multiyear business plans, including investment schedules and the likely scale and timing of revenue. What evidence confirms a ready market for these resources? Can the market leverage this technology? What staff will these programs require, what resources will be necessary for success?

3. *Think laterally:* A good association program employs any and all approaches that respond to market opportunities, member segments, subjects, learning styles, technical competencies, and so on. Look first at what and how your members want to learn, not at what seems to be the most compelling new technology offered by competitors or promoted by an aggressive salesperson. By focusing on learning rather than teaching, other forms of electronically mediated knowledge resources can be leveraged (blogs, email lists, podcasts, resource and research engines, discussion forums, wikis—the list is long and rapidly changing). Many forms of technology-based delivery don't require big investments and can have a greater, more immediate impact on members' lives.

FIGURE 26.7. ROGERS'S ADOPTION OF INNOVATION CURVE.

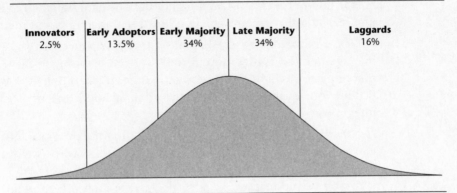

| Innovators 2.5% | Early Adoptors 13.5% | Early Majority 34% | Late Majority 34% | Laggards 16% |

Source: E. Rogers, *The Diffusion of Innovations* (New York: Free Press/Simon & Schuster, 1962), 247.

4. *Plan and manage the transition:* Markets do not react well to abrupt, ninety-degree turns; the transition must be planned and managed, and there is a consistent pattern in new technology adoption. The model developed by Everett Rodgers (Figure 26.7) suggests that early participation is limited to a very small percentage of the market ("innovators"), followed by a somewhat larger cohort of early adopters, and only then widely accepted by the majority of a population.

Planners are advised to understand the pace and scale of technology adoption, whether it be video, CBT, online learning, or some new approach as yet unimagined. A prudent business plan will acknowledge that any new technology will eventually be rendered obsolete by the Next New Big Thing.

Organizing the Professional Development Department

The education function can be thought of as a bundle of knowledge and production capacities that cluster in five KSA groups known as the ADDIE model:

Assess: Identifying the issues of specific constituencies, understanding workplace constraints, individual aspirations and preferences, and other defining factors of the prospective learners. (Frequently involves psychometrics and IT support)

Design: Defines the kinds of activities that facilitate learners' acquisition of KSAs. (Instructional design, human systems, cognitive and learning theory, andragogy, educational materials and methods)

Develop: Competencies marshaled to actually produce things—project management KSAs that move resources from planning to the marketplace. (Graphic and product design; print, online, video production; event planning; learning management system integration)

Implement: Setting the plan in motion; putting the program into the market; integrating the resources with audiences' lives—delivered in ways that are easily and successfully used by consumers. (Promotion and marketing, advertising, customer relations and commercial systems; inventory, fulfillment, record-keeping, budget administration)

Evaluate: Determines the degree of success in hitting the target. Evaluation and assessment phases are closely related—both seek to better understand learning needs and measure success at developing effective initial and subsequent resources. (Back to psychometrics and IT)

This ADDIE model is widely used to understand the education function, but it is by no means the only model. The American Society of Association Executives' (ASAE's) Professional Development Section produced several studies that describe the range of KSAs necessary for successful association education practice.

The section used its 1992 consideration of the *educator's job description* to create a self-assessment tool that clustered seventy-five competencies into three broad categories:

Practice competencies: Active application of the educator's theoretical and technical KSAs to his or her job; finding the best pathway to the most effective methods of learner success.

Production competencies: Educator as a resource manufacturer and product manager; includes development through evaluation phases.

Relationship competencies: Educator as communicator and team member or leader; market engagement, political judgment, dispute resolution, manager or mentor, advocacy, and so on.[5]

In 2010, the section conducted a similar inquiry into the typical *professional development department*, and produced a job task analysis composed of 120-plus elements grouped in eight areas:

1. Personal, member, and organizational learning
2. Program planning
3. Development and delivery
4. Marketing
5. Evaluation
6. Technology
7. Relationship management
8. Management and administration of the function[6]

All three models (ADDIE and the two ASAE studies) describe how an education function might be structured and managed, and can be adapted as planning or assessment frameworks, but no two associations are alike. What is most important is the ability of education managers to have or have access to the full complement of necessary resources. Whether they exist within or adjacent to the department is less important than whether or not they are *readily available*. It is the job of the chief staff executive to ensure that the function is appropriately equipped for success.

Summary

The following summary notes are offered to confirm the key ideas that senior association executives will find useful in guiding professional development.

We are obligated to do this work by our corporate charters and by our mission statements. The association and departmental missions guide our development choices, overlaid with our member or audience segmentation frames and segment research.

Learners are motivated by their expectation of benefit. Program development is based on a solid, authoritative, evidence-based understanding of the benefits sought by those we serve.

Effective professional development begins with authoritative learner assessments, includes clearly stated learning outcomes, uses tailored instructional methods that meet learner needs in manners appropriate to the material, and ends with evaluation of learner success.

We serve a large potential audience (greater than 56 million adults),[7] composed of different kinds of learners, with differing learning styles and participation preferences, working in widely varied employment situations, and with needs and interests that change throughout their various and varied careers. A comprehensive education program will necessarily have a broad field of view and will address a range of subjects (many more than once and in more than one format).

Learning progresses incrementally from the concrete to the abstract; the intended (measurable) learning outcomes guide the selection of methods and materials. This stepwise progress must be embodied in the resources developed.

We are more focused on creating situations in which learners can learn, and less on creating opportunities for instructors to teach; *learning* is the goal, not teaching. We meet learners where they live, creating resources that are useful, engaging, animating, and worth the effort.

Well-established principles guide effective adult education. This is especially critical in light of our provision of learning resources to credentialed practitioners charged with protecting public health, safety, and welfare, and who must undertake continuing education to assert continued competency. We have a responsibility to foster learner success.

Few things are more important to individual and organizational success than the ability to adapt and change, to acquire new knowledge and to master new skills, to respond to new situations with facility and dispatch, and to rise to meet the challenges we are certain to face. Supporting learners as they seek to improve their professional repertoires and career performance is, has been, and will continue to be the central organizing and animating focus of responsive and successful associations. If you do nothing else well, do *this* well, and you—and your association—will have achieved immeasurable success.

Notes

When possible, the primary references are cited.

1. SHRM/Achieve, *Survey: Changing Employee Skills and Education Requirements—Training Budgets, Resources and Strategies* (Alexandria, VA: Society for Human Resource Management, 2012), 9.

2. L. R. Albert and M. Dignam, *Decision to Learn* (Washington, DC: ASAE Association Management Press, 2010), 16. This provides a list of the top fifteen motivation responses cited in the ASAE's research.

3. *The Continuing Education Unit, Criteria and Guidelines* (Washington, DC: Council on Continuing Education Unit/International Association of Continuing Education and Training, 1974).

4. Albert & Dignam, *Decision to Learn*, 18.

5. ASAE, "Competencies for the Association Educator," in *Association Educator* (Washington, DC: ASAE Association Management Press, September-October 1990), 3.

6. ASAE, "Core Competencies in Professional Development," in *Professional Development Council* (Washington, DC: ASAE Association Management Press, 2010).

7. U.S. Department of Education, National Center for Education Statistics, "Table 4. Number and percentage of adults who gave selected reasons for participation in formal work-related courses or taining: 2004–05," *Adult Education Participation in 2004–05, National Household Education Surveys Program*, Washington, D.C., 2006, 13 (the last year for which the data were collected).

The Author

Donald R. Levy, MEd, is the president and CEO of the Rochelle Organization, Inc., a learning-oriented consulting firm based in Washington, D.C. The firm provides research, strategic planning, and program and product development support to major national professional societies and associations.

CHAPTER TWENTY-SEVEN

STRATEGIC LEADERSHIP

Barbara Byrd Keenan, FASAE, CAE

What is strategic leadership, and why is it so important for association executives to practice it? Strategic leadership is a process and a philosophy. As a process it is how you approach assessing the needs and opportunities for the organization and how you exercise leadership. As a philosophy, it is how you see your role as an organizational champion, leadership coach, and staff mentor. Strategic leadership is simply the most important quality for success as an association executive.

Why? Because it embodies the crucial components of your role as the chief staff executive (CSE)—thinking strategically, executing effectively, grooming and supporting volunteer leadership, developing staff talent, and ensuring that the association serves its members and society. It is your ability to align resources and talent to frame and achieve a vision for your organization that distinguishes you from an effective administrator or manager. It is not a role you can delegate to others on the staff. It is a mind-set and a competency that you want to nurture and support at all levels within your organization.

The foundations of strategic leadership include

- Demonstrating interpersonal effectiveness
- Cultivating an innovation culture
- Managing ambiguity

- Committing to social responsibility
- Developing talent
- Nurturing and sustaining trust
- Collaborating in leadership

Demonstrating Interpersonal Effectiveness

The CSE has a crucial role as "chief cat herder." You need to get volunteer members, leaders, staff, and stakeholders moving in an aligned way toward the organization's goals. How are you going to make that happen? Your ability to communicate in a clear, concise way will be an essential element of your leadership. Everyone involved with the organization needs to understand the basics:

- What are we doing?
- Why are we doing it?
- How and when will we accomplish it?

If you are not clear about the direction and process needed for future success, how will leadership and staff contribute?

We each have the ability to develop and enhance our own style of communication. We don't need to be a charismatic orator to be effective. We do, however, need to be clear, contextual, and compelling in framing the options for the organization and the implications of those various scenarios.

The ability to have "crucial conversations"[1] to manage and resolve conflicts is a key aspect of interpersonal effectiveness. Human beings are political animals, and organizations are political entities. To be effective as a strategic leader, you need to deal with the many divergent opinions and political pressures and approach them from a win-win perspective. Most of us would rather not have to deal with disagreeable people and prefer to avoid conflicts when we can. It takes courage and emotional intelligence to address problem issues and problem people in a timely way. Others in the organization will follow your lead and model your approach; they will learn from how you handle conflicts.

The willingness to discuss the "undiscussables" is a test of interpersonal effectiveness and emotional intelligence, and a hallmark of strategic leadership. This is difficult to do and very easy to avoid. We hope the issue will go away or resolve on its own so we don't have to deal with it. But how and when we deal with challenging issues and people sets the tone for the rest of the organization. If not addressed, problems undermine an innovative, productive, and fun culture. Some of the consequences of not addressing undiscussables are

- Status quo remains
- Bad news is stifled, along with innovation
- Relationships flounder and rumor mills flourish
- Mutual respect dissipates, replaced by complacency and ultimately cynicism

To successfully get critical issues and information in a safe environment so they can be addressed, you first have to be clear about the issue.

Effective listening is often the most overlooked component of interpersonal effectiveness. "Seek first to understand, then to be understood," famously framed by Stephen Covey, captures the essence of effective listening and of the ability to master crucial conversations.[2] Listening is hard work. "You're a great listener," "You really understand my viewpoint," or "Thanks for listening" are comments we should all strive to hear every day.

Resources abound on leadership. The most sage advice harvested from current literature on leadership includes

- Establish a free flow of relevant information.
- Share your perspective and facts and ask the same of others.
- Look for shared purpose and meaning.
- Maintain a respectful and safe environment and apologize as necessary.
- Commit to a decision and timetable for follow-up.

Cultivating an Innovation Culture

It is a commonly held belief that people in general are resistant to change. *Change* often becomes something to be feared and resisted. "We have always done it this or that way—why should we change what's working" is a theme that resonates in many organizations around the world.

Organizations that sustain success however, don't focus on change. They don't even use the word. They focus on creating a clear, compelling mission and continuous dialogue about how to achieve it in the most effective way. They recognize that if the world is moving faster than they are, they are falling behind.

For years, association executives have talked about the need for decision-making processes to be nimble and flexible. While nimbleness and flexibility are important elements of success, they are insufficient elements of success. Strategic leadership requires establishing and cultivating an innovation culture and mind-set, led by the CSE and actively supported by senior staff. This is a crucial area for "modeling the way,"[3] demonstrating daily a willingness and determination to continuously improve current initiatives, stretch to launch new initiatives, prune or reframe faltering programs, and consider the improbable to discern the possible.

Another step in cultivating an innovation culture includes fostering freedom of thought and expression. Consider this question: "Do I feel free and comfortable to express my viewpoints, challenge organizational assumptions, disagree with proposed programs or implementation steps or just say 'wacky' things?" What kind of environment needs to exist to say "Yes" to that question?

A technique that I have used in numerous creative development sessions has been to frame a conversation from a three-part viewpoint; given an issue to explore, what would be considered wacky? Wackier? Wackiest? Can you imagine some of the ideas that surface under the "wackiest" end of the spectrum? I can share that, with deeper dialogue and perspective, the wackiest notions have morphed into executable programs.

It also matters who's in the room. Embracing everyone in the process, not just the creative types, allows you to harvest ideas from people who have wildly divergent opinions about the issue being considered. It helps you strengthen critical thinking skills across the staff and reinforce that the entire team is responsible for the success of the organization.

Further, it requires you to reward creative thinking and risk taking. To illustrate, there is a fabled story of Thomas Watson, past head of IBM. When a prototype project failed and the lead manager thought he would be fired, Mr. Watson reportedly said, "Fire you? We just spent thousands of dollars educating you!" Cultivating an environment of "falling forward" and continuously learning from whatever happens reinforces a culture of innovation.

In *The Ten Faces of Innovation*, CEO Tom Kelley highlights specific roles or personas needed within a team to foster breakthrough thinking and creative development.[4] He organizes the ten roles into three personas: learning, organizing, and building. Examples of the roles include the Anthropologist, the Hurdler, and the Experienced Architect. Two key takeaways from this archetype approach to innovation are that

1. A broad and disparate set of perspectives is needed to foster innovation.
2. You have to intentionally design teams with this level of diversity.

It is the CSE's job to ensure that the necessary voices are in the room, whether staff or volunteer. Designing teams for innovation and building supportive teams to advance the mission are the CSE's strategic responsibilities.

Managing Ambiguity

Peter Senge's work in systems thinking has guided many organizations in their quest to achieve breakthrough results. A particular principle cited by Senge is at the core of strategic leadership—creative tension (Figure 27.1). Creative tension is created by the gap between the vision of what you want to achieve in your organization and what is the actual state of affairs. Managing this tension productively is a critical skill for CSEs.

I have always loved the rubber band analogy for creative tension—it is clean and tactile. If the ends of the bands are too far apart, it snaps; if they are too close together, the band is limp. What better way to illustrate how energy dissipates in a system—whether by lowering the vision or changing the "current reality."

Senge reminds us that the ability to harness creative tension propels us to our vision with positive energy. Solving problems might eliminate pain points and neutralizes tension but it does not move us forward.

Where is the power in the ability to manage creative tension? It is three-fold:

1. Creating and articulating a compelling vision of what can be
2. Accurately describing the current state of effectiveness or ineffectiveness
3. Managing the emotions that surface when the gap threatens to "snap the band"

If managing creative tension is central to strategic leadership, then managing the ambiguity that is continuously created within the system is a core skill. Some CSEs have a high degree of comfort dealing with "unknowns" and the absence of a clear pathway toward a goal. A key leadership skill is to be able to step boldly into uncharted territory and make sense out of disparate insights and bits of information.

FIGURE 27.1. CREATIVE TENSION.

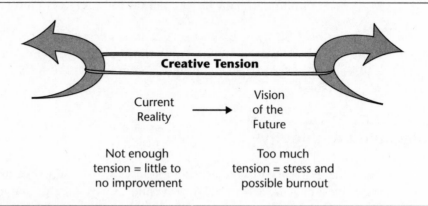

Source: Adapted from Michael Murphy, "Creative Tension." http://waremalcomb.com/wordpress/2012/11/creative-tension/

However, everyone else in the organization may not have that same tolerance for uncertainty or risk. It is your job as the leader to manage the creative tension in such a way that your team feels passion for the vision, senses the opportunities to make real progress on your goals, and develops the capacity for taking action when the options before them are less than crystal clear. Ineffective management of creative tension fosters anxiety and confusion, often leading to "analysis paralysis." When this occurs, it is the CSE's responsibility to redirect the group back to the vision, reframe a refreshed "current reality," and help frame the logical next steps. The path to the vision will be clearer and feel less onerous if you do.

One tricky aspect of managing creative tension and ambiguity is ensuring that you are truthful, comprehensive, and contextual when assessing current reality. Whether it is a traditional SWOT (strength, weaknesses, opportunities, threats) analysis, competitive intelligence audit, environmental scan, member survey data, or focus group feedback, you have to articulate the full picture of the organization. The good, the bad, and the ugly all need to be outlined. You cannot manage the creative tension in your system if you start from a false place.

The other tricky aspect of managing the creative tension is how you keep the team from getting overwhelmed and depressed about where you are versus the vision. Overwhelmed and depressed people can't easily focus on a big vision, especially if they place judgment on the things that aren't going well in the organization. You need to inspire hope and help staff and volunteers focus on the logical next steps in the journey as part of the continuum of progress. There is a need to acknowledge what is going on without fixating on the downside—it is just the place you are starting from.

Case Study: The Power of (A)

The power of (A) is ASAE's strategic platform for sharing the association communities' commitment to serving the greater good, encouraging associations to share their unique stories, and magnifying the collective accomplishments and contributions all of our organizations make every day to our members and the world. The Summit Awards, created by ASAE, showcase "how associations spotlight their unique resources to solve problems, advance industry/ professional performance, kick start innovation and improve world conditions." If you want to be inspired, go to www.thepowerofa.org and watch the videos of recent award winners. They are phenomenal and reflect the award categories:

- The power to enrich lives
- The power to create a competitive workforce
- The power to prepare for the future
- The power to innovate
- The power to make a better world

How is your organization diagramming your transition from *membership* to *movement*? Where are you harnessing the experience and expertise of your members to make a meaningful and positive difference? What are you doing to make a better world?

Case Study on Level 2 Social Responsibility: LEAD 360

What is it? LEAD 360, created and launched in 2013 by the Institute of Food Technologists (IFT), is a global leadership development experience designed for emerging leaders in food science.

What is the goal? The goal of LEAD 360 is to identify and invest in a select group of talented, high-potential young professionals from around the world who are passionate about the profession and interested in developing the leadership and stewardship skills needed to advance the profession in the twenty-first century. The expectation is that the group will establish the lifelong connections needed to foster leadership in the profession throughout the world.

Why was it created? IFT had sponsored several leadership development activities over the years; all had been successful in helping to identify and nurture new talent for the organization. The precursor to LEAD 360, the Strategic Leadership Forum, was a hybrid leadership development workshop and organizational "think tank." The rationale for LEAD 360 was the need to focus on global talent development and help "fast track" a global network for younger professionals who have not enjoyed the same level of financial support for meeting attendance or participation as more tenured leaders.

How were nominees chosen? Food science associations around the world, leading universities, and multinational food companies were asked to nominate dynamic, high-potential individuals who were excited to learn valuable leadership and stewardship skills and eager to champion the emerging issues facing the global food system. Criteria included

- Be an active member of a country-based society or research institution, such as the Chinese Institute of Food Science & Technology
- Have fewer than ten years of professional experience in industry, academia, and government
- Hold an advanced degree in food science or related discipline
- Be a champion for food science and actively support advancement of the profession

A small team of staff and volunteers selected the nominees to ensure geographic, practice setting, and demographic balance.

What was the financial model? Nominating organizations paid for travel to the event, held in conjunction with the IFT Annual Meeting & Food Expo in the United States. This co-location enabled participants to leverage the business and scientific sessions of the meeting to supplement their overall learning experience. IFT provided a complimentary meeting registration, covered all housing expenses, and acquired sponsors for the food and beverage events.

What was the agenda? Prior to the event, candidates completed a behavioral style (*DISC*) profile, answered a general survey of background and interest, and joined an online community to generate conversation before meeting face to face.

Key workshop content included discussion on

- Behavioral style (DISC) profile
- *Leadership Practice Inventory* (Kouzes and Posner 5 Practices of Exemplary Leadership)
- Leading for a networked world
- Current and energizing global trends
- Building effective global teams

In addition, participants developed a personalized plan for attending scientific sessions and the Expo.

Finally, the cohort participated in the inaugural *Power of 3 Strategic Dialogue: Food, Water, and Energy*. This mega-issue workshop was developed to help frame IFT's focused objectives in the area of food security.

What were the results of the launch of LEAD 360? Twenty-five young leaders participated in the program. They prepared a summary report with an action-packed agenda for contributing to the profession and to IFT. They have an active Facebook page, have contributed to the annual strategy retreat, helped design the 2014 LEAD

360 curriculum, and have volunteered for numerous task forces and work groups, both within IFT and their nominating groups. They have prepared reports for their sponsoring organizations as well. They are a highly energized group dedicated to their new leadership roles.

◆ ◆ ◆

Developing Talent

A strategic leader in an association knows that the organization is only as good as the talent on the team. Developing staff and volunteer talent and leadership is an important element of organizational success, no matter what business or profession you are serving. Volunteers have so many pressures on their time. How will you create the environment where they will choose to work with you and not choose elsewhere? How will you get volunteers to commit to the number of years it may take to ascend the leadership ladder?

Building a volunteer talent development platform will be a positive step in your strategic leadership. Here are some components to consider as you build a system customized to your organization:

1. Orientation for new leaders

    New leaders at all levels need to know the fundamentals of the organization—the mission, vision, value proposition, long- and short-range goals, budget, and available human resources. They also need immersion in the culture and values of the organization. Committee, task force, and work group leaders need specific orientation to their charges and how their work links to the broader organizational goals.

    Board members need to know all of the above, plus their legal responsibilities, liability exposures, and contemporary governance practices. The chief elected officer (CEO) needs additional training on how to serve as the chief spokesperson, lead the board, establish a partnership with the CSE, and manage strategic dialogue within the board.

2. Embedded leadership training

    This is an important investment that you make in volunteer leaders. Appropriate training in a variety of leadership practices will pay dividends and will reinforce the value of volunteering in your organization. The skills volunteers develop while participating in your association will translate into their daily work and should be valued by employers as a return on their investment in their employees.

Skills development you will want to incorporate into volunteer work should include

- Critical thinking and anticipatory foresight
- Scenario development
- Strategic framing of issues
- Conflict resolution
- Group facilitation
- Meeting and project management
- Change management
- Financial analysis

You will find that volunteers will appreciate your investment in them, their employers will appreciate it, and their coworkers will see it. Your organization will gain a reputation for leadership development that will serve as a magnet for attracting talent.

3. Public presence coaching

Your leaders are part of the core team representing your association around the world. They need the ability to serve as ambassadors for the organization, meeting with legislators, regulators, and heads of related organizations. Your leaders might be eminent scholars or business leaders in their field but unable to speak effectively to issues outside of their specific expertise. This presents a challenge for effectively communicating, testifying with impact, and representing the organization in highly visible arenas.

Investing in this training early in the leader's involvement will build his or her confidence and competence as leaders on a "stage."

4. Staff development

Staff will benefit from the same types of training that volunteers will—the same skills and aptitude apply. In addition, staff will need to know how to work with volunteers, support and guide committees, and develop work groups to inform staff initiative. The CSE needs to serve as the chief strategic talent officer to support the organization, since, as we know, an organization is only as strong as its talent.

Nurturing and Sustaining Trust

An association colleague has a favorite phrase that has become one of mine too:

"You operate at the speed of trust."

How do you define trust? Dictionary.com defines trust (as a noun) as the reliance on the integrity, strength, ability, surety of a person or thing and the confident expectation of something or hope. As a verb, trust is defined as—to rely upon or place confidence in someone or something, to hope and to believe.

If an organization operates at the speed of trust, then the ability to develop and nurture trust is a cornerstone of strategic leadership. Trust becomes an essential element of competitive advantage.

Trust envelops other qualities we expect from our leaders, such as strong values, ethics, rapport, interpersonal effectiveness, candor, and honesty. With trust, leaders within organizations have the flexibility and freedom to take risks, make mistakes, challenge the status quo, and move quickly toward their goals. Without trust in the environment, members, leaders, and staff can become risk averse and overly cautious, leading to missed crucial opportunities for growth or simply maintaining status quo to the detriment of the association. At the more extreme end of the spectrum, the culture becomes suspicious, riddled with gossip and ultimately toxic.

How do you build trust?

Attributes that build and nurture trust include these:

- *Reliability:* Do what you say you are going to do.
- *Openness:* Share insight and information so that people know what you are thinking and feeling (and aren't assuming).
- *Honesty:* Tell the truth, even when it is uncomfortable.
- *Fairness:* Don't play favorites.
- *Integrity:* Behave in a moral and ethical fashion.

An atmosphere and culture of trust is not sufficient for organizational health, but it certainly is necessary.

What would you add to Table 27.1?

These markers of trust, plus those you would add from your experience, occur from any organizational perspective—staff to staff, staff to volunteer, volunteer to volunteer, volunteer to leaders, staff to CSE, CSE to leaders. Moreover, levels of trust constantly shift. Trust is a dynamic state, not something you achieve and then move on to the next "thing" that needs your attention.

You undoubtedly have found yourself in a position of needing to rebuild trust after something has gone awry. Building and rebuilding trust are similar but not matching processes. It is much more difficult to regain trust once a breach is perceived. It takes additional patience,

TABLE 27.1. DEVELOPING AN ATMOSPHERE OF TRUST.

Low Trust	High Trust
Rampant gossip	Minimal gossip
Serious silos	Collaborative environment
Bureaucracy; self-preservation	People supporting one another
Risk aversion	Openness to risk
Finger pointing and blame	Nimble
Win-lose attitude	Win-win attitude

transparency, and follow-through to recalibrate relationships at any level. This is critically important for the CSE and chief elected officer. The organization can only operate at the speed of their trust in one another and in their respective leadership teams.

Committing to Social Responsibility

Association leaders have long been talking about the need for our organizations to embrace a vision beyond serving the business and professional interests of our members. While our traditional goals are the foundation of our work, they are no longer sufficient to help transform our organizations. Organizations today need to develop their unique hierarchy of goals, similar to Abraham Maslow's Hierarchy of Needs (Figure 27.2).[5]

The diagram illustrates a possible framework for evaluating your organization through a social responsibility lens. We all know that associations are well positioned to contribute to society. The question is, "What is the best way for your particular organization to make its mark on your members, the groups they serve, and the global community?"

As a practitioner of strategic leadership, the CSE has to champion the association's commitment to social responsibility, guide the conversation to develop your unique approach, and shepherd the approach to implementation.

Then you need to share with the rest of us so we can learn from your example!

Conclusion: Collaborating in Leadership

The culmination of applying the skill sets required of the strategic leadership is your ability to work collaboratively with the board to advance the mission of your organization at the pace required for success. To remain

FIGURE 27.2. MASLOW'S HIERARCHY OF NEEDS.

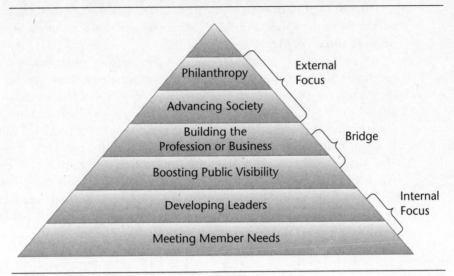

Source: Original drawing by Barbara Byrd Keenan.

relevant and purposeful, our organizations need to examine the future, seize opportunities for new program development as they emerge, shift resources fluidly to capture those opportunities, and deploy resources to implement those initiatives, and we have to do this with half of our human resource base being volunteers with tremendous demands on their time.

The foundations of strategic leadership—

- Demonstrating interpersonal effectiveness
- Nurturing and sustaining trust
- Cultivating an innovation culture
- Managing ambiguity
- Developing talent
- Committing to social responsibility
- Collaborating in leadership

—are the building blocks for collaborative leadership and will help you create the atmosphere needed to make tough choices about the future direction of your organization.

How do we build this capacity in ourselves? We do it by being curious learners and self-evaluators, and through intentional and thorough practice. This statement on practice really resonated with me: "Even world-class athletes have coaches, and they practice constantly." Think of it, what if each of us embraces that philosophy of life-long learning in our pursuit of enhancing our strategic leadership skills? It can be so easy to focus on *what* needs to get done, but *how* the environment is managed makes a big difference in the speed and depth of acceptance and commitment to move your organization forward successfully.

Here is one final characteristic that is core to strategic leadership and combines all the other traits when put into action. It is courage—the courage to have crucial conversations, the courage to address questionable ethical practices, the courage to prune the pet projects that no longer are relevant, the courage to address disagreements on role and function, and the courage to address staff performance issues. The consistency of courage can make all the difference. Uneven exercise of courage can lead to confusion, both with volunteer leaders and staff. Different situations lead to different choices. Building your personal capacity for strategic leadership will provide benefits to you, the staff, the leadership, membership, and those they serve. Isn't that why we are all here?

Notes

1. Reference to K. Patterson, J. Grenny, R. McMillan, and A. Switzler, *Crucial Conversations: Tools for Talking When Stakes Are High*, 2nd ed. (New York: McGraw-Hill, 2012).
2. Habit 5 from S. R. Covey, *The Seven Habits of Highly Effective People: Restoring the Character Ethic* (New York: Simon and Schuster, 1989).
3. The first of five practices of exemplary leadership from J. M. Kouzes and B. Z. Posner, *The Leadership Challenge*, 5th ed. (San Francisco: Jossey-Bass, 2012).
4. T. Kelley and J. Littman, *The Ten Faces of Innovation: IDEO's Strategies for Beating the Devil's Advocate & Driving Creativity Throughout Your Organization* (New York: Currency/Doubleday, 2005).
5. Abraham Maslow's "Hierarchy of Needs" model first proposed in A. H. Maslow, "A Theory of Human Motivation," *Psychological Review 50*, no. 4 (January 1943): 370–396.

Resources

Leadership

The Leadership Challenge, by James Kouzes and Barry Pozner, is in its fifth edition and is one of the best-selling leadership books of all time. In addition to the book, the authors also have developed the *Leadership Challenge Workbook*, the *Leadership Practices Inventory* and *LPI Online.* The book focuses on five practices of exemplary leadership. Derived from twenty-five years of research, the five practices are a "leadership journey" and an approach for continuous leadership growth at a personal level.

Communication

Two excellent resources for anyone wishing to improve their communication skills, manage difficult circumstances, and improve relationships are companion books by Kerry Patterson, Joseph Grenny, Ron McMillan, and Al Switzler: *Crucial Conversations: Tools for Talking When Stakes Are High* (second edition, 2012) and *Crucial Accountability: Tools for Resolving Violated Expectations, Broken Commitments and Bad Behavior* (second edition, 2013, also with David Maxfield). These best-selling books illustrate the power of framing, dialogue, and emotional intelligence in bridging the gaps between people when there is much at stake and strong emotions are fueling opposing opinions. The authors summarize the focus of their book as supporting solutions that are "our way," not "your way" or "my way."

A website, www.CrucialConversations.com, has additional resources including videos and other tools.

You might also gain important insight from *Influencer: The New Science of Leading Change,* also by Patterson, Grenny, Maxfield, McMillan, and Switzler, 2013. The premise of this book is that effective leaders must be influencers, focusing on results through attention to high leverage actions that shape behaviors they want to change, leading to better results.

Strategy and Innovation

Hundreds of books and videos have been produced on strategic planning, thinking, and execution as well on innovation—how, when, and why to pursue it. In lieu of an exhaustive list of titles to review, I would recommend the following as preeminent thinkers and prolific authors whose works are often cited as among the best:

- Larry Bossidy
- Ram Charan
- Clayton Christensen
- David Cooperider
- Daniel Goleman
- John Kao

- John Kotter
- Rita Gunther McGrath
- Daniel Pink
- Michael Porter
- Peter Schwartz
- Peter Senge
- Michael Treacy

Certainly this list could expand to include many others, and you will have your personal favorites. The key is to be a curious learner.

The Fifth Discipline: The Art and Practice of the Learning Organization, by Peter Senge, 2006, is a must-read for anyone who seeks a deeper insight into how organizations can continuously transform and perform as learning organizations.

The Author

Barbara Byrd Keenan, FASAE, CAE, based in Washington, D.C., is the chief executive officer of the Endocrine Society and the former chief executive at the Institute for Food Technologists.

CHAPTER TWENTY-EIGHT

DIVERSITY AND INCLUSION

Velma R. Hart, FASAE, CAE, and D. A. Abrams, CAE

Diversity and inclusion (D&I) has earned its place as a key business strategy in any association that is focused on sustaining successful growth and creating value for its constituents. It is critical that an association executive understands how D&I contributes to mission-driven organizations and helps a CSE meet societal imperatives, financial objectives, and legal requirements. It is also very valuable for nonprofit managers to have a solid D&I framework of their own, in order to remain competitive in the marketplace.

Why Diversity and Inclusion Matters

A CSE should understand the elements of a well-developed diversity and inclusion strategy for their association. Because of our swiftly evolving social and professional landscape, a deficiency in D&I now often leads to undesirable levels of *retention* among association volunteers, staff, membership, and customers; it is also linked to suboptimized *productivity* and low (if any) *innovation*.

Given the rapidly evolving multicultural demographics of the United States, associations now have the opportunity to expand their product and service offerings to myriad new markets and groups. The key to being successful in these efforts, however, is "an authentic understanding of the audience and a commitment to investing in their communities."[1] The *benefits* of mastering D&I are not only that you will deliver on your association's mission in more effective and comprehensive ways, but also that you will enhance your brand awareness and reputation, as well.

Associations have always needed to attract and retain the best talent, necessary skills, and essential resources. Today, diversity is a true key to accomplishing that in an effective and forward-thinking way. Due to our "demographic tsunami" plus advances in technology, communications, and globalization, diversity can be your key driver of relevance and growth.

Diversity goes hand in hand with *inclusion*, which involves the ways in which an association values and includes any and all individuals. Successful diversity strategies really rely on inclusive leadership: managers who ensure that all staff and volunteer talent have the opportunity to fulfill their potential and bring to their association-related responsibilities everything that they have to offer.

An association executive can decisively increase his or her organization's capabilities through diversity. But each organization needs to adapt to working with people who have different experiences or backgrounds, some apparent and some not so visible. The positive result, though, is that your association becomes receptive to more and different ideas. By embracing D&I, CSEs not only do the right thing; they also do the right thing *for their associations.*

The Approach: Make D&I a Strategic Priority

The following are tools to make diversity and inclusion a *key business strategy* for your association. First, establish some key objectives that pertain specifically to your association. D&I can help you to sustain successful growth and create value for your members and customers. In many organizations it has become helpful for leadership to *make diversity and inclusion a core value* of their association. As a stated commitment, D&I then stays in the forefront of decision making like any other brand promise or mission statement.

Prioritizing D&I: USTA

At the United States Tennis Association (USTA), we define diversity as "the collective mixture of our human and organizational assets characterized by our similarities and differences."* This perspective can apply to many nonprofit organizations and corporations across the spectrum. Diversity, along with inclusion—which is "leveraging the power of diversity in a respectful environment that encourages all to participate and contribute to further our mission"—is a *strategic priority* of our association. In fact, D&I is so important to delivering on our mission and succeeding in any marketplace that we have made it a *core value*.

*"USTA 2013 Diversity and Inclusion Statement." *USTA Yearbook*. (White Plains, NY: Author).

Diversity and inclusion can then be woven into the fabric of an association. We have found it helpful to include D&I right in an organization's strategic plan. The business is better off taking this approach. As with any other growth objective, you can develop and realize D&I targets on the basis of this core commitment.

D&I: Statement and Definitions

When *diversity and inclusion* is a strategic priority for any association, a CSE can then develop tactics and strategies unique to the institution, products, and services. Write a formal D&I statement that states *what will flow from diversity and inclusion* as it pertains to your association and its mission. Post the statement on the association website and LinkedIn profile, and throughout your staff handbook and volunteer publications. In addition, ensure that your partners and suppliers are aware of your D&I statement.

There is no fixed definition for "diversity" and "inclusion." Diversity may mean "a wide range of interests, backgrounds, experiences." Or "differences among groups of people and individuals based on ethnicity, race, socioeconomic status, gender, exceptionalities, language, religion, sexual orientation, and geographical area." Diversity may focus on human and institutional viewpoints, backgrounds, and life experiences, on "tolerance of thought, ideas, people with differing viewpoints, backgrounds, and life experiences." The variety reflected under the diversity umbrella also includes different opinions, backgrounds (degrees and social experience), religious and political beliefs, sexual orientation, heritage, and life experience.

You need to decide the definition, and then examine the question, "How does diversity relate to your core mission?" Do the same for inclusion. Ask, "How is the specific environment of your association designed to respect and encourage the kind of participation that will support your mission and social objectives?"

◆ ◆ ◆

Sample Diversity Statements

Some *diversity statements* are a few paragraphs long.

Teach For America, for example, "seeks to enlist our nation's most promising future leaders in the movement to eliminate educational inequity" and knows "these leaders will be diverse in ethnicity, race, and economic background." Their places on the political spectrum and their religious beliefs will be similarly varied, and we seek individuals of all genders and sexual orientations and regardless of physical disabilities. Maximizing the diversity of our organization is important so that we can benefit from the talent and energy of all those who can contribute to our effort, and also to increase the opportunity for engagement in the circles of influence in our tremendously diverse society. Moreover, we seek to be diverse because we aspire to serve as a model of the fairness and equality of opportunity we envision for our nation.

"At the same time that we value each individual who commits to our cause, we also place a particular focus on attracting and fostering the leadership of individuals who share the racial and/or economic backgrounds of the students underserved by public schools. In terms of race, we place the most significant focus nationally on ensuring the representation of African American and Latino/Hispanic individuals, given that more than 90 percent of the students we reach share these backgrounds. At the same time, we also seek to recruit Native American, Native Hawaiian, and Asian-American corps members and staff members given that we reach many students of these backgrounds in certain Teach For America regions. We emphasize racial, ethnic, and economic diversity to enhance our impact."

The American Society of Association Executives (ASAE) states that their "long-term goal is to ensure that (their) membership, volunteer leadership, and staff represent a strong, vibrant, and evolving model of diversity and inclusion for the association community." Their D&I statement reads, "In principle and in practice, ASAE values and seeks diverse and inclusive participation within the field of association management. ASAE promotes involvement and expanded access to leadership opportunity regardless of race, ethnicity, gender, religion, age, sexual orientation, nationality, disability, appearance, geographic location, or professional level. The organization provides leadership and commits time and resources to accomplish this objective while serving as a model to other associations engaged in such endeavors."

The Python Software Company speaks to "you" in its statement: "The Python Software Foundation and the global Python community welcome and encourage participation by everyone. Our community is based on mutual respect, tolerance, and encouragement, and we are working to help each other live up to these principles. We want our community to be more diverse: whoever you are, and whatever your background, we welcome you."

The College and University Professional Association for Human Resources states "WHY" they are committed to diversity, inclusion, and equitable practices as a means to achieving excellence in higher education. Their D&I statement and action plan include concise definitions right on their webpage (http://www.cupahr.org/about /diversity.aspx).

Xerox believes that "diversity breeds creativity" and states that the company "promotes a workplace culture of dignity, respect and openness to diversity which is reflected in the actions and behavior of all employees. Xerox is committed to equal opportunity of employment and all employment decisions are based on merit, qualifications, and abilities. Employment related decisions are not influenced or affected by an employee's race, colour, nationality, religion, sex, marital status, family status, sexual orientation, disability, age or membership of the travelling community. The company fully endorses a working environment free from discrimination, harassment and sexual harassment."

Other D&I position descriptions are more succinct. UCLA's chancellor states that "diversity is a core value" of the university. Google "strives to create a wholly inclusive workplace everywhere we operate in the world" because "diversity is an essential component of the culture at Google," and something that they want to celebrate.

The US Tennis Association has a business scope within the United States, and a mission that, of course, focuses on the growth of tennis. A portion of the *USTA*'s "Diversity & Inclusion Statement" states that "diversity allows us to touch 'all of America' and inclusion allows 'all of America' to touch us."

D&I: Importance

The next step is to *define why an effective diversity and inclusion strategy is critical* to achieving your essential business purposes. Review your association's top business directives or strategic direction and find the ways that your D&I strategy will be integral to the success of each one of those initiatives or business goals. Every organization has a corporate responsibility to create a respectful, inclusive workplace and commercial environment. That's important, too!

D&I: Target Audiences

The way to *identify the target audience* for your diversity initiative is to analyze your workforce, stakeholders, audience, and markets. That helps you

FIGURE 28.1. FEATURES AND ATTRIBUTES.

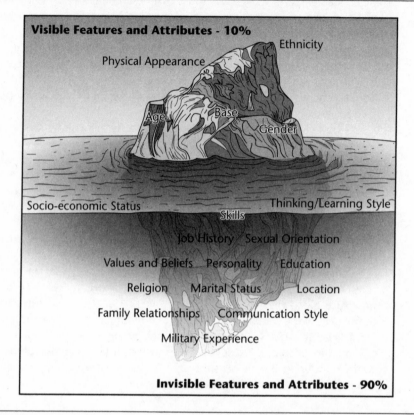

Note: Diverse associations seek balance and inclusion according to myriad factors, many of which are challenging to discern "on the surface." Are you thinking about how your stakeholders are represented?

to establish some "primary focus areas" for your services and operations, for example, ethnic, racial, ability, or sexual orientation. Figure 28.1 may inspire your thinking about the *many* dimensions of diversity: the idea is to maximize the creativity and contributions that *any* talent (volunteer and staff), market, supplier, or stakeholder can make to your operations and business success. Be inclusive!!

D&I: Philosophy

Your association has goals and objectives. It is helpful to have a range of diversity and inclusion tools and solutions that meet the overall ambitions of the organization, whether to reach your market in a new way, to improve your association image, or to better engage a diverse workforce. We will offer some suggestions in the next section about how to develop an action plan that works for your "customers."

It is becoming practical for many associations to establish a diversity and inclusion department, business unit, or strategic team that is charged to research, envision, and implement an ultimate D&I "plan of attack." It may even become *your* unique purpose as CSE to help every facet of your institution realize the strategic priority of diversity and inclusion.

Strategic Direction

As the CSE, you may need ideas and guidelines to help you to motivate your staff, volunteers, and board of directors around D&I. Goals and objectives are helpful, along with a precise understanding of how diversity will improve mission-related results. We offer the following framework as a way to develop D&I within an association, align managers and affiliates with your diversity vision, and use it to further your mission. It has six components, and is based on a strategy that has been proven across the field. It is easy to adapt to a variety of institutions, and it helps to embed diversity and inclusion into your specific workforce, workplace, suppliers, partners, and marketplace.

Talent Optimization

Including a full spectrum of diverse voices at the table making decisions within your association—from membership, products, services, marketing, human resources, and volunteer management—may sound obvious, but it takes both commitment and energy. To help your association reflect the demographics of America, it requires more than *just sprinkling the staff and volunteers with a few women and people of color.*

Talent optimization is a commitment to diverse talent on all levels, including suppliers and board members. It often leads an association to establish a set of goals for not only diverse *employment and volunteer representation,* but also diversity goals for key executives, departments, and committees, and for program areas and community managers.

Goals for talent diversification will help you to identify concrete ways to attain those goals. It may be just a dozen sentences, each one directed at a specific level of leadership, management, or governance.

Or it may be a directive to establish an annual diversity goal that is made by one component of your association (for example, the board committing vis-á-vis one program area). Sometimes you want to create financial incentives tied to D&I goals, or provide financial assistance that supports your targets directly, in order to develop diverse talent within your organization. *We recommend that CSEs look to add an annual line item to their budgets for D&I incentives.*

Image (Internal and External)

Your *association image* is that mental picture that springs to mind when someone mentions your association name. It is a fluid public perception, comprising ever-changing impressions that are based on your company's performance, coverage in the media, and what is being said about it. Examples of your image include

An actual physical image

An ad

An optic at a convention or public presentation

A logo or graphic

Simply the way that you are viewed internally and externally

Your image is changeable, but it is also something that you can influence and direct. Because it is often a major part of what sells the products or services of your association, think of *image* as the second component in your D&I strategy.

What do people *see* when they look at your organization or product, marketing materials or service offerings? What can you do to *display images that encourage a diverse audience to support what you do, make, or sell?* How can you bring the pictures, key art, photographs, optics, and photo opportunities of your association in line with your diversity sensitivity? How can your D&I strategy help you to generate a smart image for your association?

Establish a set of goals for your various executives, departments, and divisions in order to improve both your association's internal and external images among diverse communities. Then develop ways to attain your image-improvement goals. Develop marketing materials that include appropriate translations, multicultural images, and a feeling of inclusion that speaks directly to the wide complement of demographics within your target audience. Think about your online and social media presence, too.

Consider what language or translations are available for your digital assets. How do the images on your website reflect not only ethnic and racial diversity but also differences of ability, or nontraditional lesbian, gay, bisexual, and transgender (LGBT) relationships and family constellations?

Part of building a great image is to *publicize your success at D&I,* too. You can spotlight your diverse staff, commend diverse volunteer leaders, promote the diversity statistics of your programs or services, and even produce and publicize events for and with your diverse workforce, stakeholders, and community members.

Supplier Diversity

Associations spend a lot of money. They buy supplies and procure product, plus do RFPs and then award contracts for goods and services. *How you select your suppliers or commission services* can be a critical element of your D&I strategic direction. Setting goals to have more supplier diversity will both strengthen your appeal to diverse audiences *and* have a direct impact on your bottom line through new avenues and opportunities for your business, product, or service.

This point is made part of your D&I strategy because tradition and inertia work against you. The most significant reason given for why more minority- and women-owned businesses are not used as association suppliers is because of preexisting relationships or track records with male- or Caucasian-owned firms. Of course, it is often hard to move business, contracts, or commitments over to new or different firms, *but it is worth doing* for many reasons, not least of which being that it can extend your outreach and market research. Expanding your supplier diversity into new communities invites entrée and access. CSEs find that suppliers from traditionally underrepresented groups are a *great* source for new ways to reach populations whose buying power is on the rise. Use them as a resource!

Regional or Community Engagement

Your community engagement and local, regional, or sectional D&I initiatives are one of the key levers that will affect your association's ability to thrive and increase the impact of its mission. You want to explore every opportunity for your organization to engage with diverse sectors of your market on a community level, and maybe have *different strategies and programs that address the regional needs and cultural differences of the communities you serve.*

For example, your initial goal-setting around D&I may involve analyzing your cities, states, and regions; identifying the target communities within them; then matching either your goals or ways to reach them with your new intelligence. Many times, you will find both a need and an opportunity within a given local community that offers your association a great way either to reach or expand into a new or growing market segment. In addition, if your association engages in philanthropy or scholarship giving, you have an additional opportunity to connect these gifts to specific community engagement programs.

Strategic Partnerships

When associations and corporations make alliances with diverse organizations through sponsorships or partnerships, they find that they can enhance their brands, and attract new clients, customers, and social-media relationships. Through building connections with diverse partners, they also improve corporate image along with employee retention and recruitment. In addition, they gain unique insight into new, diverse markets, which enhances income and efficacy. The strategic partnerships that your association has, or could develop, are *tools to build your diverse staff, markets, suppliers, and customers.* Partnering with special-interest organizations is an essential step in fostering relationships and bolstering recruitment efforts within different demographic segments.[2]

As an association executive, you probably already know that sponsorships or partnerships with for-profit companies bring you not just increased funding but greater public recognition, a better image, and access to valuable corporate resources. And *you help the corporate donor, too.* There are management best practices for making strategic partnerships that ensure you reap the greatest rewards.

Find *a clear alignment between your goals and values, and those of any nonprofit or company you elect to partner with.* Discuss it right up front, then *identify a clear value proposition for both your association and your partner or sponsor.* When you *do a sponsorship agreement with any partners or nonprofits, define expectations and deliverables for both sides.* This may be money and advertising or promotion or other co-branded collateral materials, but also photos with key stakeholders, eBlasts, or access to digital information on members or participants. Ensure that *any partnership you undertake is coordinated with stakeholders both inside and outside of all organizations involved,* so that you secure their support and maximize your opportunities. Finally, *agree with your partners on the ways in which your contribution and outcomes can be measured, and by whom.* How will you evaluate the activities generated by the association or alliance? What system of metrics is appropriate? Ideally there are steps to your sponsorship, and points to gauge your progress as part of the deliverables.

Training and Development

CSEs need to lead and *encourage their staff and volunteers to think actively about how to promote D&I in their activities.* Oftentimes, you need to establish training and professional-development initiatives in order to orient your team members to diversity goals. Just like our other five recommendations in this action plan, we believe that your company's D&I efforts are not just the job of the human resource department. The CSE can lead the way to *make it part of association culture.* It is worth doing because your organization cannot be competitive for talent or succeed at maximum retention if you don't create a culture that attracts and retains the very best people.

D&I training should help people develop relationships with others who are not like them. Since your employees' abilities to build equitable relationships correlate directly to their effectiveness in business, this is a real *economic imperative.* It is also helpful to do a *cultural audit or assessment* of your corporate workforce including volunteers. We'll talk about some benchmarking ideas next, but if your association already does employee and volunteer surveys, you can learn a great deal as a manager by including D&I values and other cultural questions.

Let's look at some ideas for measuring diversity and inclusion within your association.

Dashboard or Scorecard

You can develop your own D&I scorecard! Take valuable measurements within these four strategic areas of your association business:

- Workforce
- Workplace
- Community
- Marketplace

Here are six steps that we use as a guide to developing a scorecard within these four areas.[3]

1. Identify what the association accomplished last year, where it's headed next year, and what budget is needed for two things: to do a *thorough measurement,* and to realize *diversity objectives.*
2. Use this scorecard to establish a baseline so that the CSE and board know where they are and what they'd like to change. Then develop the scorecard so that the D&I goals are specific and definable plus measurable; ensure that you have a fix on who is accountable for each element, as well.
3. List those annual goals as developed from the baseline, and then define strategies for making change. This is a very helpful year-end planning activity.
4. Management accountability is critical to the success of any D&I strategy success. Some associations link goals and objectives to certain bonuses or incentive programs, in order to enhance management buy-in.
5. Detailing workforce levels really helps you to develop scorecards and goals for talent diversity efforts. Collect complete details on the demographics of executives, board members, volunteers, and staff.
6. Check both your baselines and your goals implementation against any concerns that you have about either internal or external compliance (such as with EEO, Affirmative Action).

Workforce: "Who We Are"

To measure your workforce as regards the talent management of your diverse target populations, compared to nonminority men, look at your diversity breakdown in these areas:

- Recruitment
- Hiring representation
- Movement—both promotions and lateral
- Retention versus attrition and turnover
- Talent assessments, leadership development, and competency gaps
- Corporate engagement

Workplace: "How We Work Together"

Because your ultimate objective with a D&I strategy is to *build an inclusive culture* that recruits, retains, and promotes diverse individuals, see where your association is strong, and where there may be areas for improvement.

What does progress look like, given your goals for inclusion? Gallup has studied organizations and defined clear "satisfiers" and "dis-satisfiers" for employees, regardless of demographics.[4] These satisfiers include

- Getting to do what I do best
- Caring managers and supervisors
- Positive coworker relationships
- Adequate resources to do my job
- Trust and treatment by upper management
- Opportunities to learn and grow
- Clear expectations about the work requirements
- Competitive compensation, reward, and recognition

The dis-satisfiers include

- Prejudice and discrimination for arbitrary reasons
- Poor career development opportunity
- Poor work environment or climate
- Low organizational savvy on the people issues
- Pressure to conform or assimilate

The more "satisfiers," the higher your association's employee engagement. And engagement *creates better performance.* Organizations that promote a culture that produces these satisfiers and eliminates the dis-satisfiers produce better results.[5] There are a few reliable instruments from Gallup and Quantum Workforce for measuring engagement and disengagement.[6] Consider weaving them into your workplace analysis.

For smaller workplaces, you may not need to do broad polling in order to assess your employee engagement effectively. One-on-one meetings with employees might do the trick. At medium and larger workplaces, you may want town hall meetings, focus groups, or surveys. In your efforts to give voice to diverse populations and gather a snapshot of your employees' attitudes toward diversity and inclusion, develop ways to identify salient concerns. (These may include historical stereotyping baggage, social isolation, economic constraints, and the impact of role models and mentors.) Be sure that you ask all employees the same questions. This will permit you to analyze your feedback better and design more targeted action steps as a consequence.

Community: "Where You Serve"

Tie each of your goals and initiatives, identified in your D&I strategy, to a set of benchmarks, measurements, and metrics. Use your *quantitative scorecards* plus *qualitative measurements* gleaned by engaging community constituents and garnering feedback in order to measure community benefits as you enhance your community relations.

How many diverse community organizations have you partnered with? What numbers do their constituencies represent? How many association "impressions" have been made in diverse communities? How many scholarships given? Or internships, services, or donations to community members that affect these constituencies? There are a lot of helpful data for looking at your association's community impact in these ways. You can even survey awareness levels of your diversity message outside of your organization!

Marketplace: "Who You Serve"

Because D&I are good business, you will discover that improvements have an impact on your organization's marketplace just as they do your internal talent-resource management. So it is very helpful to measure that by developing benchmarks and scorecards that define diversity goals for your programs, mission success, client or constituent acquisition and retention, as mapped against your target groups. This can also affect your fundraising success, too, and give you great data for grant requests and funding pitches.

Survey the demographics and experiences of diverse attendees when you undertake programs and events, as well as the diversity of your suppliers for each one. How much of your company's total spending is attributable to spending at diverse suppliers? This will give you concrete evidence of how your policies have had impact.

While diversity scorecards are becoming an increasingly important tool in evaluating an organization's progress in D&I, the specific components of each can vary greatly. The most effective metrics include a holistic approach to the process, and assess the impact of D&I in all four strategic areas described. Cold, hard data are difficult to ignore. When you can credibly show your board of directors or senior executives that current conditions are not going to take your association to where it needs to go, they become your partners in driving change!

Conclusion

We are all familiar with the maxim, "Doing right is good business." Clearly, developing a diverse and inclusive workforce, customer or constituent base, and supplier network is the *right* thing to do. Also true, however, is that successful diversity and inclusion is your key to *great* business for your association.

As an association executive, you have an opportunity to ensure that D&I becomes a key business strategy for your organization. This framework is a proven strategy, one that can generate an accurate review of your diversity status, inspire discussion and planning, and then make D&I happen within your own association in a meaningful way. We invite you to incorporate this framework into your professional best practices.

Notes

1. Collins, Michael. "Where Marketing Meets Diversity: How D&I is Relevant to the Business." February 4, 2013. http://www.diversitybest-practices.com/news-articles/where-marketing-meets-diversity-how-di-relevant-business.
2. Diversity Best Practices Staff. "Partnerships with Special Interest Organizations," December 2011, available at www.diversitybestpractices.com.
3. Diversity Best Practices, "Diversity Scoring Tool©: Measuring Your Diversity, Diversity Best Practices," date, available at www.diversitybest-practices.com.
4. M. Robinson, C. Pfeffer, and J. Buccigrossi, *Business Case for Diversity with Inclusion* (Rochester, NY: wetWare, 2003).
5. Cumulative Gallup Workplace Studies. "State of the American Workplace Report 2013," http://www.gallup.com/strategicconsulting/163007/state-american-workplace.aspx; "State of the Global Workplace 2013," http://www.gallup.com/strategicconsulting/164735/state-global-workplace.aspx; "Majority of American Workers Not Engaged in Their Jobs," http://www.gallup.com/poll/150383/majority-american-workers-not-engaged-jobs.aspx; "Worldwide, 13% of Employees Are Engaged at Work," http://www.gallup.com/poll/165269/worldwide-employees-engaged-work.aspx.
6. J. K. Harter, F. L. Schmidt, E. A. Killham, and J. W. Asplund, "Q^{12} Meta-Analysis," Gallup Consulting, 2006, available at http://strengths.

gallup.com/private/resources/q12meta-analysis_flyer_gen_08%2008_
bp.pdf.

The Authors

Velma R. Hart, FASAE, CAE, is the chief financial officer of the Thurgood Marshall College Fund and does extensive work and education in the area of diversity and inclusiveness. She is past chairman of ASAE and also serves on several nonprofit boards. She is an author of various articles and publications, including previous chapters on diversity and finance in earlier editions of *Professional Practices in Association Management.* She is a 2005 ASAE Fellow.

D. A. Abrams, CAE, is chief diversity and inclusion officer for the United States Tennis association. He has worked for the USTA for twenty years on both the national and sectional levels. He is the author of *Diversity & Inclusion: The Big Six Formula for Success* and *Certified Association Executive Exam: Strategies for Study & Success.*

CHAPTER TWENTY-NINE

HUMAN RESOURCE MANAGEMENT

Matthew Gertzog, MBA, FASAE, CAE

Aligning resources to achieve desired results is one of the primary responsibilities of any association staff leader—dollars need to be allocated, volunteers need to be assigned to critical tasks, and metrics of achievement need to be established. But arguably the most critical—and perhaps most challenging to manage—are an association's human resources. Human resources, that is, an organization's employees, are the capital that can help associations navigate to success; or, they can be the reason that an association can get derailed from its stated mission.

In most associations, the expenses associated with salaries and benefits make up a significant portion of the annual operating budget, and for that reason, all senior-level association executives need a fundamental understanding of human resources management (HRM). While most agree that HRM is a complicated and nuanced discipline, there has been little agreement over how to define HRM. For the purposes of this chapter, HRM in its most fundamental role is *managing people to effectively and efficiently achieve an organization's mission.* This chapter is designed to outline the critical areas of HRM that a CSE, or those aspiring to become a CSE, need to understand in order to manage to success.

There are a number of areas that fall under the rubric of HRM:

- *Recruitment and retention:* Attracting the right people to the association and helping them effectively make the transition into the association.
- *Staffing management:* Creating systems, policies, and procedures that allow for and facilitate effective management.
- *Compensation and benefits:* Developing remuneration systems and policies that are fair and market competitive, and that allow for enough flexibility to achievement association goals.
- *Managing the work environment:* Enhancing employees' skill sets and creating a work environment that is conducive to effectiveness and efficiency.
- *Legal compliance:* Establishing a work environment that operates within parameters of the jurisdiction's laws and regulations.

While these areas are all interrelated, it's best to explore each of the areas in more depth.

Recruitment and Retention

The first steps in the recruitment of employees is assessing the organization's current and future needs, identifying the skill set which the organization hopes to create or enhance, and evaluating the market conditions in which the hiring will be done. Issues that executives might consider during an assessment include

- Are we hiring for a short-term or long-term need?
- What level of professional experience or academic credentials would qualify someone for the role?
- What level or type of remuneration will attract a qualified person to the job?

Once an organization completes a needs assessment, it will be in a better position to make a number of business determinations. For instance, if an organization is looking to fill a short-term need, it might consider whether it would be better to hire a temporary employee or *outsource* the function. Outsourcing allows an organization to contract with an individual or company to complete a specific assignment over a prescribed period of time rather than creating a full-time position or department. In some situations it may be helpful to outsource a function because it allows an opportunity for employers to modulate their resources depending on the organizational need.

In other situations, employers may determine that their need is only critical during a specific part of the year or that the position does not warrant an individual being employed full time. In these types of situations, organizations may evaluate whether they want to hire *part-time* or *seasonal* employees.

In some cases an association may need highly specialized skills and is looking for a *specialist* who has a precise expertise. Association executives should assess what specific qualifications would make some appropriate for the job and where or how that skill set might be identified. At the other end of the spectrum, an association may determine that it needs a *generalist*, that is, a person who has a broad array of skills but not a specific area of expertise. In these situations, HRM executives may seek potential employees who "can do it all"—from membership to meeting planning to administration.

At times, employers may look for student interns to fill certain short-term positions. Student internships provide employers with eager students who are looking to build their real-world experience at no or low cost to the associations. Internship programs can also be a resource for identifying prospective employees for the association.

A thorough needs assessment will often go hand-in-hand with a comprehensive *job analysis*. A job analysis typically will identify the reason the job exists, the duties and responsibilities of the position, the manner in which they are carried out, the knowledge or skills that are requisite for the position, as well as other personal characteristics that might be instrumental to success. A meaningful job analysis will include interviews with colleagues and managers who might interact with the potential new hire, as well as a comparison of the proposed job to other jobs in the same department or across the association at the same grade level.

Once the needs assessment and job analysis are complete, the association is better positioned to draft a clear job description and an appropriate compensation package. The package will usually include salary, benefits, and any other incentives for which the prospective employee may be eligible. Once these determinations are made, the recruiting and selection process can begin.

Association recruiting and selection processes include a number of steps: job postings, applications, interviews, tests, and references. Oftentimes, these processes may go on concurrently.

First, when drafting a job posting it is important that it be written in a way that does not incur legal liability. For example, a well-intentioned phrase such as "great job for recent college graduates," could be construed as discriminatory toward older workers. Poorly constructed job postings may also be used as evidence in wrongful termination lawsuits.

Associations should have job application forms that capture all pertinent information that an employer needs to support the recruiting and hiring process. In some situations, an application will need to be completed before an individual will be considered for a job; in other situations, job applications will only be required of finalists for the position and may inform the applicants that background checks may be conducted. Because of the laws and regulation surrounding hiring practices, it is a good idea to have your organization's job application reviewed by a lawyer familiar with HRM law.

Finalists for a position will be invited to interview with the prospective hiring manager and other key stakeholders in the hiring process, such as subordinates or potential colleagues. It is important to think of job interviews as a two-way exchange—the employer is looking to learn more about the prospective employee, while the candidate is looking to learn more about his or her prospective employer. Consequently, interviewers must design open-ended questions that elicit clues to the critical thought processes and behavioral patterns of candidates.

Candidate interviews are formal exchanges designed solely to assess a candidate's fit for a particular position. No matter how cordial the exchange, it is inappropriate and a potential legal risk if conversations wander into areas that are not relevant to the position. Because of this, it is good practice to train employee interviewers about appropriate questions to ask, or not ask, during an employment interview.

In some situations, an employer may require a test or exercise that will evaluate some of the skill sets that are being sought or are important to achieving success in the position. For instance, a candidate for a media relations job may be asked to draft a fictitious press release so that the hiring manager can see examples of job-relevant skills.

Finally, most recruiting processes will involve reference checks of final candidates. These references can be from former colleagues or employers who are prepared to attest to an individual's work product or ethic or they may come through third-parties who verify other information that may have been included in the application or required as a condition of employment.

When one final candidate emerges as the most-qualified for the position, the HR executive or hiring manager will extend a verbal offer to the successful candidate and will outline some of the specific details, ranging from salary to start date to any specific terms that may have been negotiated through the recruiting and selection process. This is usually followed up by an "offer letter," which, at a high level, outlines the terms of employment in a written form. It is good business practice to have the new employee accept the offer in writing, which can be accomplished by having the individual sign the offer letter. Keep in mind that in most cases, employment will be "at-will," which is a concept that will be reviewed later in this chapter.

The final process of recruiting and selection is an orientation for the new employee, known as "on-boarding." The on-boarding process exposes new employees to the skills, knowledge, and behaviors that will help him or her acclimate to the new organization and serves as the foundation for understanding the values that shape the organization's culture and its mission.

In most cases, the association board of directors or other volunteer leaders will not be involved in hiring practices or processes. The board of directors of an association typically will only be involved in the recruitment and selection of a chief executive and then delegate HRM oversight to him or her; in a larger association, the chief executive may extend this responsibility to others on the association staff such as the HRM professional.

Staffing Management

Whether you have two or two hundred employees, there are several HRM practices that should be developed, implemented, and monitored, including

- Drafting position descriptions
- Evaluating performance
- Establishing disciplinary and termination procedures
- Writing an employee handbook
- Considering alternative work solutions such as telecommuting and job-sharing
- Setting up human resources information management systems (HRIMS) and HRM assessment tools (such as ratios, trend analyses, and so on)

During the recruitment and selection process, the key components of a written position description will typically be identified. The key elements of a position description include

- Job title
- Reporting relationships
- Summary of the position
- Essential duties and responsibilities
- Job qualifications
- Special considerations

A well-crafted position description may serve as the basis for performance evaluation and management since it outlines what is expected of an employee and establishes the criteria against which his or her performance will ultimately be evaluated. The position description, coupled with a formal evaluation form, creates a performance management system. This system facilitates employees and employers to agree on goals, establish performance metrics, and address any areas of concern or uncertainty. It is good business practice for formal performance evaluations to occur at least once a year, but it should certainly not be the sole opportunity for employee and employer to discuss goals and performance. There are multiple perspectives on when annual evaluations should be conducted—some organizations may have explicit linkages between pay and performance and so they will conduct performance evaluation in concert with salary reviews; others may choose to disassociate the two so that the evaluation can be focused more directly on performance. Furthermore, issues related to annual scheduling or budget management may drive the decision of whether associations choose to deliver all employees' reviews at the same time each year or to do them annually according to the individual employee's date of hire.

The annual performance evaluation is not the time for an employee or employer to introduce a "surprise" issue; when this occurs, it is usually a good indication that there are communication challenges between the employee and manager that should have been addressed earlier. Ultimately, an effective performance management system allows employees and employers to reflect on the past year and plan for the new one.

Despite everyone's best intentions, there are times when employees fail to meet agreed-upon standards. Sometimes this may occur because goals were not clear, while at other times it may occur because the employee lacks the skills or knowledge to accomplish the goals. For these reasons, it is good practice for employers to establish and document disciplinary and termination procedures.

Disciplinary and termination procedures can help prevent the loss of potentially good employees and can also reduce legal liability for the employer. These procedures may be implemented in the form of an oral warning, a written warning, or as a performance improvement plan that lays out specific goals and target dates by which they must be achieved. In some cases, disciplinary action may not achieve the goal of improving an employee's performance, and in those cases, termination of employment may be appropriate.

It is good business practice to review disciplinary and termination procedures with legal counsel on a case-by-case basis because of the uniqueness of each individual situation.

As an association grows in its size, breadth, and level of sophistication, it is beneficial for an employer to compile an "employment handbook" that summarizes all employment policies, benefit programs, and other policies or procedures related to employment with the association. This handbook can address employees' questions and serve as a resource to employees and employers so that issues can be addressed fairly and consistently. It can also be the mechanism through which evolving and emerging employment issues can be addressed.

New technologies have also introduced new efficiencies in HRM. Human resources information management systems have automated many HR processes and allow for more efficient recordkeeping and easier remote access to data. Today, HRIMS allow associations to manage a wide range of HRM functions, ranging from payroll and attendance processes to performance management systems to employee self-service on benefits-related concerns.

Finally, it is important to establish metrics that help associations gauge HR performance, assess trends, and chart new approaches in HRM. Today's association professionals assess multiple trends and monitor statistics in multiple areas such as

- Employee retention rates
- Ratios that are illustrative of the association's financial performance (such as compensation as a percentage of overall association revenue)
- Market-competitiveness of benefits costs
- Return of investment (ROI) on recruitment practices

Compensation and Benefits

While it is critical to establish strong recruiting practices and a supportive work environment, it is equally important for a CSE to develop and administer a competitive compensation system and benefits program. A competitive compensation system is developed by assessing market demand for a particular position, valuing the technical skills needed for the potential or current position, and considering the professional and educational experience and credentials that are expected. It is also important to take into account *internal equity*—in other words, ensuring that the compensation principles are being applied fairly and consistently across the association.

A competitive benefits package is one that supplements salary with an attractive mix of benefit offerings that might not otherwise be available to the individual. In some cases, a benefit may be fully subsidized by the employer (for example, an employer may opt to cover 100 percent of the employee's medical insurance premium), while in other cases a benefit may take the form of preferred or discounted pricing (such as commuting or transportation subsidies or lower fees at a health club).

Potential or current employees will often focus on the straight salary as the key indicator of how much they are earning, but the more sophisticated individual will be more apt to look at the value of the "whole package"—salary, benefits, bonuses or incentives, and intangible criteria such as flexibility or growth opportunity. With that in mind, a business-savvy association executive will design an employment remuneration package that is competitive on multiple levels—salary, benefits, and as a "whole package."

Because the salary and benefits costs usually constitute one of the largest expenses in the organization operating budget, it is important to have a clear, fair, and consistent compensation management system that is based on principles that can be explained to both employees and volunteer leaders. In most situations it is not appropriate for boards to get involved with salary administration, but rather to ensure that the association compensation systems are based on solid principles and market realities. This is best achieved by objectively assessing position descriptions, benchmarking salaries and benefits against organizations with which you compete for employees, and monitoring other external forces that might influence the job market. It is recommended that associations develop a clear salary administration program with formal pay structures for jobs that are classified into different hierarchical levels.

Once these levels have been established, defined salary ranges for each of the levels can be established and individual positions can then be assigned to one of the various levels. This approach gives HRM professionals a tool to manage and administer salaries and may help employees better understand the compensation opportunities within their organization.

Compensation may come in many forms, but they fall into three broad categories: base compensation, incentives (or "at-risk") pay, and bonuses.

- *Base pay* is a fixed amount of remuneration that is agreed upon by both the employer and the employee. Base pay enables employers to better predict their salary expenses and allows employees to have a predictable cash flow.
- *Incentive pay* is a variable form of remuneration that is intended to motivate performance and is paid out only if certain agreed-upon goals are achieved. Incentive pay is most applicable when there are clearly established measureable targets and employees have the capacity to influence whether or not the goal is achieved, such as in sales functions.
- *Bonus pay* may be used when a manager or an organization wants to recognize contributions beyond what is normally expected, such as significantly exceeding goals in the strategic plan. It may be paid to an individual, to a work team, or to all the employees in an association.

Employers offer a number of benefits to supplement compensation in order to attract and retain employees. These offerings may include

- Medical, dental, and vision insurance
- Life and disability insurance
- Retirement plans
- Paid time off (PTO)
- Parking or transportation subsidies
- Wellness programs
- Professional and educational assistance programs

It is important for an association to create a package of benefits that will be meaningful to its employees and to those you may wish to attract to the association. For example, a new father may appreciate benefits such as telecommuting or increased PTO, while an employee approaching retirement age may be drawn to a more generous retirement plan.

On one hand, employee benefits can favorably supplement compensation. On the other hand, benefit offerings can be a significant expense for an association, so it is important for employers to develop a cost-effective benefits package that balances the needs of employees, the goals of the association, and the demands of the marketplace in which it operates. It is a good practice to periodically bid out individual benefit programs so you can be assured that you are getting valuable programs at a fair-market price. HRM executives also know that benefits offerings can also be time-intensive to manage, so employers need to establish systems and processes to effectively administer the programs.

Managing the Work Environment

When employees come together in the workplace—whether in-person or virtually—they create a community that must be managed and developed in order for it to reach its full potential. HRM professionals may enrich this community by creating an environment that sparks creativity, stimulates innovation, and fosters collaboration—all characteristics that are often associated with effective organizations.

A positive environment can be nurtured in a number of ways, including

- Investing in employees and recognizing achievement
- Embracing diversity in all its forms
- Accommodating work-life balance
- Supporting the communities in which the association operates
- Creating an aligned corporate culture

Investing in Employees and Recognizing Achievement

Employers who want to retain a strong workforce will invest in training programs that build employee skill sets, mentoring opportunities that cultivate leadership potential, and recognition programs that create employee loyalty.

Training programs, whether held onsite or off premises, can allow an employee to hone a technical skill or fill a knowledge gap. These types of programs, especially when paid for by the employer and held during the workday, offer concrete examples of the willingness of the employer to invest in the employee's future; employees feel rewarded and may see potential professional growth opportunities, while employers build a more competent workforce.

Mentorship programs can help new employees acclimate to a new work environment and give them a chance to interact with individuals—either inside or external to the association—that demonstrate the capacity to lead. When employers give employees an opportunity to interact with committed and successful mentors, the employees become motivated to achieve and develop new leadership skills that can propel them ahead in their careers.

Finally, recognizing employees' milestone achievements give employers the opportunity to publicly acknowledge the contributions that individuals have made to the association; those being recognized have a chance to reflect on their achievement, while other employees can see how their employer appreciates the difference one person can make.

Embracing Diversity in All Its Forms

Each of us is different and as a result brings varied skills, backgrounds, and cultural values to our employer. The progressive employer will capitalize on these differences by drawing on the unique strengths of each employee, encouraging diversity of thought and supporting a collaborative solution that taps the best that each employee has to offer. In the end, diversity creates a team-based and inclusive focus in which employees—individually and collectively—have an opportunity to excel and observe that one plus one can equal more than two. (For more on diversity, see Chapter Twenty-Eight.)

Accommodating Work-Life Balance

In a world where we are all tethered to electronic devices and the twenty-four-hour demands of society, we struggle to find a way to balance the stresses of work vis-à-vis our human instinct to be supportive partners, nurturing parents, and loyal friends.

There are a number of steps employers can take to support the quest for work-life balance, including allowing alternative working arrangements or offering self-improvement programs and benefits. Employers can ease the balancing act between home and work by instituting telecommuting policies and flexible work hours that allow employees to spend more time with their families; one emerging trend is establishing a "virtual office" setup that allows employees to work from any location by using laptop and mobile technology.

Associations can also offer work-life balance programs that are designed to provide both physical and financial fitness. Today some associations offer gym subsidies, onsite exercise programs, or nutritional seminars in order to create and nurture a healthy workforce. Similarly, some organizations may have programs put on by outside financial professionals that educate employees about the basics of financial planning and preparing for retirement. These types of programs illustrate an employer's commitment to employees' well-being outside of the workplace.

Supporting the Communities in Which the Association Operates

Associations operate in a number of communities—for example, they are part of the industry or profession they represent, they are part of the local community in which its headquarters is located, and they are corporate citizens of both the United States and the world. Today, more and more association professionals want to work for organizations that are "socially responsible," in other words, groups that act with sensitivity toward social, cultural, and environmental issues and intentionally create a positive impact on the community while doing business. With that in mind, associations should consider offering opportunities for employees to volunteer in the community, supporting recycling and other eco-friendly office-based practices, and educating employees about association initiatives that serve the underrepresented or disadvantaged.

Creating an Aligned Corporate Culture

HRM professionals understand the powerful influence corporate culture can play with regard to the ability of employees to achieve organizational goals; as a result, they know that someone with the best skills doesn't necessarily mean he or she will be the best fit. An organization's corporate culture is the set of shared values or beliefs that drive employees' behaviors in the workplace. Whether these tenets are explicitly stated or just tacitly understood, an effective HRM professional will align the association's corporate culture by learning what employees think, understanding the association's objectives, and then creating HR practices that engage and align the workforce in a manner that supports achievement of the association's goals. For instance, an association that values "innovation" might have compensation practices that more clearly reward creativity and risk-taking; associations that value "teamwork" may have professional development programs that encourage collaboration and cooperation.

Legal Compliance

Just as HRM affects every aspect of association management, so do laws and regulations—at both a federal and a jurisdictional level—affect every aspect of the practice of HRM. Furthermore, the impact of applicable laws may differ according to the size of the association's staff.

There is exhaustive, ever-evolving literature on human resources and employment law, and therefore the best course of action with regard to legal compliance of HRM practices is to work with legal counsel—with expertise in HR—to draft an employee handbook that broadly defines and documents the association's policies. Once drafted, the HRM professional is responsible for ensuring that these policies and procedures are consistently and fairly implemented; it is wise to seek legal counsel whenever the employer or employee deviates from the established practices or when an employer finds itself having to deal with unanticipated situations. Organizations may also want to periodically hire legal counsel to review the employee handbook and to audit the HR practices and procedures to ensure that they remain compliant with relevant HR laws.

It is important to keep in mind that HRM organizational policies are ultimately designed to protect the interests of the employer. While most effective association executives and HRM professionals strive to create a positive and productive work environment, they do so in the context of ensuring that the association can effectively, efficiently—and legally—meet its strategic objectives and tactical plans.

There is no way to anticipate every situation that may arise with regard to HRM practices in your association, nor is it possible to create policies and procedures that provide ironclad protection from any possible legal challenge. To the contrary, any actions taken by an employer with regard to its HRM practices can present risk; the key consideration for association executives is to have the legal foundation against which you can assess these risks and to know when to engage legal counsel to help you manage or mitigate the risk.

Following are situations in which you might want to be particularly sensitive and engage HR legal counsel.

Hiring and Recruiting Employees

During the hiring and recruiting process, association executives need to take into account a number of issues to ensure compliance with applicable laws and regulations. For instance, some of the issues one may consider include

- Characterizing a candidate as an "employee" or a "contractor"
- Classifying the position as "exempt" or "non-exempt" from certain wages or hours laws as established by the Fair Labor Standards Act (FLSA)
- Educating those who interview candidates about the permissibility or impermissibility of certain interview questions in order to avoid real or perceived discrimination as outlined by agencies such as the Equal Employment Opportunity Commission (EEOC)
- Verifying eligibility of the candidate to be employed in the United States
- Providing an explanation to a newly hired employee that he or she is employed "at-will" and as such, either the organization or the employee can terminate the employment relationship at any time, with or without cause, and with or without notice so long as it not for a reason that may be protected under law; in cases when there is an employment contract, there may not be employment at-will since the terms related to termination are more explicitly laid out
- Ensuring that employment candidates understand they may be subject to certain background checks that are allowable by laws such as the Federal Fair Credit Reporting Act (FFCRA)

Managing the Work Environment

Once an employee begins work, it is important that employers comply with laws and regulations related to safety concerns and employee rights and protections, including

- Complying with workplace safety as outlined by the Occupational Safety and Health Act (OSHA)
- Understanding the protections afforded to employees under a number of laws such as Title VII (prohibits a number of forms of discrimination in the workplace), the Americans with Disabilities Act (ADA), and the Family and Medical Leave Act (FMLA)
- Ensuring that the workplace is free of harassment, retaliation, and discriminatory practices
- Educating employees to the limits of their privacy when they are on the job, using employer-owned technology, or engaged in evolving forms of social media

Administering Salary and Benefits Programs

A number of laws and regulations have an impact on the ways in which benefit plans are administered, including the following:

- The Employee Retirement Income Security Act (ERISA), which sets standards of protection for individuals in most voluntarily established, private-sector retirement plans.
- The Consolidated Omnibus Budget Reconciliation Act (COBRA), which provides continuation of group health coverage that otherwise might be terminated.
- The Health Insurance Portability and Accountability Act (HIPAA), which has a number of provisions, including
  - The ability to transfer and continue health insurance coverage for workers and their families when they change or lose their jobs.
  - The establishment of national standards that protect the privacy of individuals' medical records and other personal health information.
- The Patient Protection and Affordable Care Act (PPACA), also called the Affordable Care Act (ACA), which was signed into law in 2010, bringing sweeping changes to the U.S. health care system. The implementation of this act is evolving and will have significant impact on the management and administration of employee health insurance plans.

All nonprofits operating in the United States are required to annually file an IRS Form 990, which is an informational tax form available for public inspection. HRM executives should be aware that there are a number of questions currently on the 990 long form related to the way compensation is determined for the chief executive officer and other key employees. For this reason, CSEs should consider benchmarking executive compensation levels against comparable market data.

Disciplining and Terminating Employees

Employee termination is a time at which an employer needs to ensure that it has followed explicitly documented procedures and that performance deficiencies have been clearly explained to the employee. It is good practice to give underperforming employees an opportunity to turn around unsatisfactory performance within a specific period of time. A *performance improvement plan* lays out a suggested path for enhancing performance and outlines conditions required for continued employment. Both employers and employees need to keep in mind that even when an employee's performance improves, there is still no guarantee of ongoing employment; the doctrine of employment-at-will usually prevails.

In some instances, the employer may sense that an involuntary termination may result in a legal action by the employee. For this reason, it is often wise to consult with legal counsel *prior to* the actual termination in order to review the course of events that led to the proposed termination, examine performance documentation, and better understand the steps the association might take to mitigate the risk.

Despite all efforts to plan, follow established policies and procedures, and comply with applicable laws, there may be situations in which employees still feel that they have been wrongfully terminated, discriminated against, harassed, or so on. *Employment practices liability insurance* is a type of coverage that protects employers against employees who file legal actions claiming that their employee rights and legal protections have been violated. HRM professionals should consult with the association's insurance broker to learn more about employment practices liability insurance coverage and determine its applicability to the association.

Hiring an HRM Executive

While the CSE needs to broadly understand HRM principles and practices, there may be a point at which it becomes necessary for the organization to hire an HRM professional. While the needs of every organization will differ, one should consider the following skill set when recruiting and selecting a qualified candidate:

- *Technical skills:* The HRM professional should possess basic or intermediate skills related to HR law, the use of HRIMS-related technology, candidate-interviewing skills and techniques, and the use of social media as they relate to recruiting and employment policies. The savvy HRM professional will know the limits of his or her technical skills and know when to supplement his or her expertise with counsel from lawyers, insurance brokers, and information technology (IT) specialists.
- *Business skills:* The HRM professional needs to be prepared to understand the strategic priorities and business of the association as well as the issues facing its membership. This understanding will help better position the HRM to recruit the appropriate candidates, facilitate performance evaluations, and assess market-based competition systems.

Furthermore, because of the uniqueness of individual employees and the challenges they face, an HRM professional must be able to evaluate a situation, identify alternative approaches, determine the best course of action, plan the intervention, execute the plan, and assess the results.

- *Human relations skills:* An effective HRM professional will have the ability to communicate with, understand, and work well with individuals and groups at all levels of the association. He or she will have an ability to be empathetic to the needs of employees while meeting the business and strategic objectives of the association.

Incorporating a full-time HRM professional into the staff will have a significant impact on the association, so it is important to carefully craft the position description, have an inclusive interview process with participants from all levels of the organization, and carefully check professional references.

Conclusion

The effective HRM executive creates an environment that invites employees to stretch beyond their initial potential and deliver results—individually and collectively—that exceed expectations. Ultimately, an association's human resources are its most valuable asset and as such, they must be managed by professionals who can balance the needs of employees while simultaneously supporting the association in pursuit of its mission. In summary, HRM—the art and science of managing people to effectively and efficiently achieve an organization's mission—is best derived by combining a sound corporate structure; a collaborative culture that celebrates individual, team, and organizationwide achievements; and an HR strategy that is aligned with both the tactical and the strategic goals of the association.

The Author

Matthew Gertzog, MBA, FASAE, CAE, joined the American Society of Hematology (ASH) in March 2003 and currently services as the deputy executive director. He is responsible for ensuring the day-to-day operations of ASH, as well as working closely with the executive director in the strategic management of the organization.

CHAPTER THIRTY

INTEGRAL TECHNOLOGY MANAGEMENT

Steve DeHaan, CAE

Nothing really stays the same. Our members' needs and demands change, key employees leave, and the business and social environments are altered constantly. It is all part of normal evolution in the workplace. However, those evolutionary, and sometimes disruptive, changes have the potential to generate a change in the heart of our organization's data-management system.

Creating a "Living System" for a Changing Work Environment

The database module is often the core from which all of the other systems "hang." Many associations use a central database to gather, manipulate, and create reports that allow staff to relate to and serve their members. Decision making about your integrated association management system (AMS) should not be taken lightly, for the systems are financially expensive. You'll want to determine the true total cost of change projects, looking at all anticipated expenses over a period of five years to understand all of the ongoing expenses. For example, new technology requires initial training of staff, upgrades, and ongoing training over that five-year period. In addition, in today's financial environment, the AMS requires considerable security to prevent fraud and identify theft.

The system when implemented well can be a relationship manager, a financial manager, an organization manager, a member manager, an event tool, a member information tool, and a help to political fundraising. It is the assistant to every manager and staff person in your organization. This organizational and administrative tool can assist in monitoring and controlling expenses on the backend operation of your organization. Then resources can be put toward serving the members in a very individualistic way. Many see the system as just hardware and software, but it is more about people, policies, procedures, and organizational culture. It is first about what is to be accomplished rather than the road of getting there.

The management and development or changing of an information management system need to consider the association's mission and its ultimate value proposition for its members. An organization should always start with its expressed desired outcomes and work back to the concrete data that can be entered into a system and the relationship of that data to all the other data.

Approaching the Prospect of New or Integrated Technology

As a CSE involved in technology decisions, it is important to keep an open, but controlled mind. We need to be able to look at new technologies, so our staff experts can do their jobs. Do not let the different vendors lead your team into something that you don't need or is too difficult for your staff.

To get started, find or create a list of questions that will support your policies, procedures, and goals, along with tools to assess your association's computer and software needs. (If you have bad policy and procedure coupled with weak goals or outcomes, it will not help you build a strong system.) If you do not write down the questions by which you will evaluate your current and future operations in the light of your goals, you will not have a method to measure your success. It all starts with where you are and where you want to be with enough concrete measure points to have confidence that you will ultimately arrive "into" the future.

Here are a few questions from the conceptual to the practical that a CSE may need to consider:

- Will I be able to pull a report while I am traveling?
- We have a five-year PAC solicitation and fundraising method; will this system manage it?

- Our bylaws note that each member's multiple locations will be put into the map for customers to find their different locations; will this system gather those locations and deliver them to the mapping or searching portion of our website?
- Will the systems tell me how many members participated in an association service in the past two years?
- Will the system tell me how we are doing in membership? Whether we are growing or shrinking? How we compare to the same month last year, year to date, and annually?
- Our strategic plan says that we want to get more next generation involvement; how do we or might we track, engage, and encourage this by using our system?

Consideration should also be given to your staff's appetite and ability for new technology, balanced with what the association can afford. Consideration should also be given to your leadership's vision of how this expense will benefit the membership and whether it really will. Technology should greatly lower the expense of all of your meeting registration expenses, your dues billing expenses, your financial accounting, and like items. Technology, effectively used, will arrange critical prospect and member information that can create systematic processes that result in great retention and recruitment of members. One of the larger expenses will likely be the ongoing education of your current and future staff. You can maximize your education investment by ensuring that your staff can get increasingly more information out of your system in ways that better serve the members. That investment should result in a more dynamic, progressive association. And you will still have a large and unrecovered investment in technology.

You will want to factor those expenses into your event registration fees, as well as the cost of recruiting and retaining members, and other revenue-generating activities so that you can recover the cash that you have invested in the technology over its estimated life and usage.

Choosing Future Hardware and Software

Technology choices are getting easier and harder!!! Do you want to invest in hardware and software, upgrades, maintenance, backup, and so on, or do you want to rent it as "cloud technology"? Businesses are doing both, with equal success. You will have setup, conversion, and education costs with each. What is right for your association will depend on the expertise of your staff and the future direction that you believe is right for the association.

Again, don't get sucked in to "this is the future" hype or hoopla. Stay true to your organizational goals and capabilities. You will need to create a set of terms and definitions, so that you and the vendors are speaking and *meaning* the same things. Typically, how an association talks about technology and how a technology vendor talks about delivering it may be similar language that, in reality, mean different things. For example, you may want different kinds of media, meaning social media and communication methods that will integrate with your system, and a vendor may be thinking in terms of clouds, drives, routers, and system components.

Involving your staff, as a team, is absolutely critical for success, for people support what they help to create. All members of your staff use your information management system. They need to be knowledgeable in its design and function in order to be effective in using it to serve the members.

Scanning to Ensure Effective Technology Solutions

With a long-term objective of positive and significant impact to both staff expense and revenue generation, a first consideration is to have an integrated system that can handle large amounts of data with an organizational structure to make it simple to use. Getting the data out of the system to be used in multiple environments and compatible with other software programs is the most important part of any database. Integration and retrieval of data are key and also create far more complexity and short-term expense.

Big Database

All people and companies that the association has or seeks as members or as purchasers of association products and events should be in the database with all of their needed and desired contact information. How many contacts are there per company, and how are you going to drill down to them? For example, can you get to the sales manager, the advertising manager, the warehouse manager, the personnel manager, or the store manager?

Relational Content

Because we want high touch with our members, notes of every member and customer contact or attempted contact should be included. If a salesperson talks to them, there are notes. If a meeting planner talks with them, there are notes. If the CSE wants to talk with them, they can see the previous conversations and record their own notes. If they are a PAC donor, we know. We can tell what events they have attended and, in effect, archive their entire purchasing, service, and communications history with the association.

Leadership and Volunteer Involvement Including Councils, Chapters, or Any Segment Within the Association

Who is serving in what role? Can I track years of service? Does it track years in the term and the total terms of office? Can I send a group letter, email, message, tweet, or something similar? Can I track attendance? Can I track spouse's or significant other's name and contact info? Do I know what the person drinks? Eats? What can I record in the database? Can I mine the database and pull reports that would help me understand the customized needs or aggregate patterns of member and customer data? What can I load on my travel computer, or can I access the database from remote locations? Does it give me their phone numbers and email addresses?

Phones

Can you dial your phone numbers directly out of your database? Do your phones (whether on your desk, via VOIP on your computer or mobile phone, or as a transfer from or to your mobile phone) connect to the database, and do you have access to the contact info at all times? Do you use Bluetooth technology to make yourself and employees hands-free and connected when in range? Are you making sure you are decreasing or eliminating phone tag?

Emails

Can you email or post messages from within the database to the contact in his or her preferred network? Can you link your emails to the contact in the database?

Websites

Are all prospect websites connected to the prospect contacts in the database for ease of finding information when making membership or program sales calls? Are they one click away?

Social Media

Which social media are you going to participate in, and are you gathering information regarding your members and prospects? Are you sending them customized information that you know they are interested in? Is there capacity to add on when the mode and media of today shifts and another media approach comes into common use?

Congressional Contacts

Do you track congressional districts and link them to the list of contact information for each congressman? Can you put critical congressional contact information into your emails, especially when you have a special message for your members to send to their legislators? Is it all in your database? Is it easily changed for newly elected legislators or redistricting? How do you make sure that your members' systems don't see your messaging as spam?

PAC Solicitations and Contributions

If you are a trade association, can your system track or offer analytics on your solicitations for funds? Can it track them if your members sign up for *x* years into the future? Does it tell you when you asked for the contribution and if they pledged an annual amount for the next five years? Does it manage your solicitations and contributions, and invoice your pledges?

Event Management

Will your system track your registrations, event revenue for people, exhibits, sponsors, and golfers? Will it handle your counts per function and generate function tickets, if needed? Will it produce a dashboard that your members may want to see to make sure the association is on track to meet its revenue goals? How does it handle online registration and credit card payments? How does it track and send statements for receivables?

Accounts Receivable

Will your system track receivables, differentiating anticipated dues dollars and past due invoices such as an exhibitor's or advertiser's invoice? Will it automatically generate statements at the appropriate times? Will it make transfer of receivable and payment information easily available for any accounting program with appropriate audit trails? Will it make sure that the staff does not miss any opportunity to invoice or collect funds, when the information is in the system? Can you put an association or personal message on invoices and statements to vendors? Can the system handle financed purchases on a monthly, bimonthly, or quarterly basis?

Knowledge Management

Will your system be able to search for key words (metatags) necessary to an effective knowledge management system? Should your system contain a platform for assessing knowledge competencies or educational efforts?

Miscellaneous Configuration and Administrative Concerns

- How are you going to do your backups? Online, in the cloud, with redundant systems, through tapes to take offsite, or something else?
- Are you going to be virtual and in the cloud with your software, files, and data?
- How will you include and integrate office productivity software?
- Remote access is paramount. Will it be via the cloud, VPN, or some other option?
- When you have a contact's financial information in your database system, how are you protecting it? Are you PCI compliant?
  - Do you have insurance to protect you?
  - How easy is it to get into your accounting system?
- What security measures are available to you, and how would you optimize the protection of member data to hacking, malicious viruses, and theft of data?

Critical Staffing Questions

There are many questions to ask approaching a project of this magnitude, but none as critical as "What can your staff really do?" If you are a large association, and you have dedicated IT people, such as a director of information systems, an analyst or programmer, a database administrator, a network administrator, and support people, they probably *can* handle the task. But that is not the case for most associations.

Many association executives have the attitude of, "My staff can do that." However, when an executive evaluates a project of great impact, senior-level staff should be involved to evaluate whether there is true ability and capacity to fulfill the project's mandates. The real questions in a project of this scope are

- Does your staff really have the time?
- Does your staff have the knowledge and skills?
- Does your leadership respect and have confidence in staff's ability to fulfill this project?

If not, seek professional guidance.

Great care should be used in consideration of hiring a consultant. The association needs alignment of the consultant's skill and knowledge sets with the desired goals of the project. The consultant's style needs to fit with the culture of the organization. A consultant's value to the project can be immense, especially if you have a small staff or do not have a large or knowledgeable technology staff.

Making the Buying Decision

Make certain that you have assembled adequate research and resources to ensure that you can have the system designed to your requirements. Vendors will want to dazzle you, but you need to recognize which technology meets your requirements. To make a smart purchase, you need to assess performance to measures that you have defined, as you evaluate the products available. Ask your prospective vendors lots of financial questions, as there are many fees that will not be discovered until the contract phase. Such questions may include

- What are your current and proposed upgrade times and fees?
- Can we share licenses for our part-timers, and do I have to have two licenses for home or travel and office computers?
- What future education have you been doing for other clients, and what has been the cost of that education?
- What other modules do you have, and what are the current installation, education, maintenance and product costs?
- What services are included in the monthly service fee, and is that in writing?
- Is the vendor firm financially stable and sustainable for long term support? (You may want to request to see evidence of financial stability.)

Planning for Implementation

Plan plenty of time to select, install, and convert to the new system. The process is logical and relatively easy to follow, but it takes research, knowledge, attention, dedication, and management to get it done right. Select a project team (which may include an external consultant) and define how it will organize and work with other groups of staff.

Cross-Functional Project Planning

Project management planning is crucial when initiatives are undertaken that require contribution from cross-functional teams. Because these projects require "part-time" resources from many functional areas, creating a shared view of the work to be done, the sequencing of the action steps, realistic timelines to enable seamless handoffs, and coordinated efforts with accountability built in must be documented and regularly evaluated throughout the life of the project.

Project management follows the scan, plan, implement, and evaluate (SPIE) pattern. For any major project, there should be appropriate project management plans in place to address preparation, roll out, change management issues, and fulfillment.

The scanning phase of project management requires considerable time and exploration. Seven steps lead to a solid project management plan. Following is the path to defining a project.

1. *Study, discuss, and analyze the problem or opportunity.* Be sure the planning team fully understands the nature of the problem or opportunity and that the team is addressing the *right* problem or pursuing the *real* opportunity. Major projects affect people from multiple departments. It is important to make sure the right people are consulted as the project is defined.
2. *Write a project definition,* which includes the following elements:
    *   Project name and description
    *   Objectives
    *   Key milestones
    *   Major steps in the plan and associated expected deliverables
    *   Start and finish dates
    For a familiar context, a project definition is nearly the same as what one might include in a request for a proposal (RFP) from a vendor.
3. *Define the desired bottom-line result.* What is it that you really want to achieve?
4. *List the essentials and desirables pertaining to the end results.* That is, list the key success measures that must be present for the project to be considered successful and outcomes that are not essential but that would add value to the project's success.

5. *Generate alternative strategies* that might lead you to your objective. (Team brainstorming is an effective method for this activity.)
6. *Evaluate the alternatives generated.* Be sure to use criteria that are realistic, that are within the human and financial capacity, and that reflect the desired outcomes.
7. *Choose a course of action* that will meet the elements of your project definition and deliver your bottom-line results.

Then you tactically plan the project, identifying the tasks to be accomplished, who will complete the task, and by when.

Business Planning for the Project

The creation of a business case, followed by an integrated business plan, is absolutely imperative for any long-term project. Replacing all critical membership and business systems will cost more, take more time, and have a bigger impact on operations than you think it should. This is true for highly skilled and knowledgeable computer project managers as well. By having a well-thought-out business plan, your association can mitigate some expense. Make sure you detail what you have, where you want to be in five years, and what you need to do to get there. Don't be afraid to adjust your plan after the first year, when you learn from experience about the investment you've made.

You will want to document where the association technology is now (point A) and what it is that you see yourselves doing in five years (point B). In the business plan, you'll want to define all of your functional requirements, attaching the budget implications for each of the value-add modules and customized features. Then you will want to prioritize the expenditures over time. You will need to establish a multiyear prioritized budget over the life of the investment, and it should be fairly detailed.

Taking the time to do excellent "due diligence" in advance of the implementation will help you understand the size and scope of the issues you will likely experience as you sell technology upgrades to your board, select your vendor, or implement the purchase, installation, conversion, and training. If you have codified it in a business plan, you will have prepared yourself and your staff for most of what they will encounter. While there will always be issues that have not been anticipated, it will make your process easier. If you can develop the plan far in advance of your implementation, you will discover some of the issues in the course of that planning work. Plan enough time (if you can), and you will have a lower cost system that performs to your association's specifications.

The Author

Steve DeHaan, CAE, is the CSE and president of the International Warehouse Logistics association. He has managed a local, two states, a national, and now an international association. These have had as few as two hundred members and as many as fourteen thousand, with staff sizes ranging from three to forty-eight. He loves networking with fellow association executives and leaders about the challenges that we all face.

CHAPTER THIRTY-ONE

LEGAL ISSUES

Jefferson C. Glassie, JD

In this complex and litigious society, chief staff executives and all staff must remain on alert to protect their associations from risks of liability and to ensure best legal practices in association operations. The integrity of the association and its brand mandates not only compliance with applicable laws but also superior programs and services. It is critical for associations to make sure their activities comport with the highest level of performance legally, ethically, and operationally. In light of the Sarbanes-Oxley inspired obligations of responsibility, transparency, and accountability, careful attention to legal issues is crucial. In addition, the Internal Revenue Service (IRS) has recently expanded its scrutiny of tax-exempt organizations, especially by revising the Form 990 annual information return to include more governance coverage. Compliance with the law and best practices will help limit liability risks for associations and maintain the association's goodwill and reputation.

Legal Audits

In a perfect world, every association would commission a formal and comprehensive legal audit to review all aspects of its programs and activities to determine whether significant legal exposure existed. Then, in that perfect world, the association would undertake a routine "legal checkup" every year or so to review ongoing and developing legal issues and problems.

Like a financial audit, a legal audit can help protect an association against unexpected liability or legal problems. In addition, a legal audit can point out trouble spots that deserve board or staff attention and may even trigger the development and implementation of key association policies that will help ensure that the association remains on the cutting edge of best practices.

Undertaking a legal audit of association activity also demonstrates the board's or CSE's good faith and due diligence in taking reasonable steps to identify and avoid potential liability. Even a less formal but thorough legal review of specific high-profile areas, such as certification programs, can highlight some of the more problematic risks and generate recommendations for minimizing those risks.

Of course, it is often not possible to have outside counsel conduct a full legal audit. Both seasoned veterans and those new to association management can use the following summary to review legal considerations important to most associations. (Note that this is not an exhaustive review and cannot replace legal advice, counsel, or a formal legal audit; it may, however, help avoid some of the legal potholes associations may encounter.)

Corporate Status

The association's corporate status offers a good starting point for a legal review. An incorporated association has articles of incorporation on file with the state or jurisdiction (such as the District of Columbia) in which incorporation occurred. Periodically, association staff or the relevant volunteer committee should review the articles of incorporation to ensure that they remain consistent with current activities. For instance, changes made in the bylaws or other structural aspects of the association—such as the number of directors and officers, membership criteria, and voting requirements—may make articles of incorporation out of date, and they should be amended by the process set out in state law to ensure consistency.

In addition, the legal status of the association in its state of incorporation must be current—otherwise known as keeping the corporation in "good standing." Most states require the filing of annual or other periodic reports in order for associations to obtain the limited liability protection available through the corporate form.

An association incorporated in one state but with offices in another state usually needs to file reports in the other state, too. Failure to file the annual reports can result in revocation of corporate status or authority, with subsequent liability exposure to the individual officers, directors, and staff members of the association. Therefore, all annual corporate filings in any jurisdictions where the association is incorporated or has offices should be made routinely and on time.

The bylaws—the general governing document that applies primarily to day-to-day association activities—should be consistent with state law and the articles of incorporation. The bylaws usually cover such organizational aspects as membership, meetings, voting, officers, directors, and committees. Provisions authorizing the existence of chapters also may be included.

Many associations have specific committees charged with ensuring that the bylaws are up to date and consistent with the association's current practices and procedures. In turn, it's important for associations to follow their bylaws. For example, membership voting and proper notice of meetings should be accomplished in accordance with the bylaws. Otherwise, failure to follow the policies and procedures of the association as outlined in the bylaws and other governing documents can result in challenges by members. Legal counsel can review preparation of notices for meetings, voting materials, and agendas to ensure compliance with legal requirements.

It is also important to address governance and board issues and ensure that meetings follow applicable law. Sarbanes-Oxley-inspired principles argue for adopting conflict-of-interest and whistleblower policies. Board and committee education and orientation sessions are also advisable. The Form 990 focus on additional policies addressing document retention, chapters, and joint ventures makes these policies also advisable.

Finances

Practically speaking, strong and healthy finances greatly influence the success of an association. Legally speaking, strong policies that protect against improper financial activities are essential as well. Legal liability can arise if association finances are mishandled, whether through incompetence, inadvertence, or deliberate fraud or embezzlement.

The board of directors generally has the responsibility for overseeing the development of budgets and for reviewing the finances. In fact, directors owe certain fiduciary duties to the organization to manage its affairs in good faith and in its best interests. The board, however, must remain apprised of important financial developments and receive periodic financial reports. Otherwise, the CSE or staff could possibly be accused of misleading the board, and liability could be imposed on individual staff members.

Accountants can help develop procedures and policies to prevent against embezzlement or other misuse or misappropriation of association funds (for instance, employees who handle funds should be bonded). Other useful policies relate to the investment of operating and surplus funds and the routine handling of deposits and writing of checks.

The preparation of audited financial reports also is recommended for associations. These reports give the board, members, and the general public confidence that the association's finances have been carefully and professionally prepared and audited. If the cost of hiring an outside professional (specifically, a certified public accountant) seems cost-prohibitive, the association should have an independent third-party review its accounting and financial policies and procedures to ensure that appropriate protections are in place. Again, Sarbanes-Oxley principles suggest that associations should have an audit committee—or an executive or finance committee—that specifically reviews and monitors the audit and interacts independently with auditors.

Tax

Carefully, correctly, and accurately compiled financial information must form the basis for annual reports to the IRS. Tax-exempt associations must file an annual information report with the IRS on Form 990. Currently, most small organizations with gross receipts of less than $50,000 annually may file the Form 990-N (ePostcard), and other organizations with annual gross receipts under $200,000 and less than $500,000 in assets may file the short Form 990-EZ. The due date is the fifteenth day of the fifth month following the end of the organization's fiscal year.

The majority of trade associations and professional societies are exempt from federal income tax under Section 501(c)(6) or Section 501(c)(3) of the Internal Revenue Code. Section 501(c)(6) covers membership organizations with professional industry interests, such as business leagues, boards of trade, and other organizations that exist to promote a specific profession, industry, or line of commerce. Section 501(c)(3) organizations have primary purposes that are charitable, educational, or scientific; because donations to such organizations are tax-deductible to the donors, additional legal requirements apply.

The determination letter from the IRS granting (c)(3), (c)(6), or other 501(c) tax status should remain part of the association's permanent records. In the absence of a determination letter, the association should immediately seek legal counsel to ensure that it fulfills appropriate filing and reporting requirements. In addition, most states require tax-exempt organizations to file annual reports, and some (such as California and the District of Columbia) even require that an association submit a formal application to obtain such an exemption.

If tax-exempt organizations fail to conduct their activities in accordance with the tax-exempt purposes described under the Internal Revenue Code, they may face the imposition of taxes, penalties, or even revocation of their tax-exempt status. In addition, if an association's non-exempt activities—such as marketing particular services for members or selling nonrelated products—become substantial, they may jeopardize the organization's tax exemption. More commonly, activities that are unrelated to the association's purpose or mission, are "regularly carried on," and constitute a "trade or business" under IRS definitions will result in unrelated business income subject to tax.

If revenues subject to unrelated business income tax (UBIT) rise to within 30 or 40 percent of the association's annual budget, the IRS may question its tax-exempt status. Associations in that situation often spin off some of their activities into a for-profit subsidiary

One way to avoid UBIT is to properly structure activities in such a manner that they will not be subjected to tax. For example, many association affinity programs can be appropriately characterized in legal agreements as generating "royalty" income for associations. Passive revenues, such as dividends, interest, and royalties, are exempt from UBIT provided certain rules are observed. In addition, sponsorships of activities can generate tax-free revenues if the association recognizes and acknowledges the sponsor in accordance with IRS guidance.

Insurance

Associations can take many steps to reduce potential liability. Yet, in the current legal environment, there is no way to prevent an aggrieved member or other person from suing the association to seek compensation or relief from allegedly harmful behavior. Therefore, associations must have adequate insurance coverage to protect against liability arising from a wide variety of legal claims. Given the sophisticated insurance policies on the market, associations do well to turn to a knowledgeable insurance agent or broker with experience in the association field for help in obtaining adequate and appropriate coverage.

It's important to adequately disclose all association activities to the insurance company when obtaining insurance and to carefully review any endorsements or exclusions in the policy. For example, the policy may exclude damages or losses from antitrust, certification or standardization programs, or even employment practices. It often is worth paying additional amounts to ensure that the coverage for the association is broad and without significant loopholes; the extra protection can pay off if a lawsuit is filed. Additional information on insurance is included in the next chapter.

Litigation

Given the potentially high cost and time-intensity of litigation, ignoring any claims made against the association can prove foolhardy. Legal counsel must be involved in the analysis and handling of any claims that might lead to litigation. The CSE or other appropriate staff person should carefully monitor, with legal counsel, any litigation in process against the association. He or she can then ensure that all aspects of the litigation are handled carefully and in a timely manner, not only to avoid potentially serious damages but also to manage legal costs.

When litigation is either expected or in progress, it's important to have policies and procedures that preserve the association's confidences and "attorney-client privilege." Association boards of directors also should be kept informed of the status of any significant claims or litigation, but board members must be clearly warned against inadvertent disclosures that may harm the association's case.

Although insurance policies tailored to association activities should cover the costs of litigation, the insurer will require proper and timely notice of any claim to obtain coverage.

Contracts

A written contract or agreement should memorialize any important legal obligation owed by, or to, an association. This is important not simply from the legal perspective, but also to confirm that the parties entering into arrangements for the sale or purchase of goods or services know exactly what is required of each. Most associations have policies stating that legal counsel must review and approve all contracts, which can be signed only by authorized officers.

All contracts are subject to negotiation. In other words, an association doesn't have to accept the exact contracts submitted by hotels, vendors, or others. In fact, it's helpful for associations to develop standard-form contracts to use with hotels, affinity program sponsors, and other vendors. A standard form makes it easier to always include contractual provisions that protect the association.

Important provisions include the following: warranties or specifications with respect to the goods or services to be provided, appropriate assignment of ownership or licenses for any intangible property (such as trademarks or copyrights), payment terms, indemnification or limited liability provisions, and termination or cancellation clauses. An "out" clause always is advisable because any relationship—no matter how good it appears at the start—can turn sour. It's better to think about termination before the contract is signed than have to fend off claims of loss or damage if a contract is terminated inappropriately without adequate terms.

Personnel

Personnel- or employment-related claims often present a difficult area for associations because personal relationships may become bitter when employees depart on the association's terms rather than on their own. Allegations of discrimination based on age, sex, or race are commonplace, whether in fact any discrimination occurred.

A well-written, clear, and legally sufficient employee manual offers the best protection against difficult disputes with employees. Courts look to a manual as the basis for the terms and conditions of the relationship between employer and employee. As such, it should govern all aspects of employment, including termination, and be kept up to date to reflect the current practices of the association. The association should also conduct objective and consistent personnel evaluations and maintain them in appropriate files.

Employment-related claims may arise in a number of areas other than discrimination. For example, some associations have been subject to legal liability for failing to pay proper overtime for nonexempt employees, instead substituting compensatory time. Vacation policies also are important; in most circumstances, unused vacation time must be paid upon termination.

A well-written employee manual, followed closely, can minimize the potential for long, expensive, and divisive lawsuits based on employment practices. At least one association employee should be specially trained in employment matters, including proper methods of hiring and firing, as well as employee benefits. Legal advice should be sought in advance of any proposals to terminate employees.

Intellectual Property

What is the most important property held by an association? Perhaps an office building—but many lease space. And most associations are not likely to own cars, boats, or extensive art collections. Therefore, "intellectual property" often represents an association's most valuable property.

Also referred to as "intangible property," intellectual property consists of patents, trademarks, service marks, trade names, certification marks, copyrights, and mailing lists (which can be considered valuable intellectual property). From a legal standpoint, the association should take all reasonable steps to protect its intangible property, such as filing registrations with appropriate state and government authorities. Registrations can enhance the value of intangible property and provide important procedural protections in the event of any litigation.

An association's name and acronym are key to an association's brand, and only authorized uses should be permitted. Associations should ensure that any use of their names, marks, or logos is appropriate. Permitting unauthorized uses can lead to diminishing legal protection for the association's marks; a license agreement should be in place for all uses. Guidelines should be in place also to govern use of association marks by members (a stipulation for only making authorized uses can be included in with dues notices to construct a binding contract).

In addition to ensuring that they use proper copyright or trademark notices, file registration applications, and properly attribute sources in association publications, staff must also make sure that the association has all rights to use anyone else's copyrighted materials that it includes in its publications or other materials. For instance, articles submitted by independent authors or speeches made at association meetings and published in conference proceedings have to be handled in a manner that grants the association adequate rights to use the material as it wishes.

For copyrighted publications, the general recommendation is to obtain full copyright assignments so that the association owns the rights to the materials. Otherwise, it is sufficient for the holder of the copyrighted work (usually the author) to grant a release or license that is broad enough to cover any potential uses by the association. It's preferable that all who write for association publications—print or online—or make presentations at association meetings submit standard-form copyright assignments or releases. Also, any agreements with independent contractors should include provisions assigning copyright to the association.

Intellectual property rights command increased attention as associations move further into the world of cyberspace with websites, home pages, bulletin boards, email lists, and social media. Special legal issues apply to Internet and social media activities, particularly in connection with intangible property rights, so associations should consult legal counsel. It is advisable to have terms of use for all social media activities to ensure appropriate online conduct when using association related media. Cybersecurity is also a significant liability concern; applicable laws impose substantial legal obligations on associations in the event of privacy or security breaches. Associations should consult legal counsel to ensure they have required protections in place (such as written information security plans) and obtain special insurance applicable to such breaches.

Association Programs

The wide range of association activities and programs, different for each profession and industry, makes a full legal review of such programs impossible here. However, several themes run through the general collection of association programs and activities.

Antitrust

The Sherman Act and other federal and state antitrust laws prohibit anticompetitive acts in restraint of trade. Among these are several commonly recognized illegal activities, such as price fixing, allocation of markets, and boycotting of competitors. But any activities considered unreasonably exclusionary or anticompetitive may give rise to problems. For instance, antitrust issues can crop up with respect to membership eligibility criteria, certification programs, availability of products and services to nonmembers, standard settings, promulgation of codes of conduct, statistical programs, and credit-reporting activities.

To avoid potential problems, associations need strong antitrust compliance policies that they routinely announce to members, particularly at association meetings. It's advisable for legal counsel to attend meetings when sensitive topics are on the agenda and to remain apprised of any activities that potentially come within the ambit of antitrust laws.

Due Process

Association actions that are inherently exclusionary or may adversely affect members and others must be taken in accordance with basic due process principles. In other words, association programs must be substantively and procedurally fair and reasonable.

Furthermore, professional or product certification programs, standards setting, and other self-regulation programs should be developed in a fair and reasonable manner. They must not unfairly exclude those who should be entitled to participate or to receive credentials or other recognition from the association.

Membership

Membership eligibility decisions and any disciplinary actions, particularly expulsion, must be undertaken in accordance with relevant due process principles. It is recommended that members have the opportunity to appeal decisions to a neutral appeal panel.

Political and Lobbying Activities

Special rules apply in the area of lobbying and political activity. For instance, organizations that are exempt under Section 501(c)(3) of the Internal Revenue Code are absolutely prohibited from any political activities, such as supporting or opposing a particular candidate during an election campaign. Section 501(c)(3) also limits the amount of lobbying that organizations can conduct; lobbying cannot exceed an "insubstantial amount" or the specific limits established under Section 501(h) of the Internal Revenue Code.

Although Section 501(c)(6) organizations have more freedom to lobby, they're subject to lobbying dues nondeductibility laws, whereby the portion of member dues allocated to fund lobbying activities are nondeductible. Associations must annually notify members what portion of dues is not deductible as a business expense or, alternatively, the association can pay a 35 percent "proxy" tax on such lobbying expenditures.

In addition, the Lobbying Disclosure Act requires registration of those lobbying the federal or executive branches of the United States government. The definitions of lobbying found in both the legislation and the Internal Revenue Code are broad and complex. To ensure compliance, associations should seek the assistance of legal counsel.

Finally, under the Federal Election Campaign Act, it is illegal for corporations to participate in federal elections, except through political action committees (PACs). The rules for participation in federal elections and solicitations for PAC contributions are complex, and some states have laws with similar restrictions. In addition, new super-PACs and the use of Section 501(c)(4) organizations have become prominent in connection with election campaigns. The applicable law and regulations are quite complex and changing. Any associations engaging in political activity should consult legal counsel.

Appropriate Protection

Association executives face numerous legal issues and obstacles in the daily course of their activities. That's why it's important for CSEs and staff to ensure that appropriate policies and procedures are in place to protect the association against potential liability. In situations when numerous, complicated, and oftentimes convoluted rules and regulations apply, however, CSEs may wish to seek legal counsel for assistance in devising appropriate steps or responses. In some cases, responding in the wrong manner may be worse than doing nothing.

Like it or not, one of the hats an association executive must wear says "Legal" on it, and he or she needs an adequate knowledge of legal issues to handle the job professionally and competently.

Resources

Glassie, J. *International Legal Issues for Nonprofit Organizations*, 2nd ed. Washington, DC: ASAE Association Management Press, 2010.

Glassie, J., Johnson, E., and Lynch, D. *Intellectual Property for Nonprofit Organizations and Associations*. Washington, DC: ASAE: Association Management Press, 2012.

Jacobs, J. A. *Association Law Handbook: A Practical Guide for Associations, Societies, and Charities*. Washington, DC: ASAE Association Management Press, 2012.

The Author

Jefferson C. Glassie, J.D., is a partner and co-chair of the nonprofit organizations and associations group at Whiteford, Taylor & Preston. He represents associations and nonprofit organizations on a wide range of legal matters, including antitrust, tax, certification, accreditation, contracts, employment, mergers, intellectual property, and corporate issues. He has significant experience in international legal issues and is the author of *International Legal Issues for Nonprofit Organizations*, published by ASAE. He is also coauthor with Jerry Jacobs of *Certification and Accreditation Law Handbook*, 2nd edition, and with his partners Eileen Johnson and Dana Lynch of *Intellectual Property for Nonprofit Organizations and Associations*. He has served on several ASAE section councils and committees and is an ASAE Fellow.

CHAPTER THIRTY-TWO

LEGAL LIABILITY RISK MANAGEMENT

Jeffrey P. Altman, JD

Legal issues are important to many areas of association manage-ment as discussed throughout this book. (See in particular Chapter Thirty-One, "Legal Issues.") This chapter focuses on activities that may expose your association to legal liability and suggests actions you can take to best protect your association.

The first step is to identify and take reasonable measures to minimize or avoid situations that may potentially expose your association to legal liability. When legal problems arise, you need to manage and resolve them with the least disruption and cost possible. You also need to be familiar with the processes for handling and responding to subpoenas, claims, and lawsuits.

Insurance is important to protect your association from having to pay legal fees as well as the cost of any settlement or judgment. You need to evaluate the particular risks that your association faces and make sure you purchase the appropriate insurance policies. To get the full benefit of the insurance protection you purchased, you also need to be aware of how insurance companies respond to and defend claims. Most important, you need to be actively involved in coordinating the defense in order to help achieve the best outcome for your association.

In addition, your members may also face unique liability risks due to the nature of their occupation or business. As their association, you have the unique opportunity to help develop a customized insurance program for your members. This can include a sponsored affinity insurance program as well as a setting up a captive insurance company.

Who and What Do You Need to Protect Against and How?

To be prepared, it is important to understand who may make claims against the association, the possible legal basis for their claims, and what you can do to try to minimize or avoid these risks.

Employees

It comes as a surprise to many association executives that the vast majority of claims against associations are employment related. This includes would-be employees, who feel that there was something wrong in the hiring process that prevented them from getting a job they felt they deserved. An example could be inappropriate questions during the interview process about the applicant's family plans, religion, or sexual preference. It also includes employees who fail to receive promotions or pay raises to which they think they are entitled. An example might be a claim by an employee who feels he or she was the subject of retaliation for reporting a hostile work environment, harassment, or other improper conduct by his or her supervisor. In the case of a disciplinary action or termination, the issues could be alleged discrimination or retaliation against a whistleblower.

This suggests that the most important thing that every association can do is to make sure it has an up-to-date employment manual. Supervisors and staff also should be trained in order to avoid these kinds of occurrences from happening. Since disputes over the termination of executives are particularly contentious and expensive to resolve, consideration should be given to negotiating employment contracts that contain no-fault termination and severance provisions that will allow a clean break without a protracted fight over what went wrong.

Although it may involve a loss to the association rather than any third-party liability, it also is important to guard against the possibility of employee embezzlement. Among other things, this means establishing appropriate financial oversight and internal control procedures.

Since employment claims are the most frequent, you should be sure to utilize an HR expert or engage employment law counsel before you take final action that may result in a claim.

Sometimes, this means postponing a termination until after the behavior forming the basis of the termination can be documented in the employee's file. Also, it may make sense to offer severance to a terminated employee that has a colorable claim in return for a release. In the long run, these efforts may be worth it in order to avoid a formal legal claim.

Members

Claims in this category may include individuals or companies who are denied membership as well as termination of existing members. The basis for these kinds of claims is varied, but may include discrimination, an antitrust violation, or breach of contract. This suggests that an association should have carefully written guidelines for who can be a member that are based on objective criteria that satisfy antitrust and other legal requirements.

Antitrust

Antitrust laws generally prohibit acts that restrain competition or trade, such as price fixing, coordinating bids, dividing up markets, and boycotts. Associations can become prime targets for antitrust claims, because of the perceived opportunity for competitors to meet and coordinate their activities that may harm nonmembers or the general public. A strong antitrust policy, articulated procedures in response to noncompliant member behavior, and documented training for staff and volunteers, as well as carefully planned agendas, meeting minutes, and monitoring of any problematic activities are all key to reducing this exposure.

◆ ◆ ◆

The process of terminating a member other than for nonpayment of dues also must be based on a violation of objective and legal criteria. Particular care must be taken if the termination is based on any alleged violation of a code of ethics or practice guidelines, since these may themselves be anticompetitive and give rise to an antitrust or other claim. Whatever the basis, there should be defined procedures for terminating an otherwise eligible member that include due process, meaning official notice of a complaint and an opportunity to respond or be heard if possible. This will make sure that all the facts are considered and the right decision is reached. It also will help with the defense if a claim is made.

Among other things, an association can increase its protection against member claims by having bylaws and other governance documents that clearly state any critical membership requirements. Also consider including language in applications and other forms whereby members confirm the accuracy of the information they provide and promise to abide by association policies and procedures, or agree that their membership can be terminated.

Certificate Holders and Accredited Bodies

If your association engages in certification or accreditation activities, your legal exposure may be to individuals or applicants who are initially denied status or who later have that status revoked. Once again, it is important that there are objective and legal criteria against which candidates initially are judged or may later have their status terminated. Unlawful antitrust restrictions, such as by denying certification or accreditation to competitors, or by enforcing overly restrictive practice guidelines or codes of ethics, should be carefully avoided. Once again, your association should include legal language in your applications and forms that will favor the association if any disputes arise.

Volunteers

Volunteers can include directors, committee members, and individuals who interact with the public. Volunteers can be a source of liability for an association when a volunteer with actual or apparent authority to speak or act on behalf of the association does something wrong, such as making a defamatory comment in public. A volunteer can also cause an accident while acting on behalf of the association that results in someone being injured or property being damaged. Also the association can be liable if a volunteer, such as a director, harasses, discriminates against, or otherwise acts inappropriately with staff. This suggests the importance of providing training, developing a code of conduct policy, and providing guidance to make sure volunteers are knowledgeable and act appropriately.

Volunteers can also be claimants, such as in cases when a director or committee member feels that he or she was wrongfully accused and that their removal from office, dismissal from a committee, retraction of an article, or other such action by the association has hurt their reputation or standing. Once again, this suggests the importance of discovering all of the facts, providing notice, and due process to hear and consider the other side of the story before the association removes, retracts, or takes other disciplinary action against a volunteer. If the association is fully informed about the circumstances before acting, it is far more likely to make a good decision that also can be more easily defended in case of a claim.

Advertisers and Exhibitors

Conflicts may arise and caution is appropriate if advertisers or exhibitors who compete with an association's members are excluded from advertising or exhibiting in association publications or at association meetings. Some exclusions may be appropriate, such as where the product or service being promoted is contrary to the purposes of the association or the advertising style is inconsistent with the standards imposed on regular advertisers and exhibitors. It is important to carefully examine the rationale for the exclusion to make sure it is objective and legally sufficient.

Nonmembers

Individuals or companies may sometimes want to purchase association products or services that the association only makes available to its members, but without wanting to pay the cost of membership. Although your initial reaction may be that someone should have to join the association, this can result in a claim. Instead, you may charge nonmembers a premium or higher price to the extent the product or service is supported by member dues dollars and other association resources. The price differential cannot be so great, however, as to economically compel membership because it is almost as much if not the equivalent of the dues it would cost to join the association. Also, if setting standards or guidelines, the association must be careful that the standards or guidelines are objective, they are widely circulated for review with multiple audiences, and they are not influenced to favor the products of members over nonmembers who were excluded from the process. Otherwise, nonmembers can claim that they were competitively harmed.

Vendors, Consultants, and Contractors

Disputes oftentimes can arise with vendors, consultants, and contractors. The best way to avoid claims in this area is to make sure that your contracts and agreements are carefully drafted to state the work to be performed, the performance schedule, and the timing of payments against measurable benchmarks. In terms of risk management, it is important for the contract to specify that the vendor, consultant, or contractor is an independent contractor, that they cannot bind or obligate the association to third parties, and that they will be legally responsible to indemnify and hold harmless the association for any claims that may arise out of their activities. The contract should also specify the insurance they carry and include a requirement that the association be named as an additional insured on their policy if possible. Also important is your right to terminate for nonperformance or breach as well as a clause indicating where and how any disputes will be resolved. Many associations develop their own contract templates and addendums that cover these and other provisions that are important to include in any agreement as well as special clauses for special kinds of agreements such as hotel and convention contracts, technology contracts, and contracts involving international activities.

IP Owners

Associations must be careful not to infringe the copyrights, trademarks, service marks, patents, and intellectual property (IP) of others during the course of their activities. This risk of claims by IP owners can be minimized by making sure that the association staff is trained and careful not to use the IP property of others. Authors, speakers, entertainers, and contractors should all be required to confirm in writing the originality of the materials and products they provide to the association or that they have obtained permission or licenses to include the IP of others. Appropriate licenses should be obtained with respect to playing music at association meetings and events as well as for this content to be streamed or communicated online, which may implicate different rules. To defend its own IP against claims, an association should consider registering its trademarks, service marks, and copyrighted materials. An association should be careful always to use a copyright notice on its published materials and a trademark symbol for its logos. It should also send timely cease-and-desist letters and otherwise object to infringing material in order to protect its IP rights.

General Internet Activities

Association Internet activities, including websites, bulletin boards, email lists, and social media all present special liability challenges since they could expose an association to a wide variety of claims, including defamation and antitrust violations for collusive communications. Association staff should be trained to make sure they understand what is appropriate. There also should be clear terms of use and rules for members and others that will prohibit offending communications and allow the association to remove improper communications, as well as bar violators from further access.

Cybersecurity and Data Privacy Breaches

One of the newer areas of potential legal exposure for associations relates to the handling of information and data that can be hacked or inadvertently released. In addition to the possible loss of data that may be costly to reconstruct, an association can face enormous liabilities in terms of the costs that must be incurred to notify the data owners of a breach as well as to provide future monitoring services. It is also possible that individuals or businesses whose data was released or stolen may make claims in case they suffer any damages from the breach. Since most associations utilize an outside vendor to develop appropriate security checks and controls, an important risk management tool is to make sure that their contracts specify appropriate security requirements and that the vendor will be legally responsible for all costs associated with the breach.

General Public

Claims by the public against an association can occur in many ways. Someone could be injured by staff or a volunteer, as mentioned earlier. They could slip and fall visiting the association's premises or attending a convention. The risk in these situations is obvious and can be guarded against with regular attention to safety issues. Perhaps more serious from an association's perspective is if a claim is made that someone was injured by a product manufactured by an association member, particularly if the association is involved in setting standards or generally promotes the product in question. This suggests extreme care to make sure that the standards are objectively and scientifically based, and are subject to wide and independent review, thereby minimizing the possibility that members of the public may be injured or try to hold the association responsible.

Government

Not to be forgotten is the legal exposure that may be incident to oversight and audits by the Internal Revenue Service (tax); the Department of Justice and Federal Trade Commission (antitrust and deceptive/unfair trade practices); Congress and the GAO (lobbying); the Federal Election Commission (election and campaign activities); state attorneys general, secretaries of state, and licensing or regulatory authorities (various state activities including fundraising and gaming). International activities also require compliance with the Foreign Corrupt Practices Act and checking the U.S. Department of State terrorist watchlists before payments are made to foreign vendors or making international grants. Associations should be sure to get advice and guidance before engaging in any activities that could trigger government intervention in any of these areas.

Chapters

If you have chapters or affiliated components, their activities can have all of the same exposures as your association. Even if your chapters or affiliates are separately incorporated and insured, your association still may be included in any claim. National or lead associations need to encourage their components to embrace all of these same risk-management techniques.

Maintaining Your Corporate Status

Do not forget that your directors, officers, staff, members, and volunteers are generally protected from liability by your corporate status, unless there is a basis to pierce the so-called corporate shield. Your tax exemption also is dependent on maintaining your corporate status. This requires that you properly register and maintain your corporate status in the jurisdiction where your association is incorporated and other states where you may have an office or are doing business. For example, most states require all corporations headquartered or registered in the state to file an annual report confirming the location and resident agent for the entity. Associations and their chapters sometimes neglect these simple filing requirements and thereby unnecessarily increase their exposure to claims and liabilities by allowing their corporate status to lapse.

Meetings and Events

Associations that have meetings and events need to guard against possible bodily injury and property damage claims to attendees and exhibitors, as well as the hotels and convention centers where their events may be held. Such liability may include a claim involving an attendee who slips and falls or possibly is served too much alcohol. Careful risk management is suggested, as is particular attention to exhibitor, vendor, and hotel or convention center contracts to make sure they properly allocate risk and insurance responsibilities and also contain appropriate indemnification, hold harmless, and insurance clauses to protect the association.

Although not a third-party liability risk, associations also need to pay careful attention to ensure room block attrition clauses and force majeure clauses in hotel and convention contracts will broadly excuse nonperformance to make sure the association is protected.

Property and Business Interruption

Although this chapter focuses on legal liability risks that may expose the association to liability to third parties, it is important to be mindful of additional risks that need to be managed and can also possibly be covered by insurance to the extent it may be available (as further discussed in the insurance sidebar). Among other things, this includes possible damages to the association facilities or property that may result from a fire or other natural disaster and the interruption of the association's business that may occur if you fail to plan for backup and the ability to work in an alternate location or remotely for an extended period.

Concluding Thoughts on Liability

Although the foregoing discussion is illustrative and far from exhaustive, it highlights the many potential sources of claims and legal liabilities while suggesting steps an association may wish to consider to minimize their risk exposure.

Managing Conflicts and Claims

It may seem obvious, but it is important to do whatever you can to deal with minor conflicts in a proactive and constructive manner. While your instinctive reaction may be to brush aside or reject an initial inquiry or complaint, you need to consider the consequences to your association if a formal claim is made. It is important to do what you can to resolve informal disputes and keep them from growing into major claims.

Generally speaking, it is important to gather all the facts and afford a member, volunteer, or applicant the opportunity to be heard before adverse action is taken. Also involve legal counsel when appropriate to advise the association and help minimize your legal exposure. This process is most likely to lead to a correct and just result and one that can be defended.

You need to do what is right and protect the association if necessary, but you also need to be mindful of the difficult process that may follow if a formal claim is made or a lawsuit is filed. This may include

- Legal fees and expenses for the defense
- Possible monetary damages for a settlement or judgment
- Staff time and the diversion of the organization's time and attention
- Possible lost members, revenue, and opportunities
- Damage to the association's reputation and ability to stay in business

Once again, you need to do the right thing in protecting the rights of your association, but be mindful of these consequences of not dealing quickly with situations or informal claims that have some basis and may be better to resolve at the outset than fight.

Dealing with Subpoenas and Lawsuits

Sometimes an association may not be directly involved in a legal dispute, but may get a request for information or a subpoena in connection with a lawsuit involving a member or the industry represented by the association. The first thing to remember to do after you receive a subpoena or other information request is to evaluate what responsive information you may have. You should also inform staff and volunteers to suspend any regular or automatic document destruction or email deletion policies in order to preserve emails and other responsive information. After that, it is best to contact the member if possible to learn more about the dispute or legal action and what role the association may play. You oftentimes can offer the member or its counsel the opportunity to intervene and block the subpoena at their expense. In the end, remember that the association itself may eventually become a target, so it is best to consult with counsel.

Another key risk management tool is to make sure that association staff, board members, and volunteers are all cautioned to be careful in their email and other written communications. Everything is potentially discoverable and can be taken out of context and used against the association. Also, information or communications with the government may be subject to public information requests. Finally, every association should have a records management policy with a document destruction and retention schedule, since the cost of reviewing millions of emails in response to a subpoena can be enormous.

If your association is sued, the first thing to do is to contact your legal counsel. If you have insurance, you must immediately give notice of a claim so that it will be covered. In this regard, it is important to carefully consider the wording of your notice to make sure it will trigger coverage and obligate the insurance company to defend your claim.

Insurance

Even if they have identified their major risks and done the best they can to minimize or avoid the possibility of a claim, a small percentage of associations are still going to be sued. Few associations have the resources readily available to defend themselves or to pay damages if they should settle or lose at trial. That is why associations can and should buy insurance.

Insurance should protect not only the association but also its directors, officers, staff, and volunteers. On the basis of the risks described earlier, the two most critical policies to obtain are association directors and officers (D&O) insurance that covers employment practices liability and protects against various economic claims and a business owners policy (BOP) that provides general liability coverage for bodily injury and property damage claims and also protects the association's property. Depending upon the unique risks posed by your association's activities and your financial resources, you should work with your insurance advisor to consider a wide range of additional property or casualty insurance coverages that may be appropriate to protect against the losses highlighted in this chapter (as described in the insurance sidebar).

◆ ◆ ◆

Protecting Your Organization Through Careful Risk Review

P. Allen Haney, CPCU, CLU, ChFC, CASL, ChHC, FASAE

Association executives must apply careful risk management to protect the association from exposures to loss. Association risk management is the practice of identifying and analyzing possible loss exposures, then implementing steps to minimize the financial impact these risks create. Property fire loss, third-party lawsuits, injury to staff, stolen private information, events cancelled because of weather, disgruntled employees, misappropriation of association assets, and disagreement with board actions are just some examples of actual events causing negative financial impact for associations. Association leadership must plan to mitigate these threats. There are five approaches to handling these exposures to loss:

- *Insurance transfer:* Buy insurance to protect you in case of loss, in effect transferring your exposure to the insuring entity.
- *Risk avoidance:* Stop the activity so you don't have the exposure.
- *Risk control:* Take measures to reduce the frequency of loss or the severity of a potential loss.
- *Contractual risk transfer:* Outsource the activity with the inherent exposure to another business and include a "hold harmless" provision in the contract to protect you.
- *Assumption of risk:* Recognize that you can't avoid all exposures to loss and you willingly accept that if there is a loss, you are responsible.

A competent association insurance broker or risk manager can guide you to the right solutions for your organization. This sidebar focuses on the insurance transfer aspect of risk management.

At a minimum all associations *must* have *basic* protection insurance in place that includes an association office package policy, association directors and officers liability coverage, workers' compensation, and umbrella liability coverage. These are each described below.

Association Office Package

Appropriate for most associations, an association office package policy combines several insurance coverages that are tailored to the nature of association activities. All associations have members, use volunteers, educate, hold meetings, raise money, travel, and create networking opportunities. By combining different coverages together in one policy, associations are able to achieve better risk protection. Coverages under an association office package normally would include general liability, property and contents, automobile, and crime and employee dishonesty.

General liability protects association assets against lawsuits for bodily injury or property damage brought by a third party. General liability is based on the law of negligence, which obligates all associations to use care in their operations so members of the public do not suffer bodily injury or property damage. This standard of care requires *reasonableness* and *prudence* on behalf of the association. General liability coverage should also include protection for products and completed operations, personal and advertising injury, fire damage to others, legal liability, convention and meeting liability, host liquor liability, medical expenses, and contractual liability. General liability is a cornerstone for all activities when holding meetings, working with outside suppliers, hotels, and convention bureaus.

Property and content coverage provides protection for physical assets such as equipment, furnishings, computers, business income, buildings, art, and improvements and betterments. Replacement cost protection should always be provided to assist in the event of a loss. Replacement cost provides coverage at a level that will *replace* lost or damaged property with similar materials and quality. Choosing "actual cash value" will only pay the depreciated value of your damaged property at the time of loss.

Crime and employee dishonesty protection has been highlighted by recent stories of embezzlement in the press. Make certain your policy offers this protection for the headquarters location *and* for meetings, conventions, and other income-producing events taking place away from the office. Crime and employee dishonesty protection covers losses caused by association employees as well as volunteers, non-employees, and meeting personnel.

Automobile coverage for personal cars, or rented or non-owned vehicles used in the course of association business should also be included under the association office package.

Association Directors and Officers Liability Coverage (D&O)

Association directors and officers liability coverage protects the organization, its directors and officers, paid and volunteer staff, and committee members from lawsuits for management decisions or nondecisions made in good faith. Often this is viewed as *malpractice protection* for errors and omissions of governance or management actions. This coverage is a *must*, particularly for board members, for board members are often concerned about the possibility of personal liability incurred through actions by the board. Some companies have expanded this coverage to meet other unique risks of associations. These companies offer additional coverages under this policy including publishers liability, fiduciary liability, employment practices liability, antitrust allegation protection, third-party coverage, and breach of contract coverage. Beware that D&O coverage uses manuscript or nonstandard forms, so each company's policy language needs to be examined carefully. The best approach to ensuring you have the coverage you need is to brainstorm about all of the association's activities and share that list with your insurance broker or risk manager to be sure you have all your bases appropriately addressed.

Workers' Compensation

Another *essential* coverage is workers' compensation. Workers' compensation insurance provides wage replacement, vocational rehabilitation, and medical benefits to employees with a work-related injury or illness acquired in the course of employment. Although workers' compensation benefits will differ among states, some benefits include life protection for employees killed during employment. This coverage protects the employer against suits brought by employees for tort negligence. Associations should also add a *voluntary compensation* and *all-states endorsement* for risk control.

Umbrella Insurance

Umbrella insurance, generally sold separately, should be part of the basic association insurance protection to provide additional liability coverage when a lawsuit for injury or property damage *exceeds* the liability limits under the association office package policy. This coverage may also provide liability coverage in some lawsuits not covered in your underlying policies. For example, if an association rents a boat for a convention or board meeting, the umbrella coverage may provide additional protection above a self-insured retention amount (deductible) should a covered loss occur. By layering an umbrella liability policy over your basic liability policies, associations are in better control of insurance costs.

Association Event Cancellation Insurance

Associations should consider additional insurance protection because of their size, activities, revenue stream, and best practice activities. Associations who derive 20 percent or more of their annual revenue from conventions, meetings, and educational activities *should* consider association event cancellation insurance. This insurance provides coverage for loss of revenue or expenses incurred to diminish the loss due to an event cancellation, interruption, or postponement. Association loss of revenue may be caused by adverse weather, labor disputes, fires, terrorism, earthquake, and non-appearance of principal speaker.

Cyber Liability

According to cyber security experts, "There are two types of companies out there: those who have been hacked, and those who will be hacked."* As ominous as this seems, addressing the digital risk is critical.

In a 2009 study, Travelers Casualty & Surety Company of America estimated that 31 percent of all breaches of information take place in organizations of *fewer than one hundred employees*, so smaller and mid-size association should be aware. According to Travelers, the cost associated with a data breach is on average $188 per compromised record. With the number of cyber-related data breach thefts of personal information increasing, cyber liability coverage should be seriously considered by associations.

Since 2003, forty-six out of fifty states have amended their state laws concerning the loss of personally identifiable information to outside parties. Hacking, phishing, outside cyberattacks, lost phones, and stolen laptops are examples of how personal identifiable information has caused severe risk for all organizations. If private information is held by outside vendors, then a contractual risk transfer should be required. This means that your vendor provides both a "hold harmless" clause and an additional insured endorsement in their contracts whereby the vendor is responsible for the loss, rather than the association.

Professional Liability and Standard Setting

If your association is involved in developing best practice guidelines, setting standards, accreditation, or certification activities, a professional errors and omissions (E&O) liability policy or a miscellaneous professional liability insurance policy for standards and specifications should be considered.

If your association provides insurance programs for members, an E&O policy is important to cover your exposure. Should the program be offered through an outside vendor or insurance company, the association needs to have a contractual risk-transfer to protect its endorsement or sponsorship. This means your outside partner or insurance company needs to protect you under an E&O policy, fiduciary liability policy, and a "hold harmless" clause. The association must be protected against suits brought by members participating in the association-sponsored insurance program.

If your association is providing an insurance program on a direct basis, not through an outside sponsored or endorsed provider, then you must have your own E&O policy, fiduciary liability policy, and cyber liability policy. At the same time, the insurance program should be listed as an additional insured on the association's general liability policy, and publisher's liability policy if applicable.

International Risks

Many associations are very active in international outreach. Specific insurance coverages should be considered for these exposures. When establishing operations internationally, the need for general liability, automobile coverage, workers' compensation, and property protection must be addressed.

U.S. insurance policies generally cover claims made worldwide, but only offers protection for those claims filed in the United States. Insurance internationally is usually very country-specific. Often, many countries around the world require insurance policies to be issued through companies licensed in their jurisdiction. To meet this requirement, organizations such as AIG, Chubb & Sons, and Lloyds of London issue *specific coverages* that combine risk exposures and comply with international jurisdiction requirements.

Associations with international exposures should review the additional protection needed for business travel accident (health insurance for hospitalization outside the United States), potential kidnap or ransom protection, and war and terrorism coverage. Expanding association activities internationally involves careful insurance review with your insurance advisor.

*Stacy Cowley, "FBI Director: Cybercrime Will Eclipse Terrorism." CNN. Available at http://money.cnn.com/2012/03/02/technology/fbi_cybersecurity.

◆ ◆ ◆

Other Insurance Issues

Beyond the list of policy types that should be reviewed and possibly purchased, there are also other important issues to consider, as follows:

- What limits should you purchase? This may depend upon whether defense costs count against the limits or are paid in addition to the limits. Litigation is expensive and sometimes can exceed $50,000 or $100,000 for a simple case (if there is any such thing) or over a $1 million for a complex case. If it can afford it, an association should purchase limits of $1 to $3 million. Larger associations with bigger risks may purchase $5 to $10 million limits.

- Who appoints your defense counsel? Some carriers allow an association to pay a higher premium for the right to select counsel, but most insurance policies give this right to the insurance company, and they usually have so-called panel counsel who are experienced in defending different kinds of claims. Depending upon the nature of the claim and the carrier's position on coverage, your regular counsel can ask the insurance carrier if he or she can represent you, but they must be willing to accept the lower billing rates normally paid by insurance carriers. In these circumstances, some associations may also negotiate an arrangement under which the association may supplement the fees paid by the carrier so it can engage counsel of its choice.

- What is a reservation of rights letter? Oftentimes, some parts of a claim are covered and other parts are not. This is why it is so important to involve your counsel or experienced insurance broker in drafting a notice letter that will be sure to trigger the broadest coverage possible. In such situations, the carrier will usually have a duty to defend the entire lawsuit but only to pay that portion of a settlement or judgment that is covered. This is oftentimes explained in a written communication from the carrier called a reservation of rights letter. If you get such a letter, it is important to discuss its implication with your legal counsel and respond in kind. Also be mindful that it may be desirable to demand that the insurance company settle the case by agreeing to pay covered claims within the policy limits and obtain a dismissal of the uncovered claims, in order to be done with the case. This avoids the risk of a trial and judgment on claims that may not be covered that the association could be required to pay. In the event of a serious coverage dispute, an association may wish to consider bringing a declaratory judgment action. These various possibilities should be discussed with your legal counsel.

- It is also important for you not to just turn over the defense of your claim to the insurer and panel defense counsel, but to be actively involved in developing the strategy for defending the claim. The association's reputation may be at stake, and the outcome may implicate future claims or lawsuits of the same nature. Also, substantial assistance from staff may be needed in order to prevail. Finally, you will need to know what is going on in order to participate meaningfully in the decision of whether to settle or proceed to trial once all the facts are discovered.

Member Insurance Programs

So far, we have focused on the needs of the association in terms of risk management, dealing with conflicts and claims, and insurance. We now turn to the needs of your members.

Many associations help their members identify their particular risks and then negotiate a special insurance program with a particular carrier that can provide customized coverage, underwriting, and discount pricing. In most cases, the association just endorses or sponsors the insurance program, including the insurance broker or program manager that may actually sell the insurance to your members. This is typically called an affinity insurance program, because the association itself is not actually involved in selling or underwriting the insurance but just passively endorses or sponsors the program. These types of programs can also be important sources of nondues revenue to the association, which may come from royalties, advertising, exhibit fees, and sponsorships paid to the association in connection with the insurance program.

A few associations also take the extra step of setting up a for-profit subsidiary that may obtain a broker's license to sell insurance. This will allow the association indirectly to be more engaged in marketing the insurance product without the association having to pay taxes on unrelated business income. The subsidiary can also earn extra revenue by being able to earn commissions that can only be paid or shared with a licensed broker.

Finally, an association may wish to consider having a subsidiary get licensed as a captive insurance company in order to be able to reinsure and share in the premiums, losses, and profits that otherwise accrue only to the insurance carrier. This also allows the association, through its captive, to have greater influence over pricing, underwriting, and claims, than just an endorsed or sponsored program. The possible share of underwriting profits is in addition to the other nondues revenue sources described above.

Each of these alternatives for member insurance programs present business opportunities and risks that you should carefully review with your insurance advisor and counsel. It also should be noted that insurance activity is regulated by each state, rather than by federal law. Associations conducting insurance operations must be well-versed in the applicable state regulations and make sure they get expert advice on their alternatives and how best to proceed.

The Authors

Jeffrey P. Altman, JD, is a partner in the law firm of Whiteford Taylor Preston LLP. One of the primary focuses of his association practice is to advise clients on insurance, liability, and alternative risk transfer issues. Mr. Altman also speaks and writes on these topics for ASAE and other groups. He is currently a director and past chair of the ASAE Insurance Company (ASAE's captive insurance company) and a past director of ASAE Business Services, Inc. (ASAE's for-profit subsidiary that develops insurance and other affinity programs for ASAE and its members), and also has served on other ASAE committees throughout his career.

Sidebar author *P. Allen Haney, CPCU, CLU, ChFC, CASL, ChHC, FASAE* is an insurance broker based in Silver Spring, Maryland. He is the only insurance broker to receive the FASAE honor from ASAE. A trusted advisor to business owners and nonprofit executives, Haney is best known for solving problems. His counsel on employee benefits, executive compensation, and retirement planning routinely vitalizes the health and sustainability of closely held businesses and associations.

CHAPTER THIRTY-THREE

FACILITY MANAGEMENT

Mike Moss, CAE

Facility management, as defined by the International Facility Management Association (IFMA), is

> A profession that encompasses multiple disciplines to ensure
> functionality of the built environment by integrating people, place,
> process and technology.[1]

So what does that mean for the association executive?

As a key driver to the association's future success, the facility and the workplace are your responsibility as the chief staff executive (CSE). Facility management for the association executive means designing the optimal work environment for your staff to support your association's mission and vision. Your organization's facility management plan will have a tremendous impact on your organization, affecting your finances, staff productivity and satisfaction, talent recruitment, corporate social responsibility, and, most important, your ability to meet the goals of your strategic plan.

Next to your human resource costs, your facility is most likely the second highest cost you are carrying in your operational budget. If you are leasing your office space, you have a contractual obligation to a set amount of space that carries a defined per-square-foot cost. If you own your space, you are most likely carrying an amortized cost that is affecting your balance sheet, plus you are carrying an operations and maintenance budget for the many vendors required to keep a facility safe and operational. In either case, unless you are a very small operation, you are budgeting and paying for a facility or space that carries a significant financial cost, as well as the secondary consequence of representing your brand image.

While the core competencies of the association executive will most likely not include facility management, it is absolutely an essential value-add knowledge set that will help distinguish your association as a leading-edge, progressive organization that is using all available resources to fulfill the mission set forth by your members and board.

◆ ◆ ◆

The Eleven Core Competencies of Facility Management

- *Communication:* Communication plans and processes for both internal and external stakeholders
- *Emergency preparedness and business continuity:* Emergency and risk management plans and procedures
- *Environmental stewardship and sustainability:* Sustainable management of built and natural environments
- *Finance and business:* Strategic plans, budgets, financial analyses, procurement
- *Human factors:* Healthy and safe environment, security
- *Leadership and strategy:* Strategic planning; organize, staff, and lead the organization
- *Operations and maintenance:* Building operations and maintenance, occupant services
- *Project management:* Oversight and management of all projects and related contracts
- *Quality:* Best practices, process improvements, audits, and measurements
- *Real estate and property management:* Real estate planning, acquisition, and disposition
- *Technology:* Facility management technology, workplace management systems

Adapted from International Facility Management Association, *Global Job Task Analysis,* 2009.

Legal Considerations

Legal considerations related to your facility management plan include, but are not limited to

- ADA compliance, both within your workplace and external access to your facility
- Real estate and lease contract considerations and issues (Always consult legal counsel prior to signing any facility- or real-estate-related contract.)

- OSHA compliance liabilities associated with providing a safe work environment such as indoor air quality, slip and fall, preventive maintenance programs, and ergonomic considerations for your workplace design
- Tax implications related to ownership versus leasing

Essential Organizationwide Considerations for Effective Facility Planning

Financial Considerations

The first, and most significant, decision your board of directors will make in developing your facility management plan is the decision to update your current space or to relocate. Whether the decision is to redesign your existing space with new furniture systems and floor plan design or to relocate to a fully redesigned workplace, the decision points outlined in the following sections are relevant to the decisions the CSE will be tasked to make.

Once the location decision has been made, the board must decide if it is in the best interest of the organization to lease or own office space. This decision will have a long-term impact on your budget planning process, as your financial obligations will likely extend anywhere from a low end of five years to a potential long-term obligation of twenty years.

There are many factors that will drive the lease or own decision, including the following:

- *Use of cash reserves:* If you choose to lease your office facility, you will have a lower up-front cost and a predictable annual cost that has been set within the terms of your contract with the building management company. But with a lease you are also subject to the potential real estate market swings when your lease expires. Purchase your facility, and you will have a much larger up-front cost but, as noted in the next bullet point, an asset for your organization's future. In either case you will also have operational costs, due at the time of relocation, related to build-out and construction, furniture and fixtures, technology, and contractors such as your workplace designer. You may want to consult with your CFO or financial consultants to determine if you have sufficient cash reserves on hand or if you will need to supplement the cost of your selected facility with financial loans or lines of credit.
- *Investment considerations:* If you choose to own your facility, your association is now an active participant in the real estate market. Land appreciation where your facility is located can add to the long-term financial

strength of the organization. The facility value is also now an asset for the organization and with a properly managed operations and maintenance plan can also appreciate in value of the ownership term. The decision that the CSE will need to make is whether the association mission is best served by participating actively in the real estate market as an owner or retaining the investment costs of ownership by leasing and using those funds within other investment vehicles.

- *Projected organization growth:* Are you growing or becoming leaner over the next five years? What about in ten years? Is your growth in multiple markets where satellite offices will provide the best service or within a region where a centralized office is the best solution? Are you supporting a mobile workforce in the future, or is your organization's culture designed for daily onsite attendance by staff? These are strategic considerations that the association executive will need to consider from a growth perspective that will have a direct impact on the facility management plan.

Board and Transparency Considerations

Following the decision to lease or own, the CSE works to align the facility management plan and workplace design with the organization's strategic plan. Considerations cross operational, human capital, and organizational culture lines and will have a strong impact on the association's future development in support of mission (Figure 33.1). As your facility is a large financial obligation, a transparent process with the membership is critical to develop support for the investment that will be required to execute the plans.

FIGURE 33.1. PLANNING CONSIDERATIONS FOR YOUR FACILITY AND OFFICE SPACE.

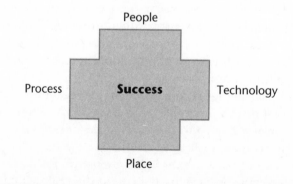

As a CSE, a large part of your responsibility is to ensure that a functional structure is implemented ensuring long-term viability for your organization. This process begins with the CSE leading an effective planning process for your facility with your board of directors. A common critical planning error by association executives is the assumption that the decision to lease or own is the end of the board participation in facility planning. In actuality, it is very important that the CSE enables a process that captures the vision of the board in alignment with the voice of the membership. For buy-in and stay-in, the CSE must ensure that the facility investment meets the vision of the organization and creates an environment that allows for development of quality product and service delivery and ongoing member support.

For a fully transparent process, the planning for your facility extends beyond the board and involves staff and membership input through several mechanisms. As you begin development of your facility management plan with the board, you can improve the long-term viability of your efforts by conducting the following scanning exercises, many of which can be most efficiently conducted through the use of consultants and other third-party resources:

- *Workplace performance survey:* Design a survey (paper or online) for your employees that asks questions about the current and ideal work conditions of your workplace. Allow the staff to provide confidential feedback on the performance of the existing office and workplace design. Specifically, ask staff to evaluate specific productivity factors that affect their ability to provide high-quality service to your members. Factors to evaluate include workspace type (private or collaborative), where staff spend their time in the office (private desk or meeting room), type of work completed (concentrative or collaborative), and technology use.
- *Time utilization study:* A time utilization study of your current facility and workplace will provide you with a strong understanding of how your current facility is supporting operational goals. As an example, if your office is 50 percent meeting rooms, but the utilization of these rooms is less than 15 percent, then you need to determine whether this is a managerial preference or a productivity reality based on heads-down work versus collaborative work requirements. The metrics gathered from the utilization study will provide the designer of your new workplace with a data set that supports the productivity requirements of your staff.
- *Member survey:* While the board provides a great perspective for the organizational voice, it is important that as a leader within the organization

the CSE has an understanding of the overall voice of the member. Allow time in your planning process for a survey to be conducted with your overall membership on their expectations for support in the future, inclusive of their expectation for local connectivity with your staff. This survey goes back to the lease-or-own decision made early in the facility planning process when the organization is determining its future growth potential for both headcount and geographic location.

- *Member and key stakeholder focus groups:* In addition to the member survey, take advantage of the onsite events you conduct as an association to facilitate focus groups with your members and key stakeholders. Run a session with your board specifically on the ten-year vision of the association's facility portfolio. Find out what the organization's vision is for its level of corporate social responsibility, as this will have an impact on your sustainability program within your facility. Run a dedicated session with a group of component officers at your annual conference, centered on expectations about staff service requirements. This feedback will provide a very good data set that can be used in combination with the member survey to truly understand the service requirements of your members, both currently and in the future.

The critical question to ask at the beginning of the planning cycle is, What are the future workplace needs for the association to support mission and vision?

Effective planning for your facility begins by ensuring the facility requirements are integrated into the strategic planning process. Aligning your facility and workplace plan within the planning exercise is very important, as it ensures that the operational costs and productivity impacts are not handled as a secondary consideration at a later date. All association functions are affected by the design and function of your facility, and as the CSE, it is your responsibility to ensure that it is given top-level strategic focus.

Workforce Considerations

The future growth expectations for your association will strongly influence the direction and funding required for your facility and workplace. Among the key decisions that the association CSE is responsible for are staffing levels and the geographic location of staff and offices. If your organization is projecting a spike in international membership growth, a decision will be necessary on whether the support of these members is handled from a

U.S.-based office or by regional or local staff. This clearly has an impact on budgetary requirements for your facility management plan as you grow or contract your workforce across your service area.

In looking at your facility portfolio, another consideration by the CSE is the allocation of expertise. If multiple offices will be in your facility portfolio, the association has the opportunity to allocate service skill sets to specific offices. For example, to optimize talent acquisition opportunities related to technology skill sets, perhaps a small satellite office in Silicon Valley will provide your members with the best IT and web support. Or if you have a large member presence in the Northeast, perhaps a customer service center in Boston will provide the best level of service while the remainder of the operation is based at your headquarters location.

Once the decision has been made on the location of staff resources (the where), the CSE will need to decide how the staff will meet the service delivery goals of the association. Will the staff be required to come into the office daily or will a mobile workforce meet the service needs of the association? Will the service and product requirements drive the need for collaborative or concentrative space? Is a hybrid solution the best approach and, if so, for how long before a facility refresh will be required given evolving strategic goals?

Workplace Considerations

As we know from a human resource perspective, a productive employee tends to be a happier employee. A happier employee tends to be more engaged and creative, providing your members with higher-quality customer service. Given the upside of happy, engaged employees, are you providing a facility and workplace that drives and creates productivity? Does the design of your workplace support or conflict with your organization's culture? Have you provided your staff with a facility that balances workstyle needs with service delivery expectations?

With the survey results conducted early in the planning process, the CSE has a set of quantitative and qualitative data to discuss the future state of the association's workplace with the board. On the basis of growth projections for both membership and geographic presence, the board can set forth a vision of the organization that the CSE can then incorporate into the facility management plan.

The design of your association's workplace has a direct effect on employee productivity, but more important, on employee satisfaction and engagement. In a study conducted by Dale Carnegie and MSW Research, the results showed that only 29 percent of the workforce is engaged, 45 percent are not engaged, and 26 percent are actively disengaged.[2] Simply stated, if you meet the workforce average, 71 percent of your staff are not actively engaged in meeting the service requirements of your membership on an ongoing basis. While there are other factors affecting employee engagement beyond the facility, it is the CSE's responsibility to provide a workplace that offers every opportunity for an employee to be fully engaged with the mission of the association and with the service requirements of the member.

In designing your workplace, provide your employees with the ability to focus, to balance work-life commitments, and to meet workstyle and service requirements. With a balanced workplace, your staff will be more creative, driving innovative approaches to your member service challenges. Choice drives performance and innovation, which in turn drive productivity. And as stated earlier, productive employees are happier employees who are more likely to engage and contribute to the member value proposition.

Other design considerations should support the multigenerational workforce that the CSE will increasingly be challenged to support. Boomers and Gen-Xers have materially different work styles than Gen-Ys in the workforce. This extends beyond the use of technology and into privacy expectations, collaboration requirements, and the need to actually be in the office. Younger employees are more comfortable with a flexible work schedule and in working in multiple workplace settings, often within the same workday. More experienced staff have spent the majority of their career in a workplace that was structured on a traditional nine to five schedule that rewarded success with large offices and other privacy-based amenities such as executive suites. The savvy CSE should think beyond the financial decision of a lease or property purchase and seize the opportunity to strategically design a workplace that supports the many needs of a diverse workforce (Figure 33.2).

As you work with the senior team on designing your workplace, focus on value ahead of expenses. As you increase your focus on member value creation, the related expenses will drop as your employees embrace the efficiencies designed into your workplace. If you are using lean practices or as the program is embraced, the use of traditional workflows will change and your staff will migrate to more efficient processes as they experience the increased flexibility that the workplace is providing and the improved satisfaction ratings of the members.

FIGURE 33.2. VARIETY OF SPACE TYPES OF DIFFERENT STAFF USES.

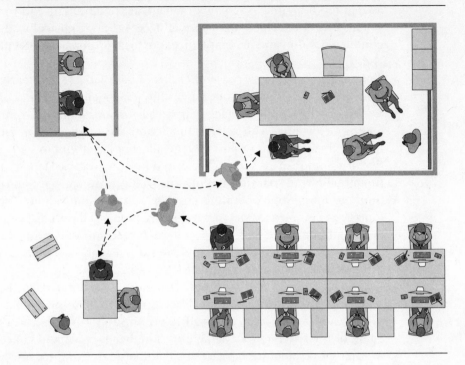

Following are some workplace design and protocol considerations that will need to be incorporated into your planning process:

- *Regulatory compliance:* Compliance with the Americans with Disabilities Act (ADA), OSHA safety regulations, local and state building codes, and a number of other workplace regulations needs to be considered before and during the workplace design phase. Whether you are tweaking your current workplace or designing for a new location, the CSE needs to engage with the appropriate legal counsel to review all construction, lease, and other contractual engagements used in the workplace planning process. Understanding the design considerations for regulatory compliance issues before implementation can potentially save the organization significant dollars. Rework and other retrofit challenges discovered during site inspections at the tail end of the implementation process are expensive and can be avoided with proper scanning and planning. The CSE should also engage with qualified professionals such as registered architects, change management consultants, and professional project managers to ensure all facets of a workplace project are conducted within and in compliance with local ordinances and building codes.

- *Optimal square footage per employee:* Usable square footage is an early decision in the development of your facility management plan. This will determine the size of the facility that your organization will commit to leasing or owning, with a large impact on the financial commitment moving forward. The square footage allocation per employee is inclusive of common areas such as break and meeting rooms. Depending on the mobility and space design of your facility, you may have an opportunity to lower your operating costs by reducing the required square footage per employee. Moving in this direction will have a direct impact on the morale of the staff; however it can be accomplished with reduced suite sizes, introduction of a mobile workforce, and encouraged use of collaborative space over private office space.

- *Number and type of meeting spaces:* Depending on the service delivery requirements of your plan, the CSE will need to determine what types of space are available for the staff to use in support of their workflow. Some of the space types available include heads-down and concentrative spaces, collaborative areas, small and large meeting rooms, phone rooms, private space, and social areas. The balance of these space types needs to be in alignment with your facility management plan, but, more important, with the culture you are establishing as the CSE. If you need to drive a collaborative culture, then a reduction in private office space and an open office plan will be to your advantage (Figure 33.3). If you need to drive more research and technical papers into the market, concentrative space will serve your organization best. For most associations, the solution will be a hybrid approach that balances the multiple product development requirements you have along with the workstyle preferences of your staff.

- *Healthy workplace considerations:* An important human resource responsibility of the CSE is providing a safe and healthy workplace. A common improvement in workplace redesign is adding increased levels of natural light, as well as integrating plants and "living walls" into your facility to provide color and to assist in providing high indoor air quality. Be sure that the HVAC systems in use are in compliance with ASHRAE standards for particulate filtration and mold spore capture.

FIGURE 33.3. INFORMAL COLLABORATIVE SPACE.

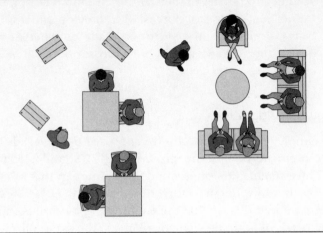

- *Corporate social responsibility:* In the design of your workplace, encourage the use of sustainable products in your office supplies and systems. Establish recycling programs and the use of reclaimed water to manage your landscape requirements.
- *Workstation ergonomics:* Select furniture systems, most specifically chairs, that provide multiple ergonomic points of support for your staff. Focus on providing furniture solutions that allow for a variety of work setting opportunities for the staff, including systems that are designed for standing versus sitting. If you use bench solutions, be sure that the desktop heights are either adjustable or supported by keyboard solutions that provide ergonomic support for long typing sessions.
- *Mobility:* As part of your facility management plan, a decision will be required on the mobility solutions available to staff that is based on your growth projections and geographic footprint. These solutions are inclusive of telecommuting, but extend beyond the traditional HR policy associated with occasional remote work. The first critical decision that will need to be made is whether your association culture requires an "all in" office, a mobile workforce, or a hybrid solution incorporating the best of both practices. If your requirement is for all staff to be at the office location, will they be internally mobile with the ability to move between workspace solutions, or will they be based in private office spaces? If they are allowed to be externally mobile using both remote locations and

the office, a decision on the technology solutions related to connectivity will need to be determined. If they are hired as remote-only employees supporting local service areas, with some potentially outside the United States, decisions will need to be made on whether they are full time or part time and what level of facility support will be provided to these employees.

Technology Considerations

Technology continues to evolve at a pace that exceeds the daily business requirements of most organizations. The CSE will need to make the strategic investment decisions around the technology that will support the strategic plan. More important, technology needs to be aligned to the facility management plan so that the technology platform is scalable to the evolving needs of both the strategic plan *and* the association's workforce. Technology, while a component of strategic success, is best viewed by the CSE as a tool supporting the mission, and not a determinant of the success of the organization. Human capital will always carry a greater importance, with technology optimized to support the staff and their requirements for workflow and member service.

Technology considerations in support of the facility management plan include the following:

- *Mobility support:* Whether you implement partial or full mobility programs for your staff, technology resources will need to be deployed that are flexible to multiple workspace types and locations. Most likely this means converting your full staff to laptops or tablet devices. With the conversion to laptops, several considerations for mobility will need to be made, including the size and weight of the device and port availability for printers, scanners, a mouse, and other productivity tools to be tethered to the computer. For productivity software, decisions will need to be made around hosted or cloud-based software packages. Additional considerations include policy-based decisions related to remote location WIFI reimbursement, home office supply support and reimbursement, remote location technical support, and replacement policies for lost or damaged laptops.
- *Connectivity:* Your facility will need high-speed, business-class connectivity to the Internet. Given that your staff will most likely be working off of mobile devices, your association will also need to invest in a high-efficiency, high-speed WIFI network for your facility. Beyond

hardware connectivity, a larger consideration will need to be made on how your staff will maintain connectivity with one another between office-based, remote, telecommuting, and other mobile staff members. Texting applications, video conferencing, email, software phones, VOIP phone systems, and cellular phone support capabilities will need to be accommodated in your annual operating budget in support of your facility management plan.

- *Meeting rooms:* Similar to the connectivity requirements for staff, your meeting rooms will need to have systems capable of hosting and receiving video conferencing, group collaboration (both in person and with virtual attendees), and voice conferencing.

- *Energy efficiency and sustainability:* As technology continues to evolve, the energy efficiency opportunities continue to grow as well. Energy-efficient hardware and other sustainable practices are widely available and should be included as a component of your facility management plan. Use of distributed and cloud-based solutions can reduce your organization's carbon footprint and contribute to your corporate social responsibility strategy.

- *Disaster recovery and business continuity:* As core technology competencies, your facility management plan should include disaster recovery and business continuity protocols in the event of the unexpected. As your association continues to grow, the impact of local service interruptions will need to be minimized as you provide services to an expanding global membership base. For business continuity, the IT infrastructure used at your workplace needs to balance onsite and hosted solutions (including third-party co-located facilities and cloud-based solutions). Critical web-facing solutions should be hosted outside your facility to reduce downtime risk. Redundancy should be implemented for your data backup systems, communication systems, and the Internet access points into your workplace. For communication and Internet access points, consider using two separate vendors operating off of a separate backbone (if available) to avoid construction- and weather-related outages caused by a severed line outside your facility.

With natural disasters or other major business interruptions, for additional continuity purposes provide key personnel with a contingency plan and the required equipment to allow the business to operate on an interim basis from remote locations including their homes or hotel locations outside of the affected area.

Emergency and Safety Considerations

The safety of your employees is one of the most important responsibilities of the CSE, if not the most important. Unfortunately, incidents of workplace violence, hazardous material spills, natural disasters, and other unpredictable events occur far too often and with serious impacts to the health and welfare of employees and the businesses that employ them. Emergency preparedness planning is extremely important to your organization and should be incorporated into your organization's facility planning process. These plans should be reviewed at a minimum of once per year to ensure that proper contacts and procedures are identified and provided to staff correctly in onboarding exercises and ongoing training.

For emergency preparedness planning, the following should be contained within your facility plan:

- Clearly posted emergency response contact numbers and procedures
- Building and facility exit plans with posted diagrams
- Building and workplace contact information
- Evacuation procedures, including emergency assembly points
- Shelter-in-place procedures and locations (in other words, when and where to take immediate shelter inside the building)
- Designated emergency personnel from your staff within the workplace
- System shutoff locations and procedures (alarms, utilities, and so on)
- Emergency equipment locations and procedures (defibrillators, eye wash stations, fire extinguishers, alarms, and so on)

If your association leases your workspace, coordinate your emergency preparedness plan with your building management company. In many cases they will have a template for your organization to use that aligns with the emergency response plan that they have coordinated and filed with first responders.

Consider using a third-party vendor to assist your human resources personnel with developing a workplace violence protocol. As rare as these incidents are, workplace violence is a circumstance you need to be prepared to handle effectively and with minimal impact to the safety of your employees. While shelter-in-place procedures and contacting police and other first responders are part of the process, third-party providers who specialize in preventing incidents and protecting organizations from workplace violence should be consulted to ensure that your procedure is designed effectively for your workplace location.

Effective Implementation of Your Facility Management Plan

As the CSE, you have successfully facilitated your planning process and developed an operating budget with the support of the board. With the budget approved, the implementation of your facility management plan can begin. And it starts with a detailed and well-managed change-management process.

Your change-management process must maintain the integrity of your association's values. If this process is unsuccessful, change will not come easily or effectively. Your change-management process will connect the workplace to your business strategy and provide staff members with the guidance they need to effectively meet the service requirements of their position.

Successful change management is driven by your management team. It is imperative that you include your senior leadership team in the process and that they serve as the mavens for the facility management plan and the resulting workplace policies. As discussed earlier in this chapter, your staff has contributed their vision of an effective workplace early in the planning process. Through the change-management process that voice must become integrated in the operating protocols of your workplace.

As your management team implements changes to the workplace, whether it is a redesigned workspace or the introduction of mobility, engagement with your staff very early in the conversation will be critical to long-term success. Start the process by focusing on the expected outcomes of your facility management plan. Walk the staff through the vision of how the facility serves as a productivity tool and not simply a destination at the end of a commute. Tout the investment that the organization is making in the employees through technology, optimized high-efficiency space, and work-life balance protocols that will allow them to work more effectively. Allow time in meetings for staff to provide their feedback throughout the process so that concerns can be addressed in real time. If staff feels that the facility management plans are being mandated, you will face a longer adaptation curve and you will likely not see the benefits of your workplace design in the short term.

Most important, for the change-management process to be effective, the CSE must walk the talk of the facility management plan and model the way. If the staff is expected to be internally mobile without assigned space, it is critical that the senior executives on staff follow the same protocols and avoid "camping" in a meeting room or other private space. Generate short-term wins to build enthusiasm for the full implementation of the plan by being the first one on staff to try the new meeting room technology or collaboration space.

Performance Evaluation

Effective success measures for your facility management plan will be based on the key performance indicators your association uses for your strategic plan. Areas to consider setting baseline performance on include

- Revenue per employee
- Response time to member inquiries
- Project delivery
- Operating ratios
- Employee and member satisfaction
- Sick time

If you redesign or relocate your facility, consider running a six-month and one-year post-occupancy study. The results of the study will provide strong empirical evidence to the performance of your workplace and insight into which protocols are working and which may be less effective.

In closing, it is the CSE's responsibility to ensure that a functional structure is implemented ensuring long-term viability for your organization. Managing the four success areas of people, process, technology, and place is critical to your organization's ongoing success. Provide your staff with a workplace that supports flexibility, focus, and balance. In turn they will be happier, more productive, and more engaged.

Notes

1. International Facility Management Association (IFMA), *IFMA Global Job Task Analysis* (Houston, TX: Author, 2009).
2. Dale Carnegie & Associates, Inc., *What Drives Employee Engagement and Why IT Matters* (2012). Available at http://www.dalecarnegie.com/assets/1/7/driveengagement_101612_wp.pdf.

The Author

Mike Moss, CAE, is the chief operating officer of the International Facility Management Association (IFMA). He has been managing association operations for over twenty years. A veteran of office relocations and construction of new association facilities, Mike has a solid understanding of the facility's role in the strategic success of an association. As a passionate supporter of lean thinking, he enjoys the daily challenges of meeting member expectations by providing staff with efficient processes, effective technology solutions, and high-performance workplaces.

CHAPTER THIRTY-FOUR

BUILDING EFFECTIVE INDUSTRY SUPPLIER PARTNERSHIPS

Brian Stevens, FASAE, and Gregg Balko, FASAE, CAE

Chief staff executives (CSEs) and senior staff must have positive relationships with the outside organizations, vendors, or suppliers that the association hires. Whether the hired firm performs your annual financial audit, manages your association management system (AMS), or does your conference registration, your association (including its members and customers) will not only succeed but thrive if the relationship between you and your suppliers is healthy, mutually beneficial, and transparent.

All businesses contract for services. In a contract, the hiring party is paying for a service or expertise they either don't have or cannot justify as a full-time salaried expense. Payroll services constitute one example. Most associations have a relationship with a vendor that not only prepares the employee's paychecks but also assures the association that all the required taxes and fees have been applied. As another example, associations often hire a conference registration contractor with the required technology and expertise to register their members and customers. By hiring outside contractors, you contract for services to improve the efficiency of your association, increase member value, or improve your association's bottom line.

Business relationships are partnerships in which everyone benefits. Any contract that is the final piece of a business partnership must be fair.

Each party has responsibilities, and associations must acknowledge that their business partners need to make a profit. There is absolutely nothing wrong with this—after all, associations have the same need.

It sounds simple. However, association executives must recognize the impact of the contracts they sign. Committing the association—and its resources—to a contract has risks. If the relationship does not work, the enforcement of the contract may significantly harm the association. We know of one association that signed a contract with a printer that if fully enforced would have caused the association to go bankrupt. The executive did not fully understand all the terms of the documents and yet signed the contract anyway.

Before the association enters into a business relationship, it must identify the association's needs *in writing*. If you, as the exec, do not completely comprehend the scope of the intended project, ask for assistance from other association executives or even a potential partner. Just because you ask a company to assist in the preparation of a request for proposal (RFP) does not obligate the association to contract with that company.

In doing your homework, the association must be able to identify all possibilities and options. Being realistic does not require any additional text. Knowing what is possible is much harder.

For example, if you are selecting a company to help you produce an app for your trade show, the association needs to identify not only the basic services an app should provide but also what other options are in the marketplace that might offer solutions. Identifying what is possible may not come from your current vendor, for that company may not be able to offer new or additional services or other functionality. The association staff stays on top by becoming informed through regular environmental scanning of market trends and by asking questions of others, comparing the scope of service your app provider is offering against those of other companies.

Another risky area for the association is to simply renew a contract because staff is familiar with the business partner. As associations compete not only with for-profit companies but also other associations, is the service you are contracting a match for the needs of the customers you serve?

The Contract

In discussion with the potential vendors, it is essential that all parties understand the scope of work desired. The association's objectives should be clearly stated in the RFP.

The vendor partner has equal responsibilities. The partner needs to ask important questions, such as

- What are the event-related needs of the association? Can they be documented? (For example, we need 100,000 square feet of exhibit space near a general session for seven thousand people.)
- What are the personal needs of the decision maker? (My contract is up, and I would like to stay at the association for another contract.)
- Do they understand that association business is different from that in the for-profit community?
- What are the business needs of the association? (We have competition from another organization, and we need to give a better overall price and experience than our competition.)

When the contract is received, it must be read—and understood—by either the CSE or the senior staff responsible for the monitoring of the project or contract. If wording is ambiguous, ask for clarification. If the vendor is unfamiliar, ask for and check references. Remember, you are about to commit the association's name and the association's resources. Be as confident as possible this is a good decision.

One topic that is hard to quantify in this process is your or your senior team's relationship with the potential business partner. How forthright is the partner in answering your questions? Are their responses handled in a timely manner? Does it feel like a good match? As in any relationship, if you do not feel comfortable with the partner, it is prudent to walk away.

Key Items for Any Contract

- Name and address of both parties
- Length of contract
- Purpose or objectives (scope of work)
- Duties of each party
- Key dates
- Prices or fees
- Terms of payment
- Dates for payment
- Limitations
- Change of ownership
- Financial stability (if the vendor files for Chapter 10 or 11)
- Termination
- Arbitration clause
- Authorized signatures

Developing the Business Relationship

In any partnership, mutual respect is essential. With respect comes expectations. Are the staff assigned to the project competent and knowledgeable enough to participate in a meaningful way? By staff, we mean staff from either of the contracting parties. Since associations may not be introduced to the vendor's staff tasked with completing the contract, it is vital to assess the association's confidence with the vendor's team. Again, if there is any hesitation at all, talk to the partner's senior manager or sales manager about the reservations the association is having. You cannot develop trust if either party to the contract is uncomfortable with the other.

Then there is the "entitled staff person." We all know an association professional staff member who views the outside agency or vendor as a subordinate. This could not be farther from reality—we work together for a mutual benefit.

Let's look at this from another perspective. If you think the hotel selected for your annual meeting only wants to take advantage of you, think again. Not only does the hotel want you, your members, and your customers to have a great experience, they want you to rebook. It's a partnership.

Companies that do business with you elect to do so. In evaluating a potential business opportunity with an association, an association with a reputation for being a fair and good partner is always attractive.

If you, as CSE, think the hotel or show decorator is trying to nickel-and-dime you (or your staff), then learn how your vendor or partner makes money. For example, let's consider the exhibit service contractor or show decorator. If your association wants free registration counters, a deeply discounted exhibit hall entrance unit, and a discount on show management freight, where is the show contractor making profit to pay for those things you want for free? As a partner, know (by asking) what is reasonable and what is not.

The most critical component to any relationship is trust. Do all the parties of the business partnership trust each other?

Monitoring the Business Relationship

While it may sound trite, success in business depends on honest and open communication between the two parties. It can also help to eliminate or diffuse potential problems. Both parties to a contract have the same end goal:

to benefit themselves and each other. To accomplish that, being candid is a requirement.

Mistakes will be made. They happen in any type of relationship. As CSE, you must dig deep to discover the root of the problem. Is the work being produced in line with the scope of work described in the contract? Have expectations by either party changed?

It may be that your staff members are unable to admit they caused the problem. There was a scenario in which one hotel was not being considered for a future meeting. After asking why, the CSE was told it was because the last time the association met at that facility, the hotel changed all their meeting rooms on the last day and did not tell the association. Upon further inquiry, it was discovered the error was not the hotel's.

Mistakes can be corrected and relationships rebuilt. Realistic expectations are the foundation of any successful long-term relationship. Look at the people in your personal life with whom you are closest. You know each other. You can anticipate your best friend's behavior. Does the problem situation seem plausible that it was just caused by the vendor party?

A relationship is give and take by both parties. As CSE, you are the final decision maker to determine whether the business practices and attitudes exhibited by your association staff produce good and healthy relationships.

Not all relationships work. If you (or your staff) feel the association is "owed something" just because you are the customer, don't expect healthy relationships with your business partners. Similarly, if you find your business partners do not approach your business as a relationship, it is time to change business partners.

As in any relationship, a sense of humor can be a terrific asset. While the disappointment or frustration is real, failure to deliver is often more annoying than life threatening. Being able to maintain a cordial relationship with your business partners who may not be meeting the association's expectations is an asset. Adding appropriate humor often helps to relieve the tension the failed business transaction has created. Further, since this is a very small community, you never know when you might cross paths with that person again. Walking away from a partnership with heads held high serves each party well.

What If a Business Relationship Is Not Working?

Be honest in your appraisal of what is working and what is not.

- Did the association conduct proper due diligence in hiring the business partner?

- Was the association's staff sufficiently trained to work with the partner?
- Were the expectations realistic?
- Did the business partner bring definable value to the relationship, or not?
- Was the relationship undermined by a staff member to his or her own benefit?
- Did the parties clearly define each other's scope of work and responsibilities?

As you monitor the business relationship, is the resulting work what was expected? Was the project delivered within a reasonable time as noted in the contract? If not, why weren't the association's expectations met? Who is to blame for the missed deadlines?

How do you find out what is going on? Talk to your staff managers about how things are going with this registration company, investment firm, or hotel. Ask questions. When you have the chance to directly interact with the business partner, ask the business partner the same questions. You might be surprised by their candor.

When Association Members Interact with Your Business Partners

If your association uses members to work with your business partners, your job is significantly harder. Volunteer members must share your vision of business relationships when they interact with the partners with whom you do business. This does not come automatically, nor does it come easily, because volunteers are not generally professional association managers.

Monitoring volunteer activity is a challenge. The well-intentioned member is not your direct report. When volunteers are engaged with your business partners, you must have open and honest relationships with your vendors. Ask the vendors how things are going. Encourage them to be honest with you. If a volunteer or member is out of line, you have to know. It is your responsibility to protect the vendor and address the issue with the member as tactfully and directly as possible.

This goes both ways. If the business partner is trying to take advantage of the volunteer or member, there must be a discussion with the business partner.

The Ethics of a Business Relationship

The hospitality industry is an attractive business. You know the life: free drinks, delicious gourmet dinners, free or upgraded hotel suites with corner ocean views, limos waiting for you at the airport.

You and your staff must make decisions (particularly hotel and venue decisions) that are sound business decisions. They must be for the betterment of the community you serve. They must be defendable. They must be transparent. Association executives and their staffs cannot create the impression that one individual is benefiting more than others.

If a hotel offers meeting planner points in their contract, it may not serve your members and customers to accept it. Hotel (and credit card) points are a particularly vexing issue. Can you explain to an auditor or to your incoming president why the points earned at your last board meeting are in your personal hotel account? Association staffs book business on behalf of the communities they represent. We do not "own" our associations, nor do we "own" the business (and the points that business generates). Personal gain is not transparent, and it does not create trust.

The literature on how unethical it is for a meeting planner to take a familiarization (FAM) trip to a destination the association will never book is well documented. Are there other ethical issues in your business relationships?

In the sales phase, does the salesperson play up to the CSE because the CSE signs the contract, when the real partnership needs to be with the planner or some other person on the association team? While it is imperative the CSE have a relationship with the salesperson and the company he or she represents, the salesperson must also develop a working relationship with the key staff member from the association.

Are perks being offered that seem wrong? Or, are you aware of the perks your staff is being offered?

As the CSE, you lead the way to establishing and codifying the standard for ethical business practices for the association. This demonstrates not only to the staff but also to your volunteer leadership that your association values ethical business. In doing so, your business partners will likely reciprocate that behavior. If they do not reciprocate, do you really want to do business with them?

Another ethical consideration is the balance of a short-term against a long-term consideration of a business decision. If either side benefits in the short term, what are the implications in the long term? As CSE, your responsibility is to leave your association in a positive position for the future good of the members.

If the core value of doing the right thing is not a sufficient motivator, remember this. The association community is a small community. People talk. Do you want all of your professional staff reputations clouded by poor ethical decisions?

Transparency Is Required

There are too many stories about CSEs, staff members, and volunteers who abuse the hospitality community.

For example, one morning during the planning of the meeting, the CSE saw a letter on the office fax machine from the hotel selected to host the association's meeting. The contract for that meeting at the hotel had already been signed. The letter was addressed to the president [chief elected officer]; the copy on the fax machine was the "cc" to the meeting planner on staff. The letter confirmed an "ocean view suite for a week for the president 'comped' for his selection of the hotel for the group's meeting."

When this matter was brought to the attention of the president of the association, he responded by saying this is a common practice in the industry.

In your contracts, is everything transparent? Would you be comfortable showing those contracts to any member of your board? Are there hidden commissions? What is the association's policy on hotel points? Is there any part of the contact that makes you wince when you read it?

If any part of your business contracts makes you even a bit nervous, something is wrong. Doing business fairly and ethically is a standard to which we aspire. The ASAE Standards of Conduct for CAEs states that we must

- Maintain exemplary standards of professional conduct
- Actively model and encourage the integration of ethics into all aspects of management of the association which employs me

In addition, to fulfill the goal of being transparent, know your association policy on how often it bids out its contracts. We do not suggest they be re-bid every year. That is a waste of your staff's time as well as the time of your vendor partners. However, having a policy to systematically re-bid contracts demonstrates to your association leadership that your staff team is continually checking to see if your members and customers are being offered the best value, service, or product.

Other Issues with Vendor Contracts: The Devil Is in the Detail

In your contracts, what are the key terms you as CSE need to be aware of? Certainly, the deliverables are obvious. But beware of unrealistic time frames. For example: If you hire a firm to do a member survey and you know your association officers want to review the questions prior to the survey's release, have you allowed sufficient time to develop the questions, review them, distribute the survey, and compile the results?

Think of it this way: Have you had contractors work on your residence? Has any project ever been completed on time and on budget? Our business relationships need to include the same "allowances" we provide the people who paint our house or install our lawn sprinklers.

If the terms of the contract change, get the changes *in writing*. It sounds so simple, but too often, changes do not get written down. Ask your staff, if we change the contract, does it affect other parts of the contract, such as payment terms? Has your business partner also agreed to the proposed changes? A contract is not enforceable unless both parties agree—*in writing*. An abundance of courtroom television shows are all about two parties who do not agree on contract terms.

Current Trends: Are You Getting the Best the Industry Offers?

In addition to these other responsibilities, as a CSE, you must be confident your association is partnering with the businesses that are not only the best fit or the best value, but also one that provides the best service to the association and its members or consumers of a product or attendees at your events.

Earlier in this chapter we talked about the importance of staff members doing their homework. With so many technological changes, which of the new technologies or programs is the best fit for your customers—and your bandwidth? And is your staff on top of those trends?

What are the current trends in what a vendor and his or her competitors offer? Is this business partner an industry leader or just a business partner your staff knows and has a comfortable working relationship with? This is difficult, because you need to know if your staff is current with trends in that business segment.

Acknowledging Your Business Partners

Just as you acknowledge your staff members for their good work, it is recommended business practice to express your gratitude both verbally and with a written thank you to the business partners who help your association succeed. After all, it is a relationship, and showing appreciation is a component of that relationship.

Summary

A successful business relationship is not difficult. It has to be a good, sound business deal for both parties. Neither group should have the upper hand. If the balance of scales is tipped, the relationship is not healthy. Next, the association must have staff knowledgeable of the trends in the industry the business partner is servicing. Although clichéd, "Let the buyer beware" is fundamentally sound. Then there's the question, "Is it ethical?" Can you share or describe your business relationship to your board of directors and feel good about it? Last, what's in the contract? Are the terms clear? Are the expected deliverables appropriate and realistic?

As CSE, your personal integrity is at risk if the business you or your staff conducts does not meet a high standard of ethics. As a leader, doing business in a fair and ethical manner will not only serve all the partners in the transaction well but also the membership and customers you represent.

The Authors

Brian Stevens, FASAE, is the president and CEO of meetings services company ConferenceDirect, Los Angeles.

Gregg Balko, FASAE, CAE, is the chief executive officer of the Society for the Advancement of Material and Process Engineers, a global membership society based in Greater Los Angeles.

CHAPTER THIRTY-FIVE

KNOWLEDGE MANAGEMENT

Richard V. Lawson and Robert C. Nedbal

Knowledge is at the very core of an association's value to its stakeholders. Consider, for example, the power of a knowledge-sharing program in the health care profession. The program might connect highly skilled nurses to individuals wanting to enter the field. They form mentor-protégé relationships in which guidance and sharing of real-world know-how is provided against defined learning objectives. The program could be measured on the successful completion rate and its impact on shortening the learning curve of the protégés. This might lead to a shortened time frame for earning a credential and increasing the throughput of qualified talent entering a field with recognized job growth opportunities. In this example, knowledge is a focal point around which members share information, collaborate, and become smarter and more skilled as professionals. There are opportunities as well in the case of trade associations in which know-how is shared among companies or other organizations.

From the perspective of association leadership and staff, knowledge is a critical factor in maintaining organizational relevance to all stakeholders. It is central to the successful delivery of products and services that members value. It can strengthen an organization's relationships with key partners. Knowledge sharing and knowledge management (KM) can also enhance the human resource capacities of an association. All of this to say that knowledge is a key source of competitive advantage, and in an increasingly disruptive and competitive environment, is of strategic importance in distinguishing those associations that falter, sustain, or thrive.

In practical terms, nonprofit organizations differ only in nuance from any other enterprise that excels by making smart strategic business decisions, leveraging historical experience in the context of salient market information. To be successful, every enterprise must be agile in its synthesis of information into knowledge to inform and enable innovation to strengthen its relationship with customers. In the case of nonprofit organizations, leveraging KM to improve operational performance is valuable. However, consider the impact of leveraging communities of practice or intellectual property to positively affect the advancement of the organization's purpose, be it social, scientific, philanthropic, or otherwise—this will likely be the greatest positive outcome you may realize.

What Exactly Is Knowledge?

Let's start with the basics. A simplified evolution to knowledge begins with data. Data become information when we notice patterns and trends within and attach meaning to what we see. The more information-rich a process is (with information from multiple sources confirming the same patterns), the more context it provides. Knowledge is information in context to produce an *actionable* understanding.

Keep in mind the distinction between "information" and "knowledge." Knowledge requires human interaction. *Merriam Webster's Dictionary* defines the terms as follows:

- *Information:* Facts provided or learned about something or someone
- *Knowledge:* Facts, information, and skills acquired by a person through experience or education; the theoretical or practical understanding of a subject

Distinctions should also be made among various *types* of knowledge. In general, knowledge is a result of human capacity applying information, experience, and intuition in context to solve a problem or create value in some fashion. Information and knowledge transfer are inputs to the creation of new knowledge in a given context or decision-making process.

Documented processes and procedures are a form of *explicit* knowledge and are relatively easy to store and retrieve. While they are necessary and important, they are not usually the highest-value opportunities in a knowledge management effort.

Implicit knowledge is known, but not documented. An example of implicit knowledge might be the procedures that a seasoned employee follows to complete a task more quickly. Those procedures are known by the employee but not documented so that others might learn from that efficiency. Implicit knowledge is fairly easy to document, but might require an intentional scan of what people habitually do that produces a desirable result and recognition that there is no accessible documentation or training on those procedures. Moving implicit knowledge to explicit is an effective way to grow operational knowledge in an organization.

Tacit knowledge or expertise is not readily documented and turned into information for many reasons. Tacit knowledge evolves with experience and becomes something "we just know." For example, how is it that some people are more effective teachers than others? The effective ones "just know" how to relate to various groups and adapt their presentations on the basis of the audience that is before them. When asked, those teachers are hard-pressed to define how they learned to be so effective because it evolved from experience. The wisdom of experience is embedded in our thought processes.

What Exactly Is Knowledge Management?

Intuitively, knowledge management is something that all of us do. We all use knowledge management systems, whether that knowledge simply resides in our brains, in a paper filing system, in a complex software system, or in the context of today's hyperconnected world—perhaps across social media networks.

As a side note, as the Internet continues to evolve into the "Internet of Things," social media at their core are about connecting people in various contexts without the constraints of space or time. The essence of this is more important than the phrase "social media."

KM happens continuously throughout our everyday lives. What makes this a meaningful topic is that the ultimate driver for your association remains the same: "How do you create a culture that values knowledge sharing and creates, acquires, and transfers knowledge effectively for the benefit of your stakeholders, and depending on the scope of your mission, potentially society at large?"

There are numerous definitions that vary with respect to the scope entailed in KM efforts. The Gartner Group created a definition that is both broad and deep in scope:

> Knowledge management is a discipline that promotes an integrated approach to identifying, capturing, evaluating, retrieving, and sharing all of an enterprise's information assets. These assets may include databases, documents, policies, procedures, and previously un-captured expertise and experience in individual workers.[1]

This is a comprehensive description offering a great deal of process and procedure to evaluate. Alternatively, if an organization considers what is essential, a more contemporary definition of knowledge management is "delivering the right information to the right people at the right time."

Borrowing a quote from Stephen Denning, a *Forbes Magazine* contributor, author, and consultant on leadership, innovation, and radical management who previously spearheaded the KM efforts of the World Bank:

> Overall, whatever the term employed to describe it, knowledge management is increasingly seen, not merely as the latest management fashion, but as signaling the development of a more organic and holistic way of understanding and exploiting the role of knowledge in the processes of managing and doing work, and an authentic guide for individuals and organizations in coping with the increasingly complex and shifting environment of the modern economy.[2]

KM has three primary elements:

- An organization must introduce values, practices, processes, and tools to identify know-how, expertise, and other intellectual capital for reuse in the organization.
- Success is measured by how well these activities contribute institutional learning and improved outcomes.
- The key outcome of KM is knowledge transfer and resulting decisions and actions contributing to advancement for the organization or its stakeholders.

How do you develop an organizational culture to enable knowledge sharing and delivery? For success, your organization must be committed to becoming a *learning organization*. The concept was inspired by Peter

M. Senge's book *The Fifth Discipline* and a variety of other sources in the mid-1990s.[3] An organization's culture is central to the success of achieving the outcomes desired from KM.

A learning organization is one that is skilled at creating, acquiring, and transferring knowledge, and at modifying its behavior to reflect new knowledge and insights.

The players in a learning organization master

- Systematic problem solving
- Experimentation
- Learning from past experience
- Learning from others
- Transferring knowledge

A learning organization incorporates an iterative approach that embraces short cycles of "do, learn, pivot." The concept of a pivot means "a change in strategy without a change in vision,"[4] when the decision to change the strategy comes from real-time learning that indicates the current strategy is not working. It supports the notion of empowering your team(s) to take risks and experience small failures, learn, adapt, and continue the process sharing successes along the way. Your association will experience progress, while minimizing the financial and organizational impact of failures. In the following example, all three types of knowledge are used in a virtual, collaborative environment to create new knowledge and standards for the association.

Scrum Alliance is a global certification and membership organization with the mission to promote widespread adoption and effective practice of Scrum to transform the world of work through increased employee engagement and improved business results. The organization seeks to fulfill its mission through advocacy, community, and education. Scrum is the most widely adopted Agile framework used for product development in software and non-software settings, with over three hundred thousand members worldwide.

The Scrum Alliance education staff works with member volunteers to establish learning objective committees (LOCs). The volunteers are subject-matter experts in the training and coaching of individuals, teams, and organizations on adopting and embedding scrum within their culture. The LOCs collaborate with staff to establish learning objectives (LOs) for approved training programs and tests. Through iterative discussion, draft materials, and considerable debate, the collective expertise (explicit, implicit, and tacit knowledge) of the LOCs and staff result in reviewed and accepted learning objectives. These LOs set the expected outcomes which "Certified Scrum Trainers" and "Registered Education Providers" are to achieve in training their students. The work product of this knowledge sharing and collaboration forms the foundation for large groups of individuals to be trained on the values, roles, practices, and guidelines of this agile framework.

The tools used to complete this important work include online collaboration tools for virtual meetings and screen sharing, standard Microsoft Office documentation and phone calls. Not fancy or expensive, but the knowledge sharing creates significant value. The important takeaways from a KM program perspective include

- The culture of collaboration
- A clear goal (effective learning objectives for global use) that support expected outcomes of the cross-functional team of staff and volunteers
- New knowledge becoming embedded in the education program through the organization's website and in policy and procedure documents within the education function

Financial Considerations

For associations that consider taking a more comprehensive systems approach and think technology investment might be the bulk of the financial commitment because a new "system is required," consider this advice from Steve Denning:

> The provision of financial resources for sharing knowledge is often an unambiguous signal to staff that the organization has definitely decided to incorporate knowledge sharing into the way the organization functions. Funding will be needed to cover the incremental costs of the coordinating function, the technology, the communities [of practice] and [support]. The main focus of the financial provisioning should be on support to operations. [As a rule of thumb], if more than 20% of the resources are being spent on technology, a review may be warranted as to whether knowledge sharing has become confused with information management.[5]

Leadership Considerations

Motivations that often lead organizations to KM include the desire to

- Gain competitive advantage by creating new relevance for members
- Promote greater innovation
- Provide better member experiences
- Maintain consistency in best practices
- Provide knowledge access for global organizations
- Create a network effect between employees to increase the quality of shared information
- Facilitate organizational learning
- Manage intellectual capital

It is crucial that the CSE signal to staff the organization's commitment to knowledge management and establish a vision for the organization and sustain it throughout the transformation. A clear vision will reflect the benefits to the organization and stakeholders.

To be successful in this cultural shift, the CSE must

- Lead by example and embrace a culture of learning.
- Establish sound priorities with respect to investment as noted earlier, using checks and balances to ensure you reinforce valuing individuals and interactions over processes and tools.
- Explore and describe the possible tangible benefits to stakeholders and the organization.
- Work with staff to organize strategic priorities of knowledge collection and empower them to make decisions according to those priorities. Should it be an internal initiative focused on knowledge for staff and volunteers? Or should effort be focused on knowledge that members need to grow professionally and in their agility to respond effectively in new situations?

How could your organization enable opportunities for sharing knowledge or expertise to enrich the decision-making process, power the learning organization, and create greater relevance and value for your members? Your KM culture might include new forms of member engagement such as self-organizing "communities of practice" to discuss solutions for professional challenges. Maybe you develop a concise body of knowledge for the field that includes a self-assessment for career progression. Maybe you launch a mentoring program coupling a seasoned professional with a young rookie with documented lessons learned. Consider integrating your print and digital publications, credentialing, and education efforts as key pieces of the KM puzzle.

As alluded to earlier, the knowledge economy continues to evolve rapidly. One fascinating area is the proliferation of social networks. Many capable collaboration and social networking tools are available today along with a growing base of individuals adopting and realizing their potential. Associations must leverage these opportunities, demonstrating leadership and commitment to further develop their membership networks to enrich knowledge sharing for new ideas and new value creation.

KM Principles and Process

Once a vision is established, the next step is to decide what knowledge is mission critical and how the organization can gain a quantifiable benefit from its reuse.

Here is a mission-critical example: evaluate the impacts on a major, long-term public service campaign due to an unexpected change in capital reserve requirements. By connecting expense data from the financial system with campaign performance data from an enterprise marketing system in month over month and year over year comparisons, the CSE is able to make better decisions about funding to the campaign.

Here is a non-mission-critical example: a cross-functional staff team evaluates call center records to identify opportunities to answer member questions in a more timely fashion. The result is the creation of a call center FAQ developed by various program staff throughout the organization. This simple example might save time for staff and members, improve performance for the call center, and improve member perception of the association.

Aligning KM assets typically involves an analysis of existing knowledge repositories—this might include scholarly journals, financial systems, meeting content—and the creation of new knowledge-generating activities. Priorities need to be assigned and measured against organizational goals. For example, knowledge existing in paper form will need to be analyzed to determine the need and associated cost with digitizing it and potentially integrating it with other electronic assets. Once knowledge assets have been identified and prioritized, management can begin to assess what form a KM system might take.

◆ ◆ ◆

Human Resource Considerations for a Knowledge Management Initiative

In developing a knowledge management discipline and the supporting systems, an important consideration is whether or not the implementation should be undertaken solely by staff. Obviously there is a lot at stake, and nonprofit organizations vary considerably in size, structure, staff expertise, and resources. In most cases, it's probably wise to engage a consultant specializing in knowledge management and social networking to assist in the strategic and tactical discovery and decision-making steps. Many of the interfacing areas could require special expertise, so you might need a consultant well versed in taxonomy, for example, to assist with the very rigorous exercise of developing your KM architecture.

Another example of highly specialized knowledge that resides outside most associations is search functionality expertise. The necessity for a capable search function across your various information stores and social networks is crucial. This will be covered later in this chapter.

While you will likely rely on outside expertise for some of the elements of knowledge management system development, many tasks can be done by staff and typically will reduce out-of-pocket cost. For instance, it's always a good idea to appoint a dedicated project manager on staff to interface with the consultant and drive major milestones and deliverables. Also consider enabling staff to self-form into teams that can discuss and identify possible solutions for the challenges they have that KM could resolve. Staff insights would also be well suited to identify opportunities for integration across systems to allow seamless access to related information living in different places. They are the best resources for determining opportunities within a given context, for example, improving access to information to enhance member services support. A final example would be staff functioning as liaisons to volunteers to explain the intent of the effort if it includes them as project resources or beneficiaries of the work.

A commitment to knowledge management requires ongoing planning, development, and maintenance. To facilitate the capture and reuse of knowledge assets, many larger organizations now have a knowledge management office and even a chief knowledge officer. The purpose is to have the individual(s) function as stewards and champions of the process, not as prescriptive staff managers. Their stewardship aids in maintaining a high commitment level to the practice of KM throughout the organization, and their role contributes to the competitive advantage as a learning organization. It is doubtful that many smaller associations have sufficient resources to dedicate solely to the practice of KM. Often, however, identifying a staff person with the appropriate skill set and experience to function in a facilitator role can contribute to successful KM initiatives. For example, in the learning objectives scenario early in the chapter, a KM facilitator could share the experience and artifacts of success with other teams, he or she could monitor, report on, and evaluate the overall program; develop good or best practices specific to the organization's culture; and act as a KM subject-matter expert with staff and volunteers working on a project expected to produce valuable knowledge for the organization.

While you are likely to rely on outside expertise at least in the initial development of a KM system, it is important to understand the principles and the process. At a high level, keeping your organization focused on the vision is foremost in importance. Consider this: in an IBM study of seventeen hundred CEOs from eighteen industries, "encouraging employee collaboration to mobilize the organization's collective brainpower" and "responding to customers with greater relevance and immediacy" were two of the top issues.[6] As an association executive, you can no doubt relate. For example, in the case of a professional membership association, good knowledge management and knowledge sharing can positively affect both the volume and quality of knowledge that is shared among members focused on having the most contemporary knowledge about their field. Likewise, effective knowledge management could enable the association to identify gaps in knowledge and provide new services to members to fill those gaps.

First, and foremost, keep in mind that, as noted by Steve Denning,

> One of the major risks in knowledge management programs is the tendency for organizations to confuse knowledge management with some form of technology, whether it be a [knowledge management system, document management system, or a web-based solution of some sort]. In the process, the essentially ecological concept of knowledge management becomes degraded into a simple information system that can be engineered without affecting the way the work is done. It is not that information systems are bad. Rather, it is important to recognize that knowledge management is a different and better way of working which affects people, and requires social arrangements like communities to enable it to happen on any consistent and sustained basis.[7]

At the process level, developing a knowledge management program begins with a discovery phase in which you and your team will look for answers to the following questions:

- Does your existing organizational culture support the concepts of the "learning organization"? A common hurdle is stove-piped organizations, in which departments feel compelled for whatever reason to retain the knowledge amongst themselves as a form of power. To effectively change the culture, these issues must be addressed. Who are key people suited to work with cross-functional teams to reinforce the values and principles of knowledge management?
- How can the relevant groups of people develop and agree to social arrangements or contracts that describe new ways of working together?
- What are the paper-based knowledge sources? This includes sources such as archives of journals and other publications that are considered relevant to the current market. It could also be meeting minutes, election results, financial statements, or any myriad of historical information.
- What are the electronic-based knowledge sources? Website content is obvious. How about other electronic applications such as financial systems, journal manuscript and submitted paper systems, user-generated content such as posts on association discussion forums, and membership directories? Also, consider evolving technologies that rapidly become knowledge repositories on their own, such as social networks, podcast archives, Wikis, and intra-society information networks.
- How will knowledge be reused, and how will knowledge transfer be facilitated? The answers to these are related to the size and scope of the effort and the focus of your program—are you focused internally between staff or reaching outward to engage volunteers and members?
- What are the technology requirements and costs? Keep in mind that this is not a technology-driven program. Technology enables the program but does not drive it; otherwise, you are dealing in the information management realm, not knowledge management.
- What technological improvements need to be made to enable knowledge sharing? Is there a taxonomy or key word system in place that can help organize and describe the knowledge assets? This is like creating your own Dewey Decimal System, as found in libraries. Taxonomy is simply a hierarchical classification system that defines an organization's information, disciplines, and activities that it undertakes as part of its routine business. In a geoscience association example, a taxonomy key word might be *tectonic*. The use of this key word in the taxonomy would identify tectonic-related content in disparate systems. The search functionality could then utilize that key word to structure the search results. For example, a result from a professional journal entry and another

from a community of practice entry could be displayed in a meaningful and usable fashion for the individual searching on the term. Without an understanding of the knowledge assets and how they can be organized and classified, information chaos ensues.

KM Repositories and Retrieval

Once your knowledge management environment is established, search technologies may become just as important as the knowledge repositories themselves. They are important tools for knowledge use, as anyone using Google search today can attest.

Knowledge management enablers, or repositories, come in some familiar names. Organizations leverage expert systems, knowledge bases, help desk tools, and document management software to organize and distribute knowledge. More recently, these enablers have increased in number to include such evolving technologies as e-learning, web conferencing, collaboration, content management, directories, Wikis, social media, and blogs. Implicit to all the systems is an enterprise search and, oftentimes, a portal application that ties in the search and various knowledge sources into an easy-to-use interface. Managing the proliferation of data and information sources in increasingly complex environments and still allowing your members and staff efficient and intuitive access, remains KM's most challenging call.

The most typical reuse of knowledge is top-down. For example, staff or volunteer leaders working on a business objective could evaluate knowledge assets to make their effort more efficient and productive. Using search information or information portals, users like these search across knowledge assets to access and retrieve relevant information. There are evolving efforts to make the collection and distribution of knowledge more organic, using a bottom-up approach, but in practice one typically finds the top-down strategy far more common. This is the classic debate between pushing information and pulling it.

Conclusion

Ultimately, the challenge for most of our organizations will be two-fold. First, inspiring the collaborative, learning organization culture. Second, connecting our disparate systems in strategically meaningful ways and developing a knowledge repository that serves the staff, leadership, and membership effectively. To achieve this, the CSE must inspire the team and marshal the financial resources to undertake and then make successful the KM practice. In most cases, the wiser course is to take smaller iterative steps as describe earlier, keeping your people top-of-mind and instilling the values of knowledge sharing, rather than viewing it from a purely systems and IT perspective. Knowledge management and knowledge sharing are about people. Remember the distinction between information and knowledge. Knowledge requires human interaction.

Maximize your return on investment by leveraging KM in areas where the outcomes are measurable. Look to activities centered around your members and your member services. Executives should look to sources of information that exist and to places where members are already using electronic tools to facilitate the creation of content within their disciplines. Look to e-learning and your website, web conferences, and collaboration. Extend existing information systems in logical ways to enrich content. For example, most all nonprofit organizations have membership directories. Such directories can become valuable sources of knowledge if the members are allowed to enhance their listings beyond the usual point-of-contact information. This is the place to start when evaluating your organization's social network. Association management system vendors are beginning to incorporate social functionality into their products. Examine them for viability depending on your priorities. Also, evaluate where your members are gathering on public social networks. There are search software products that enable you to leverage these external sources and incorporate them into your internal knowledge repository.

Most important, look for the low-hanging fruit aligned with your priorities. Identify existing, valuable electronic assets, then develop approaches to organize the information, and deploy. Simple search technologies remain the quickest and most cost-effective approaches to reaping the rewards of information collection and reuse.

In summary, knowledge management is a constantly evolving discipline centered on people and their social agreements to leverage know-how, in the case of association work—in support of its mission and to the benefit of its stakeholders. From its strictest definition, there's value to be gained from capturing, storing, and repurposing knowledge to make more agile, strategic changes to your products and services. Big KM solutions don't easily fit into the nonprofit world, and the organizational overhead of maintaining them is burdensome. Smart, agile association executives will understand the basic premise of KM and the impact it can have in creating a learning organization as an enabler of higher performance and innovation. As is true with most things, targeted, limited scope implementations have the greatest chance of success and reap the maximum return on investment. Understand the sources of knowledge within your organization and, more important, how to access and leverage them. Last, don't underestimate the cultural and technology barriers to enhancing organizational learning and do so only with clear objectives and strategies.

Notes

1. B. Duhon, "It's All in Our Heads," *Inform* 12, no. 8 (September 1998): 8–13.
2. http://www.stevedenning.com/Knowledge-Management/default.aspx.
3. P. M. Senge, *The Fifth Discipline: The Art and Practice of the Learning Organization,* 2nd ed. (New York: Doubleday/Currency, 2006).
4. "Do, learn, pivot" is a concept drawn from E. Ries, *The Lean Startup: How Today's Entrepreneurs Use Continuous Innovation to Create Radically Successful Businesses* (New York: Crown Business, 2011).
5. http://www.stevedenning.com/Knowledge-Management/what-is-knowledge-management.aspx.
6. Coveo, "Driving Radically Better Returns on Collective Enterprise Knowledge in a Big Data World." Available at http://coveosc.coveo.com/~/media/Files/WhitePapers/Part%201%20-%20Why%20Knowledge%20is%20Becoming%20a%20C-Level%20Discussion.ashx.
7. http://www.stevedenning.com/Knowledge-Management/what-is-knowledge-management.aspx.

The Authors

Richard V. Lawson is the executive director of the Marine Technology Society in Washington, D.C. Prior to this position he directed the American Association of Pharmaceutical Scientists Internet and career services strategies. Lawson has also previously served as a technology strategist and consultant in the for-profit and government sectors.

Robert C. Nedbal is the director of operations for Scrum Alliance in the Greater Denver Metro area. Prior to this, he served as the director of information technology at both CFP Board and the American Educational Research Association, in Washington, D.C. Before entering the nonprofit sector he established a successful technology consulting practice for Sytel, Inc., in Bethesda, Maryland, that served federal government and nonprofit clients.

CHAPTER THIRTY-SIX

RESEARCH AND EVALUATION

Marc Beebe, CAE, and Elena Gerstmann, PhD, FASAE, CAE

In the words of Sherlock Holmes, "Data! Data! Data! I can't make bricks without clay!" There are some situations that gut instincts are wise not to ignore (watch out for the tiger behind you), but in most other situations, the quizzical and questioning mind should be fed with data, knowledge, and information. *Research* is a broad term used for any gathering of information. It ranges from a quick web search on tomorrow's weather to conducting a multistaged research project with focus groups and questionnaires with two thousand members. Yes, the first one is quick and free and the latter takes time and some money, but both are research and both allow the "learner" to make a better decision.

It isn't surprising that scholarly research shows that businesses that rely on research to make data-driven decisions are more successful than businesses that do not. This point is underscored in literature specific to our field. One of the five criteria of a great association identified in *7 Measures of Success: What Remarkable Associations Do That Others Don't* is "data-driven strategies."[1] This is true of all sizes of associations, regardless of membership, revenue, or staff size.

For associations to be strong and sustainable organizations, leaders must either (1) understand how to read, interpret, and implement research findings or, at minimum, (2) appreciate the value of research and rely on teammates or partners to bring the power of data to their association. It is critical to respect research enough to know that research isn't done for the sake of doing research. It is done to make decisions and have an impact on decision making. The link between research and association strategy must be solid and significant.

External versus Internal Research

Although overly simplistic, one can separate association research into two categories. One is external, which focuses on the industry that the association serves. The second is internal, which focuses on how the association serves its community. Examples of external research include salary surveys, trend analysis of future job growth, and guidelines for regulatory agencies. Examples of internal research include membership satisfaction, needs assessment, and conference evaluations.

Most associations house the functions of external and internal research in the same team (or individual) because the skill set is similar, but some larger associations may divide the two. Regardless of where these functions are placed, both are important. The creation and distribution of external research typically serves a mission of the association while producing member value or extra revenue. Conducting internal research allows the association to make data-driven decisions in its pursuit of continuous improvement, financial stability, and member and customer engagement and satisfaction.

Setting the Research Agenda

You could choose to research many questions, so how do you decide? You can deal with each potential research question as it comes up, but a more effective approach is to develop a research agenda that outlines what projects you will undertake on a longer-term basis. One logical way to develop such an agenda is to base it on the strategic goals and priorities as set by your association's leadership. In addition, some research may need to be conducted on a regular basis. For example, you may want to conduct a general member satisfaction survey every year, a survey of nonrenewing members every two years, a general needs assessment every three years, and a broader member segmentation survey every four years.

Specific Types of Research Projects

Benchmarking

A benchmarking project allows you to compare one set of data to another set. The comparison set is typically a data set collected by someone else that depicts best practices or industry norms, or it could be a data set that you have previously collected. One recent example is a set of benchmarking studies that were part of the ASAE "Decision to ... " series. The resultant books provided information from tens of thousands of association members on issues related to belonging to a membership organization and deciding whether to give, volunteer, and learn. While the books summarizing the research provided a general norm, individual associations could conduct their own research project using the same questions and then compare (that is, benchmark) themselves to the results in the book that represented the general norm.

Comparison data are available from numerous sources, including sister associations; national polls (such as Pew Research Center, Conference Board); and research projects conducted by academia, government agencies, and vendors that focus on associations.

At times it may be important to compare yourself to another point of time within your own organization. For example, if you plan to roll out a series of new membership offerings, you may want to conduct a specific survey on how your members view your offerings, including general satisfaction questions. This first study is usually called the "baseline" study, which captures a specific point in time before an action is taken that allows you to then "benchmark" future studies to these baseline results. Once you roll out your new program, you will want to use the same set of questions and query your membership again. Did the change in your membership offerings increase or decrease satisfaction or have no impact? Your research study will give you this answer.

Predictive Data Analysis

If you looked at your databases from five years ago, do you think you could use the information you have about your members to "predict" who stayed and who did not renew? On the basis of our previous research and research conducted by ASAE, the odds are you will discover that those individuals who were more active (for example, buying products, attending a conference, and so on) were more likely to stay members. However, what are the specifics for *your* association? Are some events, products, or services "stickier" than others? If yes, what can you do to leverage this sticky strength? If you identify some offerings that are weaker, should you consider reallocating resources from these? This type of analysis is not restricted to the membership area but can be used for conference attendance, employee retention, subscription businesses, and so forth.

Satisfaction and Engagement Research

This primary research (that is, done with people who have direct experience) is one of the most frequently conducted types of data collection at for-profit and not-for-profit organizations. This research can be a basic member satisfaction survey (how satisfied are you with your membership?), readership survey (how happy are you with our magazine, what are you reading from it?), conference attendee (how satisfied were you with the keynote speaker?), and your own slice-and-dice of your business. There are many appealing aspects of a satisfaction survey:

- The cost is relatively low, especially for those that can be conducted online.
- It is typically quantitative (that is, based on numbers, not words), so statistics can be performed and analyzed and interpreted (for example, speakers at your conference had an average satisfaction rate of 9.2, which was 2 points higher than regular attendees who had an average satisfaction rate of 7.2).
- You already have the sample because you know who your members are, who attended your conference, and so on.
- It is easy to do year after year, so trend data are available and goals can be set for future years.
- It provides a quick temperature of the state of affairs (are you doing great, okay, or ugh?) while allowing you to ask some specific follow-up questions to pinpoint areas of joy or pain. (Please think about the key takeaway messages from the keynote speaker at Tuesday's lunch session. How applicable are they to your current job?)

Needs Assessment and Product Development Research

This broad area of research covers areas related to delivering more value to your customers and members. The primary goal of needs assessment research is to uncover needs of your target market that you can match with programs, products, and services that you can deliver. If there is a gap between what they need and what you and your competition offer them, you may have an opportunity to develop a new program, product, or service or expand a current one. A savvy researcher will also be on the lookout for the reverse. If you see your association has an offering that does not address a need, you will want to consider eliminating or repositioning this existing program, product, or service.

While a well-structured needs assessment is critical in product development, research can also help other important areas. (These methods are best practice for products but can be used for programs and services.) Following are some common research techniques used in product development:

- *Competitive analysis:* Identifying and understanding the environment in which your association competes typically involves secondary research because it relies on information already available in the world. If you are unsure of your competitors, you may also need to do some primary research to ask your potential customers so that you can understand the marketplace. The objective of competitive analysis is to understand who your competitors are but, more important, help you gauge where you have opportunity (in other words, your competitor's vulnerability).
- *Pricing analysis:* Pricing is not only about what you will charge for something but also includes what it costs you to deliver and the value it provides to the market. It is best to have a pricing strategy (for example, value-based pricing or cost-recovery pricing) first to allow you to test certain price points and understand the features and attributes of your offering that the market finds value in and thus is willing to pay for.
- *Detailed features and attributes:* For large product releases, associations may require a more detailed and specialized research project (yes, this also means more expensive) that relies on conjoint analysis or discrete choice modeling. Using one of these advanced statistical methods will allow the product development team to understand the features and attributes that your target market wants and what trade-offs the market is willing to make.
- *User testing:* Decades ago, testing with real users was cost prohibitive for many associations, but now with many products and services being electronic only, the costs may be within reach. It is beneficial to have a small sample of possible users participate in a usability study in which they are interacting with either a prototype or the actual end product. Doing

so will allow you to detect possible problems or opportunities with the product before launch.

- *Market share:* Most product development teams will ask for research to help with determining the potential market share for a new or expanded product. Market share relies on both secondary research and primary research. The secondary research will allow you to determine how many people in the population may fit your key demographic for your product. For example, if you are considering developing a new certification for organic landscapers for your state, you could rely on state data for how many registered landscapers there are in your state. You would then want to survey a sample of these landscapers to determine if there is a key segment that may be more interested. For example, you may find that landscapers with fewer than three employees are not interested, but those with more than three are interested and the more employees the landscaper has, the more interested they are in this certification. This will then allow you to better predict your true market. Using results from your primary research, calculate how many landscapers have more than three employees and this will be your more refined target market. You can then review your results on how interested they are and make predictions on how many certifications you may sell.

Member and Customer Segmentation

Segmentation studies are useful when you have the ability to target smaller groups for marketing or product development. Many associations (and businesses) treat all members and customers the same, sending them the same emails and promotional materials and developing one-size-fits-all products and services. For some small, niche associations, this approach may work well, but for many associations, segmenting their customer base may lead to more value creation and better resource allocation.

Segmentation studies collect data that can be used to divide a broad target group into smaller subsets (that is, segments). Segments are composed of individuals who share common needs. There are many different segment types, but the most frequently used are segments based on demographics, behavior, or both. For example, if you work for an association working with retired individuals, valuable demographic segments may include segments such as "younger, Hispanic retirees" or "over-ninety retirees" or behavioral-based segments such as "independent, solo retirees who like to travel" or "grandparents first, retiree second." Could you imagine writing different promotional materials targeted at each of these groups and how the language you select and the features you decide to highlight might be different?

Environmental Scanning

Environmental scanning is an important part of research, as it is related to strategic planning. To determine where you want to go, you usually need to know what forces and trends may affect your future. A well-researched environmental scan will provide your association leaders with the information they need to form the basis of a data-driven strategic plan. There are several formats of environment scans. Regardless of the model, environmental scanning allows the reader to get a 360-degree view of the climate the association and its represented industries are operating in.

Research Process

The first part of the chapter reviewed types of research projects. The second half will dive deeper into the process of research itself.

The general research process has a number of key steps, each described in more detail as follows.

Scanning

The first step in the research process is to understand what you need to study and the context around it. As mentioned earlier, what key business decisions do you need to make given the results of your research? Different kinds of answers will call for different types of research.

For example, a membership director may be concerned about why overall membership numbers have declined. Or you may want to understand the business models your competitors use for their continuing education products. These broad questions will need to be expanded and formulated in a way that will guide how you conduct your research.

In addition, in your planning phase, think about the realities of your research project. What resources do you have to conduct the research, including budget, human resources, and time? Are there key dates by which you need to complete the research? For example, you may need results to report at your next board meeting or before your next membership renewal cycle starts.

Formulate the Research Question

Next, formulate the specific research question and develop the data-collection instruments. The first major part of this is determining what specific question you're trying to answer, essentially the hypothesis you have about your general concerns. For example, you might have a hypothesis that increasing your annual dues will *not* have a significant effect on your renewal rate. With a specific hypothesis, you can better determine which research will be most effective in answering it.

If the question is about developing new products to better serve members, you might want to do some exploratory focus groups to understand their needs. On the other hand, if you want to conduct some predictive data analysis and understand what benefits are the "stickiest" and how that varies across different segments of members, a survey with large numbers of respondents in key segments would generate more useful insights.

◆ ◆ ◆

Legal Issues and Research

How you conduct research may create legal concerns in several areas. Three key ones are antitrust, privacy, and incentives for participants. As in many association activities, think about any potential antitrust implications of how you collect data and distribute the results. The U.S. Federal Trade Commission and Department of Justice have published guidelines to assist antitrust issues, which are available at http://www.ftc.gov/os/2000/04/ftcdojguidelines.pdf. Associations should seek professional legal counsel about all activities that may involve possible antitrust risks.

In addition, when you conduct research, you inevitably collect data about people, and you should be aware of laws regarding data and privacy. At the time of writing of this chapter, the European Union in particular has stronger laws on personal privacy, but this is an evolving area.

Finally, researchers frequently use incentives to boost research, and sweepstakes may be an option. However, the rules and regulations vary from U.S. state to state, and from country to country.

 ◆ ◆ ◆

Methodology and Data Collection

During this phase you're determining the most effective method to collect the data and then doing that data collection. This could be, for example, an online survey emailed to all attendees of your annual meeting, in-depth interviews of former members, or collecting annual reports of all your corporate members for secondary research.

There are many methods to collect data, but they are broken into two categories. Simply, *quantitative* is generally more conclusive and uses numbers and statistics, while *qualitative* is more exploratory and descriptive and based on words. Quantitative methods rely on a large, representative sample and allow the researcher to use statistics to make strong generalizations. Qualitative methods rely on a smaller number of participants and allow the researcher to gain very rich and in-depth knowledge.

The prototypical quantitative research project is the survey. You ask people a number of questions, most commonly in a close-ended format (for example, "On a scale of 1 to 5, how satisfied or not are you with your membership in this association?").[2] These can have as few as one question (like the polls you see on many websites) to over a hundred (but don't do that!).

Data for surveys can be collected in a number of different ways: in person, though the mail, on the phone, via email, on the web, or even through text message or smartphone app. With most quantitative research, the goal is to have the data you collect be representative of the larger population you are interested in. As for the specific method you use, depending on the particular population you are interested in, any one of these could work.

Combining multiple techniques of collecting data (called mixed-mode research) can yield more complete results. For example, you could email an invitation to a sample of members, then follow up with a mail survey to those who don't respond to the email. This can enable you to have a more representative sample but will increase the time and expense of the research project.

For focus groups and other forms of qualitative research, there are also many ways of collecting data. The traditional focus group, often with a moderator in a room with eight or so participants and you, the client, watching from behind a one-way mirror, is still used. But you can conduct traditional focus groups in variety of settings, from your association's conference room to a meeting room at a conference hotel.

Beyond the traditional in-person focus group, you can conduct real-time focus groups online or by teleconference or web conferencing. Another effective technique for online focus groups is a bulletin board focus group, which is not conducted in real time, but instead the moderator posts questions on a special site for participants' responses. These are typically conducted over a three- or four-day period, and respondents participate each day at the time that is best for them. This method works particularly well for groups that are spread across multiple time zones. As with traditional focus groups, the moderator can probe on participants' responses and observers can see how fellow participants respond.

Many other ways of collecting qualitative data exist. These vary in scope considerably. If your association has a Facebook page or LinkedIn group, you can collect data by asking questions to the group. At the more elaborate end, you can develop market research online communities (MROCs), effectively private social networking sites that allow you, on an ongoing basis, to ask questions of a group of between fifty and a thousand or more people. You can also conduct ethnographic research, in which a researcher observes participants in their "natural habitat" (for example, following members around in their day-to-work efforts to better understand their work habits so you can have better insight into their needs).

No matter what methods you choose, all research requires you to develop your research instrument, pilot or test it, and actually collect the data.

◆ ◆ ◆

Sample Size

The size of the sample is normally much less important than how representative that sample is. We're often asked if a sample of four hundred people can really represent all the members in our association. The answer is generally yes, given the trade-offs needed between our desired margin of error and confidence interval and the costs of collecting more responses.

The typical example in research classes of a survey that had a lot of responses but did not provide accurate information was the Literary Digest survey of 1936, which (incorrectly) predicted that Alf Landon would beat Franklin Roosevelt for U.S. president. This survey had 2.4 million respondents but drew its sample from subscribers to the magazine, car registrations, and telephone users. Amidst the Great Depression, this led to a sample that was, on average, much wealthier than the average American voter of the time. Here the size of the sample was fine but it wasn't representative at all. You never want to be in this position.

Similarly, polls on the websites of many news sites these days may get tens of thousands of responses, but those who respond are unlikely to be representative of the population.

Typical choices are a margin of error of plus or minus 5 percentage points and a confidence level of 95 percent (see table 36.1). This means one can be 95 percent confident that the true answer lies within plus or minus 5.0 percentage points of the finding. For a large population, that means you need around 384 respondents (using the formula for the margin of error that we won't bore you with here). Notice 381

TABLE 36.1. LEVELS OF CONFIDENCE BY SAMPLE SIZE.

Sample Sizes	
95% Confidence	
Population Size (N)	**Plus or Minus 5%**
500	218
1,000	278
1,500	306
2,000	322
4,000	351
5,000	357
10,000	370
20,000	377
50,000	381
100,000	383

and 383 are the number of respondents you need, respectively, for a population size of 50,000 and 100,000 so around 384 is what you need for a very big sample. So, if your membership is 5,000, you only need 357 respondents to achieve a margin of error of plus or minus 5 percentage points and a confidence level of 95 percent.

For small populations (for example, less than two hundred people), the general rule of thumb is that you want at least half of the population to respond.

So how do you ensure that your sample is representative of the population you want to study? Most commonly, you want to make sure that those asked to participate in the survey are a random representative sample from your population. This means that every person in the population has an equal chance of being asked to participate in the survey. This is known as a simple random sample. You can also do "stratified random samples," in which you separate the population into different groups (for example, males and females) and then do a separate simple random sample of each group. This can reduce the amount of statistical error in your final results. There are many other ways to conduct sampling, some of which are very complex.

Once you collect the data, you want to try to assess if those who actually gave you information still reflect the population as a whole. You can often compare basic demographic data on your respondents with that of the population and see how well these match. For example, you may find that those who responded to your survey were, on average, younger than the population as a whole. If that's the case, you should statistically weight those who responded, or try to increase the number of respondents, or simply be aware of this issue as you try to understand your results.

Qualitative research rarely looks to represent the population, so a perfect, representative, sample is less important to generate ideas or test out concepts. You may want to have a broad range of participants with a range of opinions or target a specific group of individuals.

Data Analysis and Interpretation

Naturally, the type of analyses conducted varies with the type of research that you've done. The way you would analyze a focus group of eight people will be significantly different from an online survey with five hundred respondents.

However, whatever the data-collection method, the analysis should focus on answering the questions that you developed in the second phase of the research process.

For example, let's go back to our example of our director of membership who wanted to know why overall membership has declined. If she refined the actual research question to try to understand what segments are most prone to not renew their membership and why, the analyses would flow from these questions. She might do an analysis that looks at the statistical relationship between what segment a person is in and what their satisfaction is for various products and services (for example, do younger members value continuing education more?).

For any project, you could use a wide variety of types of analysis, but a few are most effective for most of the kinds of projects we see. These include

- *Frequencies and basic statistics:* One of the first things you'll likely do for a quantitative project is to look at the results of every question, how frequently people gave each answer, measures of central tendency (such as mean, median) and dispersion (for example, standard deviation).
- *General statistical techniques:* Much of the power of good research comes from understanding how issues or items relate to one another. Use techniques such as correlations, cross-tabs, and more sophisticated methods such as linear regression to do so.
- *Visualization:* Graphical displays of the results can be incredibly useful, both for analysis and for dissemination of the results. This can be as simple as graphing the responses to individual questions to as elaborate as the sophisticated infographics that many organizations now create using graphics, numbers, and words to tell a complete and more engaging story.
- *Advance techniques:* To answer specific types of questions (for example, pricing products to maximize revenue or reach or statistically segment

your members), special techniques such as segmentation, discrete choice analyses, and conjoint analysis yield the most powerful results. Due to the sophistication of these techniques, you should probably seek out expert advice.

- *Text analysis:* Many surveys have open-ended questions for which respondents are able to write a response. Qualitative research is mostly all open-ended. Text analysis allows you to bring some order and clarity to open-ended responses by grouping similar responses into common groups. An easy way to group general comments is to label each comment as positive, neutral, and negative. More elaborate text analysis requires the researcher to create "buckets" of similar responses, allowing you to see how many of the open-ended comments fall into a certain bucket. We generally just use Microsoft Excel to organize and classify open-ended responses, but companies such as SAS, IBM, and Clarabridge have a wide range of sophisticated (and often expensive) software options.

Data Dissemination and Use

So you've completed your research on reasons for the decline in membership, you look at the results, you say to yourself, "Well, I can check off that project on my goals for the year," and then you go on to your next project. Uh, no—that's not a good way to use your research. Research is only effective if it gets used in your decision-making process. And that means reporting and disseminating the results in effective ways.

Going back to your goals for the research, you want to make sure your reporting succinctly provides understanding that can be acted upon. You can write a fifty-page report, or produce a 150-slide PowerPoint deck, but these likely won't lead to implementation of your results. Often, researchers order reports by the way the questions are ordered in a questionnaire, and this is rarely the most effective approach. In general, successful reports are those that clearly and directly answer the research questions that you started with, and are organized and ordered by important priorities.

Different audiences may need different styles of reports. For example, a product manager may want the fifty-page report along with all the data. A chief staff executive will more likely value a very brief executive summary, with key results and recommendations.

In addition, you may want to distribute the results of the survey beyond those who originally asked for the research. Other internal stakeholders may have similar questions, and you may save the effort of repeating very similar research.

Finally, research may have a clear external audience. Your goal may be to inform public policy (for example, research briefings for government leaders), or it may be a product that you want to sell to members and nonmembers (such as a salary survey). If it has a clear external audience, share it.

In conclusion, quality research can significantly improve association decision making. Quality research requires thought and planning. It starts with understanding what decisions you are going to make and how research can inform those decisions, and then paying careful attention to how you collect data, who participates in the research, and how you analyze and distribute the results.

◆ ◆ ◆

Responsible Conduct of Research

When conducting research, we always need to ensure that it's conducted ethically.

While little of the research conducted by associations may be covered by formal regulations, such as those from the U.S. federal government, it is essential for the stature and reputation of associations that we voluntarily practice ethical research practices.

What does responsible conduct of research mean? We think of the responsible conduct of research as three subtopics:

- Protection of those participating
- Ensuring that research is done correctly
- Credit where credit is due

The Belmont Report, prompted in large part by the infamous Tuskegee syphilis study, highlights three principles for ethical research:*

- *Respect for persons:* People are treated as autonomous agents and those with diminished autonomy are given protection.
- *Beneficence:* Maximizing the benefits of the research while minimizing the risks to the participants. This often includes keeping the names of those who responded confidential.
- *Justice:* The costs and the benefits of participating in research are fairly distributed.

Another component of responsible research is ensuring that the research is actually done correctly. Poor research fails on two fronts. First, badly done research wastes the time of the participants. The implicit trade-off respondents make when participating in your research is that they will take the time to give you their information and you will take that information and do something useful with it. Second, bad research will lead to faulty recommendations, which will lead to bad decisions that could cost you money and members.

One final aspect of the responsible conduct of research is the idea that credit needs to go where it is due. In research, this is not just about the writing, but ensuring that those who conceive the research, actually conduct the research and analyze it, as well as those that do the writing are properly credited.*

*Note: The historical background for current views of the responsible conduct of research lies with three major documents—the Nuremberg Code (1947), the Declaration of Helsinki (1964) and the Belmont Report (1978), from what is now the U.S. Department of Health and Human Services but at the time was the U.S. Department of Health Education and Welfare (http://www.hhs.gov/ohrp/humansubjects/guidance/belmont.html).

Notes

1. ASAE, *7 Measures of Success: What Remarkable Associations Do That Others Don't* (Washington, DC: ASAE Association Management Press, 2006).
2. People can obsess over the right scale to use—should it be a 3-point scale or 7-point scale or even a 100-point scale? Should it have an odd number of points (which allows for a neutral option) or an even number (which forces people to favor one end of the scale or the other)? The short answer is, it doesn't matter that much. There's some evidence that a 7-point scale does best at balancing the need to provide enough points to allow people to make meaningful distinctions without having so many points that respondents can't really make accurate judgments. But overall these differences are very slight, and making sure the questions are well worded and in the right order is far more important. Also, do your best not to change scales within one questionnaire. If you are using a 5-point scale (our favorite), use a 5-point scale for all your questions.

Resource

Slater, S. C., and Moss, S. *The Informed Association: A Practical Guide to Using Research for Results.* Washington, DC: ASAE Association Management Press, 2013.

The Authors

Marc Beebe, CAE, is the director of strategic research for IEEE, where he has managed research since 2005. Prior to coming to IEEE, Marc worked as the internal evaluator for a number of precollege math and science education projects at Rutgers University. Marc is an active member of ASAE, the American Psychological Association, and the Marketing Research Association.

Elena A. Gerstmann, PhD, FASAE, CAE, is staff executive, corporate activities at IEEE. Elena's background in social psychology provides a great framework for her work at IEEE and her volunteer work for the research industry and the global association industry. She currently serves on the board of directors for ASAE and the ASAE Foundation.

CHAPTER THIRTY-SEVEN

GOVERNMENT RELATIONS, PUBLIC POLICY, AND COALITION BUILDING

Stefanie Reeves, MA, CAE

Everything that happens on Capitol Hill will affect you, your association, and the people your members serve. Just look at the impact of the Affordable Care Act (ACA). Under the ACA, most individuals are now responsible for purchasing health insurance or risk a penalty. For associations that provide health coverage, the ACA will affect everything from the cost of providing such coverage to which employees an association may choose to cover. This has the potential of affecting an industry's bottom line, its workforce, and the people it serves.

When it comes to advocacy, the squeaky wheel definitely gets the oil on Capitol Hill. The groups that achieve legislative success are the ones who are constantly pushing their issues using their lobbyists, their association members, and their PAC to drive home the message to their representatives. Members of Congress and their staff stand behind the belief that if they don't hear about an issue, it's not considered a priority. If associations are not involved on Capitol Hill, your priorities do not exist in the halls of Congress.

On average, over six thousand bills are introduced during the two-year congressional session. Of that six thousand, only three hundred will become law. And that number is shrinking. By the end of 2013, only sixty-five bills became law.[1] Competition for Congress's limited time and attention will only continue to grow. If your association is not actively participating, it runs the risk of negative consequences.

If You're Not at the Table, You're On the Menu!

This chapter seeks to increase your understanding of government relations and how to see this domain from the mind-set of a chief staff executive (CSE). It focuses on government relations from a federal perspective. It deserves to be noted that executives working at the state level basically operate the same as on the federal level. State advocacy requires advance planning with a touch of flexibility, knowledgeable staff, and a supportive membership. The big difference is that state legislature sessions are typically shorter with issues particular to that state.

First, some terminology. Advocacy. Lobbyist. Government relations. What do they all mean?

- *Advocacy* for our purposes refers to efforts to influence policymakers.
- One way to influence is lobbying. A *lobbyist* is one who makes direct contact with an elected official (or their staff) with the expressed purpose of advocating for or against a particular issue.
- *Government relations* (GR) is an umbrella term that includes advocacy work. You may also hear the phrase *public policy* instead of *government relations.*

The Role of the Chief Staff Executive in Association Government Relations

Even with a top-notch, in-house government relations office, the CSE plays an important role in government relations beyond reporting the association's GR activities to the board. The CSE's actual role in GR may depend on a number of factors. For example, if you're the CSE of a small staff association, you may likely be the GR staff. If you're the CSE of a very large association, your job may be as the sounding board for your GR staff. Regardless, the successful association is one that has a CSE that understands and cares about government relations. You may be saying to yourself, "Isn't it a given that the CSE should care about GR?" Not necessarily. Remember, GR is related to politics and many people, including those in a CSE position, have strong feelings about politics.

Working with Your Board

It's important for the CSE to get buy-in from the board on your GR activities. If your board isn't enthusiastic about your plan, how can you convince your rank-and-file member to get excited about it? For best results and buy-in, the CSE should be sure to do the following:

- Present the advocacy plan to your board with an annual review and update.
- Make the GR update a regular part of your board agendas.
- Keep the board aware of what is coming down the pike on Capitol Hill.
- Continue to communicate with the board throughout the year.
- Most important, train your board members on being advocates. Take them to the Hill. Board members with firsthand account of lobbying for an important issue will understand and encourage others to participate.

Whether it's participating in your association's advocacy day or responding to a grassroots alert, your board members have a responsibility to be front and center. The success of an association's advocacy effort is due in part to member participation with their volunteer leadership leading the charge.

Board and Member Engagement

No matter how great your GR staff is or how much money is raised by your PAC, you need to get your members involved and engaged in your efforts. As I mentioned, you must get your board buy-in on your advocacy plan. You also need to get your rank and file involved as well.

Get Your Members to Care About the Issues

If your members don't have a vested interest in your legislative issues, why should they bother participating in your annual event at the Capitol, sometimes called "Hill Day"? Make it plain. Talk about the repercussions of inactivity. Talk about the financial and human costs. Make it relevant so that your members take ownership of the issue. If you tell them that Congress is debating legislation that would increase funding for health care, the response may be "Okay, that's good." If you tell them that same bill would fund up to ten thousand new jobs for the industry the association represents, the response is going to be a bit more enthusiastic.

Get Them Involved; Think Outside the Box. While action alerts, Hill Days, and government relations updates in the newsletter are great tools in any advocacy plan, there's more that can be done to get your members involved. Associations can

- Host a Twitter chat to educate your members about the association's legislative agenda.
- Encourage your volunteer leaders to blog about their experience on Capitol Hill.
- Create a Facebook page highlighting your advocacy efforts.
- Create legislative activities for your student members, including their own Hill Day.
- Recognize your top grassroots members at the annual conference.
- Encourage your members to invite members of Congress to tour their facility.

When it comes to getting your members involved, don't be afraid to think outside the box. Keeping your members involved is only the first step. You need to keep them engaged. Emphasize to your members that your legislative priorities will likely be a multiyear effort. The association will need them to keep these issues in the forefront.

Using Social Media and Technology for Government Relations

The majority of the House and Senate utilize at least one social network such as Facebook or Twitter. According to the Congressional Management Foundation, congressional staff are increasingly seeing social media as a way to gauge public opinion on important issues. In addition, lobbyists follow the action on the House and Senate floor live via their Twitter feeds. Associations are doing a better job of utilizing social media in their advocacy efforts, but not to the same extent as Congress. However, some associations are still reluctant to utilize social media as part of the government relations agenda. We can no longer continue to ignore the validity of these platforms in the work that we do.

◆ ◆ ◆

The Association Government Relations Team

Your government relations team is the association's lifeline to everything legislative. They are responsible for making sure the association's interests are protected on Capitol Hill. They are charged with developing and implementing the association's advocacy plan.

Who makes up a GR team? GR staffs can take on many forms. If you're a 501(c)(3), your staff may consist of lobbyists and a grassroots director as well as a legislative assistant. If you're a 501(c)(6), you may also have a PAC director. If you're a small staff association, you may contract with an outside consultant who will lobby on behalf of the association. In a few instances, the CSE also serves as the association's chief lobbyist.

Associations most often have at least one in-house lobbyist. However, there are times when associations will look outside the organization for additional assistance. Contract lobbyists work for firms (or are self-employed) where the association is a client. As such, these lobbyists usually work hand and hand with the in-house lobbyists on Capitol Hill. Outsourced lobbyists can be most beneficial if they have a certain expertise or have relationships to congressional leaders or a specific political party that the in-house lobbyist lacks. Contract lobbyists can also be used to provide assistance during major lobbying efforts.

The Role of the Association Lobbyist

Just what does a lobbyist do? For the most part, lobbyists meet with members of Congress or their staff to encourage the support or defeat of a particular bill or issue. Successful lobbying takes relationship building, strategic planning, community outreach, and a lot of patience to accomplish your goals. No two days are ever alike. One day, your lobbyist may be giving an issue briefing to association members. The next, they're in a pressured environment, meeting with legislative staff at the Capitol. It's never a dull moment when 535 unique personalities stand between you and legislative success for your association. It is the lobbyist's responsibility to keep the CSE informed on all legislative developments affecting the association.

In recent years, the job of a lobbyist has expanded. So much so, that lobbyists are taking on the moniker of *government relations professional* rather than *lobbyist*. Besides actual lobbying, some give presentations to association members on advocacy, organize congressional briefings, draft congressional testimony, organize grassroots efforts, and even manage their legislative office.

Developing Your Advocacy Plan

A successful association's public policy outreach follows the SPIE model: scan, plan, implement, and evaluate. For example, you cannot do public policy without some type of plan that anticipates rather than reacts to what's going on legislatively. Your plan should include issues of importance to the association, position statements, advocacy training, and, of course, participation from your members. The approach to public policy must be strategic, take into account judgment-based decision making, and include relationship building.

Government relations require a plan. In preparation for legislative activity, a thorough scan and analysis is recommended. How did your issues fair in this congress? What's happening in the current congress that may affect future congresses? How will upcoming elections affect your issues? How many issues can we adequately cover? The scanning process should incorporate the issues that you monitor, follow, and rank for priority, for example, highest priority, priority, and monitoring.

Identifying the issues that resonate with the membership is a group effort between the CSE, the government relations committee and the GR staff. For some associations, it may be pocketbook issues, those that would have a positive or negative impact on the financial well-being of your industry. For others, it may be issues that affect the clients or patients your members serve. How can you identify those issues? For the most part, the government relations staff and committee will work collaboratively to identify which issues the association should focus on.

Most important, you must decide which issues will have the biggest impact on your membership and industry.

- *High-priority* issues are ones that will receive the most time, attention and resources. An example of a high-priority issue would be funding request.[2]
- A *regular-priority* issue could be one that may see some action in the House or Senate, but is not expected to go far.
- A *monitoring* issue is one that will likely see little to no legislative action. By remaining nimble, you can move issues around as needed on the basis of legislative action, staff time, and resources.

Once the priority issues have been identified, tactical decisions need to be made. Advocacy plan considerations include

- How will you engage your members and leadership?
- How will you identify and prioritize legislative issues?
- What resources will you need?
- What does success look like for the community, volunteer leadership, and membership?

- How can you best utilize association resources such as social media and your website to promote advocacy efforts? What technology (grassroots advocacy software, for example) could you use?
- How might coalitions be utilized?

Once tactical plan elements have been determined, then it is time to allocate resources. When developing a budget for GR activities, take into account the priorities and the strategy that will be used on each priority. For example, for a high-priority activity, an association may implement a full campaign, including direct lobbying, grassroots advocacy, and (if applicable) PAC fundraisers for your key congressional champions. Obviously, high-priority activities will likely utilize the majority of your financial and staff resources.

Grassroots advocacy involves engaging your members in the process. This includes encouraging your members to meet with their legislators in their home districts (with talking points in hand!). However, the most common way is to have your members send messages (in person or electronically) to their members of Congress in response to email action alerts and congressional fly-ins or Hill Days.

Email Action Alerts

With the increased scrutiny of snail mail to Capitol Hill, associations had to find different ways to get letters from their members to Capitol Hill. Email became an ideal alternative. Thanks to software vendors such as Cap-Wiz, associations are able to send thousands of messages to the Hill with a few simple keystrokes. Email alerts also allow associations to be nimble in response to Capitol Hill activities. If an association knows a bill is coming to the floor that afternoon, an alert can be timed to go out to their membership that morning.

Congressional Hill Days involve bringing your association members to Washington, D.C., to meet face to face with their members of Congress. Typically, the Hill Day is preceded by a full or half-day training session for association members on how to conduct a meeting with legislators and their aides. Many associations specify one day per year (usually in the spring) to gather as many of their members at the Capitol as possible. Strength in numbers can show legislators that your issue is very important to the association (and their voting constituency).

With so much email and visits being made to the Hill, associations are finding new ways to differentiate themselves. Some are turning to social media as another way to amplify their message beyond email and personal visits. Regardless of whether you utilize email action alerts or congressional Hill Days, content is what matters. Association members are encouraged to stay on message to provide a unified voice over a particular issue.

◆ ◆ ◆

Factors Associations Should Keep in Mind When Evaluating Their GR Plan

- *Consistency with the association's mission & strategic plan:* Do our legislative priorities align with our mission? Do they help accomplish goals within our strategic plan?
- *Recognized expertise on policy issue:* Do we have members or staff who are experts on our legislative priorities?
- *Uniqueness and importance of contribution:* Do we have research or valuable data that can be used to develop legislative priorities?
- *Support of governance and membership:* Do our leaders and members support these initiatives?
- *Prospects for success:* In the midst of congressional partisanship and a short schedule, how successful will our priorities be? How do we measure success given these variables?
- *Availability of resources:* Do we have the financial and staff resources to work on our priorities?

◆ ◆ ◆

Coalitions

Coalitions are a very important part of any association government relations plan. Associations understand the value of strength in numbers. Regardless if you're a small staff association of five or a large association of five hundred, coalitions are a valuable tool in bringing attention to your issue. Coalitions are typically a group of organizations that form behind a common purpose. For government relations, that purpose is usually a large piece of legislation with multiple parts centered on a common theme.

While coalitions may form to support a common purpose, occasionally groups align with groups that may not share common philosophy on all matters. "Cross-functional" coalitions serve as a message to legislators that the issue of focus has wider public appeal, which leads to better public policy.

The power in numbers gained by forming a coalition can also benefit by adopting a few simple guidelines for effectiveness.

What goes into an effective coalition?

- *Clear goals and objectives:* Understand what you want to gain from joining or forming a coalition and what the roles of the other coalition members will be.
- *Strategic alignment of coalition members:* This includes how many groups should be part of your coalition and whether you can support every group working on this issue or you need a more exclusive group.
- *Understanding and commitment:* Even within a coalition, all parties won't agree to everything. The goal and common purpose of the coalition should take precedence over an individual organization's goals.
- *Evaluation:* As with all things, it's hard to improve if you don't evaluate. In addition to improving, it also helps to let you know when to leave a coalition. Some coalitions outlast their usefulness. There's no shame in leaving.

Section 501(c)(3) Versus Section 501(c)(6) Organizations: Lobbying and Political Activities

There seems to be a long-standing myth that if you're a 501(c)(3) charitable organization, you're not allowed to lobby. That is not true. 501(c)(3)s are free to lobby Congress, but must abide by some restrictions. Table 37.1 offers a basic comparison between (c)(3)s and (c)(6)s when it comes to lobbying and political activity.

Ethical Considerations of Lobbying

People take a very cynical view of the political system and those who take part in it. Many think negatively of lobbyists as those who bribe politicians to get them to vote favorably on their issue. The very nature of the job of a lobbyist makes it extremely important to maintain high ethical standards, and most lobbyists adhere to these standards. There have always been laws on the books to address permissible action between members of Congress and lobbyists. However, with the Jack Abramoff scandal in 2007 that saw lobbyists, congressional staff, and even a member of Congress convicted of bribery, fraud, and conspiracy, there were renewed calls to update these laws.

The Honest Leadership and Open Government Act (HLOGA) of 2007 was enacted. HLOGA instituted a ban of gifts and travel offered by lobbyists

TABLE 37.1. LOBBYING AND POLITICAL ACTIVITY BY ORGANIZATION TYPE.

Activity	501(c)(3)	501(c)(6)
Lobbying	Lobbying is allowed, but restricted depending on the total revenue of the organization. Some large associations qualify to spend up to $1 million annually.	Lobbying is unrestricted. Associations must inform members that a portion of their dues is not tax deductible as a business expense because it is used for lobbying activities.
Political Activity	The association cannot establish a PAC. It cannot engage in political campaigns.	Associations can establish a PAC and engage in political campaigns.
Nondeductibility of Member Dues for Lobbying	Deductibility of dues.	The percentage of dues that is used for lobbying expenses is not deductible on personal income tax filings but may be applied as a business deduction. The 501(c)(6) must report that percentage to the membership or pay a flat 35 percent proxy tax on that year's lobbying expenses.

and organizations that employ lobbyists to members of Congress. HLOGA also increased the frequency of reports from lobbyists documenting their legislative activities as well as requiring a new disclosure report of political contributions.

Lobbying Registration

Associations that employ lobbyists are required to file a single registration form with the secretary of the Senate and the clerk of the House. There is no fee for filing the form LD-1. Associations must register when lobbyists meet two criteria. First, the lobbyist must make more than one lobbying contact with an elected official or staff. Second, the lobbyist must spend at least 20 percent of his or her time on lobbying activities. Such activities include any background work done to prepare for a lobbying visit. Once those conditions are met, lobbyists have forty-five days to register.

If your association uses in-house lobbyists, it is advisable to annually confirm current registrations for all personnel who meet the two-pronged requirement. If your association uses contract lobbyists, it's likely that they have registered with the House and Senate, but it is prudent to verify that the registrations are current.

Lobbying Disclosure

Previously, organizations were required to report on lobbying activities and any expenses on a semiannual basis. With HLOGA, those reports are now filed quarterly. HLOGA also requires this report, the LD-2, to be filed electronically with the House and Senate in January, April, July, and October of each year. In addition, any organization that employs lobbyists as well as the lobbyists themselves are required to file a new semiannual report, the LD-203. The LD-203 captures any political contributions made by the lobbyist or the association's political action committee over $200. The report also reaffirms that the lobbyist and the association are aware of HLOGA regulations and have complied with them. These reports are filed in January and July of each year.

Political Action Committees

Corporations and associations are prohibited by law from contributing directly to political campaigns. Therefore, political action committees or PACs are formed to serve this function. What is a PAC? A political action committee is an entity formed by corporations and associations for the sole purpose of raising funds and making contributions to political candidates. A PAC can be a valuable asset to an association's government relations operation. The ability to contribute to candidates who are supportive of the association's issues can enhance the efforts made by direct lobbying and grassroots advocacy.

Association PAC solicitations are limited to their *restricted class*. The restricted class of individual membership associations are their individual members. For a trade association, the restricted class typically consists of the members of the board plus executive and administrative staff of the member company.[3] In addition, trade associations must also adhere to the prior approval requirement. Prior *approval* is a written request for permission from the trade association PAC to its member companies to solicit for PAC contributions. A member company can only give prior approval to one

TABLE 37.2. PAC CONTRIBUTION LIMITS.

	Contribution from Individuals to the PAC	Contributions to Political Candidates	Contributions to National Political Parties	Contributions to Other PACs
Political Action Committees (PACs)	$5,000 annually	Up to $5,000 for the primary election; up to $5,000 for the general election	Up to $15,000 annually	Up to $5,000 annually
These prohibitions also apply to PAC operations.		PACs cannot solicit contributions from outside their restrictive class. PACs cannot accept contributions from foreign nationals. Associations cannot reimburse employees for PAC contributions. Coercion cannot be used to encourage participation in a PAC.		

trade association PAC annually. In addition, approval must be given before the trade association PAC personnel can solicit employees of the member company. Table 37.2 offers some examples of PAC contribution limits.

Requirements to Starting a PAC

PACs are required to file a "Statement of Organization" with the Federal Election Commission (FEC) with ten days of formation. Though not required, it is recommended that a PAC have a treasurer who is responsible for the management of PAC finances as well as financial reports to the FEC. Depending on the association, many of the PAC financial transactional functions are carried out by the association's finance department in coordination with the treasurer.

Just as you plan for your GR efforts, it's a good idea to develop guidelines or policies for your PAC. These PAC guidelines should address the following questions.

• How and how often will you solicit your restrictive class? Associations have a number of options for soliciting their members for PAC contributions, from direct mail to fundraisers during annual conferences. Be aware that state components also solicit funds for state PACs; it is recommended to coordinate with the state PAC on timing.

- Which political candidates will receive your PAC contributions? Many associations set PAC guidelines as to who qualifies for a contribution. Some focus on congressional leadership, others on committees of jurisdiction for the issues they follow.
- Will you support incumbent candidates, or will you reserve funds for challengers?
- Will your PAC spend money during the non-election year or build up coffers for the election year?

Working with Your Other Association Staff

A government relations department can sometimes operate as its own island within an association. However, there are definite benefits to working collaboratively with other departments within your association.

Research

Congressional staff love data. They want to know how many members you have, who your members are, and where they live or work. Why? Members of your association are also constituents, and every constituent over the age of eighteen is a potential voter. Who has the data in your association? Your research department? Your membership department? Both?

Communication

The GR staff typically write for different audiences, from congressional staff to the general public. Your communications department can work with staff to ensure that the message gets across without getting bogged down with jargon.

Public Relations

Have a big event coming up on Capitol Hill? You need to engage your public relations department. They have the media contacts and can issue press releases and media advisories ahead of your event.

Information Systems

More and more government relations departments are looking for software specifically designed for such functions as developing action alerts or maintaining and generating lists of congressional staff for outreach. Before you make any software purchases, contact your IT staff. It is quite possible that your association management system can handle the functions you seek for advocacy. Discuss your goals and what you hope to accomplish. Ideally, the software should be simple enough for your GR staff to use on a daily basis.

Using Social Media for Government Relations

The majority of the House and Senate members utilize at least one social network. According to the Congressional Management Foundation, congressional staff is increasingly seeing social media as a way to gauge public opinion on important issues.[4] However, some associations are still reluctant to utilize social media as part of the government relations agenda.

◆ ◆ ◆

How the American Speech-Language-Hearing Association (ASHA) Uses Social Media for Their GR Initiatives

ASHA is a great example of how to utilize social media in government relations efforts. Caroline Goncalves, ASHA's associate director of federal advocacy had this to say about using social media.

"You should be using every platform at your disposal to be engaging members in advocacy and social media is an easy and effective way to do so. Many people have email overload and it can be harder to reach them through a traditional email message because you may be sent straight to the trash with the other twenty emails they are sorting through and don't have time to read.

"However, if someone is already on social media and happens to see your post while scrolling, you might catch them and get them interested and involved in advocacy. Even better if our post is shared by a friend or colleague of theirs because it seems more authentic coming from a trusted source. If their friend thinks it's important, maybe they should too. We're also building an educated audience and letting them know about issues as they're happening, not just when we need them to do something."*

* *Source*: Caroline Goncalves.

◆ ◆ ◆

Advocacy is a marathon, not a sprint. That *Schoolhouse Rock* cartoon that taught us how a bill becomes a law? It's no longer that easy. Most legislation introduced in Congress will never become law. If something does, it's usually years after it was first introduced. The legislative system is becoming more unpredictable by the minute, as shifting priorities leave once-promising bills languishing under committee review and constant campaign fundraising takes more and more of lawmakers' time and attention. As a CSE or government relations professional, you will inevitably find this to be a frustrating ordeal. However, with the right planning, staff, and cooperation from your members, your path to legislative success becomes a bit easier.

Notes

1. D. Desilver, "Congress Ends Least-Productive Year in Recent History," Pew Research Center, December 23, 2013, available at http://www. pewresearch.org/fact-tank/2013/12/23/congress-ends-least-productive-year-in-recent-history.
2. Appropriations bills, either as stand-alone bills or as part of an omnibus bill or continuing resolution, fund the government and must be passed every year.
3. Staff must be salaried employees with policymaking, managerial, professional, or supervisory responsibilities.
4. The Partnership for a More Perfect Union, "#SocialCongress: Perceptions and Use of Social Media on Capitol Hill." Congressional Management Foundation (2011). Available at http://www.congressfoundation. org/storage/documents/CMF_Pubs/cmf-social-congress.pdf.

The Author

Stefanie Reeves, MA, CAE, has over fifteen years of experience as an association government relations professional. She is the founder of Generation Advocacy as well as a lobbyist for the American Psychological Association. She has also held government relations positions with the American Speech-Language-Hearing Association, National Telecommunications Cooperative Association, and the American Association of Colleges of Nursing.

CHAPTER THIRTY-EIGHT

MARKETING AND COMMUNICATIONS

Tom Quash, CAE

Picture this: your association has developed a new product, added a highly anticipated member benefit, or crafted a topical press release. Then *presto!*—push the magical marketing and communications button and along comes immediate success and positive response, complete with overperforming revenue and critical accolades from your members.

Well, if that were the case, every organization would adopt such a proven formula and realize instant engagement and overnight profits. And while a successful marketing and communications strategy can indeed feel, well, magical, when all things come together according to plan, sound marketing, communications, and public relations strategies are rooted in trends analysis, data mining, goal setting, planning, execution, innovation, and evaluation.

The disciplines of marketing, communications, and public relations (see sidebar for definitions and key functions) overlap somewhat and complement one another, and the key to distinguishing the functions and ensuring their integration in an association lies in both understanding and valuing the role each function plays in association management. Likewise, each should be integrated into your communications plans, considered together as a core strategic approach that is critical to maintaining your association's competitive edge and relevance while supporting its mission.

Think of it this way. Throughout the course of just one year, your association has a series of "stories" it needs to share. It may be a new membership category. Or your association's reaction to a poignant public policy issue. Some stories may even be perennial: attend the annual convention, purchase this year's edition of a popular publication, renew membership. Together, marketing, communications, and public relations act as your association's "storyteller."

◆ ◆ ◆

Definitions and Key Functions

Marketing is the activity, set of institutions, and processes for creating, communicating, delivering, and exchanging offerings that have value for customers, clients, partners, and society at large (American Marketing Association, 2013).

Key Functions of Marketing*

- Marketing strategy and planning
- Direct mail (brochures, postcards, promotional letters, posters, booklets, flyers, catalogs)
- Electronic communication (email, e-newsletters, e-brochures, e-postcards, fax)
- Web-based (website content, social media platforms, search engine optimization)
- Advertising (print, web banners, social media, radio, TV, billboards and signage, product placement)
- Video and film (short form, long form, infomercial)
- Sales activities (premium, trade shows and exhibits, displays, talent)

The discipline of *communications* focuses on how people use messages to generate meanings within and across various contexts, cultures, channels, and media (National Communication Association, 2014).

Key Functions of Communications*

- Communications strategy and planning
- Oral presentations, speeches
- Articles (print and online), publications, newsletters, magazines, journals
- Advocacy, grassroots efforts, public policy initiatives

Public relations is a strategic communication process that builds mutually beneficial relationships between organizations and their publics (Public Relations Society of America, 2011–2012).

Key Functions of Public Relations*

- Public relations strategy and planning
- Press releases

- Media relations
- Press conferences
- Media tours, paid media placement, advertorials

*Not all-inclusive.

American Marketing Association. "Definitions of Marketing." (July 2013). Available at https://www.ama.org/AboutAMA/Pages/Definition-of-Marketing.aspx.
National Communication Association. "Communications Discipline." (2014). Available at https://www.natcom.org/discipline/.
Public Relations Society of America. "Public Relations Defined." (2011–2012). Available at http://www.prsa.org/aboutprsa/publicrelationsdefined/.

For example, let's say your association has just secured a leading and well-known business owner for your annual convention as the opening keynote speaker. Her company's new product will likely make your association's members more efficient and profitable. She wants to use your convention to launch the new product. You want to leverage the exposure to build greater awareness and relevancy for your organization, bringing in more members, increasing convention attendance, securing new industry partners, and generating publicity. Your marketing efforts might include prominently displaying the keynote on direct mail pieces, and in emails and in ads, including placement with competitors. The communications function can support your goals through a preconvention Q&A with the keynote speaker in your association's publication. During the convention itself, your public relations strategy would ensure national publicity and media pickup of the new-product launch announcement, exposing your association to new audiences.

In this case, by combining the efforts of marketing, communications, and public relations, your association can use an integrated approach to achieve a variety of goals and to connect with a host of audiences . Whatever the story, you'll want to tap into the benefits of each discipline before moving forward and consider the questions you'll need to ask, such as those that follow, which you should consider in the example just shared.

- How do I best disseminate my story to all of the diverse audiences that are in my association's scope? What do I share with those audiences who are unfamiliar with us?
- What is the call to action I want to achieve for each activity? What are my goals?

- How can I leverage this story to also expand my reach and demonstrate my association's influence and credibility?
- What tools and resources can I use to measure my success for marketing, communications, and public relations?

Analysis and Data

Before the implementation of any integrated campaign, there are critical "first steps" that should be taken. To put it simply, you must look before you leap. That is, conduct a communications audit, perform data mining, and examine trend analysis.

A communications audit is a comprehensive evaluation of how you are currently sending and receiving information and then observing what is being done with this information, both on the recipient's end and that of the sender. An audit measures the effectiveness of your association's communications and reveals any strengths or weaknesses. It is imperative that the association make any necessary adjustments in improving communications as uncovered by the audit. For example, let's say the communications audit finds that your group's customer service function is poor and member queries are not answered in a timely fashion. Before executing any subsequent major campaigns, you'll need to ensure that questions and queries receive speedy responses and give more attention to the individuals and tools and resources on the front line.

Another key step during the earliest stages of developing a plan is to perform data mining. Even the best of campaigns are at risk if your data are not strong or valid. Data mining involves evaluating the data you already have and are collecting with your varied audiences. It is one thing to collect basic demographic information, but a complete data-mining exercise should help you predict behaviors. For example, if you learn that the majority of your new members choose not to renew because they have not found the value in your association, but the long-time members are strong advocates, how might this change the onboarding process you have in place for new members during the first few weeks or months of joining? Similarly, are you tracking the types of articles or content that get the most traction in the press? How might this alter your public relations efforts?

In addition, it is critical to examine trend analysis before jumpstarting your campaign—this would consider both internal and external influences. Here, you are looking at the historical information to predict future patterns. It's important to note that trend analysis is an ongoing activity. Your current results may no longer ring true even one year later. Let's say, for example, your members were slow to adapt to a new technology that was far more used throughout other segments of society. It makes sense that you might not use the technological platform as your primary means for communication to all members today, but if you were to find a greater percentage of your new members were indeed early adopters to the technology, you might be better able to predict how your communications might change six months or a year later and how you might segment the new member target for different communication activities.

Setting Goals

Your association likely has gone through strategic planning and has a future-focused plan in place. The strategic plan acts as a blueprint for your organizational marketing and communications plan. Every organization should have one. The organizational marketing and communications plan acts as the "umbrella" for the dissemination and management of your organization's messaging.

It's likely that your organizational marketing and communications plan is not overly tactical. Indeed, it should remain more global and high-level in its approach. But, of course, there are revenue, sales, and publicity goals to achieve that may be aligned with specific products, resources, and services. For example, are you trying to increase member retention? If so, how much of a percentage increase are you seeking? Do you need to promote your annual convention to new audiences? If so, what's a reasonable expectation for increased attendance? Are you trying to gain participation in a new affinity partner program? If so, how much revenue do you anticipate the first year? While these goals are specific to individualized areas of the association, they funnel upward to relate to the goals of your overall campaign. Here, the organization marketing and communications campaign is focused on the *what* (increase membership revenue, build better awareness, demonstrate member value) while the respective plans related to core products and services are addressing the *how* (focus on greater member retention, target the convention to new audiences, add new member programs).

Developing the Plan

Once you've performed the audit, mining, and analysis, you'll need to consider how your story can be tied into effectively reaching your target audiences and achieve the established goals and reasonable projections for your association.

It is important that the goals remain measurable. Some might be quite obvious: grow membership by a certain percentage, achieve a designated dollar amount of product sales or event attendance. You must not overlook that there are also measurable goals tied to the marketing, communications, and PR functions. You may want to increase the number of social media engagements, web impressions, or audience reach. While these goals may not always directly relate to revenue streams, they certainly enhance your association's visibility and brand, which can translate to stronger credibility. In short, you increase your association's participation, support, and perceived value.

Marketing and communications should always have a seat at the strategic table, but it is also important to include the other tablemates throughout the planning process:

- *Financial:* Identify the budget parameters needed to support the marketing and communications plan.
- *Technology:* Explore how technology may help or hinder the execution of the plan.
- *Legal or ethics:* Review any legal or ethical concerns surrounding the plan.
- *Volunteer leaders:* Examine how volunteer leaders may play a part in the widespread dissemination of the plan.
- *Relationships:* Identify suppliers, partners, like-minded organizations, and the media, all of which may play a key role (or serve as an adversary).

Smart planning also relies on transparency and organizational communication. Integrating the interests and concerns of your association colleagues during the planning stages helps to secure buy-in. The plan that was born through silos is often the one positioned to miss the mark. Marketing and communications plans are designed to blossom through the spirit of collaboration.

◆ ◆ ◆

Key Components: An Abbreviated Sample Marketing and Communications Plan

Overview of Association XYZ's Member Recruitment Campaign

Theme: Determine the basis of a theme that can be used for the overall marketing and communication strategy. It should be consistent, constant, and carried throughout all activities and channels. Through data mining and trends analysis, you may determine what the value proposition is for prospects. What is the sticking point? This should be supported by an overarching goal in the strategic plan.

Objectives of the Plan

- To grow membership revenue by at least 2 percent annually over the next year.
- To create unique and measurable marketing and communication messaging and resources that inform all target audiences of the benefits and relevancy of membership in Association XYZ.
- To develop a series of sound and consistent sales messages that can be tailored for integration throughout all of the marketing and communication efforts.
- To customize and segment messages to best fit specific audiences.

Data and Analytics

To support the direction of the plan, here is where you would include any vital information from a communications audit, your data mining, or trends analysis. Before implementation, there may be a need to conduct additional market research, such as member and nonmember surveys, telemarketing, or face-to-face or virtual focus groups.

Target Audiences

- Lapsed members
- Nonmember attendees of events
- Nonmember purchasers of products
- Nonmembers working at the same organizations as members
- Subscribers to competitive publications
- Purchased list of key prospects

Key Messages

Association XYZ is the recognized leading authority for its profession, and your membership demonstrates your professional commitment.

Membership in Association XYZ offers exclusive access to proven resources and services and allows you to directly connect with a powerful network of your colleagues.

With Association XYZ member discounts and member-only publications, you'll stay on top of the latest industry research and news while saving yourself time and money.

Segmentation by Audience

In looking at your target audiences, you would develop marketing and communications efforts for each group. For example, you may easily reach subscribers to a competitive publication through print or web advertising (providing the competitor accepts your ad reservation form and advertisement). In addition, when developing messaging to lapsed members, you may spend more time promoting what's new at your association than introducing them to who you are, since they have already been a member at some point in time. In developing your plan, you would typically create subcategories of the intended audiences and list the supporting activities or efforts under each. It's likely that several efforts would be repeated under a number of targeted audiences (such as a major direct mail campaign or using existing members to recruit new ones). It's acceptable to use the same efforts for different audiences, and this segmentation of the core activities for all of the audiences is typically the largest portion of your plan and deserves a great deal of attention.

Examples

- Lapsed members
- Virtual focus group
- Targeted email
- Phone calls
- Direct mail postcard
- Letter from the association's chair
- Subscribers to competitive publication
- Print ad
- Web banner ad
- Direct mail postcard with special discount offer
- Testimonial flyer
- Letter from the association's chair

Schedule and Budget

This area is reserved for an overview of the plan's timeline and budget. Launch dates and milestones can be captured adjacent to the respective activities in the plan and, separately, financial oversight of these efforts should be scrutinized on an ongoing basis to ensure the plan remains within the budgetary parameters set.

Evaluation

A marketing and communications plan is just that: a plan. It should remain fluid in function and flexible in execution. That is, you are continuing to evaluate its success throughout the stages of the plan. Sometimes, messaging may have to be modified or new activities added, while other efforts may be eliminated. But none of this can be done without proper evaluation of your efforts as they are happening and should continue with a comprehensive assessment of all of the key components of the plan after it has been fully executed.

◆ ◆ ◆

The Message

The storyteller is nothing without *the story*. What is the story that you want to share? While your story will likely emphasize slightly different points to diverse audiences and through varied channels, the story itself needs to remain consistent and all of the messaging must support the initial idea.

Using the preceding abbreviated marketing and communications sample, let's assume that Association XYZ has determined from its own communications audit and data mining that the organization's primary member value proposition is its online member community portal that connects their 20,000 members with each other and averages 550 communications a day. This network allows members to query each other, post rich discussions, and connect from around the world in a safe, professional environment. To leverage this for member recruitment, messaging can be created to read: "200,000 conversations a year. 20,000 XYZ Professionals. One Resource: Association XYZ."

This message conveys three thoughts, and can be supported in other areas of the plan: the volume of engagement is very active, the size of the membership is identified, and the association is positioned as the resource for the profession. To make your message strong, you will need qualifiers to support it. It's not as effective to state "the best" or "the leading" alone, in your messaging. Here, you've demonstrated the size of the professional membership in your association and identified the number of engagements or conversations that they are holding each year. Professionals in your industry who are not members will feel left out.

The Brand

As you read in a quote from Seth Godin in Chapter Six, branding "is the set of expectations, memories, stories, and relationships that, taken together, account for a consumer's decision to choose one product or service over another." Perform a quick "reality check" throughout your planning process, asking yourself, "Does this plan support the mission?" and "Does this plan stay true to our brand?" The answers must always be "yes."

Market Segments

Many associations fall into the ease of blanketing entire memberships or constituents with blast messaging. If, for example, you are promoting your annual convention, a new member who has joined three months prior should not be treated exactly as the eleven-year vet who attends the conference religiously each year. People often conjure up "Amazon.com" or "Nordstrom's" as the quintessential models of business-to-consumer engagement. At the core of their reputations is the delivery of superior customer experiences. With so many organizations and companies vying for our attention as consumers, we want those who we have a relationship with to make us feel valued. Associations must act accordingly and establish interactions with members on the basis of those expectations.

Going back to our marketing sample, let's look at two markets that Association XYZ wants to target for membership: lapsed members and non-members who have attended their events. In this case, both groups have been engaged with the association: one as former members and the other as event participants. Since these groups have already had direct engagement with Association XYZ, they are considered "hot prospects."

However, you would market to each segment differently. After you've gone through data mining and analysis and eliminated lapsed members who have left the profession or will not likely join for other reasons, you can craft messaging that hopes to "win back" the members by promoting your association's new benefits since they left and leveraging the online data portal discussed earlier, which is no longer accessible to them. Since the second group has already interacted with your association, you are trying to encourage them to take the next step of engagement and demonstrate all else that there is to offer beyond their experience as an event attendee. In this example, your messaging must acknowledge their past participation, but showcase the other points of value they are missing by not enjoying the benefits of membership.

Marketing and Communications Channels

As storyteller, you must ensure you use the proper distribution channels when communicating your message. It might be easy to just send an email and check this off the "to do" list, but for some associations direct mail may deliver a better return on investment. You must weigh the ROI when orchestrating your "marketing mix," accepting how your messaging presence would play on different platforms and channels. Following are some examples of the more popular channels for sharing your story.

Direct Mail

Production and distribution costs are factors, but typically consumers will react more readily to direct mail than email. It is a mistake to think that email and the web are "shoe-in" replacements for direct mail. While the CAN-SPAM Act (national standards for sending commercial email, enforced by the Federal Trade Commission) upheld content and behavior compliance, it arguably did not curb the volume of emails, unsolicited or otherwise. The disorder of the mailbox has been replaced by the clutter of the inbox, allowing direct mail to stand out as a near novelty in this digital age—and direct mail does not always have to be the flashy brochure. A well-written letter may also deliver your results, depending on the outcomes you hope to achieve.

Email

Associations are attracted to the quickness, low cost, and ease of using email. Email allows you to personalize and target messages, while tracking valuable data in real time. However, consider how much time you spend managing just your own internal emails and how effortless it is to either delete a message or save it to a folder to read for another day (which we may never do). As email becomes the communication of choice, it becomes trickier to stay above the fray.

This is where personalization, customization, and creativity come into play. By using the metrics from your association's database, you should be able to address your members' past history and behaviors. ("Hi Lisa, we're happy that you were able to attend your first annual convention last year, and we hope that you'll join us again this year, especially since this year's event is a short driving distance from you.") A robust database and smart software allow for strong market segmentation. In the earlier example, the association may have used email to send messages to attendees from any of the conventions of the past five years, while long-time members who have not attended during the past five years may not be specifically targeted through email.

Advertising

Advertising is among the most difficult marketing and communications activities to track, primarily in print medium, but not impossible. Implementing source codes or quick surveys are good ways to test the awareness and responsiveness of your ad campaigns. You might also use special URLs that are only made available to subscribers to the publication that features your advertising.

Web

Online advertising has grown in its appeal to associations. The cost is traditionally cheaper than print advertising, and associations may customize their audiences according to self-selected criteria offered by many websites. Web banner ads placed on an industry website, partner organization, or through an e-publication or e-newsletter can embed hyperlinks that allow your members to directly connect with your association. Many search engine sites offer customized advertising and search engine optimization (SEO), designed to help you tell your story to like-minded individuals.

But there's more to your website than advertising. For those members who cannot attend an annual convention or local event, your website may be the only real touch point for them. As you integrate a web presence in your marketing and communications plan, the content must be positioned for the medium. Brochure copy will not work on websites, ordinarily, until they are revised for the web user. Consider adding copy to your website that may have been left on the "cutting room floor" from your publication. The website is a great resource to leverage video and photography to convey your story in a more aesthetically pleasing way than even great copy can convey.

Press and Publicity

Not every communication will warrant a press release, but when you can offer a newsworthy story, a press release is an effective way to ensure that your content reaches news media outlets. The press release should act as a conversation starter for your association. Hopefully, it will generate interest from news publications and resources. Ideally, your association's spokesperson will then be contacted to further discuss the subject matter through an in-depth interview or news item.

The resources for news and publicity continue to grow beyond the traditional news media and industry publications. Today, many bloggers and other online outlets that have grown in popularity organically sometimes wield just as much influence as the major news resources. Still, whether it's a homegrown one-person entity or an internationally known newspaper, the media will only demonstrate interest if your issue is newsworthy. What unique story do you have to share that most people might find interesting?

Just as we explored the concept of capturing your members' attention in your email, direct mail, communications, and advertising, so too must you do so with your reporters and the media, with attention-grabbing content.

Social Media

Social media's applicability and value are growing cornerstones of marketing and communications. However, just as other channels should be leveraged on the basis of their corresponding strengths, it is also true of social media platforms. In deciphering all of the social media choices, you must first determine which of these platforms make the most sense for your association's story. What are the social media preferences of your members? Of your other constituents? How would you leverage each? How do they like to engage on each? Each social media channel has its own personality, and it's just as essential that your story is fashioned to fit the dynamics of each applicable platform.

Telemarketing

Telemarketing may be underutilized by many associations, but in these busy times, the unexpected phone call may be a needed touch point, especially if your members are not interacting with your association regularly. Telemarketing may prove beneficial for such needs as member renewals or when incentivizing attendance at events. With telemarketing, you must remain especially vigilant in order to delicately achieve your goals without behaving intrusively.

Ready? Set? Execute!

Now that you've performed the auditing, done the data and trends analysis, established your goals, and planned for your messaging on the different channels, it's time to execute the marketing and communications plan. It's worth repeating that marketing and communications do not happen in a vacuum—all other stakeholders are affected and should be aware of the efforts involved in your strategy.

Key Stakeholders

Customer and Member Relations

Does your member relations team know what is going out to members and other audiences? What are some of the questions they might receive as follow up to the marketing or communications activities? Do they have a cheat sheet or list of FAQs to help them respond to anticipated questions?

The Board of Directors and Other Volunteer Leaders

Your board and other volunteer leaders are likely engaged and visibly recognized by other professionals in your association's industry. You want to make sure they too can address general questions they might be asked as they are out in the field. By not preparing your volunteer leader team effectively, you risk placing them in awkward positions and presenting your association as disorganized.

Spokesperson(s)

Primarily when the marketing and communications plan employs press and publicity measures, a spokesperson should be identified and briefed. However, it's always good to plan for a spokesperson to respond to queries that might come from the press or industry trade resources. Typically, the chief staff executive, board chair, or VP or director of communications at the association serves in this capacity.

Association Staff

Ensure that the staff stay on message and that your story is consistent. It is feasible that one or more of your members may reach out to those staff that they have a relationship with—the bookkeeper, the research assistant, or the education manager—to inquire about a related email or postcard they received. Talking points and key FAQs should be made available to your association's staff.

Members

While it is likely that members will be on your list of key targets, in some cases, that might not be true. But depending on the communication and purpose, it will be wise to share the milestones of your marketing and communications plan with the membership. For example, you may want to inform your members of a press release or provide them access to it through a link on your site. Some of your members will have stronger relationships with local press and can act as champions for your story and position.

The Media

News outlets want a good story and you have a story you want to share. Perfect combination, right? Well, not necessarily. Like other partnerships in associations, cultivating a relationship with the press relies on credibility and a mutual understanding and respect for each other's interests. Once you've determined the preferences of the news outlets, whether they are bloggers, industry trades, or general interest publications, you can better target the types of stories that are applicable to them. Just as you would target messages to your members that are based on your own data mining, an analysis of your prospective press partners will reveal the topics and styles they find most appealing.

Even when your marketing and communications plan is being well-executed, consider it fluid. Constant evaluation can clue you in on where adjustments are needed. Are there parts of your story that are not clear? If so, what revisions can be completed so that your story is presented and applied the way you prefer? Some areas to evaluate include the following:

- *Open rates and click through rates on email or online advertising:* The beauty of electronic marketing is the real-time results. If you find results are below expectations, supplemental efforts can be made. Consider A-B testing—that is, looking at the same audience, but sending alternate messages to demonstrate if one has a higher interest.
- *Press pick up:* If you are generating little interest from your press releases, how newsworthy might your content be? Learn the reporters and trades that periodically will cover your industry and stay connected to them.

- *Direct mail:* Are you finding the response rates you expect from your direct mail? If not, is the call to action clear? Is the message compelling? Does your message address a need identified in your environmental scan?

Back to the Goals

You've journeyed through the key steps in your marketing and communications plan. A key component of the evaluation process is determining if you were able to achieve goals and meet sales projections. While there is still no magic button for achieving global success, through a comprehensive, data-driven, well-planned, and nimble marketing and communications strategy, your association will better understand the high-level role marketing, communications, and public relations play in delivering results and maintaining relevance.

The Author

Tom Quash, CAE, is the vice president of marketing, communications, and publications at the Association of Women's Health, Obstetric and Neonatal Nurses (AWHONN). He has held marketing positions at major publishing companies before overseeing marketing and communications divisions at several associations.

CHAPTER THIRTY-NINE

PUBLISHING AND MEDIA

Debra J. Stratton and Angela Hickman Brady

Association publications and media have the power to create and maintain an association's image, enhance its credibility within the industry or profession, and establish it as a valuable source of information. Media in all formats, whether print or digital, provide an essential link to members, supporting member value, visibility, and brand equity, all critically important as competition for member attention and engagement explodes. In addition, media can provide much-needed nondues revenue from advertising, subscriptions, sponsorships, content licensing, and more.

The most effective association communication programs include a variety of media and formats that appeal to members' special interests and needs. Arriving at the right mix of communications for your organization means adapting to the ever-changing interests and concerns of members and the rapidly evolving technology for content delivery. Some members look for an in-depth magazine or scholarly journal coupled with a brief and timely electronic newsletter; others seek out a lively blog, a comprehensive textbook, or opportunities to interact with their peers via discussion groups and social media. Hitting on the right mix of communication vehicles can be a challenge and requires a depth of understanding about members and their information needs, a clear vision of the association's goals and mission, well-defined objectives and business plans for operations, and an integrated strategic communications plan for achieving those objectives.

General Guidelines for Media Operations

Most professional societies and trade organizations promote their publications as a major benefit of membership—with good reason. When asked to rank important association services, members typically place publications at or near the top of the list. The association's content—delivered via magazines, journals, e-newsletters, or websites, for instance—represents a tangible benefit to members and reminds them of what the association accomplishes on their behalf. Media and publications may, in fact, be the only link some members have with an association or society. Given their important role, media sources must be timely, authoritative, credible, well-designed or formatted, highly readable, and carefully tuned to members' needs.

Publishing with a Purpose

Every publication or regular communication—whether a magazine, e-newsletter, blog, monograph, or other media—needs a written statement of purpose: three or four sentences that describe the target audience, the type of content to be included, and the overall goals of the publication. A statement of purpose is the basis for determining what content goes into a communication vehicle and evaluating how effective that vehicle is in meeting its objectives.

To avoid misunderstandings and unneeded conflicts, and to ensure staff know what is expected of them, develop a written statement of purpose for each vehicle; review and update it regularly; and share it with readers, staff, and volunteers. Then use it to evaluate what editorial content is most appropriate for each publication.

It is not uncommon for association staff and leadership to disagree on a publication's purpose, especially if the publication is advertiser-supported. Some prefer a "house organ" that reports on association activities and services, while others believe strongly in the need for an independent trade or professional publication. Clarifying the distinction between a house organ and an independent magazine is critical for publications that carry advertising and for those that serve a broader audience than just members. Is the publication primarily promotional, reporting on the association? If so, an e-newsletter is generally an appropriate format. Or is the publication independent, reporting on the industry or profession? In that case, a magazine or journal is a better format.

Matching Needs and Formats

Content and the frequency of communication required will help determine the best format. If members are looking for the latest legislative news affecting their profession or their companies, a brief, weekly e-newsletter might be the perfect format. But if members want in-depth case studies and practical advice on how to apply practices in their own settings, a bimonthly or monthly magazine may be more on target. Consider the function of the communication vehicle as well as members' preferences for print versus electronic communications as you review your current publication mix.

E-newsletters continue to be a common format for associations. Associations may publish several e-newsletters, each directed to a specialized segment of the membership or to nonmember subscribers, in addition to a general membership e-newsletter. Some associations are moving to a more customized approach to content delivery, allowing members to create their own profile of interests and indicate the type of news and information they want to receive on a regular basis. This trend toward customized content is expected to continue.

Weekly e-newsletters that provide a combination of association and breaking industry and professional news are a common format, as are targeted e-newsletters for a particular job function or area of interest, such as legislative updates. The most effective e-newsletters are concisely written and attractively designed and formatted, with multiple entry points for busy readers. Brief, engaging headlines and teaser copy will then link readers to full stories. Readers should be able to easily scan an e-newsletter for specialized content of interest.

Nearly three-quarters of associations (73 percent) generate advertising or sponsorship revenue from their e-newsletters, offering button and banner ads or sponsorships as part of integrated plans of print and electronic advertising.[1]

Magazines and journals are a more formal means of communicating with members and may be published in print or digital format or a combination of both. Although magazines and journals may contain news sections, their primary purpose is to provide in-depth coverage of selected topics. They vary in size, from as few as twenty-four pages to more than two hundred pages, and often are supported by advertising.

Electronic publications, especially newsletters, are common among associations as a quick and relatively inexpensive way to deliver timely information that can be customized to meet specialized needs. The advantage of online publications is their timeliness and relatively low production cost; the disadvantage is that with the glut of electronic communications, they can easily be overlooked and considered one more marketing solicitation. Some technical and medical societies have opted for digital journals that provide interactivity, video, and other enhancements, enabling organizations to communicate technical information in multiple formats.

Other formats, including blogs, social media channels, Internet TV, and electronic discussion groups, are also gaining ground, providing easy access for communicating 24/7 with today's members, who are used to constant access to news and information. These formats provide an opportunity for associations to drive conversations among members and, in some cases, create user-generated content. Electronic delivery formats are largely dependent on members' needs and preferences, something continually evolving as technology expands.

Every organization has different communication needs at different times. The formats and frequencies selected must balance members' needs with the association's financial and staff resources. Furthermore, what's valuable to members must also be efficient for the association. A society of professional photographers, for example, may sacrifice other publications to produce a monthly four-color magazine that showcases its members' work. An organization of scientists, on the other hand, might have staff produce a bimonthly e-newsletter, but rely on volunteers to prepare a book or eBook containing specialized research findings.

Is It Still Relevant?

A publication's format, and even its reason for being, may change over time and must regularly be assessed to ensure the publication remains on target. Staff should periodically review each communication channel or publication to determine relevance and effectiveness: Is this publication or vehicle still relevant? Would it be more effective to integrate several e-newsletters into one single e-newsletter? Is another format better suited to members' needs? Or has the publication outlived its purpose? Should it be published more often—or less frequently? Would the e-newsletter content be better suited for a magazine? How could the publication be repositioned?

Regular, systematic review helps ensure that media and publications remain healthy. This may include using an outside specialist to conduct a readership study every two years or so or undergoing a broader communication audit review of all member communications and media. An objective outside advisor can provide insights into how to structure communications programs to be most effective.

Content Development

Most associations publish a mix of periodicals, from journals and newsletters to magazines, directories, conference reports, and bulletins. No matter how many communications are produced, the staffs of all successful periodicals must first establish an editorial niche and develop appropriate content to fill that niche.

An association can identify industry trends and information of interest to readers in several ways. For example, track what information members ask for. Interview readers or conduct focus groups or "straw polls" at conventions or meetings. By reading other trade publications, association publishers can stay one step ahead of the competition. This informal research, combined with editorial brainstorming sessions as well as more formal readership research, will help identify the topics and article formats that readers find most useful and appealing.

Some publications may be well served to use an editorial group to keep them in touch with a technical field or to serve as a sounding board. Scholarly, scientific, or technical journals commonly use an editorial board, sometimes elected by the membership, whose members function almost as editors to "peer review" articles before publication. Scholarly journals usually require at least three qualified reviewers to look at a manuscript before sending it to the editor—often a paid outside practitioner—for a final decision. This peer-review process helps protect a publication's credibility and integrity.

Even some nontechnical publications turn to an advisory board of volunteers for help in developing editorial content and locating expert authors and interviewees. A board, however, can't effectively manage a publication. Ultimately, decisions regarding what is published rest with a well-qualified, professional editor and staff—the people who know the readers and know the publication the best.

Just as a publication's statement of purpose serves as its foundation, the articles filling its pages represent the bricks. Consistently well-written, high-quality content builds reader interest and loyalty more than award-winning designs and colorful graphics. To generate the content, an association may rely on a staff of editors and writers, freelance writers, members and suppliers, academicians, government leaders, and others. The content-development process should be continual, with the editor always on the lookout for new topics and different angles.

Although feature articles are the main attraction in a magazine or journal, departments devoted to ongoing issues are equally important. Departments, or standing columns, form the framework for a magazine, giving the reader a familiarity and consistency that helps build reader loyalty. Readers know they can turn to a regular department each month for the latest on legal issues, technology trends, legislative updates, or a calendar of events.

Design for Readability

Packaging and presentation of media—layout and design, paper stock, typeface, use of photos and illustrations, electronic formats and styles—are critical to readership. Good design and layout get a publication noticed; valuable content keeps readers coming back. Effective design employs easy-to-read type fonts, effective use of white space, and other design elements—such as color choices, headlines, art and photos, decks, callouts, and sidebar boxes—to draw readers into the publication and keep them moving from one article to another.

Every publication needs a professional design as a starting point, including a logo and templates and style sheets for articles and recurring departments and columns. Because design can easily become dated and ineffective, reexamine your publication's design every few years and study trends in consumer magazine design to ensure readers do not become complacent.

Staffing and Policy Considerations

Larger associations may hire a full-time graphic designer or art director. Smaller associations might contract with a design firm for each issue or by hiring an outside designer to develop an attractive, readable format and design approach. The association may then choose to implement that design with in-house editorial or production assistants or outsource the complete design and production operation.

With technology advances, in-house design capability is common in many associations, yet many associations may still choose to outsource ongoing design of their publications to design professionals. The advantage of in-house design operations is increased control and the potential for reduced costs and quicker turnaround. The downside can be that in-house design may put design in the hands of untrained editors and production personnel, resulting in reduced quality and delayed production due to competing priorities.

Today's all-digital printing technology requires designers to also preflight and place ads and ensure all content is in appropriate press-optimized formats, all of which require more time and technical proficiency by design staffs. Be sure to provide appropriate training and support to ensure in-house designers are skilled in technical requirements. Seek the advice and services of professional designers to create templates and overall formats that can then be used by in-house production staff to execute the layout.

Digital versions of print publications are another consideration. A wide range of digital providers offer services to publishers today. The right approach for any organization depends on its audience. Do they prefer a page-flipping replica, an HTML version with added content, or other version? This may have an impact on design and content choices.

For print publications, decisions related to paper stock, scheduling, and distribution are the responsibility of the production manager, editor, or art director or designer. This area of publishing represents a key financial function and requires knowledgeable staff to identify and work with printers, mailing houses, and fulfillment companies. Selecting the most cost-effective ways to produce and distribute publications while ensuring consistent quality and timely distribution are critical roles. To fulfill these needs, staff need appropriate financial and publishing training to prepare and compare print specifications, determine press runs, and keep current with continually evolving digital print technology and postal and distribution issues.

To maintain credibility with their members and compete with commercial publications, associations must base their production decisions on financial data and strictly adhere to schedules. Making last-minute alterations at proof stage, for example, is costly and may delay distribution. A realistic production schedule accommodates many factors, allowing time for submissions from volunteers and outside writers, fact checking, proofreading, and alterations. The entire media and communications staff should be well acquainted with the production process so they understand how any deviation from their deadlines affects the entire process.

The Business Considerations

Financial Management

As a business, association publishing needs a financial plan to set goals. Financial management begins with preparing a business plan and budget that establish financial and profit goals for each publication. Clarify the financial goals of your publications to avoid misunderstandings:

- Is the association's intent to break even or to make money?
- How much revenue is expected?
- Will overhead be assigned to the publication?
- Will a portion of member dues be allocated to the publication?
- What level of investment in an existing publication or a startup publication is the association willing to make over how many years to ensure a high-quality, member-valued publication?

Build a budget for each publication that takes a fresh look at the entire operation each year. Zero-based budgeting makes staff annually reconsider how they are approaching the publishing process. To be effective, get as much input from staff and outside sources as possible, review the past performance of established publications, and keep informed on possible developments that could affect overall costs or income during the coming year, such as postage increases, format changes, freelance writing requirements, fees for digital versions, or other expenses.

Once the budget is established, use it as a management tool for controlling expenses and making key decisions. At any given time, the editor should know the numbers: production costs for each publication, the per-copy cost, and the dues subsidy and advertising revenue for each publication. Sound financial management may employ regular quarterly reviews of performance goals, financial income and expense reports, and monitoring of significant variances with accompanying revised year-end budget projections. Some associations offer incentives to key staff for reaching or exceeding budgets. Ultimately, it is the publisher—who also may hold the editor role—who is responsible for ensuring the publishing operation meets its financial goals.

Tax Considerations

Adding advertising to a publication introduces tax and legal issues. Selling advertising does not jeopardize the tax-exempt status of an organization, but it may make the association liable for taxation. Advertising sold by tax-exempt organizations is considered unrelated business income and is therefore subject to the unrelated business income tax (UBIT).

Discuss the tax implications with an accountant well versed in association matters. It is critical that an association's financial records clearly differentiate between advertising and editorial income and expense. On the advertising side, include all advertising income and all the costs associated with generating that income, including commissions and sales materials. On the editorial side, include income from nonmember subscriptions, royalties, reprints, licensing agreements, supplements, and other editorial sources as well as all costs of producing the editorial portion. To reduce potential tax liability, ensure that appropriate expenses are charged against the advertising portion of the publication, including a percentage of printing and distribution costs, salaries, overhead, and direct sales expenses. The more that can be legitimately claimed as an advertising expense, the more net advertising revenue can be offset.

Advertising

The decision to sell advertising is a complex one. If you are considering selling advertising in a publication, conduct a feasibility study first to determine whether the potential revenue would sufficiently offset the investments of time and money involved in launching an advertising program.

Adhering to a predetermined advertising-to-editorial ratio in periodicals ensures that advertising revenues will help offset production costs. Even if a magazine or journal does not rely solely on advertising to meet its income goals, having an established advertising-to-editorial ratio adds structure and balance to a publication. Publishers who seek to generate a net profit on their publications will generally adhere to a ratio of 45 to 50 percent advertising and 50 to 55 percent editorial in most issues. Controlling the advertising-to-editorial ratio is an important factor in containing expense.

With the pressures to sell advertising, conflicts may develop between the editorial and the advertising portions of the publication. The greatest conflict is over issues of editorial integrity and whether to run editorial content that is in some way supportive or promotional of advertisers. Credible association publications avoid any suggestion of advertising influence in editorial content. However, general topic areas of interest to advertisers as well as readers are usually identified in an annual editorial calendar, which is provided to advertisers in a media kit. To avoid conflicts, clarify editorial and advertising policies in advance.

In addition, here are some other areas in which conflicts may arise that can be addressed by clear editorial policy:

- *Ad placement:* Will all the ads be "stacked" in the back pages of the publication or integrated into the editorial pages? Will ads and editorial be clearly separated? Generally, integrating ads throughout the publication is the most attractive and most appealing approach both for advertisers and readers.
- *Positioning:* Covers and other premium positions are specially priced at rates substantially higher than the page rate. Some publishers also sell positions opposite well-read departments or columns at a slightly higher rate than regular space costs. Determine if you will offer special positions and how to structure and promote these to advertisers.
- *Pricing:* Associations often undervalue their publications when setting advertising rates. Ensure you are selling a quality publication and then price advertising space for value. Sell your "specialness"—your exclusive niche—to potential advertisers. Pricing is often measured on a cost per thousand readers (CPM) basis, which should be considered in pricing a publication among competitors. Association publications can often command a higher CPM, based on the quality of its audience. Although association staffs and resources may be considerably smaller than a commercial counterpart, associations have a number of advantages over general trade publications. Price and position your publication to take advantage of the association's inherent strengths:
  - *Clout of organization:* As the official publication of the association, the periodical not only enjoys the recognition and visibility of the association but can also draw on its many resources. Promote this tie-in.
  - *Highly targeted readership:* Association members form a highly specialized group of potential buyers. Advertisers are willing to pay a premium to reach the top players in the industry or profession.
  - *Quality of editorial content and level of readership by members:* Traditionally, association publications are well read. Conduct research to back up this claim and sell it to advertisers.
  - *Paid circulation (by virtue of membership dues) as opposed to controlled circulation:* Association publications that are distributed as a part of membership dues are considered paid circulation and therefore represent a higher quality of distribution than controlled or free circulation trade and professional publications.

The Audit Bureau of Circulations or Business Publications Audit or a similar program whereby an outside firm regularly verifies the quality and accuracy of circulation figures may be an option for some association publications, particularly those that compete with large for-profit trade publishers. The decision to pursue audited circulation depends on a number of factors, including expense, whether the audit will improve the publication's chances to secure advertising, and whether the association has the data available for the audit.

To compete successfully, associations must do more than decide to "accept" whatever advertising and subscriptions come in. Instead they must incorporate a strategy for aggressive sales growth into a marketing plan designed for long-term results. To implement the marketing plan, hire experienced, trained salespeople or contract with an outside sales firm. Many associations begin by using a sales firm, paid on commission only. According to recent research, about one-third of associations staff their sales operation with in-house staff, while 29 percent use outside reps or contractors, 21 percent use a combination of in-house staff and reps, and 17 percent use no sales staff.[2]

Both in-house and outside sales staff arrangements have advantages, depending upon the size of the publication, the geographic areas to be covered, and the revenue generated. You might consider the sales needs throughout the association. Increasingly, associations are moving to integrated marketing plans in which all marketing opportunities are integrated into one plan to encourage use of multimedia platforms and formats, both print and online. In addition to selling display advertising, sales staff can also sell print or electronic classified advertising; sponsorships in print publications or monographs; buyer's guide listings; electronic sponsorships; web advertising; and convention-related advertisements, sponsorships, and exhibits. Staffing considerations are critical to success, so be sure to conduct a careful analysis of the costs and benefits of your options before you make the final decision.

Circulation and Distribution

While most consumer publications rely on subscription income to help underwrite the costs of publishing, associations usually equate circulation with membership. Typically, a member's dues entitle him or her to receive a basic newsletter or magazine. However, in most cases, the publishing department does not receive part of those dues to apply toward publication expenses.

In recent years, however, more association publishers that have "unbundled" member benefits offer customized subscription services to members. Moreover, many associations are looking to nonmember subscriptions as a means of not only expanding their reach but also generating additional revenue.

Several factors should be reviewed before embarking on a campaign to solicit nonmember subscribers, including the following:

- *Competition with the membership department:* The keenest competition for prospects usually arises between an association's publishing department and its membership department. The membership department may believe that selling an association benefit separately undermines membership recruitment. Often, however, when nonmember subscriptions are offered, subscribers convert to membership within the first year. In addition, exposing nonmembers to information about the organization's work on members' behalf, marketing messages for meetings and conferences, and other services can support additional revenue generation.
- *Not limiting promotions to potential members:* Suppliers to the industry or profession, government officials, the media, universities, libraries, and members of related organizations are all potential audiences. Purchasing commercial mailing lists will help define the universe of prospective subscribers.
- *Conducting a small sample mailing to test the potential for subscription sales:* Increasing nonmember circulation in increments, such as 10 percent per year, may be more realistic than a one-time effort to increase it 30 percent.
- *Evaluating additional expenses:* The cost of boosting circulation goes beyond a larger print run and increased mailing costs. Adjusting or expanding editorial content to attract nonmembers might require additional staff or outside writers, in addition to the costs of producing and sending direct-mail promotion pieces, purchasing mailing lists, entering subscriber data, and sending renewal notices.
- *Analyzing the long-term pay-offs:* Paid subscriptions translate into more revenue, and higher circulation figures attract more advertisers—but not immediately. Consider whether the association can wait several years before its investment in nonmember subscriptions pays off.

A program to attract nonmember subscribers is just one component of a publication's overall marketing plan. Although the plan will vary according to the type of publication and its audience, the plan should include an analysis of the market (including the competition), an analysis of the product (the publication), short- and long-term objectives, and strategies for accomplishing those goals.

◆ ◆ ◆

Digital Disruption: A Survival Guide

Julie Shoop

If your association is in the business of distributing content, you're like every media company in the world in at least one respect: you've been digitally disrupted.

The tectonic shift from print-only publishing to the multichannel approach brought on by new digital technologies has shaken everyone in the information business, including associations. Print advertising revenue in general has been declining for years and, for many associations, has not been fully replaced by digital revenue. Reader expectations are constantly evolving. And competition, especially from nontraditional sources such as social media and content aggregator apps, is rising rapidly. The next innovation that will upset the publishing model is hard to predict.

This is challenging territory, especially for organizations with leaders, members, or staff who may have trouble seeing past their print publishing tradition. But for associations that produce industry news, practical member resources, and other valuable content—in other words, just about all of us—this is also a land of opportunity.

Associations can survive digital disruption. There's no secret formula—even the biggest names in the media business are still trying to figure this out—but organizations that adopt a flexible, integrated approach to publishing, with the right channels in print and online, can position themselves to thrive.

This takes a few shifts in thinking.

Give up the idea that you can cut your way to sustainability. Many discussions about publishing strategy in associations start with the red ink on the bottom line of the magazine budget. Unless your board has determined that your organization should get out of the content business altogether, you need a plan for sustainability. That plan surely will look at reducing print expenses, but without more steps, this approach inevitably leads to death by a thousand cuts. A growth strategy needs to include revenue analysis and an assessment of the association's position against other content providers that serve the same audience. What do you, or can you, offer that no one else does, or does well? What subject matter or audiences can you "own"? And how can you get that high-value content to your readers more cost-effectively, and with more engagement potential, using digital channels?

Consider how to allocate resources differently. Don't assume that starting something new will cost you more. Consider whether you can be smarter with your current budget (or even with a smaller budget) by shifting resources from work you can discontinue to new projects. Can you reduce your magazine's print frequency and redeploy editorial and design resources, both staff and budget, to new digital products that will help you achieve goals like building web traffic and providing additional options for advertisers? You may need to fill gaps in your team's skill set, but many skills are transferable among content channels. Don't miss opportunities to use your team's talents to best advantage.

Accept that change has become a constant. It's unlikely that any publishing plan you devise today will look exactly the same a year or two from now. Like any solid strategy, the one guiding your publishing program should be flexible, allowing for adjustments to your tactics as needed to respond to audience demands, cost and revenue realities, and changes to the competitive landscape. You're on the right track if your strategy is moving the publishing operation toward its goals; to maintain your progress, you'll need to stay informed of your members' delivery preferences and what information they need, and keep tinkering. It helps to get comfortable with that.

Reinventing *Associations Now*

This is the path ASAE has taken with its flagship publication, *Associations Now*, since a 2012 relaunch. Well into the digital publishing revolution, AN had remained almost entirely a print product, and although surveys confirmed that members valued and trusted the content, they also reported that they were increasingly turning to digital information sources and had less and less time to read. With that writing on the wall (along with declining print ad revenues and increasing costs), it was clear that ASAE needed to reinvent *Associations Now* for the digital age.

The strategy: ASAE set out to leverage the trusted monthly magazine into a multi-channel media brand that would more fully engage existing audiences—largely ASAE members—and attract new readers who were interested in news and information about associations but who had not chosen to join (or renew with) ASAE. This larger audience would build web traffic and drive digital ad revenue, and new readers eventually could be put on a path to higher engagement with ASAE. Although converting new readers to members would clearly be a desirable outcome, signing up new members was not an explicit goal of the publishing strategy.

The structure: the print magazine would remain the backbone of the recharged *Associations Now* brand, but ASAE saw an opportunity for digital expansion—no one was producing and distributing daily news about associations. This is where ASAE chose to put its stake in the ground, launching AssociationsNow.com in 2012 as a stand-alone media website updated several times a day with news stories and blog posts about current happenings in and around associations. That content reaches readers via email in *Associations Now Daily News* every morning. A year later, ASAE's fourteen section e-newsletters, which had been published for years under different names and at different frequencies, were brought into the *Associations Now* brand and relaunched as *Associations Now Plus*, a single email newsletter delivering premium, customized content for members only that complements the wide-reaching, free-to-all *Daily News*. The magazine, meanwhile, was reduced to bimonthly, providing a more sustainable business model for continued print publishing in a digital world.

The result: ASAE now has a series of distinct content channels unified under the *Associations Now* name. The digital channels have seen significant growth in both traffic and ad revenue in the first two years, and by right-sizing the magazine ASAE has preserved a valuable physical touch point with members and a premium opportunity for advertisers to reach their target market.

Content channels will keep evolving, for ASAE and every association publisher. Associations that can let go of past publishing models and get comfortable with a constant state of flux will be in a strong position to succeed in this digitally disrupted business.

◆ ◆ ◆

Books

Unlike periodicals, which contain news that quickly becomes dated, books have a sense of permanence. An association that publishes books can influence a trade or profession for years to come by setting standards, preparing members for the future, and establishing itself as the main source for information. Books and content licensing are valuable sources of nondues revenue for some associations. Books can also be an expensive undertaking if they are not well planned and marketed.

Before accepting or rejecting any idea for a book, association staff members, in conjunction with a publications or special-projects committee, should follow several steps:

1. *Assess the need:* Many book publishing projects have their roots in other association activities, such as the results of a professional research survey, requests to the information department, or comments made during informal and formal discussions with members. What is the reason for publishing a book? What can a book do that an article in the association's magazine or journal cannot?
2. *Define the potential market:* Before any work begins, understand the proposed book's market. Is the book targeted exclusively to the association's members, or to other audiences as well? How large is the potential market? What is the book's shelf life—will the topic still appeal to buyers three or five years later?
3. *Examine the financial considerations:* As a business, a book publishing operation needs financial goals. Can the association afford to heavily subsidize or break even on the project? Some associations are willing

to lose money on one book, calculating that sales of another book will more than offset the losses. In addition to financial resources, does the association have enough staff to devote to producing and marketing the final product?

For long-term projects, associations often turn to consultants and free-lance writers to draft original copy. To ensure consistency in copy, provide manuscript guidelines that discuss deadlines, style, length, tone, and the book's target audience. Be sure to require signed copyright release forms from all contributors and paid authors.

A staff member or an outside expert coordinates the book project. Typically, this editor ensures that deadlines are met, keeps copy moving through the review process, and assembles all the pieces before production. If your association does not wish to maintain complete control of a book project, sign a publishing contract with a book manufacturer. Companies that specialize in these book-publishing partnerships usually give the association editorial control but handle all the other production, distribution, and promotion details.

Setting the Price

Book pricing depends on demand for the material, the size of the market, production costs, and the association's goals. Most associations start with the book's direct costs—author's fees, illustration, design and layout, and printing—and calculate the per-copy cost. Next, they apply a multiplier that ranges from three to ten times the per-copy cost. Because their smaller print runs represent higher per-copy costs, associations usually use smaller multipliers.

For example, 3,500 copies of a hard-cover book may cost $45,000 to produce, or just under $13 per copy. Having researched what the market will bear, an association may price the book at $39 (a multiplier of three) or at $65 (a multiplier of five). Or it may use both prices: it's common to establish different prices for members and nonmembers, with the latter group paying more to account for the fact they don't pay dues. The difference in the member and nonmember price should relate to the proportion of dues income or other resources that support the product, and the non-member price should not be set so high as to compel the customer to join the association.[3]

As with subscription and advertising rates, book prices should be competitive in the marketplace. Pricing a 150-page soft-cover book at $3.50 to encourage sales could have the opposite effect. Would-be purchasers may not perceive value in a book that carries a low price tag.

A Strong Link

A well-planned and highly integrated publications program strengthens the link between an association and its members. To vie for members' attention in this world of increasingly sophisticated communications, associations must make professional communications a priority. A successful publishing program can ensure a healthy association.

Notes

1. Angerosa Research Foundation, *Association Media Nondues Revenue Metrics & Trends* (Alexandria, VA: Stratton Publishing & Marketing, 2014).
2. Angerosa Research Foundation, *Association Media Nondues Revenue Metrics & Trends* (Alexandria, VA: Stratton Publishing & Marketing, 2014).
3. J. A. Jacobs, *Association Law Handbook: A Practical Guide for Associations, Societies, and Charities* (Washington, DC: ASAE Association Management Press, 2012).

Resources

Angerosa Research Foundation. *Association Publishing Benchmarking Study.* Alexandria, VA: Stratton Publishing & Marketing, 2005.
Angerosa Research Foundation. *E-Publishing Trends & Metrics.* Alexandria, VA: Stratton Publishing & Marketing, 2007.
Angerosa Research Foundation. *Web 2.0: How Associations Are Tapping Social Media* Alexandria. VA: Stratton Publishing & Marketing, 2009.

The Authors

Debra J. Stratton is president and founder of Stratton Publishing & Marketing, Inc., a leader in the development of media strategies and solutions for associations and other organizations. The company has worked with hundreds of organizations over the past thirty years to create strategies that leverage resources to better engage members, enhance the bottom line, and support the organization's goals.

Angela Hickman Brady is senior consultant and publishing strategist with Stratton Publishing & Marketing, Inc., and president of Hickman Brady Media LLC, a custom media company. Over the past eighteen years she has managed and edited nearly a dozen different association print publications as well as several e-newsletters, while also directing several strategic communication audits and research studies each year.

Sidebar author *Julie Shoop* is vice president and editor-in-chief for ASAE: The Center for Association Leadership.

INDEX

Page references followed by *fig* indicate an illustrated figure; followed by *t* indicate a table.